"This is a well written, well structured introductory textbook covering the most current literature in the field. Throughout the chapters, complex phenomena are described and explained in a comprehensible way that applies directly to the students' everyday lives. The authors manage to provide both in breadth and depth across this wide and fascinating discipline."

Dr Torun Lindholm, Stockholm University

"Hogg and Vaughan's book is clear in its explanations and contemporary in its examples. An excellent text in both its critique and analysis, I will be recommending this as the ideal core text to parallel my teaching for undergraduate students in social psychology."

Paul Muff, University of Bradford

"Hogg and Vaughan have managed to yet again produce a great social psychology book. The text should prove useful for students who wish to learn about the key aspects of social psychology. It is an engaging read that clearly and concisely introduces the reader to the world of social psychology!"

Dr Cathrine Jansson-Boyd, Anglia Ruskin University

"Hogg and Vaughan successfully capture the essence of what is all around, all the time and what concerns us all: social psychology. Each topic is captivating and the format is easy-to-grasp yet instructive. I strongly recommend this volume."

Professor Pär Anders Granhag, Göteborg University

"*Essentials of Social Psycholology* is no doubt the most creative, exciting, and inspired textbook on the market. It reminded me of how exciting it is to learn."

Dr Bjarne Holmes, Heriot-Watt University

"For any introductory psychology text to succeed it must strike the right balance between academic rigour and accessibility for the naïve reader. The authors of *Essentials of Social Psychology* have drawn of their wealth of writing experience to walk this tightrope with considerable aplomb, producing a book that leads you by the hand through the contemporary landscape of social psychology in a way that never feels overly challenging or daunting. Pitched with the introductory market always in mind, by journey's end the reader will have accumulated a comprehensive understanding of contemporary, international social psychology, and critically, will have enjoyed the trip as well."

Dr John Kremer, Queen's University Belfast

"This is a very comprehensive volume and, compared to many competitors, has increased relevance to contemporary issues, including more than enough material to generate hours of critical discussion about the role of (social) psychology in the contemporary world. It's not only a good text book for students but a useful reference work for postgraduates and academic staff."

Dr Ron Roberts, Kingston University

D1089263

PEARSON

We work with leading authors to develop the
strongest educational materials in psychology
bringing cutting-edge thinking and best learning
practice to a global market.

Under a range of well-known imprints, including
Prentice Hall, we craft high-quality print and
electronic publications which help readers
to understand and apply their content, whether
studying or at work.

To find out more about the complete range of our
publishing, please visit us on the World Wide Web at:
www.pearsoned.co.uk.

Essentials of Social Psychology

Michael A. Hogg
Claremont Graduate University

Graham M. Vaughan
University of Auckland

Prentice Hall
is an imprint of

PEARSON

Harlow, England • London • New York • Boston • San Francisco • Toronto • Sydney • Singapore • Hong Kong
Tokyo • Seoul • Taipei • New Delhi • Cape Town • Madrid • Mexico City • Amsterdam • Munich • Paris • Milan

Pearson Education Limited
Edinburgh Gate
Harlow
Essex CM20 2JE
England

and Associated Companies throughout the world

Visit us on the World Wide Web at:
www.pearsoned.co.uk

First published 2010

ISBN 978-0-13-206932-8

British Library Cataloguing-in-Publication Data
A catalogue record for this book is available from the British Library

Library of Congress Cataloging-in-Publication Data
Hogg, Michael A., 1954–
    Essentials of social psychology / Michael A. Hogg, Graham M. Vaughan.
-- 1st ed.
        p. cm.
    ISBN 978-0-13-206932-8 (pbk.)
    1. Social psychology. I. Vaughan, Graham M. II. Title.
    HM1033.H644 2010
    302--dc22

                                            2009036150

10 9 8 7 6 5 4 3 2 1
13 12 11 10 09

Typeset in 10/12.5 Sabon by 30
Printed and bound by Rotolito Lombarda, Italy

The publisher's policy is to use paper manufactured from sustainable forests.

Brief contents

Contents

Chapter 4 Attitudes and persuasion   92

Chapter 7 Prejudice and intergroup relations   192

Chapter 8 Hurting other people   228

Chapter 9   Helping other people   260

Chapter 10 Attraction and close relationships 286

Chapter 11 Culture and communication 320

Supporting resources

Visit **www.mypsychlab.co.uk** for valuable learning resources.

MyPsychLab for students
- Complete student self-assessment and revision centre including diagnostic tests, a customised study plan, multiple choice and essay questions
- Media library for quick access to video and audio resources of interviews with experts, re-enactments of classic experiments, and extended examples of social psychological concepts in action.
- Annotated links to relevant websites for further research
- Key term flashcards and an online glossary

For instructors
- Comprehensive Instructor's Manual
- Extensive test bank of question material
- PowerPoint slides
- Additional video and audio-based Media Assignments

For more information please contact your local Pearson Education sales representative or visit **www.mypsychlab.co.uk**

List of figures and tables

List of figures

List of tables

Guided tour

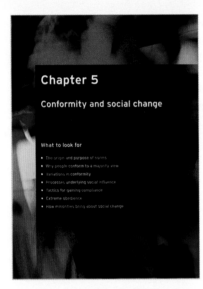

Each chapter begins with **What to look for** – a quick outline of the key terms, concepts and theories to be covered in the chapter.

Essentials of Social Psychology is accompanied by **MyPsychLab**, which contains a wealth of online resources designed to support and extend your learning and enrich your journey through the text.

Wherever you see this icon: visit **www.mypsychlab.co.uk**, where you will find additional resources, including video and audio clips, expanding on the topic in question.

Focus questions are a series of thought-provoking statements, questions and vignettes that are designed to get you thinking about some of the areas that social psychology can shed light on. As you read through each chapter, you will be asked to reflect back on these questions to see how your new understanding of social psychology might inform, and possibly change, your initial reactions. You will find additional resources to accompany this feature, including video and audio clips, on the MyPsychLab at **www.mypsychlab.co.uk**.

Research and applications boxes emphasise the wider relevance of social psychological insights, giving detailed examples of contemporary research and practice in social psychology and related areas, such as organisational, health and criminal justice settings.

Real world boxes present everyday examples of social psychology in action, applying social psychological principles to familiar real world scenarios.

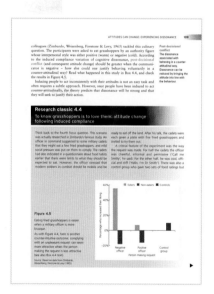

Research classic boxes summarise classic research studies, highlight their continuing relevance and discuss new developments. These are influential studies that represent turning points in the development of social psychology.

All chapters are **richly illustrated** with diagrams and photographs. Clear and concise definitions of **key terms** can be found in the margins and in a comprehensive Glossary at the end of the book. You can test your knowledge of the key terms using the **Flashcards** feature available at **www.mypsychlab.co.uk**.

Literature, film and TV offers the opportunity to explore key social psychological concepts using examples from popular media.
A mixture of classic and contemporary examples is included, from the disintegration of social norms in *Lord of the Flies* to attitude change and persuasion tactics in *Frost/Nixon*.

At the end of each chapter the **Summary** pulls together key points to help you consolidate your knowledge and understanding and to provide an excellent starting point for revision.

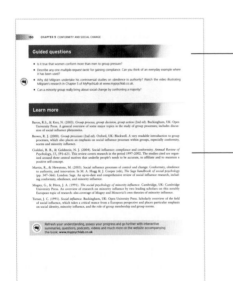

Guided questions enable readers to test their knowledge and prepare for assessment with essay questions based on the chapter content. Further guidance on how to answer these questions can be found on MyPsychLab at **www.mypsychlab.co.uk**, along with links to additional resources.

Learn more sections provide annotated further reading lists, guiding you towards the right resources to help you take your learning further.

MyPsychLab: resources for students

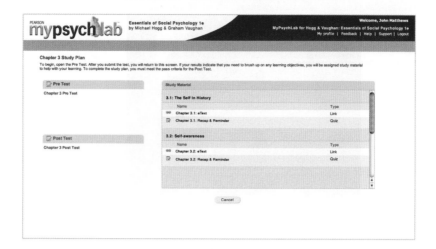

The **Study plan** section of MyPsychLab is a comprehensive student self-assessment and revision centre, which puts you in control of your learning, to help you to test your knowledge, identify areas for further study and generate a personalised study plan. The study plan includes:

● Pre-test and post-test questions

● Self-assessment multiple choice questions

● Recap and reminder materials

● Revision questions

● eText.

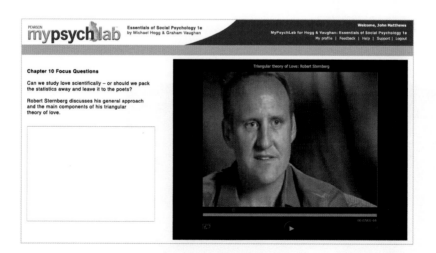

Focus questions provide video and audio clips that help you explore the focus questions at the start of each chapter in more depth.

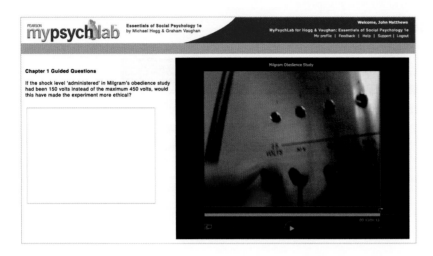

Guided questions provide additional guidance on how to answer the essay-style questions that are found at the end of each book chapter. Additional resources are provided to improve your understanding, including video and audio clips.

Annotated links to relevant websites for further research.

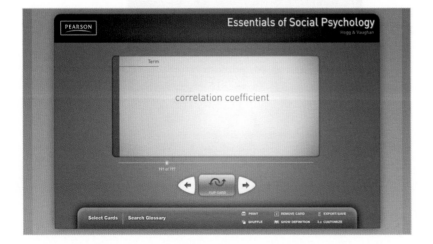

Flashcards of all the key terms found in the book, and an online Glossary.

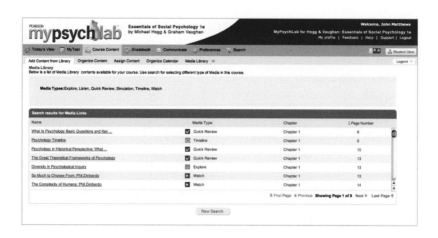

The MyPsychLab **Media library** contains a wealth of video and audio clips to support learning and teaching. You can choose from:

- Key figures in contemporary social psychology discussing their field of expertise and their research. For example:

    Robert Cialdini discussing the 'low-ball technique'
    Phil Zimbardo on the Stanford Prison experiment
    Mahzarin Banaji on the Implicit Association Test
    Robert Rosenthal on the 'Pygmalion effect'
    Robert Sternberg on his Triangular Theory of Love.

- Illustrations or re-enactments of classic social psychology studies, such as:

    Albert Bandura's Bobo Doll experiment
    Stanley Milgram's studies on obedience to authority.

- Discussions and extended examples exploring key themes in social psychology, including:

    Evolutionary approaches to selecting a mate
    Cognitive processing and stereotypes
    Children's self knowledge
    Low self esteem
    Justifying our actions
    Group loyalty
    Prejudice against minority groups
    The relation between exposure to TV violence and aggression
    Prosocial behaviour and reactions to bullying
    Attachment styles and insecure attachment
    Bilingualism and cultural identity.

For lecturers: the teaching and learning package

A full suite of lecturer support material is provided with this textbook, including:

- Comprehensive, downloadable Instructor's Manual
- Multiple choice question test bank
- PowerPoint slides
- Additional video and audio-based 'Media Assignments' and an online Media Library.

Contact your local Pearson Education sales consultant for more details about these resources or to arrange a demonstration. Sales consultant details can be found at **www.pearsoned.co.uk/replocator**.

Preface

We are all social psychologists – trying to understand why people do, say and think the things they do and why our social interactions play out as they do. We examine and dissect our relationships, other people's personalities and our sense of who we are, and are amazed at how selfish and cruel people can sometimes be. We all gain a working understanding of social psychology through day-to-day life, which we need in order to function as human beings. However, our keen interest in ourselves and in the way we interact with others is rarely satisfied.

Not surprisingly, social psychology is an extraordinarily popular subject of informal and formal study and a major focus of scientific research. Like other sciences, social psychology has its own specialist language, arcane technical terms, subtle distinctions, sophisticated research methods and arid statistical analyses. It can at times seem dry. Introductory textbooks in this field are often weighty tomes designed to train students to be scientific social psychologists. They are usually pitched at those specialising in social psychology. But what about those of us who need or would like to learn just the most important principles and general approach of social psychology – perhaps as a feature of a wider focus of study, or perhaps as a truly first introduction to the topic?

This is why we have written this book – to provide a concise and accessible yet scholarly introduction to the essentials of social psychology. We hope we are rather well qualified to do this – between the two of us we have taught social psychology at all levels in Europe, North America, South East Asia and Australasia for a scary total of some 70 years! We have also written one of those weighty books mentioned above – first published in 1995, our *Social Psychology* is now being revised for its 6th edition. It is also the leading social psychology text in Britain and Europe. That book is configured and written for British and European university students who are studying social psychology as their major focus, most likely as part of a psychology degree. It is nearly twice the size of *Essentials* with more chapters and substantially more detail, with a broader coverage, and assumes more background familiarity with fields of psychology. In contrast, *Essentials* has fewer chapters: as the title conveys, it focuses on the main phenomena, theories and research findings in social psychology, and occasionally other social sciences.

Over the years, Mike and Graham have talked a number of times about writing a shorter and simpler book. We explored the idea of *Essentials* more seriously at Pearson's marketing meeting in Bristol in September 2005 – there were discussions between Mike and Morten Fuglevand, from Pearson, that generated a proposal. In April 2006 Graham and Mike spent a few delightful days holed up in Noosa (a small beach town north of Brisbane in Australia) to flesh out the details of the project. Graham had a further discussion with Janey Webb and Stephanie Poulter in the unlikely context of a dinner at a Heathrow hotel airport and lunched with Morten in

Oslo. Then in May 2007 Janey and Stephanie bravely ventured north to Birmingham to meet with Mike to finalise details – a memorable meeting in stormy weather at Aston University. Graham visited Mike's home in the Santa Monica Mountains outside Los Angeles in late October 2007. There, we spent a busy week planning and configuring the chapters, broken by occasional sorties to nearby wineries where amateur but enthusiastic judgements were pronounced. By the time that Mike met Janey and Stephanie in London in June 2008 there had been enough intercontinental travel and talk. The book was written over that autumn/winter and into the late spring of 2009.

In writing *Essentials* we have been guided by the British Psychological Society's requirements for a course of study in social psychology ensuring that these are met. Although the chapters can be read separately, there is a logical structure to the book. Chapter 1 describes what social psychology is and how scientists 'do' social psychology. This is a short chapter that sets the scene for the nine main content chapters that follow. Chapter 2 describes how we think about and 'know' other people and what the causes and consequences are of thinking about people in certain ways. Chapter 3 focuses on how we think about and know ourselves – the causes, consequences and nature of our sense of self and our identity in society.

People have attitudes that can influence what they do and say. In Chapter 4 we explore the nature of attitudes – what they are, how they change, how they relate to what people actually do, and how they might be changed. The theme of change continues in Chapter 5 where we look at how people can be induced to obey orders, how they conform to group norms, and how a minority can sway the attitudes of a majority. The discussion of social influence flows into Chapter 6 where we deal with the psychology of groups – how groups influence behaviour, why and how people join groups, how groups are structured, how groups make decisions, and how people lead groups. The focus on groups is widened in Chapter 7 – we look at what happens between groups, featuring the nature of prejudice, discrimination, group conflict, collective protest, and ask how intergroup relations might be improved.

Studying intergroup conflict raises the question why people can be so nasty and aggressive. In Chapter 8 we discuss human aggression directly, followed by Chapter 9 where we explore the more positive side of human behaviour – the psychology of when people help others even at great cost to themselves. Warming to this uplifting theme, Chapter 10 explores friendship, love, romance and close personal relationships. Our final chapter, Chapter 11, examines the role of culture in social life – with a particular emphasis on the cultural context of modern society, and on how culture is tightly intertwined with language and communication. What is culture, how deep does it go, and how can different cultures live together in harmony?

Book writing is not a stroll in the park. It requires long hours concentrating in front of a computer screen – time that could be spent with one's family and friends. So of course we owe a huge debt of gratitude to the support provided by our partners – Alison Mudditt and Jan Vaughan. Graham enjoyed the encouragement of his extended family, while Mike's kids, Jessica, Jamie, Sam and Joe, kept him laughing through it all; and of course his mother is entirely to blame for encouraging him to read and study in the first place. We would also like to thank Janey Webb, Stephanie Poulter and Claire Lipscomb, our editors at Pearson in beautiful Harlow. They have been incredibly patient, carefully attentive to detail and enthusiastically involved in all stages of the enterprise. As a team they provided individual feedback on all parts of the book. Claire coordinated the constructive reviews and suggestions from a panel of colleagues in Europe and Joe Vella set the wheels of production into motion.

We would also like to thank the reviewers for their valuable time, patience and comments:

Ute Gabriel, Norwegian University of Science and Technology, Norway
Nicolas Geeraert, University of Essex, UK
Steffen R. Giessner, Rotterdam School of Management, Erasmus University, The Netherlands
Dr Cathrine Jansson-Boyd, Senior Lecturer, Anglia Ruskin University, UK
Dr John Kremer, Reader in Psychology, Queen's University, Belfast
Torun Lindholm, Department of Psychology, Stockholm University, Sweden
Paul Muff, University of Bradford, England, UK
Dr Lovemore Nyatanga, Principal Lecturer in Psychology, University of Derby, UK
Kerry John Rees, Senior Lecturer in Psychology, University of Gloucestershire, UK
Rob Ruiter, Maastricht University, The Netherlands.

How to use this book

Our book is a new and up-to-date introduction to social psychology as an international scientific enterprise, written from the perspective of European social psychology and in the context of people living in Britain and Europe.

It has a range of pedagogical features to facilitate independent study. Each chapter has the following features:

- *What to look for*: a compact list of topics covered.
- *Focus questions*: These pose issues that might challenge one's preconceptions, often with an applied flavour. They are re-visited in the course of the chapter.
- *Summary*: A detailed set of the main, need-to-know points that have been covered.
- *Literature, film and TV*: Social psychology is part of everyday life – so, not surprisingly, social psychological themes are often creatively and vividly explored in popular media. We have chosen some classic and contemporary works we feel have a particular relevance.
- *Guided questions*: This is a new feature consisting of topics that can be explored by consulting the Companion Website. We provide enough detail to write an essay, including starting points, references and web links.
- *Learn more*: This is a fully annotated list of further reading, usually books, and occasionally review articles.
- *Figures and tables*: We have sampled both historically important and modern studies whose data or theory illustrates a major point in the chapter.
- *Text boxes*: We identify three kinds of material. A research classic is a study that has been highly cited and sometimes was a turning point in the field; research and applications summarises the findings of a contemporary study, or gives an example relevant to kindred fields including organisational, health and the criminal justice settings; real world illustrates a social psychological principle that helps us to understand a topical issue or an everyday experience.

Essentials has a logical structure, with earlier chapters leading into later ones – however, it is not necessary to read it from beginning to end. Each chapter stands on its own and is carefully cross-referenced so that sections in chapters can be consulted should the need arise. Chapter 1, of course, is an introduction, but it also defines social psychology, its aims, its methods, a little of its history, and its peace in the scheme of things. For these reasons it might benefit from being reread after you have studied some of the other chapters and have become familiar with some of the theories, topics and issues of social psychology.

The primary target of our book is the student who is new to the field, though we intend it and its supplements to be of use also to teachers and more senior students of social psychology. We will be grateful to any among you who might take the time to share your reactions with us.

Michael Hogg, Los Angeles
Graham Vaughan, Auckland
December 2009

About the authors

MICHAEL HOGG was educated at Bristol Grammar School and Birmingham University and received his PhD from Bristol University. Currently Professor of Social Psychology at Claremont Graduate University, in Los Angeles, and an Honorary Professor of Social Psychology at the University of Kent, he has held teaching appointments at Bristol University, Princeton University, the University of Melbourne and the University of Queensland. He is a Fellow of the Society for Personality and Social Psychology, a Fellow of the Society for the Psychological Study of Social Issues, a Fellow of the Western Psychological Association, and a Fellow of the Academy of the Social Sciences in Australia. His research interests are group behaviour, intergroup relations and social identity processes. In addition to publishing about 270 scientific books, chapters and articles, he is an associate editor of the *Journal of Experimental Social Psychology*, foundation editor with Dominic Abrams of the journal *Group Processes and Intergroup Relations*, and senior consulting editor of the SAGE Social Psychology Program. Two of his books are citation classics, *Rediscovering the Social Group* (1987) with John Turner and others, and *Social Identifications* (1988) with Dominic Abrams.

GRAHAM VAUGHAN has been a Fulbright Fellow and Visiting Professor at the University of Illinois at Champaign-Urbana, a Visiting Lecturer and a Ford Foundation Fellow at the University of Bristol, a Visiting Professor at Princeton University, a Visiting Directeur d'Etudes at the Maison des Science de l'Homme, Paris, a Visiting Senior Fellow at the National University of Singapore, a Visiting Fellow at the University of Queensland and a Visiting Fellow at Churchill College, Cambridge. A Professor of Psychology at the University of Auckland, he also served twelve years as Head of Department. He is an Honorary Fellow and past President of the New Zealand Psychological Society, and a past President and Life Fellow of the Society of Australasian Social Psychologists. Graham Vaughan's primary areas of interest in social psychology are attitudes and attitude development, group processes and intergroup relations, ethnic relations and identity, culture and the history of social psychology. He has published widely on these topics. His 1972 book, *Racial Issues in New Zealand*, was the first to deal with ethnic relations in that country, and his two introductory social psychology texts co-authored with Michael Hogg and now in their fifth editions are the market leaders in the UK and in Australasia.

Publisher's acknowledgements

We are grateful to the following for permission to reproduce copyright material:

Figures

Figure 5.8: From *Obedience to authority*. London: Tavistock. (Milgram, S., 1974). Reproduced with permission from HarperCollins and Pinter and Martin; Figure 6.6: Adapted from Socialization in small groups: temporal changes in individual-group relations. In L. Berkowitz (ed.), *Advances in experimental social psychology*. Vol. 15, pp. 137–192. New York: Academic Press. (Moreland, R. L. & Levine, J. M., 1982). Copyright © 1982 Elsevier, Ltd. Reproduced with permission; Figure 9.1: Adapted from Some neo-Darwinian decision rules for altruism: weighing cues for inclusive fitness as a function of the biological importance of the decision, *Journal of Personality and Social Psychology*, 67, 773–789. (Burnstein, E., Crandall, C., & Kitayama, S. 1994). Copyright © 1994 by the American Psychological Association. Reproduced with kind permission from Professor Eugene Burnstein; Figure 10.2: From The evolutionary psychology of facial beauty, *Annual Review of Psychology*, 57, pp. 199–226 (Rhodes, G., 2006). Copyright © 2006 by Annual Reviews (www.annualreviews.org). Reproduced with permission from Annual Reviews and Professor Gill Rhodes; Figure 10.5: After *The triangle of love*. New York: Basic Books. (Sternberg, R. J., 1988). Reproduced with permission from Professor Robert J. Sternberg; Figure 11.5: After *Social identifications: a social psychology of intergroup relations and group processes*. London: Routledge. (Hogg, M. A., & Abrams, D., 1988). Reproduced with permission.

Photos

The publisher would like to thank the following for their kind permission to reproduce their photographs:

Page 1: Rex Features / ITV; 8, 11: Pearson Online Database (POD); 12: iStockphoto / Andreas Reh; 17: Corbis / MM Productions; 25: DK Images / Neil Lukas / © Dorling Kindersley; 28: Alamy Images / Mark Harmel; 33 (left, right), 45: Pearson Online Database; 53: Getty Images / Daniel Berehulak; 56: Press Association Images / Cathal McNaughton / PA Archive; 63, 67: Pearson Online Database (POD); 73: Reuters / Fred Prouser; 78, 87: Pearson Online Database (POD); 93: ABACA / Press Association Images; 98: Pearson Online Database (POD); 101: Mohamad Torokman / Reuters; 104: Pearson Online Database (POD); 111: Imperial War Museum, London / DK Images; 123: Graham Vaughan; 131: Ricardo Azoury / Corbis; 140: AP Photo / Wathiq Khuzaie, Pool / Press Association Images; 145: Scanpix / Bertil Ericson Reuters; 153: Jim Young / Reuters; 155: Graham Vaughan; 158, 163, 171, 175: Pearson Online Database (POD); 186: Julien Behal / PA Archive / Press Association

Images; 193: Tsvangirayi Mukwazhi / Press Association Images; 202: Pearson Online Database (POD); 208: Wolfgang Rattay / Reuters; 211: Bob Strong / Reuters; 219 Janine Wiedel Photolibrary / Alamy Images; 223: Matty Stern / U.S. Embassy / Handout / Reuters; 229: Charles Platiau / Reuters; 237: BAE Inc. / Alamy Images; 240: Pearson Online Database (POD); 251: The Advertising Archives; 253: Peter Schols / GPD / Handout / Reuters; 261: Reuters; Ismail Zaydah; 269, 271, 276: Pearson Online Database (POD); 281: The Advertising Archives; 287: Alamy Images: Blend Images; 295, 304: Pearson Online Database (POD); 311: Rex Features / © Focus / Everett; 314: Rex Features / Everett Collection; 321: Photofusion Picture Library / Janine Wiedel; 332: Graham Vaughan; 335: Reuters / Asim Tanveer; 337: Pearson Online Database (POD); 340: Godfrey Boehnke; 345: Michael Hogg.

In some instances we have been unable to trace the owners of copyright material, and we would appreciate any information that would enable us to do so.

Chapter 1

What is social psychology?

What to look for

- Defining social psychology
- Social psychology's use of the scientific and other empirical methods
- Ethical issues for researchers
- The history of social psychology
- Social psychology in Europe

Focus questions

1. Should we replace a course in social psychology with a course in evolutionary social psychology? Students describe major qualities with some evolutionary significance that they would look for in a mate in Chapter 1 of MyPsychLab at www.mypsychlab.co.uk.

2. Would it ever be ethically acceptable to conceal aspects of the truth from a person volunteering to take part in a psychological experiment?

3. Many texts in social psychology imply that it is an American rather than an international discipline. Do you have a view on this?

Source: ITV / Rex Features

What is social psychology?

Social psychology
Scientific investigation of how the thoughts, feelings and behaviour of individuals are influenced by the actual, imagined or implied presence of others.

Social psychology is the part of psychology that studies human interaction: its manifestations, its causes, its consequences, and the psychological processes involved. A widely used and more technical definition given by Gordon Allport is that social psychology is 'the scientific investigation of how the thoughts, feelings and behaviours of individuals are influenced by the actual, imagined or implied presence of others' (Allport, 1954a, p. 5).

What does this mean? It's actually more straightforward than it seems. Social psychology is, like the rest of psychology, a science (more on this below): it develops psychological theories to explain human behaviour and tests these theories empirically through experiments and observation. Social psychology's focus is on what people think, what they feel, and what they do – the latter includes physical movement, but also what people say and how they say it. It is difficult to know directly what people are thinking and feeling (they are unobservable, internal and private) without inferring it from what they say and do (publicly observable behaviour) – one of social psychology's great challenges is to make reliable inferences about internal states from overt behaviour.

What makes social psychology distinctive from the rest of psychology is the last bit of the definition, to do with being 'influenced by the actual, imagined or implied presence of others'. Actual presence is easy. You are physically in the presence of other people – they may be close by or far away, you can see or hear them, and you may actually be interacting with them. Imagined presence is also easy – it is imagining being in the presence of other people, like anticipating giving a class presentation, playing a football match in a huge stadium, spending an evening with your friends.

Implied presence is more tricky – it refers to the way that human interaction assigns meaning to things. Typically this 'social meaning' is constructed and transferred through language (see Chapter 11) – we tend to think with words, words derive from language and communication, and language and communication would not exist without social interaction. A good example of implied presence is norms (see Chapter 5). For example, most of us do not drop litter, even when no one is watching and even if there is no possibility of ever being caught. This is because there are societal norms or conventions that have emerged through social interaction that proscribe littering. Such a norm implies the presence of other people and 'determines' behaviour even in the absence of other people.

Norms
Attitudinal and behavioural uniformities that define group membership and differentiate between groups.

Armed with this description, we can see how *social* psychology might differ from neighbouring or related disciplines. We have seen that it is different from general psychology because it focuses on social interaction, between individuals and within and between groups, and on how products of social interaction (the notion of implied presence) influence thought and behaviour. It differs from sociology and anthropology in that it focuses on the role of psychological processes that occur within the head of the individual person. In contrast sociology focuses on how groups, organisations, social categories and societies are organised, how they function and how they change. Anthropology is similar but focuses on culture; and traditionally non-industrial societies, in particular – what we might call 'exotic' cultures. In both cases the disciplines are mainly dealing with the group as a whole rather than the individual people who compose the group. There is a fine line in research in choosing the most suitable kind of data to collect as well as selecting the appropriate level of theory to account for what is found. We turn to this problem next.

Levels of explanation

Reductionism is the practice of explaining a phenomenon in terms of the language and concepts of a lower level of analysis. Society is explained in terms of groups, groups in terms of interpersonal processes, interpersonal processes in terms of intrapersonal cognitive mechanisms, cognition in terms of neuropsychology, neuropsychology in terms of biology, and so on. A problem of reductionist theorising is that it can leave the original scientific question unanswered. For example, the act of putting one's arm out of the car window to indicate an intention to turn can be explained in terms of muscle contraction, or nerve impulses, or understanding of and adherence to social conventions, and so on. If the level of analysis (or explanation) does not match the level of the question, then the question remains, in effect, unanswered. In researching interpersonal relations, to what extent does an explanation in terms of social neuroscience (dealt with below) really address how one person interacts with another?

Although a degree of reductionism is possibly necessary for theorising, too great a degree is undesirable. Social psychology has been criticised for being inherently reductionist because it tries to explain social behaviour in terms that are not social, such as cognitive and motivational processes (e.g. Moscovici, 1972; Taylor & Brown, 1979). Recent trends in social psychology towards social cognitive neuroscience and evolutionary psychology, explaining behaviour in terms of neural activity and genetic predisposition, can be criticised on the same grounds. Reflect now on the first focus question.

The problem is most acute when social psychologists try to explain group processes and intergroup relations. By tackling these phenomena exclusively in terms of personality, interpersonal relations or intra-psychic processes, social psychology may leave some of its most important phenomena inadequately explained – for example, prejudice, discrimination, stereotyping, conformity and group solidarity (Billig, 1976; Hogg & Abrams, 1988).

The Belgian social psychologist Willem Doise (1986) has suggested a way around this problem: accept that different levels of explanation exist but to make a special effort to construct theories that formally integrate concepts from different levels (see Table 1.1). One of the more successful attempts is social identity theory (Tajfel & Turner, 1979), in which both individual cognitive processes and large-scale social forces are used to explain intergroup behaviour (see Chapter 7). Doise's ideas have also been employed to reinterpret group cohesiveness by Michael Hogg (1992), attribution theories by Miles Hewstone (1989) and social representations by Doise and his colleagues (Doise, Clémence & Lorenzi-Cioldi, 1993). All of these researchers come from the European tradition in social psychology.

Social psychology and its close neighbours

Social psychology has developed in such a way that it sits at the intersection of disciplines (see Figure 1.1). It is influenced by and has influence on developments and perspectives outside social psychology – this interdisciplinary potential is one of the strengths of social psychology. Studies in social cognition (see Chapter 2) draw on experimental cognitive psychology. What is sometimes called individual psychology contributes personality tests and other diagnostic tests that can be used as correlates of social processes. Research dealing with social norms (see Chapter 5) and groups (see Chapter 6) brings social psychology into contact with sociology and social anthropology. Sociology has also influenced how the self is studied in social

Reductionism
A phenomenon in terms of the language and concepts of a lower level of analysis, usually with a loss of explanatory power.

Level of analysis (or explanation)
The types of concepts, mechanisms and language used to explain a phenomenon.

Table 1.1 Levels of explanation in social psychology

I. Intrapersonal
Analysis of how people organise their experience of the social environment (e.g. research on how we form an impression of another person – see Chapter 2).

II. Interpersonal and situational
Analysis of interpersonal interaction. Positional factors that are external to the situation, such as status, are not considered. The object of study is the dynamics of the relations at a given moment by given individuals in a given situation (e.g. meeting a total stranger for the first time on the Internet – see Chapter 10).

III. Positional
Analysis of interpersonal interaction in specific situations, but with the role of social position (e.g. status, identity) outside the situation taken into account (e.g. some research on social identity between groups who differ in status on the toss of a coin – see the study of minimal groups in Chapter 7).

IV. Ideological
Analysis of interpersonal interaction that considers the role of general social beliefs, and of social relations between groups (e.g. studies of natural groups in real life and some laboratory contexts, such as some research dealing with social representations and minority influence in Chapter 5 or with social identity in Chapter 7).

Source: Based on Doise (1986); Hogg (1992).

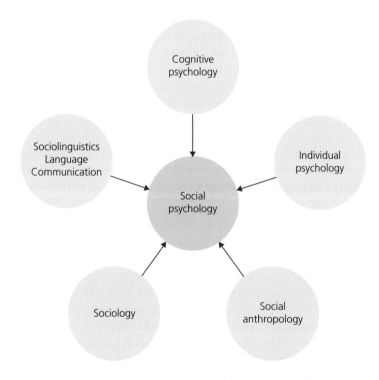

Figure 1.1

Social psychology and some close scientific neighbours.

Social psychology draws on a number of subdisciplines in general psychology for concepts and methods of research. It also has fruitful connections with other disciplines, mostly in the social sciences.

psychology (see Chapter 3) through *symbolic interactionism* associated with the work of G. H. Mead (1934) and Herbert Blumer (1969). There are also lines of research in social psychology (see Chapter 11) that interact with the subdisciplines of sociolinguistics, language and communication.

Social psychology has been influenced by Freud's psychodynamic analysis of the human mind – particularly the extension of his theory to groups, as described in his 1921 work 'Group psychology and the analysis of the ego'. As Michael Billig (1976) observed, psychodynamic notions have left a special and enduring mark on social psychology in the explanation of prejudice (see Chapter 7).

Social psychology has always been strongly influenced by general psychology, particularly cognitive psychology. Indeed *social cognition* (see Chapter 2), which is a cognitive perspective on social behaviour that employs cognitive methods (e.g. reaction time) and concepts (e.g. memory) to explain a wide range of social behaviours, is in many ways the dominant paradigm in social psychology (Devine, Hamilton & Ostrom, 1994; Fiske & Taylor, 2008). In recent years this focus on the cognitive dimension of social behaviour has, in the guise of *social neuroscience*, investigated the role of brain structures and processes in social cognition (e.g. Harmon-Jones & Winkielman, 2007).

Contemporary social psychology also abuts sociolinguistics and the study of language and communication as seen in the work of Howard Giles, and in some cases even literary criticism as used by Jonathan Potter (Giles & Coupland, 1991; Potter, Stringer & Wetherell, 1984). It also feeds a variety of applied areas of psychology, such as sports psychology, health psychology and organisational psychology.

Social psychology's location at the intersection of different disciplines is part of its intellectual and practical appeal. However, it is also a cause of vigorous debate about what constitutes social psychology as a distinct scientific discipline. If we lean too far towards individual cognitive processes, then perhaps we are pursuing individual psychology or cognitive psychology. If we go further and spend too much time gazing at neuro-imaging pictures perhaps we are neuroscientists. If we lean too far towards the role of language, then perhaps we are being scholars of language and communication. If we overemphasise the role of social structure in intergroup relations, then perhaps we are being sociologists. Social psychologists enjoy metatheoretical debate – that is, arguing over what constitutes social psychology, what kinds of theories social psychology should develop, and about what level of explanation social psychology should pursue.

Doing social psychology

Another way to define social psychology is in terms of what social psychologists study. Social psychologists generally do not study animals – they study people. Some principles of social psychology may be applicable to animals, and research on animals may provide evidence for processes that generalise to people. However, social psychologists believe that the study of animals does not take us very far in explaining human social behaviour, unless we are interested in its evolutionary origins (e.g. Schaller, Simpson & Kenrick, 2006).

What social psychologists do study can readily be gleaned from the contents of this book. We cover an enormous range of topics, including conformity, persuasion, power, influence, obedience, prejudice, prejudice reduction, discrimination, stereotyping, bargaining, sexism and racism, small groups, social categories, inter-group relations, crowd behaviour, social conflict and harmony, social change, overcrowding, stress, the physical environment, decision making, the jury, leadership, communication, language, speech, attitudes, impression formation, impression management, self-presentation, identity, the self, culture, emotion, attraction, friendship, the family, love, romance, sex, violence, aggression, altruism and prosocial behaviour (acts that are valued positively by society).

One problem with defining social psychology in terms of its topics, however, is that it overlooks the distinctive level of explanation that social psychology provides – as discussed above it focuses on social interaction and psychological processes in the head of the individual person. Another problem is that a focus on topics fails to capture *how* social psychology studies the phenomena it is interested in.

Science

Science
Method for studying nature that involves the collecting of data to test hypotheses.

Social psychology is a science. It is a science not because of what it researches but because of the way it researches. Science is a *method* for studying nature, and it is the method – not the people who use it, the things they study, the facts they discover nor the explanations they propose – that distinguishes science from other approaches to knowledge. In this respect, the main difference between social psychology and, say, physics, chemistry or biology is that the former studies human social behaviour, while the others study non-organic phenomena and chemical and biological processes.

Just as physics has concepts such as electrons, quarks and spin to explain physical phenomena, social psychology has concepts such as dissonance, attitude, categorisation and identity to explain social psychological phenomena. The scientific method dictates that no theory is 'true' simply because it is logical and seems to make sense, or because one simply believes it to be true. On the contrary, the validity of a theory is based on its correspondence with publicly verifiable fact. So, social psychologists develop hypotheses or predictions based on theories or past observations. They then collect data to test if the hypothesis is correct.

Theory
Set of interrelated concepts and principles that explain a phenomenon.

For example, let us propose that people are faster and more accurate at texting when others are watching them. This is our hypothesis and we could test it very simply by having some people text alone and other people texting when they are being closely watched. If our hypothesis was upheld we might go on to qualify our theory by predicting that this social facilitation effect on texting only occurs when people are already proficient at texting, and inept texters actually go more slowly when being watched. We could then go further to test this more complex hypothesis by having: (a) two kinds of people, proficient and inept texters; and (b) two contexts or conditions, texting alone or in front of an audience. If our elaborated hypothesis was supported we might go on to generate even more fine-grained hypotheses to test. This is a simple example of how an experimental science is developed.

Hypotheses
Empirically testable predictions about what goes with what, or what causes what.

But how do you know if any of your hypotheses are supported? Social psychologists analyse the data they collect to come to this conclusion. In general they are trying to determine that the effect they have found is not a chance event but a bona fide effect. In order to do this they conduct statistics.

Testing hypotheses

Some statistics are relatively straightforward but many are immensely complicated – the stuff of nightmares for undergraduate psychology students. In the simple examples above the data might be something like the number of correct text words typed in a given time – and statistical tests would generate a number, a statistic based on the size of the difference between the groups and the difference among individuals in each group, that allows the experimenter to know the probability that the effect was a chance phenomenon. The magic probability number in psychology is 0.05. If statistical tests show that the effect has a probability of less than 0.05 (i.e. less than 1-in-20) of being a chance event then one can consider it a true effect – one's hypothesis is supported. If the probability is greater than 0.05 then one's hypothesis is not supported and it is back to the drawing board – the hypothesis needs to be tested differently and/or reframed, or the theory needs to be modified (see Figure 1.2).

A key advantage of the scientific method is that when observed effects can be replicated by someone else it guards against fraud. If your team claims to have discovered X by doing Y, then another team can repeat Y to also discover X. The alternative to science is dogma or rationalism, where understanding is based on authority: something is true ultimately because an authority (e.g. the ancient philosophers, charismatic leaders or religious scriptures) says so. Valid knowledge is acquired by pure reason: that is, by learning well, and uncritically accepting, the pronouncements of authorities. Even though the scientific revolution, championed by such luminaries as Copernicus, Galileo and Newton, occurred in the sixteenth and seventeenth centuries, dogma and rationalism still exist as influential alternative paths to knowledge.

As a science, social psychology has in its toolbox an array of different methods for empirically testing hypotheses. There are two broad types of method, *experimental*

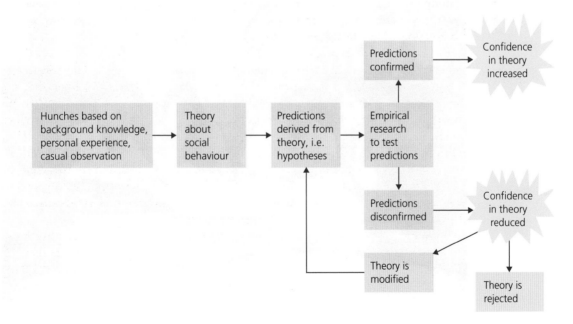

Figure 1.2

How social psychologists use the scientific method.

and *non-experimental*: each has advantages and limitations. The choice of an appropriate method is influenced by factors to do with the nature of the hypothesis under investigation, the resources available for doing the research (e.g. time, money, research participants) and the ethics of the method. Confidence that our hypothesis is true is greatly enhanced if the hypothesis has been supported a number of times by different research teams using different methods. Methodological pluralism helps to minimise the possibility that the finding is an artefact of a particular method, and replication by different research teams helps to avoid confirmation bias – a tendency for researchers to become so personally involved in their own theories that they lose some objectivity in interpreting data.

Experiments

An experiment is a hypothesis test in which something is done to see its effect on something else. Take the case of Henrietta who is both environmentally aware and keen to save some money. She hypothesises that her car greedily guzzles too much petrol because the tyres are under-inflated, so she conducts an experiment. She notes the petrol used over an average week. Then she increases the tyre pressure and again notes how petrol is used over an average week. If consumption is reduced, then her hypothesis is supported. Casual experimentation is one of the commonest and most important ways in which people learn about their world. It is an extremely powerful method because it allows us and Henrietta to identify the causes of events and thus to gain control over our destiny.

Not surprisingly, systematic experimentation is social psychology's most important research method. Social psychology is largely experimental, in that most social psychologists would prefer to test hypotheses experimentally if at all possible, and much of what we know about social behaviour is based on experiments. The

Experimental data. These students collected data in a social psychology experiment. They are now studying the results.

Source: Pearson Online Database (POD)

experimental method involves *intervention* in the form of *manipulation* of one or more independent variables, and then measurement of the effect of the manipulation on one or more dependent variables. Variation in the dependent variable is *dependent* on variation in the independent variable. In Henrietta's experiment the independent variable is tyre inflation, which was manipulated to create two experimental conditions (lower versus higher pressure). Henrietta's dependent variable is petrol consumption, which was measured on refilling the tank at the end of the week.

Experimentation is not easy. Much has been written about how to conduct successful experiments and how to avoid pitfalls that make it difficult to infer what causes what, as Eliot Aronson and others have explained (e.g. Aronson, Ellsworth, Carlsmith & Gonzales, 1990; Rosnow & Rosenthal, 1997). For example, it is important to make sure that when you manipulate a variable you do not inadvertently manipulate something else that might cause the effect. Say you wanted to test the hypothesis that people are more likely to donate money to a charity if requested in a quiet street than a noisy street, and you had one research confederate, Mary, do the requesting in the quiet street, and the other, John, doing it in a noisy street, you would not know if the effect was due to the noisiness of the street or the gender of the requester – gender and ambient noise are examples of confounding. Another potential problem might be that the request was so extreme (to donate 6 hours a week for 6 months) that no one would be likely to say yes no matter where asked or by whom – there is a *floor effect*. If the request had been to donate 20p then everyone would probably have said yes irrespective of requester or noisiness – there is a *ceiling effect*. A third problem is that participants might be able to discern what your hypothesis is and then intentionally behave in ways to confirm or refute your hypotheses. Martin Orne (1962), a pioneer in the experimental study of hypnosis, called these demand characteristics, after wondering if some of his patients were really hypnotised. In a university corridor he casually asked some individuals if they would take part in a brief experiment. When they agreed, he asked them to perform five push-ups. They typically replied 'Where?', not 'Why?'.

The word 'experiment' conjures up an image of white lab-coated experimenters clutching clipboards or sitting at consoles, and research participants wired up to machines in a high-tech laboratory, a place where you might see contraptions that beep and flash and benches with test tubes. Some social psychology experiments might have this flavour, though white coats are a very rare sight, and laboratories are rarely like this. Laboratories are typically just classrooms or rooms with tables and chairs, and experiments usually involve participants reading, watching or doing things and then filling out questionnaires.

The advantage of a laboratory experiment is that you or I can control the situation so that our manipulations are pure and not confounded. Experiments are intended to be clever, to create artificial situations that are rare in the outside world. In this way we can investigate psychological processes and cause–effect relationships that are difficult to isolate in natural circumstances. Experimenters intend their manipulations to be low on mundane realism – how similar the conditions are to those usually encountered by participants in natural circumstances. However, their aim is high on experimental realism – the manipulations must be full of psychological impact and charged with meaning for the participants.

Because lab experiments necessitate bringing people to a laboratory it has over time become expedient and cost effective to use university undergraduates as participants (Sears, 1986). Critics have suggested that this overreliance on students is creating a 'social psychology of the college sophomore' and not easily generalised

Experimental method
Intentional manipulation of independent variables in order to investigate effects on one or more dependent variables.

Independent variables
Features of a situation that change of their own accord, or can be manipulated by an experimenter to have effects on a dependent variable.

Dependent variables
Variables that change as a consequence of changes in the independent variable.

Confounding
Where two or more independent variables covary in such a way that it is impossible to know which has caused the effect.

Demand characteristics
Features of an experiment that seem to 'demand' a certain response.

Mundane realism
Similarity between circumstances surrounding an experiment and circumstances encountered in everyday life.

Experimental realism
Psychological impact of the manipulations in an experiment.

to other sectors of the population. In their defence, experimental social psychologists point out that theories, not experimental findings, are generalised, and that replication and using a variety of other methods will ensure that social psychology is about people, not just about psychology students.

It is difficult to perform experiments on some phenomena in the lab and some manipulations can actually be more powerful outside the lab. Very often, we want to do research on populations that one cannot easily bring into the lab – field experiments provide the answer. The charity donation example given earlier is a field experiment – a manipulation is conducted in the field. Field experiments have high mundane and experimental realism and, as participants are often unaware that an experiment is taking place, few demand characteristics are present. However, there is less control over extraneous variables and random assignment of participants to experimental conditions is sometimes difficult. It can also be difficult to record data accurately or measure subjective feelings: often, overt behaviour is all that can be measured.

Other research methods

Doing an experiment is usually the preferred research method in social psychology. However, there are circumstances where it is very difficult or impossible to properly test a hypothesis experimentally. For example, theories about the relationship between biological sex and decision making are not amenable to experimentation – we cannot manipulate biological sex in an experiment and see what effects emerge. Social psychology also confronts ethical issues that can prevent experimentation. For instance, hypotheses about the effects on self-esteem of being a victim of violent crime are not at all easily tested experimentally – we would not be able to assign participants randomly to two conditions and then subject one group to a violent crime and see what happened! We revisit ethical issues in the next section.

Where experimentation is impossible or inappropriate, social psychologists have a range of non-experimental methods from which to choose. We should note now that these methods do not involve the manipulation of independent variables against a background of random assignment of participants to condition. You might well ask: so what? The problem is that we will find it almost impossible to draw reliable cause–effect conclusions. Take an example. Suppose we try to compare the self-esteem of people who have been victims of violent crime with those who have not. We might like to think that any differences will be due to violent crime, but unfortunately they could be due to *other* differences between the two groups. We can only conclude that self-esteem and being the victim of violent crime are correlated. There is no evidence that one causes the other – being a victim may lower self-esteem or having lower self-esteem may increase the likelihood of becoming a victim. It is also possible that there is actually no causal relationship at all – a third variable such as chronic unemployment might both reduce self-esteem and expose one to violent crime. In general, non-experimental methods involve the examination of correlation between naturally occurring variables and as such do not permit us to draw causal conclusions. We should note that scientists often employ non-experimental methods. For example, the use of clinical diagnosis is important in medicine and observational data are crucial in astronomy.

Archival research is a non-experimental method that is useful for investigating large-scale, widely occurring phenomena that may be remote in time – for example a stock market crash, or a disastrous decision made by a government, such as groupthink, an idea explored by Irving Janis (1972; see Chapter 6). The researcher

Correlation
Where changes in one variable reliably map onto changes in another variable, but it cannot be determined which of the two variables *caused* the change.

Archival research
Non-experimental method involving the assembly of data, or reports of data, collected by others.

Archival research. Stored records can be a useful source of research data in social psychology.

Source: Pearson Online Database (POD)

has to make do with whatever is there – assembling data collected by others, often for reasons unconnected with those of the research project. Archival methods are often used to make comparisons between different cultures or nations regarding things such as suicide, mental health or child-rearing strategies. Archival research is of course not subject to demand characteristics, but can be unreliable because the researcher has no control over the primary data collection, which might be biased or unreliable in other ways (e.g. missing vital data).

Case studies are another non-experimental method. They involve in-depth analysis of a single case (a person, a group or an event) and are well suited to the study of unusual or rare phenomena that could not be created in the laboratory: for instance, mass murderers, bizarre cults or terrible disasters. Case studies employ a variety of data collection and analysis techniques involving structured and open-ended interviews and questionnaires, and the observation of behaviour. They are useful as a source of hypotheses, but findings can be compromised by the bias of the researcher, who is not blind to the hypothesis. Another issue is participant bias, such as demand characteristics discussed earlier as well as evaluation apprehension that people feel when they are the object of attention. Finally, findings of a case study may not easily be generalised to other cases.

A variant of the case study is discourse analysis, an approach that is popular in the United Kingdom and is associated with Margaret Wetherell and other researchers (Wetherell, Taylor & Yates, 2001). Here the focus is on what people actually say in naturally occurring conversation or 'discourse' and what is behind the mere words to detect underlying discursive themes. Effective discourse analysis requires a great deal of skill and expertise and is prone to subjectivity – the interpretation of the discourse resting heavily on the perspective and expertise of the researcher. However, when well executed it can be very effective at detecting attitudes and feelings that people are careful to hide – for example racist attitudes in western societies (van Dijk, 1987).

Another common non-experimental method is survey research. All of us have undoubtedly been surveyed at some point. A survey can involve a researcher interviewing us and noting down our responses, or it can be a questionnaire in which

Case study
In-depth analysis of a single case (or individual).

Evaluation apprehension
A concern about being evaluated by others who are present can lead to social facilitation

Discourse analysis
A set of methods used to analyse text, in particular, naturally occurring language, in order to understand its meaning and significance.

Survey research
Method in which a large and representative sample of people answer direct questions about their attitudes or behaviour.

we write down our own responses to questions on scales or in an open-ended format. Surveys can obtain a lot of data from a large sample of participants that is representative of the general population as a whole. Anonymous and confidential surveys that are well designed can measure people's true attitudes and feelings.

We have already described field experiments. The non-experimental equivalent is the field study, in which a non-intrusive and 'invisible' researcher simply observes, records and codes naturally occurring behaviour. Field studies are excellent for investigating spontaneous action sequences in a natural context. However, they are prone to observer bias and to distortions by the unintended impact of the researcher on the people being investigated. Field studies also lack objectivity and make for poor generalisations. On the other hand, they can be really exciting! Would you like to be an undercover cop in a drug bust sting or join a terrorist cell?

Field study
The gathering of animal or human behavioural data in a natural setting.

Doing research ethically

As researchers, social psychologists confront ethical issues. For instance, is it ethical to expose experimental participants to a treatment that is embarrassing or has potentially harmful effects on their self-concept? If such research is important, what are the rights of the person, what are the ethical obligations of the researcher, and what guidelines are there for deciding? A question of ethics arises most often in the psychological experiment. But they can also confront non-experimental researchers. For example, if you were a professional observer of crowd behaviour and witnessed a violent assault are you ethically obliged to at least try to intercede? It is not only the social psychologist who must think this kind of problem through. Journalists, doctors, lawyers and counsellors live with professional ethical issues as well.

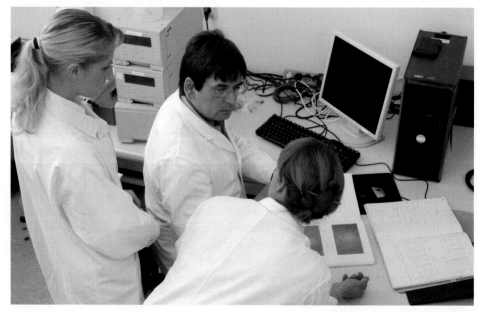

Human research ethics. Researchers know that people who volunteer to participate as subjects in research have clear rights specified by the APA's code of research ethics.

Source: Andreas Reh / iStockphoto

To guide researchers, the American Psychological Association established, in 1972 and updated in 2002, a set of principles for ethical conduct in research involving humans. In western countries universities do not permit research to go ahead unless it has been checked to conform to these principles. There are five ethical principles that have received most attention: protection from harm, right to privacy, deception, informed consent and debriefing.

Although it is pretty obvious that you should not *harm* your participants, much hinges on what is defined as 'harm'. Splinters under the fingernails is clearly harm, but what about telling participants they have done badly on a word-association task? It may have long-term effects on self-esteem and could therefore be considered harmful, but on the other hand, the effects may be so minor and transitory as to be insignificant. *Privacy* is more straightforward. Because research participants often give personal information and sometimes embarrassing and intimate information, researchers do their best to ensure confidentiality so that data cannot be traced back to individual participants.

Perhaps the most contentious issue is the use of deception in experiments. In experiments participants need to be unaware of the manipulations and the hypotheses being tested otherwise data would reflect deliberative responses rather than automatic reactions, and it would be impossible to study many psychological processes. A degree of deception is therefore often necessary – a review published in 1982 (Gross & Fleming, 1982) reported that over the previous twenty years between 50 and 75 per cent of published experiments involved some deception.

Because the use of deception seems to imply 'trickery', 'deceit' and 'lying', it has attracted a frenzy of criticism – ignited in the early 1960s by Diana Baumrind's (1964) attack on Stanley Milgram's (1963) studies of destructive obedience that you will read about in Chapter 5. Social psychologists have even been urged to abandon experiments altogether in favour of simulations or role-playing exercises (e.g. Kelman, 1967).

This is clearly too extreme, as social psychological knowledge has been enriched enormously by classic experiments that have used deception (many are described in this book). Although some experiments have used excessive deception, in practice the deception used in the overwhelming majority of social psychology experiments is trivial. For example, an experiment may be introduced as a study of group decision making when in fact it is part of a programme of research into prejudice and stereotyping. In addition, no one has yet shown any long-term negative consequences of the use of deception in social psychology experiments (Elms, 1982), and experimental participants themselves tend to be impressed, rather than upset or angered, by cleverly executed deceptions, and they view deception as a necessary withholding of information or as a necessary ruse (Sharpe, Adair & Roese, 1992). How would you address the second focus question?

One way to safeguard people's rights in experiments is to tell them 'the truth, the whole truth and nothing but the truth' about the experiment and that they are free to withdraw at any point, and then obtain in writing their *informed consent* to participate. In practice, however, 'full information' can be difficult to define, and, as we have just seen, experiments often require some deception in order that participants remain naive. Participants should also be fully *debriefed* after taking part in an experiment – they should learn all about the research and the research procedures so that they leave the laboratory with an increased respect for and understanding of social psychology.

A short history of social psychology

Although classical social and political philosophy considered such questions as the nature–nurture controversy, the origins of society and the function of the state, it was mostly a speculative exercise and devoid of fact gathering. A systematic empirical approach to the study of social psychology did not appear until the latter part of the nineteenth century.

The early days

The very earliest stirrings of social psychology can be traced to a group of scholars in Germany who were influenced by the philosopher Hegel. They called themselves *folk psychologists*. In 1860, Steinthal and Lazarus founded a journal devoted to this *Völkerpsychologie* that published theoretical and factual articles. Unlike general psychology, which was developed later by Wilhelm Wundt to focus on the individual mind, folk psychology dealt with the study of the *collective* mind. This concept of collective mind was interpreted in conflicting ways by Steinthal and Lazarus, meaning on the one hand a societal way of thinking within the individual and on the other a form of trans-individual mentality that could encompass a whole group of people.

Group mind
McDougall's idea that people adopt a qualitatively different mode of thinking when in a group.

This idea has been called the group mind and gained popularity in the 1890s and early 1900s through the work of the French writer Gustav LeBon (1896/1908) and later the English psychologist William McDougall (1920). Both, in slightly different ways, argued that people in crowds and perhaps some other collective or group situations behave antisocially and aggressively because they are under the control of a group mind. This notion that people are transformed by group situations is a theme that has pervaded social psychology, in different ways, ever since. For example Muzafer Sherif (1935) showed how social interaction produces norms that endure to regulate people's behaviour (Chapter 5). Henri Tajfel and John Turner (1979) distinguished between social identity which is associated with group processes and personal identity which is associated with interpersonal processes (Chapter 7). Philip Zimbardo (1970) described the way that people in groups can lose their sense of individuality and personal responsibility and regress to a more primitive and impulsive state and then behave aggressively (Chapter 8).

An early issue was whether social psychology should be a 'top-down' science, where the focus was on how societal processes influence the individual's psychology. Or should it be a 'bottom-up' science where the focus was on how individual psychology influences societal level phenomena? Two French sociologists debated this – Emile Durkheim (1898) championed the former approach, Gabriel Tarde (1898) championed the latter. Tarde's approach anticipated the subsequent tone of social psychology more accurately – he proposed that a science of social behaviour must derive from laws that deal with the individual case.

The two earliest writers of English language social psychology textbooks were the psychologist William McDougall (1908) in Britain and the sociologist E. A. Ross (1908) in America. Neither looks much like a modern social psychology text – their main topics were the principal instincts, the primary emotions, the nature of sentiments, moral conduct, volition, religious conceptions and the structure of character.

Social psychology as science

Things were changing, however. Social psychology, which as we have seen above, seemed to have its roots originally in sociology and, as historian Robert Farr (1996) observed, the study of society was being seduced by psychology as a whole that was quickly establishing itself as an experimental science. Willem Wundt had set up a psychological laboratory at Leipzig in 1879 to provide an experimental basis for psychology in Germany, and by 1910 there were 31 such laboratories across the United States (Ruckmick, 1912). These developments allowed the behaviourist John Watson to publish with confidence his classic scientific manifesto for psychology in 1913.

For social psychology the watershed publication was Floyd Allport's (1924) agenda for social psychology. Building on Watson, Allport argued that social psychology would flourish only if it became an experimental science. Shortly after, Gardner Murphy and Lois Murphy (1931/1937) felt justified in producing a book actually entitled *Experimental Social Psychology*. As a matter of both interest and controversy, social psychology's first experiment is often identified as Norman Triplett's (1898) study of how people can put more effort into a task when other people are present as observers or competitors (Chapter 6).

Over the past eighty years or so, social psychology as a science has developed astronomically. For example, social psychology's two main scientific bodies, the Society for Personality and Social Psychology and the European Association of Social Psychology, have between them a membership of over 5500 university academics.

The growth of the discipline has been marked by a number of trends, watersheds and classic research programmes. An early and enduring focus has been on people's attitudes – how to measure them, how they are structured in mind, how they are related to behaviour and how to change them (Chapter 4). Indeed, in the early days some scholars (e.g. Thomas & Znaniecki, 1918) even equated social psychology with the scientific study of attitudes. More modestly, one of social psychology's classic research programmes was all about attitudes. The Yale *attitude change* programme, led by Carl Hovland, was designed to uncover the theory and techniques of propaganda (Hovland, Janis & Kelley, 1953). Another line of research, associated with Leon Festinger's enormously popular theory of cognitive dissonance, focused on how inconsistencies between one's attitudes and behaviour can change one's attitudes (Festinger, 1957). Attitudes are still a key focus of social psychology (Eagly & Chaiken, 1993; Maio & Haddock, in press).

Another early and very influential focus has been on the behaviour of people in groups (Chapters 6 and 7, and to an extent Chapter 5). Kurt Lewin, often considered the 'father' of experimental social psychology, played a key role in the study of group processes (Marrow, 1969). He conducted early classic studies of leadership in groups (Lewin, Lippitt & White, 1939) and went on to found in 1945 a research centre devoted to the study of group dynamics (which still exists, in a different guise and now at the University of Michigan). Lewin is often quoted as saying 'there is nothing so practical as a good theory', and as being a passionate advocate of a tight link between basic and applied laboratory and field research – positions that have helped create an enduring bridge between social psychology and the organisational sciences.

See Box 1.1 for a summary of crucial contributions that paved the way for the development of social psychology. Most of the studies mentioned are covered in more detail in other chapters.

Research classic 1.1
Early breakthroughs in social psychology

In 1898, Norman Triplett published a study on the effects of competition on physical performance. Track cyclists were clocking faster speeds in paced events or races than they did when racing alone, as in modern time trials. He mimicked this effect among children. They raced in pairs, or else went as fast as they could alone, by winding a loop of cord quickly several times around a set of reels. Although not strictly a study of *social facilitation*, it paved the way for later work by Floyd Allport (1924) that dissected how the presence of others influences the way people perform tasks. Robert Zajonc (1965) added a modern slant, suggesting that having an audience energised people to try harder, just as it did for cockroaches when watched by other cockroaches!

The study of attitudes flourished in the 1930s after Louis Thurstone (1928) developed an ingenious scale for measuring attitudes. Following this, there was interest in assessing religious and racial beliefs, but the most dramatic application was in politics, and in predicting elections. At this time, Muzafer Sherif (1936) was first to ask how it is that *norms* control the way we interpret what we see, providing the impetus for Solomon Asch (1951) to find out why we often conform to group pressure. In another field, Kurt Lewin discovered that work groups most often performed better when the leader was democratic rather than autocratic (Lewin, Lippitt & White, 1939) – a finding that did not fit well with the assumptions of fascist regimes. Later explorations of *leadership* owed much to this seminal study.

In 1946 Asch reported that people used a few simple strategies to form a first impression of another person. This work was supplemented by Fritz Heider's (1958) research into how the way we perceive others contributes to the nature of our relationships with them. This was a springboard for later studies in *social cognition*. The same line of work is not far removed from the contributions made by Ned Jones (Jones & Davis, 1965) and Harold Kelley (1967) to the study of *attribution*, and more generally to understanding the human need to give life meaning.

The wartime use of propaganda was a starting point for research into the most effective ways to use mass persuasion techniques. Carl Hovland was first contracted by the US War Department to investigate how propaganda could be used to support the American war effort. This was followed by a series of studies featuring how a message should be framed, the role of the audience, and why some communicators fare better than others (Hovland, Janis & Kelley, 1953). Around this time Leon Festinger (1957) developed his influential theory of cognitive dissonance: we get bothered when our attitudes are inconsistent and also try hard to ensure that our attitudes are in line with our actions.

Perhaps the most dramatic psychological studies ever conducted were those by Stanley Milgram (1963). Like many people, he reacted strongly to the many horrors of the Second World War, of which the holocaust was a massive symbol. A major perpetrator within the Nazi regime was Adolf Eichmann, and his defence that he was actually just carrying out his Fuehrer's orders was a trigger for research. He commenced his work on what he called destructive obedience – the willingness of ordinary people to inflict suffering upon other ordinary people when ordered to do so by a legitimate authority. More than any other line of research, this contributed to the establishment of an ethical research code for psychologists.

All of these studies originated in the United States and this reflects the reality of how social psychology developed. It emerged as an organised discipline with the rapid establishment of American psychology departments at the turn of the nineteenth and twentieth centuries (Ruckmick, 1912). It was not until the 1970s that social psychology 'came of age' in Europe (Jaspars, 1980).

The group dynamics tradition of focusing on interaction within small groups continues to flourish but has in the past two decades been expanded into a broader and more integrated social psychology of group processes and intergroup relations (e.g. Hogg, Kelley & Williams, in press; Stangor, 2004). The intergroup relations component has a long tradition of focusing on cooperation, competition and conflict between groups (Sherif & Sherif, 1953), on the roles of categorisation and

Intergroup discrimination. An early study by Sherif showed that competition led to conflict and then discrimination among groups of children. This is heightened when the groups compete for a goal that only one group can win.

Source: MM Productions / Corbis

identity in group life (Tajfel & Turner, 1979), on the role of authoritarianism in prejudice and discrimination (e.g. Adorno, Frenkel-Brunswik, Levinson & Sanford, 1950), and on prejudice and discrimination in general (Dovidio, Hewstone, Glick & Esses, in press). This intergroup dimension has generated some classic studies – for example, Muzafer Sherif's studies of competition and cooperation among groups at a boys' summer camp in the United States (Sherif, Harvey, White, Hood, & Sherif, 1961), and Henri Tajfel's (1970; Tajfel, Billig, Bundy & Flament, 1971) classic experiment showing that merely being categorised into groups was sufficient to cause people to discriminate between groups.

Another central theme in social psychology has been a focus on how people influence one another and on how groups develop norms that influence members (Chapter 5). We will look in detail at several famous experiments in this field. Muzafer Sherif (1935) conducted a classic experiment in which small laboratory groups developed norms to guide how they judged the apparent movement of a pinpoint of light (the autokinetic illusion); Solomon Asch (1951) showed how an individual could be persuaded to make completely erroneous judgements just because the rest of the group did; Stanley Milgram (1963) was able to make ordinary people obey commands to inflict what they thought were severe, even deadly, shocks to other research participants just because they made mistakes on a learning task; Philip Zimbardo (1971) showed how students assigned to the role of prisoner or guard in a simulated prison went overboard in adhering to their roles; and Serge Moscovici (1980) described how people could be swayed by a minority. One intriguing experiment in the minority influence tradition, on colour perception, showed how a consistent minority could actually bring people apparently to see 'blue' as 'green'. Research on influence is still a central topic of social psychology.

Many of us come to social psychology to try to make sense of our interpersonal relationships and important experiences – friendship and love, romance and despair. John Thibaut and Harold Kelley (1959) developed a far-reaching and influential social exchange approach to interpersonal relationships that characterised them as based on relatively rational exchanges of valued resources, including liking and support, among people. Interpersonal relations are discussed in Chapter 10.

Social psychologists have always been interested in how we perceive and think about other people – indeed social cognition (Chapter 2) is probably the dominant way in which social psychologists approach social psychology (Fiske & Taylor, 2008; Hamilton & Stroessner, in press). This approach has its roots in early classic research on how we perceive people, social perception, by Fritz Heider (1946) and Solomon Asch (1946). In the 1960s, it was driven by Ned Jones (Jones & Davis, 1965), and focused on the causes and consequences of the sorts of causal explanations we make of people's behaviours – attribution theories. In 1980 Richard Nisbett and Lee Ross published a classic book that broadened the remit of social cognition to concentrate on the mental short cuts (heuristics) we use when we make cognitive inferences about people and groups. Most recently, social cognition researchers have started investigating the neuropsychology of social behaviour (e.g. Harmon-Jones & Winkielman, 2007).

Europe

Although, as our historical overview has shown, the beginnings of social psychology, and psychology as a whole, were in Europe, the United States quickly assumed leadership in terms not only of idea but also of journals, books and organisations. Part of this was simply because of the nineteenth-century rise of the United States as an economic power in the world. However, the 1930s rise of Fascism that culminated in the Second World War had a uniquely destructive effect – it decimated European social psychology so that by 1945 it was effectively non-existent. During an approximately fifteen-year period there was a massive exodus of Jewish and liberal German academics, mainly to the United States. This decisively shifted the centre of gravity for the developing discipline of social psychology.

From 1945 into the 1950s the United States provided resources (e.g. money and academic links) to (re-)establish centres of European social psychology. These centres were linked to the United States rather than to one another. There were few links among European social psychologists, who were often unaware of one another. Europe was largely an outpost of American social psychology. Gradually, however, European social psychologists did learn more about each other. They also became conscious that European and American interests in, and approaches to, social psychology were not the same. For instance, the recent European experience was one of war and conflict, while America's last major conflict within its own borders was its Civil War in the 1860s. Not surprisingly, Europeans felt they were more concerned with intergroup relations and groups, while Americans seemed more interested in interpersonal relations and individuals. Europeans pushed for a more *social* social psychology.

The first step towards this intellectual and organisational independence from the United States was to begin to integrate European social psychology from within Europe. A series of meetings took place; in Sorrento in 1963, Frascati in 1964 and Royaumont/Paris in 1966. The 1966 meeting established the European Association of Experimental Social Psychology. Ever since, this acted as the organisational mechanism to promote social psychology in Europe – it holds a conference every three years, sponsors a summer school, funds an array of scientific meetings across Europe, and in 1971 launched the now highly influential *European Journal of Social Psychology*. European social psychology also has a prestigious theory and review journal – the *European Review of Social Psychology*, launched in 1990 and published annually.

Since the early 1970s European social psychology has undergone a powerful and continuing renaissance (Jaspars, 1986). Initially, it set itself up in opposition to American social psychology and adopted an overtly critical stance. However, since the late 1980s European social psychology, although not discarding its critical orientation, has attained self-confidence. In the light of substantial international recognition it 'grew up'. Its impact, particularly on American social psychology, is now significant and well acknowledged. These days the flow of ideas (and academics and students) across the Atlantic is genuinely in both directions.

Europe is a continent of many languages and a historical diversity of national emphases on different aspects of social psychology: for example, the study of social representations in France, political psychology and small-group processes in Germany, social justice research and social cognition in the Netherlands, social development of cognition in French-speaking Switzerland, goal-oriented action in German-speaking Switzerland, applied and social constructionist approaches in Scandinavia, and discourse analysis and intergroup relations in the United Kingdom. However, it is through work on social representations (Chapter 2), minority influence (Chapter 5) and social identity and intergroup behaviour (Chapter 7) that Europe has had its most visible and significant international impact.

Historically, there are two figures that have particularly shaped European social psychology: Henri Tajfel and Serge Moscovici. Tajfel (1974), at the University of Bristol, developed a new approach to the study of intergroup relations. His *social identity theory* focused on intergroup relations emphasising the role of categorisation and how people's identity is defined in terms of the groups they belong to. It questioned Sherif's argument that a clash of interests or competition over resources was necessary for intergroup conflict (Chapter 7). Moscovici (1961), at the Maison des Sciences de l'Homme in Paris, resuscitated an interest in the work of the nineteenth-century sociologist Emile Durkheim with his idea of *social representations* (Chapter 2). In addition, he developed a radical perspective on social influence and conformity that focused on the role of active minorities in changing the attitudes of the majority and thus producing social change (Chapter 5). In reflecting on what you have just read, do you think that Europe has contributed something to international social psychology (see the third focus question)?

Back to the future

Where is social psychology headed? When making predictions it can be difficult to dissociate genuine trends from fads, or developments that are effectively old ideas dressed in new clothing. However, there are a handful of more reliable trends, many tied to events in our social world.

Research on intergroup behaviour continues to develop – social identity theory has a high profile here, but there is, not surprisingly, a growing focus on religion, extremism, terrorism and the psychology of 'evil'. Related to the study of intergroup behaviour is a concern that theories are too dry and cognitive to account for the passion and emotional heat of, for example, prejudice, bigotry and genocide – there is a growing focus on emotions.

Social cognition remains a dominant perspective in social psychology; however, there is an explosion of interest in mapping the physiological brain activity associated with social cognition. Social neuroscience is a clear new trend in social psychology. Another trend over the past decade has been an interest in the evolutionary dimension of social behaviour – interest has grown but there is now some evidence that it may have reached a plateau. Finally, the study of social dimensions of health behaviour is a very strong applied theme – quite likely set to become stronger as global health problems (e.g. obesity) assume a higher profile.

Two other areas that are quite likely to take off are the study of electronic communication (via computer and mobile phone), and the study of social issues revolving around mass immigration.

Summary

- Social psychology is the scientific study of how people's thoughts, feelings and behaviour are influenced by the actual, imagined or implied presence of others. Although social psychology can be described in terms of what it studies, it is more useful to describe it as a way of looking at human behaviour.

- Social psychology employs the scientific method to study social behaviour. Although this involves a range of empirical methods to collect data to test hypotheses and construct theories, experimentation is preferred as it is the best way to discover what *causes* what. Nevertheless, methods are yoked to research questions, and methodological pluralism is highly valued.

- Social psychology is enlivened by fierce and invigorating debates about the ethics of research methods, the appropriate research methods for an understanding of social behaviour, the validity and power of social psychology theories, and the type of theories that are properly social psychological.

- Although having origins in nineteenth-century German folk psychology and French crowd psychol-

ogy, modern social psychology really took off in the United States in the 1920s with the adoption of the experimental method.

- Despite its European origins, social psychology became dominated by the United States – a process accelerated by 1930s European Fascism and the subsequent Second World War.

- Since the 1960s there has been a rapid and sustained renaissance of European social psychology. Europe has a set of distinctive intellectual and sociohistorical priorities to develop a more *social* social psychology with an emphasis on intergroup relations. Social psychology in Europe is now a dynamic and well-established discipline and its research makes it an equal but complementary partner to zthat in the United States.

- Current and possible future directions in social psychology include intergroup behaviour, extremism, emotions, social neuroscience, social psychology and health, immigration, and possibly evolutionary social psychology and electronic communication.

Literature, film and TV

Das Experiment

This 2001 Oliver Hirschbiegel film, in German with English subtitles, starts with a fairly accurate treatment of Zimbardo's Stanford prison experiment. It engages with ethical issues associated with the research, but deteriorates rapidly into a dramatisation that would do Hollywood proud. This is a good example of how the popular media can seriously distort science and scientific issues and debates. A more recent 2008 film, again German, that builds on Zimbardo and shows how science can go wrong, is *Die Welle* (*The Wave*). A school teacher's attempt to demonstrate to his class what life is like under dictatorship spins horribly out of control as the class takes on a life of its own.

The Double Helix

James Watson's (1968) book is an account of how Francis Crick and James Watson identified the structure of DNA, for which they won the Nobel Prize. The book is very readable, engrossing and even thrilling. It shows how science is conducted – the rivalries, the squabbles, the competition, set against the backdrop of great minds and great discoveries. It captures the excitement of doing science.

Bad Science

A weekly column in *The Guardian* in which Ben Goldacre skewers those who distort and misrepresent science for the sake of spin, promotion or a headline.

Lord of the Flies

William Golding's (1954) classic novel about the disintegration of civilised social norms among a group of boys marooned on an island. A powerful portrayal of a whole range of social psychological phenomena, including leadership, intergroup conflict, norms and cultures, conformity, deviance, aggression. A very social psychological book!

War and Peace

Leo Tolstoy's (1869) masterpiece on the impact of society and social history on people's lives. It does a wonderful job of showing how macro- and micro-levels of analysis influence one another, but cannot be resolved into one another. A wonderful literary work of social psychology – how people's day-to-day lives are located at the intersection of powerful interpersonal, group and intergroup processes. Other classic novels of Leo Tolstoy, Emile Zola, Charles Dickens and George Eliot, accomplish much the same social psychological analysis.

Reality TV

At the opposite end of the spectrum from *War and Peace* is reality TV (e.g. *Big Brother; I'm a Celebrity, Get Me Out of Here*), which is actually all about social psychology. Themes include human interaction in groups, interpersonal relations, aggression and helping others.

Guided questions

- What do social psychologists study? Can you give some examples of interdisciplinary research?

- Sometimes experiments are used in social psychological research. Why?

- What do you understand by *levels of explanation* in social psychology? What is meant by *reductionism*?

- If you or your lecturer were to undertake research in social psychology you would need to gain ethical approval. Why is this, and what criteria would be required?

- If the shock level 'administered' in Miligram's obedience study had been 150 volts instead of the maximum 450 volts, would this have made the experiment more ethical? Watch the video illustrating this pivotal research in Chapter 1 of MyPsychLab at www.mypsychlab.co.uk.

Learn more

Baumeister, R., & Vohs, K. (eds) (2007). *Encyclopedia of social psychology*. Thousand Oaks, CA: Sage. An excellent place to go to find relatively short and accessible bite-sized coverage of topics in social psychology.

Crano, W. D., & Brewer, M. B. (2002). *Principles and methods of social research* (2nd ed). Mahwah, NJ: Erlbaum. A nice and accessible but scholarly coverage of social psychology research methods.

Fiske, S. T., Gilbert, D. T., & Lindzey, G. (eds) (in press). *The handbook of social psychology* (5th ed). New York: Wiley. Now in its fifth edition this two-volume tome is considered the 'gold standard' of social psychology; it is comprehensive and very detailed – a dense read, but everything you ever wanted to know about social psychology is here.

Hogg, M. A., & Cooper, J. (eds) (2007). *The Sage handbook of social psychology: Concise student edition*. London: Sage. A very readable series of scholarly chapters by leading social psychologists – it covers the main topics of social psychology, including the history of social psychology.

Hogg, M. A., & Vaughan, G. M. (2008). *Social psychology* (5th ed). London: Prentice Hall. A text written for university students studying social psychology as their main focus, this is a detailed and comprehensive introduction to social psychology that goes well beyond the essentials.

 Refresh your understanding, assess your progress and go further with interactive summaries, questions, podcasts, videos and much more on the website accompanying the book: **www.mypsychlab.co.uk**.

Chapter 2

Social thinking

What to look for

- How we process social information
- Forming impressions of other people
- Social schema and social categories
- Encoding persons in memory
- Biases and mental short cuts in social inference
- How thinking interacts with feelings and emotions
- Explaining our own and other people's behaviour
- Attributing the causes of behaviour
- The nature of biases in attribution
- Attributions made about groups
- Social representations, rumour and conspiracy theories

Focus questions

1. You have just been interviewed for a job. Ms Jones in the personnel department has decided that you are intelligent, sincere and helpful. However, you did not laugh readily at one of her jokes – she may suspect you don't have a sense of humour! How would she form an overall impression of you?

2. John's hair is multi-coloured and the colours change every couple of weeks. Would others spot him immediately at a student–staff meeting in your university department? What about at a board meeting of your capital city's largest accountancy firm?

3. Aaron comes to mind rather differently for Julie and Rosa. Julie remembers him mostly when she thinks of the various lawyers whom she knows. Rosa thinks about his quirky smile and his knowledge of best-selling novels. Why might their memories differ in these ways?

4. Helen is angry with her husband Lewis who avoids approaching his boss for a pay rise. Lewis argues that the timing is not right. Helen says he simply fails to face up to people. How are these attributions different in kind? Watch Helen and Lewis debate this in Chapter 2 of MyPsychLab at www.mypsychlab.co.uk.

5. You read a newspaper report about a rape case in which the defence lawyer pointed out that a young woman was actually dressed provocatively. What attributional bias is involved here?

6. The job market was tight and Rajna began to worry that she might be made redundant. Then she heard a rumour that the worst had come – several staff were about to be fired. She was itching to pass this on to the next colleague that she saw. Why would Rajna want to spread the rumour further?

As we saw in Chapter 1, social psychology studies how human thoughts, feelings and behaviours are influenced by and have influence on other people. Within this broad definition, thought has occupied a pivotal role: people think about their social world, and on the basis of thought they act in certain ways. Psychologists use another term in their treatment of our thinking processes. While thought and cognition are often used interchangeably in popular language, there are some differences in emphasis made within psychology. *Thought* is very much the internal language and symbols we use. It is often conscious, or at least something we are or could be aware of. The term *cognition* has another connotation since it also refers to mental processing that can be largely automatic. We are unaware of it and only with some effort notice it, let alone characterise it in language or shared symbols. In this sense, cognition acts like a computer program: it operates in the background, running all the functions of the computer that we are aware of.

Cognition is a mental activity that occurs in one's mind to process, make sense of and store perceptual information, and to plan and programme what we do and say. Cognition cannot be observed directly, so we infer it from people's expressions, actions, writings and sayings. If we can understand cognition, we can also gain an understanding of how and why people behave in the ways they do.

In this chapter we look in some detail at thought itself. We introduce the topic of social cognition, doing so within the context of how we form impressions of people. We deal with the ways we organise these impressions to construct apparently real mental pictures (*schemas*) of them, and the short cuts (*cognitive heuristics*) we use as we do this. We then consider how humans seek to explain behaviour. Finally, we ask an intriguing question: are people merely driven by curiosity when they try to uncover causes, as if they are amateur scientists, or are they searching for an account of life that makes living seem reasonably predictable?

Social cognition
Cognitive processes and structures that influence and are influenced by social behaviour.

Cognitive consistency
A model of social cognition in which people try to reduce inconsistency among their cognitions, because they find inconsistency unpleasant.

Naive scientist (or psychologist)
Model of social cognition that characterises people as using rational, scientific-like, cause–effect analyses to understand their world.

Forming impressions of people

Social psychology has always developed theories of cognitive activity to explain social behaviour (Jones, 1998; Taylor, 1998), and since the late 1970s this approach, called social cognition (e.g. Fiske & Taylor, 2008; Hamilton & Stroessner, in press; Moskowitz, 2005), has dominated the field and had an enormous impact on social psychology (Devine, Hamilton & Ostrom, 1994).

Social cognition has taken different forms over the years. For example, Kurt Lewin, who is often considered the 'father' of experimental social psychology (Marrow, 1969), believed that behaviour is best understood as a function of how people perceive their world and manipulate and interrelate these mental representations (e.g. Lewin, 1951). During the 1940s and 1950s social psychologists researching attitude change produced a number of theories sharing an assumption that people strive for cognitive consistency. These theories assumed that people feel uncomfortable when their thoughts are contradictory, and engage in all manner of behaviours and rationalisations, including changing their attitudes, to resolve the inconsistency (e.g. Abelson *et al.*, 1968; Festinger, 1957; Heider, 1958; see Chapter 4).

Consistency theories lost popularity in the 1960s as it became clear that people are remarkably tolerant of cognitive inconsistency. Researchers next adopted a naive scientist model, which characterised people as having a need to attribute causes to behaviour and events in order to render the world a meaningful place in which to act. This model underpins the attribution theories of social behaviour that dominated social psychology in the 1970s – we look at these later in this chapter. The naive scientist model assumed that people are rational and scientific when they analyse cause and effect.

By the late 1970s, however, research was suggesting that people are either very poor scientists who are compromised by limited cognitive capacity, or are irrational and motivated by self-interest, or both. All sorts of errors and biases creep in. Even in ideal circumstances people are not very careful scientists and they take cognitive short cuts. Richard Nisbett and Lee Ross (1980) used the colourful phrase cognitive misers to describe how we are often economic rather than accurate when jumping to a conclusion. However, the various errors and biases in our social thinking are not motivated departures from some ideal form of information processing – they are actually intrinsic to social thinking. In this account, the term 'motivation' had almost disappeared from the description of the cognitive miser. However, as Carolin Showers and Nancy Cantor (1985) noted in their review, the cognitive miser perspective matured further and motivation regained its prominence. The social thinker was now a motivated tactician who was:

> a fully engaged thinker who has multiple cognitive strategies available and chooses among them based on goals, motives, and needs. Sometimes the motivated tactician chooses wisely, in the interests of adaptability and accuracy, and sometimes . . . defensively, in the interests of speed or self-esteem. *(Fiske & Taylor, 1991, p. 13)*

In social psychology today, social cognition focuses on how cognition is affected by both wider and more immediate social contexts and on how cognition affects our social behaviour. Social cognition is also an approach to research that uses an array of methods, largely borrowed and refined from cognitive psychology.

A recent development in social cognition is social neuroscience (Harmon-Jones & Winkielman, 2007). It is largely a methodology where cognitive activity is monitored by functional magnetic resonance imaging (fMRI), which detects and localises electrical activity in the brain associated with cognitive activities or functions. Social neuroscience is increasingly being applied to many social psychological phenomena. For example, different parts of the brain may 'light up' when people are thinking positively or negatively about friends or strangers or social categories, and in general about interpersonal processes. Matthew Lieberman and his associates have outlined how social neuroscience can be applied to the study of how people look for causes of behaviour (Lieberman, Gaunt, Gilbert & Trope, 2002), a field known as causal attribution that is discussed later in this chapter. Other studies have pursued a search for a so-called 'God spot': has the human brain evolved in such a way that believing in God might improve our chances of survival? A research team led by Jordan Grafman and his colleagues (Kapogiannis *et al.*, 2009) has reported that neural activity increased when people think about God's involvement in our daily lives. Researchers in neuroscience are nothing if not inventive in the topics they now choose to investigate!

Joseph Forgas and Craig Smith (2003) have described another recent development that has gathered momentum – a focus on how feelings (affect, emotion, mood) influence and are influenced by social cognition. Different situations (funeral, party) evoke different emotions (sad, happy), but also the same situation (examination) can evoke different emotions (anxiety, challenge) in different people

Attribution
The process of assigning a cause to our own behaviour, and that of others.

Cognitive miser
A model of social cognition that characterises people as using the least complex and demanding cognitions that are able to produce generally adaptive behaviours.

Motivated tactician
A model of social cognition that characterises people as having multiple cognitive strategies available, which they choose among on the basis of personal goals, motives and needs.

Social neuroscience
The exploration of the neurological underpinnings of the processes traditionally examined by social psychology.

Social neuroscience. Increased neural activity in specific areas of the brain may indicate that the person is having a particular thought or a particular feeling.

Source: © Mark Harmel / Alamy

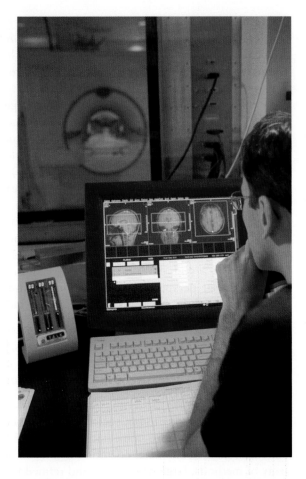

(weak student, competent student). Research suggests that people continually appraise their hopes, desires and abilities, and the situation they find themselves in (see Box 2.1).

These cognitive *appraisals* generate or are associated with specific emotions (such as fear, anger or guilt) and physiological reactions (such as elevated heart rate and trembling) that together ready one to take some form of action. There is also some evidence, from Forgas's (1995) affect-infusion model, that the way we think about people is most infused by the mood we are in when: (1) we need to think longer and more constructively; and (2) we actively elaborate the details of a stimulus (e.g. another person or our health) and can draw on details from memory.

There is no doubt that social cognition has advanced social psychology immensely – as you will see below. However, critics have felt that some aspects of social cognition focus too much on cognitive activity and brain functioning within the head of the isolated individual and too little on social interaction among individuals and processes within and between groups. Make up your own mind as you read on.

Affect–infusion model
Cognition is infused with affect such that social judgements reflect current mood.

Which impressions are important?

People spend a great deal of time thinking about other people. We form impressions of people we meet, have described to us or encounter in the media. We communicate these impressions to others, and we use them as bases for deciding

Research and applications 2.1
Appraisals leading to emotional responses

According to Smith and Lazarus (1990), emotional response rests on seven appraisals that can be framed as questions that people ask themselves in particular situations.

Primary appraisals

1 How relevant (important) is what is happening to my needs and goals?

2 Is this congruent (good) or incongruent (bad) with my needs or goals?

Secondary appraisals

1 How responsible am I for what is happening?

2 How responsible is someone or something else?

3 Can I act on this situation to make or keep it more like what I want?

4 Can I handle and adjust to this situation however it might turn out?

5 Do I expect this situation to improve or to get worse?

These appraisal dimensions produce an array of emotional and behavioural responses. For example, if something were important and bad and caused by someone else, we would feel anger and be motivated to act towards the other person in a way that would fix the situation. If something were important and bad, but caused by us, then we would feel shame or guilt and be motivated to make amends.

---

how we will feel and act. Impression formation and person perception are important aspects of social cognition (Schneider, Hastorf & Ellsworth, 1979).

Control impressions

We are very quick to use personality traits when we describe other people, even those we have just met (Gawronski, 2003). However, the impressions we form are influenced by some bits of information more than others. Very early on, Solomon Asch (1946) argued that some attributes are strongly related in our minds to a large number of other attributes – knowing someone has one of these attributes allows one to infer a great deal about a person and readily form an integrated impression of that person. These attributes he called central traits, to distinguish them from less diagnostic attributes that he called peripheral traits.

To investigate this idea, Asch had students read one of two lists of seven adjectives (traits) describing a hypothetical person. The lists differed only slightly – embedded in one was the word *warm* and in the other the word *cold*. The students then evaluated the target person on a number of other dimensions, such as generous/ungenerous, happy/unhappy, reliable/unreliable. Students who read the list containing *warm* formed a much more favourable impression of the target than did those exposed to the list containing the trait *cold* (see Figure 2.1). When the words *warm* and *cold* were replaced by *polite* and *blunt*, the difference in impression was far less marked. Asch argued that warm/cold is a central trait dimension that has more influence on impression formation than polite/blunt, which is a peripheral trait dimension.

Perhaps you are now wondering how ordinary people, or social psychologists for that matter, decide which traits are central and which peripheral. Asch believed that central traits are ones that are intrinsically highly correlated with other traits.

Central traits
Traits that have a disproportionate influence on the configuration of final impressions, in Asch's configural model of impression formation.

Peripheral traits
Traits that have an insignificant influence on the configuration of final impressions, in Asch's configural model of impression formation.

Figure 2.1

Impressions of a hypothetical person, based on central and peripheral traits.

Asch (1946) presented students with a 7-trait description of a hypothetical person in which either the word *warm* or *cold*, or *polite* or *blunt* appeared. The percentage of students assigning other traits to the target was markedly affected when *warm* was replaced by *cold*, but not when *polite* was replaced by *blunt*.

Source: Based on Asch (1946).

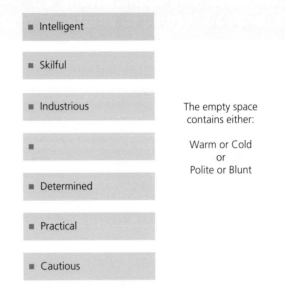

The empty space contains either:

Warm or Cold
or
Polite or Blunt

% assigning additional traits as function of focal trait inserted:

Additional traits	Focal traits inserted in the list			
	Warm	Cold	Polite	Blunt
Generous	91	8	56	58
Wise	65	25	30	50
Happy	90	34	75	65
Good-natured	94	17	87	56
Reliable	94	99	95	100

Personal constructs
Idiosyncratic and personal ways of characterising other people.

Implicit personality theories
Idiosyncratic and personal ways of characterising other people and explaining their behaviour.

However, others such as Mark Zanna and David Hamilton (1972) argued that what makes a trait central is influenced by context. In Figure 2.1, a trait that is distinctive (e.g. *warm*) and semantically linked to the other judgement dimensions (e.g. *good-natured*) will be more central than one that is non-distinctive or not obviously related to the other dimensions. Yet others have suggested that people have their own idiosyncratic and enduring beliefs, which the personality psychologist George Kelly (1955) called personal constructs, about which attributes are most important in making judgements of people – for example, you might organise your impressions around *humour* while your partner anchors it on *intelligence*. Arising from his research in person perception, David Schneider (1973) suggested that people may also have more integrated implicit personality theories, or philosophies of human nature, which are enduring general principles about what sorts of characteristics go together to form certain types of personality. Implicit personality theories are widely shared within cultures but differ between cultures, according to Hazel Markus and her colleagues (Markus, Kitayama & Heiman, 1996), and can sometimes be quite idiosyncratic.

First and last impressions

Impressions are also influenced by the order in which bits of information about the person are encountered. There is a primacy effect in which the first things you learn about a person disproportionately affect your overall impression. For example, Asch (1946) found that people had a more favourable impression of a hypothetical person described as being *intelligent, industrious, impulsive, critical, stubborn, envious* (i.e. positive traits first, negative traits last) than when the order of the traits was reversed. He speculated that early information functions in the same way as central traits. There is also evidence for a recency effect where later information has more impact than earlier information – this is most likely to occur if you are distracted (e.g. overworked, bombarded with stimuli, tired) or you have little motivation to attend to someone. Overall, however, primacy is more common (Jones & Goethals, 1972) – first impressions really do count!

Primacy
An order of presentation effect in which earlier presented information has a disproportionate influence on social cognition.

Recency
An order of presentation effect in which later presented information has a disproportionate influence on social cognition.

Physical appearance counts

Given that in forming impressions of strangers often the first bit of information we have is what they look like, maybe appearance has a primacy effect. Although we would like to believe that we are way too sophisticated to be swayed in our impressions by mere physical appearance, research suggests otherwise – physical appearance has a huge influence on impressions. According to Leslie Zebrowitz and Mary Ann Collins (1997), people *do* tend to 'judge a book by its cover'. This may not necessarily always be a bad thing, as appearance-based impressions can be surprisingly accurate. Indeed, as you will find in Chapter 10, impressions based on physical appearance play a critical role in romantic attraction. Now try answering the first focus question.

However, forming impressions based on appearance can also have undesirable implications. For example, Mark Knapp (1978) found that professional men taller than 1.88 m had 10 per cent higher starting salaries than men under 1.83 m. In her research conducted in work settings, Madeline Heilman found that attractive male executives were considered more able than less attractive male executives. She also found that this effect was reversed for female executives; participants suspected that attractive female executives had been promoted because of their appearance, not their ability (Heilman & Stopeck, 1985; also see Chapter 7).

Another problem with appearance-based first impressions is that because racial, ethnic and gender cues are highly visible, people rapidly categorise others and generate impressions based on these cues, effectively stereotyping them, sometimes in negative ways (again, see Chapter 7). Negative impressions formed in this way are difficult to change.

Indeed a review of research shows that we usually give more weight to negative information when we form impressions than we do to positive information (Skowronski & Carlston, 1989). Even a positive view of a stranger that we have just formed can be dramatically reversed by just a small negative 'fact', such as appearing to avoid eye contact a couple of times. Unfortunately, positive information seems to have little impact on a negative impression. Negative information has this effect because it is unusual and distinctive; it may also have survival value because it signals potential danger.

Schemas and categories

In this section we explore how schemas flow from the categories we form, and how these are related to two technical concepts – prototypes and stereotypes.

A mental activity common to us all is that we store information about ourselves and about other people, events and places as schemas. A schema is a circumscribed and coherent set of interrelated cognitions (e.g. thoughts, beliefs, attitudes) that allows us quickly to make sense of a person, situation, event or place on the basis of limited information. Typically, certain cues activate a schema and the schema then 'fills in' missing details to provide a rich set of perceptions, interpretations and expectations.

Once activated, schemas facilitate what is called *top-down*, concept-driven or theory-driven processing – that is, they rapidly generate an overall impression based on preconceptions and prior knowledge. The converse is *bottom-up* or data-driven processing in which an impression is painstakingly put together from separate bits of information gleaned directly from the immediate context.

There are many types of schema, all of which influence the encoding (internalisation and interpretation) of new information, memory of old information and inferences about missing information.

- *Person schemas* are idiosyncratic schemas we have about specific people: for example, a close friend (she is kind and intelligent but is shy and would rather frequent cafes than go mountain climbing).
- *Role schemas* are knowledge structures about role occupants: for example, airline pilots (they fly the plane and should not be seen swigging whisky in the cabin) and doctors (although often complete strangers, they are allowed to ask intimate questions and get you to undress). Role schemas can sometimes be better understood as schemas about social groups, in which case if such schemas are shared, they are social stereotypes.
- *Scripts* are schemas about events (Abelson, 1981): for example, attending a lecture, having a party, giving a presentation or eating out in a restaurant.
- *Self-schemas* are schemas about your self – they are often more complex and varied than schemas about other people. They form part of a person's concept of who they are, the self-concept, and are discussed in Chapter 3 when we deal with self and identity.
- *Content-free schemas* do not describe specific people or categories, but are 'rules' about how to process information: for example, a content-free schema might specify how to attribute causes to people's behaviour (see discussion of attribution theories below); or that if you like John and John likes Tom, then in order to maintain balance you should also like Tom (Heider, 1958).

Categories and prototypes

To apply a particular schema, you first need to categorise an instance that fits. It might be a specific person, event or situation. A key question is how do we identify an instance as being a member of one category not another, and how do we cognitively organise information about a category?

Research shows that people view categories as collections of instances that are not identical but have a general family resemblance (Rosch, 1978) – categories are fuzzy sets of related attributes, called a prototype, rather than a rigid checklist of essential attributes. Although prototypes often represent the average or typical

Schema
Cognitive structure that represents knowledge about a concept or type of stimulus, including its attributes and the relations among those attributes.

Family resemblance
Defining property of category membership.

Fuzzy sets
Categories are considered to be fuzzy sets of features organised around a prototype.

Prototype
Cognitive representation of the typical/ideal defining features of a category.

Are prototypes accurate? What is your idea of a typical mother? The woman on the left is probably closer to your prototype than the woman on the right – but some mothers do like climbing big rocks!

Source: Pearson Online Database (POD)

category member (e.g. the typical environmentalist), this may not always be the case (Chaplin, John & Goldberg, 1988). Under some circumstances, for example when social categories are in competition (e.g. environmentalists versus developers), the prototype may be an extreme member (the most radical environmentalist).

In addition to representing categories as prototypes (essentially an abstraction from many instances), people may also represent them in terms of exemplars, specific concrete instances they have encountered (Smith & Zárate, 1992). For example, many Americans may represent the category 'British' in terms of the actors Hugh Grant or Colin Firth.

What determines whether we represent a category as a prototype or an exemplar? As people become more familiar with a category, they shift from using prototypes to exemplars. This shift is most clear-cut when people represent outgroups (Klein, Loftus, Trafton & Fuhrman, 1992).

Once a person, event or situation is categorised, the relevant schema is invoked. Schemas and prototypes are similar and indeed are often used interchangeably by social psychologists. One way to distinguish them is that prototypes are more nebulous and fuzzy whereas schemas are much more organised (Wyer & Gordon, 1984).

Exemplars
Specific instances of a member of a category.

Categories and stereotypes

Stereotypes are essentially schemas of social groups, and those applied to out-groups are ethnocentric, and are often associated with prejudice, discrimination and conflict between groups (see Chapter 7). They featured in Gordon Allport's (1954b) famous book *The Nature of Prejudice*, and as Susan Fiske (1998) noted in her review, nearly a century of social psychological research means that we now know a great deal about them.

- Stereotypes are simplified images of members of a group; they are often derogatory when applied to outgroups; and they are often based on, or create, clearly visible differences between groups (e.g. in terms of physical appearance; Zebrowitz, 1996). They are usually shared by group members characterising members of another group; and can also be shared images of one's own ingroup.
- People readily describe vast human groups using a few fairly crude shared features. Stereotyping is an adaptive cognitive short cut that allows one to form quick impressions of people. Stereotypes are not inaccurate or wrong, and they may or may not have a kernel of truth; but the key point is that they serve to make sense of particular intergroup relations.
- Because stereotypes are cognitively adaptive they are slow to change. When they do, it is generally in response to wider social, political or economic changes. However, stereotypes of the same group can vary from context to context – they are selected to fit situational demands and our own goals and motives. Stereotypes will usually persist if we can readily access them in memory, because we use them a great deal and they are important to who we are. Changes in accessibility or fit will change the stereotype.
- Some stereotypes are acquired at an early age, often before the child has any knowledge about the groups that are being stereotyped, while others crystallise later in childhood, after age 10 (e.g. Rutland, 1999).
- Stereotypes become more pronounced and hostile when social tensions and conflict arise between groups, and then they are extremely difficult to modify.

Stereotypes and accentuation

There is a respect in which stereotypes are more than schemas associated with social categories. The actual process of categorising can lead to perceptual 'distortion' that lends stereotyping some of its distinctive features. The famous European social psychologist Henri Tajfel (1959) argued that when we judge a stimulus (for example, how long a line is, how aggressive a person is) we draw on any and all other information we believe may help us make the judgement.

Tajfel and Wilkes (1963) used a visual perception task to test this. The stimuli were eight lines that differed in length by a constant percentage increment. A simple manipulation in an experimental condition caused the eight lines to be categorised into two groups of four, and their estimated lengths were different from those judged in a control condition. In the experimental condition, the four shorter lines were labelled *A* and the four longer lines are labelled *B*, whereas in the control condition the *A* and *B* labels were random. In the experimental condition, length was therefore correlated with the labels and the lines were perceived to be in two categories or groups, a shorter one and a longer one. Further, the participants accentuated the difference between the categories: the *A*-lines were judged a little shorter and the *B*-lines a little longer than they really were.

Relying on categories to clarify perception is a very basic human activity, but it also produces a widespread cognitive perceptual bias. Tajfel (1959, 1969) introduced the term accentuation principle to describe how we accentuate: (1) similarities among instances within the same category; (2) differences between instances from different categories; and (3) differences between different categories as a whole. This effect is enhanced when people are uncertain about how to judge something, and when they think that what they are categorising is very important, relevant or valuable. Shelley Taylor and her colleagues found that, in practice, we tend to make more errors within a category than between categories (Taylor, Fiske, Etcoff & Ruderman, 1978). For example, British people attending a meeting in London would more likely remember whether it was an Italian or a Greek delegate who said something than remember which specific Italian or Greek delegate it was.

In summary, the categories we use are basic to stereotypes. However, a deeper understanding of stereotypes requires recognising that they are developed by one group to characterise another group and that they are closely connected to the nature of the relations between the groups involved (Oakes, Haslam & Turner, 1994). In this respect stereotypes are grounded in and sustained and shaped by intergroup relations. They define identities, reduce uncertainty and justify the status quo (see Chapter 7). They also provide an explanation of complex social phenomena such as social representations (see below).

How we use and acquire schemas

Our social world is overflowing with information that we can use as the basis for categorisation. For instance, Juan is a British, male, Catholic from Aberdeen who is witty, well read, not very sporty and works as a nurse. How would we categorise him – what determines which cues serve as a basis for categorisation and schema use?

Using schemas

According to the cognitive psychologist Eleanor Rosch (1978), people tend to default to basic-level categories that are neither too big nor too small (see Figure 2.2). They use subtypes such as 'career woman', rather than superordinate categories such as 'woman' or subordinate categories such as 'female astronaut'. They also access social stereotypes and role schemas such as 'politician', rather than trait schemas such as 'intelligent'. According to optimal distinctiveness theory (Brewer, 1991), basic-level categories and subtypes balance people's need to see people as similar to others but also as different from others. People also readily categorise on the basis of distinctive cues such as skin colour, dress or physical appearance (Zebrowitz, 1996), or standing out from the crowd (a single man in a group of women), and on the basis of subjectively important schemas and schemas that are easily retrieved from memory because they use them a lot or have used them recently (Bargh, Lombardi & Higgins, 1988).

Schemas that we use automatically are usually accurate enough for immediate day-to-day interaction – they have *circumscribed accuracy* that optimises the trade-off between rapid top-down theory-driven cognition and accurate bottom-up data-driven cognition (Swann, 1984). A key factor that governs this trade-off is how costly people feel it is to be wrong or to be indecisive.

If the costs of being wrong are high, we are more attentive to data and use more accurate schemas. The costs of being wrong become important when our rewards and punishments are heavily dependent on the actions of others, and when we feel

Accentuation principle
Categorisation accentuates perceived similarities within and differences between groups on dimensions that people believe are correlated with the categorisation. The effect is amplified where the categorisation and/or dimension has subjective importance, relevance or value.

Basic-level categories
Middle range categories that have cognitive priority because they are the most useful, e.g. a 'chair' rather than 'furniture' or a 'rocker'.

Optimal distinctiveness
People strive to achieve a balance between conflicting motives for inclusiveness and separateness, expressed in groups as a balance between intragroup differentiation and intragroup homogenisation.

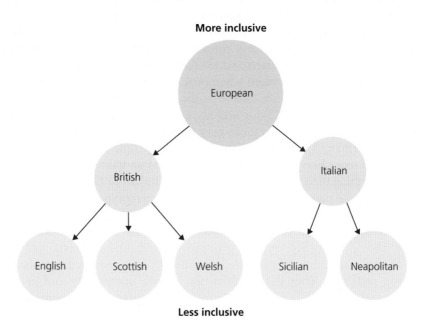

Figure 2.2

Categories organised by level of inclusiveness.

Categories are organised hierarchically so that less inclusive categories are nested beneath more inclusive categories.

that we should account for their actions (see Neuberg & Fiske, 1987; Tetlock & Boettger, 1989). If the costs of being indecisive are high, people make quick decisions and form quick impressions – indeed, any decision or impression, however inaccurate, may be preferable to no decision or impression, so people rely heavily on schemas. The costs of being indecisive become important when people perform a task under time pressure, or when people are anxious or distracted (Jamieson & Zanna, 1989; Wilder & Shapiro, 1989).

People are often aware that schemas can be inaccurate, and in the case of social groups can also be undesirable. Thus William may refrain from calling Mary a housewife, since it is a schema suggesting he is sexist. Some people are better at avoiding being too dependent on schemas – for example, those who think deeply and complexly about things and can entertain ambiguity and a variety of explanations of their world. However, attempts to buffer or circumvent the automatic processes described above are typically not very successful (Ellis, Olson & Zanna, 1983).

Acquiring schemas

Where do our schemas come from? People can simply tell you or you can read about them, but more typically we acquire or modify our schemas through encounters with instances that fit the category (directly or through various media). Take an example when the schema is of an individual person. According to Bernadette Park (1986), as you encounter more instances of a category, in this case a person, your schema becomes more general and abstract. For example, your impressions of

Roberta might evolve from descriptions such as 'dyes her hair pink' and 'is boisterous in class' to character traits such as 'extraverted'. A schema can also become richer, more complex and more tightly organized into a single compact mental structure that can be activated in an all-or-nothing manner. Thus an experienced university student is more likely than a first-year student to have a more detailed schema of someone who would make a good roommate. Schemas formed in this way are quite resilient – they are able to incorporate exceptions, rather than disregard them simply because they might threaten the validity of the schema (Fiske & Neuberg, 1990). One paradoxical feature of such schemas is that they are relatively 'accurate' in so far as they closely map social reality.

Changing schemas

Because schemas *appear* to be accurate they suggest a sense of order, structure and coherence to a social world that would otherwise be highly complex and unpredictable. For this reason schemas do not easily change. Ross, Lepper and Hubbard (1975) investigated how people deal with information that is not consistent with a schema. They told their participants that information they had received, that a target person had made either good or poor at making decisions, was entirely false. Despite this correction, participants held on to their original impression that the target was a good or poor decision maker. Trial lawyers take advantage of this. They introduce inadmissible evidence, which the judge immediately instructs the jury to disregard. But of course an impression formed from inadmissible evidence will not vanish just because the judge has instructed jurors to disregard it (Thompson, Fong & Rosenhan, 1981). The impression lingers.

People think a lot about their schemas, marshalling all sorts of supportive evidence. The original basis of the schema is lost in the mists of time and is rarely unearthed, let alone critically re-examined (e.g. Schul & Burnstein, 1985).

Schemas can, and do, change, however, if they are really inaccurate. For example, a schema that characterised lions as cuddly, good-natured and playful pets as seen in a fun TV programme would, if you encountered one on foot in the wild, change rather dramatically – assuming that you survived the encounter! Mick Rothbart (1981) has studied extensively how social categorisation works, and suggested three ways in which schemas can change:

1. *Bookkeeping* – they can change slowly in the face of accumulating evidence.
2. *Conversion* – they can change suddenly once a critical mass of disconfirming evidence has accumulated.
3. *Subtyping* – they can form a subcategory to accommodate disconfirming evidence.

Subtyping is probably the most common way that a schema adapts to disconfirming evidence (Weber & Crocker, 1983). For example, a woman who believes that men are violent might, through encountering many who are not, form a subtype of non-violent men to contrast with violent men.

Perceiving and remembering people

Social encoding

Social encoding is the process of representing external social stimuli in our minds. There are at least four key stages (Bargh, 1984):

1. *Pre-attentive analysis* – an automatic, non-conscious scanning of the environment.
2. *Focal attention* – once noticed, stimuli are consciously identified and categorised.
3. *Comprehension* – stimuli are given meaning.
4. *Elaborative reasoning* – the stimulus is linked to other knowledge to allow complex inferences.

Social encoding depends heavily on what captures our attention. In turn, attention is influenced by salience and accessibility.

Salience

Salience
Property of a stimulus that makes it stand out in relation to other stimuli and attract attention.

Salience is the property of a stimulus that makes it stand out relative to other stimuli in a particular context – for example, a single male is salient in a group of women but not a mixed sex group, and someone wearing a bright T-shirt is salient at a funeral but not on the beach. Consider the second focus question. People can be salient because they are novel and stand out against the background, because their appearance or behaviour does not fit your expectations of them, or because they are important to you (e.g. because of their rank) in a particular context. Salient people attract attention and are considered more influential in a group, more personally responsible for their behaviour (e.g. choosing to dress differently from others), and less influenced by the situation. We usually attend closely to them and form coherent impressions of them. People do not necessarily recall more about salient people; rather, they find it easier to hold a coherent mental picture of them.

Accessibility
Ease of recall of categories or schemas that we already have in mind.

Attention is often directed not so much by stimulus properties 'out there' but by the accessibility of categories or schemas that we already have in our heads (Higgins, 1996). Because accessible categories are ones we often use and are consistent with our goals, needs and expectations, they are very easily activated or primed by things we see or hear – priming takes place. For example, people who are concerned about racial discrimination (i.e. it is an accessible category) may see racism everywhere: it is readily primed and used to interpret the social world.

Priming
Activation of accessible categories or schemas in memory that influence how we process new information.

Once primed, a category interprets stimuli, particularly ambiguous stimuli, in a *category-consistent* manner. However, when people become aware that a category has been primed, they may try to counteract it. For example, Charles Stangor (1988) has shown that gender is often an accessible category that is readily primed and used to interpret behaviour; but if you knew that gender had been primed, you might make a special effort to interpret behaviour in a non-gendered way.

Memory for people

Associative network
Model of memory in which nodes or ideas are connected by associative links along which cognitive activation can spread.

What we remember about people is our person memory, and how this is organised influences our behaviour, sometimes profoundly (Fiske & Taylor, 2008; Hastie & Park, 1986). Typically, however, we tend not to rely on memory but instead form impressions of people *on-line*, relying on incoming data that are assimilated by schemas to produce an impression. Our memory of Bill, let us say, depends on what engages our attention in interacting with him, in particular about his behaviour and personality. According to Thomas Srull and Robert Wyer (1989), the more we focus, the more deeply we process and store information about Bill.

Memory operates as an associative network (e.g. Anderson, 1990) – specific ideas or items of memory, called *nodes*, are linked to (i.e. *associated* with) other nodes. Associative links vary in strength. Links become stronger the more they are activated by cognitive rehearsal and a node is more likely to be recalled (i.e. activated) if there are many strong links to it. There are two levels of memory:

long-term memory, which is the vast store of information that can potentially be brought to mind, and *short-term memory* (or working memory), which is the much smaller amount of information that you actually have in consciousness, and is the focus of your attention, at a specific time.

This basic model of memory applies to person memory (Srull & Wyer, 1989), with one important feature – information that is inconsistent with an impression we have of someone attracts attention and generates cognition, and is therefore better recalled. This is most likely if we do not already have a well-established impression, if the inconsistency is evaluative rather than descriptive, and if the judgement task is simple and we cannot deliberate carefully about our impression.

Contents of person memory

What we remember about Bill will vary in concreteness, from concrete appearance through behaviour to abstract traits, and in valence, from positive and desirable to negative and undesirable. Memory for Bill's *appearance* is usually based on directly observable concrete information and is stored like a picture in the mind – for example, both of his tweed jackets have leather patches on the elbows. We are phenomenally accurate at remembering faces, often with 100 per cent accuracy over very long periods of time (Freides, 1974). Bill has a long nose and wide-set piercing blue eyes.

However, we are less accurate at remembering outgroup faces, most likely because we pay less attention to them; indeed, a general remedy for poor memory for faces is simply to pay more attention. We are also pretty bad at remembering appearances in natural contexts where eyewitness testimony is required; probably because the witness or victim is frightened and doesn't get a clear look, and the event is unexpected, confusing and quick. However, eyewitness testimony is more accurate if certain conditions are met (see Box 2.2).

Unlike people's appearance, we store *trait* memories as propositions that can be quite abstract ('Mary is mean and nasty'). They are based on causal inferences drawn from behaviour and situations (Park, 1986; see below), and tend to be coded in terms of social desirability (e.g. *warm*, *pleasant*, *friendly*) and competence

Real world 2.2
Factors that make eyewitness testimony more accurate

Although eyewitness testimony is often unreliable, there are various ways in which its accuracy can be improved.

The *witness*:

- mentally goes back over the scene of the crime to reinstate additional cues;
- has already associated the person's face with other symbolic information;
- was exposed to the person's face for a long time;
- gave testimony a very short time after the crime;

- is habitually attentive to the external environment;
- generally forms vivid mental images.

The *person*:

- had a face that was not altered by disguise;
- was younger than 30 years old;
- looked dishonest.

Sources: Based on Shapiro & Penrod (1986); Valentine, Pickering & Darling (2003); Wells, Memon & Penrod, (2006).

(e.g. *intelligent, industrious, efficient*; see Schneider, Hastorf & Ellsworth, 1979). Although we can observe *behaviour* directly, how we remember an act is influenced by our inferences about its purpose or goal. For example, we would remember running differently if we thought its purpose was to catch a bus rather than to escape with a stolen wallet (Hoffman, Mischel & Mazze, 1981).

Organising person memory

There are two distinct ways in which we can organise information about people – by *person* or by *group*. In most situations we remember people as a cluster of information about their traits, behaviour and appearance. Organising person memory by person in this way produces rich and accurate person memories that are easily recalled – it is most common when people are significant to us because they are familiar, real people with whom we expect to interact across many specific situations (Sedikides & Ostrom, 1988). (Now consider the third focus question.) We can also store information about people by clustering people under groups or schemas of groups (see Figure 2.3).

Organising person memory by group is most likely in first encounters with strangers: the person is pigeon-holed, described and stored in terms of stereotypical attributes of a salient social category. Think of when you meet a new psychology lecturer whom we'll call Dr MacIlroy. Does she dress and speak like an academic? Over time and as you become more familiar with her, the category of *academic* recedes to an extent – it becomes less salient – and Penny the human being emerges. However, the two ways of representing your lecturer can coexist and can be primed by different contexts (Srull & Wyer, 1989). In a group context such as a lecture room your lecturer assumes a social identity as Dr MacIlroy, whereas sitting in the cafeteria with a few of your friends you say 'Hi Penny!'. Her personal identity has been primed (see social identity theory in Chapter 7).

Figure 2.3

Person memory organised by person or by group.

We can organise information about people in two quite different ways. We can cluster attributes under individual people, or we can cluster people under attributes or groups.

Source: Based on Fiske & Taylor (1991).

Person information

> Giovanna is a movie buff.
> Ling is a swimmer.
> David is a medical student.
> Giovanna is a medical student.
> David is a swimmer.

Organised by person

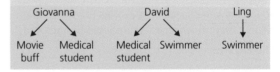

Organised by group

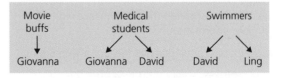

Social inference

Social inference lies at the heart of social cognition. It refers to the way we process social information to form impressions of people and make judgements about them. A key distinction that has already surfaced in different guises in this chapter is between (a) bottom-up processing in which we construct impressions piecemeal from specific bits of information and (b) top-down processing in which we automatically draw inferences from general schemas or stereotypes.

Related distinctions abound, such as in treatments of impression formation. For example, Marilyn Brewer (1988) distinguished between two kinds of processing: one that uses categories and is relatively automatic; and one based on a person's attributes and is more deliberate. Susan Fiske and Steven Neuberg (1990) pointed to a difference between inferences based on schemas and those based on data. Alice Eagly and Shelley Chaiken (1993) argued that we use two different processing routes whenever our attitudes come into play. We can choose a heuristic/peripheral route for rapid top-of-the-head decisions based on stereotypes, schemas and other cognitive short cuts, or a systematic/central route when we need to think carefully and deliberately. We call on one of these two routes when we respond (i.e. process) persuasive messages such as TV advertisements (see Chapter 4).

Whichever process we use, our inferences are generally less accurate than they could be and not very scientific. Indeed, we are prey to quite a range of biases and errors, and our focus is on one of these next.

The illusory correlation

A well-known bias that is difficult to avoid is the illusory correlation (e.g. Hamilton & Gifford, 1976). When we make an inference we essentially make a judgement that a correlation exists – for example, if you believe that obesity and poor education are correlated then if you met an obese person you would infer that he or she was also poorly educated. The illusory feature is the tendency to overestimate the degree of correlation or to even see a correlation where none actually exists.

Loren Chapman (1967) observed that an illusory correlation can justify a belief in magic, e.g. it is more likely to rain after a rain dance. He demonstrated how this bias can intrude into the way we make verbal associations:

- Chapman showed students lists of paired words such as *lion/tiger*, *lion/eggs*, *bacon/eggs*, *blossoms/notebook* and *notebook/tiger*, who then had to recall how often each word was paired with each other word.
- Although every word was paired an equal number of times with every other word, participants overestimated meaningful pairings (e.g. *bacon/eggs*); and distinctive pairings (e.g. *blossoms/notebook* – words that were much longer than all the other words in the list).
- He concluded that there are two bases for illusory correlation: associative meaning (items are seen as belonging together because they 'ought' to, on the basis of prior expectations) and paired distinctiveness (items are thought to go together because they share some unusual feature).

Although associative meaning is clearly related to stereotyping, it has also been suggested that illusory correlation based on distinctiveness is involved in stereotyping. In an experimental demonstration, Hamilton and Gifford (1976) had participants recall statements describing two groups, A and B. There were twice as many statements about group A as there were about group B, and there were twice as many positive as

Bottom-up processing
Information is processed synthetically from specific bits of data.

Top-down processing
Information is processed analytically from psychological constructs or theories.

Illusory correlation
Cognitive exaggeration of the degree of co-occurrence of two stimuli or events, or the perception of a co-occurrence where none exists.

negative statements about each group. So the actual ratio of positive and negative statements was the same for both groups. Participants erroneously recalled that more negative statements (the less common and more distinctive statements) were paired with group B (the less common and more distinctive group). When the experiment was replicated but with more negative than positive statements, participants now overestimated the number of positive statements paired with group B.

In real life, negative events are distinctive because they are perceived to be more rare than positive events (Parducci, 1968), and minority groups are distinctive because people have few contacts with them. As a result, an illusory correlation based on distinctiveness will occur and produce negative stereotyping of minority groups. If you reckon that a green-haired man cheated you out of money on a card game, you might be inclined to keep an eye on the next green-haired man you play with!

Short cuts in making inferences

People are inferentially challenged when making inferences because they have limited short-term memory available to work with, i.e. for on-line processing, but an enormous capacity for long-term memory. So, it pays for us to store information as schemas in long-term memory and call up these as needed. Social inference is thus heavily schema-driven, and it means that we draw conclusions that support schemas we already have. Why accumulate new knowledge when you can be lazy and muddle through? Most of the time, our day-to-day inference processes seem adequate, if occasionally wrong or even unfair on others.

Cognitive heuristics

Heuristics
Cognitive short cuts that provide adequately accurate inferences for most of us most of the time.

These 'adequate' rather than optimal processes are based on cognitive short cuts, called heuristics, that reduce complex problem solving to simpler judgemental operations. Amos Tversky and Daniel Kahneman (1974) have researched extensively on how humans make decisions and on their tolerance of getting some of these wrong. Here are three heuristics that have been explored:

Representativeness heuristic
A cognitive short cut in which instances are assigned to categories or types on the basis of overall similarity or resemblance to the category.

- Representativeness heuristic – we assess how similar we think an instance, say a person, is to a typical member in a given category, and if we feel the level of similarity is sufficient we infer that the person has all the category attributes. If Jane, whom you have just met, has short hair, wears overalls and talks loudly, you might mull over whether she might be one of 'those radical protestor types'.

Availability heuristic
A cognitive short cut in which the frequency or likelihood of an event is based on how quickly instances or associations come to mind.

- Availability heuristic – events or associations that come readily to mind are considered to be more common and prevalent than they really are. And so in sizing Paul up, who has even shorter hair than Jane, wears big boots and carries a cane, you would overestimate the likelihood that he will also be violent because you had just seen that old film *A Clockwork Orange*. Availability is adequate as a basis for making inferences (after all, things that come to mind easily are probably fairly plentiful), but it fails to control for the odd exposure to events or associations that may actually be rare.

Anchoring and adjustment
A cognitive short cut in which inferences are tied to initial standards or schemas.

- Anchoring and adjustment – impressions are tied to earlier perceptions that are a starting point, much like the primacy effect we discussed earlier. Inferences about other people are often anchored in beliefs about ourselves. We might therefore decide how intelligent, artistic or kind someone else is by referring to our own self-schema. 'Because I think *I* am bright, smart Fred must have a giant brain!' Another example – your dislike for Mary can act as an anchor from which only small adjustments are made, even in the light of subsequent overwhelming evidence that she is actually absolutely delightful!

Should we be worried about our cognitive biases? Although social inference is not as good as it could be, it is generally adequate and well adapted to everyday life – so 'remedies' for our shortcomings may not actually be necessary (Funder, 1987). For example, on encountering a pit bull terrier in the street, it might be very adaptive to rely on availability (media coverage of attacks by pit bull terriers) and to flee automatically rather than think long and deeply about what to do: an error in the laboratory might be a disaster in the field.

Of course, not being accurate can have some undesirable consequences. One of these is when people form inaccurate impressions of others, or develop stereotypes of minorities. However, it is possible to improve on our intuitive inferential strategies, for example, through formal education in scientific and rational thinking and in understanding statistical techniques (Nisbett, Krantz, Jepson & Fong, 1982).

Seeking the causes of behaviour

A key motive behind social inference is to gain sufficient understanding of other people to predict how they will behave, how they will treat us, how we should behave and more generally how the course of interaction will play out. All of us are in the business of constructing a representation of our social world that makes it a predictable and controllable – a place in which we can reliably make things happen.

The most powerful way to do this is to have an understanding of what causes what, being able to attribute causes to behaviour and events (Forsterling & Rudolph, 1988). This is the business of formal science, but not surprisingly we also do this automatically and informally almost all the time. The famous Austrian psychologist Fritz Heider (1958) thought of humans as 'naive' or lay psychologists who constantly construct their own informal theories to explain and predict how people will behave.

How do we attribute causality, why is it important?

People as naive psychologists

Fritz Heider (1958) drew the attention of social psychologists to the importance of studying people's naive, or commonsense, psychological theories. He believed that these theories are important in their own right because they influence behaviour. For example, people who believe in astrology are likely to have different expectations and are likely to act in different ways from those who do not. Heider believed that people are intuitive psychologists who construct causal theories of human behaviour, and because such theories have the same form as systematic scientific social psychological theories, people are actually intuitive or naive psychologists.

Heider made a lasting distinction between personal factors (e.g. personality, ability) and environmental factors (e.g. situations, social pressure) in the way that we account for the causes for behaviour. The former are examples of an internal (or dispositional) attribution and the latter of an external (or situational) attribution. So, for example, it might be useful to know whether someone you meet at a party who seems aloof and distant is an aloof and distant person or is acting in that way because she is not enjoying that particular party. Heider believed that because internal causes, or intentions, are hidden from us, we can infer their presence only if there are no clear external causes. However, as we see below, people tend to be biased in preferring internal to external attributions even in the face of evidence for

Internal (or dispositional) attribution
Process of assigning the cause of our own or others' behaviour to internal or dispositional factors.

External (or situational) attribution
Assigning the cause of our own or others' behaviour to external or environmental factors.

external causality. It seems that we readily attribute behaviour to stable properties of people. Klaus Scherer (1978), for example, found that people made assumptions about the stable personality traits of complete strangers simply on the basis of hearing their voices on the telephone.

People as everyday scientists

Covariation model
Kelley's theory of causal attribution – people assign the cause of behaviour to the factor that covaries most closely with the behaviour.

A well-known theory of how attributions are made is Harold Kelley's (1967) covariation model. A key question that people ask themselves is whether someone's behaviour is caused by the person's internal disposition to behave in that way (their personality) or by external situational factors. This allows us to know whether the person will always behave in a certain way or whether the behaviour is tied to the situation – is Jane being nice to me because she likes me (an internal dispositional cause) or because we are working on something together and being nice helps get the task done (an external situational cause)? This much is in line with what Heider had observed.

Kelley went on to argue that in order to discover a cause of someone's behaviour people act much like scientists, rather than naive psychologists. They identify what factor covaries with the behaviour and then assign that factor a causal role. People use this covariation principle to decide whether to attribute a particular act to internal dispositions (e.g. personality) or external environmental factors (e.g. social pressure). To make this attributional decision people consider three types of information: consistency, distinctiveness and consensus.

If Jane only sometimes behaves in a particular way, for example giggles, in a given situation then *consistency* is low and we look for alternative causes. If on the other hand Jane always giggles in the same situation consistency is high but we still don't know whether the giggling reflects Jane's personality or the situation. Assuming high consistency, people can assess the *distinctiveness* of the behaviour (distinctiveness is low if Jane giggles all the time, high if Jane only giggles in this situation) and whether there is high *consensus* (every one giggles in this situation) or low consensus (only Jane giggles in this situation). The conjunction of high distinctiveness and consensus leads to an external attribution (Jane's giggling is due to the situation), and the conjunction of low distinctiveness and consensus leads to an internal attribution (Jane's giggling is due to Jane – she is simply the sort of person who giggles).

Research shows that people certainly can make causal attributions for behaviour in this way (Kassin, 1979; McArthur, 1972), however, they under-use consensus information and are generally not very good at assessing covariation. Also, just because people *can* perform these laborious attributional analyses, it does not mean that in everyday life they actually do it or do it all the time.

Acts that are stable and controlled

Bernard Weiner (1979, 1986) was interested in the causes and consequences of the sorts of attribution people make when they succeed or fail on a task – for example, how students interpret their performance in examinations. He believed that in making an achievement attribution, we consider three performance dimensions. The first is locus, which once again features internal and external causes. The next two are new and interesting: stability and controllability.

Let us say that your classmate Helga fails in her psychology examination, and we think this was caused by 'unusual hindrance from others' (the top right-hand box in Figure 2.4). Now, you know that Helga is intelligent (therefore, failure in this case is an external factor). You also know that she was seriously disturbed by Bevan. He should never have been there – his eyes were running from a bout of hay fever, he

	Internal		External	
	Stable	Unstable	Stable	Unstable
Controllable	Typical effort	Unusual effort	Consistent help or hindrance from others	Unusual help or hindrance from others
Uncontrollable	Ability	Mood	Task difficulty	Luck

Figure 2.4

Achievement attributions as a function of locus, stability and controllability.

How we attribute someone's task achievement depends on:

* *Locus* – is the performance caused by the actor (internal) or the situation (external)?
* *Stability* – is the internal cause a stable or unstable one?
* *Controllability* – to what extent is future task performance under the actor's control?

kept sneezing throughout, and he was sitting next to poor Helga. So let us look to the future: in future examinations Bevan might not be present (an unstable factor), or Helga could choose to sit well away from Bevan if he turns up (a controllable factor). In total, there are eight different ways of explaining task performance.

Controllability. According to Weiner's attribution model, these athletes may attribute their success to unusually hard training – an internal but unstable attribution.

Source: Pearson Online Database (POD)

Weiner's model is a dynamic one, in that people first assess whether someone has succeeded or failed and accordingly experience positive or negative emotion. They then make a causal attribution for the performance; further, people can experience specific emotions (e.g. pride for doing well due to ability) and expectations that influence future performance.

Weiner's model is relatively well supported by experiments that provide participants with performance outcomes and locus, stability and controllability information, often under role-playing conditions (e.g. de Jong, Koomen & Mellenbergh, 1988). However, critics have suggested that the controllability dimension may be less important than was first thought. They have also wondered to what extent people outside controlled laboratory conditions really analyse achievement in this way.

Causal attribution in action

In this section we look first at the way we make attributions about ourselves, and in particular about explaining our emotions. Next we note that people can differ in their emotional styles. We close by considering how our attributions for other people's motives can impact our close relationships.

Self-perception

If you can attribute an act internally to a person's disposition you now know something about that person – his or her personality. Daryl Bem (1972) pinpointed an interesting implication of this in his self-perception theory. He argued that: (1) we make attributions for our own behaviour in the same way as we make attributions for others' behaviour; and (2) it is through internal attribution of our own behaviour that we gain knowledge about ourselves, our self-concept and identity (see Chapter 3).

Self-perception theory
Bem's idea that we gain knowledge of ourselves only by making self-attributions: for example, we infer our own attitudes from our own behaviour.

Explaining our emotions

Making attributions also plays a role in defining emotions. Our emotions have two distinct components: a state of physiological *arousal,* and *cognitions* that we use to label the arousal as an emotion, such as fear or excitement. Although the arousal and label usually go hand-in-hand and our thoughts can generate the associated arousal, in some cases unexplained arousal could be experienced as different emotions depending on what kind of attributions we make for what we are experiencing. A major contributor to theory and research in this area is Stanley Schachter (1964; for a review of his work see Reisenzein, 1983). One of his experiments dealt with 'emotional lability'. See Box 2.3 and Figure 2.5 to see the components in the process of attributing an emotion in this experiment.

Being emotionally labile can help in therapy. Valins and Nisbett (1972) wondered if the process of making attributions could be used to treat emotional disorders. For example, might someone who is chronically anxious learn to re-label the arousal as happiness, transform depression into contentment, or attribute shyness to external factors rather than their own social anxiety? While some experiments suggest this could work (e.g. Olson, 1988), in general what is a misattribution effect is limited to the laboratory, unreliable and short-lived (Forsterling, 1988; Parkinson, 1985).

Research classic 2.3
The context affects how we label an emotion

In the late nineteenth century the famous psychologist William James turned the usual account of how we experience an emotion on its head. As ordinary folk, we might believe that our mental images cause the body to react, and define our feelings as an emotion. However, James argued that first the body responds automatically to a stimulus, and then we interpret our bodily responses on the basis of what is going on around us: if we see a bear, we run, and a little later our pounding heart tells us that we are afraid.

One of Stanley Schachter's experiments dealing with 'emotional lability' brought this idea into the laboratory and gave it an attributional flavour. The key condition was one in which adrenalin was administered to male volunteers causing them to feel aroused (an increase in

heart rate), but were not informed what the drug was or what would happen. The aim was to show that the drug-induced arousal would be interpreted differently according to the context, of which there were two. In the first context, a confederate in the same room engaged in silly antics and made paper aeroplanes, which led the volunteers to report feeling euphoric. In the second context, the confederate ripped up papers and stomped around the room, which led the students to report feeling angry.

Given that the arousal brought on by the drug was unexpected, the confederate's actions provided sufficient cues to attach a label to what the volunteers thought was actually an 'emotion'.

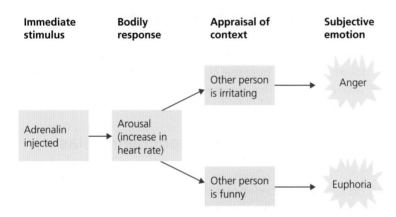

| Immediate stimulus | Bodily response | Appraisal of context | Subjective emotion |

Figure 2.5

Attributing a likely cause to an experimentally induced emotion.

Source: Based on Schachter & Singer (1962).

Styles of attribution

We all engage in attributions, but it appears that we differ in our **attributional style**. According to the eminent clinical psychologist Julian Rotter (1966), those of us who are *internals* tend to make internal attributions; believing we have a great deal of personal control over our destiny – things happen because we make them happen. Those of us who are *externals* tend to make external attributions; believing that we have little control over what happens to us – things simply occur by chance, luck or the actions of powerful external agents. We can also differ in the

Attributional style
An individual (personality) predisposition to make a certain type of causal attribution for behaviour.

extent to which they attribute behaviour or events to very general, diffuse and widespread causes (e.g. 'the economy') to explain redundancy, or to more narrowly defined causes (e.g. a company closing down).

Close relationships and attribution

Attributions also play an important role in close interpersonal relationships where attributions are *communicated* to fulfil a variety of functions: for instance, to explain, justify or excuse behaviour, as well as to assign blame and instil guilt (Hilton, 1990; see Chapter 10). A key finding is that attributional conflict, where partners in a relationship disagree over attributions (e.g. one exclaiming, 'I withdraw because you nag', the other, 'I nag because you withdraw'), is strongly associated with and plays a causal role in relationship dissatisfaction and distress (Fincham & Bradbury, 1993). In good relationships people credit their partners for positive behaviour by citing internal, stable, global and controllable factors to explain them, and explain away negative behaviour by ascribing it to external, unstable, specific and uncontrollable causes. Distressed couples behave in exactly the opposite way. Women tend fairly continuously to engage in attributional thought about the relationship, but men do so only when the relationship becomes dysfunctional. In this respect, and contrary to popular opinion, men's attributional behaviour is a better barometer of relationship dysfunction.

Biases in attributing motives

A central theme in social cognition is that people only do as much social thinking as is necessary for an adequate outcome – they are not in the business of optimal thought, as we noted earlier in this chapter. The same is true of the way we make attributions – there is an array of biases and errors (Nisbett & Ross, 1980).

From acts to dispositions: correspondence bias

Correspondent inference

Correspondent inference
Causal attribution of behaviour to underlying dispositions.

Ned Jones and his colleagues developed a theory of theory of correspondent inference to explain that people infer that a person's behaviour corresponds to an underlying disposition or personality trait (Jones & Davis, 1965; Jones & McGillis, 1976). For example, if we saw Alex make a donation to charity we might infer that he has an underlying disposition to be charitable. People like to make correspondent inferences. A dispositional cause is a stable cause that renders people's behaviour predictable: it increases our own sense of control over our world. There are several cues that suggest a correspondent inference will be made. One cue is whether an act seems to be *freely chosen* rather than a response to external threats, inducements or constraints. Another cue is whether an act appears to be *socially desirable*, i.e. controlled by social norms. If so, it does not tell us much about a person's disposition. A better basis for a correspondent inference is socially undesirable action, because this would be in breach of a social norm.

Correspondence bias

Correspondence bias
A general attribution bias in which people have an inflated tendency to see behaviour as reflecting (corresponding to) stable underlying personality attributes.

Perhaps the best-known attribution bias is correspondence bias (also called the *fundamental attribution error*). This a tendency for people to attribute behaviour internally to stable underlying personality dispositions, even in the face of strong evidence for external causes (Gilbert & Malone, 1995; Ross, 1977). It is called *correspondence bias* because it is a bias in viewing behaviour as corresponding to internal dispositions rather than external situations. Check the fourth focus question.

Correspondence bias was the focus of a classic study by Jones and Harris (1967). American participants read speeches about the Cuban leader Fidel Castro ostensibly written by fellow students – at the time Castro was very unpopular in the United States. The speeches were either pro-Castro or anti-Castro, and the writers had ostensibly either freely chosen to write the speech or been instructed to do so. Where there was a choice, participants not surprisingly reasoned that those who had written a pro-Castro speech were in favour of Castro, and those who had written an anti-Castro speech were against Castro – an internal, dispositional attribution was made (see Figure 2.6).

However, a dispositional attribution was also made even when the speech writers had been *instructed* to write the speech! Although there was overwhelming evidence for an exclusively external cause, participants seemed largely to overlook this information and to prefer a dispositional explanation – they were victims of the fundamental attribution error or correspondence bias.

Correspondence bias has been widely demonstrated as a common inferential error that we all make (Gilbert, 1998). It is, however, less pronounced in relatively collectivist, East Asian cultures where people are more inclined to adjust their behaviour to the social context of other people and of situational norms (Morris & Peng, 1994; Smith, Bond & Kağitçibaşi, 2006; see Chapter 11). Correspondence bias arises primarily because people tend automatically to focus on the person against the background of the situation. The other person is the focus of their attention and is therefore more salient in information processing (e.g. Rholes & Pryor, 1982). Clearly, the bias will be weakened if one focuses more on the situation, as is the case in Eastern cultures.

Nick Haslam has pointed out that, in some situations, correspondence bias can take an extreme form called essentialism. People not only attribute behaviour to underlying dispositions but regard these dispositions as immutable and often innate

Essentialism
Pervasive tendency to consider behaviour to reflect underlying and immutable, often innate, properties of people or the groups they belong to.

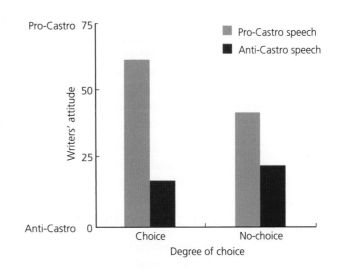

Figure 2.6

The correspondence bias: attributing attitudes in the absence of freedom of choice.

- Students who freely chose to write a pro- or an anti-Castro speech were attributed with a pro- or anti-Castro attitude, respectively.
- Although less strong, this same tendency to attribute the speech to an underlying disposition (the fundamental attribution error) prevailed when the writers had no choice and were simply instructed to write the speech.

Source: Based on data from Jones & Harris (1967).

properties of the person or the group the person belongs to. Essentialism is particularly troublesome when it causes people to attribute negative stereotypes of outgroups to essential and immutable personality attributes of members of that group (e.g. Haslam, Rothschild & Ernst, 1998; Haslam, Bastian, Bain & Kashima, 2006).

The actor–observer effect

Actor–observer effect
Tendency to attribute our own behaviours externally and others' behaviours internally.

Correspondence bias only occurs reliably when we make an attribution of others' behaviour. When seeking causes for our own behaviour we are more likely to attribute it externally to situational factors. This asymmetry, for which there is substantial empirical support, is called the actor–observer effect (Jones & Nisbett, 1972; Watson, 1982). The most likely causes of the actor–observer effect are the following:

- *Focus of attention* – when other people are the focus we judge them against the background of the situation. However, when we consider our own actions we focus outwards on the situation rather than inwards on our self: the situation is causally more salient.
- *Asymmetry of information* – we know more about ourselves and therefore know that our behaviour is influenced by situational factors, because we behave differently in different situations. At least *we* think we do!

Not surprisingly, the actor–observer effect can be reduced or even disappear if the actor becomes the observer. One way that you might begin to see your dispositional side is to watch videotape of yourself recorded in a natural situation. Now, you become like others – you are the observer of *you* (Storms, 1973).

False consensus

False consensus effect
Seeing our own behaviour as being more typical than it really is.

A third attributional bias is called the false consensus effect. People tend to overestimate how typical their own behaviour is – assuming that others behave in the same way as they do. This egocentric bias was first demonstrated by Ross, Greene and House (1977) who asked students if they would agree to walk around campus for 30 minutes wearing a sandwich board carrying the slogan 'Eat at Joe's'. Those who agreed estimated that 62 per cent of their peers would also have agreed, while those who refused estimated that 67 per cent of their peers would also have refused.

False consensus is very prevalent (Marks & Miller, 1987), and arises because:

- we usually seek out similar others and so should not be surprised to find that other people are similar to us;
- our own opinions are so salient to us that they eclipse the possibility of alternative opinions;
- we are motivated to ground our opinions and actions in perceived consensus in order to validate them and build a stable world for ourselves.

False consensus is stronger for important beliefs that we care about, for beliefs we feel certain about, when we feel under external threat, and where we feel others are similar to us and we are members of a minority status group.

Self-serving biases

In keeping with the motivated tactician model of social cognition (Fiske & Taylor, 1991) discussed earlier in this chapter, attribution is influenced by our desire for a favourable image of ourselves. We are very good at producing self-serving biases. Overall, we take credit for our positive behaviours as reflecting who we are and our intention and effort to do positive things (the *self-enhancing bias*), while we explain away our negative behaviours as being due to coercion, normative constraints and other external situational factors that do not reflect who we 'really' are (the *self-protecting bias*). This is a robust effect that holds across many cultures (Fletcher & Ward, 1988).

Self-enhancing biases are more common than self-protecting biases (Miller & Ross, 1975) – partly because people with low self-esteem tend not to protect themselves by attributing their failures externally; rather, they attribute them internally (Campbell & Fairey, 1985). However, self-enhancement and self-protection can sometimes be muted by a desire not to be seen to be boasting over our successes and lying about our failures (e.g. Schlenker, Weingold & Hallam, 1990). A fascinating self-serving bias, which most of us have used from time to time, acts in anticipation – self-handicapping, a term described by Edward Jones and Steven Berglas:

> The self-handicapper, we are suggesting, reaches out for impediments, exaggerates handicaps, embraces any factor reducing personal responsibility for mediocrity and enhancing personal responsibility for success. *(Jones & Berglas, 1978, p. 202)*

People use this bias when they anticipate failure, whether in their job performance, in sport, or even in therapeutic settings when being 'sick' allows one to drop out of life. What a person often will do is to intentionally and publicly make external attributions for a poor showing even before it happens. Check the experiment about choosing between drugs in Box 2.4 and Figure 2.7.

Self-serving biases are also framed by our need to believe the world is a just place in which we have some control over our destiny. We cling to an illusion of control (Langer, 1975) by having a belief in a just world (Furnham, 2003) in which 'bad things happen to bad people', 'good things to good people' (i.e. people get what they deserve), and people have control over their outcomes. Refer back to the fifth focus question. This pattern of attributions makes the world seem a controllable and

Self-serving biases
Attributional distortions that protect or enhance self-esteem or the self-concept.

Self-handicapping
Publicly making advance external attributions for our anticipated failure or poor performance in a forthcoming event.

Illusion of control
Belief that we have more control over our world than we really do.

Belief in a just world
Belief that the world is a just and predictable place where good things happen to 'good people' and bad things to 'bad people'.

Research classic 2.4
Self-handicapping: explaining away your failure

Imagine that you are waiting to take an examination in a subject you find difficult and that you fully anticipate failing. You might well make sure that as many people as possible know that you have done no revision, are not really interested in the subject and have a mind-numbing hangover to boot. Your subsequent failure is thus externally attributed without it seeming that you are making excuses to explain away your failure.

To investigate this idea, Berglas and Jones (1978) had introductory psychology students try to solve some problems where the problems were either solvable or not solvable. They were told that they had done very well, and before continuing with a second problem-

solving task they were given the choice of taking either a drug called 'Actavil', which would ostensibly improve intellectual functioning and performance, or 'Pandocrin', which would have the opposite effect. As predicted, those students who had succeeded on the solvable puzzles felt confident about their ability and so chose Actavil in order to improve further (see Figure 2.7). Those who had succeeded on the not-solvable puzzles attributed their performance externally to luck and chose Pandocrin in order to be able to explain away more easily the anticipated failure on the second task.

Source: Based on data from Berglas & Jones (1978).

Figure 2.7

Self-handicapping: choosing a drug depends on a puzzle's solvability.

- Students who had done well on a solvable puzzle could attribute their performance internally (e.g. to ability): anticipating an equally good performance on a second similar task, they chose a performance-enhancing drug, Actavil, rather than a performance-impairing drug, Pandocrin.
- Students who had done well on a not-solvable puzzle could only attribute their performance externally (e.g. to luck): with little prospect of an equivalent performance on the second task they chose the performance-impairing drug, as the self-handicapping option.

Source: Based on data from Berglas & Jones (1978).

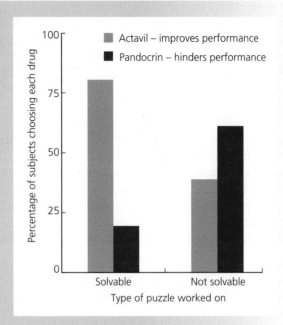

secure place in which we can determine our own destiny. One consequence of this is that we often blame others for their misfortunes, such as unemployment, stigma or victimisation. We can even blame ourselves for bad things that happen to us; for example, victims of incest or rape can experience such a strong sense that the world is no longer stable, meaningful, controllable and just that they may reinstate an illusion of control by taking some responsibility for the event (Miller & Porter, 1983).

Explaining our social world

When we talk of an illusion of control and a belief in a just world we have travelled a long way from attribution theory's initial focus on how an individual painstakingly attributes a cause to another individual's behaviour. Often, it is groups or even our society that construct causal explanations to explain events and justify actions, and we as members of particular groups subscribe to these *social explanations*. People do not wake up every morning and causally reconstruct their world anew. In general we rely on causal scripts, group stereotypes, cultural belief systems, and wider ideologies (see Box 2.5). We stop, think and make causal attributions only when events are unexpected or inconsistent with expectations (Hastie, 1984), when we are in a bad mood (Bohner, Bless, Schwarz & Strack, 1988), when we feel a lack of control (Liu & Steele, 1986), or when we are actually asked or expected to proffer a causal explanation.

Intergroup attribution

Miles Hewstone (1989) has observed that groups develop causal explanations for themselves as group members and others as either ingroup or outgroup members (also see Chapter 7). For example, the British tend to attribute crime and economic

Real world 2.5
A very strange custom: the cultural context of causal attribution

Gün Semin tells a fictitious story about a Brazilian aborigine who visits Rio de Janeiro and then returns home to his tribe deep in the Amazonian rainforest to give an account of the visit (Semin, 1980, p. 292).

On particular days more people than all those you have seen in your whole lifetime roam to this huge place of worship, an open hut the size of which you will never imagine. They come, chanting, singing, with symbols of their gods and once everybody is gathered the chanting drives away all alien spirits. Then, at the appointed time the priests arrive wearing colourful garments, and the chanting rises to war cries until three high priests, wearing black, arrive. All priests who were running around with sacred round objects leave them and at the order of the high

priests begin the religious ceremony. Then, when the chief high priest gives a shrill sound from himself they all run after the single sacred round object that is left, only to kick it away when they get hold of it. Whenever the sacred object goes through one of the two doors and hits the sacred net the religious followers start to chant, piercing the heavens, and most of the priests embark on a most ecstatic orgy until the chief priest blows the whistle on them.

This is, of course, a description of a football match by someone who does not know the purpose or rules of the game! It illustrates an important point. For causal explanations to be meaningful they need to be part of a highly complex general interpretative framework that constitutes our socially acquired cultural knowledge.

ills to minority outgroups, such as Eastern European immigrants in Britain. In making attributions for the behaviour of outgroups, people often attribute negative behaviour dispositionally and positive behaviour externally – Thomas Pettigrew

Intergroup attributions. These are usually negative when applied to an outgroup, and in the case of gangs can lead to murder.

Source: Daniel Berehulak / Getty Images

Ultimate attribution error
Tendency to internally attribute bad outgroup and good ingroup behaviour, and to externally attribute good outgroup and bad ingroup behaviour.

Intergroup attributions
Process of assigning the cause of one's own or others' behaviour to group membership.

(1979) called this the ultimate attribution error. When you also build in attributions for ingroup behaviour you get true ethnocentric intergroup attributions – a group level manifestation of self-serving biases, in which socially desirable (positive) behaviour by ingroup members and socially undesirable (negative) behaviour by outgroup members are internally attributed to dispositions, and negative ingroup and positive outgroup behaviour are externally attributed to situational factors.

Don Taylor and Vaishna Jaggi (1974) studied intergroup attributions in southern India, against a background of intergroup conflict between Hindus and Muslims. Hindu participants read vignettes describing Hindus or Muslims acting towards them in a socially desirable way (e.g. offering shelter from the rain) or socially undesirable way (e.g. refusing shelter), and then chose one of a number of explanations for the behaviour. As predicted, Hindus made more internal attributions for socially desirable than socially undesirable acts by Hindus (ingroup), and this difference disappeared when Hindus made attributions for Muslims (outgroup). Other studies have shown that intergroup attributions are more pronounced where a group has a negative stereotype of an outgroup and less pronounced where outgroup attitudes are more favourable (e.g. Hewstone & Ward, 1985; Islam & Hewstone, 1993).

Intergroup attributions are ethnocentric. They reflect ethnocentric differences between ingroup and outgroup schemas and stereotypes that we hold: our evaluations are biased in favour of our own group. People often accentuate these perceived differences to achieve a positive self-image as a group member (Hogg & Abrams, 1988; Tajfel & Turner, 1979). We are biased to attribute internally good things about the ingroup and bad things about the outgroup, and likewise to attribute externally bad things about the ingroup and good things about the outgroup.

At the societal level, group attributions furnish us with explanations for poverty, wealth and unemployment. In the political sphere, conservatives tend to make internal attributions for poverty (Pandey, Sinha, Prakash & Tripathi, 1982), wealth (Furnham, 1983) and unemployment (Feather, 1985); liberals are inclined more towards external explanations. These attributions are quite clearly framed by ideology, as are explanations of social unrest, riots and even widespread disease. Conservatives will identify deviance, or personal or social pathology as the cause, while liberals will identify extenuating circumstances (Reicher & Potter, 1985; Jost, Federico & Napier, 2009). You will probably get a sense of this in media releases by party spokespersons and sometimes in letters to a newspaper editor.

Ideology
A systematically interrelated set of beliefs whose primary function is explanation. It circumscribes thinking, making it difficult for the holder to escape from its mould.

Level of education level may lead people to arrive at intergroup attributions. Paul Sniderman and his colleagues investigated explanations for racial inequality and preferences for government policies. They found that less educated American Whites employed an 'affect-driven' reasoning process; starting with (mainly negative) feelings about Blacks, then proceeding directly to advocate minimal government assistance. Having done this, they 'doubled back' to fill in the intervening link to justify their advocacy – that Blacks were personally responsible for their own disadvantage. In contrast, better-educated Whites adopted a 'cognition-driven' reasoning process, in which they reasoned both forwards and backwards. Their policy recommendations were based on causal attributions for inequality, and in turn their causal attributions were influenced by their policy preference (Sniderman, Hagen, Tetlock & Brady, 1986).

Social representations

One way in which cultural knowledge about the causes of things may be developed is described by the eminent social psychologist Serge Moscovici in his theory of social representations (Lorenzi-Cioldi & Clémence, 2001; Moscovici, 1988). These are commonsense explanations of the world we live in, which are shared among members of a group. They develop through everyday informal communication among people to transform the unfamiliar and complex into the familiar and straightforward. Social representations are simplified and often ritualised 'distortions' of the real nature of the world.

Everyday commonsense understandings of evolution, global warming, the economy, globalism, and diet and health are all examples of social representations. We also have social representations of the nature of particular groups in society (what they do and believe, and why) – for example, Muslims, Americans and rich people. Carmen Huici and her colleagues gave the European Union as an excellent example of a social representation (Huici *et al.* 1997). The EU is a relatively new and quite technical idea that has its roots in complex economic matters such as free trade and subsidies. But the EU is now an accepted and commonplace part of European discourse which often emphasises more emotive issues of national and European identity rather than economic and trade matters.

Social representations research is popular in France. It uses a variety of methods that includes qualitative and quantitative analyses of interviews, questionnaires, observational data and archival material (Breakwell & Canter, 1993). A good example of this pluralism is Denise Jodelet's (1991) classic work *Madness and Social Representations* that centred on how mental illness is described and represented in the small French community of Ainay-le-Chateau. Her research used questionnaires, interviews and ethnographic observation.

Social representations
Collectively elaborated explanations of unfamiliar and complex phenomena that transform them into a familiar and simple form.

Rumour

The way that social representations are developed through informal communication resembles the way rumours develop and spread. The transmission of rumours is characterised by levelling, sharpening and assimilation: the rumour becomes shorter and less detailed and complex, at the same times as certain features are selectively exaggerated to conform to people's pre-existing schemas (Allport & Postman, 1945; Rosnow, 1980).

Rumours are most likely to develop in a crisis when people are uncertain, anxious and stressed. When we pass a rumour on to others we are actually helping to reduce the uncertainty and stress we feel and to build social integration. (Check the sixth focus question. Here is one reason why Rajna wanted to pass a rumour on.) Rumours also have a source, and often this source purposely elaborates the rumour for a specific reason – someone might be trying to discredit individuals or groups. For example, an organisation can spread a rumour to undermine a competitor's market share (Shibutani, 1966), or a social group can spread a rumour to blame another group for a widespread crisis. A popular instance is the fabrication and promulgation of conspiracy theories.

Rumours
Unverified accounts passed between individuals who try to make sense of events that are uncertain or confusing.

Conspiracy theories

Conspiracy theories are convoluted causal theories. They attribute widespread natural and social calamities to the intentional and organised activities of certain

Conspiracy theories
Explanations of widespread, complex and worrying events in terms of the premeditated actions of small groups of highly organised conspirators.

Conspiracy theories. As an adherent to a convoluted causal theory, Mohamed Al Fayed would not relinquish it easily.

Source: Cathal McNaughton / PA Archive / Press Association Images

social groups, depicted as conspiratorial bodies out to ruin and then dominate the rest of humanity. Conspiracy theories wax and wane in popularity. They were particularly popular from the mid-seventeenth to the mid-eighteenth centuries:

> Everywhere people sensed designs within designs, cabals within cabals; there were court conspiracies, backstairs conspiracies, ministerial conspiracies, factional conspiracies, aristocratic conspiracies, and by the last half of the eighteenth century even conspiracies of gigantic secret societies that cut across national boundaries and spanned the Atlantic. *(Wood, 1982, p. 407)*

One well-known conspiracy theory is the myth of the Jewish world conspiracy which surfaces periodically and is often associated with persecution of Jews (Cohn, 1966); another is of the role of the CIA in the 1963 assassination of John F. Kennedy. The accomplished conspiracy theorist can, with consummate skill and breathtaking versatility, explain even the most arcane and puzzling events in terms of the devious schemes and inscrutable machinations of hidden conspirators. Michael Billig (1978) believed it is precisely this that can make conspiracy theories so attractive – they are incredibly effective at reducing uncertainty. They provide a causal explanation in terms of enduring dispositions that can explain a wide range of events. It is much more fun to suggest and solve a devious mystery in simple terms. The reality of dealing with complex situational factors is both less widely applicable and more boring. Furthermore, 'uncovering' a conspiracy renders worrying events controllable and easily remedied. They are caused by small groups of highly visible people rather than arising from sociohistorical circumstances that may be difficult to comprehend.

Not surprisingly, conspiracy theories are almost immune to disconfirming evidence. For example, in December 2006 the outcome of a three-year, £3.5 million enquiry into the death in 1997 of Princess Diana was reported. Although there was absolutely no evidence that the British Royal family conspired with the British Government to have her killed to prevent her marrying an Egyptian Muslim, this conspiracy theory still persists. Take another recent example, emerging as a clash of civilisations. In his book *The Crisis of Islam: Holy War and Unholy Terror*, the historian Bernard Lewis (2004) described how the Muslim world portrayed President Bush's war on terror as a religious war. There is another even more convoluted conspiracy theory that Israel, or perhaps even the US Government itself, perpetrated the 9/11 terrorist attacks in the United States in 2001.

The basic cognitive and attributional processes we have discussed in this chapter are important for numerous sections in the chapters that follow. To take a few examples: we make attributions about our self and an intimate partner (Chapters 3 and 10); cognitive heuristics are involved in how we attend to persuasive messages (Chapter 4); schemas are fundamental to stereotypes and prejudice (Chapter 7); priming is sometimes involved in the way aggressive thoughts arise (Chapter 8); and cognitive biases can vary across cultures (Chapter 11). We expect that you will revisit this chapter many times as you progress further in this book.

Summary

- Social cognition deals with how our thinking processes and structures interact with the social context. People are limited in how they process information. Sometimes they are cognitive misers who take all sorts of cognitive short cuts. At other times they are motivated tacticians who choose, on the basis of their goals, motives and needs, between an array of cognitive strategies.

- The overall impressions that we form of other people are dominated by stereotypes, unfavourable information, first impressions and idiosyncratic personal constructs.

- Schemas are cognitive structures that represent knowledge about people, objects, events, roles and the self. Once a schema is invoked, our biases ensure that it is not undermined by the way we process information and make inferences.

- Categories are fuzzy sets of features organised around a prototype. They are hierarchically structured in terms of inclusiveness. Less inclusive categories are subsets of broader, more inclusive categories. When we categorise we aim to accentuate similarities within a category and differences between categories. Accentuation is a basis for stereotyping. To really work, a stereotype needs to

- be connected with the way that groups relate to each other.

- In processing information about others, we rely mostly on schemas relating to subtypes, stereotypes, current moods, easily detected features, accessible categories and information relevant to our self. However, we depend less on schemas when the cost of making a wrong inference is increased, when the cost of being indecisive is low, and when we believe that using a schema can lead to errors.

- Schemas become more abstract, complex, organised, compact, resilient and accurate over time. A schema is hard to change but can be modified when information is inconsistent with it. One kind of change occurs when we form subtypes.

- The way we encode information is heavily influenced by salient stimuli and by existing schemas that are easy to access.

- We remember people mainly for their traits but also their behaviour and appearance. They can be stored as individuals, or as members of a category.

- Our inferences fall far short of ideal. Our schemas dominate us, we disregard regression effects and base-rate information, and we perceive illusory

▶

correlations. We use cognitive short cuts (heuristics) such as representativeness, availability, and anchoring and adjustment, rather than process information accurately.

- Our needs, goals, being accountable and capacity to cope underpin affect and emotion. In turn, affect can influence social cognition. It infuses social cognition only when we need to put effort into processing information, such as actively elaborating stimulus details and retrieving information from memory.

- People are commonsense psychologists trying to understand the causes of their own and other people's behaviour.

- Much like scientists, we take account of consensus, consistency and distinctiveness information when we attribute behaviour either internally to personality traits and dispositions, or externally to situational factors.

- Our attributions can have a profound impact on our emotions, self-concept and relationships with others. People can differ in their tendencies to make internal or external attributions.

- We are actually poor scientists who show biases when making attributions. Two biases stand out. One is our tendency to attribute the actions of others internally but our own actions externally. The other is our tendency to protect our self-concept, attributing our failures externally but successes internally.

- Attributions for the behaviour of the people acting as group members are ethnocentric and stereotyped, a bias that is affected by the real or perceived nature of intergroup relations.

- Stereotypes may originate in a need for groups to attribute the cause of large-scale distressing events to outgroups we have already stereotyped and seem relevant to such events.

- People resort to causal attributions only when there is no readily available social knowledge (e.g. scripts, ideologies, social representations, cultural beliefs) to explain things automatically.

Literature, film and TV

The Reader

A 2008 film directed by Stephen Daldry and starring Ralph Fiennes, Jeanette Hain and David Kross. A teenage boy, Michael, in post-World War II Germany develops a passionate relationship with an older woman, Hanna, which profoundly affects him. Hanna suddenly disappears, but reappears 8 years later in Michael's life when she is on trial for war crimes. The impression of Hanna that Michael has cherished for so long is dramatically and upsettingly turned upside down. One way in which Michael deals with this is by focusing on a positive aspect of his former impression of her – her vulnerability in one aspect of her life.

Billy Elliot

The 2000 film by Stephen Daldry, and with Julie Walters, is set in a north of England mining town against the backdrop of the very bitter 1984 miners' strike. Billy Elliot is an 11-year-old boy who rejects the traditional male activity of boxing – preferring to become a ballet dancer. The film shows what happens when people violate social scripts and behave out-of-role in counter-stereotypical ways.

Reality TV

In shows such as *I'm a Celebrity, Get Me Out of Here*, minor celebrities attempt to gain publicity by projecting particular images of themselves to the public. These programmes show how people construct, manage and project impressions about themselves, and form impressions of other people.

About a Boy

This feel-good 2002 comedy by Chris and Paul Weitz, stars Hugh Grant. One of the themes in this light-hearted film is the embarrassment felt by the young boy, Marcus (Nicholas Hoult), because of the weirdness of his mother Fiona (Toni Collette), an ex-hippie depressive who tries to commit suicide and dresses Marcus strangely for school. Marcus is made to stand out and be salient at an age where one simply wants to fit in and be ordinary and part of the crowd.

The Third Policeman

Flan O'Brien's (1967) book is a wacky, bizarre and magical book about the absurd. It has a very funny section that is relevant to social representations. There is an hilarious account of how bizarre social representations (in this case about atomic theory) can be formed and sustained.

JFK

The 1991 film by Oliver Stone stars Kevin Costner as a New Orleans district attorney who reopens the case to find out who really assassinated JFK on 22 November 1963, in Dallas, and what the process/plot behind it was. This is a wonderful encounter with conspiracy theories and people's need to construct a causal explanation, however bizarre, of a disturbing event. The film also stars Tommy Lee Jones and Sissy Spacek.

The Devils

Harrowing 1971 Ken Russell cult classic about the inquisition and political intrigue in the church/state.

The scenes are grotesque, evocative of the paintings of Hieronymus Bosch. The film is based on an Aldous Huxley novel and stars Vanessa Redgrave and Oliver Reed. It shows the awful lengths to which a group can go to protect its ultimate causal explanation – any divergence is seen as heresy or blasphemy, and is severely punished in order to make sure that everyone believes in its explanation of the nature of things.

Macbeth

Shakespeare's 1606/07 tragedy in which three witches prophesise a string of evil deeds committed by Macbeth during his bloody rise to power, including the murder of the Scottish king Duncan. The causal question is whether the prophecy caused the events – or was there some other complex of causes.

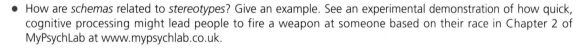

Guided questions

- You have heard the saying that people sometimes 'judge a book by its cover'. Use this idea as a springboard to outline how we form our first impressions of another person.

- *Stereotypes* are notoriously resistant to change. Why is this?

- How reliable is witness testimony? Apply what you know about *person memory* to this issue.

- Sometimes our mental short cuts lead us into error. One of these is *correspondence bias*. Describe and illustrate this concept.

- The term *conspiracy theory* has entered everyday language. Can social psychology help us understand what purpose these theories serve?

- How are *schemas* related to *stereotypes*? Give an example. See an experimental demonstration of how quick, cognitive processing might lead people to fire a weapon at someone based on their race in Chapter 2 of MyPsychLab at www.mypsychlab.co.uk.

Learn more

Devine, P. G., Hamilton, D. L., & Ostrom, T. M. (eds) (1994). *Social cognition: Impact on social psychology*. San Diego: Academic Press. Leading experts discuss the impact that social cognition has had on a wide range of topics in social psychology.

Fiske, S. T., & Taylor, S. E. (2008). *Social cognition: From brains to culture*. New York: McGraw-Hill. Fully updated edition of perhaps *the* classic text on social cognition. It is comprehensive, detailed and very well written.

Hewstone, M. (1989). *Causal attribution: From cognitive processes to collective beliefs*. Oxford: Blackwell. A comprehensive and detailed coverage of attribution theory and research, which also includes coverage of European perspectives that locate attribution processes in the context of society and intergroup relations.

Hilton, D. (2007). Casual explanation: From social perception to knowledge-based causal attribution. In A. W. Kruglanski & E. T. Higgins (eds), *Social psychology: Handbook of basic principles* (2nd ed, pp. 232–253). New York: Guilford. A recent overview of how and why we make causal attributions for behaviour, and how this relates to basic social cognition.

Moskowitz, G. B. (2005). *Social cognition: Understanding self and others*. New York: Guilford. A comprehensive social cognition text written in a relatively accessible style as an introduction to the topic.

Tesser, A., & Schwarz, N. (eds) (2001). *Blackwell handbook of social psychology: Intra-individual processes*. Oxford: Blackwell. A collection of twenty-eight chapters by leading scholars on intra-individual processes. It includes many chapters covering social cognition topics.

Trope, Y., & Gaunt, R. (2007). Attribution and person perception. In M. A. Hogg & J. Cooper (eds), *The Sage handbook of social psychology: Concise student edition* (pp. 176–194). London: Sage. A recent, comprehensive and very readable overview of attribution research.

 Refresh your understanding, assess your progress and go further with interactive summaries, questions, podcasts, videos and much more on the website accompanying the book: **www.mypsychlab.co.uk.**

Chapter 3

Self, identity and society

What to look for

- Origins of the Western self and the impact of the 'looking-glass' self

- What do we mean by 'I' or 'We'?

- When do we become consciously aware of ourselves?

- How we develop schemas about ourselves

- Self-guides that regulate what we do

- Different forms of self and identity

- Motives for developing a concept of self

- Why we pursue self-esteem

- How we present ourselves to others

Focus questions

1. To what extent is your identity unique, distinguishing you from all other human beings?

2. Would you accept that you are overwhelmingly driven to look good in other people's eyes?

3. Manfred poses a dilemma: if people generally want to feel good about themselves, have those with low self-esteem failed in their quest? Could you clarify this apparent anomaly for Manfred? You can get some help by watching a video based on the work of Dianne Tice in Chapter 3 of MyPsychLab at www.mypsychlab.co.uk.

4. Andrea has found out that you are studying social psychology. She asks your advice for presenting herself in the best possible light to others. Can you give her some tips?

Who are you? Take a look in your wallet. You will probably find numerous cards and pieces of paper that have your name on them, and probably a rather gruesome photograph of yourself. What happens when you meet someone socially? Very early in the piece you discover each other's name, and soon after that you establish such things as their occu-pation, their attitudes and what they like to do. You also try to identify mutual acquaintances. In more formal contexts, people sometimes display their identity through uniforms, name or role badges and business cards.

Social interaction, and social existence itself, depends on people knowing who they are and who others are. Your identity and your self-concept underpin your everyday life – knowing who you are allows you to know what you should think and do, and knowing who others are allows you to predict what they think and what they do. Knowing our identity regulates and structures how we interact with others; and in turn, there are ways of interacting and structures in our society that provide identities for us.

Many scholars have argued that it is reflexive thought – that is, the ability to think about ourselves thinking – that separates us from almost all other animals. Reflexive thought means that we can think about ourselves, about who we are, how we would like to be and how we would like others to see us. These days, humans have a highly developed sense of self. Self and identity, then, are fundamental parts of being human. We should not be surprised that social psychologists in particular have become intrigued with the self.

In this chapter, we explore the self – where it comes from, what it looks like and how it influences thought and behaviour. Self and identity are cognitive constructs that influence social interaction and perception and are themselves influenced by society. As a result, the material in this chapter connects to virtually all other chapters in this book. In recent years, there has been an explosive revival of research on the self, exemplified in the work of Constantine Sedikides and Marilynn Brewer (2001). We discuss their contributions below.

Constructs
Abstract or theoretical concepts or variables that are not observable and are used to explain or clarify a phenomenon.

The self in history

The very idea that you or I might have a self is relatively new. Roy Baumeister (1987) paints a picture of medieval society in which social relations were fixed and stable and legitimised in religious terms. People's lives and identities were tightly mapped out according to their position in the social order – by visible attributes that go with birth, such as family membership, social rank, birth order and place of birth. In many ways, what you saw was what you got, so the idea of a complex individual self lurking underneath it all was difficult to entertain and probably superfluous.

This started to change in the sixteenth century and has gathered momentum ever since. The forces for change included the following:

- *Secularisation* – the idea that fulfilment would occur in the afterlife was replaced by the idea that you should actively pursue personal fulfilment in this life.
- *Industrialisation* – people were increasingly seen as units of production who would move from place to place to work, and thus would have a portable personal identity that was not locked into static social structures such as the extended family.

- *Enlightenment* – people felt that they could organise and construct different, better, identities and lives for themselves by overthrowing orthodox value systems and oppressive regimes (e.g. the French and American revolutions of the late eighteenth century).
- *Psychoanalysis* – Freud's theory of the human mind crystallised the notion that the self was unfathomable because it skulked in the gloomy depths of the unconscious.

Together, these and other social, political and cultural changes caused people to think about self and identity as highly complex. Theories of self and identity propagated and flourished in this fertile soil.

The psychodynamic self

Psychoanalysis created a problem: the self and identity were connected to complex dynamics that are hidden deep within our sense of who we are. Freud (e.g. 1921) believed that unsocialised and selfish libidinal impulses (the *id*) are repressed and kept in check by norms internalised from our society (the *superego*), but that, from time to time and in strange and peculiar ways, repressed impulses surface. You might say that the superego was there to spoil the id's fun! Freud's view of the self is one in which you can only truly know yourself, or indeed others, when special procedures, such as hypnosis or psychotherapy, are put in place to reveal repressed thoughts. Freud's ideas about self, identity and personality are far-reaching in social psychology: for example, Adorno, Frenkel-Brunswik, Levinson and Sanford's (1950) influential authoritarian personality theory of prejudice is a psychodynamic theory (see Chapter 7).

The self: 'I' or 'We'?

Freud, like many other psychologists, viewed the self as very personal and private – the high point of individuality: something that uniquely describes an individual human being. When someone says '*I am . . .*' they are describing what makes them different from all other human beings.

But think about this for a moment. When Bud Flanagan sang the post-war 'buck-up' lyrics of *Maybe it's because I'm a Londoner* in 1946, he made a significant point. It is more than an 'I' statement. Today there more than 12 million people in the greater metropolitan area in and around London who could truthfully sing along with Bud – with a formidable variety of accents! It is in this sense that the self can also be a shared or collective self – a 'we' or 'us'. Sometimes these two aspects are breathtakingly close. Think of the moment that an athlete stands on a Olympic podium, wearing a medal as an individual, 'I', and listening to an anthem for a nation, 'we'.

Social psychologists argued long and hard for more than a century about what to make of this. Is the self an individual or a collective phenomenon? For much of this time, advocates of the individual self have tended to prevail. This is largely because social psychologists have considered groups to be made up of individuals who interact with one another rather than individuals who have a collective sense of shared identity. Individuals interacting in aggregates make up the province of social psychology, whereas groups as collectives are the province of several other social sciences, such as sociology and political science (see Chapters 1 and 7).

This perspective on groups, summed up by Floyd Allport's legendary proclamation that 'There is no psychology of groups which is not essentially and entirely a psychology of individuals' (1924, p. 4), has made it difficult for the collective self to thrive as a research topic. However, in recent years the field has loosened up – as we shall see during the course of this chapter.

The view that the self draws its properties from groups is shared by many other early social psychologists: for example, early theorists of collective behaviour and the crowd, such as Gustav LeBon (1908); also see Chapter 7. In his book *The Group Mind*, William McDougall (1920) argued that out of the interaction of individuals there arose a 'group mind', which had a reality and existence that was qualitatively distinct from the isolated individuals making up the group. There was a collective self that was grounded in group life. Although phrased in rather old-fashioned language, this idea has a direct line of descent to subsequent experimental social psychological research, which confirms that human interaction has emergent properties that endure and influence other people: for example, Muzafer Sherif's (1936) research on how norms emerge from interaction and are internalised to influence behaviour, Solomon Asch's (1952) research on conformity to norms, and more recent research stimulated by Serge Moscovici (1982) on the emergence of social representations out of social interaction. These ideas are explored in Chapters 2 and 5.

In recent years, the notion of a collective self has been elaborated in social identity theory, which is discussed in Chapter 7.

The self and social interaction

Another twist to the idea of the collective self is recognising that the self emerges and is shaped by social interaction. Early psychologists such as William James (1890) distinguished between self as stream of consciousness, 'I', and self as object of perception, 'me'. In this way, reflexive knowledge is possible because 'I' can be aware of 'me', and people can thus know themselves. However, people's self-knowledge is not particularly accurate. People tend to reconstruct who they are without being aware of having done it, as Tony Greenwald (1980) has noted. Although people may be aware of who they are in terms of their attitudes and preferences, they are rather bad at knowing how they arrived at that knowledge (Nisbett & Wilson, 1977).

Nevertheless, people do have a sense of 'me'. According to symbolic interactionism, associated with the work of the sociologist G. H. Mead (1934), the self arises out of human interaction. Mead believed that human interaction is largely symbolic. When we interact with people it is mainly in terms of words and non-verbal cues that are rich with meaning because they symbolise much more than what is available in our actions alone (see Chapter 11). Mead believed that society influences individuals through the way they think about themselves, a process that is continually updated as we interact with other people. We use symbols that must have shared meaning if we want to communicate effectively. If you say to your friend 'let's eat out tonight' you both know what this means and that it opens up a variety of choices that each of you know about.

Interacting effectively also rests on being able to take the role of the other person. More specifically, this entails seeing oneself as others do – as a social *object*, 'me', rather than a social *subject*, 'I'. Because others often see us as representatives of a category (e.g. a student), the 'me' is probably more often seen as a collective 'me' – we might even think of it as 'us'. The representations, or views, that our society has of the world are traded through interacting symbolically with

Collective behaviour
The behaviour of people en masse – such as in a crowd, protest or riot.

Social representations
Collectively elaborated explanations of unfamiliar and complex phenomena that transform them into a familiar and simple form.

Social identity theory
Theory of group membership and intergroup relations based on self-categorisation, social comparison and the construction of a shared self-definition in terms of ingroup-defining properties.

Symbolic interactionism
Theory of how the self emerges from human interaction that involves people trading symbols (through language and gesture) that are usually consensual, and represent abstract properties rather than concrete objects.

others. We are effective only if we can take the role of the other, and thus see ourselves as others do. In this way, we construct a self-concept that reflects the society
we live in; we are socially constituted.

Symbolic interactionism offers a quite sophisticated and complex model of how
the self is formed. And yet it generates a very straightforward prediction. Because
forming our concept of self comes from seeing ourselves as others see us, which is
the idea of the looking-glass self, how we rate ourselves should be closely connected to how others rate us. Sidney Shrauger and Thomas Schoeneman (1979)
reviewed sixty-two studies to see if this was true. What they found was that people
did *not* tend to see themselves as others saw them but instead saw themselves as
they *thought* others saw them.

Looking-glass self
The self derived from
seeing ourselves as
others see us.

Dianne Tice's study provides an example (Tice, 1992). Her participants were
undergraduate students who were asked to act as 'stimulus persons' for postgraduate clinical psychology trainees. Their task was to answer verbal questions using an
intercom system in a way that would reflect an aspect of their personality.
Effectively, they were to describe themselves so that they would come across as
either consistently *emotionally stable* (implying *not responsive*) or *emotionally
responsive* in different situations. There were two conditions in the experiment:
(a) a private condition, in which they believed no one was watching them; (b) a
public condition, in which they believed a clinical psychology trainee was closely
monitoring their behaviour. (This was a ruse, since there was no one actually monitoring the students.) In the next phase, they were asked to rate themselves in terms
of how responsive they really were. They made their ratings on a 25-point scale
ranging from 1 (stable = not responsive) to 25 (responsive).

Tice intended the public condition to be the one that would engage the looking-
glass self. As predicted, subsequent descriptions of self were more radically altered
under public conditions than private conditions (see Figure 3.1).

The looking-glass self. G. H. Mead argued that our
self-concept derives from seeing ourselves as others see us.

Source: Pearson Online Database (POD)

Figure 3.1

Private self or public self? Effect of seeming to be either emotionally responsive or not responsive (stable).

- People who were instructed to present themselves as either less emotionally responsive (i.e. more stable) or more emotionally responsive.
- Next, they rated themselves for their 'true' level of emotionality on a 25-point scale, ranging from a low score (less emotionally responsive) to a high score (more emotionally responsive).
- When they believed that their earlier behaviour had been public, their self-conception moved in the direction of their action: closer to a score of 1 for those who had been less emotionally responsive, or closer to a score of 25 for those who had been more emotionally responsive.

Source: Based on data from Tice (1992), Study 1.

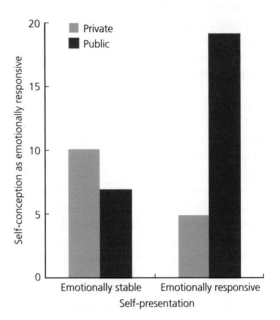

The idea coming through in studies like Tice's is that people do not see themselves as others see them, but instead see themselves as they *think* others see them. So we do not actually take the role of the other in constructing a sense of self. We are mostly unaware of what other people really think of us (Kenny & DePaulo, 1993), perhaps fortunately so. A sage person once said: 'If you really want to hear how much people like you, you'd better listen to what they say at your funeral!'

As we discover below, our concept of self is linked to how we go about enhancing our self-image. People normally overestimate their good points, overestimate their control over events and are unrealistically optimistic – Sedikides and Gregg (2003) call this the *self-enhancing triad*.

Self-awareness

If the truth be known, you do not spend all your time thinking about yourself. Self-awareness comes and goes for different reasons and has an array of consequences.

In their book *A Theory of Objective Self Awareness*, Shelley Duval and Robert Wicklund (1972) argued that self-awareness is a state in which you are aware of yourself as an object, much as you might be aware of a tree or another person. Thus they speak of objective self-awareness. When you are objectively self-aware you make comparisons between how you actually are and how you would like to be – an ideal, a goal or some other standard. The outcome of this comparison is often a sense that you have shortcomings, along with negative emotions associated with this recognition. People then try to rectify their faults by bringing the self closer into line with ideal standards. This can sometimes be very difficult, and people can give up trying, experience reduced motivation, and feel even worse about themselves.

Objective self-awareness is generated by anything that focuses your attention on yourself as an object: for example, being in front of an audience (see Chapter 6) or catching your image in a mirror. Indeed, a very popular method for raising self-awareness in laboratory studies is precisely this – place participants in front of a mirror. Charles Carver and Michael Scheier (1981) elaborated self-awareness theory. They distinguished between two types of self that we can be aware of:

1. the *private self* – your private thoughts, feelings and attitudes;
2. the *public self* – how other people see you, your public image.

Private self-awareness leads us to match our behaviour with our internalised standards, whereas public self-awareness is oriented towards presenting yourself to others in a positive light.

Being self-aware can be very uncomfortable. We all feel self-conscious from time to time and are only too familiar with how it affects our behaviour – we feel anxious, we become tongue-tied, or we make mistakes on tasks. We can even feel slightly paranoid (Fenigstein, 1984). However, sometimes being self-aware can be a terrific thing, particularly on those occasions when we have accomplished a great feat. In early December 2003, having won the Rugby World Cup, the England team paraded through London and ended up in Trafalgar Square in front of three-quarters of a million people – standing in an open-topped bus, the team looked freezing, but certainly did not suffer from the crowd's adulation.

Self-awareness can also make us feel good when the standards against which we compare ourselves are not too exacting: for example, if we compare ourselves against standards derived from 'most other people' or from people who are less fortunate than ourselves (Taylor & Brown, 1988). Self-awareness can also improve introspection, intensify emotions and improve performance of controlled effort-sensitive tasks that do not require undue skill, such as checking over an essay you have written.

The reverse side of being objectively self-aware is being in a state of reduced objective self-awareness. Because elevated self-awareness can be stressful or aversive, people may try to avoid this state by drinking alcohol, or by more extreme measures such as suicide (Baumeister, 1991). Reduced self-awareness has also been identified as a key component of deindividuation, a state in which people are blocked from awareness of themselves as distinct individuals, fail to monitor their actions, and can behave impulsively. Reduced self-awareness may be implicated in the way that crowds behave and in other forms of social unrest. Read how this comes about in both small groups and crowd settings (Chapters 7 and 8).

Deindividuation
Process whereby people lose their sense of socialised individual identity and engage in unsocialised, often antisocial, behaviours.

Self-knowledge

When people are self-aware, what are they aware of? What do we know about ourselves and how do we gain a sense of who we are? Self-knowledge is constructed in much the same way and through many of the same processes as we construct representations of other people. We looked at some of these general processes when we discussed social thinking and attribution in Chapter 2.

Self-schemas

By using a number of *schemas*, we store information about the self in a way that is similar to what we do for other people (see Chapter 2). However, the outcome is much more varied.

According to Helen Markus, the self-concept is neither a 'singular, static, lump-like entity' nor a simple averaged view of the self – it is complex and multi-faceted, with a relatively large number of discrete self-schemas (Markus, 1977; Markus & Wurf, 1987). People tend to have clear conceptions of themselves (i.e. self-schemas) on some dimensions but not others – i.e. they are schematic on some but aschematic on others. People are self-schematic on dimensions that are important to them, on which they think they are extreme and on which they are certain the opposite does not hold. For example, if you think you are sophisticated, and being sophisticated is important to you, then you are self-schematic on that dimension – it is part of your self-concept. If you do not think you are sophisticated, and if this does not bother you, then being *sophisticated* is not one of your self-schemas.

We try to use our self-schemas strategically. Patricia Linville (1985) used a colourful phrase to describe what we usually do: 'Don't put all your eggs in one cognitive basket'. Having a variety of self-schemas provides a buffer from some of life's misfortunes: we can always pull some self-schemas out of other baskets to derive some satisfaction.

Self-schemas that are rigidly compartmentalised have disadvantages (Showers, 1992). If some self-schemas are very negative and some are very positive, events may cause extreme mood swings according to whether a positive or negative self-schema is primed. Generally, more integrated self-schemas are preferable. For example, if James believes that he is a wonderful cook but an awful musician, he has compartmentalised self-schemas – contexts that prime one or the other self-schema will produce very positive or very negative moods. Contrast this with Sally, who believes that she is a reasonably good cook but not a great musician. She has self-schemas where the boundaries are less clear – context effects on mood will be less extreme.

Learning about the self

One of the most obvious ways to learn about who you are is to examine your private thoughts and feelings about the world – knowing what you think and feel about the world is a very good clue to the sort of person you are.

However, when these internal cues are weak we may make inferences about ourselves from what we do – our behaviour. This idea underpins Daryl Bem's *self-perception theory* (Bem, 1967, 1972). Bem argued that we make attributions not only for others' behaviour (see Chapter 2) but also for our own, and that there is no essential difference between self-attributions and other attributions. Furthermore, just as we construct an impression of someone else's personality on the basis of being able to make internal dispositional attributions for their behaviour, so we construct a concept of who we are, not by introspection but by being able to attribute our own behaviour internally. So, for example, I know that I enjoy eating curry because, if given the opportunity, I eat curry of my own free will and in preference to other foods, and not everyone likes curry – I am able to make an internal attribution for my behaviour.

How we perceive ourselves can also be based on simply imagining ourselves behaving in a particular way. For example, sports psychologist Geraldine van Gyn and her colleagues divided runners into two groups; one group practised power training on exercise bikes, the other did not. Half of each group used imagery, i.e. also imagined themselves sprint training, whereas the others did not. Of course, the sweaty business of power training itself improved subsequent performance; but, remarkably, those who imagined themselves sprint training did better than those who did not. The researchers concluded that imagery had affected self-conception, which in turn produced performance that was consistent with that self-conception (van Gyn, Wenger & Gaul, 1990).

Self-attributions have important implications for motivation. The theory predicts that if someone is induced to perform a task by either enormous rewards or heavy penalties, task performance is attributed externally and thus motivation to perform is reduced. In the absence of external factors to which performance can be attributed, we will instead look to enjoyment or commitment as causes, so motivation increases. This has been called the overjustification effect (see Figure 3.2), for which there is now substantial evidence (Deci & Ryan, 1985).

For example, Mark Lepper and his colleagues had nursery-school children draw pictures. Some of the children simply drew of their own free will, while the rest were induced to draw with the promise of a reward, which they were subsequently given. A few days later, the children were unobtrusively observed playing; the children who had previously been rewarded for drawing spent half as much time drawing as did the other group. Those who had received no extrinsic reward seemed to have greater intrinsic interest in drawing (Lepper, Greene & Nisbett, 1973).

In fact, a review by John Condry (1977) showed that introducing external rewards can backfire by reducing motivation and enjoyment of a task that was

Overjustification effect
In the absence of obvious external determinants of our behaviour, we assume that we freely choose the behaviour because we enjoy it.

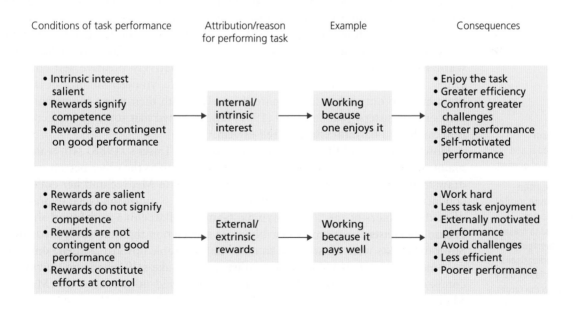

Figure 3.2

The overjustification effect.

Our motivation to perform a task can be reduced, and performance of the task impaired, if there are obvious external causes for task performances – an overjustification effect that is reversed if performance can be internally attributed.

previously intrinsically motivated. This has clear educational implications. Parents generally love to tell their children stories and in time encourage the young ones to enjoy stories by learning to read themselves. However, if reading is accompanied by rewards their intrinsic joy is put at risk. Is it possible for rewards to play any useful role? The answer is yes. The trick is to reduce a reliance on rewards that are *task-contingent* and make more use of those that are *performance-contingent*. Even a task that people find boring can be enlivened when they shift their attention to features of their performance (Sansone, Weir, Harpster & Morgan, 1992). Consider how you look for ways to maintain interest in a monotonous physical fitness programme, especially when you need to work out alone. You could of course listen to music or watch television. However, a performance-contingent strategy is to set targets using measures such as 'distance' covered on an exercycle, checking your heart rate and how many calories you expended.

We turn now to the impact that other people have on how our self-concept develops.

Social comparison and self-knowledge

Are you bright? How do you know? There are aspects of ourselves that call for a yardstick: we can learn by comparing ourselves with other people. Indeed, Leon Festinger (1954) developed social comparison theory in just this way, to describe how people learn about themselves through comparisons with others. People need to be confident about the validity of their perceptions, attitudes, feelings and behaviour, and because there is rarely an objective measure of validity, people ground their cognitions, feelings and behaviour in those of other people. In particular, they seek out similar others to validate their perceptions and attitudes, which can, to some extent, be read as meaning that people anchor their attitudes and self-concept in the groups to which they feel they belong.

According to Thomas Wills (1981), when it comes to performance we try to compare ourselves with people who are slightly worse than us – we make downward social comparisons, which deliver an evaluatively positive self-concept. Often, however, our choices are limited: for example, younger siblings in families often have no option but to compare themselves with their more competent older brothers and sisters. Joanne Wood (1989) has suggested that some upward comparison can have a harmful effect on self-esteem.

How can we avoid this? According to Abraham Tesser's (1988) self-evaluation maintenance model, we try to downplay our similarity to the other person or withdraw from our relationship with that person. Victoria Medvec and her colleagues conducted an intriguing study along these lines. They coded the facial expressions of medal winners at the 1992 Olympic Games in Barcelona and found that the bronze medallists expressed noticeably more satisfaction than the silver medallists! Silver medallists were constrained to make unfavourable upward comparisons with gold medallists, whereas bronze medallists could make self-enhancing downward comparisons with the rest of the field, who received no medal at all (Medvec, Madley & Gilovich, 1995).

Downward comparisons also occur between groups. Groups try to compare themselves with inferior groups in order to feel that 'we' are better than 'them'. Indeed, intergroup relations are largely a struggle for evaluative superiority of one's own group over relevant outgroups (Hogg, 2000). This in turn influences self-conception as a group member – social identity (Tajfel & Turner, 1979). According

Social comparison Comparing our behaviours and opinions with those of others in order to establish the correct or socially approved way of thinking and behaving.

Self-esteem Feelings about and evaluations of oneself.

Self-evaluation maintenance model People who are constrained to make esteem-damaging upward comparisons can underplay or deny similarity to the target, or they can withdraw from their relationship with the target.

to self-categorisation theory, an extension of social identity theory, the underlying process is one in which people who feel they belong to a group categorise themselves as group members and automatically internalise as a self-evaluation the attributes that describe the group – if the group is positive, the attributes are positive, and thus the self is positive (see Chapter 7).

Sport provides an ideal context in which the outcome of this process can be seen. Few Italians will not have felt enormously positive when their team beat Germany in the finals of the 2006 football World Cup. Robert Cialdini and his associates have referred to this phenomenon as 'basking in reflected glory', or BIRGing (Cialdini *et al.*, 1976). To illustrate the effect, they conducted experiments in which they raised or lowered self-esteem via feedback on a general knowledge test; and student participants were then, seemingly incidentally, asked about the outcome of a recent football game. Participants who had had their self-esteem lowered tended to associate themselves with winning and not with losing teams – they tended to refer to the teams as 'we' in the former case and as 'they' in the latter.

Self-regulation

Do you find it easy to stick to a diet? Many people do not, and yet they may really want to. Self-schemas not only describe what we are but what we want to be. Markus and Nurius (1986) have suggested that we have an array of possible selves: future-oriented schemas of what we would like to have happen, or of what we fear we might become. For example, a postgraduate student may have hopes of becoming a university lecturer or a successful executive – or a fear of being unable to get a job.

Another perspective is offered by Higgins's (1987) self-discrepancy theory. Higgins suggests that we have three types of self-schema:

Self-categorisation theory
Turner and associates' theory of how the process of categorising oneself as a group member produces social identity and group and intergroup behaviours.

BIRGing
Basking In Reflected Glory – that is, name-dropping to link yourself with desirable people or groups and thus improve other people's impression of you.

Self-discrepancy theory
Higgins' theory about the consequences of making actual–ideal and actual–'ought' self comparisons that reveal self-discrepancies.

Self-discrepancy theory. Oprah has reported some concern that her body weight fluctuates. No doubt, her actual self in this picture is far from her ideal self.

Source: Fred Prouser / Reuters

1. *actual self* – how we currently are;
2. *ideal self* – how we would like to be;
3. *'ought' self* – how we think we should be.

The latter two are 'self-guides' that mobilise different types of self-related behaviours. The same goal – for example, prosperity – can be constructed as an ideal (strive to be prosperous) or an 'ought' (strive to avoid not being prosperous). Discrepancies between actual, and ideal or 'ought' can motivate change to reduce the discrepancy – in this way we engage in self-regulation. (In Chapter 10 we discuss self-regulation in the context of close relationships.) Failure to resolve the actual–ideal discrepancy can make us feel dejected, whereas failure to resolve the actual–ought discrepancy tends to make us agitated. Read about a test of self-discrepancy theory in Box 3.1 and see the results in Figure 3.3.

Self-regulation
Strategies that we use to match our behaviour to an ideal or 'ought' standard.

Research classic 3.1
Self-discrepancy theory: the impact of using self-guides

Tory Higgins and his colleagues measured self-discrepancy by comparing the differences between attributes of the *actual* self with those of either the *ideal* self or with those of the *'ought'* self.

In this study, they used questionnaires to identify students who were either high in both kinds of discrepancies or else low in both. Several weeks later, the same students participated in an experiment in which a range of emotions that reflected dejection or agitation were measured, both before and after a priming procedure. For their ideal prime they were asked to discuss their own and their parents' hopes for them; for their 'ought' prime they discussed their own and their parents' beliefs about their duties and obligations.

It was hypothesised that an actual-ideal discrepancy would lead to feeling dejected (but not agitated), whereas an actual–'ought' discrepancy would lead to feeling agitated (but not dejected). These predictions were supported, as the results in Figure 3.3 show.

Figure 3.3

Priming the ideal self can lead to dejection, whereas priming the 'ought' self can lead to agitation.

People with a high actual–ideal and actual–ought self-discrepancy experienced:

- an increase in dejection but not agitation emotions after being primed to focus on their ideal self, and
- an increase in agitation but not dejection emotions after being primed to focus on their 'ought' self.

Source: Based on Higgins, Bond, Klein & Strauman (1986), Experiment 2.

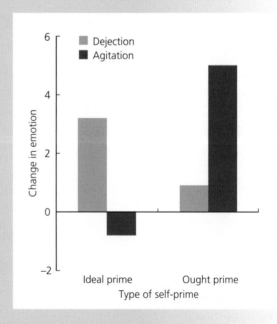

Self-discrepancy theory and the general notion of self-regulation have recently been elaborated into regulatory focus theory. Higgins (1997) made it clear that he wanted to go beyond Freud's *pleasure-pain principle*, that we are bent on procuring the first and avoiding the second. At the root of this simplistic proposition, argued Higgins, is a motivational principle with two separate self-regulatory systems related to the pursuit of different types of goals. Consider the case of students:

- The *promotion system* – you are motivated to attain your hopes and aspirations: your *ideals*. You will be on the lookout for positive events. When you focus in this way you adopt an *approach strategy* to attain your goals – e.g. you might try to improve your grades, find new challenges and treat problems as interesting obstacles to overcome.
- The *prevention system* – you are motivated to fulfil your duties and obligations: your *oughts*. You will be on the lookout for negative events. When you focus in this way you adopt an *avoidance strategy* to attain your goals – e.g. you might try to avoid new situations or new people, and concentrate more on avoiding failure than achieving the highest possible grade.

Some people are habitually more promotion-focused and others more prevention-focused, a difference that can arise during childhood. A promotion-focus is encouraged when children are habitually hugged and kissed for behaving in a desired way, or when love is withdrawn as a form of discipline. A prevention-focus can arise when children are encouraged to be alert to potential dangers or when punished and shouted at for acting badly (Higgins & Silberman, 1998). Research by Penelope Lockwood and her associates shows that people who are promotion-focused look for inspiration to positive role models who emphasise strategies for achieving success. People who are prevention-focused behave quite differently – they are most inspired by negative role models who highlight strategies for avoiding failure (Lockwood, Jordan & Kunda, 2002).

We now move to a real poser: do you ever feel you are more than one person?

Many selves, multiple identities

It is probably inaccurate to characterise the self as a single undifferentiated entity. In his book *The Concept of Self*, Kenneth Gergen (1971) depicts the self-concept as containing a repertoire of relatively discrete and often quite varied identities, each with a distinct body of knowledge. My identities probably grew from the many different social relationships in my life. These are anchoring points ranging from close personal relationships with friends and family, from relationships and roles defined by work groups and professions, and from relationships defined by ethnicity, nationality and religion.

As we noted earlier, we differ in self-complexity (Linville, 1985). Some of us have a more diverse and extensive set of selves than others who have only a few, relatively similar, aspects of self.

Social identity theorists (e.g. Tajfel & Turner, 1979; see below) have argued that there are two broad classes of identity that define different types of self:

1. social identity, which defines self in terms of group memberships;
2. personal identity, which defines self in terms of idiosyncratic personal relationships and traits.

Now check the first focus question.

Regulatory focus theory
People use self-regulation to bring themselves into line with their standards and goals, using either a promotion system or a prevention system.

Social identity
That part of the self-concept that derives from our membership of social groups.

Personal identity
The self defined in terms of unique personal attributes or unique interpersonal relationships.

Marilynn Brewer and Wendi Gardner (1996) asked the question 'Who is this "we"?' and distinguished three forms of self:

1. the *individual self* – based on personal traits that differentiate the self from all others;
2. the *relational self* – based on connections and role relationships with significant others);
3. the *collective self* – based on group membership that differentiates 'us' from 'them'.

The relational self is interesting. Although in one sense it is an interpersonal form of self, it can also be considered a particular type of collective self. As Masaki Yuki (2003) observed, some groups and cultures (notably East Asian cultures) define groups in terms of networks of relationships. Not surprisingly, Elizabeth Seeley and her colleagues found that women place a greater importance than men on their relationships with others in their groups (Seeley, Gardner, Pennington & Gabriel, 2003).

The way that culture is entwined with the self is discussed more fully in Chapter 11.

Distinguishing selves and identities

How can we distinguish between our selves and our identities? Table 3.1 shows one way that different types of self and self-attributes intersect with level of identity (social versus personal) and type of attributes (identity versus relationship).

Evidence for the existence of multiple selves comes from research where contextual factors are varied to discover that people describe themselves differently, and may even behave differently, in different contexts. For example, Russell Fazio and his colleagues were able to get participants to describe themselves in very different ways. They did this by asking them loaded questions that made them search through their stock of self-knowledge for information that presented the self in a different light (Fazio, Effrein & Falender, 1981).

Other researchers have found, time and time again, that experimental procedures that focus on group membership lead people to act very differently from procedures that focus on individuality and interpersonal relationships. Consider 'minimal group' studies in which participants are either: (a) identified as individuals; or (b) explicitly categorised, randomly or by some trivial criterion as group members

Table 3.1 Self and self-attributes are related to levels of identity: social identity versus personal identity

	Identity attributes	Relationship attributes
Social identity	*Collective self* Attributes shared with others that differentiate the individual from a specific outgroup, or from outgroups in general.	*Collective relational self* Attributes that define how the self as an ingroup member relates to specific others as ingroup or outgroup members.
Personal identity	*Individual self* Attributes unique to self that differentiate the individual from specific individuals, or from other individuals in general.	*Individual relational self* Attributes that define how the self as a unique individual relates to others as individuals.

(Tajfel, 1970; see Chapter 7). A consistent finding is that categorisation makes people discriminate against an outgroup, conform to ingroup norms, express attitudes and feelings that favour the ingroup, and indicate a sense of belonging and loyalty to the ingroup.

We now need to address the question of how we get our selves together!

The search for self-coherence

Although we may have a diversity of relatively discrete selves, we also have a quest: to find and maintain a reasonably integrated picture of who we are. Coherence provides us with a continuing theme for our lives – an 'autobiography' that weaves our various identities and selves together into a whole person. People who have highly fragmented selves (e.g. some people with schizophrenia, amnesia or Alzheimer's disease) find it extraordinarily difficult to function effectively.

People use many strategies to construct a coherent sense of self (Baumeister, 1998). Here are some tricks you can use:

- Restrict your life to a limited set of contexts. Because our various selves come into play as contexts keep changing, by reducing their number you will protect yourself from self-conceptual clashes.
- Keep revising and integrating your 'autobiography' to accommodate new identities. Along the way, get rid of any worrisome inconsistencies. In effect you are rewriting your history to make it work to your benefit.
- Attribute changes in the self externally to changing circumstances, rather than internally to fundamental changes in who we are. This is an application of the actor–observer effect (see Chapter 2).

We can also develop a self-schema that embodies a core set of attributes that we feel distinguishes us from all other people – that makes us unique. We then tend to recognise these attributes disproportionately in all our selves, and as Nancy Cantor and John Kihlstrom (1987) have argued, provide a link that delivers a sense of a stable and unitary self.

In summary, people find ways to construct their lives such that their self-conceptions are both steady and coherent.

Actor–observer effect
Tendency to attribute our own behaviours externally and others' behaviours internally.

Self-motives

Because selves and identities are such critical reference points for the way we adapt to life, people are enthusiastically motivated to secure self-knowledge. Entire industries are based on this search for knowledge, ranging from personality tests to dubious practices such as astrology and palmistry. However, people do not go about this search in a dispassionate way; they have an idea about what they want to know and can be dismayed when the quest unearths things they did not expect or did not want to find.

Social psychologists have identified three classes of motive that may interact to influence self-construction and the search for self-knowledge. We pursue:

- self-assessment to validate ourselves;
- self-verification to be consistent;
- self-enhancement to look good.

Self-assessment and self-verification

Self-assessment
The motivation to seek out new information about ourselves in order to find out what sort of person we really are.

Self-verification
Seeking out information that verifies and confirms what we already know about ourselves.

Self-enhancement
The motivation to develop and promote a favourable image of self.

Self-affirmation theory
The theory that people reduce the impact of threat to their self-concept by focusing on and affirming their competence in some other area.

We have a simple desire to have accurate and valid information about ourselves – there is a self-assessment motive, as an overview by Yaacov Trope (1986) has shown. People strive to find out the truth about themselves, regardless of how unfavourable or disappointing the truth may be. But people also like to engage in a quest for confirmation – to confirm what they already know about themselves they seek out self-consistent information through a self-verification process, as Bill Swann (1987) has described. So, for example, people who have a negative self-image will actually seek out negative information to confirm that image.

Self-enhancement

Above all else, people like to learn things about themselves that make the self look good. We like to learn new things that are favourable about ourselves as well as finding ways to revise existing views that are unfavourable. People are guided by a self-enhancement motive (e.g. Kunda, 1990). Using self-affirmation theory, David Sherman and Geoffrey Cohen (2006) described how this motive reveals itself. People strive publicly to affirm positive aspects of who they are; this can be done blatantly by boasting or more subtly through rationalising or dropping hints. The urge to self-affirm is particularly strong when an aspect of one's self-esteem has been damaged. So, for example, if someone draws attention to the fact that you are a lousy artist, you might retort that while that might be true, you are an excellent dancer. Self-affirmation rests on people's need to maintain a global image that they are competent, good, coherent, unitary, stable, capable of free choice and capable of controlling important outcomes.

Self-affirmation theory. Publicly affirming a positive aspect of oneself sometimes conceals other aspects that are less positive. Perhaps this young man's biceps are more impressive than his grades!

Source: Pearson Online Database (POD)

See how Claude Steele put the process of self-affirmation in a test of adherence to religious faith in Box 3.2.

Which motive is more fundamental and more likely to prevail in the pursuit of self-knowledge – self-assessment, self-verification or self-enhancement? In a series of experiments, Constantine Sedikides (1993) pitted the three motives against one another. His participants used a self-reflection task in which they ask themselves questions. Some of these involved central traits that applied their selves whereas other questions related to more peripheral traits about their selves. The degree of self-reflection should depend on which of the three self-motives is operating:

- *Self-assessment* – greater self-reflection on *peripheral* than central traits of self, whether the attribute is desirable or not, indicates a drive to find out more about self (people already have knowledge about traits that are central for them).
- *Self-verification* – greater self-reflection on *central* than on peripheral traits, whether the attribute is positive or not, indicates a drive to confirm what one already knows about oneself.
- *Self-enhancement* – greater self-reflection on *positive* than on negative aspects of self, whether the attribute is central or not, indicates a drive to learn positive things about self.

Sedikides found that self-enhancement was strongest, with self-verification a distant second and self-assessment an even more distant third. The desire to think well of ourselves reigns supreme; it dominates both the pursuit of accurate self-knowledge and the pursuit of information that confirms self-knowledge. (Does this apply to you? See the second focus question.)

Because self-enhancement is so important, people have developed a formidable repertoire of techniques to pursue it. People engage in elaborate self-deceptions to

Research and applications 3.2
Self-affirmation in Salt Lake City

Claude Steele (1975) reported a study in Salt Lake City in which Mormon women who were at home during the day were telephoned by a female researcher posing as a community member. She asked them if they would be willing to list everything in their kitchen to assist the development of a community food cooperative; those who agreed would be called back the following week. Because community cooperation is a very strong ethic among Mormons, about 50 per cent of women agreed to this time-consuming request.

In addition to this baseline condition, there were three other conditions in the study arising from a previous call, two days earlier, by an entirely unrelated researcher posing as a pollster. In the course of this call, the pollster mentioned in passing that it was common knowledge that as members of their community, they were either:

- uncooperative with community projects (a direct threat to a core component of their self-concept), or
- unconcerned about driver safety and care (a threat to a relatively irrelevant component of their self-concept), or
- cooperative with community projects (*positive reinforcement* of their self-concept).

Consistent with self-affirmation theory, the two threats greatly increased the probability that women would subsequently agree to help the food cooperative – about 95 per cent of women agreed to help. Among women who had been given positive reinforcement of their self-concept, 65 per cent agreed to help the cooperative.

Self-serving bias
Attributional distortions that protect or enhance self-esteem or the self-concept.

enhance or protect the positive aspects of their self-concepts (Baumeister, 1998). See Box 3.3 for examples of esteem-enhancing and esteem-protecting behaviours; and Box 3.4 and Figure 3.4 for an applied example of self-enhancement among young drivers.

The sheer power of the self-enhancement motive leads us naturally to our next topic, self-esteem.

Real world 3.3
Techniques people use to enhance or protect positive aspects of the self

You may have noticed how people (perhaps you!) sometimes wish to boost themselves. Here are some of the tricks that folk get up to:

- They take credit for their successes but deny blame for their failures – this is a self-serving bias (see Chapter 2).

- They forget failure feedback more readily than success or praise.

- They accept praise uncritically but receive criticism sceptically.

- They try to dismiss interpersonal criticism as being motivated by prejudice.

- They perform a biased search of self-knowledge to support a favourable self-image.

- They place a favourable spin on the meaning of ambiguous traits that define self.

- They persuade themselves that their flaws are widely shared human attributes but that their qualities are rare and distinctive.

Research and applications 3.4
Self-enhancement in young drivers

How able and cautious young drivers think they are predicts their level of crash-risk optimism, along with one other measure – perceived luck in avoiding crashes!

Can people accurately judge how good they are as drivers? Niki Harré and her colleagues asked this question in studying self-enhancement bias and crash optimism in young drivers. More than three hundred male and female technical institute students (aged 16–29 years) compared their driving attributes to their peers on a series of ten items. A self-enhancement bias was found for all items. An analysis showed that the ten items were based on two underlying dimensions, perceived driving ability and perceived driving caution. Here are examples of items, one for each factor (italics ours):

- Perceived ability: 'Do you think you are more or less *skilled* as a driver than other people your age?'

- Perceived caution: 'Do you think you are more or less *safe* as a driver than other people your age?'

The students responded to all items on seven-point rating scales that ranged from 'much less' to 'much more' with a mid-point labelled 'about the same'. The results for the *skilled* and *safe* items are shown in Figure 3.4. Most rated themselves as above average or well above average, both on skill and safety. Although there was no age difference within the range sampled, there was a gender difference: when comparing with their peers, men gave slightly higher skill ratings while women gave slightly higher safety ratings.

Crash-risk optimism was another variable investigated. These young drivers estimated the likelihood of being involved in a crash, again relative to their peers. How they perceived ability and their degree of caution were significant predictors of crash-risk optimism, in combination with another measure – believing that luck would help them avoid crashes!

Harré and her colleagues noted that their study was not designed to identify which young drivers are biased, since to do so would require measuring a person's actual skill and actual safety when driving. Nevertheless, these young drivers had an overly optimistic view of themselves. Other research suggests that optimistic drivers may, for example, ignore safety messages because they do not believe they are relevant. This is a concern, given that safe-driving campaigns are a major strategy used to reduce the road toll.

Source: Based on Harré, Foster and O'Neill (2005).

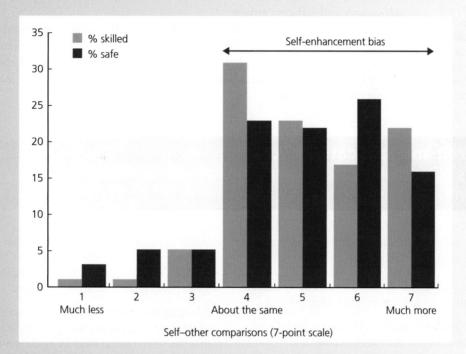

Figure 3.4

Self-enhancement bias: rating one's driving as above average.

- Young drivers compared attributes of their individual driving behaviour (skilled, safe) with their peers.
- Most showed a self-enhancement bias, using above-average ratings of 5, 6 or 7.

Source: Based on data from Harré, Foster & O'Neill (2005), Study 1.

Self-esteem

Why are people so strongly motivated to think well of themselves – to self-enhance? Research suggests that people generally have a rosy sense of self – they see, or try to see, themselves through 'rose-tinted spectacles'. For example, people who are threatened or distracted often display what Del Paulhus and Karen Levitt (1987) called *automatic egotism* – a widely favourable self-image. In their review of a link between illusions and a sense of well-being, Shelley Taylor and Jonathon Brown (1988) concluded that people normally overestimate their good points, overestimate their control over events and are unrealistically optimistic. Sedikides and Gregg (2003) call these three characteristics of human thought the *self-enhancing triad*.

In one study (Kruger & Dunning, 1999), very low achieving students (in the bottom 12 per cent) thought they were relatively high achievers (in the top 38 per cent). According to Patricia Cross (1977), your lecturers show positivity bias too, with 94 per cent convinced that their teaching ability is above average! A positivity bias, based on positive illusions, is psychologically adaptive. People without these psychological props tend towards depression and some other forms of mental illness (Tennen & Affleck, 1993). Box 3.5 describes some health aspects of self-esteem and self-conception.

An inflated sense of how wonderful I am can, however, not only nauseate but also be maladaptive. It does not match reality. Having an accurate sense of self is important but, as we have seen, is less important than feeling good about oneself. A positive self-image and associated self-esteem is a significant goal for most people most of the time.

Self-handicapping
Publicly making advance external attributions for our anticipated failure or poor performance in a forthcoming event.

Research and applications 3.5
Threats to your self-concept can damage your health: ways of coping

There are three major sources of threat to our self-concept and all can affect our sense of self-worth:

1 *Failures* – ranging from failing a test, failing a job interview, to a marriage ending in divorce.

2 *Inconsistencies* – unusual and unexpected positive or negative events that make us question the sort of person we are.

3 *Stressors* – sudden or enduring events that can exceed our capacity to cope, including bereavement, a sick child and over-commitment to work.

Threats to our self-concept not only arouse negative emotions that can lead to self-harm and suicide, they also contribute to physical illness. They can affect our immune responses, nervous system activity and blood pressure. For example, one study found that when people were reminded of significant self-discrepancies, the level of natural killer cell activity in their bloodstream decreased (Strauman, Lemieux & Coe, 1993). These cells are important in defending the body against cancers and viral infections.

There are several ways in which people try to cope with self-conceptual threats.

● *Escape* – people may remove themselves physically from the threat situation.

● *Denial* – people may take alcohol or other drugs, or engage in risky 'just for kicks' behaviour. This is not a particularly constructive coping mechanism, since it can create additional health problems.

● *Downplay the threat* – this is a more constructive strategy, either by re-evaluating the aspect of self that has been threatened or by reaffirming other positive aspects of the self (Steele, 1988).

● *Self-expression* – this is a very effective response to threat. Writing or talking about one's emotional and physical reactions to self-conceptual threats can work. It reduces emotional heat, reduces headaches, muscle tension, and a pounding heart, and improves immune system functioning (Pennebaker, 1997). Most benefits come from communication that enhances understanding and self-insight.

● *Attack the threat* – people can directly confront threat by discrediting its basis ('This is an invalid test of my ability'), by denying personal responsibility for the threat ('The dog ate my essay'), by setting up excuses for failure before the event (on the way into an exam, announcing that you have a terrible hangover – **self-handicapping** (see Chapter 2)) – or by taking control of the problem directly, such as seeking professional help or addressing any valid causes of threat.

In concluding this section, we should note that self-esteem is closely associated with social identity – by identifying with a group, that group's prestige and status in society attaches to one's self-concept. Take a modern example: Bill is so over-weight that he is on a severe warning to lose a lot or face major health consequences. This is a physical risk, but there is a psychological risk as well. Being identified as a member of a group stigmatised by their obesity is not likely to mediate positive self-esteem for Bill. Bill and others like him will probably experience negative self-esteem when they compare themselves with the 'slim and the beautiful' in their community. Helga Dittmar and her colleagues have shown how the spread of consumerism in contemporary Western culture has had a major negative effect on people's sense of self-worth (Dittmar, 2008). Their analysis points to media hype as chief culprit in creating a potent mix of goals that are unrealisable for most: the pursuit of the body beautiful, material goods and an affluent lifestyle.

The framework in which we have presented these ideas suggest a personal self-image is at centre stage: this is an individual level of explanation. However, we can also subject the phenomenon to an intergroup explanation, and we explore this more fully in Chapter 7. We will see that the outcome can hinge on which groups are normally used by disadvantaged people when they make a social comparison.

Individual differences

We all know people who seem to hold themselves in very low regard and others who seem to have a staggeringly positive impression of themselves. Do these differences reflect enduring and deep-seated differences in self-esteem? The main thrust of research on self-esteem as a trait is concerned with establishing individual differences in self-esteem and investigating the causes and consequences of these differences.

One view that has become somewhat entrenched, particularly in the United States, is that low self-esteem is responsible for a range of personal and social problems such as crime, delinquency, drug abuse, unwanted pregnancy and underachievement in school. This view has spawned a huge industry, with accompanying mantras, to boost individual self-esteem, particularly in child-rearing and school contexts. However, critics have argued that low self-esteem may be a product of the stressful and alienating conditions of modern industrial society, and that the self-esteem 'movement' is an exercise in rearranging deck chairs on the *Titanic* that merely produces selfish and narcissistic individuals.

So, what is the truth? American research suggests that individual self-esteem tends to vary between moderate and very high, so that most people feel relatively positive about themselves (Baumeister, Tice & Hutton, 1989). However, Shinobu Kitayama and his colleagues reported lower self-esteem in Japanese students studying in Japan or the United States (Kitayama, Markus, Matsumoto & Norasakkunkit, 1997).

Even if we focus on those people who have low self-esteem, there is little evidence that low self-esteem causes the social ills that it is purported to cause. For example, Baumeister, Smart and Boden (1996) searched the literature for evidence for the popular belief that low self-esteem causes violence. They found quite the opposite. Violence was associated with high self-esteem; more specifically, violence seems to erupt when individuals with high self-esteem have their rosy self-images threatened.

However, we should not lump together everyone who happens to have high self-esteem. Consistent with common sense, some people with high self-esteem are quietly self-confident and non-hostile, whereas others are arrogant, conceited and overly assertive (Kernis, Granneman & Barclay, 1989). These latter individuals also

Table 3.2 Characteristics of people with high and low self-esteem

High self-esteem	Low self-esteem
Persistent and resilient in the face of failure	Vulnerable to impact of everyday events
Emotionally and affectively stable	Wide swings in mood and affect
Less flexible and malleable	Flexible and malleable
Less easily persuaded and influenced	Easily persuaded and influenced
No conflict between wanting and obtaining success and approval	Want success and approval but are sceptical of it
React positively to a happy and successful life	React negatively to a happy and successful life
Thorough, consistent and stable self-concept	Sketchy, inconsistent and unstable self-concept
Motivated towards enhancing the self	Motivated towards protecting the self

feel 'special' and superior to others, and they actually have relatively volatile self-esteem – they are narcissistic (Rhodewalt, Madrian & Cheney, 1998). One study has shown that narcissistic individuals were more aggressive towards people who had provoked and offended them (Bushman & Baumeister, 1998). (Knowing this, you might want to learn a bit more about Manfred. See the third focus question.)

Overall, research into self-esteem as an enduring individual trait provides quite a clear picture of what people with high and low self-esteem are like (Baumeister, 1998; see Table 3.2).

In pursuit of self-esteem

Why do people pursue self-esteem? This may initially seem a silly question – the obvious answer is that having self-esteem makes you feel good. There is probably a grain of truth here, but on the other hand there are causality issues to be addressed. Being in a good mood, however caused, may provide a rosy glow that distorts the esteem in which people hold themselves. So, rather than self-esteem producing happiness, feeling happy may inflate self-esteem.

Fear of death

Terror management theory
The notion that the most fundamental human motivation is to reduce the terror of the inevitability of death. Self-esteem may be centrally implicated in effective terror management.

Jeff Greenberg and his associates suggested an intriguing, but somewhat gloomy, reason why people pursue self-esteem: it is to overcome their fear of death. In their terror management theory, they argue that knowing death is inevitable is the most fundamental threat that people face, and therefore it is the most powerful motivating factor in human existence. Self-esteem is part of a defence against that threat. Through high self-esteem, people can escape from the anxiety that would otherwise arise from continual contemplation of the inevitability of one's death – the drive for self-esteem is grounded in terror of death. High self-esteem makes people feel good about themselves. They feel immortal, and positive and excited about life.

In support of this analysis, Greenberg and his colleagues conducted an experiment in which self-esteem was shown to act as a buffer to anxiety. Participants did or did not receive success and positive personality feedback (manipulation of self-esteem) and then either watched a video about death or anticipated painful electric shocks (Greenberg *et al.*, 1992). They found that participants who had had their self-esteem raised experienced lower physiological arousal and reported less anxiety (see Figure 3.5).

Is self-esteem a sociometer?

Another reason why people pursue self-esteem is that self-esteem is a very good index, or internal monitor, of being accepted by others and belonging, rather than rejected and excluded. Mark Leary has referred to this aspect of self-esteem as a 'sociometer'. Leary and his colleagues conducted a series of experiments to support this view. They found that high self-esteem participants reported greater inclusion in general and in specific real social situations. They also found that social exclusion from a group for personal reasons depressed participants' self-esteem (Leary, Tambor, Terdal & Downs, 1995).

Before you proceed to the next section, we would like you to try out the questions in Table 3.4. The eight statements in the table deal with your personal reactions to a number of different situations. No two statements are exactly alike, so consider each statement carefully before answering. If a statement is TRUE or MOSTLY TRUE as applied to you, circle 'T' next to that number. If a statement is FALSE or MOSTLY FALSE as applied to you, circle 'F' next to that number.

Figure 3.5

How positive feedback about self and viewing a death video can reduce anxiety.

People felt less anxious (on a 0–60 scale) after having watched an explicit video about death if their self-esteem had previously been elevated through positive feedback, than if their self-esteem had previously not been elevated.

Source: Based on data from Greenberg *et al.* (1992), Experiment 1.

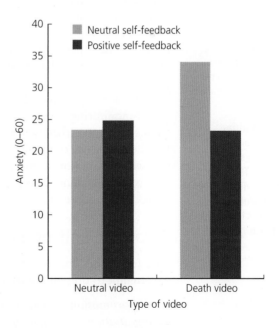

Table 3.3 How do you interact with other people?

T	F	1. I guess I put on a show to impress or entertain people.
T	F	2. In different situations and with different people, I often act like very different persons.
T	F	3. I can only argue for ideas that I really believe.
T	F	4. I'm not always the person I appear to be.
T	F	5. I may deceive people by being friendly when I really dislike them.
T	F	6. At parties and social gatherings I do not attempt to do or say things that others will like.
T	F	7. I would not change my opinions (or the way I do things) to please someone or win their favour.
T	F	8. I can look anyone in the eye and tell a lie with a straight face (if for a right end).

Note: After you have made your choices read the explanation and use the scoring key provided at the end of this chapter.

Self-presentation

Impression management
People's use of various strategies to get other people to view them in a positive light.

Self-monitoring
Carefully controlling how we present ourselves. There are situational differences and individual differences in self-monitoring.

Selves are constructed, modified and played out in interaction with other people. Since the self that we project has consequences for how others react, we try to control the self that we present. In *The presentation of self in everyday life*, the sociologist Erving Goffman (1959) likened this process of impression management to theatre, where people play different roles for different audiences. There is a vast amount of evidence that people behave differently in public from the way they do in private (Leary, 1995). There are two general classes of motive for self-presentation: strategic and expressive. Research by Mark Snyder (1974) into individual differences in self-monitoring suggests that high self-monitors adopt strategic self-presentation strategies because they typically shape their behaviour to project the impression they feel their audience or the situation demands, whereas low self-monitors adopt expressive self-presentation strategies because their behaviour is less responsive to changing contextual demands. Check Table 3.3 again for items that sample self-monitoring. How did you score on this test?

Strategic self-presentation

Ned Jones and Thane Pittman (1982) identified five strategic motives in the way we attempt to present ourselves:

1. *self-promotion* – trying to persuade others that you are competent;
2. *ingratiation* – trying to get others to like you;
3. *intimidation* – trying to get others to think you are dangerous;
4. *exemplification* – trying to get others to regard you as a morally respectable individual;
5. *supplication* – trying to get others to take pity on you as helpless and needy.

Strategic self-presentation. You could try self-promotion to persuade others that you are competent!

Source: Pearson Online Database (POD)

You or others that you know may have acted in ways that reflect these motives (see Chapter 5 on persuasion tactics). In fact, ingratiation and self-promotion serve two of the most common goals of social interaction: to get people to like you and to get people to think you are competent (Leary, 1995).

Research suggests that ingratiation has little effect on an observer's liking for you but a big effect on the target – flattery can be hard to resist (Gordon, 1996). (Use Box 3.6 to help advise Andrea. See focus question 4.)

Real world 3.6
Some tips on how to present yourself so that others like you

The key to getting people to like you through strategic self-presentation is to be subtle enough so that it does not look too obviously like ingratiation. According to Jones (1990), there are four principal strategies you should adopt:

1 Try to agree with people's opinions (similarity enhances attraction – see Chapter 10). When you do so make it credible: (a) agree on important issues but keep disagreement to trivial issues and (b) balance forceful agreement with weak disagreement.

2 Be selectively modest, but be careful by (a) making fun of your standing on unimportant issues and (b) putting yourself down in areas that do not matter very much.

3 Try to avoid appearing too desperate for others' approval. Try to get others to do the strategic self-presentation for you. If it is left up to you, use the strategy sparingly. Do not use it when it would be expected.

4 Basking in reflected glory really does work. Make casual references to your connections with winners. Only make links with losers when the links cannot be turned against you.

Source: Based on Jones (1990).

Expressive self-presentation

Self-presentation
A deliberate effort to
act in ways that create
a particular impression,
usually favourable, of
ourselves.

Strategic self-presentation focuses on manipulating others' perceptions of you. Expressive motives for self-presentation involve demonstrating and validating our self-concept through our actions – the focus is more on oneself than on others (Schlenker, 1980). But we are not naive: we usually seek out people who would validate who we are. The expressive motive for self-presentation is a strong one, because a particular identity or self-concept is worthless unless it is recognised and validated by others – it is of little use to me if I think I am a genius but no one else does. Identity requires *social validation* for it to persist and serve a useful function.

For example, research by Nicholas Emler and Steve Reicher (1995) shows that delinquent behaviour among boys is almost always performed publicly, or in forms that can be publicly verified, because its primary function is identity validation – validation of possession of a delinquent reputation.

Social validation of expressed behaviour also seems to be implicated in self-concept change. Refer back to Tice's experiment in Figure 3.1, in which she asked her participants to act as if they were either emotionally stable or emotionally volatile. Half of them performed the behaviour publicly and half privately. They all then completed ratings of what they believed their 'true self' was like. Tice found that only publicly performed behaviour was internalised as a description of their self. What is important in self-concept change is that other people perceive you in a particular way – this is social validation. It is not enough for you, and only you, to perceive your self in a particular way.

Summary

- The modern Western idea of the self has gradually crystallised over the past two hundred years. It is a product of social forces, including secularisation, industrialisation, enlightenment and psychoanalysis.

- An early challenge in the twentieth century to the idea that we are unique individuals was the view that the self merges through social interaction, typified in G. H. Mead's notion of symbolic interactionism.

- People are not continuously consciously aware of themselves. Self-awareness can sometimes be very uncomfortable and at other times very uplifting – it depends on what aspect of self we are aware of and on how relatively favourable that aspect is.

- We know who we are and we store this information as special schemas, i.e. self-schemas.

- People learn something about who they are by introspection, searching inwards. They can also observe what they say and do, and infer their 'true' self from their actions. This is called self-attribution. Again, they can learn by making social comparisons, grounding their attitudes, feelings and behaviour in those of other people.

- Important self-schemas include our actual self, our ideal self and our 'ought' self. These are self-guides that regulate our behaviour. Sometimes we compare these self-schemas. If our actual self is discrepant from our ideal self it can make us feel dejected. If our actual self is discrepant from our ought self it can make us feel anxious.

- Self and identity take different forms. Unique attributes define the individual self. The collective self shares attributes with ingroup members that make them distinct from outgroups. The relational self is defined in terms of relationships with significant other people.

- Although we experience different selves in different contexts, we also work towards a coherent self-concept that integrates our selves.

- Three major motives underpin our self-concept: we self-assess (to find out what sort of person we are), we self-verify (to confirm this) and we self-enhance (to prove how wonderful we are). We are overwhelmingly motivated to self-enhance. Self-enhancement services self-esteem, and self-esteem is a key feature of self-conception.

- Some people are generally higher in self-esteem than others. High self-esteem people have a clear and stable sense of self and aim to enhance themselves; low self-esteem people have a less clear self-concept and aim to protect themselves.

- We pursue self-esteem for many reasons. It shows that we are socially integrated, accepted and belong. It can also show that we have overcome loneliness and rejection.

- We protect and enhance our self-esteem by managing the impression we project. We can do this strategically by manipulating how others see us, or expressively by projecting our self positively.

Literature, film and TV

The Handmaid's Tale

Margaret Atwood's (1986) novel and the 1990 film starring Natasha Richardson portrays a dystopian future where most of humanity is sterile, a young woman is kept in reproductive servitude because of her fertility. This story explores the destruction of individual identity and the creation of a group self that demands conformity. In the service of the state, the protagonist's identity is submerged as she is demoted to a faceless child-bearing machine while the rest of the women, all sterile, are forced to be passive housewives.

The Beach

Alex Garland's (1997) novel (also a 2000 film starring Leonardo DiCaprio) is about backpackers in Thailand who drop out to join a group that has set up its own society on a remote island. They are expected to submerge their own identity in favour of the group's identity. This is a dramatic book that engages with many social psychological themes to do with self and identity – the tension between individual and relational self and collective self/social identity. The book could be characterised as *Apocalypse Now* meets *Lord of the Flies*.

Samuel Beckett's classic trilogy

Molloy (1951), *Malone Dies* (1951) and *The Unnameable* (1953) are ultimately about a person's frenzied and purgatorial quest throughout life for a sense of identity and an understanding of self – a quest for the true self among the many selves of one's life.

Witness

A 1985 film by Peter Weir, with Harrison Ford, is an exciting thriller in which Ford's character hides out in an Amish community to protect a young Amish boy who witnessed a brutal crime in New York. From a self and identity point of view the rugged individualist, Ford, has to fit in to the ultra-collectivist Amish society in which self is deeply integrated with and subservient to the group, and expression of individuality is not valued – is even punished.

Waco: The Rules of Engagement

1997 documentary by William Gazechi. In February 1993 the US Bureau of Alcohol and Tobacco raided and lay siege for 51 days to the compound, in Waco, Texas, of the Branch Dravidian sect, led by David Koresh. All 80 sect members were killed. This documentary is a chilling account of just how far a cult can go in controlling one's self and identity.

The Departed

Starring Leonardo DiCaprio, Matt Damon and Jack Nicholson, this is a dramatic and violent 2006 film about Irish-American organized crime in Boston. But it is also a study of the strain of nourishing multiple identities and living an all-consuming double life – Billy Costigan is an undercover cop who has infiltrated the mob, and Colin Sullivan is a hardened criminal who has infiltrated the police.

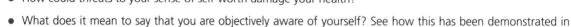

Guided questions

- Do you have a *looking-glass self*? How and why might you present yourself differently in public and in private?

- If the way you actually are is different from the way you would like to be, or how you think you should be, how might this be revealed?

- What are the usual ways that people try to enhance their sense of self-worth?

- How could threats to your sense of self-worth damage your health?

- What does it mean to say that you are objectively aware of yourself? See how this has been demonstrated in children in Chapter 3 of MyPsychLab at www.mypsychlab.co.uk.

Learn more

Abrams, D., & Hogg, M. A. (2001). Collective identity: group membership and self-conception. In M. A. Hogg & R. S. Tindale (eds), *Blackwell handbook of social psychology: Group processes* (pp. 425–60). Oxford, UK: Blackwell. Detailed discussion and overview of the relationship between the self-concept and group membership, with an emphasis on the collective self and social identity.

Leary, M. R., & Tangney, J. P. (2003). *Handbook of self and identity*. New York: Guilford. A wide-ranging and completely up-to-date selection of chapters from leading scholars of self and identity.

Sedikides, C., & Gregg, A. P. (2003). Portraits of the self. In M. A. Hogg & J. Cooper (eds), *The Sage handbook of social psychology* (pp. 110–138). London: Sage. A comprehensive and up-to-date overview of research and theory on self and identity. Sedikides is one of the world's leading self researchers.

Swann, W. B. Jr (in press). The self. In D. T. Gilbert, S. T. Fiske, & G. Lindzey (eds), *Handbook of social psychology* (5th ed). Hoboken, NJ: Wiley. A comprehensive and detailed review of the social psychology of the self by a current leading self researcher – the 'handbook' is one of the most authoritative references in social psychology.

Key to Table 3.3

The items in **Table 3.3** are slightly modified examples from Mark Snyder's (1974) *self-monitoring scale*. Use the key below to score yourself. According to Snyder, a high score suggests a more 'chameleon' character, a person who is careful to create an impression that suits the audience. A low score characterises people who focus on just expressing themselves, regardless of the audience.

Key: A maximum score on self-monitoring is gained as follows: 1 T, 2 T, 3 F, 4 T, 5 T, 6 F, 7 F, 8 T

Refresh your understanding, assess your progress and go further with interactive summaries, questions, podcasts, videos and much more on the website accompanying the book: **www.mypsychlab.co.uk.**

Chapter 4

Attitudes and persuasion

What to look for

- The structure and purpose of attitudes

- How attitudes are learned and role of socialisation

- Measuring attitudes: explicit and implicit techniques

- From attitudes to behaviour: improving prediction

- When attitudes are accessible, strong and rational

- Cognitive dissonance: effort justification, induced compliance and free choice

- Being persuaded: source, message and audience effects

- Dual-process routes to persuasion: elaboration-likelihood and heuristic-systematic models

- How to resist persuasion

Focus questions

1. What meanings do you give to *attitude*? An animal lover says that an attitude is the body posture a hunting dog assumes when indicating the presence of a prey. A sports coach says that a certain team player has an 'attitude problem', which presumably is something to do with the player's state of mind. Is the term worth keeping in our psychological dictionary if it has several quite different everyday meanings?

2. Rita polls people's attitudes and believes she knows what makes them tick. Her advice to psychologists is: if you want to find out what people's attitudes are, ask them! Is she right?

3. Citizens sometimes say that paying research companies to ask folk about their political attitudes is a waste of money. One poll may contradict another carried out around the same time, and poll predictions of who will be voted into power has not always been very good. Is there any use, therefore, in trying to link people's attitudes to people's behaviour?

4. You have just joined the army. Along with other cadets you listen to an amazing talk by an officer skilled in the use of survival techniques in difficult combat conditions. Among other things, he asks you to eat some fried grasshoppers. 'Try to imagine this is the real thing! You know, you might have to do this to save your life one day,' he says. What would be the most effective way to get you not only to eat them but actually to like them as well?

5. The university doctor wants your classmate Joseph to stop smoking. She thinks she might ask him to look at a large jar containing a chemical solution and a diseased lung. Why might this not work very well? Watch real-life clips of people justifying why they smoke, or do not smoke, in Chapter 4 of MyPsychLab at www.mypsychlab.co.uk.

I n this chapter we explore what attitudes are, how they are structured and how they work. Attitudes are our evaluations of people, objects and events in our world. They are based on our beliefs and feelings. Sometimes, but not always, our attitudes are revealed in the ways we act. While some attitudes are quite strong, come to mind easily and seem unlikely to change, others may be vulnerable to persuasion and therefore can be reshaped.

What are attitudes?

Attitude
(a) A relatively enduring organisation of beliefs, feelings and behavioural tendencies towards socially significant objects, groups, events or symbols. (b) A general feeling or evaluation – positive or negative – about some person, object or issue.

Attitude is a word that is part of our commonsense language. It was derived from the Latin *aptus*, which means 'fit and ready for action'. This ancient meaning refers to something that is directly observable, such as the way a fighter moves in a boxing ring. However, attitude researchers now view 'attitude' as a construct that, although not directly observable, precedes behaviour and guides our choices and decisions for action. Many years ago, the social psychologist Gordon Allport (1935) referred to attitude as social psychology's most indispensable concept. He was not to know that such a fashionable term would become the centre of much controversy in the decades ahead, for example, in not being an effective predictor of behaviour.

Research in this field has generated enormous interest and hundreds of studies covering almost every conceivable topic about which attitudes might be expressed. In recent years, the rise of interest in social cognition (see Chapter 2) has impacted on cutting-edge attitude research. For example, perhaps we infer that an attitude is 'strong' if we can recall relevant facts quite easily. In an analysis of what social psychologists generally do in their research, Abraham Tesser and Jinn Bau (2002) concluded that the study of attitudes continues to have a very high profile.

In this chapter, we take the view that attitudes are basic to and pervasive in human life. Without attitudes, it would be difficult for us to construe and react to events, to make decisions and to make sense of our relationships with others. Let us now look at the anatomy of an attitude.

Attitudes have a structure

Three-component attitude model
An attitude consists of cognitive, affective and behavioural components. This three-fold division has an ancient heritage, stressing thought, feeling and action as basic to human experience.

A widely held view of an attitude's anatomy is the three-component attitude model, consisting of:

- *a cognitive (thinking) component* – beliefs about the object of an attitude;
- *an affective (feeling) component* – positive or negative feelings associated with the object of an attitude;
- *a behavioural (acting) component* – a state of readiness to take action.

This model can be traced at least as far back to the work of Milton Rosenberg and Carl Hovland (1960). As well as the three components, this approach also emphasised that attitudes are:

- relatively *permanent*: that is, they persist across time and situations – a momentary feeling is not an attitude;
- limited to *socially significant* events or objects;
- *generalisable* and at least somewhat abstract – if you drop a book on your toe and find that it hurts, this is not enough to form an attitude, because it is a single event in one place and at one time, but if the experience makes you dislike books or libraries, or clumsiness in general, then that dislike is an attitude.

Each attitude, then, is made up of thoughts and ideas, a cluster of feelings, likes and dislikes, and behavioural intentions.

Despite the appeal of the 'trinity', this model presents a problem by prejudging a link between attitude and behaviour, as we shall see below. Based on what you have read so far, try to answer the first focus question.

Attitudes have a purpose

If attitudes have a structure they must also have a function. As M. Brewster Smith observed, an attitude saves energy, as we do not have to figure out 'from scratch' how we should relate to the object or situation in question (Smith, Bruner & White, 1956), a purpose that parallels the usefulness of stereotypes (see Chapter 2). An attitude enables us to maximise our chances of having positive experiences and minimise having aversive ones.

Russell Fazio (1989) later argued that the main function of any kind of attitude is utilitarian: that of object appraisal. This should hold regardless of whether the attitude has a positive or negative valence (i.e. whether our feelings about the object are good or bad). Merely possessing an attitude is useful because of the orientation towards the object that it provides for the person. For example, having a negative attitude towards snakes (by believing they are dangerous) is useful if we cannot differentiate between safe and deadly varieties. However, for an attitude truly to fulfil this function it must be accessible. We develop this aspect of Fazio's thinking about how attitudes work when we deal with the link between attitude and behaviour.

Where do attitudes come from?

Attitudes are learned as an integral part of becoming socialised. They can develop through our experiences or vicariously through interactions with others, or be a product of cognitive processes. Generally, social psychologists have researched the nature of attitude formation rather than the content of attitudes that people develop. The study of these processes usually involves experiments rather than survey research or public opinion findings.

Experience

Many attitudes arise from our *direct experience* with attitude objects, and there are several explanations for its effect: mere exposure, classical conditioning, operant conditioning, social learning theory and self-perception theory.

Direct experience informs us about the attributes of an object and helps to shape beliefs that influence how much we like or dislike it. According to Stuart Oskamp (1977), even a mildly traumatic experience can trigger a negative attitude and make some beliefs more salient. If your first visit to the dentist is painful, you may conclude that dentists hurt rather than help you, despite their friendly smile.

Simply experiencing something several times can affect how we evaluate it – the mere exposure effect (see Zajonc, 1968). The first time you hear a new song, you may find you neither strongly like nor dislike it, but with repetition your response in either direction will probably strengthen. However, the effect of continued exposure diminishes. For example, an increased liking for people based on their photos levels off after about ten repetitions (Bornstein, 1989). Mere exposure has most

Attitude formation
The process of forming our attitudes, mainly from our own experiences, the influences of others and our emotional reactions.

Mere exposure effect
Repeated exposure to an object results in greater attraction to that object.

impact when we lack information about an issue. Sitting members of a government or an opposition party, for example, usually have an advantage over other candidates in an election simply because their names are more familiar.

Conditioning

Repeated association may cause a formerly neutral stimulus to elicit a reaction that was previously elicited only by another stimulus. This is *classical conditioning*, and it can be a powerful, even insidious, form of attitude learning. A study by Irvin Janis and his colleagues demonstrated the power of background stimuli by reinforcing some participants with soft drinks at a time that they were reading a persuasive message (Janis, Kaye & Kirschner, 1965). Those given soft drinks were more persuaded by what they read than those who were not.

Behaviour with positive consequences is reinforced and is more likely to be repeated, whereas behaviour with negative consequences is not. This is *instrumental conditioning*. For example, parents use verbal reinforcers to encourage acceptable behaviour in their children – quiet, cooperative play wins praise. However, when they fight, a reward is withheld or a punishment such as scolding is introduced. When parents reward or punish their children they are shaping their attitudes on many issues, including religious or political beliefs and practices.

Both classical and instrumental conditioning emphasise the role of direct reinforcers in how behaviour is acquired and maintained.

Attitudes can also be formed through *social* learning and can occur in the absence of direct reinforcers. Albert Bandura (1973) concentrated his research on modelling, where one person's behaviour is a template for another's. Modelling requires observation: individuals learn new responses, not by directly experiencing positive or negative outcomes but by observing what happens to others. Having a successful working mother, for instance, is likely to influence the future career and lifestyle choices of a daughter. Likewise, ethnic attitudes can be instilled in otherwise naive children if the models are significant adults in their lives. As Gordon Allport (1954b) noted, young children learn to use ethnic slurs and insults despite being unable to define the group correctly or have factual knowledge about its members.

Modelling
Tendency for a person to reproduce the actions, attitudes and emotional responses exhibited by a real-life or symbolic model. Also called *observational learning*.

Sources of learning

A crucial source of our attitudes is the actions of other people around us. For the child, parents are a powerful influence, involving the kinds of learning you have just read about (classical conditioning, instrumental conditioning and observational learning). Although the attitudes held by parents and their children are not usually highly correlated, there are some exceptions. One study reported correlations between children's political preferences and choice of religion on one hand and those of their parents, 0.60 and 0.88 respectively (Jennings & Niemi, 1968).

The mass media, in particular television, have a major influence on people's attitudes and those of their children – especially so when attitudes are not strongly held (Goldberg & Gorn, 1974). Communication scientist Steven Chaffee found that, before age 7, American children get most of their political information from television (Chaffee, Jackson-Beeck, Durall & Wilson, 1977). Paul Kellstedt (2003) made an extensive statistical analysis of changes in Americans' racial attitudes over the last half-century. He found that media coverage does more than reflect public opinion – it has helped mould it. Long periods of liberalism have been followed by periods of conservatism, and these eras have responded to cues in the American media.

The impact of commercials on children's attitudes has also been investigated. Charles Atkin (1980) reported that two-thirds of a group of children who saw a circus strong man eat a cereal believed it would make them strong too! These findings are of particular concern in the light of murders sometimes committed by young children (e.g. the murder in Liverpool in 1993 of 2-year-old James Bulger by two 10-year-old boys), and carried out in ways similar to those portrayed in certain films. Media effects on aggression are discussed further in Chapter 8.

Self-perception theory

A less obvious way of forming an attitude is to deduce what we think or feel about an attitude object by searching our behaviour. This was the basis of Daryl Bem's (1967) self-perception theory (also see Chapter 2). He proposed that people gain knowledge about who they are, and their attitudes, by examining their own actions and asking: 'Why did I do that?' A person may act for reasons that are not really clear and so determine their attitude from the most readily available cause. For example, if you often go for long walks, you may conclude that 'I must like them, as I'm always doing that'. But there may be other reasons not taken into account – e.g. wanting to escape temporarily from the house. Bem's theory suggests that people act, and form attitudes, without much deliberate thinking.

Self-perception theory
Bem's idea that we gain knowledge of ourselves only by making self-attributions: for example, we infer our own attitudes from our own behaviour.

How attitudes are revealed

One way to find out what people's attitudes are is to ask them and this is the aim of some questionnaires. These are still used today and there is an entire area of social psychology dedicated to constructing attitude scales. However, people lie, sometimes to avoid embarrassment or criticism. There has been a recent trend to circumvent a person's defences by using less obtrusive methods.

Clues from our body

Does your heart beat faster each time a certain person comes close? Perhaps your pupils dilate as well. If so, we might surmise you have an attitude of some intensity! Physiological measures have one big advantage over self-report measures: people may not realise that their attitudes are being assessed and, even if they do, they may not be able to alter their responses. This is why a polygraph or 'lie detector' is sometimes used in criminal investigations.

Physiological measures, however, have some drawbacks. Most are sensitive to factors other than attitudes, as John Cacioppo and Richard Petty (1981) have noted. For example, trying to solve a problem often raises heart rate, while being vigilant so as not to miss a signal usually lowers it. Further, these measures provide limited information: they can indicate intensity of feeling but not direction. Two, totally opposed people who feel equally strongly about an issue cannot be distinguished.

Action clues

Counts of empty beer and wine bottles in dustbins are examples of unobtrusive measures of attitudes towards alcohol in your neighbourhood, while chemists' records show which doctors prescribe new drugs. In a museum, Eugene Webb and

Unobtrusive measures
Observational approaches that neither intrude on the processes being studied nor cause people to behave unnaturally.

Revealing an attitude. Counting bottles yields a clue to a neighbourhood's alcohol consumption.

Source: Pearson Online Database (POD)

his colleagues (Webb, Campbell, Schwartz & Sechrest, 1969) noted that the number of prints made by noses or fingers on a display case could show how popular the display was – and the height of the prints could indicate the viewers' ages! Webb also reported that interpersonal distance can imply an emotion. In one instance, adults told ghost stories to young children seated in a circle. The size of the circle of children grew smaller with each successive scary story!

Such measures are, of course, rough and ready rather than convincing. Is it possible to have an obtrusive measure that will work? One instance is the bogus pipeline technique which sets out to convince participants that they cannot hide their true attitudes. People are connected to a machine said to be a lie detector and are told that it measures both the strength and direction of emotional responses, thus revealing their true attitudes and implying that there is no point in lying. Roger Tourangeau and his colleagues found that people usually find this cover story convincing and are more willing to 'spill the beans', such as drinking to excess, snorting cocaine and having frequent oral sex (Tourangeau, Smith & Rasinski, 1997). So take care when you trial psychological equipment at the next university open day!

Bogus pipeline technique
A measurement technique that leads people to believe that a 'lie detector' can monitor their emotional responses, thus measuring their true attitudes.

Implicit attitudes

Sometimes an unobtrusive measure can tell us about an implicit attitude – one that a person may not actually be aware of. Here are three recent measures that have been researched:

- *Bias in language use*. Attitudes can be linked to the way that people use words. Anne Maass (1999) found that when a member of our own group does something good, we use an abstract adjective or noun to describe it, making it both a positive stereotype and an *internal attribution* (e.g. *John is honest*). However, a good action by an outgroup person is described using a concrete verb, suggesting that the action was determined by the situation and is an *external attribution* (e.g. *Hanif helped the old lady to cross a street*). The reverse logic applies to undesirable characteristics. Other techniques based on communication include *discourse analysis* and non-verbal cues to reveal hidden attitudes.

- *Attitude priming.* Russell Fazio used *priming*, noting we can respond more quickly when an underlying attitude is congruent with a 'correct' response (Fazio, Jackson, Dunton & Williams, 1995). While looking at a series of photos of Black and White people, participants decided by pressing a button whether an adjective (from a series of positive and negative adjectives) that followed very quickly after a particular image was 'good' or 'bad'. White participants were slower in rating a positive adjective as good when it followed a Black image, and Black participants were slower in rating a positive adjective as good when it followed a White image.

- *Implicit association test.* In a similar way to attitude priming, Tony Greenwald and his colleagues developed the implicit association test using a computer display coupled with responding on a keyboard (Greenwald, McGhee & Schwartz, 1998). Check Box 4.1 and visit the website provided there to try this method for yourself. (Then check the second focus question and think how you might respond to Rita.)

Implicit association test
Reaction-time test to measure attitudes – particularly unpopular attitudes that people might conceal.

Can attitudes predict actions?

Most of us expect people's attitudes to help us predict their behaviour. But do they? Bill Crano and Radmila Prislin suggested in their review that 'because attitudes predict behavior, they are considered the crown jewel of social psychology' (2006, p. 360). Perhaps so, but let us consider why a number of social scientists have questioned this assumption, and then reassess the conditions when it could be valid.

Research and applications 4.1
The implicit association test

A research method has been applied from the field of social cognition as an ingenious way of measuring attitudes that people may want to conceal, or even not appreciate that they hold – the implicit association test (IAT). The IAT has participants press either of two computer keys to match a series of concepts to a target, such as an ethnic group. Where an attitude already exists, one's reaction is much faster when the concept is already strongly associated in the mind. It is automatically activated.

If attitudes are mental networks, associations are stronger if the attitude exists than if it doesn't. It follows that people will more quickly link concepts that are related than those that are not. Suppose that you are being tested for your concealed attitudes towards property developers. You might be asked to look at photos of property developers, paired one at a time with a positive word (e.g. *nice*) or a negative word (e.g. *nasty*). Your task is to press the left key if the word you see is positive and the right key if it is negative. If you do not like property developers, you will press the right key more quickly when a photo is paired with *nasty*, but take longer to press the left key when a photo is paired with *nice*. Hence your prejudice against property developers is revealed!

The IAT is now popular as a way of measuring prejudice in liberal Western societies such as the United States. It is correlated with, and often superior to, other measures of prejudice and implicit attitudes, according to Tony Greenwald.

Try the demonstration test at this website: https://implicit.harvard.edu/implicit/

Attitude scales were developed by the early 1930s and used to measure people's views on issues that were fundamental – then as now – such as politics, religion and race. These scales were questionnaires that asked people what they thought and felt about these issues and how they might act in various situations. An early study of ethnic attitudes by Richard LaPiere (1934) revealed a glaring inconsistency between what people do and what they say (see Box 4.2).

LaPiere's provocative study questioned the validity of attitude questionnaires. In a later review, Allan Wicker (1969) concluded that the correlation between attitudes and actions is seldom as high as 0.30 (which, when squared, indicates that only 9 per cent of the variability in an action is accounted for by an attitude). In fact, Wicker found that the average correlation between attitudes and behaviour was only 0.15. This view was seized upon during the 1970s as critical evidence that the attitude concept is not worth a fig, since it has little predictive power. A sense of despair settled on the field (Abelson, 1972). In fact, this pessimism is unnecessary. LaPiere's study showed that people's behaviour changed across two situations, one where an act was public (e.g. in a hotel's reception area) and the other where it was private (responding to a letter). This difference does not mean that the underlying attitude had changed.

Later work was to show that there are attitude characteristics, as well as situational factors, which can promote or disrupt the connection between an attitude and an action. We consider two of these next: attitude accessibility and attitude strength.

Availability heuristic
A cognitive short cut in which the frequency or likelihood of an event is based on how quickly instances or associations come to mind.

When attitudes are accessible

Accessible attitudes are those that can be recalled from memory more easily and are expressed more quickly. This is an instance of the availability heuristic (see Chapter 2). Russell Fazio's work has indicated that accessible attitudes exert a strong influence on behaviour, improve the link between attitude and behaviour,

Research classic 4.2
Do people do as they say?

The sociologist LaPiere (1934) tested the difference between prejudiced attitudes towards Chinese in general and discriminatory behaviours towards a Chinese couple in particular. In the early 1930s, anti-Asian prejudice was known to be quite strong among Americans. LaPiere embarked on a 10 000-mile sightseeing tour of the United States, accompanied by two young Chinese friends. They visited 66 hotels, caravan parks and tourist homes and were served in 184 restaurants. As they went from place to place, LaPiere was concerned that his friends might not be accepted but, as it turned out, they were refused service only once. So far so good.

LaPiere later sent a questionnaire to the places visited, asking, 'Will you accept members of the Chinese race as guests in your establishment?' Of the 81 restaurants and 47 hotels that replied, 92 per cent said that they would *not* accept Chinese customers! Only 1 per cent said they would accept them, and the remainder checked 'Uncertain, depends on circumstances'. These written replies from the erstwhile hosts directly contradicted the way they had actually behaved.

This study was not, of course, scientifically designed – perhaps the people who responded to the letters were not those who dealt face-to-face with the Chinese couple; they might have responded differently in writing if they had been told that the couple was educated and well dressed; attitudes may have changed in the six months between the two measures. Nevertheless, the problem that LaPiere had unearthed provided an early challenge to the validity of the concept of attitude.

and are also more stable, more selective in judging relevant information and more resistant to change (Fazio, 1986, 1995).

Most studies in this field have focused on highly accessible attitudes, drawing on Fazio's model of attitudes as an association in memory between an object and an evaluation. The degree to which an attitude is 'handy' or functional and useful for the individual depends on the extent that it can be automatically activated from memory. The likelihood of automatic activation depends on the strength of the association between the object and the evaluation. Strong object–evaluation associations should therefore be highly functional by helping us make decisions.

Accessible attitudes can affect the way we categorise. When choosing from a number of possible categories to describe an object, we are more likely to select the one that is most accessible. For example, Eliot Smith and his colleagues found that when participants rehearsed their attitudes towards dairy products, yoghurt was more likely to cue as a *dairy product* (Smith, Fazio & Cejka, 1996). On the other hand, if attitudes towards health food were experimentally enhanced, and therefore made more accessible in memory, yoghurt was more likely to cue as a *health food* (Eagly & Chaiken, 1998).

An attitude becomes more accessible as *direct experience* with the attitude object increases. Attitudes formed through actual experience are more consistently related to behaviour (Regan & Fazio, 1977). Suppose Mary has participated in several psychology experiments but William has only read about them. We can predict that Mary's willingness to participate in the future more accurately than William's.

When attitudes are strong

You would expect that strong attitudes guide behaviour. Indeed, in a Dutch study of attitudes towards the Greenpeace movement, Rob Holland and his colleagues found that people with very positive attitudes were much more likely to make a

Attitude strength. The attitudes of these young people near the West Bank city of Jenin are very strong and highly accessible.

Source: Mohamad Torokman / Reuters

donation to the cause than those with weak positive attitudes (Holland, Verplanken & Van Knippenberg, 2002).

Almost by definition, strong attitudes must be highly accessible. They will come to mind more readily and exert more influence over behaviour than will weak attitudes. Fazio argued that attitudes are evaluative associations with objects. These associations can vary in strength from 'no link' (i.e. a non-attitude), to a weak link, to a strong link. Only an association that is strong allows the automatic activation of an attitude (Fazio, 1995; see Figure 4.1). Note that the way that 'strength' is used in Fazio's model is really in relation to the association itself, and does not mean that a strong attitude is necessarily an extreme attitude.

Direct experience of an object and having a vested interest in it (i.e. something with a strong effect on your life) make the attitude more accessible and increase its effect on behaviour. For example, people who have had a nuclear reactor built in their neighbourhood will have stronger and more clearly defined attitudes regarding the safety of nuclear reactors. These people will be more motivated by their attitudes – they may be more involved in protests or more likely to move to another part of the country.

The more often you *think* about an attitude, the more likely it is to resurface and influence your behaviour and ease decision making. Martha Powell applied this idea to attitudes towards issues such as legalised abortion, retirement age and gun control, finding that people's views became more accessible simply by asking questions on six different occasions compared with asking them only once (Powell & Fazio, 1984). Accessing general attitudes can affect behaviour in specific situations. If the general attitude is never accessed, it cannot affect behaviour. Therefore, the activation step of Fazio's model is critical, since only activated attitudes can guide

Automatic activation
According to Fazio, attitudes that have a strong evaluative link to situational cues are more likely to automatically come to mind from memory.

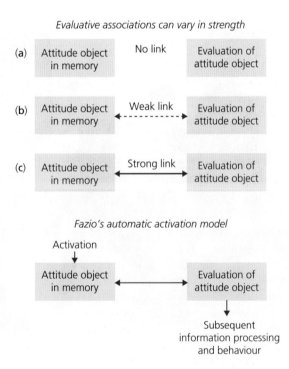

Figure 4.1

When is an attitude accessible?

A stronger attitude is more accessible than a weaker attitude. It can be automatically activated and will exert more influence over behaviour.

subsequent information processing and behaviour. Think of a sports coach priming a team by asking the question 'Which is the greatest team?', demanding a shouted response of 'We are!', and repeating this scenario a number of times before the match begins.

Attitudes and being rational

Not all classes of social behaviour can be predicted accurately from verbally expressed attitudes. We look now at two theories that gave new leads on how to get a better fit between attitudes and behaviour: the theory of reasoned action and the theory of planned behaviour.

The theory of reasoned action (TRA) was the first to deal explicitly with the quandary of the rather poor attitude–behaviour link that we referred to earlier. Developed by Martin Fishbein and Icek Ajzen (1974), it dealt specifically with how someone's beliefs and intentions are critically involved in how they act, and included the following components:

* *Subjective norm* – an outcome of what the individual thinks others believe. Significant others provide a guide about 'the proper thing to do'.
* *Attitude towards the behaviour* – based on the individual's beliefs about the specific behaviour and how these beliefs are evaluated. This is an attitude towards an act (e.g. taking a birth control pill), not towards an object (e.g. the pill itself).
* *Behavioural intention* – an internal declaration to act.
* *Behaviour* – the action performed.

Usually, an action will be performed if (1) the person's attitude is favourable; and (2) the social norm is supportive. A crucial link in this chain is intention, and Fishbein underlined the need to have a measure of a person's intention to act if the act is to be predicted. In one study he found a fairly strong correlation (0.80) between the intention and the action in the 1976 American presidential election (Fishbein, Ajzen & Hinkle, 1980).

The TRA emphasises not only the rationality of human behaviour but also the belief that it can be controlled: for example, 'I can stop smoking if I really want to'. However, some actions are less under people's control than others. Ajzen (1989) went on to emphasise the role of *volition* in a modified model, the theory of planned behaviour (TPB). Perceived behavioural control is the extent to which the person believes it is easy or difficult to perform an act. In deciding, we think of past experiences and present obstacles. For example, Ajzen and Madden (1986) found that students, not surprisingly, want to achieve A grades in their courses: A grades are highly valued by the students (attitude), and they are the grades that their family and friends want them to achieve (subjective norm). However, predicting an A grade will be unreliable unless we measure how the students rate their own abilities. The two theories, TRA and TPB, are not in conflict. The concepts and the way in which they are linked in each theory are shown in Figure 4.2.

Debbie Terry used both models to study safe sex behaviour in the face of the threat of contracting HIV (Terry, Gallois & McCamish, 1993; see Box 4.3). Specifically, the target behaviours encouraged were monogamous relationships, nonpenetrative sex and the use of condoms. All of the variables shown in Figure 4.2 can be applied here. Practising safe sex will depend on an individual's degree of perceived behavioural control – neither sex partner may be really confident of controlling the wishes of the other person. For example, will a woman be very confident that a condom will be used at a passionate moment in her next sexual encounter?

Theory of reasoned action
Fishbein and Ajzen's model of the links between attitude and behaviour. A major feature is the proposition that the best way to predict a behaviour is to ask whether the person intends to do it.

Theory of planned behaviour
Modification by Ajzen of the *theory of reasoned action*. It suggests that predicting a behaviour from an attitude measure is improved if people believe they have control over that behaviour.

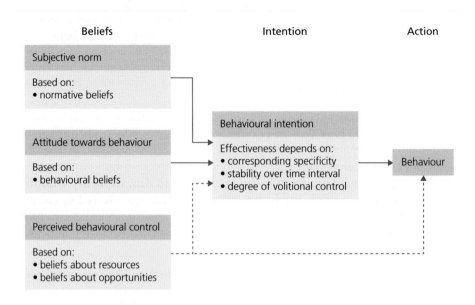

Figure 4.2

The theory of planned behaviour (TPB).

- The original theory of reasoned action did not include the component perceived behavioural control.
- By adding this component, the accuracy of an attitude measure in predicting behaviour can be improved. (See dotted lines.)

Perceived behavioural control. The search for physical fitness includes the belief that 'I can do this!' Having company adds a supportive social norm.

Source: Pearson Online Database (POD)

Research and applications 4.3
Reasoned action, planned behaviour and safe sex

In recent years, health professionals have shown intense concern about the spread of HIV and the deadly spectre of AIDS. In this context, social psychologists have mounted a concerted programme of research promoting condom use, safe sex and monogamous relationships. Several researchers, including Debbie Terry, have explicitly recognised Fishbein and Ajzen's theories of reasoned action and planned behaviour to account for variability in people's willingness to practise safe sex (Terry, Gallois & McCamish, 1993). Studies of this kind start by measuring whether people feel they can actually control their state of health. A woman who feels she can is more regular in wearing a seat belt, examining her breasts, using a contraceptive, having sex in an exclusive relationship, and discussing her partner's sexual and intravenous drug-use history.

A problem with practising safe sex with one's partner is that it is not a behaviour that comes completely under one individual's *control*, whereas going for a jog usually is. TRA and TPB (see Figure 4.2) provide a framework that targets factors with the potential to encourage safe sex, as well as other health behaviour.

Habit is also a predictor of future behaviour. We have already seen in Fazio's work that an action can become relatively automatic, and therefore operate independently of the reasoning process underlying TPB. David Trafimow (2000) found that male and female students who were in the habit of using condoms before sex reported that they would continue to do so on the next occasion. In effect, habitual users do not 'need' to use reasoned decisions, such as thinking about what their attitudes might be or about what norms are appropriate.

Both the TRA and TPB models have implications for how we can strive for a healthy lifestyle. We look at this in more detail again when we discuss *protection motivation theory* (see Box 4.6 and Figure 4.6). Meantime, try to answer the third focus question.

Attitudes can change: experiencing dissonance

People are allowed to change their minds, and as you know they do. In this section we will deal with research dealing with attitude change, with a focus on the theory of cognitive dissonance. The fact that attitudes and behaviour can often be inconsistent has a far-reaching consequence and can be one of the most powerful forces leading people to change their attitudes. Cognitive dissonance is one of a family of cognitive consistency theories. These assume that people wish to believe that they *are* consistent in how they think, feel and behave. This assumption has been most completely explored by the theory of cognitive dissonance, developed by the famous social psychologist Leon Festinger (1957), and it became the most studied topic in social psychology during the 1960s.

Cognitive dissonance is that unpleasant state of mental tension generated when a person has two or more cognitions (bits of information) that are inconsistent or do not fit together. Cognitions are thoughts, attitudes, beliefs or states of awareness of behaviour. For example, if a woman believes that monogamy is an important feature of her marriage and yet is having an extramarital affair, she may experience a measure of guilt and discomfort (dissonance).

Attitude change
Any significant modification of an individual's attitude. In the persuasion process this involves the communicator, the communication, the medium used, and the characteristics of the audience. Attitude change can also occur by inducing someone to perform an act that runs counter to an existing attitude.

Cognitive dissonance
State of psychological tension, produced by simultaneously having two opposing cognitions. People are motivated to reduce the tension, often by changing or rejecting one of the cognitions. Festinger proposed that we seek harmony in our attitudes, beliefs and behaviours, and try to reduce tension from inconsistency among these elements.

Cognitive consistency
A model of social cognition in which people try to reduce inconsistency among their cognitions, because they fine inconsistency unpleasant.

Festinger proposed that we seek harmony in our attitudes, beliefs and behaviour, and try to reduce tension from any inconsistency. People will try to do this by changing one or more of the inconsistent cognitions (e.g. in the case of the unfaithful wife, 'What's wrong with a little fun if no one finds out?'), by looking for additional evidence to bolster one side or the other ('My husband doesn't understand me'), or by derogating the source of one of the cognitions ('Fidelity is an outcome of religious indoctrination'). The maxim is: *The greater the dissonance, the stronger the attempts to reduce it.* Experiencing dissonance leads people to feel 'on edge' – as evidenced by changes in the electrical conductivity of the skin that can be detected by a polygraph.

Research has distinguished three ways that produce dissonance: effort justification, induced compliance and free choice. Let us see how these lines of investigation, called research paradigms, differ.

Effort justification

Now here is a surprise. The moment you choose between alternatives, you invite a state of dissonance. Suppose you need some takeaway food tonight. You make the momentous decision to go to the hamburger bar rather than to the stir-fry outlet. You keep mulling over the alternatives even after making your choice. Tonight's the night for a hamburger – you can taste it in your mouth already! The hamburger will be evaluated more favourably, or perhaps the stir-fry becomes less attractive, or maybe both. You have just experienced effort justification, and tomorrow is another day.

Effort justification
A special case of cognitive dissonance: inconsistency is experienced when a person makes a considerable effort to achieve a modest goal.

In an early study by Elliot Aronson and Judson Mills (1959) students who volunteered to join a discussion group were told that they must first pass a screening test for their capacity to speak frankly – in effect, an initiation. Those who agreed were assigned to one of two conditions, one 'severe' and the other 'mild'. Next, they listened over headphones to a sample discussion held by a group with a view to joining in during the following week. What they heard was incoherent and plain boring.

According to dissonance theory: (a) the act of volunteering to be initiated should cause dissonance; and (b) the severe initiation should lend to a sense of suffering and increase the degree of dissonance experienced. Consequently, the severe initiation with high dissonance should also increase interest in what was otherwise a boring discussion. This was confirmed when the two conditions were compared. It was those who went through the severe initiation condition who thought that both the group discussion (and also the other group members heard on tape) were much more interesting.

Joel Cooper and Danny Axsom (1982) used a similar design to study effort expenditure by women who wanted to lose weight and were willing to try a 'new experimental procedure'. The women came to a laboratory, were weighed and listened to the plan of action. In a high-effort condition, some were told that they needed to perform several time-consuming tasks, including reading tongue twisters aloud for a session lasting forty minutes. These tasks required psychological endeavour rather than physical exercise. When the effort was low, the tasks were shorter and easier; and in a control condition, the volunteers did not participate in any tasks at all but were simply weighed and asked to report again at a later date. The high-effort and low-effort groups came to the laboratory for five sessions over a period of three weeks, at which point they were weighed again. The results are shown in Figure 4.3.

Figure 4.3

Losing weight after expending psychological effort.

You may think that physical effort should reduce weight. This study suggests that mental effort is an important ingredient in a programme's effectiveness.

Source: Based on data from Cooper and Axsom (1982).

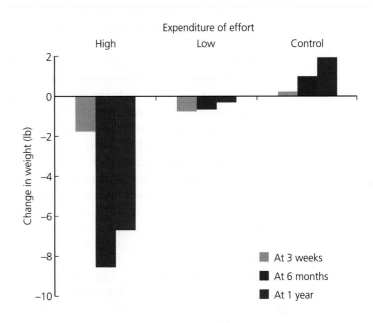

Cooper and Axsom were encouraged to find that the weight loss effect in the high-effort group was not simply an artefact of the interest shown in the women during the time of the five-week study. After six months, a remarkable 94 per cent of the high-effort group had lost some weight, while only 39 per cent of the low-effort group had managed to do so.

Induced compliance

Occasionally people are induced to act in a way that is inconsistent with their beliefs. An important aspect of the induced compliance, our second dissonance paradigm, is that the inducement should not be perceived as being forced against one's will. Leon Festinger and J. Merrill Carlsmith (1959) carried out an often-quoted experiment in which student volunteers for a psychology experiment were asked to perform an extremely boring task for an hour, believing that they were contributing to research on 'measures of performance'.

Imagine that you are the volunteer and that in front of you is a board on which there are several rows of square pegs, each one sitting in a square hole. You are asked to turn each peg a quarter of a turn to the left and then a quarter of a turn back to the right. When you have finished turning all the pegs, you are instructed to start all over again, repeating the sequence over and over for twenty minutes. (This was not designed to be fun!) When the twenty minutes are up, the experimenter tells you that you have finished the first part, and you can now start on the second part, this time taking spools of thread off another peg board and placing them all back on again, and again, and again. Finally, the mind-numbing jobs are over.

At this point, the experimenter lets you in on a secret: you were a control participant, but now you can be of 'real' help. It seems that a confederate of the experimenter has failed to show up. Could you help out? All you have to do is tell the next person that the tasks are really very interesting. The experimenter explains

Induced compliance
A special case of cognitive dissonance: inconsistency is experienced when a person is persuaded to behave in a way that is contrary to an attitude.

that he is interested in the effects of preconceptions on people's work on a task. Later, he offers money if you would be on call to help again at some time in the future. Luckily, you are never called.

The participants were paid just $1 in one condition for cooperating, but were paid $20 in another condition. The study's design also included a control group of participants who were not asked to tell anyone how interesting the truly boring experience had been, and they were paid no incentive. On a later occasion, all were asked to rate how interesting the task had been. According to the idea of induced compliance, dissonance follows when you have agreed to say things about what you have experienced knowing that the opposite is true. You have been induced to behave in a *counter-attitudinal* way.

The variation in levels of incentive adds an interesting twist. Participants who had been paid $20 could explain their lie to themselves with the thought, 'I did it for the $20. It must have been a lousy task, indeed.' Perhaps dissonance did not exist in this condition. (We should point out that $20 was a sum of money not to be sneezed at by a student in the late 1950s.) On the other hand, those who told the lie and had been paid only $1 were confronted with a dilemma: 'I have done a really boring task, then told someone else that it is interesting, and finally even agreed to come back and do this again for a measly $1!' Herein lies the dissonance. A way of reducing the continuing arousal is to believe that the experiment was actually quite interesting. See the results of this classic study in Figure 4.4.

Note that the $1 group rated the task as fairly interesting whereas the $20 group found it slightly boring (while control participants found it even more so). For $1 participants were also more willing to take part in similar experiments in the future. The use of a smaller reward to bring about a larger attitude change has been replicated several times. To modify an old saying: 'If you are going to lead a donkey on, use a carrot – but make it a small one if you want the donkey to enjoy the trip.'

Talking of carrots, how would you now respond to the fourth focus question? An intriguing experiment carried out in a military setting by Phil Zimbardo and his

Figure 4.4

Reducing incentives can make a boring task seem more interesting.

One of social psychology's counter-intuitive findings: Commitment to return to repeat a boring task is maximised, as is dissonance, by offering a very small reward.

Source: Based on data from Festinger & Carlsmith (1959).

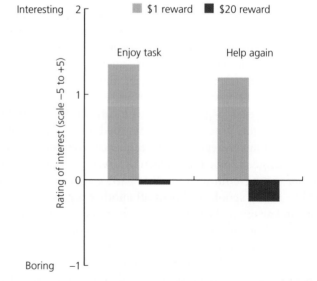

colleagues (Zimbardo, Weisenberg, Firestone & Levy, 1965) tackled this culinary question. The participants were asked to eat grasshoppers by an authority figure whose interpersonal style was either positive (warm) or negative (cold). According to the induced compliance variation of cognitive dissonance, post-decisional conflict (and consequent attitude change) should be greater when the communicator is negative – how else could one justify behaving voluntarily in a counter-attitudinal way? Read what happened in this study in Box 4.4, and check the results in Figure 4.5.

Inducing people to act inconsistently with their attitudes is not an easy task and often requires a subtle approach. However, once people have been induced to act counter-attitudinally, the theory predicts that dissonance will be strong and that they will seek to justify their action.

Post-decisional conflict
The dissonance associated with behaving in a counter-attitudinal way. Dissonance can be reduced by bringing the attitude into line with the behaviour.

Research classic 4.4
To know grasshoppers is to love them: attitude change following induced compliance

Think back to the fourth focus question. This scenario was actually researched in Zimbardo's famous study. An officer in command suggested to some military cadets that they might eat a few fried grasshoppers, and mild social pressure was put on them to comply. The cadets had also indicated in a questionnaire about food habits earlier that there were limits to what they should be expected to eat. However, the officer stressed that modern soldiers in combat should be mobile and be ready to eat off the land. After his talk, the cadets were each given a plate with five fried grasshoppers and invited to try them out.

A critical feature of the experiment was the way the request was made. For half the cadets the officer was cheerful, informal and permissive ('Call me Smitty', he said). For the other half, he was cool, official and stiff ('Hallo, I'm Dr Smith'). There was also a control group who gave two sets of food ratings but

Figure 4.5

Eating fried grasshoppers is easier when a military officer is more brusque.

As with Figure 4.4, here is another counter-intuitive outcome: complying with an unpleasant request can seem more attractive when the person making the request is less attractive (see also Box 4.4 text).

Source: Based on data from Zimbardo, Weisenberg, Firestone & Levy (1965).

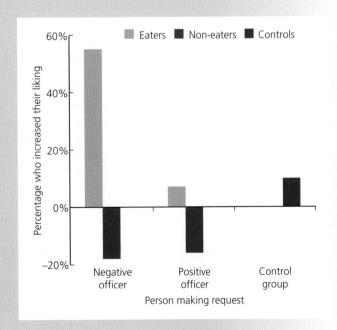

▶

never had the chance to eat the crunchy critters. The pressure on the experimental participants had to be subtle enough for them to feel they had freely chosen whether or not to eat the grasshoppers. Indeed, an order to eat would not arouse dissonance, because a cadet could say 'He made me do it'. Again, those who listened to the positive officer might justify complying by thinking 'I did it as a favour for Smitty'. However, those who ate the grasshoppers for cold Dr Smith could not justify their actions in this way. They should experience dissonance, and the easy way to reduce this would be to change their rating of grasshoppers as food.

About 50 per cent actually ate some grasshoppers, eating about two of the five hoppers sitting on their plate. The results in Figure 4.5 show the percentage who changed from liking or disliking grasshoppers as food. In both the negative and positive officer conditions, eaters were more favourable and non-eaters less favourable. It is likely that self-justification was needed for an act that was voluntary but aversive. However, most interest is in the negative officer condition in which dissonance should be maximal. It was here that the biggest change towards liking the little beasties was recorded.

Sources: Based on Zimbardo, Ebbesen & Maslach (1977); Zimbardo, Weisenberg, Firestone & Levy (1965).

Free choice

Suppose that your choices between courses of action are fairly evenly balanced, and that you are committed to making some kind of decision. This applies to numerous situations in our everyday lives: whether to buy this product or that; go to this tourist spot or another for a holiday; take this job offer or some other one. Based on Festinger's blueprint of the process of conflict in decision making, the pre-decision period is marked by uncertainty and dissonance, and the post-decision period by relative calm and confidence.

In our third dissonance paradigm, free-choice reduction of conflict is likely to be a feature of bets laid on the outcome of sporting events, horse racing, gambling and so on. Once a person has made a choice between decision alternatives, dissonance theory predicts that the person making a bet will become more confident about a successful outcome. Jonathan Younger approached people at a fair ground who were either about to bet or had just placed their bets, on carnival games such as bingo and wheel of fortune, and asked them to rate their confidence in winning (Younger, Walker & Arrowood, 1977). They found that both men and women who had already made their bet were more confident of winning.

Cognitive dissonance theory has had a chequered history in social psychology (see Visser & Cooper, 2003) and its critics have suggested various other explanations for some of the results. Despite this, cognitive dissonance theory remains one of the most widely accepted explanations of attitude change and much other social behaviour. It has generated over 1000 empirical studies and will probably continue to be an integral part of social psychological theory for many years.

Next we look at how techniques of persuasion have been used to bring about changes in attitudes and behaviour.

The science of persuasion

The receptive powers of the masses are very restricted, and their understanding is feeble. On the other hand, they quickly forget. Such being the case, all effective propaganda must be confined to a few bare essentials and those must be expressed as far as possible in stereotyped formulas. These slogans should be persistently repeated until the very last individual has come to grasp the idea that has been put forward. If this principle be forgotten and if an attempt be made to be abstract and general, the propaganda will turn out ineffective; for the public will not be able to digest or retain what is offered to them in this way. Therefore, the greater the scope of the message that has to be presented, the more necessary it is for the propaganda to discover that plan of action which is psychologically the most efficient. *(Hitler, Mein Kampf, 1933)*

Has there ever been a more dramatic, mesmerising and chilling communicator than Adolf Hitler? His massive audiences at the Nazi rallies of the 1930s and 1940s might not have been so impressed had they known what he thought of them. At a more day-to-day level, social psychological research on the relationship between persuasive communication and attitude change is more narrowly focused. Two well-researched areas of application are advertising and the promotion of health behaviours.

Persuasive communication Message intended to change an attitude and related behaviours of an audience.

Communicating persuasively

The insights and aphorisms of Bernbach are famous among advertising executives. Here is one from a collection titled *Bill Bernbach Said*:

An important idea not communicated persuasively is like having no idea at all. *(Bernbach, 2002)*

Towards the end of the Second World War, Carl Hovland was contracted by his government to investigate how propaganda could be used to support the American war effort – as it already had for the German cause by Hitler and the Nazi party. After the war, he set up the first coordinated research programme dealing with the social psychology of persuasion at Yale University. The main features of this

Persuading the masses. Hitler felt that the content of an effective public message should be simple. Slogans were a key ingredient of Nazi propaganda.

Source: Imperial War Museum, London

pioneering work were outlined in the research team's book, *Communication and Persuasion* (Hovland, Janis & Kelley, 1953). They suggested that the key to understanding why people would attend to, understand, remember and accept a persuasive message was to answer the question 'Who says what to whom and with what effect?' This general research structure can still be seen today. The three variables involved in persuasion are:

Source
The point of origin of a persuasive communication.

Message
Communication from a source directed to an audience.

Audience
Intended target of a persuasive communication.

1. the source or communicator (*who*);
2. the message (*what*);
3. the audience (*to whom*).

A taste of research over many years that has a real life flavour is shown in Box 4.5. If you were planning to make a public campaign as persuasive as possible, there are points to bear in mind: some communicators, message strategies and speech styles are more effective than others; and the nature of the audience needs to be accounted for.

The persuasion process requires that an audience attends to some extent to a message and understands at least part of the content. A message is more likely to be accepted if it arouses favourable thoughts but rejected if it triggers strong counter-arguments.

The three links in the persuasion chain (who, what and to whom) are always present and often more than one of these plays an important part. We will look more closely at a message factor that has been studied intensively for its power to change both attitudes and behaviour – *fear*. Not surprisingly, fearful advertise-

Real world 4.5
Persuasive communications that can lead to attitude change

WHO: source factors

- Experts are more persuasive than non-experts. The same arguments carry more weight when delivered by someone who seems to know all the facts (Hovland & Weiss, 1952).

- Popular and attractive communicators are more effective than unpopular or unattractive ones (Kiesler & Kiesler, 1969).

- People who speak rapidly are more persuasive than people who speak slowly. Rapid speech gives an impression of 'I know what I'm talking about' (Miller, Maruyama, Beaber & Valone, 1976).

WHAT: message factors

- We are more easily persuaded if we think the message is not deliberately intended to manipulate us (Walster & Festinger, 1962).

- A message in a powerless linguistic style (frequent hedges, tag questions, hesitations) is less persuasive than one in a powerful linguistic style. A powerless style gives a negative impression of both the arguments and the speaker (Blankenship & Holtgraves, 2005).

- Messages that arouse fear can be very effective. For example, to stop people smoking we might show them pictures of cancerous lungs (Leventhal, Singer & Jones, 1965).

TO WHOM: audience factors

- People with low self-esteem are persuaded more easily than people with high self-esteem (Janis, 1954).

- People are sometimes more susceptible to persuasion when they are distracted than when paying full attention, at least when the message is simple (Allyn & Festinger, 1961).

- People in the 'impressionable years' are more susceptible to persuasion than those who are older (Krosnick & Alwin, 1989).

ments have been used for decades to induce people to obey the law or to care for their health, based on fear. Does fear work?

In an early study, Irving Janis and Seymour Feshbach (1953) used three message variations to encourage people to practice good dental hygiene:

- *Low-fear message* – they were told of the painful outcomes of diseased teeth and gums.
- *Moderate-fear message* – the warning about oral disease was more explicit.
- *High-fear message* – they were told that the disease could spread to other parts of their body, and saw very unpleasant slides of decayed teeth and diseased gums.

There was an inverse relationship between degree of (presumed) fear arousal and change in dental hygiene practices. The low-fear participants were taking the best care of their teeth after one week, followed by the moderate-fear group and then by the high-fear group.

Although other research has not been so clear-cut, the use of high-fear messages has been cogently questioned. William McGuire (1969) suggested that as the fear content in a message increases, so does arousal, interest and attention to what is going on. However, a very frightening way of presenting an idea may arouse so much anxiety, even a state of panic, that we become distracted and miss some of the factual content of the message. Disturbing TV images, for example, may distract people from the intended message or, even if attended to, so upset people that the advertisement is avoided.

Ideas developed in health settings have cast further light on the use of fear. Protection motivation theory has offered insights into the way fear appeals may succeed or fail in eliminating dangerous health practices (see Box 4.6 and Figure 4.6).

Protection motivation theory
Adopting a healthy behaviour requires cognitive balancing between the perceived threat of illness and one's capacity to cope with the health regimen.

Self-efficacy
Expectations that we have about our capacity to succeed in particular tasks.

Research and applications 4.6
Can we protect ourselves against major diseases?

Cardiovascular disease and cancer have been the leading causes of death in most affluent Western countries. Preventive behaviour includes routine medical examinations, regular blood pressure readings, exercising aerobically for at least twenty minutes three times per week, eating a well-balanced diet that is low in salt and fat, maintaining a healthy weight level and choosing not to smoke. A major challenge is to uncover a robust model of health promotion, particularly to lower the incidence of these major killer diseases.

Inspired by the work of Fishbein and Ajzen that we have noted earlier, protection motivation theory was developed by Ron Rogers to explain the effects of fear appeals on maladaptive health attitudes and behaviour.

In their *meta-analysis* of sixty-five health studies and more than twenty health issues, Floyd, Prentice-Dunn and Rogers (2000) concluded that intentions to make a change are facilitated by:

- an increase in the perceived severity of a health threat;
- the vulnerability of the individual to that threat;
- the perceived effectiveness of taking protective action; and
- self-efficacy.

In considering why Joe Six Pack, for example, might either continue to smoke or quit, the theory includes two mediating cognitive processes:

1 *Threat appraisal* – smoking has intrinsic rewards (e.g. taste in mouth, nicotine effect) and extrinsic rewards (e.g. his friends think it's cool). These are

▶

weighed up against what Joe thinks about the risk to his health (e.g. after reading the latest brochure in his doctor's waiting room) and how vulnerable he thinks he is (e.g. because a close relative who smoked died of lung cancer).

2   *Coping appraisal* – Joe estimates response efficacy (whether nicotine replacement therapy might work)

and self-efficacy (whether he thinks he can adhere to the regime).

The trade-off when Joe compares his appraisals of threat and coping determines his level of protection motivation and whether he decides to quit smoking (see Figure 4.6). Now is the time to answer the fifth focus question.

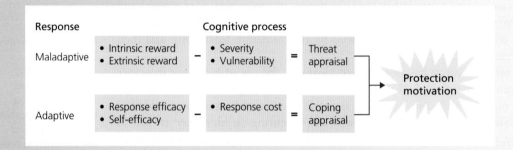

Figure 4.6

Mediating cognitive processes in protection motivation theory.

This theory grew from psychological research into health promotion. Adopting a healthy practice will depend on several cognitive processes that lead to a balancing up of perceived threat versus the capacity to cope with a health regime.

Source: Based on Floyd, Prentice-Dunn & Rogers (2000).

Dual-process routes to persuasion

Within social psychology in particular, cognitive processes that are fundamental to how we respond to the content of persuasive messages have been clarified in the last two decades. Slightly different approaches have emerged: the elaboration–likelihood model and the heuristic–systematic model. Both postulate two processes and both deal with persuasion cues. Sometimes it may not be the quality and type of the persuasion cues that matter but rather the quantity of message processing that underlies attitude change. Let us see what these models entail.

Elaboration-likelihood model

Elaboration–likelihood model
Petty and Cacioppo's model of attitude change: when people attend to a message carefully, they use a central route to process it; otherwise they use a peripheral route. This model competes with the heuristic–systematic model.

According to Richard Petty and John Cacioppo's elaboration–likelihood model (ELM), when people receive a persuasive message they think about the arguments it makes. However, they do not necessarily think deeply or carefully about the arguments, because to do so requires considerable cognitive effort. The ordinary person is a *cognitive miser* who is motivated to expend cognitive effort only on issues that are important to them (see Chapter 2). Persuasion follows two routes, depending on whether people expend a great deal or very little cognitive effort on the message.

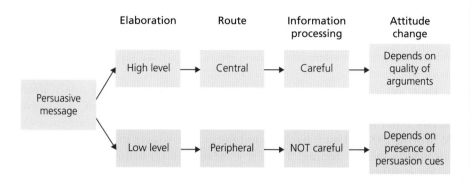

Figure 4.7

The elaboration–likelihood model of persuasion.

Source: Based on Petty & Cacioppo (1986).

If the arguments of the message are followed closely, a *central route* is used. We digest the arguments in a message, extract a point that meets our needs and even indulge mentally in counter-arguments if we disagree with some of them. If the central route to persuasion is to be used, the points in the message need to be put convincingly, as we will be required to expend considerable cognitive effort – that is, to work hard – on them. For example, suppose that your doctor told you that you needed major surgery. The chances are that you would take a considerable amount of convincing, that you would listen carefully to what the doctor says, read what you could about the matter and even seek a second medical opinion. On the other hand, when arguments are not well attended to, a *peripheral route* is followed. By using peripheral cues we act in a less diligent fashion, preferring a consumer product on a superficial basis, such as an advertisement in which the product is used by an attractive model. The alternative routes available according to the elaboration–likelihood model are shown in Figure 4.7.

Heuristic-systematic model

Shelley Chaiken's (1980) heuristic–systematic model (HSM) deals with the same phenomena using slightly different concepts, distinguishing between *systematic* processing and *heuristic* processing. Systematic processing occurs when people scan and consider available arguments. In the case of heuristic processing, we do not indulge in careful reasoning but instead use cognitive heuristics, such as thinking that longer arguments are stronger. Persuasive messages are not always processed systematically. This is when people will sometimes employ cognitive heuristics to simplify the task of handling information. You will recall that heuristics are a variety of simple decision rules or 'mental short cuts', the tools that cognitive misers use. So, when we are judging the reliability of a message, we may resort to such truisms as 'statistics don't lie' or 'you can't trust a politician' as an easy way of making up our minds. As previously discussed, this feature of judgement is actively exploited by advertising companies when they seek to influence consumers by portraying their products as supported by scientific research or expert opinion. For instance, washing detergents are often advertised in laboratory settings, showing

Heuristic–systematic model
Chaiken's model of attitude change: when people attend to a message carefully, they use systematic processing; otherwise they process information by using heuristics, or 'mental short cuts'. This model competes with the elaboration–likelihood model.

technical equipment and authoritative-looking people in white coats. At what point would we switch from heuristic to systematic processing? According to Petty, people have a *sufficiency threshold*: heuristics will be used as long as they satisfy our need to be confident in the attitude that we adopt (Petty & Wegener, 1998). When we lack sufficient confidence, we resort to the more effortful systematic mode of processing.

How well we concentrate on the content of a message can be subtly affected by something as transient as our *mood*. Diane Mackie, for example, has shown that merely being in a good mood changes the way we attend to information (Mackie & Worth, 1989). Using background music is a widely used advertising ploy to engender a mellow feeling. There is a sneaky reason behind this – feeling 'good' makes it difficult for us to process a message systematically. When time is limited, which is typical of TV advertising, feeling really good leads us to flick on to auto-pilot, i.e. to use a peripheral route (ELM) or heuristic processing (HSM).

However, Duane Wegener demonstrated that people who are already happy do not always scrutinise messages superficially. If the message content is in line with our attitudes (therefore congruent with our already good mood), then being happy as well leads to more extensive processing (Wegener, Petty & Smith, 1995). What is involved here is an interaction between two of the three major persuasion factors noted in the Yale programme: a supportive message and a happy audience.

Think again about how advertisers present everyday merchandise: cues like feel-good background music have an additional and longer-term 'benefit'. Marketing strategists George and Michael Belch (2007) noted that, through classical conditioning, a product repeatedly associated with a good mood can come to be evaluated positively – in time, in the absence of music or other positive contextual cues.

A question remains. Can we arm ourselves against the manipulators?

Resisting persuasion

When we feel strongly about an issue we can be quite stubborn in resisting attempts to change our position. However, much of the material presented in this chapter highlights factors that are conducive to altering our attitudes, very often beyond a level of direct awareness. Even so, far more attempts at persuasion fail than ever succeed. Researchers have identified three major reasons: reactance, fore-warning and inoculation.

Reactance

Reactance
Brehm's theory that people try to protect their freedom to act. When they perceive that this freedom has been curtailed, they will act to regain it.

We noted in Box 4.5 that we are more easily persuaded if we think the message is not deliberately intended to be persuasive. Think back to an occasion when someone obviously tried to change your attitudes. Perhaps you found it unpleasant and possibly hardened your existing attitude. Jack Brehm (1966) referred to this process as reactance. We can think of this as a rebound response.

Recall the biblical story in the Garden of Eden. God said 'I forbid you to eat that apple'. Eve (egged on by the serpent) thought 'Right! Let's see how it tastes'. Brad Bushman and Angela Stack (1996) tested this idea in an interesting study of warning labels for television films with violent content. Two kinds of labels were compared: (a) *tainted fruit* labels, in which a warning is lower key, suggesting that a film's content could have harmful effects; and (b) *forbidden fruit* labels, in which the warning seems like censorship – the very thing that a network could be anxious to avoid. Perhaps you will not be surprised that strong warnings increase interest in the violent films and viewers in this study, like Eve, responded in kind. The underlying cause of reactance is a sense of having our personal freedom infringed.

Forewarning

Forewarning is prior knowledge of persuasive intent – telling someone that an attempt will be made to influence them. Bob Cialdini and Richard Petty (1979) concluded that, when we know this in advance, persuasion is less effective, especially with respect to attitudes and issues that we consider important. When people are forewarned, they have time to rehearse counter-arguments that can be used as a defence. From this point of view, forewarning can be thought of as a special case of inoculation.

Forewarning
Advance knowledge that one is to be the target of a persuasion attempt. Forewarning often produces resistance to persuasion.

The inoculation effect

> The Chinese Communists have developed a peculiar brand of soul surgery which they practice with impressive skill – the process of 'thought reform'. They first demonstrated this to the American public during the Korean conflict. . . . And more recently we have seen . . . Western civilians released from Chinese prisons, repeating their false confessions, insisting upon their guilt, praising the 'justice' and 'leniency' which they have received, and expounding the 'truth' and 'righteousness' of all Communist doctrine. *(R. J. Lifton, 1956; cited in Bernard, Maio & Olson, 2003, p. 63)*

As the term suggests, inoculation is a form of protection. In biology, we can inject a weakened or inert form of disease-producing germs into the patient to build up resistance to a more powerful form. In social psychology, we might seek an analogous method of providing a defence against persuasive ideas. The technique of inoculation is initiated by exposing a person to a weakened counter-attitudinal argument.

Inoculation
A way of making people resistant to persuasion. By providing them with a diluted counter-argument, they can build up effective refutations to a later, stronger argument.

Bill McGuire and his associates (e.g. McGuire & Papageorgis, 1961; Anderson & McGuire, 1965) became interested in the technique following reports of 'brainwashing' of American soldiers imprisoned by Chinese forces during the Korean War of the early 1950s. Some of these made public statements denouncing the American Government and saying they wanted to remain in China when the war ended. McGuire reasoned that these soldiers were mostly inexperienced young men who had not previously been exposed to attacks on the American way of life and were not forearmed with a defence against the Marxist logic.

McGuire applied the biological analogy to the field of persuasive communications, distinguishing two kinds of defence:

1. *The supportive defence* – This is based on attitude bolstering. Resistance could be strengthened by providing additional arguments that back up the original beliefs.
2. *The inoculation defence* – This employs counter-arguments, and may be more effective. A person learns what the opposition's arguments are and then hears them demolished.

McGuire and Papageorgis (1961) put both forms of defence to the test. Students were asked to indicate their agreement on a 15-point scale with a series of truisms relating to health beliefs, such as:

- It's a good idea to brush your teeth after every meal if at all possible.
- The effects of penicillin have been, almost without exception, of great benefit to mankind.
- Everyone should get a yearly chest X-ray to detect any signs of TB at an early stage.
- Mental illness is not contagious.

Before the experiment began, many of the students thoroughly endorsed these propositions by checking 15, at one extreme on the response scale. The main variables of interest were the effects of introducing defences and attacks on these health beliefs in the form of essays offering arguments for or against the truisms. Students who were in the defence groups were in either (a) a *supportive* defence group (the students received support for their position), or (b) an *inoculation* defence group (their position was subjected to a weak attack, which was then refuted). There were also two control groups, one in which the students were neither attacked nor defended, and another that read essays that strongly attacked the truisms but none defending them.

Not surprisingly, control participants who had been neither attacked nor defended continued to show the highest level of acceptance of the truisms. The crucial findings shown in Figure 4.8 were:

- Students equipped with a supportive defence were a little more resistant to an attack when compared with the control group who had been attacked without any defence (compare the data in columns 2 and 4).

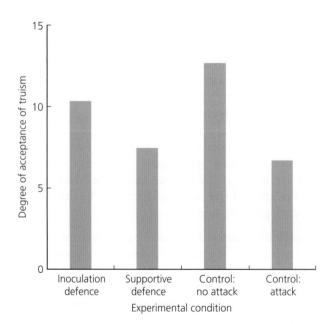

Figure 4.8

An inoculation defence can be effective in resisting an attack on one's attitude.

One of the best forms of defence against counter-arguments is to be exposed to small doses of these arguments.

Source: Based on data from McGuire & Papageorgis (1961).

- Students who had been inoculated were substantially strengthened in their defence against a strong attack compared with the same control group (compare the data in columns 1 and 4).

A study by Julia Jacks and Kimberly Cameron (2003) added further weight to the power of inoculation defence: overall, using counter-arguments may be the most effective solution. The inoculation phenomenon has been used in some kinds of advertising. An example is issue/advocacy advertising in which a company protects consumer loyalty from 'attitude slippage' by issuing media releases on controversial issues (see Burgoon, Pfau & Birk, 1995). For example, a chemical company may issue a statement about environmental pollution in order to inoculate its consumers against allegations of environmental misconduct from competing companies, or from other 'enemies' such as a local green party. This practice is now widespread: an alcohol company may fund alcohol research and alcohol-moderation campaigns, and a fashion company may support the protection of wildlife.

In general, research in the field of resistance to persuasion has expanded during the last decade, as documented in Eric Knowles and Jay Linn's book *Resistance and Persuasion* (2004).

Summary

- Attitudes are lasting, general evaluations of socially significant objects, including people and issues, based on organised beliefs and tendencies to act in a particular way.

- Attitudes are learned. They can be formed by direct experience, by conditioning, by observational learning and sometimes by drawing an inference from what we do (self-perception). Attitude learning in children is highly dependent on their parents and the mass media.

- Traditionally, attitudes have been measured by using questionnaires. There is a recent and high interest in less obvious measures, such as the implicit association test. These measures aim to probe attitudes that people would rather not reveal, in particular, their prejudices.

- The link between attitudes and behaviour has been controversial. The apparently poor predictive power of attitude measures led to a loss of confidence in the concept itself.

- Highly accessible attitudes are those that are easily recalled, and are more likely to be automatically activated. Strong attitudes are usually highly accessible, and are more clearly linked to action.

- The interrelated theories of reasoned action and planned behaviour introduced the idea that predicting a specific behaviour required measuring a person's intention to perform the act in question. Prediction is also improved by knowing what are relevant norms provided by others and how much control the individual has over the act.

- Inconsistency between attitudes and behaviour is a core issue in the theory of cognitive dissonance. This theory addresses not only conflict between a person's beliefs but also discrepancy between behaviour and underlying attitudes. It includes three variations on the way in which dissonance is brought about: effort justification, induced compliance and free choice.

- The Yale research programme was a major approach to the study of communication and persuasion. It focused on three kinds of factors: the source of a message (*who* factors), the message itself (*what* factors) and the audience (to *whom* factors).

- A well-researched message variable is an appeal based on fear. Protection motivation theory has concentrated on ways that people's fears may be exploited to promote health practices.

- Advertising is now a constant and unavoidable life experience. Two theoretical models have addressed how people attend to a persuasive message. The elaboration–likelihood model proposes that when people attend to a message carefully, they use a central route to process it; otherwise they use a peripheral route. The heuristic–systematic model suggests that people use systematic processing when they attend to a message carefully; otherwise they use heuristic processing. The models are not in conflict.

- Reactance is an increase in resistance to persuasion when the communicator's efforts to persuade are obvious. Techniques for building up resistance include forewarning and the inoculation defence. In recent years, manufacturing companies have used inoculation in media releases to protect consumer loyalty.

Literature, film and TV

1984

George Orwell's 1949 novel about life in a fictional totalitarian regime, is based on Stalin's Soviet Union. The book, which places an emphasis on the role of ideology, illustrates how such a regime can control all aspects of life. Through the creation of a new language, 'Newspeak', the regime is able to determine how people think and how they view the world. The book touches on the relationship between language and thought (see Chapter 11), and on how language constrains and reflects what we can easily think about.

The Office

TV series in which David Brent (played by Ricky Gervais) and Gareth Keenan (played by Mackenzie Crook) are both prejudiced in old-fashioned and modern ways. Their antics are acutely embarrassing, and a wonderful illustration of how prejudiced attitudes reveal themselves in behaviour – all played out in a suburban British office environment.

Pride and Prejudice

Jane Austen's classic 1813 novel is about life and love in the genteel rural society of the day. The focal characters are Elizabeth and Darcy. One of the key features of this society is the possibility of misunderstanding based on the fact that there are strong normative pressures that inhibit the expression of one's true attitudes.

Glengarry Glen Ross

A 1992 film directed by James Foley, written by David Mamet, and starring Jack Lemmon, Al Pacino, Ed Harris, Kevin Spacey, Alec Baldwin and others. The film is about a real estate office and the different ways in which salesmen under pressure try to sell, and to persuade others.

Holy Smoke

This 1999 film by Jane Campion follows Kate Winslet's Ruth, a young girl who is obsessed with a charismatic Indian guru and is subsequently captured by P. J. Waters (played by Harvey Keitel), an 'anti-programmer', hired by her family to bring her back to 'normality'. They spend four days in the desert together locked in a battle of wills but despite trying every tactic in the book, P. J. realises that Ruth is just as persuasive as him in changing his views and attitudes to life. An intense demonstration of the power of persuasion and the different methods used to change attitudes.

The Godfather trilogy: 1901–1980

All three Godfather movies together (1992), directed by Francis Ford Coppola, and with stars such as Marlon Brando, Al Pacino, Robert Duvall, James Caan, Robert de Niro, Diane Keaton and Andy Garcia. A trilogy all about the persuasive power exerted by the Mafia through fear, and the actual, implied or imagined presence of the Godfather.

Frost/Nixon

In the summer of 1977 ex-president Richard Nixon, three years after being forced from office in disgrace for the Watergate scandal, decides to put the record straight and reinstate his legacy through a televised interview. He chooses the breezy young jet-setting British interviewer David Frost. What follows, in this 2009 film, is an exercise in persuasion and attitude change as Nixon cleverly seems to prevail over Frost for most of the interview and surrounding events.

Guided questions

- What we do does not always follow from what we think. Why not? Are there ways that our underlying attitudes may be uncovered?

- What is the theory of *planned behaviour*? How can it be used to improve the predictive power of an attitude measure? Give an example from research.

- What are the odds that you could be persuaded to eat fried grasshoppers?

- If your aim was to 'inoculate' someone against an upcoming propaganda campaign how would you go about it?

- Are there ways in which attitudes that are beyond awareness may be uncovered? Mahzarin Banaji outlines the nature of implicit attitudes and introduces the Implicit Association Test (IAT), a technique that has been used to reveal them in Chapter 4 of MyPsychLab at www.mypsychlab.co.uk.

Learn more

Belch, G. E., & Belch, M. A. (2007). *Advertising and promotion: An integrated marketing communications perspective* (7th ed). New York: McGraw-Hill/Irwin. This latest edition of a well-known textbook uses a communications theory approach (source, message, receiver) to show how social psychological principles can be applied to change consumer attitudes and behaviour. It is rich with examples and illustrations of advertisements.

Bohner, G., & Wänke, M. (2002). *Attitudes and attitude change*. Hove, UK: Psychology Press. A useful monograph with a treatment of persuasion, including dual-process models of information processing.

Eagly, A. H., & Chaiken, S. (2005). Attitude research in the 21st century: The current state of knowledge. In D. Albarracín, B. T. Johnson & M. P. Zanna (eds), *The handbook of attitudes* (pp. 742–767). Mahway, NJ: Lawrence Erlbaum Associates. An up-to-date coverage of attitude components and dimensions, and the attitude–behaviour link.

Knowles, E. S., & Linn, J. A. (eds) (2004). *Resistance and persuasion*. Mahwah, NJ: Erlbaum. Contributors deal not only with how people can withstand persuasive assaults, but also how resistance can be used to deter persuasive attempts.

Visser, P. S., & Cooper, J. (2003). Attitude change. In M.A. Hogg & J. Cooper (eds), *The Sage handbook of social psychology* (pp. 211–31). London: Sage. An up-to-date, comprehensive and accessible overview of research and theory on persuasion and attitude change.

 Refresh your understanding, assess your progress and go further with interactive summaries, questions, podcasts, videos and much more on the website accompanying the book: **www.mypsychlab.co.uk.**

Chapter 5

Conformity and social change

What to look for

- The origin and purpose of norms

- Why people conform to a majority view

- Variations in conformity

- Processes underlying social influence

- Tactics for gaining compliance

- Extreme obedience

- How minorities bring about social change

Focus questions

1. Jennifer read a story about a tribe of people in a faraway country who lived on a river with a jungle nearby. They didn't wear clothes and thought crocodiles were sacred. She wondered 'why they don't have norms to guide their behaviour?' Is Jennifer being fair?

2. While playing Trivial Pursuit, Sarah simply agrees with Paul and John when they decide which plane first broke the sound barrier. They say she is a typical conformist female. What do you say?

3. Someone offers you a sum of money for your prized racing bike, which you believe is a fair price. After they have checked their bank balance, the offer is reduced by 15%, saying that's all they can afford. Could such a tactic work? This is the low-ball technique and is discussed by Robert Cialdini in Chapter 5 of MyPsychLab at www.mypsychlab.co.uk.

4. While serving in the army on combat duty, Private Milkins is ordered to set booby traps in a neighbourhood that is also used as a playground by small children. Although he feels very distressed about doing this, he sees that other members of his unit are already obeying the order. What is Private Milkins likely to do and how will he feel about it? What factors might make it easier for him to disobey this order?

5. Aleksei and Ivan work for a large multinational corporation. They agree that many conditions of their employment are highly exploitative. Aleksei wants to take the corporation on, but Ivan exclaims 'how can we possibly succeed – there are only two of us up against the system'. What tips would you give Aleksei and Ivan to improve their chance of success?

Source: Michael Hogg

Social psychology was defined by Gordon Allport as 'an attempt to understand and explain how the thoughts, feelings, and behaviours of individuals are influenced by the actual, imagined, or implied presence of others' (Allport, 1954a, p. 5). This has been a widely accepted and commonly quoted definition of social psychology (see Chapter 1), but reality is that the discipline has evolved considerably, as the chapters of our book attest. We shall address the topic of social influence in a more particular and focused way. As Robert Cialdini and Noah Goldstein (2004) have observed, there are explicit social forces that people are conscious of and which aim to influence them. At other times these forces are subtle and far from obvious.

In the sections that follow we deal with several questions. What purpose do social norms have and why do people conform to them? Does compliance with the demands of others mean that we accept their views? Why do people obey commands that can be extreme and sometimes destructive? Finally we ask: if, as social beings, our actions can be so constrained by conforming, complying and obeying, how can social change arise?

Social influence
Process whereby attitudes and behaviour are influenced by the real or implied presence of other people.

Norms

Norms
Attitudinal and behavioural uniformities that define group membership and differentiate between groups.

Norms are shared beliefs about what is the appropriate conduct for a group member: they are both descriptive ('is' statements) and prescriptive ('ought' statements). As such, norms describe the uniformities of behaviour that characterise groups, while normative discontinuities provide the contours of different social groups. For example, the behaviour of students and lecturers in a university is governed by very different norms: knowing whether someone is a student or a lecturer establishes clear expectations of appropriate normative behaviour.

Norms and stereotypes are closely related – the terms 'normative behaviour' and 'stereotypical behaviour' mean virtually the same thing, even though research traditions have generally separated the two areas: norms referring to behaviour that is shared in a group, and stereotypes to shared generalisations about other groups (also see Chapters 2, 6 and 7).

Norms can take the form of explicit rules that are enforced by legislation and sanctions (e.g. societal norms to do with private property, pollution and aggression), or they can be the implicit, unobserved, taken-for-granted background to everyday life). The sociologist Harold Garfinkel believed that these latter norms are hidden because they are so integral to everyday life, and that they account for much behaviour that is often labelled native, instinctive and innate.

Ethnomethodology
Method devised by Garfinkel, involving the violation of hidden norms to reveal their presence.

Garfinkel (1967) devised ways to detect these background norms – ethnomethodology. One was to deliberately violate norms to attract people's attention. For example, Garfinkel had students act at home for fifteen minutes as if they were boarders: to be polite, speak formally and only speak when spoken to. Their families reacted with astonishment, bewilderment, shock, embarrassment and anger, backed up with charges of selfishness, nastiness, rudeness and lack of consideration! An implicit norm for familial interaction was revealed, and its violation provoked a strong reaction.

Group norms can have a powerful effect on people. For example, Theodore Newcomb (1965) conducted a well-known study of norms in the 1930s at a small American college with progressive and liberal norms but which drew its students from conservative, upper-middle-class families. The 1936 American presidential election was an opportunity for Newcomb to conduct a confidential ballot. First-year students strongly favoured the conservative candidate, while third-year and fourth-year students had shifted their voting preference towards the liberal and communist/socialist candidates. It is likely that prolonged exposure to liberal norms had produced the change in political preference (see Figure 5.1).

Norms are inherently resistant to change. This is not surprising, because their function is to provide stability and predictability. However, norms initially arise to deal with specific circumstances. They endure as long as those circumstances prevail but ultimately change with changing circumstances. (Check the first focus question. How would you approach the topic of norms with Jennifer so as not to hurt her feelings?) Norms vary in their 'latitude of acceptable behaviour': some are narrow and restrictive (e.g. military dress codes) and others wider and less restrictive (e.g. dress codes for university lecturers). In general, norms relating to group loyalty and to central aspects of group life have a narrow latitude of what is acceptable, while norms relating to more peripheral features of the group are less restrictive. We look at the way norms operate within groups again in Chapter 6.

How norms form

We have seen that norms specify a limited range of behaviour that is acceptable in a certain context. Muzafer Sherif (1936) explored this idea in one of the classic experiments in social psychology. He showed that when people made perceptual judgements alone, they relied on their own estimates as a reference frame; however, when they were in a group, they used the group's range of judgements to converge quickly on the group mean.

Because people need to be certain and confident that what they are doing, thinking or feeling is correct and appropriate, Sherif argued that people use the behaviour of others to establish the range of possible behaviour — the frame of reference,

Frame of reference
Complete range of subjectively conceivable positions that relevant people can occupy in that context on some attitudinal or behavioural dimension.

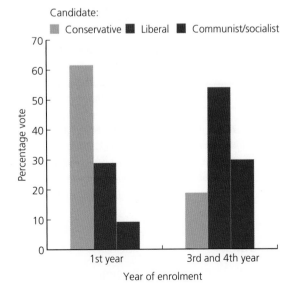

Figure 5.1

Newcomb's 1965 Bennington study: how liberal norms affected voting preferences in the 1936 US presidential election.

First-year students at Bennington College in the USA showed a traditionally conservative voting pattern during the 1936 presidential election, while third- and fourth-year students, who had been exposed for longer to the college's liberal norms, showed a significantly more liberal voting pattern.

Source: Based on data from Newcomb (1965).

which we use to make social comparisons in that context. Average, central or middle positions in such frames of reference are perceived to be more correct than fringe positions, thus people tend to adopt them. Sherif believed that this explained the origins of social norms and the concomitant convergence that accentuates consensus within groups.

Autokinesis
Optical illusion in which a pinpoint of light shining in complete darkness appears to move about.

To test this idea, he conducted his classic studies using autokinesis (see Box 5.1 and Figure 5.2 for details), in which small groups who made estimates of physical movement. Individuals quickly converged over a series of trials on the mean of the group's estimates and remained influenced by this norm even when they made later estimates alone.

Research classic 5.1
Sherif's autokinetic study: the creation of arbitrary norm

Muzafer Sherif (1936) believed that social norms emerge in order to guide behaviour under conditions of uncertainty. To investigate this idea, he took advantage of a perceptual illusion – the autokinetic effect. Autokinesis is an optical illusion where a fixed pinpoint of light in a completely dark room appears to move: the movement is actually caused by eye movement in the absence of a physical frame of reference (i.e. objects). People asked to estimate how much the light moves find the task very difficult and generally feel uncertain about their estimates. Sherif presented the point of light a large number of times (i.e. trials) and had participants, who were

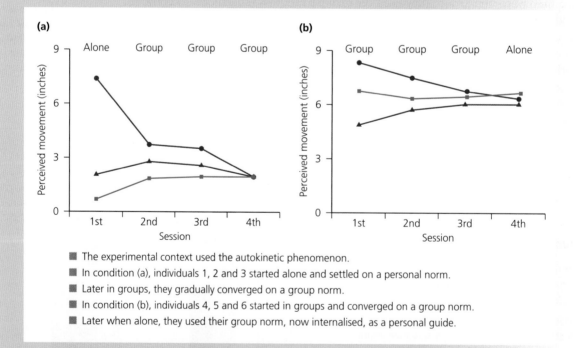

- The experimental context used the autokinetic phenomenon.
- In condition (a), individuals 1, 2 and 3 started alone and settled on a personal norm.
- Later in groups, they gradually converged on a group norm.
- In condition (b), individuals 4, 5 and 6 started in groups and converged on a group norm.
- Later when alone, they used their group norm, now internalised, as a personal guide.

Figure 5.2

Experimental induction of a group norm.

Source: Based on data from Sherif (1936).

unaware that the movement was an illusion, estimate the amount the light moved on each trial. He discovered that they used their own estimates as a frame of reference: over a series of 100 trials they gradually focused on a narrow range of estimates, with different people adopting their own personal range, or norm (see session 1 in Figure 5.2a, when participants responded alone).

Sherif continued the experiment in further sessions of 100 trials on subsequent days, during which participants in groups of two or three took turns in a random sequence to call out their estimates. Now the participants used each other's estimates as a frame of reference, and quickly converged on a group mean, so that they all gave very similar estimates (see sessions 2–4 in Figure 5.2a).

This norm seems to be internalised. When participants start and then continue as a group (sessions 1–3 in Figure 5.2b), the group norm is what they use when they finally make autokinetic estimates on their own (session 4 in Figure 5.2b).

Note: The results shown in Figure 5.2 are based on two sets of three participants who made 100 judgements on each of four sessions, spread over four different days.

Sherif showed that a norm was an emergent property of interaction between group members, but once created it acquired a life of its own. Members were later tested alone and still conformed to the norm.

This was strikingly demonstrated in a follow-up study (MacNeil & Sherif, 1976). In a group comprising three confederates, who gave extreme estimates, and one true participant, a relatively extreme norm emerged. The group went through a number of 'generations', in which a confederate would leave and another true participant would join, until the membership of the group contained none of the original members. The original extreme norm still powerfully influenced the participants' estimates. It was as if the group itself is carried in the head of the individual in the form of a norm.

Conformity

Yielding to the majority

Solomon Asch (1952) was impressed by Sherif's experiment. He believed that conformity reflects a relatively rational process in which people construct a norm from other people's behaviour in order to determine correct and appropriate behaviour for themselves. Clearly, if you are already confident and certain about what is appropriate and correct, then others' behaviour will be largely irrelevant and thus not influential. In Sherif's study, the object of judgement was ambiguous: participants were uncertain, so a norm arose rapidly and was highly effective in guiding behaviour. Asch argued that if the object of judgement was clear-cut, then the views of others would have no effect on behaviour: an individual should remain entirely independent of group influence.

To test this idea, Asch (1951) created a classic experimental paradigm. Male students, participating in what they thought was a visual discrimination task, seated themselves around a table in groups of seven to nine. They took turns in a fixed order to call out publicly which of three comparison lines was the same length as a standard line (see Figure 5.3). There were eighteen trials. In reality, only one person was a naive (real) participant, and he answered second to last. The others were experimental confederates instructed to give erroneous responses on twelve focal trials: on six trials they picked a line that was too long and on six a line that was

Conformity
Deep-seated, private and enduring change in behaviour and attitudes due to group pressure.

Figure 5.3

Sample lines used in conformity experiment.

Participants in Asch's conformity studies had simply to say which one of the three comparison lines was the same length as the standard line.

Source: Based on Asch (1951).

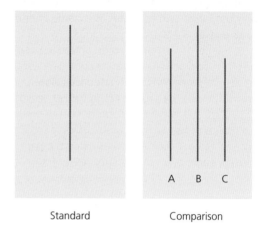

Standard   Comparison

too short. There was a control condition in which participants performed the task privately with no group influence; as less than 1 per cent of the control participants' responses were errors, it can be assumed that the task was unambiguous.

The experimental results were intriguing. Participants varied greatly, with about 25 per cent of participants remaining steadfastly independent throughout, about 50 per cent conforming to the erroneous majority on six or more focal trials, and 5 per cent conforming on all twelve focal trials. The average conformity rate was 33 per cent: computed as the total number of instances of conformity across the experiment, divided by the product of the number of participants in the experiment and the number of focal trials in the sequence.

After the experiment, Asch asked his participants why they conformed. They said that at first they were uncertain and experienced self-doubt. The naive participants had each disagreed often with the group, became self-consciousness, feared disapproval, and felt anxious and even lonely. Different reasons were given for yielding. Most knew they saw things differently from the group but felt that their perceptions may have been inaccurate and that the group was actually correct. Others did not believe that the group was correct but simply went along with the group in order not to stand out. A few reported that they actually saw the lines as the group did. Those who remained independent were either confident in their own judgements or were emotionally affected but guided by a belief in individualism or in doing the task as directed (i.e. being accurate and correct).

These subjective accounts tell us that one reason why people conform, even when the correct choice is clear-cut, may be to avoid censure, ridicule and social disapproval. This is a real fear. In another version of his experiment, Asch had sixteen true participants facing one confederate who gave incorrect answers. This time the participants found the confederate's behaviour ludicrous and openly ridiculed him and laughed at him. Even the experimenter found the situation so bizarre that he could not contain his mirth and also ended up laughing at the poor confederate!

Perhaps, then, if participants were not worried about social disapproval, there would be no subjective pressure to conform? Asch tested this idea in another variation of the experiment. This time, the incorrect majority called out their judgements publicly but the single true participant wrote his down privately. Conformity dropped to 12.5 per cent. Later research by Morton Deutsch and Harold Gerard (1955) confirmed that pressure to conform could be reduced if the participant responded privately and therefore felt anonymous.

Who conforms?

The existence of large individual differences in conformity led some social psychologists to search for personality attributes that predispose some people to conform more than others. Those who conform tend to have low self-esteem, a high need for social support or social approval, a need for self-control, low IQ, high anxiety, feelings of self-blame and insecurity in the group, feelings of inferiority, feelings of relatively low status in the group, and a generally authoritarian personality (Costanzo, 1970; Crutchfield, 1955). However, contradictory evidence suggested that people who conform in one situation do not conform in another, suggesting that situational factors may be more important than personality in conformity (Barron, 1953; Vaughan, 1964).

A similar conclusion can be drawn from research into sex differences in conformity. Although women often conform slightly more than men in conformity studies, this probably derives from the kinds of conformity tasks employed – ones with which women have less familiarity and expertise, experience more uncertainty, and thus are influenced more than men are. A good example of this effect was a study by Frank Sistrunk and John McDavid (1971) in which men and women were pressured to agree with group choices as they tried to identify various stimuli. For some, the stimuli were traditionally masculine items (e.g. identifying a special type of wrench), for some, traditionally feminine items (e.g. identifying types of needlework), and for others the stimuli were neutral (e.g. identifying rock stars). As expected, women conformed more on masculine items, men more on feminine items, and both groups equally on neutral (non sex-stereotypical) items – see Figure 5.4. (Perhaps you could shed some light on the comment by the males in the second focus question).

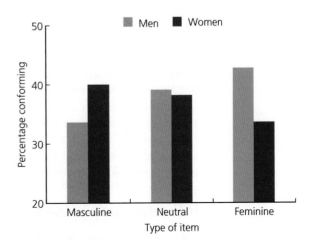

Figure 5.4

Conformity among men and women in relation to tasks that are sex-stereotyped.

When a task is related to a male stereotype, more women conform. When the task is related to female stereotype, more men conform.

Source: Based on data from Sistrunk & McDavid (1971).

Culture and conformity

Do cultural norms affect conformity? In a review of conformity studies using Asch's general paradigm, Peter Smith and his colleagues found significant intercultural variation (Smith, Bond & Kağitçibaşi, 2006). The level of conforming (i.e. incorrect responses) ranged from a low of 14 per cent among Belgian students to a high of 58 per cent among Indian teachers in Fiji, with an overall average of 31 per cent. Conformity was lower among participants from individualist cultures in North America and north-western Europe (25 per cent) than among participants from collectivist or interdependent cultures in Africa, Asia, Oceania and South America (37 per cent).

This kind of cultural variation suggests that collectivist peoples conformed more to their group than did those from individualistic peoples. According to Hazel Markus and Shinobu Kitayama (1991), conforming to group norms is viewed favourably in Eastern or interdependent cultures – it is a form of social glue. What is perhaps more surprising is that although conformity is lower in individualist Western societies, it is still remarkably high; even when conformity has negative overtones, people find it difficult to resist conforming to group norms.

Context and conformity

People are more inclined to conform in some contexts but remain independent in others. Two factors that have been well researched are *group size* and *group unanimity*. Imagine that you felt that your university lecturer has given your class too little time to hand in a report. Your sense of grievance is diminished, however, if the first few people you check for support disagree with you. Maybe it is your problem! In reviewing studies using the Asch paradigm, Vernon Allen (1975) concluded that, provided a majority remained unanimous, conformity began to level off when the size of the majority reaches about 3 or 4. However, only one other 'deviant opinion' ruins the effect. Asch found that a correct supporter (i.e. a member of the majority who always gave the correct answer, and thus agreed with and supported the true participant) reduced conformity from 33 to 5.5 per cent.

It seems that support for remaining independent is not the crucial factor in reducing conformity. Rather, any sort of lack of unanimity among the majority seems to be effective. For example, Asch found that a dissenter who was even more wildly incorrect than the majority was equally effective. Allen and Levine (1971) conducted an experiment in which participants, who were asked to make visual judgements, were provided with a supporter who had normal vision or a supporter who wore such thick glasses as to raise serious doubts about his ability to see anything at all, let alone judge lines accurately. In the absence of any support, participants conformed 97 per cent of the time. The 'competent' supporter reduced conformity to 36 per cent, but most surprising was the fact that the 'incompetent' supporter reduced conformity as well, to 64 per cent (see Figure 5.5).

Supporters, dissenters and deviates may be effective in reducing conformity because they shatter the unanimity of the majority and thus raise or legitimise the possibility of alternative ways of responding or behaving.

Influence processes

Social psychologists generally believe that two processes of social influence are responsible for conformity: informational influence and normative influence

Figure 5.5

Conformity rates drop when a supporter is present, even one who is incompetent.

Social support on a line judgement task reduced conformity, even when the supporter was patently unable to make accurate judgements because he was visually impaired.

Source: Based on data from Allen & Levine (1971).

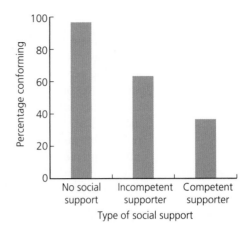

(Deutsch & Gerard, 1955). Our tendency to accept the views of others as evidence about reality is called informational influence. We need to feel confident that our perceptions, beliefs and feelings are correct. Informational influence comes into play when we are uncertain, either because stimuli are intrinsically ambiguous or because there is social disagreement. When this happens, we initially make objective tests against reality; otherwise, we make social comparisons, as Leon Festinger (1954) argued. Effective informational influence causes true cognitive change.

Informational influence was probably partially responsible for the convergence effects in Sherif's study that we have already discussed. Reality was ambiguous,

Informational influence
An influence to accept information from another as evidence about reality.

Normative influence. This peer group in Rio de Janeiro exerts powerful pressure to conform, even in a context as dangerous as train surfing.

Source: Ricardo Azoury / Corbis

and participants used other people's estimates as information to remove the ambiguity and resolve subjective uncertainty. In that kind of experimental setting, when participants were told that the apparent movement was in fact an illusion, they did not conform (e.g. Alexander, Zucker & Brody, 1970); presumably, since reality itself was uncertain, their own subjective uncertainty was interpreted as a correct and valid representation of reality, and thus informational influence did not operate. On the other hand, Asch's stimuli were designed to be unambiguous in order to exclude informational influence. However, Asch did note that conformity increased as the comparison lines were made more similar to one another and the judgement task thus became more difficult. The moral? Informational influence rules in moments of certainty, not times of doubt.

Normative influence
An influence to conform with the positive expectation of others, to gain social approval or to avoid social disapproval.

Our tendency to conform to the positive expectations of others is called normative influence. Our need for social approval and acceptance leads us to 'go along with' the group and avoid censure or disapproval. Normative influence comes into play when we believe the group has the power and ability to reward or punish us according to what we do. For this to be effective we also need to believe we are under surveillance by the group. The reality is, however, that normative influence creates surface compliance rather than true cognitive change.

There is little doubt that normative influence was the principal cause of conformity in the Asch paradigm – the lines being judged were unambiguous (informational influence would not be operating), but participants' behaviour was under direct surveillance by the group. We have also seen that privacy, anonymity and lack of surveillance reduce conformity in the Asch paradigm, presumably because normative influence was weakened.

Referent informational influence
Pressure to conform to a group norm that defines oneself as a group member.

The distinction between informational and normative influence underemphasises the role of group belongingness. This has been addressed by *social identity theory* which proposes a separate social influence process responsible for conformity to group norms, called referent informational influence (Hogg & Turner, 1987). When group membership is salient, we feel a sense of belonging and we define ourselves in terms of the group. We recruit from memory and we use information in the social context to decide the relevant group norms and attributes. The most immediate sources of information are the actions of fellow ingroup members. In a real group, a developing ingroup captures and accentuates not only similarities among ingroup members but also differences between our group and relevant outgroups. According to *self-categorisation theory*, we come to see ourselves in group terms and assimilate our thoughts, feelings and behaviour to the group norm (Turner *et al.*, 1987; see Chapter 6). If members of the group construct a similar group norm, self-categorisation produces intragroup convergence on that norm and increases intragroup uniformity – the typical conformity effect.

Referent informational influence differs from normative and informational influence in a number of important ways. For example, people conform because they are group members, not to validate physical reality or to avoid social disapproval. People do not conform to other people but to a norm: other people act as a source of information about the appropriate ingroup norm. Because the norm is an internalised representation, people can conform to it in the absence of surveillance by group members, or for that matter anybody else.

Compliance

The literature on social influence sometimes uses the term compliance interchangeably with conformity. This can happen when 'conformity' is broadly defined to include a change in behaviour, as well as beliefs, as a consequence of group pressure. We use compliance to refer to a *behavioural* response to a *request by another individual*, whereas conformity refers to the influence of a group upon an individual.

We are confronted daily with demands and requests. Often they are put to us in a straightforward and clear manner, such as when a friend asks you to dinner, and nothing more is requested. At other times, requests have a 'hidden agenda': for example, an acquaintance invites you to dinner to get you into the right mood to ask you to finance a new business venture. The result is often the same – we comply.

What are the factors and situations that make us more compliant, and why is it that we are more influenced on some occasions than others? Generally, people influence us when they use effective tactics or have powerful attributes.

Tactics for enhancing compliance

To persuade people to comply with requests to buy certain products has been the cornerstone of many economies. It is not surprising, therefore, that over the years many different tactics have been devised to enhance compliance. Salespeople, especially, have designed and refined many indirect procedures for inducing compliance, as their livelihood depends on it. Nearly all of us have come across these tactics.

Take ingratiation. You might try to influence others by first agreeing with them and getting them to like you. Next, various requests are made. You would be using ingratiation if you agreed with target people to appear similar or to make them feel good, made yourself look attractive, paid compliments, dropped names of those held in high esteem or physically touched target people. In a study by Leasel Smith and colleagues (Smith, Pruitt & Carnevale, 1982), shoppers who were approached to sample a new food product were more likely to sample and buy the item when they were touched in a socially acceptable way (although they did not think the food tasted any better!). However, ingratiation that is transparent can backfire, leading to the 'ingratiator's dilemma': the more obvious it is that an ingratiator will profit by impressing the target person, the less likely it is that the tactic will succeed (see Gordon, 1996, for a meta-analysis).

Using the reciprocity norm is another tactic, based on the principle that 'we should treat others the way they treat us'. If we do others a favour, they feel obliged to reciprocate. Judith Regan (1971) showed that people would comply more often if they had previously received a favour. Similarly, *guilt arousal* produces more compliance. People who are induced to feel guilty are more likely to comply with a later request: for example, to make a phone call petitioning to save native trees (Carlsmith & Gross, 1969), to agree to donate blood (Darlington & Macker, 1966), or at a university to participate in an experiment (Freedman, Wallington & Bless, 1967).

Have you had your car windscreen washed while waiting at traffic lights? If the cleaner washes it before you can refuse, there is subtle pressure on you to pay for the service. In some cities (e.g. in Portugal), people guide you into parking spaces that one could have easily located and then ask for money. These are real-life examples of persuasion to give money that involves activation of the reciprocity norm.

Compliance
Superficial, public and transitory change in behaviour and expressed attitudes in response to requests, coercion or group pressure.

Ingratiation
Strategic attempt to get someone to like you in order to obtain compliance with a request.

Meta-analysis
Statistical procedure that combines data from different studies to measure the overall reliability and strength of specific effects.

Reciprocity norm
The principle of 'doing unto others as they do to you'. It can refer to returning a favour, mutual aggression or mutual help.

Multiple request tactics

There are several very effective tactics based on the use of multiple requests. Instead of a single request, a two-step procedure is used, with the first request functioning as a set-up or softener for the second, real request. The three classic variations, recently reviewed by Bob Cialdini and Noah Goldstein (2004), are the foot-in-the-door, the door-in-the-face and low-balling tactics (see Figure 5.6).

According to the foot-in-the-door tactic, if someone agrees to a small request, they will be more willing to comply with a later, large request. Some salespeople use this approach. At first they might telephone you to ask just a few questions 'for a small survey that we are doing' and then entice you to join 'the hundreds of others in your area' who subscribe to their product.

In a study by Freedman and Fraser (1966), people were first contacted in their home to answer a few simple questions about the kind of soap they used at home. Later, they were more willing to comply with the larger request of allowing six people to make a thorough inventory of all the household items present. Only 22 per cent complied when they received the larger request 'cold', but 53 per cent complied when they had been softened up by the initial questions about soap.

The foot-in-the-door tactic may not always work. If the initial request appears too small or the second too large, the link between the multiple requests breaks down (Foss & Dempsey, 1979). Nevertheless, a review by Michael Saks (1978) suggested that if the technique is tuned carefully, people can even be induced to act as donors for organ and tissue transplants.

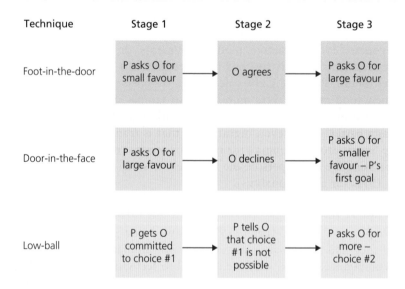

Figure 5.6

Three classic techniques for inducing compliance.

These are three, widely studied techniques that have been used in everyday settings to induce compliance. Each involves three stages. Stages 1 and 2 are preliminary steps designed to increase the probability of achieving the ultimate goal in Stage 3. Evidence shows that each technique has been used with some success.

In a refinement of the tactic, people agreed to a series of graded requests rather than jumping from a small to a large request. They were presented with two preliminary requests, increasingly demanding, prior to an ultimate request (Goldman, Creason & McCall, 1981). This has proved more effective than the classic foot-in-the-door technique. Think of this, perhaps, as the 'two-feet-in-the-door technique'! Graded requests occur often, such as when someone asks someone out on a 'date'. At first, a prospective partner might not agree to go out with you on a 'date' but might well agree to go with you to study in the library. Your next tactic is to request another meeting, and eventually a proper date.

In a Polish field experiment using the foot-in-the-door tactic, Dariusz Dolinski (2000) arranged for a young man to ask people in the city of Wrocław for directions to Zubrzyckiego Street. There is no such street. Most said they did not know, although a few gave precise directions! Further down the street, the same people were then asked by a young woman to look after a huge bag for five minutes while she went up to the fifth floor in an apartment building to see a friend. A control group was asked to look after the bag, but not for the street directions. Compliance with the second, more demanding request was higher in the experimental group (see Figure 5.7; also see Chapter 9 for a discussion of altruism).

Since there is reasonable evidence across a variety of studies that the foot-in-the-door technique actually works, what psychological process could account for it? A likely candidate is Daryl Bem's (1967) *self-perception theory* according to William DeJong (1979). (Also see Chapter 4.) By complying with a small request, people become committed and develop a picture of themselves as 'giving'. The subsequent large request compels them to appear consistent. Dolinski explained his results in

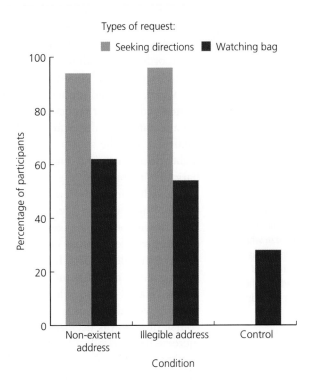

Figure 5.7

The foot-in-the-door technique: complying when an impossible request is followed by one that is possible.

Percentage of participants who answered 'I do not know' when asked about a non-existent (or else an illegible address) and of those who then complied with the request to keep an eye on the confederate's bag.

Source: Based on data from Dolinski (2000), Experiment 2.

the same way. In trying to help a stranger, although unsuccessfully, his participants would have inferred that they were altruistic. They were therefore more susceptible to a later influence – even if that request was more demanding.

Similarly, Cialdini and Trost (1998) refer to *self-consistency*, i.e. we try to manage our self-concept so that if we are charitable on one occasion then we should be charitable again on the second occasion. Donald Gorassini and James Olson (1995), however, are sceptical that something as dramatic as self-conceptual change mediates the effect. Instead, they proposed an explanation with fewer assumptions. The foot-in-the-door tactic alters people's interpretation of situations that activate attitudes enhancing compliance. The self is left out of the loop.

What happens if an attempt to get a foot in the door fails? Common sense suggests that this should reduce the likelihood of future compliance. Surprisingly, the opposite strategy, the door-in-the-face tactic, can prove successful (Cialdini *et al.*, 1975; Patch, 1986). Here a person is asked a large favour first and a small request second. Politicians especially are masters of this art. To illustrate, say that the government warns the media that student fees will need go up 30 per cent. Are you angry? Later, however, it announces officially that the increase will 'only' be 10 per cent – the actual figure planned. You probably feel relieved and think 'that's not so bad', and consequently are more accepting.

Cialdini *et al.* (1975) tested this tactic by approaching students with a huge request: 'Would you serve as a voluntary counsellor at a youth offenders' centre two hours a week for the next two years?' Virtually no one agreed. However, when the researchers then asked for a considerably smaller request, 'Would you chaperone a group of these offenders on a two-hour trip to the zoo?', 50 per cent agreed. When the second request was presented alone, less than 17 per cent complied. For the tactic to be effective, the researchers noted that the final request should come from the same person who made the initial request. According to them, participants perceive the scaled-down request as a concession by the influencer, and consequently they feel pressure to reciprocate. If some other person were to make the second request, reciprocation would not be necessary.

According to Cialdini, the door-in-the-face technique may well capitalise on a contrast effect: just as lukewarm water feels cool when you have just had your hand in hot water, a second request seems more reasonable and acceptable when it is contrasted with a larger request. This procedure is prevalent in sales settings. Suppose you tell an estate agent that you would like to spend quite a lot of hard-earned money on a small flat and she shows you a few run-down and overpriced examples. Then the higher-priced flats (the ones she really wants to show you!) look like extremely good bargains. In doing this, the estate agent has used the door-in-the-face tactic.

The other multiple-request technique used in similar situations is the low-ball tactic. (Check the third focus question. Could this tactic work successfully on you?) Here the influencer changes the rules halfway and manages to get away with it. Its effectiveness depends on inducing the customer to agree to a request before revealing certain hidden costs. It is based on the principle that once people are committed to an action, they are more likely to accept a slight increase in the cost of that action. Shaul Fox and Michael Hoffman (2002) noted that this tendency for people to stick with decisions is also captured in the notion of *sunk costs*, where once a course of action is decided on, people will continue to invest in it even if the costs increase dramatically.

Suppose you shop around for a car and are confronted with the following chain of events. The car salesperson makes you a very attractive offer – a high trade-in price for your old car – and suggests a reduction on the marked purchase price for

Door-in-the-face tactic
Multiple-request technique to gain compliance, in which the focal request is preceded by a larger request that is bound to be refused.

Low-ball tactic
Technique for inducing compliance in which a person who agrees to a request still feels committed after finding that there are hidden costs.

the car you have set your heart on. You decide to buy it and are ready to sign the papers. The salesperson then goes off to check the agreement with the boss, comes back, looks very disappointed and informs you that the boss will not sanction it because they would lose too much money on the deal. You can still have the car, but at the marked price. You have been tricked, but perhaps you don't know it. What should you do? Surprisingly, many customers still go ahead with the deal. It seems that once you are committed, you are hooked and reluctant to back out. A commonplace example of low-balling is when someone asks 'Could you do me a favour?' and you agree before actually knowing what will be expected of you.

The effectiveness of low-balling was demonstrated by Cialdini and his colleagues. They asked half their participants to be in an experiment that began at 7 a.m. The other half were asked first to commit to participating in an experiment and then were informed that it would start at 7 a.m. The latter group had been low-balled and complied more often (56 per cent) than the control group (31 per cent) and also tended to keep their appointments (Cialdini, Cacioppo, Bassett & Miller, 1978).

Obedience to authority

Not all social psychologists were impressed by the results of Asch's classic study of conformity (discussed earlier). They noted that the task, judging line length, was trivial, and there were no significant consequences for self and others of conforming or resisting.

Stanley Milgram (1963, 1974) was one of these critics; he tried to replicate Asch's study, but with a task that had important consequences attached to the decision to conform or remain independent. He decided to have experimental confederates apparently administer electric shocks to another person to see whether the true participant would conform. Before being able to start the study, Milgram needed to run a control group to obtain a base rate for people's willingness to shock someone *without* social pressure from confederates. For Milgram, this almost immediately became a crucial question in its own right. In fact, he never actually went ahead with his original conformity study, and the control group became the basis of one of social psychology's most dramatic research programmes.

A wider social issue influenced Milgram. Adolf Eichmann was the Nazi official most directly responsible for the logistics of Hitler's 'Final Solution', in which six million Jews were systematically slaughtered. Hannah Arendt (1963) reported his trial in her book *Eichmann in Jerusalem*, bearing the riveting subtitle *A report on the banality of evil*. This captures a scary finding, one that applied to Eichmann and later to other war criminals who have been brought to trial. These 'monsters' may not have been monsters at all. They were often mild-mannered, softly spoken, courteous people who repeatedly and politely explained that they did what they did not because they hated Jews (or Muslims, etc.) but because they were ordered to do it – they were simply obeying orders. Looks can, of course, be deceiving. Peter Malkin, the Israeli agent who captured Adolf Eichmann in 1960, discovered that Eichmann knew some Hebrew words, and he asked:

'Perhaps you're familiar with some other words,' I said. '*Aba. Ima.* Do those ring a bell?'

'*Aba, Ima,*' [Eichmann] mused, trying hard to recall. 'I don't really remember. What do they mean?'

'Daddy, Mommy. It's what Jewish children scream when they're torn from their parents' arms.' I paused, almost unable to contain myself. 'My sister's boy, my favorite playmate, he was just your son's age. Also blond and blue-eyed, just like your son. And you killed him.'

Genuinely perplexed by the observation, he actually waited a moment to see if I would clarify it. 'Yes,' he said finally, 'but he was Jewish, wasn't he?' *(Malkin & Stein, 1990, p. 110)*

Milgram's obedience studies

Agentic state
A frame of mind thought by Milgram to characterise unquestioning obedience, in which people as agents transfer personal responsibility to the person giving orders.

Milgram brought these strands together in a series of experiments with the underlying feature that people are socialised to respect the authority of the state. If we enter an agentic state, mentally we can absolve ourselves of responsibility for what happens next. Participants in his experiments were recruited from the community by advertisement and reported to a laboratory at Yale University to participate in a study of the effect of punishment on human learning. They arrived in pairs and drew lots to determine their roles in the study (one was the 'learner', the other the 'teacher'). See Box 5.2 for a description of what happened next, and check how the shock generator looked in Figure 5.8.

Research classic 5.2
Milgram's procedure in an early study of obedience to authority

Together with the experimenter, there was a teacher (the real participant) and a learner (actually, a confederate). The learner's role was to learn a list of paired associates, and the teacher's role was to administer an electric shock to the learner every time the learner gave a wrong associate to the cue word. The teacher saw the learner being strapped to a chair and having electrode paste and electrodes attached to his arm. The teacher overheard the experimenter explain that the paste was to prevent blistering and burning, and overheard the learner telling the experimenter that he had a slight heart condition. The experimenter also explained that although the shocks might be painful, they would cause no permanent tissue damage.

The teacher was now taken into a separate room housing a shock generator (see Figure 5.8). He was told to administer progressively larger shocks to the learner every time the learner made a mistake – 15 V for the first mistake, 30 V for the next mistake, 45 V for the next, and so on. An important feature of the shock generator was the descriptive labels attached to the scale of increasing voltage. The teacher was given a sample shock of 45 V, and then the experiment commenced.

The learner got some pairs correct but also made some errors, and very soon the teacher had reached

75 V, at which point the learner grunted in pain. At 120 V the learner shouted out to the experimenter that the shocks were becoming painful. At 150 V the learner, or now more accurately the 'victim', demanded to be released from the experiment, and at 180 V he cried out that he could stand it no longer. The victim continued to cry out in pain at each shock, rising to an 'agonised scream' at 250 V. At 300 V the victim ceased responding to the cue words; the teacher was told to treat this as a 'wrong answer'.

Throughout the experiment, the teacher was agitated and tense, and often asked to break off. To such requests, the experimenter responded with an ordered sequence of replies proceeding from a mild 'please continue', through 'the experiment requires that you continue' and 'it is absolutely essential that you continue', to the ultimate 'you have no other choice, you must go on'.

A panel of 110 experts on human behaviour, including 39 psychiatrists, were asked to predict how far a normal, psychologically balanced human being would go in this experiment. These experts believed that only about 10 per cent would exceed 180 V, and no one would obey to the end. These predictions, together with the actual behaviour of the participants are shown schematically in Figure 5.9.

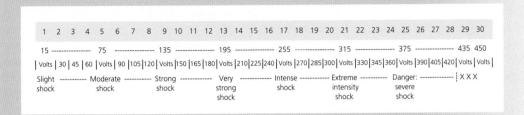

Figure 5.8

Milgram's shock generator.

Participants were confronted with a 15–450 volt shock generator that had different descriptive labels, including the frighteningly evocative 'XXX', attached to the more impersonal voltage values.

Source: Milgram, S. (1974) *Obedience to authority*. London: Tavistock. Reproduced with permission.

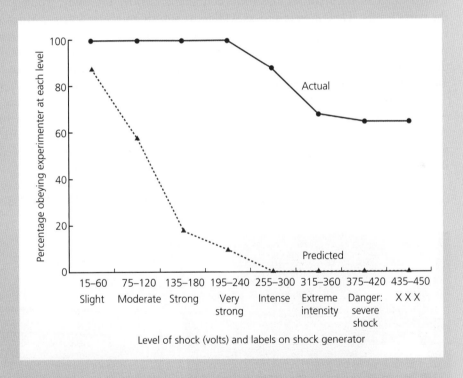

Figure 5.9

Predicted versus actual levels of shock given to a victim in Milgram's study.

'Experts' on human behaviour predicted that very few normal, psychologically balanced people would obey orders to administer more than a 'strong' electric shock to the 'incompetent' learner in Milgram's experiment – in actual fact 65 per cent of people were obedient right to the very end, going beyond 'danger: severe shock', into a zone labelled 'XXX'.

Source: Based on data from Milgram (1974).

In a slight variant of the procedure described above, in which the victim could not be seen or heard but pounded on the wall at 300 V and 315 V and then went silent, almost everyone continued to 255 V, and 65 per cent continued to the very end – administering massive electric shocks to someone who was not responding and who had previously reported having a heart complaint!

The participants in this experiment were quite normal people – forty 20–50-year-old men from a range of occupations. Unknown to them, however, the entire experiment involved an elaborate deception in which they were always the teacher, and the learner/victim was actually an experimental stooge (an avuncular-looking middle-aged man) who had been carefully briefed on how to react. No electric shocks were actually administered apart from the 45 V sample shock to the teacher.

Note: See extracts from Milgram's work at www.panarchy.org/milgram/obedience.html.

Factors influencing obedience

Milgram conducted eighteen obedience experiments to isolate various contributing factors. In all but one, the participants were 20–50-year-old males, not students, from a range of occupations and socioeconomic levels. In one study, women were the participants. They proved just as willing to punish an errant learner. Milgram's experiment has been replicated in Italy, Germany, Australia, Britain, Jordan, Spain, Austria and the Netherlands (see Smith, Bond & Kağitçibaşi, 2006). Complete obedience ranged from over 90 per cent among Spanish and Dutch, over 80 per cent among Italians, Germans and Austrians, to less that 40 per cent among Australians.

One reason why people continue to administer electric shocks may be that the experiment starts very innocuously with quite trivial shocks. Once people have committed themselves to a course of action (i.e. to give shocks), it can be difficult subsequently to change their mind. The process may be similar to that involved in the foot-in-the-door technique of persuasion that we discussed earlier.

An important factor in obedience is *immediacy of the victim* – how close or obvious the victim is to the participant. Milgram varied the level of immediacy

Obedience to authority. Torture and prisoner abuse at the Abu Ghraib prison provide a recent reminder of Milgram's lesson to the world.

Source: AP Photo / Wathiq Khuzaie, Pool / Press Association Images

across a number of experiments. We have seen above that 65 per cent of people 'shocked to the limit' of 450 V (see Figure 5.9) when the victim was unseen and unheard except for pounding on the wall. In an even less immediate condition in which the victim was neither seen nor heard at all, 100 per cent of people went to the end. However, as immediacy increased obedience decreased: when the victim was visible in the same room, 40 per cent obeyed to the limit; and when the teacher actually had to hold the victim's hand down on to the electrode to receive the shock, obedience dropped to a still frighteningly high 30 per cent.

Another important factor is *immediacy of the authority figure*. Obedience was reduced to 20.5 per cent when the experimenter was absent from the room and relayed directions by telephone. When the experimenter gave no orders at all, and the participant was entirely free to choose when to stop, 2.5 per cent still persisted to the end. Perhaps the most dramatic influence on obedience is group pressure.

The presence of two disobedient peers (i.e. others who appeared to revolt and refused to continue after giving shocks in the 150–210 V range) reduced complete obedience to 10 per cent, while two obedient peers raised complete obedience to 92.5 per cent. *Group disobedience* probably has its effects because the actions of others help to confirm that it is either legitimate or illegitimate to continue administering the shocks.

The *legitimacy of the authority figure* allows people to abdicate personal responsibility for their actions. For example, Brad Bushman (1984, 1988) had confederates, dressed in uniform, neat attire or a shabby outfit stand next to someone fumbling for change for a parking meter. The confederate stopped passers-by and 'ordered' them to give the person change for the meter. Over 70 per cent obeyed the uniformed confederate (giving 'because they had been told to' as the reason) and about 50 per cent obeyed the non-uniformed confederate (generally giving altruism as a reason). These studies suggest that mere emblems of authority can create unquestioning obedience.

The original experiments, conducted by lab-coated scientists at prestigious Yale University, were packaged as the pursuit of scientific knowledge. What would happen if these trappings of legitimate authority were removed? Milgram ran one experiment in a run-down inner-city office building. A private commercial research firm ostensibly sponsored the research. Obedience dropped, but to a still remarkably high 48 per cent.

Milgram's research addresses one of humanity's great failings – the tendency for people to obey orders without first thinking about (1) what they are being asked to do and (2) the consequences of their obedience for other living beings. However, obedience can sometimes be beneficial: for example, many organisations would grind to a halt or would be catastrophically dysfunctional if their members continually painstakingly negotiated orders. Think about crisis decisions taken by an emergency surgery team, a flight crew or a commando unit. (Now consider the plight of Private Milkins in the fourth focus question.)

However, the pitfalls of blind obedience, contingent on immediacy, group pressure, group norms and legitimacy, are also many. For example, medication errors in some American hospitals have been attributed to the fact that nurses overwhelmingly defer to doctors' orders, even when metaphorical alarm bells are ringing (Lesar, Briceland & Stein, 1977). In other research focusing on organisational obedience, 77 per cent of participants who were playing the role of board members of a pharmaceutical company advocated continued marketing of a hazardous drug merely because they felt that the chair of the board favoured this decision (Brief, Dukerich & Doran, 1991).

Before moving on to deal with ethical concerns of Milgram's experiments, we should note that reservations have been raised about their logic. The connection between destructive obedience as Milgram conceived it and the holocaust itself has been questioned. In Cialdini and Goldstein's (2004) review of social influence research, they pointed out that:

- Milgram's participants were opposed to the orders they were given, whereas many of the perpetrators of Holocaust atrocities did so willingly and sometimes sadistically.
- Although the Nazi chain of command and the experimenter in Milgram's studies had apparent legitimate authority, the experimenter had expert authority as well.

Some ethical considerations

Milgram's earliest study in 1963 had barely been published when Diana Baumrind (1964) fired the first shots in an ethical uproar. Recall that Milgram's participants really believed they were administering severe electric shocks that were causing extreme pain to another human being. Milgram was careful to interview and, with the assistance of a psychiatrist, to follow up the more than 1000 participants in his experiments. There was no evidence of psychopathology, and 83.7 per cent of those who had taken part indicated that they were glad, or very glad, to have been in the experiment (Milgram, 1992: p. 186). Only 1.3 per cent were sorry or very sorry to have participated.

The ethical issues really revolve around three questions concerning the ethics of subjecting experimental participants to short-term stress:

1. Is the research important? However, it can be difficult to assess the 'importance' of research objectively.
2. Is the participant free to terminate the experiment at any time? In one sense they were free to do so, but this was never made explicit. In fact, the purpose of the study was to persuade them to remain!
3. Does the participant freely consent to being in the experiment? Milgram's participants did not give fully informed consent: they volunteered to take part, but the true nature of the experiment was not fully explained to them.

This raises the issue of deception in social psychology research, one of several ethical issues that have been examined by Herbert Kelman. There are two reasons for deceiving participants in a psychological experiment: the first is to induce them to take part in an otherwise unpleasant experiment. This is, ethically, a highly dubious practice. The second reason is that in order to study the automatic operation of psychological processes, participants need to be naive regarding the hypotheses, and this often involves some deception concerning the true purpose of the study and the procedures used (Kelman, 1967). The fallout from this debate has been a code of ethics to guide psychologists in conducting research. The principal components of the code are:

- participation must be based on fully informed consent;
- participants must be explicitly informed that they can withdraw, without penalty, at any stage of the study;
- participants must be fully and honestly debriefed at the end of the study.

It is unlikely that a modern university ethics committee would approve the impressively brazen deceptions that produced many of social psychology's classic research programmes of the 1950s, 1960s and early 1970s. What is more likely to be endorsed is the use of minor and harmless procedural deceptions enshrined in clever cover stories that are considered essential to preserve the scientific rigour of much experimental social psychology. The main ethical requirements in all modern research involving human participants are also discussed in Chapter 1, and see the American Psychological Association's (2002) Code of Ethics at http://www.apa.org/ethics/code2002.html.

Minority influence and social change

Our discussion of social influence, particularly conformity, has dealt with how individuals yield to direct or indirect social influence, most often from a numerical majority. Dissenters have been of passing interest. However, there is a different kind of influence: in a group setting, sometimes an individual or a small minority can change the views of the majority. Why and how does this occasionally work?

From the outset, Asch (1952) did show interest in the deviate: someone who would not conform. In one of his experiments a solitary confederate, who made incorrect responses, was ridiculed and laughed at by the true participants – a majority who made correct responses. However, a minority that has little or no legitimate power can be influential and ultimately sway the majority to its own viewpoint. For example, in a variant of the solitary deviate study, Asch (1952) found a quite different response. When a correct majority of eleven true participants was confronted by a deviant/incorrect minority of *nine* confederates, the majority remained independent (i.e. continued responding correctly) but took the minority's responses far more seriously – no one laughed. Clearly, the minority had some influence over the majority, albeit not enough in this experiment to produce manifest conformity.

History illustrates the power of minorities. Think of it this way: if the only form of social influence was majority influence, then social homogeneity would rule. Social change would be very difficult to explain without the mediating effect of minority influence. For example, American anti-war rallies during the 1960s had an effect on majority attitudes that hastened withdrawal from Vietnam. Similarly, the suffragettes of the 1920s gradually changed public opinion so that women were granted the vote, and the Campaign for Nuclear Disarmament rallies in Western Europe in the early 1980s gradually shifted public opinion away from the 'benefits' of nuclear proliferation. An excellent example of an active minority is Greenpeace: the group is numerically small (in terms of 'activist' members) but has important influence on public opinion through the high profile of some of its members and the wide publicity of its views.

Important questions are whether minorities and majorities gain influence via different social practices, and, more fundamentally, whether the underlying psychology is really different.

Beyond conformity

Serge Moscovici (1972) argued that researchers unwittingly fell prey to a conformity bias, in which social influence was an adaptive requirement of human life – we should always adapt to the status quo, be uniform and remain stable. Clearly this

Minority influence
Social influence processes whereby numerical or power minorities change the attitudes of the majority.

Conformity bias
Tendency for social psychology to treat group influence as a one-way process in which individuals or minorities always conform to majorities.

is a valid and important need for individuals, groups and society. However, altered circumstances sometimes require a *change* in norms.

Moscovici and Faucheux (1972) suggested that in fact it is minority influence that Asch observed in his classic studies. The Asch paradigm appears to pit a lone individual (true participant) against an erroneous majority (confederates) on an unambiguous physical perception task. Surely the task used was clear-cut, with no room for ambiguity, as Asch had intended. Perhaps the true participant had room for doubt after all.

How certain our views are depends a good deal on how much we agree with the views of others. Doubts about the properties of objects 'out there' may require that others do not disagree with us. In this sense, Asch's lines were *not* 'unambiguous' – there was actually disagreement between confederates and participants over the length of the lines. Furthermore, Asch's lone participant can be considered to be a member of a rather large majority (those people outside the experiment who would call the lines 'correctly': that is, the rest of humanity) confronted by a very small minority (the confederates who called the lines 'incorrectly'; see Tajfel, 1972). Moscovici highlighted an irony. The solitary participant represented humanity but had been influenced by a minority (the confederates).

In contrast to traditional conformity research, Moscovici believed that there is often conflict within groups, and that people can respond in one of three ways:

1. *Conforming* – the majority persuades the minority (the deviates) to adopt the majority viewpoint.
2. *Normalising* – a mutual compromise leading to convergence.
3. *Innovating* – a minority creates and accentuates conflict, trying to persuade the majority to adopt the minority viewpoint.

Being consistent

Moscovici wanted to understand how the dynamics of social conflict produces social change. People do not like social conflict. An active minority capitalises on this by going out of its way to create, draw attention to and accentuate conflict. Moscovici and his colleagues believed that this can be very effective in winning over the majority, but it hinges on just *how* the minority goes about its task – on the *behavioural style* it adopts.

The single most important behavioural style is consistency. A *consistent minority*, one in which all members repeatedly promulgate the same message, has the following effects:

* It disrupts the majority norm and produces uncertainty and doubt.
* It draws attention to itself as an entity.
* It conveys that there is an alternative coherent point of view.
* It demonstrates certainty and an unshakable commitment to its point of view.
* It shows that the only solution to the conflict is espousal of the minority viewpoint.

(Considering these points, might Aleksei and Ivan have a chance against the system in the fifth focus question?)

Moscovici and his colleagues demonstrated the effectiveness of consistency in a series of ingenious experiments built around the colours blue and green. In one of these, four true participants and two confederates made judgements of colour involving blue slides that varied only in intensity. The confederates were either con-

An active minority. These Sami people in Stockholm know that to be effective they must be visible and also consistent in espousing their views.

Source: Scanpix / Bertil Ericson / Reuters

sistent, always calling the slides 'green', or inconsistent, calling the slides 'green' two-thirds of the time and 'blue' one-third of the time. There was also a control condition with no confederates, just six true participants. Figure 5.10 shows that the consistent minority had significantly more influence than the inconsistent minority. Although the conformity rate is much lower compared with a consistent

Figure 5.10

Conforming to a consistent minority.

Although not as effective as a consistent majority, a consistent two-person minority in a six-person group was more influential than an inconsistent minority. It is remarkable that four people were influenced by two.

Source: Based on data from Moscovici, Lage & Naffrechoux (1969).

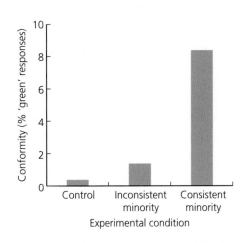

majority, it is nevertheless remarkable that a minority of two influenced a majority of four.

Moscovici and Lage (1976) employed the same blue–green perception task to compare consistent and inconsistent minorities with consistent and inconsistent majorities. There was also a control condition. As before, the only minority to produce conformity was the consistent minority (10 per cent conformity). Although this does not compare well with the rate of conformity to the consistent majority (40 per cent), it is comparable with the rate of conformity to the inconsistent majority (12 per cent). However, the most important finding was that the *only* participants in the entire experiment who actually changed their blue response to a green response were those in the consistent minority condition.

In summary, effective minorities are consistent. They also need to show a consensus, be distinct from the majority, unmotivated by self-interest or external pressures, and flexible in style. This combination of factors suggests that the minority has chosen its position freely. It is therefore difficult to explain away its position in terms of being 'way out' individuals, or in terms of external inducements or threats. Perhaps, then, there is actually some intrinsic merit to its position. This encourages people to take the minority seriously (even though social forces work against this) and at least consider its position; such cognitive work is an important precondition for subsequent attitude change (also see Chapter 4).

Being included

Groups in society that promulgate minority viewpoints are often stigmatised by the majority as social outgroups, or are labelled as deviant individuals. Their views are, at best, rejected as irrelevant, but they are often ridiculed and trivialised in an attempt to discredit them. For example, think of the treatment sometimes meted out to gays, environmentalists and intellectuals (see Chapter 7 for a discussion of discrimination against outgroups). This level of resistance by the majority makes it even more difficult for minorities to be effective.

It follows that minorities might be more effective if they not only promote a consistent viewpoint that differs from the majority position, but are also viewed as members of the majority. Indeed, Anne Maass and her colleagues have confirmed that minorities do exert more influence if the majority perceive them as an ingroup (Maass, Clark & Haberkorn, 1982). How can minorities successfully have it both ways – be thought of as an ingroup *and* hold an unwavering outgroup position? According to John Turner (1991), the trick seems to be that effective minorities need to be able to establish their legitimate ingroup credentials before they draw undue critical attention to their distinct minority viewpoint.

Doing this generates what Bill Crano (2001) calls a 'leniency contract' in which the majority is sufficiently lenient towards the minority's viewpoint not to reject it outright. The logic is that disagreement between people who define themselves as members of the same group is both unexpected and unnerving. This raises uncertainty about themselves and their attributes and motivates people to reduce this feeling (Hogg, 2007b). Where common ingroup membership is important and 'inescapable', members may try to redefine some attributes of their group to bring it into line with the minority. And so the minority has been effective. Where common ingroup membership is unimportant and easily denied, there will be no such redefining and the minority will be ineffective.

Is minority influence actually different?

Moscovici (1980) argued that majorities and minorities exert social influence through different processes. *Majority influence* brings about direct public compliance for reasons of normative or informational dependence. Majority views are accepted passively without much thought. In contrast, *minority influence* brings about indirect, often latent, private change in opinion due to the cognitive conflict and restructuring that deviant ideas produce. Minorities produce a conversion effect as a consequence of active consideration of the minority point of view.

An experiment by Maass and Clark (1983) investigated people's public and private reactions to majority and minority influence regarding the issue of gay rights. They found that publicly expressed attitudes were in line with the expressed views of the majority (i.e. if the majority was pro-gay, then so were the participants). However, their privately expressed attitudes shifted towards the position espoused by the minority (see Figure 5.11).

Charlan Nemeth (1986) has argued that minority dissent usually stimulates divergent, novel, creative thinking, and more active information processing. Likewise, Angelica Mucchi-Faina found that students at the University of Perugia generated more original and creative ideas for promoting the international image of the city of Perugia when they had been exposed to a conventional majority and a creative minority than vice versa, or where the majority and the minority were both original or both conventional (Mucchi-Faina, Maass & Volpato, 1991).

Although majorities and minorities can be defined in terms of power, they also refer to numbers of people. Although 'minorities' are often both less powerful and less numerous (e.g. West Indians in Britain), they can be less powerful but more numerous (e.g. Tibetans versus Chinese in Tibet). Perhaps not surprisingly, an attempt has been made to explain the social influence of minorities purely in terms of their relative numbers.

Conversion effect
When minority influence brings about a sudden and dramatic internal and private change in the attitudes of a majority.

Figure 5.11

Majority versus minority influence on attitudes: change can be public or private.

Relative to a no-influence control condition, heterosexual public attitudes towards gay rights closely reflected the pro- or anti-gay attitudes of the majority. However, private attitudes reflected the pro- or anti-gay attitudes of the minority.

Source: Based on data from Maass & Clark (1983).

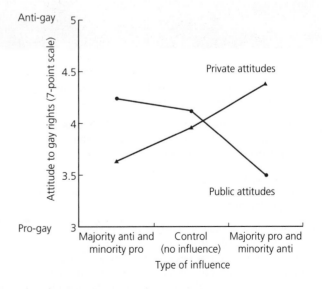

Social impact
The effect that other people have on our attitudes and behaviour, usually as a consequence of factors such as group size, and temporal and physical immediacy.

Bibb Latané drew on social impact theory to argue that as a source of influence increases in size (number), it has more influence (Latané & Wolf, 1981). However, as the cumulative source of influence gets larger, the impact of each additional source is reduced – a single source has enormous impact, the addition of a second source increases impact but not by as much as the first, a third even less, and so on. A good analogy is switching on a single light in a dark room – the impact is enormous. A second light improves things, but only a little. If you have ten lights on, the impact of an eleventh will be negligible.

Evidence does support this idea: the larger the source of influence, the more impact it has, with incremental changes due to additional sources decreasing with increasing size (see Tanford & Penrod, 1984). But how does this account for the fact that minorities can actually have influence?

There is a sense in which the effect of a large majority on an individual majority member has reached a plateau: additional members or 'bits' of majority influence have relatively little impact. Although a minority viewpoint has relatively little impact, it has not yet attained a plateau: additional members or 'bits' of minority influence have a relatively large impact. In this way, exposure to minority positions can, paradoxically, have greater impact than exposure to majority viewpoints.

The remaining question is whether we need to postulate two processes when comparing majority influence and minority influence. Moscovici argued that we should do so. However, we have already noted that the distinction between informational and normative influence by Deutsch and Gerard underemphasised the role of group belongingness. Instead, whether minorities or majorities are influential or not may be a matter of social identity dynamics. In a given situation, can people define themselves as members of the minority group or the majority group – or not? In essence, people strive for attitudes that are consistent with those that typify their ingroup. This is a fundamental aspect of *self-categorisation theory* and is addressed in Chapter 6.

Summary

- Social influence can mean several things: internalised conformity to group norms, surface compliance with requests, and obedience to commands.

- Group norms are enormously potent sources of social influence. They provide us with stable and predictable guides for thinking and behaving.

- Group norms emerge as group members interact. They provide a guide to an individual's behaviour beyond the group context.

- Conformity is a change in beliefs or behaviour in line with the view of a majority. It reduces if the task is clear and we are not under surveillance, although even under these circumstances there is often residual conformity. Lack of unanimity among the majority is particularly effective in reducing conformity.

- People may conform in order to feel sure about the objective validity of their perceptions and opinions, to obtain social approval and avoid social disapproval, or to express or validate their social identity as group members.

- Compliance is a form of surface conformity that we show in responding to requests and orders. There are several well-known compliance tactics that people use to 'get their way'.

- Given the right circumstances, we all have the potential to obey commands blindly, even if the consequences of such obedience include harm to others.

- Obedience is affected by the proximity and legitimacy of authority, by the proximity of the victim, and by the degree of social support for obedience or disobedience.

- Active minorities can sometimes influence majorities: this may be the very essence of social change.

- To be effective, minorities should be consistent but not rigid, should be seen to be making personal

sacrifices and acting out of principle, and should be perceived as being part of the ingroup.

- Unlike majority influence, which encourages 'mindless' compliance, minorities can cause more thinking and latent cognitive change as a reaction to the challenge of the novel minority position.

Literature, film and TV

American Beauty and *Revolutionary Road*

Two powerful films by Sam Mendes that explore conformity and independence. Set in American suburbia, the 1999 film *American Beauty*, starring Kevin Spacey, is a true classic about suffocating conformity to social roles, and what can happen when people desperately try to break free. *Revolutionary Road* is a 2008 film, starring Leonardo DiCaprio and Kate Winslet, which explores the same theme with a focus on the drudgery and routine of adult life and the lost dreams of youth, and again on the challenge and consequences of change.

Little Miss Sunshine

A hilarious 2006 film directed by Jonathan Dayton and Valerie Faris. A breathtakingly dysfunctional family sets out in their decrepit VW van to drive from Arizona to Los Angeles for their daughter Olive (Abigail Breslin) to appear in an absolutely grotesque children's beauty pageant. Featuring Toni Collette, Steve Carell, Greg Kinnear and Alan Arkin, this is a film about interpersonal relations and families (relevant to Chapter 9) but also about non-conformity and violation of social conventions.

Eichmann in Jerusalem: A report on the banality of evil

A 1963 book by H. Arendt on the Nuremberg war trials of the Nazis, it shows how these people came across as very ordinary people who were only following orders.

Rebel without a Cause

The 1955 film directed by Nicholas Ray, and with James Dean and Natalie Wood is an all-time classic about non-conformity, counter-conformity and independence. James Dean stands out against social and group roles and expectations, and sets the mould for teenage 'rebellion' in future decades.

Town Bloody Hall

1979 documentary by D. A. Pennebaker and Chris Hegedus. Pennebaker and Hegedus simply filmed a 1971 public debate between grizzly Norman Mailer (representing conservative male attitudes of the early 1970s) and a group of radical feminists including Germaine Greer, Susan Sontag and Jill Johnston. The film illustrates the clash of attitudes and how dominant groups often do not hear or simply ridicule the position taken by active minorities who are trying to change the status quo. What characterises this film is that the speakers are, for the most part, highly intelligent and articulate advocates for their positions.

Che

A two-part 2008 dramatisation of Che Guevara's role in Fidel Castro's toppling of the Cuban Dictator Fulgencia Batista in 1959. The films, directed by Stephen Soderbergh and starring Benicio del Toro as the now legendary Che Guevara, bring to life the nature of social change through revolution.

Guided questions

- Is it true that women conform more than men to group pressure?

- Describe any one *multiple-request tactic* for gaining compliance. Can you think of an everyday example where it has been used?

- Why did Milgram undertake his controversial studies on *obedience to authority*? Watch the video illustrating Milgram's research in Chapter 5 of MyPsychLab at www.mypsychlab.co.uk.

- Can a *minority group* really bring about social change by confronting a majority?

Learn more

Baron, R.S., & Kerr, N. (2003). *Group process, group decision, group action* (2nd ed). Buckingham, UK: Open University Press. A general overview of some major topics in the study of group processes; includes discussion of social influence phenomena.

Brown, R. J. (2000). *Group processes* (2nd ed). Oxford, UK: Blackwell. A very readable introduction to group processes, which also places an emphasis on social influence processes within groups, especially conformity, norms and minority influence.

Cialdini, R. B., & Goldstein, N. J. (2004). Social influence: compliance and conformity. *Annual Review of Psychology, 55*, 591–621. This review covers research in the period 1997–2002. The studies cited are organised around three central motives that underlie people's needs to be accurate, to affiliate and to maintain a positive self-concept.

Martin, R., & Hewstone, M. (2003). Social influence processes of control and change: Conformity, obedience to authority, and innovation. In M. A. Hogg & J. Cooper (eds), *The Sage handbook of social psychology* (pp. 347–366). London: Sage. An up-to-date and comprehensive review of social influence research, including conformity, obedience, and minority influence.

Mugny, G., & Pérez, J. A. (1991). *The social psychology of minority influence*. Cambridge, UK: Cambridge University Press. An overview of research on minority influence by two leading scholars on this notably European topic of research: also coverage of Mugny and Moscovici's own theories of minority influence.

Turner, J. C. (1991). *Social influence*. Buckingham, UK: Open University Press. Scholarly overview of the field of social influence, which takes a critical stance from a European perspective and places particular emphasis on social identity, minority influence, and the role of group membership and group norms.

Refresh your understanding, assess your progress and go further with interactive summaries, questions, podcasts, videos and much more on the website accompanying the book: **www.mypsychlab.co.uk**.

Chapter 6

People in groups

What to look for

- How being in a group affects how well you perform a task
- What makes a group cohesive
- How groups socialise their members
- How groups are structured by roles and status
- The way that transactional and transformational leaders differ
- Why there is a gender gap in leadership
- The need for followers to trust their leader
- How groups combine information to make group decisions
- Whether brainstorming works
- What groupthink is and how groups become polarised
- Things that affect how juries make decisions

Focus questions

1. Alone in his room, James can reliably play a tricky guitar riff really well – precise and clear. When his friends ask him to play it for them, it all goes horribly wrong – sounding like he has overcooked spaghetti for fingers. Why do you think this happens?

2. You want to make sure that new members of the small organisation you run are totally committed to it and its goals. You could make the experience of joining smooth, easy and pleasant; or you could make it quite daunting with a bewildering array of initiation rites and embarrassing hurdles to clear. Which would be more effective, when and why?

3. Andrea writes very quickly and neatly and is good at taking notes. She works for a large corporation and is very ambitious to rise to the top. She finds it flattering that her boss assigns her the role of taking notes in important executive meetings. She is keen to please and so always agrees – leaving her sitting at the back scribbling away on her notepad while others talk and make decisions. Was this a wise move – why, or why not?

4. The design group at Acme Aerospace meets to design a rocket for a Mars landing. There are eight of you. Because decisions have to be made quickly and smoothly, your charismatic and powerful group leader has selected members so that you are all very much of one mind. This is a very difficult task and there is a great deal of competitive pressure from other space agencies. Will this arrangement deliver a good design?

5. Is it possible for a highly cohesive group to become oblivious to the views and expectations of the wider community? Watch the video in Chapter 6 of MyPsychLab at www.mypsychlab.co.uk where students explain why they join certain groups, and whether loyalty to a group would lead them to act dangerously or unethically.

We spend lots of time in groups. We work in groups, we play in groups and of course our families are groups. Groups influence our lives enormously; not just the groups we work, play, and interact in, but also those larger groups that we belong to because of our gender, ethnicity, nationality, socioeconomic status and career choices. They determine who we are in society – our identity. Groups that we are not 'in' can also profoundly affect our lives through the decisions they make and the actions they take; for example, selection panels, juries, parliament and other official bodies.

What are groups?

Groups are actually categories, though of people rather than things (see the discussion of *categories and prototypes* in Chapter 2). Being a category, there are attributes that identify who is 'in' the group and who is not. These attributes in isolation are not necessarily precise. If we identify the French simply as people who 'speak fluent French' and distinguish them in this way from non-French we'd be in trouble – Quebecois in Canada, many Belgians, and many people in some north and west African countries speak fluent French. To more accurately identify people as French we might need a combination of attributes – e.g. language, location, family background, cuisine and customs. Social psychologists believe that human groups are actually characterised by these fuzzy sets of related and overlapping attributes that on the whole distinguish between those in the group and those outside the group.

Fuzzy sets
Categories are considered to be fuzzy sets of features organised around a prototype.

Although groups have this common feature, they can still vary in many different ways, as Kay Deaux and her colleagues have noted (Deaux, Reid, Mizrahi & Ethier, 1995). Some are large, some small; some are short-lived, some endure for thousands of years; some are concentrated in one place, others geographically dispersed; some are highly structured and organised, others are more informally organised; some have highly specific purposes, others are more general; some are relatively autocratic and others relatively democratic. The social committee for your sports club or local council is a group, even if its life is one year. A succession of Chinese dynasties is also a kind of group since it imbedded a continuing culture featuring, for example, a written language and a patriarchal power system.

Entitativity
The property of a group that makes it seem like a coherent, distinct and unitary entity.

More generally, some groups are more clearly so than others – social psychologists such as David Hamilton and Jim Sherman (1996) use the term entitativity or more simply, perceived unity, to describe this property of groupiness. A highly entitative group is relatively homogeneous and clearly structured internally, and has sharp boundaries that make it distinct from other groups.

Not all collections of people are groups in a psychological sense. For example, people with green eyes, strangers in a dentist's waiting room, folk sitting on a beach, children waiting for a bus – are these groups? More likely these are merely aggregates of unrelated individuals, with no future or a past together – not groups at all. The important social psychological question is what distinguishes groups from aggregates; it is not an easy question to answer, and social psychologists differ in what they say. We will talk more about what makes a group below.

In this chapter we discuss how people are affected by being in a group, how groups are structured, why people join groups and how people are socialised into groups. We also focus on the role of leaders, and on how groups make decisions. In

Entitativity. A group comprises individuals, but sometimes it may seem to be an indivisible entity. Do these Las Ramblas troubadours qualify?

Source: Graham Vaughan

Chapter 7, and in the context of prejudice of discrimination, we recognise that groups do not exist in isolation. Where there is an ingroup (the group you are 'in') by definition there are outgroups (groups that you are not in) – this is the study of intergroup behaviour; how we perceive and treat outgroups.

The presence of others

One way in which groups affect us is that they develop norms, and we conform to these norms – we discussed this in Chapter 5. However, there is an even more fundamental way in which groups affect us – just the mere presence of other people may influence how we behave.

Performing in public

You are playing a musical instrument, texting, reciting a poem or exercising in the gym, and someone comes to watch. Does your performance improve or deteriorate when you know you have an audience?

An early psychological experiment by Norman Triplett (1898) addressed this question, though it was in the context of competition. Triplett had children wind a line around two pulleys, set a few metres apart, as quickly as they could, alone or in a kind of race with another child doing the same – he found that children who were trying to win rather than acting alone usually competed more quickly. Triplett also found that some children did not do so well when competing: he observed that they 'went to pieces'. Working at Harvard University, Floyd Allport (1920) later

Social facilitation
An improvement in the performance of well-learned/easy tasks and a deterioration in the performance of poorly learned/difficult tasks in the mere presence of members of the same species.

Drive theory
Zajonc's theory that the physical presence of members of the same species instinctively causes arousal that motivates performance of habitual behaviour patterns.

Evaluation apprehension
A concern about being evaluated by others who are present can lead to social facilitation.

demonstrated a social facilitation effect in which the mere presence of others who were not participating at all generally improves the performance of a task, though not always.

Social facilitation has been extensively researched, much of it with an exotic array of animals. For example, we now know that cockroaches run faster, chickens, fish and rats eat more and pairs of rats copulate more when being 'watched' by members of their own species or when members of their own species are also running, eating or copulating! However, research has also revealed that social presence, such as this, can produce quite the opposite effect – social inhibition, or impairment of task performance.

How do we explain this contradiction? One of the most enduring explanations is drive theory (Zajonc, 1965; see Figure 6.1). Because people are unpredictable (you can rarely know for certain what they are going to do) there is an advantage to the species for people to be alert and ready for action when others are present. Increased arousal or motivation is thus an instinctive reaction to social presence. This arousal energises or 'drives' our dominant response – those actions that are best learned and most habitual in that situation. If the dominant response is correct, e.g. because it is well practiced and therefore easy, then social presence improves performance; but if it is incorrect perhaps because the task is difficult, then the presence of others impairs performance. For example, if you find texting easy (the dominant response is to make no mistakes) the presence of others will make you faster and more accurate; if you find it difficult (the dominant response is to make many mistakes) the presence of others will make you miserably slow and inaccurate.

Although drive theory is reasonably well supported (Guerin, 1993), there is some debate about what brings arousal about. Zajonc (1965) felt it was simply the mere physical presence of others, whereas Cottrell (1972) felt that apprehension about being evaluated by others was the culprit. Cottrell's evaluation apprehension model argues that people learn that the social rewards and punishments (e.g.

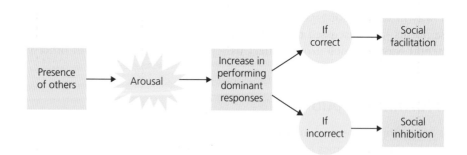

Figure 6.1

Zajonc's drive theory of social facilitation.

- The presence of others automatically produces arousal, which 'drives' dominant responses.
- Performance improves if the dominant response is 'correct', but gets worse if the dominant response is 'incorrect'.

Source: Based on Zajonc (1965).

approval and disapproval) we receive are based on how others evaluate us. Social presence produces an acquired arousal (drive) based on evaluation apprehension.

A number of studies have tested and compared these two explanations. Bernd Schmitt and his colleagues were intrigued by Zajonc's claim that mere presence of others was the trigger to arousal (Schmitt, Gilovich, Goore & Joseph, 1986). They had participants perform a task they thought was incidental and not of interest to the experimenter. This involved typing one's name into a computer (a simple task), and then entering a code name by typing one's name backwards interspersed with ascending digits (a difficult task). These tasks were performed (1) *alone* after the experimenter had left the room; (2) in the *mere presence* of only a confederate who was blindfolded, wore a headset and was allegedly participating in a separate experiment on sensory deprivation; or (3) under the close *observation of the experimenter*, who remained in the room carefully evaluating the participant's performance. The results in Figure 6.2 show that mere presence accelerated performance of the easy task and slowed performance of the difficult task, and that evaluation apprehension had little additional impact. Mere presence is a sufficient cause of, and evaluation apprehension not necessary for, social facilitation effects. (Check James's guitar playing problem in the first focus question.)

How do we know that 'drive' has a role in social facilitation? Drive is difficult to measure. Physiological measures of arousal such as sweating palms may monitor drive, but the absence of arousal is no guarantee that drive is not operating. Drive is actually a psychological concept and could even mean alertness in the context we are discussing. So we should not be surprised that several non-drive explanations of social facilitation have been proposed.

One of these is *self-discrepancy theory* developed by Tory Higgins (1987), who has researched extensively on the topic of self-concept, and whose main ideas are dealt with in detail in Chapter 3. When people become self-aware and focus their attention upon themselves, for example by being in front of a mirror or in the presence of other people, they compare their actual self (their actual task performance) and their ideal self (how they would like to perform). The discrepancy between actual and ideal self increases motivation and effort to bring actual into line with

Figure 6.2

Having an audience can help on an easy task but hinder on a difficult task.

- Participants typed their name on a computer (easy task) or typed it backwards interspersed with digits (difficult task), alone, with an incidental audience present or with an attentive audience present.
- There was a drive effect on both the easy and the difficult task.
- The incidental audience improved performance on the easy task and impaired it on the difficult task.
- The attentive audience had no additional effect.

Source: Based on data from Schmitt, Gilovich, Goore & Joseph (1986).

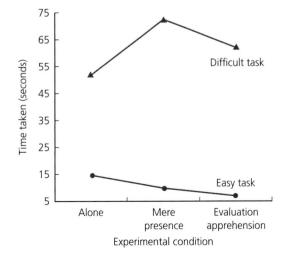

Social facilitation. He has been practising hard at home. What will determine whether he will soar or crash in front of an audience?

Source: Pearson Online Database (POD)

ideal, so on easy tasks performance improves. On difficult tasks the discrepancy is too great, so people give up trying, and performance deteriorates. Another possibility was put forward by Charles Bond (1982), a methodologist who often used meta-analysis to clarify social psychological issues: is that in the presence of others, people are concerned with making the best possible impression. On easy tasks this is achievable, so social presence improves performance. On difficult tasks, people make, or anticipate making, errors; this creates embarrassment, and embarrassment impairs task performance.

An obvious feature of social presence is we find other people distracting and this affects our task performance. Robert Baron (1986) believes that people have a finite capacity for attention, which can be overloaded by the presence of an audience. Attention overload makes people narrow their attention, figure out what they think is important and focus on a small number of central cues. Difficult tasks are those that require we attend to a large number of cues. When we narrow our attention on difficult tasks we may miss cues that we really ought to attend to: thus social presence impairs performance. Simple tasks are ones that require we attend to only a small number of cues. When we narrow our attention on simple tasks we can eliminate the distraction of extraneous cues and focus on central cues: thus social presence improves performance. Data collected by Pascal Huguet and his colleagues (Huguet, Galvaing, Monteil & Dumas 1999) has added weight to these findings.

Meta-analysis
Statistical procedure that combines data from different studies to measure the overall reliability and strength of specific effects

Social facilitation research mainly focuses on the most elementary type of group situation – one in which people are simply in the presence of others, rather than working with or interacting with others. This 'group' situation is very common and can be quite impactful – much of our behaviour occurs in the physical presence of others as an audience, and a survey by Borden (1980) revealed that people feared speaking in front of an audience more than heights, darkness, loneliness and even death! However, the effect of mere presence on behaviour is small – a meta-analysis of 241 social facilitation experiments involving 24 000 participants, found that mere presence accounted for less than 3 per cent of variation in behaviour (Bond & Titus, 1983).

Social presence has more impact when people really interact with each other, e.g. on how much they eat! C. P. Herman, who has researched what we commonly call hunger, found in a review of studies that: (a) when the others were friends or family and also eating, people ate more because they spent more time at the table; (b) in the presence of strangers who were eating, people followed the norm set by the others – if others ate more, they did also; and (c) in the presence of others who were not eating, people ate less because they were concerned that others would evaluate them negatively for overeating (Herman, Roth & Polivy, 2003).

Loafing in groups

We now move away from non-interactive contexts to interactive groups. We have all been in groups where we feel one or more members simply don't pull their weight – they put in little or no effort and sit back leaving the rest of the group to do all the work. We can be gracious in explaining this – it may be difficult for several individuals to coordinate their behaviour effectively, so some become distracted and their input is drowned by the input of others who are more influential. This does happen, and has been called coordination loss by Ivan Steiner (1976), a major figure in research on group performance. However, on other occasions there is a motivation loss in which group members simply put in less effort.

Coordination loss
Deterioration in group performance compared with individual performance, due to problems in coordinating behaviour.

An ingenious study by Alan Ingham and his colleagues (Ingham, Levinger, Graves & Peckham 1974) compared coordination and motivation losses in groups. In one condition real groups of varying size pulled on a rope. The other condition had 'pseudo-groups' with only one true participant and a number of confederates. The confederates were instructed only to pretend to pull on the rope while making realistic grunts to indicate exertion. The true participant was in the first position and so did not know that the confederates behind him were not actually pulling. As Figure 6.3 shows, what transpired was that in pseudo-groups participants reduced their effort. Because there was no coordination possible, no loss can be attributed to it; the decrease can be attributed only to a loss of *motivation*. In real groups, there was an additional decrease in individual performance that we could attribute to coordination loss.

This loss of motivation was called social loafing by the eminent social psychologist Bibb Latané and his colleagues (Latané, Williams and Harkins 1979) who replicated the effect using shouting, cheering and clapping tasks. In one experiment, they had students cheer and clap as loudly as possible alone or in groups of two, four or six. As real groups became larger, the noise levels per person clearly fell away. In a second experiment, the students were asked to shout as loud as possible, either alone or in two-person or six-person real groups, or in pseudo-groups (wearing blindfolds, and headsets transmitting 'white noise'). As in the Ingham

Social loafing
A reduction in individual effort when working on a collective task (one in which our outputs are pooled with those of other group members) compared with working either alone or co-actively (our outputs are not pooled).

Figure 6.3

Losses in motivation and coordination in groups pulling ropes.

- As group size increased from 1 to 6, there was a decrease in each person's output.
- In pseudo-groups, this is due to reduced effort, i.e. motivation loss.
- In real groups, this is more marked as a result of coordination loss.

Source: Based on data from Ingham, Levinger, Graves & Peckham (1974).

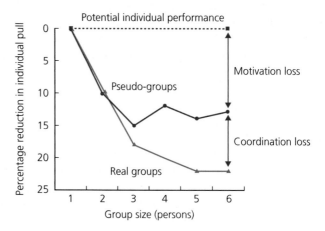

experiment, as group size increased the level of effort in pseudo-groups reduced, pointing to motivation loss. Once more, there was a greater reduction in real groups, again indicating coordination loss (see Figure 6.4).

Social loafing is a tendency for people to work less hard (i.e. loaf) on a task when they believe others are also working on the task. A change from being alone to having one other person present had the biggest impact. As the group gets bigger, the impact of each additional member on one's performance decreases – e.g. the impact of a third person joining a two-person group is large, while the impact of an additional member on a twenty-person group is small.

Social loafing is extraordinarily prevalent (Williams, Harkins & Karau, 2003). Loafing has been found in the laboratory as well as in the field, and in Western and Asian cultures. The effect has been recorded using physical tasks (e.g. clapping,

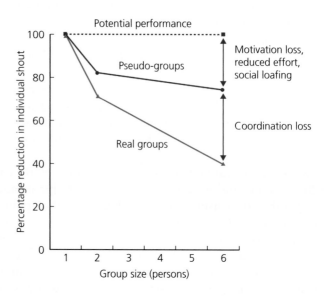

Figure 6.4

Losses in motivation and coordination in groups making noise.

- Social loafing: individual students shouted less loudly as group size increased.
- As in Figure 6.3, this demonstrates a loss of motivation in pseudo-groups and an additional loss due to a lack of coordination in real groups.

Source: Latané, Williams and Harkins (1979), Experiment 2.

rope pulling and swimming), cognitive tasks (e.g. generating ideas), evaluative tasks (e.g. quality ratings of poems) and perceptual tasks (e.g. maze performance). People even loaf when tipping in restaurants! In one study, 20 per cent of people gave tips when seated alone, but only 13 per cent tipped when seated in groups of five or six (Freeman, Walker, Bordon & Latané, 1975).

In a review of research dealing with social motivation, Russell Geen (1991) concluded that there are three reasons why we loaf when we are in a group:

1. *Output equity* – we believe that others loaf; so to maintain equity and avoid being a 'sucker' we loaf too.
2. *Evaluation apprehension* – we worry about being evaluated by others; but when we are anonymous and cannot be identified, we hang back and loaf, especially when a task is not engaging.
3. *Matching to standard* – often, we do not have a clear sense of the group's standards or norms; so we hang back and loaf.

But surely being in a group can sometimes motivate us to work even harder than when we are alone. The New York columnist James Surowiecki (2004) describes scores of such instances, and of course we have all had this experience and witnessed it in others – professional football players certainly don't loaf when playing a match; at least, if they are in the team we support, we hope they don't. There is one situation when being in a group increases individual motivation and effort. This happens when the task and the group are so important that the individual feels a need to compensate for anticipated loafing by other members of the group – there is a social compensation effect (Williams & Karau, 1991). In a study by Stephen Zaccaro (1984), participants each folded pieces of paper to make little tents in two- or four-person groups – the usual loafing effect emerged (see Figure 6.5). However, other participants who believed they were competing against an outgroup, and for whom the attractiveness and social relevance of the task were accentuated, behaved quite differently. The loafing effect was actually reversed: they constructed more tents in the larger group.

Social compensation
Increased effort on a collective task to compensate for other group members' actual, perceived or anticipated lack of effort or ability.

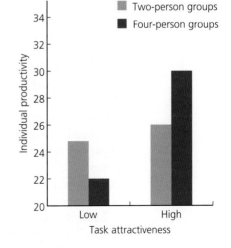

Figure 6.5

Individual effort varies with the attractiveness of the task and the size of the group.

- Social compensation: participants performing a relatively unattractive paper-folding task loafed.
- Individual productivity was lower in four-person than in two-person groups.
- For an attractive task, the loafing effect was reversed: individual productivity was higher in four- than two-person groups.

Source: Based on data from Zaccaro (1984).

As well as the social compensation effect, people work harder in groups than alone when they:

- come from a collectivist culture rather than individualist culture, a finding reported in China (Earley, 1989) and Japan (Matsui, Kakuyama & Onglatco, 1987);
- believe and expect that the group will be able to achieve important goals (Sheppard, 1993);
- identify strongly with the group and consider their actions actually define group membership (Fielding & Hogg, 2000; Worchel Rothgerber, Day, Hart & Butemeyer, 1998);
- are in a group with high levels of solidarity and cohesiveness (Karau & Hart, 1998).

To this point we have focused on how individuals respond in a group context, in particular, on how the quality of a group's performance can change and how this can become evident in its output. Our attention now shifts from the behaviour of individuals in groups to the business of the group itself.

How groups work

Why do groups need to pull together, how do they induct their members and in what ways are they structured? We address these questions and then examine people's motives for being in a group at all.

Group cohesion

Cohesiveness
The property of a group that affectively binds people, as group members, to one another and to the group as a whole, giving the group a sense of solidarity and oneness.

We often talk of groups, teams or cliques as being cohesive rather than being a fragmented rabble. Cohesiveness is a basic property of a group that causes it to 'hang together' as a tightly knit, self-contained entity characterised by uniformity of conduct, mutual support between members, solidarity, *esprit de corps*, team spirit and morale. We noted earlier in this chapter that a group is a category and has, in some degree, the property of entitativity (i.e. a perceived unity). Cohesiveness also captures feelings and relations among people in the group. Indeed, psychologically, cohesiveness has been attributed primarily to the development of bonds of mutual liking among people – where there are strong mutual bonds of liking you have not only a group but a cohesive group (Festinger, Schachter & Back, 1950).

When we characterise cohesiveness in terms of interpersonal liking we should not be surprised that factors that increase liking (e.g. similarity, cooperation, interpersonal acceptance, shared threat) generally raise cohesiveness. Further, elevated cohesiveness generates conformity to group standards, accentuated similarity, improved intragroup communication and enhanced liking (Lott & Lott, 1965). However, others have argued that there may be more to cohesiveness than interpersonal liking (Hogg, 1993; Mudrack, 1989). For example, cohesiveness has many dimensions (Dion, 2000) – e.g. in terms of how effective a group's structure is or how high its morale is – which poses a challenge when we try to measure it.

Mutual liking among members may be a relatively reliable index of cohesiveness in small groups where people know one another (e.g. a team or work group). However, there is a significant problem – mutual liking is a less reliable index in large groups where people cannot all know each other as individuals (e.g. a nation

Group cohesiveness. A cohesive group 'pulls together'
– it shows solidarity and team spirit.

Source: Pearson Online Database

or corporation). How then do we capture, psychologically, the cohesiveness of
large groups? To resolve this, Hogg (1993) distinguished between *personal attraction* and *social attraction*. James might feel personal attraction to his long-term
partner, his old friends and a few regulars at his local pub. He would feel social
attraction when his liking for someone is based only on shared group membership,
such as another supporter of his football team; or for someone who embodies the
defining attributes of a membership group, such as a personal trainer at James's
gymnasium.

Social attraction is the liking aspect of groups of all shapes and sizes and is
derived by identifying with a group. By categorising yourself as a group member,
you perceive, define and evaluate yourself and others in terms of the group's prototypical, attributes (Hogg, 2006; Turner, Hogg, Oakes, Reicher & Wetherell, 1987).
It is an irony that you can like someone as a group member but not as an individual, and vice versa (Mullen & Copper, 1994).

Group socialisation

A key feature of groups, small and large, is that they develop over time – members
become socialised into the beliefs, customs and practices of the group, and groups are
often quite active in socialising their members. In Chapter 5 we saw how group
norms develop and change and how people conform to norms. In Chapter 4 we also
saw how individuals can persuade people to change their attitudes and behaviours.

Here, we focus on how groups as a whole develop and socialise their members
over time. We feature a particular model of group socialisation as developed by
John Levine and Dick Moreland, with a focus more on individuals than on groups.
They described the passage of individuals through groups over time as they experience three basic ongoing processes: *evaluation*, *commitment* and *role transition*

Group socialisation
Dynamic relationship
between the group and
its members that
describes the passage
of members through a
group in terms of
commitment and of
changing roles.

(Levine & Moreland, 1994). An individual compares the group in terms of the rewards that it bestows with different rewards from other potential groups or relationships. At the same time, the group evaluates individuals in terms of their contribution to the life of the group which, if favourable, leads to approval of the individual. The group and the individual are partners: commitment requires both to agree on goals and values, to feel positive ties, to be willing to exert effort, and to desire to continue membership. Asymmetry may arise at any point: the individual might be more committed to the group or the group more committed to the individual. This creates instability because the less committed party has power over the more committed party, and creates pressure towards an equal level of commitment. See Figure 6.6.

Group socialisation moves people through different roles, transitions that are a central aspect of group life. There are three general types of role: (1) *non-member* – this includes prospective members who have not joined the group and ex-members who have left the group; (2) *quasi-member* – this includes new members who have not attained full member status, and marginal members who have lost that status; and (3) *full member* – people who are closely identified with the group and have all the privileges and responsibilities associated with actual membership (see Box 6.1).

Role transitions are smooth and easy when individual and group are equally committed and share the same ideas about what a transition means, e.g. when a student commences postgraduate studies. Otherwise, conflict can occur over whether a role transition should or did occur, e.g. whether an employee's performance justifies a promotion rather than a bonus. For this reason, transition criteria often become formalised and public, and ritualised rites of passage or

Research and applications 6.1
Phases of group socialisation

Moreland and Levine distinguished five phases of group socialisation (see Figure 6.6):

1 *Investigation*. The group recruits prospective members, who in turn reconnoitre the group. This can be more formal, involving interviews and questionnaires (e.g. joining an organisation), or less formal (e.g. associating yourself with a student political society). A successful outcome leads to a *role transition*: entry to the group.

2 *Socialisation*. The group assimilates new members, educating them in its ways. In turn, new members try to get the group to accommodate their views. Socialisation can be unstructured and informal, but also quite formal (e.g. an organisation's induction programme). Successful socialisation is marked by *acceptance*.

3 *Maintenance*. Role negotiation takes place between full members. Role dissatisfaction can lead

to a role transition called *divergence*, which can be unexpected and unplanned. It can also be expected – a typical group feature (e.g. university students who diverge by graduating and leaving university).

4 *Resocialisation*. When divergence is expected, resocialisation is unlikely; when it is unexpected, the member is marginalised into a deviant role and tries to become resocialised. If successful, full membership is reinstated – if unsuccessful, the individual leaves. Exit can be marked by elaborate retirement ceremonies (e.g. the ritualistic stripping of insignia in a court martial).

5 *Remembrance*. After the individual leaves the group both parties reminisce. This may be a fond recall of the 'remember when . . .' type or the more extreme exercise of a totalitarian regime in rewriting history.

Source: Moreland & Levine (1982).

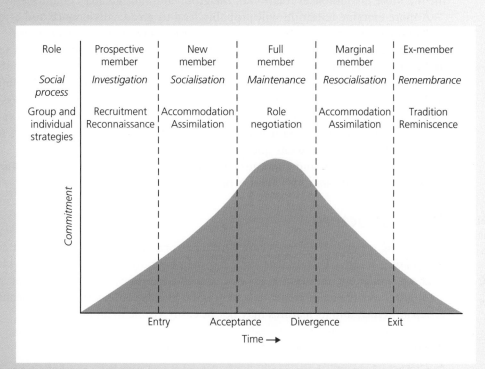

Figure 6.6

A model of the process of group socialisation.

Group socialisation: the passage of an individual member through a group is accompanied by variation in commitment and is marked by role discontinuities.

Source: Moreland, R. L., & Levine, J.M. (1982). Socialization in small groups: *Temporal changes in individual-group relations*. In L. Berkowitz (ed), *Advances in experimental social psychology* (Vol. 15, pp. 137–192). New York: Academic Press. Copyright © Elsevier Ltd. Reproduced with permission.

initiation rites become a central part of the life of the group that serve three important functions:

- *symbolic* – they allow consensual public recognition of a change in identity;
- *apprenticeship* – some rites help people to become accustomed to new roles and normative standards;
- *loyalty elicitation* – pleasant initiations with gifts and special dispensations may elicit gratitude, which should enhance commitment to the group.

Initiation rites can be pleasant events, such as graduation or a wedding. Surprisingly, they can also involve pain, suffering or humiliation, such as circumcision. This is odd – surely people would avoid joining groups with severe initiations, and if unfortunately unable to do so, then at least they should later hate the group and feel no sense of commitment.

We can make sense of this anomaly in terms of *cognitive dissonance* (Festinger, 1957), a theory discussed in Chapter 4. An aversive initiation creates dissonance between the two thoughts: 'I knowingly underwent a painful experience to join this group' and 'Some aspects of this group are not that great' (since group life is usually a mixture of positive and negative aspects). As an initiation is public and cannot be denied, I can reduce dissonance by revising my opinion of the group –

Initiation rites
Often painful or embarrassing public procedure to mark group members' movements from one role to another.

downplaying negative aspects and focusing on positive aspects. The outcome for me is a more favourable evaluation of the group and thus greater commitment.

A more extreme initiation will probably lead to greater dissonance and a more favourable evaluation of the group. This is precisely what has been found. For example, Harold Gerard and Grover Mathewson (1966) had students listen to an audiotape and rate what was a very boring discussion group that they were about to join. They were given mild or severe electric shocks, either explicitly as an initiation or under some other pretext completely unrelated to the ensuing discussion. As cognitive dissonance theory predicted, the painful experience improved evaluation of the group only when it was perceived to be an initiation (see Figure 6.7). (Now answer the second focus question.)

A group that is 'up and running' has a structure, whether evolved or planned, that helps it operate smoothly. This is our next topic.

Group structure
Division of a group into different roles that often differ with respect to status and prestige.

Roles
Patterns of behaviour that distinguish between different activities within the group, and that interrelate to one another for the greater good of the group.

Group structure

In very few groups are all members equal, performing identical activities or communicating freely. Differences between members are reflected in roles, status relations and communication networks, as well subgroups, and the central or marginal group membership credentials of specific members. This is what is meant by group structure, and its features may not be easily visible to an outsider.

Roles

In Chapter 5 we saw how norms both describe and prescribe the behaviour of a group as whole. Roles do likewise, but they are similar to a job description, focusing on what an individual or a subgroup does within the group. Roles govern how

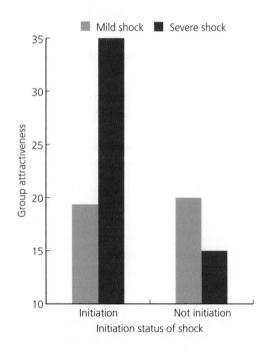

Figure 6.7

When an initiation is severe a group can become more attractive.

- Cognitive dissonance and the effectiveness of initiation rites.
- Students about to join a boring group discussion were given a mild or severe electric shock.
- When the shock was billed as an initiation, participants given the severe shock rated the group as more attractive than participants given the mild shock.

Source: Based on data from Gerard & Mathewson (1966).

they relate to and interact with another subgroup within the group, often for the greater good of the group as a whole – e.g. how waiters and cooks behave, and expect each other behave, in a busy and successful restaurant.

Roles can be informal and implicit. For example, in groups of friends at someone's flat, James might be the quiet one, Sally can be relied on to tell the latest jokes and Juanita usually gets the coffee going. They can also be formal and explicit, such as the duties of the pilots and flight attendants in a passenger airliner. We can also think of *leadership* in terms of playing out one or more roles. Indeed, in one group a leader may take the role of the task specialist who is the 'ideas' person and who will get things done. However, in another group the leader may take the role of the socioemotional specialist and so focuses on fostering supportive relationships between group members. (We discuss this in more detail on page 174.) Roles can sometimes be associated with larger category memberships that are outside the immediate context. For example, a hospital committee could include individuals representing different professional groups such as doctors and nurses. At times, such a committee is a crucible for role conflict that manifests a wider intergroup conflict.

Roles emerge in groups to represent a division of labour. They should provide clear expectations about how members will behave in relation to each other, and give members a self-definition and a place within the group. Typically, roles facilitate group functioning. However, an inflexible role can be detrimental to the group. Take a real-life example. Rigid role differentiation (who does what) in preflight checks by the flight crew of a passenger airliner caused the crew to fail to engage a de-icing device, with the tragic consequence that the plane crashed shortly after take-off (Gersick & Hackman, 1990).

Although people can move in and out of different roles, we often see them in only one role and infer that that is how they really are. When we attribute in-role behaviour to a person's dispositions and personality we fall prey to *correspondence bias*, discussed in Chapter 2. There is an irony here: if people continually treat you as though the role is you, you will gradually come to see yourself in this way – your identity and concept of self may change (Snyder, 1984). This implies that you should avoid low-status roles in groups, or you will subsequently find it difficult to escape their legacy. The most powerful and well-known social psychological illustration of the power of roles to modify behaviour is Zimbardo's (1971) simulated prison experiment (see Box 6.2).

Status

All roles are not equal – some have higher status than others. Those with high status are valued and considered prestigious by the group, and enable the role occupants to be innovative and influential. In most groups the highest status role is that of leader. Status hierarchies in groups can vary over time and across situations. For example, in an orchestra the lead violinist may have the highest status role at a concert, while the union representative has the highest status role in negotiations with management.

According to expectation states theory (see Ridgeway, 2001) status within a group derives from two distinct set of characteristics:

* *Specific status characteristics* are attributes that relate directly to the person's ability on the group's task (e.g. being a good athlete in a sports team, a good musician in a band).

Status
Consensual evaluation of the prestige of a role or role occupant in a group, or of the prestige of a group and its members as a whole.

Expectation states theory
Theory of the emergence of roles as a consequence of people's status-based expectations about others' performance.

Research classic 6.2
Guards versus prisoners: role play in a simulated prison

Philip Zimbardo was interested in how people adopt and internalise roles to guide behaviour. He was also interested in whether it is the prescription of the role rather than the personality of the role occupant that governs in-role behaviour. In a famous role-playing exercise, twenty-four psychologically stable male Stanford University student volunteers were randomly assigned the roles of prisoners or guards. The prisoners were arrested at their homes and initially processed by the police, then handed over to the guards in a simulated prison constructed in the basement of the Psychology Department at Stanford University.

Zimbardo had planned to observe the role-playing exercise over a period of two weeks. However, he had to stop the study after six days! Although the students were psychologically stable and those assigned to the guard or prisoner roles had no prior dispositional differences, things got completely out of hand. The guards continually harassed, humiliated and intimidated the prisoners, and they used psychological techniques to undermine solidarity and sow the seeds of distrust among them. Some guards increasingly behaved in a brutal and sadistic manner.

The prisoners initially revolted. However, they gradually became passive and docile as they showed symptoms of individual and group disintegration and an acute loss of contact with reality. Some prisoners had to be released from the study because they showed symptoms of severe emotional disturbance (disorganised thinking, uncontrollable crying and screaming); and in one case, a prisoner developed a psychosomatic rash all over his body.

Zimbardo's explanation of what happened in the simulated prison was that the students complied (too well!) with the roles that they thought were expected of them (see Haney, Banks & Zimbardo, 1973). This has been challenged. Steve Reicher and Alex Haslam (2006) argue that the participants were confronted by a situation that raised their feelings of uncertainty about themselves. In order to reduce this uncertainty they internalised the identities available (prisoners or guards), and adopted the appropriate behaviours to define themselves. The process was one of group identification and conformity to group norms motivated by uncertainty about their self-concept (see Hogg, 2007b).

- *Diffuse status characteristics* are attributes that do not relate directly to ability on the group task but are generally positively or negatively valued in society (e.g. being wealthy, having a white-collar occupation, being white).

Typically, specific status and diffuse status each make their own contribution to a person's overall status in a newly formed group. So, if your town was assembling a cast for a musical in the local theatre, Brenda may well play a part because of her rich contralto voice (specific status) and Rudolf could be chosen because of his dreamy looks (diffuse status). But star billing will no doubt accrue to Sophie, the soprano – she has been a successful soprano in other productions (specific status); plus, she looks stunning in most costumes (diffuse status).

Diffuse status characteristics are interesting. They create favourable expectations that are generalised to all sorts of situations, even those that may not be relevant to what the group does. Group members simply assume that someone with high diffuse status (e.g. a medical doctor) will be more able than others to promote the group's goals (e.g. analysing trial transcripts in order to render a verdict) and therefore has higher *specific* status (see the third focus question). A study by Strodtbeck, James and Hawkins (1957) illustrates this. They assembled mock juries to consider and render a verdict on transcripts of actual trials, and found that the high-status role of jury foreman almost always went to people who had higher occupational status outside the context of the jury (e.g. teachers or psychologists rather than janitors or mechanics).

Next we look at how a group shares its information.

Communication networks

No matter what their roles, people in a group typically coordinate their actions. We know they do this by communicating with one another, but are some ways more helpful than others? The answers to this lie in a variety of communication networks. You will be familiar with some very obvious instances, such as IT networks at your institution. Not too long ago, information sharing has been more restricted, such as by way of notice boards or circulated notices in the mail. Networks in large organisations and bureaucracies, such as a university or government office, are often rigidly formalised ones, even when email is the medium. For example, reminders arriving on your laptop to get your work in on time are not things that good dreams are made of. Are some network *structures* better than others?

In his classic work on communication networks, Alex Bavelas (1950) observed that they differed in how centralised they are. In centralised networks all communications go through a communication hub or centre point, whereas in decentralised networks every role can communicate directly with every other role. For simple tasks, centralisation improves group performance: the hub person is able to receive, integrate and pass on information efficiently while allowing peripheral members to concentrate on their allotted roles. For complex tasks, a de-centralised structure works better. The quantity and complexity of information would overwhelm a hub person who would be unable to integrate, assimilate and pass it on efficiently – peripheral members would experience delays and miscommunication, and coordination and group performance would suffer. However, a centralised network for complex tasks may pay off in the long run once procedures have been well established, well learned and judged acceptable by group members.

There is a general problem with centralisation. Because all communication goes through the hub, peripheral members can feel they have less autonomy and power. This often reduces overall satisfaction, harmony and solidarity, and can produce group conflict. Research on organisations confirms that job satisfaction and organisational commitment are influenced by the amount of control that employees feel they have, and that control is related to communication networks, in particular to how much participation employees feel they have in decision making (Evans & Fischer, 1992).

In almost all organisational groups the formal or official communication network is complemented by an informal but work-related communication 'grapevine' (Simmonds, 1985; Cooper & Kurland, 2002). The explosion of computer-mediated communication (CMC) in organisations since the early 1990s has created virtual teams and a communication environment that is typically less centralised (Hackman, 2002) and perhaps more open to transactive memory – and grapevine-related communication.

Groups within groups

Groups are not only structured into different roles that members occupy, but they also contain subgroups. These subgroups can be nested within the larger group (e.g. different departments in a university, different divisions in a company), or they can represent social categories that have members outside the larger group (e.g. social psychologists in a psychology department are also members of the group of social psychologists at large). In this case the subgroups are not nested but are crosscutting categories (Crisp & Hewstone, 2007).

Unlike roles, which usually cooperate for the greater good of the group, subgroups often compete and come into conflict with one another and thus harm the

Communication network
Set of rules governing how communication will take place between different roles in a group.

larger group. For example, divisions in a company can take healthy competition too far and slip into outright conflict, and merged organisations are often marred by subgroup conflict between the pre-merger organisations (Terry, Carey & Callan, 2001), and ideological factions can engineer a schism that ruptures the larger group (Sani & Reicher, 2000). The problem of subgroup conflict is often most evident and harmful when larger groups contain sociodemographic subgroups that have destructive intergroup relations in society as a whole – for example, Protestants and Catholics working together in a Northern Irish business (Hewstone *et al.*, 2005).

Why do people join groups?

In answering this question we need to remember that 'why' people join groups (reasons and motives) is not the same as 'how' people join groups (cognitive and social processes), and that the degree of choice we have in belonging to a group can vary a great deal. We have little choice in what sex, ethnic, national or social class groups we 'join'; we have some choice, possibly less than we might think, in what occupational or political group we join; and we have substantial choice in what clubs, societies and recreational groups we join. However, in all groups we can have more or less opportunity to decide or change what the group means for us – what its norms and practices might be.

Reasons and motives

We can join or form groups for many reasons. Physical proximity is a very common one. We get to like, or at least put up with, people we are in close proximity with, and proximity can reveal similar interests, attitudes and beliefs – together this can produce cohesion, shared norms and a sense of common identity (Festinger, Schachter & Back, 1950; Tyler & Sears, 1977). Another very common reason for joining or forming a group is to accomplish goals that we cannot accomplish alone – cooperative interdependence and action to satisfy shared goals produces group norms, mutual liking and a sense of being a group, separate from other groups that one is competing against (Sherif, 1966). People also join groups for the pleasure of human company and to avoid loneliness, for self-protection and personal safety (e.g. adolescents joining gangs and mountaineers climbing in groups), and for emotional support in times of stress (e.g. a wake, or a support group for AIDS sufferers and their relatives and friends).

The question 'why do people join groups?' can be reframed as 'what basic motivations cause people to affiliate?' Roy Baumeister and Mark Leary (1995) believe that people simply have a basic and overwhelming need to belong, and this causes them to affiliate and to join and be members of groups. Furthermore, the sense of belonging and being successfully connected to other human beings, interpersonally or in groups, produces a powerful and highly rewarding sense of self-esteem and self-worth (Leary, Tambor, Terdal & Downs, 1995).

Uncertainty-identity theory
People are motivated to reduce uncertainty about who they are, or about their thoughts or actions that reflect on who they are.

According to uncertainty-identity theory (Hogg, 2007b) people do not like to feel uncertain about who they are, or about attitudes and behaviours that reflect on who they are. Joining or identifying with a group is an effective way to reduce uncertainty about our self. Groups provide us with a recognised way to define and evaluate who we are, how we should behave and how we will interact with and be treated by others. When we identify with a group we categorise ourselves as group members and internalise the group's prototypical attributes (Turner, Hogg, Oakes,

Reicher, & Wetherell, 1987). It is these group attributes (e.g. political beliefs, language, ethnicity or sporting prowess) that define who we are, how we should behave and generally reduce uncertainty.

Perhaps all of us have asked the existential question what is life all about? It also intrigued Jeff Greenberg and his associates. According to terror management theory, the most fundamental threat that people face is the inevitability of death, and therefore people live in perpetual terror of death (Greenberg, Solomon & Pyszczynski, 1997). Fear of death is the most powerful motivating factor in human existence. People affiliate and join groups in order to reduce their fear of death – this happens most markedly when people's mortality becomes salient to them. Affiliation and group formation are highly effective terror management strategies because they raise self-esteem and make people feel good about themselves – they feel immortal, and positive and excited about life.

Terror management theory
The notion that the most fundamental human motivation is to reduce the terror of the inevitability of death. Self-esteem may be centrally implicated in effective terror management.

Exclusion, rejection and deviance

Not being a member of a group can be a lonely existence: we lose social interaction, emotional support, social and physical protection, the ability to achieve complex goals, a stable sense of who we are, and confidence in how we should behave. Not surprisingly, being excluded from a group can be a very painful experience – particularly when group members engage in social ostracism to intentionally exclude you.

Social ostracism
Exclusion from a group by common consent.

Kip Williams, who has worked extensively on social influence and group processes, devised a clever paradigm to investigate this (Williams, 2002; Williams, Shore & Grahe, 1998). Students in groups of three, ostensibly waiting for an experiment to begin, fill in time by throwing a ball to one another across the room. After a while two of the students (who are actually confederates of the experimenter)

Social ostracism. This girl feels the loneliness of exclusion – a loneliness that is amplified when the ostracism is intentional.

Source: Pearson Online Database (POD)

exclude the third student (the true participant) by no longer throwing the ball to them. It is very uncomfortable even to watch the video of this study (imagine how the participant felt!). True participants appear self-conscious and embarrassed, and many try to occupy themselves with other activities such as playing with their keys, staring out of the window or meticulously scrutinising the contents of their wallets. Williams adapted this method for the Internet: a person could log on to a web site and take part in an animated ball game with two other players (actually simulated). He found that ostracism in cyberspace, 'cyberostracism', had much the same effect as face-to-face ostracism (Williams, Cheung & Choi, 2000).

In almost all groups it is not actually being a member that counts, but a matter of whether you or your group *consider* that you are. You might be a core member who closely embodies the group's defining attributes, i.e. a prototypical member; or you might be a peripheral or marginal member who is not very prototypical of the group at all. Highly prototypical members often have significant influence over the group and may have leadership roles (Hogg, 2001). Marginal members are a different story (see Box 6.3).

Leadership
Getting group members to achieve the group's goals.

Subjective group dynamics
A process in which deviant group members threaten a group's norms and its unity.

Schism
Division of a group into subgroups that differ in their attitudes, values or ideology.

Leadership

Almost all groups have leaders: people who have the 'good' ideas that everyone else then agrees on; people whom everyone follows; people who have the power to persuade and to make things happen. Leaders enable groups, ranging from small teams to entire nations, to function as productive and coordinated wholes. Not surprisingly the study of leadership spans social psychology, political science and the organisational sciences (Hogg, in press; Northouse, 2007; Yukl, 2005).

Research and applications 6.3
Being a marginal group member

Marginal members have little influence over a group. José Marques and his colleagues have focused on the nature of marginality in a group's life. A marginal member is commonly disliked, and can be treated as a 'black sheep' (Marques & Páez, 1994). In fact, people who have attributes that place them right on the boundary between ingroup and outgroup are actually disliked more if they are ingroup members than outgroup members – they are treated as deviants or even traitors. One reason for this, proposed by the theory of subjective group dynamics, is that marginal ingroup members are viewed as undermining normative consensus within the group and thus threatening the integrity of the group (Marques, Abrams & Serodio, 2001).

However, marginal members can play an important role in and for a group. For example, groups, particularly their leaders, can publicly vilify marginal members to throw into stark relief what the group is and what the group is not. Marginal members can also be an active force for social change within a group. Research suggests that if they speak out as critics of the group's normative practices they can have an impact on the group – groups are more accepting of criticism from ingroup than outgroup members (Hornsey, 2005). Ingroup critics, of course, have an uphill struggle to be heard if they are treated as deviant individuals. However, the task is made easier if a number of dissenters unite and speak with one voice as an organised subgroup. This makes them an active minority within the group – a schism – with the capacity to effect some change (Hogg, in press; also see the power of minorities in Chapter 5).

Leadership is 'a process of social influence through which an individual enlists and mobilizes the aid of others in the attainment of a collective goal' (Chemers, 2001, p. 376). It requires an individual or clique to influence the behaviour of another individual or group of individuals – where there are leaders there must be followers. So, what is *not* leadership? Typically the use of power, through reinforcement and the threat or use of punishment, to make people do things is not leadership. This is why prison guards are not likely to spring to mind as leaders. Likewise if people simply comply with norms or obey regulations they are not being led. However, it *is* leadership if people are persuaded to internalise group norms that they then enact as an expression of their own beliefs and commitment to the group.

We need to distinguish between *effective* and *good* leadership. An *effective* leader is someone who is successful in setting new goals and influencing others to achieve them. Here, the evaluation of leadership is largely an objective matter of fact – how much influence did the leader have in setting new goals and were the goals achieved? In contrast, evaluating whether the leader is good or bad is largely a subjective judgement based on one's preferences, perspectives and goals, and on whether the leader belongs to one's own group or another group. We evaluate leaders in terms of their character (e.g. nice, nasty, charismatic), the morality of the means they use to influence others and achieve goals (e.g. persuasion, coercion, oppression, democratic decision making), and the nature of the goals that they lead their followers towards (e.g. saving the environment, reducing starvation and disease, producing a commodity, combating oppression, engaging in genocide). *Good* leaders are those who have attributes we applaud, use means we approve of, and set and achieve goals we value.

Great leaders

Because leaders often seem to have special and distinctive capabilities that mark them off from the rest of us, we might think that effective leadership rests on innate abilities or possession of particular personality attributes. There is no evidence that leadership effectiveness is innate in any direct sense. No leadership gene has been found, and there are few if any reliable physiological (and so genetic) correlates of great leaders – for example, although American male corporate leaders tend to be somewhat above average height, an equal number of 'great leaders' are below average height (e.g. Napoleon, Thatcher).

Perhaps effective leaders have an enduring constellation of personality attributes, acquired very early in life, which imbues them with charisma and a predisposition to lead (e.g. House, 1977). This idea has been explored exhaustively. Early on, a pioneer in the development of scales to measure of leadership, Ralph Stogdill, concluded that leadership is not the 'mere possession of some combination of traits' (Stogdill, 1948, p. 66). More recently, others have exclaimed that the search for a leadership personality is simplistic and futile (e.g. Conger & Kanungo, 1998). In general, correlations among traits, and between traits and effective leadership, are low. Stogdill (1974) reported an average correlation of 0.30, pointing to an association on only 9 per cent of the cases.

A more fruitful line of research has explored leadership in relation to what are called the Big Five dimensions, which are broader and more stable measures of personality. A researcher in individual differences, Timothy Judge, and his colleagues reported an overall correlation of 0.58 using a meta-analysis of data from seventy-

Big Five
The five major personality dimensions of extraversion/surgency, agreeableness, conscientiousness, emotional stability, and intellect/openness to experience.

three samples (Judge, Bono, Ilies & Gerhardt, 2002). The best predictors of effective leadership were being extraverted, open to experience, and conscientious.

We now consider some recent and productive theories of leadership and their implications.

Theories about kinds of leaders

Contingency theories

However one looks at it, stable personality traits are at best not a complete explanation of leadership. We all know that some people, including ourselves, can lead and do so effectively in some situations and not others. For example, in their classic studies of intergroup relations at boys' summer camps in the United States (see Chapter 7), Sherif and his colleagues (Sherif *et al.*, 1961) first divided the boys into groups. When the groups later met in competition, a boy in one group displaced the original leader because of his greater physical prowess and other qualities suggesting he was better equipped to lead the group successfully in a confrontation. In a 1949 study, Carter and Nixon (not the US presidents!) found the same effect when pairs of school pupils performed three different tasks – an intellectual task, a clerical task and a mechanical assembly task. Those who took the lead in the first two tasks rarely led in the mechanical assembly task.

An effective leader has the right attributes to deal with the situation. In a general way, we can distinguish between two leadership styles, one that concentrates on the group's task and on getting things done, and one that pays attention to the members' relationships. For example, Robert Bales, a pioneer in the study of small group communication, identified two key leadership roles – *task specialist* and *socioemotional specialist* (Bales, 1950; Slater, 1955). Task specialists concentrate on reaching solutions, often making suggestions and giving directions; socioemotional specialists are alert to the feelings of other group members. A single person rarely occupies both roles – rather, the roles devolve onto separate individuals, and the person occupying the task-specialist role is more likely to be the dominant leader.

Contingency theories recognise whether a particular leadership style is effective depends on the properties of the situation. For example, different behavioural styles are suited to an aircrew in combat, an organisational decision-making group, a ballet company or a nation in economic crisis. We deal with two contingency theories, the first in some depth and the second more briefly.

The first and best-known contingency theory is that of an eminent leadership researcher, Fred Fiedler (1964). Like Bales, Fiedler distinguished between *task-oriented leaders* who are authoritarian, value group success and derive self-esteem from task accomplishment rather than being liked by the group; and *relationship-oriented leaders* who are relaxed, friendly, non-directive and sociable, and gain self-esteem from happy and harmonious group relations. He also classified leadership situations in terms of situational control, which can vary from *high* (good leader–member relations, a clearly defined task, and a high degree of authority vested in the leadership role) to *low* (poor leader–member relations, a poorly defined task and little authority vested in the leadership role).

Fiedler measured leadership style in a rather unusual way; with his least preferred co-worker (LPC) scale in which respondents rated the person they least preferred as a co-worker on a number of dimensions (e.g. pleasant–unpleasant, boring–interesting, friendly unfriendly).

Contingency theories
Theories of leadership that consider the leadership effectiveness of particular behaviours or behavioural styles to be contingent on the nature of leadership situation.

Situational control
Fiedler's classification of task characteristics in terms of how much control effective task performance requires.

Least-preferred co-worker (LPC) scale
Fiedler's scale for measuring leadership style in terms of favourability of attitude towards one's least-preferred co-worker.

A task-oriented leader. 'Our purpose is to make money, right?' Such a leader defines group success by reaching a target rather satisfying the aspirations of members.

Source: Pearson Online Database (POD)

In a first step, the resultant LPC scores were used to divide the respondents at the two extremes into separate groups with different leadership potential:

- An extremely low score is at one end of the scale. It indicates a *task-oriented* style, with a harsh attitude towards a poorly performing co-worker.
- An extremely high score is at the other end of the scale. It indicates a *relationship-oriented* style, with a benign attitude towards a co-worker even when not performing well.

In a second step, situational control enters the scene:

- Task-oriented leaders are most effective when situational control is low (the group needs a directive leader to focus on getting things done) *and* when situational control is high (the group is doing just fine, so there is little need to worry about morale and relationships within the group).
- Relationship-oriented leaders are more effective when situational control lies between these extremes.

This prediction is illustrated in Figure 6.8, which also shows a composite of correlations between LPC scores and group performance reported by Fiedler (1964) from published studies. The results match the prediction rather well. Reviews of other studies have also supported Fiedler's theory (e.g. Schriesheim, Tepper & Tetrault, 1994).

The second contingency theory is path-goal theory (PGT) (House, 1996). This assumes that a leader's main function is to motivate followers by clarifying the paths (i.e. how to behave) that will help them reach their goals. There are two classes of leader behaviour: *structuring* (the leader directs task-related activities) and *consideration* (the leader addresses followers' personal and emotional needs). Structuring is most effective when followers are unclear about their goals and how to reach them – e.g. the task is new, difficult or ambiguous. When tasks are well understood, structuring is less effective. It can even backfire because it seems like meddling and micro-management. Consideration is most effective when the task is boring or uncomfortable, but not when followers are already engaged and motivated, because being considerate can seem distracting and unnecessary.

Path-goal theory (PGT)
A contingency theory of leadership that can also be classified as a transactional theory – it focuses on how 'structuring' and 'consideration' behaviours motivate followers.

Figure 6.8

Using LPC scores to plot variations in group performance: relationship-oriented versus task-oriented leaders.

- When situational control is very high or very low, contingency theory predicts a negative correlation between LPC scores and quality of group performance.
- A group performs poorly for a relationship-oriented leader (high LPC score), but well for a task-oriented leader (low LPC score).
- When control is intermediate a positive correlation is predicted: relationship-oriented leaders are more effective. The obtained correlations came from a series of supportive studies.

Source: Based on data from Fiedler (1964).

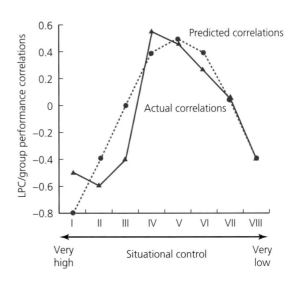

Transactional leadership

Transactional leadership
Approach to leadership that focuses on the transaction of resources between leader and followers. Also a style of leadership.

Idiosyncrasy credit
Hollander's transactional theory, that followers reward leaders for achieving group goals by allowing them to be relatively idiosyncratic.

Leader–member exchange (LMX) theory
Theory of leadership in which effective leadership rests on the ability of the leader to develop good-quality personalised exchange relationships with individual members.

Though popular, contingency theories are rather static. They do not capture the dance of leadership – leaders and followers provide support and gratification to one another, which allows leaders to lead and encourages followers to follow (Messick, 2005). This limitation is addressed by theories of transactional leadership that view leadership as a process of exchange. Followers provide the leader with social approval, praise, prestige, status and power (the trappings of effective leadership) in exchange for the leader's role in leading the group towards valued goals and in providing followers with recognition and rewards for completing the task (Bass, 1985).

The social and organisational psychologist Edwin Hollander (1958) made an interesting proposal. Leaders need to earn idiosyncrasy credit from the group. To be effective, leaders need their followers to allow them to be innovative, to be able to experiment with new ideas and new directions – to be idiosyncratic. A leader can accumulate idiosyncrasy credits by (a) initially conforming closely to group norms, (b) making sure the group feels it has democratically elected you as leader, (c) making sure you are considered competent to fulfil the group's objectives, and (d) being seen to identify with the group, its ideals and its aspirations. A good credit rating creates legitimacy in the eyes of the followers and allows the leader to exert influence over the group and to deviate from existing norms – in other words, to be idiosyncratic, creative and innovative.

Perhaps the best-known transactional theory of leadership is leader–member exchange (LMX) theory (e.g. Graen & Uhl-Bien, 1995; Sparrowe & Liden, 1997). Leaders develop exchange relationships with individual subordinates. These relationships can be of high or low quality. The former are based on mutual trust, respect and obligation; the latter are mechanically based on the terms of the formal employment contract between leader and subordinates. In high-quality relationships, subordinates are favoured by the leader and receive many valued resources, which can include material benefits (e.g. money, privileges) as well as psychological benefits (e.g. trust, confidences). These relationships go beyond the formal employment contract: managers show support, and give the subordinate greater autonomy. They also motivate subordinates to internalise the group's and the leader's goals. In low-quality relationships, however, subordinates are not favoured and receive fewer valued resources. The leader–member exchanges adhere to the terms of the employment contract, with little attempt by the leader to develop or motivate the subordinate. Subordinates simply comply with the leader's goals, without necessarily internalising them as their own.

An effective leader develops high-quality relationships. These enhance the well-being and work performance of subordinates, and bind them to the group more tightly through loyalty, gratitude and a sense of inclusion. Because leaders usually have to relate to a large number of subordinates, they cannot develop high-quality relationships with everyone – it is more efficient to select some subordinates in whom to invest a great deal of interpersonal energy, and to treat the others in a less personalised manner.

Transformation and charisma

As a style, transactional leadership can be contrasted to an extent with transformational leadership, which is now the gold standard of leadership theories. It is an approach with great appeal in management and organisational psychology (Antonakis & House, 2003).

Transactional leaders appeal to followers' self-interest, whereas transformational leaders literally want to transform a group. They inspire followers to adopt a vision that involves more than individual self-interest and works hard to convince followers 'to get on board' (Judge & Bono, 2000). Transformational leaders aim to: raise the aspirations of followers; improve their abilities; challenge their basic thinking to help them develop better mindsets and practices; and provide energy and a sense of urgency (Bass & Riggio, 2006). Such leaders can change how followers think, behave and conform to the leader's vision. They inspire their followers to identify with them and their vision, to identify with the organisation's core values, and to internalise the group as a part of their identity (Dvir, Eden, Avolio & Shamir, 2003; Hogg & van Knippenberg, 2003).

Charisma plays a key role in transformational leadership. For leaders to be transformational they need to have charm and attractiveness and be able to exercise charismatic leadership. Charismatic and transformational leaders have high levels of some *Big Five* personality dimensions: they are extraverted, agreeable and intellectually open to experience (Judge, Bono, Ilies & Gerhardt, 2002). A leader with charisma is said to be visionary – a special person who can identify attractive future goals and objectives for a group and mobilise followers to internalise these as their own. A person with vision and who is emotionally expressive, enthusiastic, driven, eloquent, self-confident and responsive to others is likely to become an effective leader (Riggio & Carney, 2003). These are the attributes that allow someone to be influential and persuasive, enabling others to buy their vision and sacrifice personal goals for collective goals.

The role of charisma is viewed differently by the *social identity theory of leadership* (discussed below). Charisma may be a consequence rather than a cause of effective leadership. Consider the following: (a) sometimes members identify strongly with a group; (b) the leader is highly prototypical of the group (embodies its defining attributes); the members view the leader as influential, attractive, trustworthy and innovative. Consequently, they attend closely to their leader, and finally attribute the leaders' actions internally – to the leader's personality (an instance of *correspondence bias*, described in Chapter 2; Gilbert & Malone, 1995) – and thus construct a charismatic leadership personality.

Transformational leadership
Approach to leadership that focuses on the way that leaders transform group goals and actions – mainly through the exercise of charisma. Also a style of leadership based on charisma.

Charismatic leadership
Leadership style based upon the leaders (perceived) possession of charisma.

Leaders lead groups

Leader categorisation theory
We have a variety of schemas about how different types of leaders behave in different leadership situations. When a leader is categorised as a particular type of leader, the schema fills in details about how that leader will behave.

Social identity theory of leadership
Development of social identity theory to explain leadership as an identity process in which in salient groups prototypical leaders are more effective than less prototypical leaders.

Leaders lead groups, and so leadership rests on the extent to which the group allows the leader to lead. This in turn depends on how followers perceive their leader. According to leader categorisation theory our perceptions of leadership play a central role in decisions we make about selecting and endorsing leaders, and thus the leader's ability to influence others and to lead effectively (Lord & Brown, 2004). There are different categories of leadership (e.g. military generals, prime ministers, chief executive officers, chefs, football club managers) that people represent as *schemas* or *prototypes* (see Chapter 2). In any given leadership situation people investigate how well their leader's characteristics and actions match the relevant leadership prototype. The better the match the more favourably the leader is perceived and the more likely you are to endorse and follow the leader. For example, if your leadership schema favours 'intelligent', 'organised' and 'dedicated' as core leadership attributes, you are more likely to endorse a leader who seems to be intelligent, organised and dedicated.

The role of group perceptions is treated somewhat differently by the social identity theory of leadership (Hogg, 2001; Hogg & van Knippenberg, 2003). Groups provide people with a social identity – a sense of who they are, how they should behave and how others will treat them. Sometimes a group, and the identity it provides to its members, is important or salient to them at a moment in time. In these circumstances, people want to know more about the group's norms, and look to internalise a prototype of the group to guide their actions. The most direct and reliable source of this comes from others in the group who already seem to be highly prototypical. This kind of person who embodies the prototype is the focus of group attention and respect and is highly influential – they are or can be a leader. This perspective acknowledges that leadership has an important identity function – people look to their leaders to express and epitomise their identity, to clarify and focus their identity, to forge and transform their identity, and to consolidate, stabilise and anchor their identity.

The more salient a group is and the more strongly people identify with the group the more that group prototypicality becomes a basis for effective leadership. A number of studies have demonstrated this (van Knippenberg, van Knippenberg, De Cremer & Hogg, 2004).

For example, Hains, Hogg and Duck (1997) conducted an experiment in which participants were either explicitly categorised or merely aggregated as a group (group membership salience was therefore either high or low). Before interacting as a group, they rated the leadership effectiveness of a randomly appointed leader, who was described as being either a prototypical or a not prototypical group member and as possessing or not possessing characteristics of very general schemas of leadership. As predicted, leaders who were consistent with a schema were considered more effective than those who were not. However, when group membership became salient, being prototypical of the group increased the perceived effectiveness of a leader (see Figure 6.9).

In salient groups, prototypical leaders are more influential than those who are not because of the following:

- They embody the group's attributes and are viewed as the source not the target of influence – they are the ones with whom other members align their behaviour.
- They are liked and are popular, qualities which increase their social influence (Hogg, 1993).
- They are trusted because their identity and fate are so closely tied to the group. Paradoxically, this trust allows them to diverge from group norms and to innovate and be transformational (cf. Hollander's notion of idiosyncrasy credit).

Figure 6.9

A leader is seen as more effective when the group is salient and the leader is prototypical of the group.

- When group salience is high, features of the leader that are prototypical for the group became important in determining how effective the leader is perceived.
- When group salience is low, being prototypical does not have this impact.

Source: Based on data from Hains, Hogg & Duck (1997).

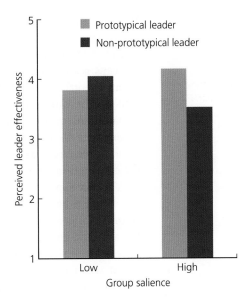

- They have legitimacy and can act in the best interests of the group, even when this may not appear to be so (Tyler, 1997).
- They acquire charisma that is constructed by the group members. Groups attribute the positive actions of their leaders to their personality, further strengthening their position (Haslam & Platow, 2001).
- They maintain their position by managing their prototypicality. By communicating and talking they can construct, reconstruct or change the group prototype to protect or promote their central position – a process of 'norm talk' (Hogg & Tindale, 2005). See Box 6.4.

Real world 6.4
Norm talk and identity entrepreneurship

There are five ways in which you as a leader can protect and enhance how group prototypical your followers think you are:

1 Talk up your prototypicality and talk down your behaviours that are non-prototypical.

2 Identify deviants or marginal members to highlight your own prototypicality or to construct a particular prototype for the group that enhances your prototypicality.

3 Secure your own leadership position by vilifying contenders for leadership and casting them as non-prototypical.

4 Identify groups as relevant comparison outgroups that cast the most favourable light on your own prototypicality.

5 Raise or lower the salience of the group. If you are highly prototypical then raising salience provides you with the leadership benefits of high prototypicality; if you are not very prototypical lowering salience protects you from the leadership pitfalls of not being very prototypical.

Trust, justice and leadership

We have noted that leaders need their followers to trust them if they wish to be innovative and transformational. An important basis of trust is that a leader attends to *procedural justice*, that an outcome is based on a fair process, since this conveys respect for group members. This encourages followers to feel positive about the group, to identify with it and to be cooperative and compliant (Tyler, 2003). The outcome itself is not the most important factor: in organisational research, *distributive justice* is usually much less important than procedural justice (Alexander & Ruderman, 1987). In effect, people can live with uneven distributions of resources as long as they are confident that the procedures used to make the distribution were fair and just.

A recent experimental study in the Netherlands by David De Cremer and Daan van Knippenberg (2003) addressed this point in the context of the role of leadership. At different points in time, individuals made several contributions earmarked for a public good. Their contributions were described as a group effort and they believed that there was a group leader. As time progressed and they learned that a leader was trustworthy they became more generous. This trust grew from the perception that the leader was acting in a procedurally fair manner.

Men, women and leadership

Throughout the world, men and women both lead and exercise authority in different domains of life. However, in the worlds of work, politics and ideology it is typically men who occupy top leadership positions. Take the case of liberal democracies such as those in Western Europe, where more progressive gender attitudes have developed over the past forty years. Although women are now well represented in middle management in many of these countries, they are still underrepresented in senior management and 'elite' leadership positions.

Alice Eagly, who has published several studies dealing with the role of gender in organisations, pinpointed a glass ceiling or gender gap (Eagly, Makhijani & Klonsky, 1992). Eagly has used role congruity theory to explain how the glass ceiling works (Eagly & Karau, 2002). Social stereotypes in general characterise men as agentic (e.g. being assertive, controlling and dominant) and women as communal (e.g. being affectionate, gentle and nurturant). In the context of leadership, people's schemas, i.e. mental pictures, characterise leaders as being agentic and this is a male stereotype. This puts a woman in a tricky position – if she is communal she may not fit the schema of being a leader so well; if she is agentic she runs the risk, like Margaret Thatcher, of being the 'Iron Lady', 'Her Malignancy' or 'Attila the Hen' (Genovese, 1993).

There is another reason for the gender gap in leadership: women claim authority less effectively than men, while men claim and hold many more leadership positions than women. Bowles and McGinn (2005) propose four main barriers to women claiming authority. The first is role incongruity, as discussed above. The second is lack of management experience. The third is family responsibility, which compromises a woman's ability to commit the time required of leadership positions. The fourth is lack of motivation – women are not as 'hungry' for leadership as men. They shy away from self-promotion and take on less visible background roles with informal titles like 'facilitator' or 'coordinator'.

One reason for this may be stereotype threat (Steele, Spencer & Aronson, 2002) – women fear that negative stereotypes about women and leadership will be

Glass ceiling
An invisible barrier that prevents women, and other minorities, from attaining top leadership positions.

Role congruity theory
Mainly applied to the gender gap in leadership – because social stereotypes of women are inconsistent with people's schemas of effective leadership, women are evaluated as poor leaders.

Stereotype threat
Feeling that we will be judged and treated in terms of negative stereotypes of our group, and that we will inadvertently confirm these stereotypes through our behaviour.

DECISION MAKING IN GROUPS

confirmed, and so they feel less motivated to lead. In addition, a woman who promotes herself and claims leadership has to contend with popular stereotypes of women. She runs the risk of being seen as 'pushy', attracting negative reactions from both men and women (Rudman & Glick, 2001). (We re-visit the topics of the glass ceiling and of stereotype threat in Chapter 7.)

In concluding this section, the great challenge of leadership is often not merely to transcend individual differences, but to bridge profound group divisions and build an integrative vision and identity. Consider the challenge of providing integrative leadership in Iraq – a country divided into Sunnis, Shi'ites and Kurds. Most studies of leaders deal with single-group leadership, whereas many contexts involve intergroup relations (Pittinsky & Simon, 2007). If I am a student at university A, I may see the Vice Chancellor at university B as someone to distrust, especially if the government decides to merge the two. Being an intergroup leader can be a big challenge (Terry, Carey & Callan, 2001).

Decision making in groups

One of the most significant functions of groups is to make decisions. Our lives are enormously impacted by group decisions – those made by parliament, juries, selection committees, committees of examiners and groups of friends. We might think that humans come together to make decisions because groups would probably make better decisions than individuals – two heads are better than one. However, as we have already learned in this chapter, groups can impair and distort performance in many ways.

In this section we first consider the process, i.e. which of several rules, by which a group can make a decision. We look at how a group that lasts uses a special kind of memory. We touch on the phenomenon of brainstorming – does an 'open slather' approach to generating ideas lead to good decision making? We ask what if a group sometimes make an unexpected decision, one that is more risky or conservative than we might have thought. Finally, we explore decision making in a particular court setting: the jury.

Rules for making decisions

How does an assembly of individuals with initially diverse opinions reach a united group position? One of the best-known models is a set of rules described by Davis – social decisions schemes. We can apply these to institutionalised groups, such as a parliament, but also to informal groups, such as where your sports team will spend a rest-and-recreational holiday (see Table 6.1).

The particular rule that a group adopts can be influenced by the nature of the decision-making task. For example, if the task is to solve a mathematical problem where there is a right answer the group is likely to adopt truth wins. If the task is to decide which colour to re-paint your clubroom at the university, which is a matter of preference, the group might adopt majority wins.

Decision rules differ in terms of how much agreement is required (in this respect unanimity is much stricter than majority wins). In general, stricter rules are more egalitarian in that decision-making power is better distributed across the group (unanimity is very strict but very low in power concentration, while two-thirds majority is less strict but has greater power concentration. The strictness and

Social decisions schemes
Explicit or implicit decision-making rules that relate individual opinions to a final group decision.

Table 6.1 Social decisions schemes: ways that a group can reach a decision

---

James Davis distinguished between several explicit or implicit decision-making rules that groups can adopt:

- *Unanimity* – discussion is aimed at pressurising deviants to conform.
- *Majority wins* – discussion confirms the majority position, which is then adopted as the group position.
- *Truth wins* – discussion reveals the position that can be demonstrated to be correct.
- *Two-thirds majority* – unless there is a two-thirds majority, the group is unable to reach a decision.
- *First shift* – the group ultimately adopts a decision in line with the direction of the first shift in opinion shown by any member of the group.

Sources: Based on Davis (1973); Stasser, Kerr & Davis (1989).

power distribution of the rule affect both group functioning and member satisfaction (Miller, 1989). For example, stricter rules can make final agreement in the group slower, more exhaustive and difficult to attain, but it can enhance liking for fellow members and satisfaction with the quality of the decision.

Group memory

When a group makes a decision it needs a memory to be able to recall and marshal information. For instance, juries recall testimony to arrive at a verdict, and selection committees recall data that differentiate candidates in order to make an appointment. Some groups even meet primarily to remember; for example, groups of old friends who gather to reminisce.

Key questions here are whether groups can remember more information and do so more accurately than individuals. Clearly, different people recall different information. When they come together as a group to share this information each person's memory is expanded and the group has remembered more. Unshared information is now shared (Clark & Stephenson, 1995). Because the group recognises 'true' information, particularly when the memory task is a simple factual one, shared information is more likely to be accurate (Lorge & Solomon, 1995).

However, group remembering is more than a collective regurgitation of facts. Typically it is a highly complex constructive process in which people who differ in power and influence within the group bring different memories to the table. A subjective version of the truth is shaped by both the group and by its members through discourse and argument (Middleton & Edwards, 1990). Group memory operates in accordance with the entire range of group processes discussed in this chapter, and is subject to the social influence processes discussed in Chapter 5.

Another perspective on group remembering is that different members remember different things (memory specialisation is distributed), but everyone also needs to remember 'who remembers what' – who to go to for information. This is called transactive memory, a term suggesting that group members have transacted an agreement (Wegner, 1987; also Moreland, Argote & Krishnan, 1996). Transactive memory allows a group to remember significantly more information than if no transactive memory system was present (Hollingshead, 1998).

Transactive memory
Group members have a shared memory for who within the group remembers what and is the expert on what.

In new groups, transactive memory is often based on stereotypical expectations about who is most likely to know what – the 'geeky' looking person will know about computers, the adolescent girl will know about texting, the macho male will know about cars and the older person will know how to negotiate. In practice, most groups go on to develop more sophisticated memory-assignment systems. A group can negotiate over who will remember what, or they can assign responsibility for memory domains on the basis of who has demonstrated most knowledge and competence or who has easiest access to specific sources of information.

There is however a pitfall to transactive memory – because memory is unevenly distributed, when a member leaves, some group memory is temporarily lost or reduced (see Box 6.5). This can be disruptive, but groups recover quickly if there are other members with the expertise and information to step in. The problem is more serious in close relationships where the departure of a lifelong partner, through death, illness or separation, effectively wipes out a now irretrievable section of memory. The depression usually associated with bereavement is, at least in part, due to this. Happy memories are lost, our sense of who we are is undermined by lack of information, and we have to take responsibility for remembering a variety of things we did not have to remember before.

What a group remembers is a significant part of the group's culture (Moreland, Argote & Krishnan, 1996). Consider the culture of work groups in organisations: such groups develop detailed knowledge about norms, allies and enemies, cliques, working conditions, motivation to work, performance and performance appraisal, who fits in, and who is good at what.

Research and applications 6.5
Groups that learn together stay together

Transactive memory: combating its loss and facilitating its development

In dealing with the loss of transactive memory, the organisational psychologist Linda Argote and her colleagues performed an experiment in which laboratory groups met over a number of consecutive weeks to produce complex origami objects (Argote, Insko, Yovetich & Romero, 1995). Member turnover did indeed disrupt group learning and performance, and its impact grew worse over time, presumably because more established groups had more established transactive memories. Attempts to reduce the problem by providing newcomers with individual origami training were unsuccessful.

The implications for the productivity of work groups and organisations are serious, given that staff turnover is a fact of organisational life and that new members are almost always trained individually. Moreland, Argote and Krishnan (1996) argue that transactive

memory systems develop more rapidly and operate more efficiently if group members learn together rather than individually. Thus new members of organisations or work groups should be trained together rather than apart. Moreland and associates reported a series of laboratory experiments in which group training is indeed superior to individual training for the development and operation of transactive memory.

A natural example of loss of transactive memory comes from the 2000 Davis Cup tennis tournament. The British doubles team comprised Tim Henman and Greg Rusedski, who had trained together as a smoothly operating team for which Britain had high hopes. Immediately before the doubles match against the Ecuadorian team, Rusedski had to drop out and was replaced by Arvind Parmar. Henman and Parmar had not teamed up before and so had not developed a transactive memory system. The pair went down to a wholly unexpected straight-sets defeat by Ecuador.

Brainstorming

Brainstorming
Uninhibited generation of as many ideas as possible in a group, in order to enhance group creativity.

Some decision-making tasks require groups to come up with creative and novel solutions. A common technique is brainstorming (Osborn, 1957). Group members try to generate lots of ideas very quickly and to forget their inhibitions or concerns about quality – they simply say whatever comes to mind, be non-critical, and build on others' ideas when possible. Brainstorming is supposed to facilitate creative thinking and thus make the group more creative. Popular opinion is so convinced that brainstorming works that it is widely used in business contexts.

However, research tells us otherwise. Although brainstorming groups do generate *more* ideas than non-brainstorming groups, the individuals in the group are no more creative than if they had worked alone. In their review, the Dutch social psychologists Wolfgang Stroebe and Michael Diehl (1994) concluded that *nominal* groups (i.e. brainstorming groups in which individuals create ideas on their own and do not interact) are twice as creative as groups that actually interact.

Production blocking
Reduction in individual creativity and productivity in brainstorming groups due to interruptions and turn-taking.

There are many possible reasons why brainstorming groups are not very effective (Paulus, Dzindolet, Poletes & Camacho, 1993). For example, as we learned earlier, people can feel less motivated in groups (they loaf) or they can be apprehensive about being evaluated by others. However, in the context of brainstorming the most significant problem is production blocking – it is difficult to be creative and to get your ideas out because everyone else is calling out ideas at the same time. It can get awfully distracting and rowdy in a brainstorming group. A way to minimise production blocking is to brainstorm electronically. This reduces much of the interference caused by listening to others or waiting for a turn to speak (Hollingshead & McGrath, 1995); groups that brainstorm electronically via computers can produce more ideas than non-electronic groups, and more ideas than nominal electronic groups. Another way to minimise production blocking is to make the group as stimulating as possible. One way to do this is to make sure the group's membership is heterogeneous and diverse in terms of members' knowledge about the brainstorming topic (Stroebe & Diehl, 1994).

Illusion of group effectivity
Experience-based belief that we produce more and better ideas in groups than alone.

Given convincing evidence that face-to-face brainstorming does not actually improve individual creativity, why do people so firmly believe that it does? One answer is the illusion of group effectivity – based on our own experience in idea-generating groups we simply feel that we were more creative and productive (Stroebe, Diehl & Abakoumkin, 1992). There are three reasons for this illusory belief:

1. People are exposed to some ideas they had not heard before, but forget whether these were their own or those of others, and so exaggerate their own contribution.
2. Brainstorming is generally great fun – people enjoy the exercise in a group more than being alone and so feel more satisfied with their performance.
3. People recognise production blocking but think it only applies to themselves – they feel that they had lots of good ideas that did not get heard, or that someone else called out first. Thus they feel they were potentially more creative and productive than the others. Nevertheless, being in a group had enhanced their own level of performance, even if this was unrecognised by others.

Groupthink

Groups sometimes make really poor decisions with disastrous consequences. Irving Janis (1972) had a background in analysing the workings of propaganda. He compared a number of American foreign policy decisions that had unfavourable outcomes (e.g. the 1961 Bay of Pigs fiasco, the 1941 defence of Pearl Harbor) with others that had favourable outcomes (e.g. the 1962 Cuban missile crisis), and coined the term groupthink to describe what went on in the decision-making groups that made the poor decisions.

Groupthink is a mode of thinking in which the desire to reach unanimity overrides the motivation to adopt logical and rational decision-making procedures. The main cause of groupthink is excessive group cohesiveness, but there are other antecedents that relate to structural faults in the group and to the immediate decision-making context (see Figure 6.10). Together, these factors generate a range of symptoms pointing to defective decision-making procedures: e.g. there is inadequate and biased discussion and consideration of objectives and alternative solutions, and a failure to seek the advice of experts outside the group (see the fourth focus question).

Research on groupthink and the role of cohesiveness was stimulated by Janis's model, though later research pointed to some restrictions (Aldag & Fuller, 1993; Kerr & Tindale, 2004). As discussed earlier in this chapter, cohesiveness itself needs to be unpacked into group-based attraction (social attraction) and true interpersonal attraction (personal attraction). When this is done, social attraction is the better predictor of groupthink. For example, Hogg and Hains (1998) studied four-person discussion groups involving nearly 500 participants to find that symptoms

Groupthink
A mode of thinking in highly cohesive groups in which the desire to reach unanimous agreement overrides the motivation to adopt proper rational decision-making procedures.

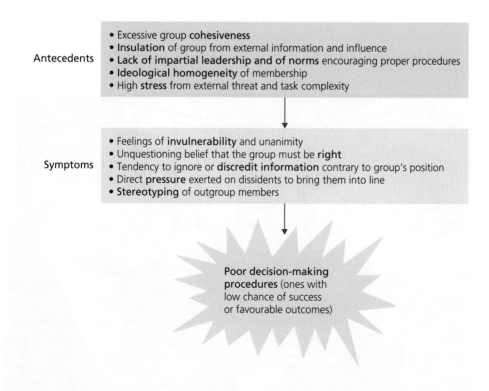

Figure 6.10

Antecedents, symptoms and consequences of groupthink.

Source: Janis & Mann (1977).

of groupthink were associated with cohesiveness – but only where cohesion represented group-based liking, not friendship or interpersonal attraction.

A radical suggestion is that groupthink is not a group process at all, just an aggregation of individual coping responses to excessive stress (Callaway, Marriott & Esser, 1985). Because group members are under decision-making stress they adopt defensive coping strategies and inadequate procedures to make decisions, which are symptomatic of groupthink. Individuals' suggestions and ideas are too often simply endorsed by other members because they are under pressure, and a group's decisions suffer.

Group polarisation

Group polarisation
Tendency for group discussion to produce more extreme group decisions than the mean of members' pre-discussion opinions, in the direction favoured by the mean.

Persuasive arguments theory
View that people in groups are persuaded by novel information that supports their initial position, and thus become more extreme in their endorsement of their initial position.

Folk wisdom has it that groups, committees and organisations make more conservative decisions than individuals would. This view assumes that individuals are likely to take risks, whereas group decision making is a tedious averaging process that errs towards caution. This is consistent with much of what social psychologists know about conformity and social influence processes in groups (see Chapter 5).

However, groups can sometimes make risky decisions (to some extent groupthink can be considered an example of this) or simply adopt very extreme positions. This phenomenon has been labelled group polarisation (Moscovici & Zavalloni, 1969). For example, group discussion among a collection of people who already slightly favour capital punishment is likely to produce a group decision that is strongly in favour. Several explanations of group polarisation have been put forward:

• Persuasive arguments theory – when we hear novel arguments that support our position on an issue we become more entrenched in our view (Burnstein & Vinokur, 1977). Suppose that the group initially leans in a particular direction.

Group polarisation. Things are going from bad to worse as pensioners in Leinster 'chat' with a government spokesperson. Intergroup conflict accentuates intergroup differences.

Source: Julien Behal / PA Archive / Press Association Images

The discussion that follows generates precisely these novel arguments and we become even more committed and extreme: the group as a whole becomes polarised (Gigone & Hastie, 1993). Further, thinking about an issue strengthens our opinion, as does the public repetition of our own and others' arguments (Brauer, Judd & Gliner, 1995).

- Social comparison/cultural values – being human, we seek social approval and avoid social censure (Sanders & Baron, 1977). Group discussion reveals which views are socially desirable or culturally valued, so in groups that already lean in one direction we shift further to gain approval and avoid disapproval from others. There is often a *bandwagon effect* in which once members identify the socially desirable pole towards which the group is leaning people compete to appear to be stronger advocates of that pole. Jean-Paul Codol (1975) called this the *primus inter pares* (first among equals) effect. Social comparison may also work through pluralistic ignorance (Miller & McFarland, 1987). Because we sometimes behave publicly in ways that do not reflect what we actually think, we can be ignorant of what everyone really thinks. However, group discussion can dispel pluralistic ignorance. If Gustav has an extreme attitude but believes that others are moderate, group discussion can reveal how extreme others' attitudes really are. This will liberate Gustav to be true to his underlying belief. Polarisation is not so much a shift in attitude as an expression of true attitudes.

- Social identity theory – as group members we identify with, construct and conform to an ingroup norm. This norm captures similarities within the group but also accentuates differences between their group and other groups (Hogg, 2006; Tajfel & Turner, 1979; Turner & Oakes, 1989). In discussion, we assemble elements into a representation of the group norm. These elements are the positions of ingroup members relative to those supposedly held, or actually are held, by outgroup members. The resulting norms minimise variability within the ingroup and distinguish it from outgroups. However, they are not necessarily the mean ingroup position: they can be polarised away from an explicit or implicit outgroup position. When individuals categorise themselves as members of a group they also identify with it. This leads them to conform to the ingroup norm. If the norm is polarised, the group as a whole is polarised. If the norm is not polarised, self-categorisation leads to convergence on the mean group position (Mackie, 1986; Turner, Wetherell & Hogg, 1989).

Social comparison/cultural values
Through group discussion people shift their views towards what others think or what is culturally valued.

Pluralistic ignorance
A situation where people in a group privately reject a norm but assume that others accept it.

Social identity theory
Theory of group membership and intergroup relations based on self-categorisation, social comparison and the construction of a shared self-definition in terms of ingroup-defining properties.

Juries are groups too

A jury is a special kind of group. It consists of lay people and, in criminal law, is charged with making a crucial decision involving someone's innocence or guilt. In this function, juries are an alternative to judges and are fundamental to the legal system of various countries around the world. They are most often associated with British law, but other countries (e.g. Argentina, Japan, Russia, Spain and Venezuela) have changed to include an input from lay citizens (Hans, 2008). In some cultures a group of lay people symbolise a just society. Not surprisingly they are the focus of numerous novels and movies – John Grisham's novel *The Runaway Jury* dramatically highlighted important social psychological points about how a jury reaches a decision. Because they are groups, juries can be prey to the deficiencies in decision making that we have outlined – which decision schemes to use, who should lead and why, leadership, the risk of groupthink when under stress and group polarisation (Kerr, Niedermeier & Kaplan, 1999; Tindale, Nadler, Krebel & Davis, 2001). There are also some issues specifically related to what a jury has to do.

Physically attractive defendants are more likely to be acquitted or to receive a lighter sentence (Michelini & Snodgrass, 1980; Stewart, 1980). However, biases can be reduced by furnishing sufficient factual evidence or by presenting the jury with written rather than spoken, face-to-face testimony (Baumeister & Darley, 1982; Kaplan & Miller, 1978). In the United States, race has been shown to influence the jury – Blacks are more likely to be found guilty of crimes that carry a prison sentence (Stewart, 1980). Further, people who murder a White have been more than twice as likely than those who murder a Black to receive the death penalty, a sentence which is determined by the jury in the United States (Henderson & Taylor, 1985).

Brutal crimes often stir up a call for draconian measures. However, the introduction of harsh laws with stiff penalties (e.g. the death penalty) can backfire – it discourages jurors from convicting (Kerr, 1978). Consider the anguish of a jury deliberating on a case in which the defendant has vandalised a car, and where a conviction would carry a mandatory death penalty.

Juries often have to remember and understand enormous amounts of information. Its sheer quantity encourages a *recency* effect: evidence delivered later in the trial is more heavily weighted (Horowitz & Bordens, 1990). In addition, evidence that a judge rules inadmissible, such as an interjection by a lawyer, is likely to affect a jury's deliberation (Thompson & Fuqua, 1998). As well, the complexity of evidence, the legal system and language conspire to challenge a jury and reduce the quality of decision making (Heuer & Penrod, 1994).

Strodtbeck and Lipinski (1985) reported that the 'foreman' or leader appointed by a jury is likely to have higher socioeconomic status, an instance of diffuse status characteristics discussed earlier. The foreman is also likely to have had previous experience as a juror, or may even simply occupy the seat at the head of the table at the first sitting of the jury!

With respect to decision schemes, if two-thirds or more of the jurors initially favour one alternative, then that is likely to be the jury's final verdict (Stasser, Kerr & Bray, 1982). Without such a majority, a hung jury is the likely outcome. The two-thirds majority rule is modified by a tendency for jurors to favour acquittal, particularly where evidence is not highly incriminating; under these circumstances, a minority favouring acquittal may prevail.

Jury size can matter, according to a meta-analysis by Saks and Marti (1997). Larger juries, of twelve rather than six members, are more likely to include people from minority groups, if selected at random; and if minority or dissident viewpoints matter, they have more impact in larger than in smaller juries (see the power of the minority in Chapter 5). Larger juries also deliberate longer, hang more often, and possibly recall trial testimony more accurately.

Summary

- At the very least, a group is a collection of people who define themselves as a group and whose attitudes and behaviour are governed by the norms of the group. Being a group member usually entails shared goals, interdependence, mutual influence and face-to-face interaction.

- People tend to perform easy, well-learned tasks better, and difficult, poorly learned tasks worse, in the presence of other people than on their own. We may be affected in this way because the presence of others may energise or drive habitual behaviour, lead us to worry about being evaluated, make us distracted, or make us self-aware.

- We tend to socially loaf in groups more than when we are alone. This is less common when the task is involving and interesting, when our contribution is clearly identifiable, or the group is important to our self-definition.

- Members of cohesive groups tend to feel more favourably towards one another as group members and are more likely to identify with the group and conform to its norms.

- Being a group member is a dynamic process. Our sense of commitment varies, we occupy different roles at different times, we endure sharp transitions between roles, and we are socialised by the group in many different ways.

- Groups have a structure, with roles that regulate interaction and serve the collective interest of the group. Some roles are more desirable and provide status. Groups can include subgroups, and members who are central or marginal.

- We join groups to get things done that cannot be done alone, to gain a sense of identity, to obtain social support or simply for the pleasure of social interaction.

- Leaders enable groups to function productively. Effective leadership is correlated with a few personality attributes (e.g. being extraverted, open to experience and conscientious), but personality alone is not sufficient.

- A *contingency* theory of leadership highlights the fit between a leader's style and the nature of a task. A *transactional* leader takes followers towards their goal, and in exchange, followers provide the leader with privileges. A *transformational* leader inspires followers with a vision that transcends self-interest and can be charismatic. According to *social identity theory*, followers look to their leader to express and anchor their identity.

- Trust plays an important role in leadership. Leaders who use fair methods to make decisions are trusted more.

- According to the glass ceiling effect, women often achieve middle management roles in many Western countries, but are underrepresented in senior management positions.

- Group decisions can sometimes be predicted accurately from the pre-discussion distribution of opinions in the group, and from the decision-making rule that prevails in the group at that time.

- Some believe that group brainstorming enhances individual creativity, but a group does not do better than the same number of individuals working alone. This illusion may be due to distorted perceptions of how ideas are generated during brainstorming and to the enjoyment people get from the experience.

- Well-established groups have a transactive memory and are often more effective than individuals at remembering information. Highly cohesive groups with directive leaders are prone to groupthink – poor decision making based on an overzealous desire to reach consensus.

- Some groups are prone to a risky (or conservative) shift in making a decision. This occurs when individuals with a somewhat extreme position before group discussion become even more extreme after discussion.

- Juries are not free from the usual range of group decision-making biases and errors.

Literature, film and TV

A League of Their Own

The 1992 film directed by Penny Marshall, and starring Madonna, Tom Hanks and Geena Davis is about a women's baseball team during the Second World War. The film shows how a rabble of very different people is forged into a cohesive team. The film also confronts issues of non-stereotypical role behaviours – in America, women don't play baseball.

Brassed Off

Mark Herman's (1996) film with Ewan McGregor about how the local Grimley Colliery Brass Band is central to life in a small northern English coal-mining town. The mine is closing down and the conflict between strikers and non-strikers spills over into the band and almost all other aspects of life. A wonderful illustration of the impact of intergroup relations on intragroup dynamics.

Castaway

The 2000 film directed by Robert Zemeckis, starring Tom Hanks, is about the consequences of exclusion, and loneliness. Tom Hanks is abandoned on an island. He uses pictures, and decorates a volleyball to look like a person whom he calls 'Wilson' – Wilson allows him to remain socially connected.

Lost

J. J. Abrams's incredibly popular TV show follows the survivors of a plane crash who have to work together to survive on an island. This series explores almost all aspects of group dynamics. A small community is formed with the common goal of survival and each character is encouraged to assume a role. Problems always arise when people are unwilling to cooperate for the good of the group.

Twelve Angry Men and The Runaway Jury

Two films based on books that highlight jury decision making. *Twelve Angry Men* is a classic 1957 film directed by Sidney Lumet and starring Henry Fonda – set entirely in the jury room it is an incredibly powerful portrayal of social influence and decision-making processes within a jury. *The Runaway Jury* is a 2003 film by Gary Fleder, with John Cusack, Dustin Hoffman and Gene Hackman, that dramatises the way that juries can be unscrupulously manipulated.

Thirteen Days

This 2000 film by Roger Donaldson is about the Cuban missile crisis that lasted for two weeks in October 1962 and was about as close as we got to all-out nuclear war between the West and the Soviet Union. The focus is on Kennedy's decision-making group. Is there groupthink or not? Wonderful dramatisation of presidential/high-level decision making under crisis. Also relevant to our coverage of intergroup behaviour in Chapter 7.

The Last King of Scotland

This 2006 film by Kevin MacDonald, based on the novel by Giles Foden, is a complex portrayal of the 1970s Ugandan dictator Idi Amin (played by Forest Whitaker) – an all-powerful and charismatic leader who can be charming interpersonally but will go to any lengths to protect himself from his paranoia about forces trying to undermine him. Amin was responsible for great brutality – 500 000 deaths and the expulsion of all Asians from the country.

Autobiographies

Autobiographies by Margaret Thatcher (*The Downing Street Years*, 1993), Nelson Mandela (*Long Walk to Freedom*, 1994), Richard Branson (*Richard Branson*, 1998) and Barak Obama (*Dreams from my Father*, 1995) – all great leaders but in quite different ways and domains.

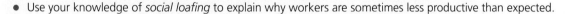

Guided questions

- Use your knowledge of *social loafing* to explain why workers are sometimes less productive than expected.

- Roles have an important function in groups – but can role-play be dangerous? Phil Zimbardo sets the scene for his famous guards vs. prisoners experiment in Chapter 6 of MyPsychLab at www.mypsychlab.co.uk.

- How is a *transformational* leader different from a *transactional* leader?

- When might *groupthink* lead to poor decision making?

- Sometimes a group makes a decision that is even more extreme than any of its individual members might have made. How so?

Learn more

Baron, R. S., & Kerr, N. (2003). *Group process, group decision, group action* (2nd ed). Buckingham, UK: Open University Press. A relatively easy to read general overview of some major topics in the study of group processes, with a good coverage of group decision making.

Forsyth, D. R. (2006). *Group dynamics* (4th ed). Pacific Grove, CA: Brooks/Cole. A comprehensive and accessible coverage of the social psychology of processes within groups.

Hogg, M. A. (2007). Social psychology of leadership. In A. W. Kruglanski & E. T. Higgins (eds), *Social psychology: A handbook of basic principles* (2nd ed). New York: Guilford. Up-to-date overview of research for social psychology and organisational science on leadership.

Hogg, M. A. (in press). Influence and leadership. In S. T. Fiske, D. T. Gilbert, & G. Lindzey (eds), *The handbook of social psychology* (5th ed). New York: Wiley. A detailed and up-to-date overview of leadership in the most recent edition of the handbook of social psychology. It views leadership as an influence process within groups, and takes a social psychological rather than organisational science perspective.

Stangor, C. (2004). *Social groups in action and interaction*. New York: Psychology Press. A comprehensive and accessible coverage of the social psychology of processes within and between groups.

Refresh your understanding, assess your progress and go further with interactive summaries, questions, podcasts, videos and much more on the website accompanying the book: **www.mypsychlab.co.uk.**

Chapter 7

Prejudice and intergroup relations

What to look for

- The functions of targets of prejudice and its targets
- Subtle forms of racism and how racism is detected
- Gender and the glass ceiling
- Genocide: discrimination in its ultimate form
- A personality-based account of prejudice
- The effect of relative deprivation on social unrest
- What brings a collective group to protest
- Intergroup theories of prejudice and discrimination
- Strategies that might reduce intergroup conflict

Focus questions

1. A neighbourhood group in the United Kingdom proposes to send the children of new immigrants into a special school, where first they can learn to speak English and later continue the rest of their education. The group says that this is for the good of the children. Would you have any concerns about this? See some real-life footage of negative comments about minority groups in Chapter 7 of MyPsychLab at www.mypsychlab.co.uk.

2. Erasmus is Dutch and very traditional in his politics and religion. He does not like the Mollucans, who came to the Netherlands years ago from Indonesia. He recalls how they highjacked a train at De Punt in 1977. But actually, he doesn't like any immigrants. How might you explain his views?

3. Jean and Alison have been close school friends. When they first arrive at university they are assigned to different but adjoining halls of residence. The halls have very different cultures and are in fierce competition with each other. What will happen to their friendship, and why?

4. Inspired by Eliza Doolittle's success in *My Fair Lady*, Katrina is determined to attend a speech production class. If she can get close to speaking posh she might be able to leave her working-class background behind. What must she be thinking?

he human importance of the material in this chapter was noted long ago by the eminent social psychologist Gordon Allport in his treatise *The Nature of Prejudice* (1954b). In some respects, the social psychology of prejudice and discrimination might seem to have an ordinary face. Prejudice and discrimination are each particular – one is a kind of attitude that is dominated by cognitive biases and the liberal use of stereotypes (see Chapter 2); the other is a kind of behaviour based on the unjust treatment of certain groups of people. The link between prejudice and discrimination is not simple. Recall that our attitudes are not always reflected in our actions (see Chapter 4); likewise, discrimination does not always follow from an underlying prejudice. When we scrutinise more carefully, the topics of prejudice and discrimination are not benign. Prejudice is built around strong and highly accessible negative attitudes, and discrimination is usually detrimental, hurtful and sometimes extremely damaging to members of minority groups.

In this chapter we define prejudice and deal with two particular kinds, one based on race and the other on gender. We also examine an influential theory from the 1950s that located the cause of prejudice in the person – if people rear their children in an autocratic way the result is an authoritarian personality, and this is manifested as a tendency to discriminate widely against members of minorities. This theory is at an *individual* level of analysis. We also touch on derivative theories that are politically based and are more sensitive to the origins of prejudice in the *groups* to which an individual belongs.

There are other theories that have located prejudice explicitly in the nature of intergroup relations and are therefore expressed at an *intergroup* level of analysis. To help understand this, we develop aspects of group behaviour not already covered in Chapter 6, and explore the negative consequences for human conduct. Studies of intergroup relations have provided an overarching view of prejudice and discrimination. Underpinning these studies are two major theories stressing an intergroup perspective that have set social psychology on its current path: realistic conflict theory and social identity theory.

Finally, we ask several difficult questions – can prejudice be reduced, are there ways of combating discrimination, and what methods are available to improve intergroup cooperation?

Prejudice
An unfavourable and sometimes hostile attitude towards a social group and its members.

Level of analysis
The types of concepts, mechanisms and language used to explain a phenomenon.

The nature of prejudice and discrimination

Prejudice and its manifestation in discrimination is a major impediment to enlightenment, and an understanding of its causes and consequences is one of our great challenges. We can put people on the moon, we can genetically modify living organisms, we can replace dysfunctional organs, we can whizz around the world at an altitude of 10 000 metres, and we can communicate with almost anyone anywhere via the Internet. But, in recent history, we have seemed helpless in preventing the Palestinians and the Israelis from fighting over Jerusalem, murders and assassinations based on religion in Northern Ireland, and tribal conflict in various African countries. In Chapter 8 we will see that prejudice is a 'normal' accompaniment of large-scale aggression, including war.

What is prejudice?

An awful aspect of prejudice occurs when it involves the dehumanisation of another group of people. If an outgroup can be viewed as less than human, then atrocities against its members become essentially no different to squishing an insect. Dehumanisation is commonplace. Europeans, who had extensive commerce with China by the sixteenth century, apparently thought that the Oriental was a 'strange and wondrous creature'. After meeting some Jesuit priests, a Confucian scholar in China offered a more damning contrary view in a letter to his son:

> These 'Ocean Men' are tall beasts with deep sunken eyes and beak-like noses . . . Although undoubtedly men, they seem to possess none of the mental faculties of men. The most bestial of peasants is far more human . . . It is quite possible that they are susceptible to training, and could with patience be taught the modes of conduct proper to a human being. *(cited by LaPiere & Farnsworth, 1949, p. 228)*

Prejudice is associated with much of the pain and human suffering in the world, ranging from restricted opportunities for employment of new immigrants to physical violence against minority group citizens and even genocide. It has always been with us and, depressingly, it may remain as a fundamental part of the human condition.

Herein lies a paradox: prejudice is socially undesirable, yet it pervades social life. Even in societies where prejudice is institutionalised, sophisticated justifications are used to deny that it is actually prejudice that is being practised. Apartheid in South Africa was a classic case of institutionalised prejudice, yet it was packaged publicly as recognising and respecting cultural differences (see Nelson Mandela's fascinating autobiography, 1994).

In our theoretical treatment we will deal with forms and consequences of prejudice and discrimination, and increase our understanding by looking at their origins in relationships between groups. Our subject is related to other chapters in this book. Prejudice rests on negative stereotypes of groups (see Chapter 2); there is a similar link between prejudice and discrimination as there is between attitudes and behaviour with respect to an outgroup (see Chapter 4); and prejudice often translates into aggression towards an outgroup (see Chapter 8). Social psychology is uniquely placed to help us understand prejudice. Prejudice involves people's feelings about and actions towards other people. It is guided by the groups to which we belong and given a context by the nature and history of particular intergroup relations.

As Gordon Allport pointed out long ago, the term 'prejudice' literally means 'prejudgement' from the Latin *prae* and *judicium* (Allport, 1954b). He also defined prejudice as 'thinking ill of others without sufficient warrant', which clearly points to its cognitive nature ('thinking'), but includes an evaluation as well ('ill'). These are two components of an attitude that we have discussed in detail in Chapter 4. If prejudice is an attitude is discrimination an inevitable outcome? Not necessarily. You will see in Box 7.1 a fanciful account of how prejudice may arise and *could* become the basis for discrimination. Fictional it may be, but it captures many of the principal features of prejudice that need to be explained. We need to address the relationship between prejudiced beliefs and the practice of discrimination, or more generally, between attitudes and behaviour.

Recall Richard LaPiere's (1934) study in Chapter 4. He travelled extensively across the United States with a young Chinese American couple, visiting 250 hotels, caravan parks, tourist homes and restaurants. They were refused service only once; it seemed there was little anti-Chinese prejudice. In response to a later

Dehumanisation
Stripping people of their dignity and humanity.

Genocide
The ultimate expression of prejudice by exterminating an entire social group.

Research and applications 7.1
The emergence of a fictional 'stigmatised group'

The social psychologist Joseph Forgas (1983) has shown that students have clear beliefs about different campus groups. One such target group was 'engineering students', who were described in terms of their drinking habits (beer, and lots of it), their cultural preferences (sports and little else) and their style of dress (practical and conservative). Think of this in terms of the *three-component attitude model* discussed in Chapter 4. We have a prejudgement that all engineering students are like this. If these beliefs (a *cognitive* component) are not associated with any strong feelings (an *affective* component) or any particular intention to act (a *behavioural* component), then no real problem exists and we would probably not call this a prejudice – simply a harmless generalisation.

However, if these beliefs were associated with strong negative feelings about engineering students because of their characteristics, then a pattern of discrimination would almost inevitably arise. If you hated and despised engineering students and their characteristics, you would probably intend to avoid them, perhaps humiliate them whenever possible, and even dream of a brave new world without them.

This is now quite clearly prejudice, but it may still not be much of a social problem. Strong pressures would

exist to inhibit expression of such views or the realisation of conation in action, so people with such prejudices would probably be unaware that others shared their views. However, if people became aware that their prejudices were widely shared, they might engage in discussion and form organisations to represent their views. Then more extreme intentions to act could arise, such as suggestions to isolate engineering students in one part of the campus and deny them access to certain resources on campus (e.g. the bar, or the whole student union). Individuals or small groups might now feel strong enough to discriminate against individual engineering students, although wider social pressures would probably prevent widespread discrimination.

However, if the students gained legitimate overall power in the university, they would be free to put their plans into action. They could indulge in dehumanising engineering students: deny them their human rights, degrade and humiliate them, herd them into ghettos behind barbed wire, and systematically exterminate them. Prejudice would have become enshrined in, and legitimated by, the norms and practices of the community.

questionnaire, only 1 per cent of these establishments said they would accept Chinese customers (refer to Box 4.2 in Chapter 4). This pointed to an intriguing conundrum – why would apparent acceptance of Chinese guests (the behaviour) be contradicted by overwhelming prejudice against Chinese (the response to the questionnaire)? We return to this issue when we consider later research that explores the meaning of *new racism*.

What is discrimination?

It is likely that in your community prejudice is expressed in subtle and often hidden ways and that crude discrimination is now less common. Here we briefly note three kinds of behaviour that may conceal underlying prejudices: reluctance to help, tokenism and reverse discrimination.

1. *Reluctance to help*: this is a failure to help other groups improve their position in society. Examples include landlords who are reluctant to rent accommodation to ethnic minorities, and organisations that omit to provide new mothers with flexible working hours or opportunities for job sharing. In an American study by Gaertner and Dovidio (1977), White bystanders in an emergency situa-

tion discriminated more against a Black victim when they believed that their failure to help would not be attributed to race.

2. **Tokenism**: this refers to a relatively small or trivial positive act, a token, towards members of a minority group. This token allows one to appear unprejudiced and decline to engage in more meaningful positive acts – 'Don't bother me, I've already done enough' (Rosenfield, Greenberg, Folger & Borys, 1982). On a larger scale, organisations may employ minorities as tokens to help deflect accusations of prejudice.

3. *Reverse discrimination*: this is a more extreme form of tokenism. People with residual prejudiced attitudes may sometimes go out of their way to favour members of a group against which they are prejudiced more than members of other groups. Because reverse discrimination favours a minority group member, it can have beneficial effects in the short term, but in the long run it may have some harmful consequences for its recipients (Fajardo, 1985). There is as yet no evidence that reverse discrimination reduces or abolishes the deep-seated prejudices of the discriminator.

> **Tokenism**
> Practice of publicly making small concessions to a minority group in order to deflect accusations of prejudice and discrimination.

Tokenism can have damaging consequences for the self-esteem of those who are employed as token minorities. In his research on human resource practices, Thomas Chacko (1982), who has researched extensively in management practices, found that women managers who felt that they had been hired only as token women were less committed to their organisation and less satisfied in their job. Likewise, reverse discrimination can also reduce self-esteem.

Educationist Daniel Fajardo (1985) arranged for White teachers to grade four essays that were reliable examples (drawn from college entrance records) of poor, average or excellent quality. The teachers understood that the essays were written by either Black or White high school students applying to enter university. Teachers evaluated an essay more favourably when they believed that it was written by a Black student, especially if the essay was of average quality (see Figure 7.1). The practice of reverse discrimination may furnish minority students with self-confidence: it could also foster an unrealistic opinion of their ability and future

Figure 7.1

White teachers' evaluations of student essays of varying quality as a function of student race.

White teachers evaluated Black students' essays more favourably than White students' essays, particularly where the essays were of average, rather than poor or excellent, quality. An unintended consequence of reverse discrimination such as this is that Black students would be less likely to seek or be given guidance to improve their actually very average performance.

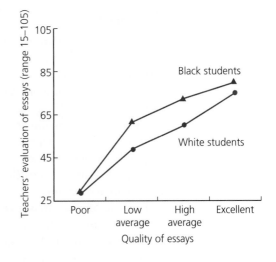

Source: Based on data from Fajardo (1985).

prospects, resulting in damage to self-esteem when such hopes collide with reality. We can distinguish between reverse discrimination and affirmative (equal opportunities) action. Fajardo noted that for affirmative action to be effective, it should be based on a teacher's guidance, honest evaluation and cultural acceptance of a minority student.

Two 'isms': race and gender

Prejudice knows no cultural or historical boundaries. Human beings are remarkably versatile in being able to make almost any social group a target of prejudice. However, certain groups are the enduring victims of prejudice. They are based on social categories (discussed later) that are vivid, omnipresent and have a social purpose. They also feature people who almost always occupy low power positions in society. Victimised groups that have been studied include gays and lesbians (Herek, 2000), people who have physical or mental disabilities (Fishbein, 2002) and the elderly, i.e ageism (Kite, Stockdale, Whiteley & Johnson, 2005). Two of the most exhaustively researched are racism and sexism and these are the targets we will deal with.

Racism

Discrimination on the basis of race or ethnicity is responsible historically for some of the most appalling acts of mass inhumanity. While sexism is responsible for the continuing practice of selective infanticide, in which female babies (and foetuses) are killed, this is largely restricted to a handful of developing countries (Freed & Freed, 1989). Genocide is universal. For example, in recent times it has been carried out in Germany, Cambodia, Iraq, Bosnia and Rwanda.

Racism
Prejudice and discrimination against people based on their ethnicity or race.

Most research on racism has focused on anti-Black attitudes and behaviour in the United States where historically Blacks have been perceived negatively – descendants of rural, enslaved, manual labourers (Plous & Williams, 1995). John Dovidio, who has researched extensively in the field of prejudice, and his colleagues have suggested that anti-Black attitudes have become much less marked since the 1930s (see Figure 7.2).

New racism

Can we conclude that racial prejudice is dying out in Western industrial nations? Probably not. What Figure 7.2 shows is a decline over sixty years in characterising African Americans as superstitious, lazy and ignorant. What this figure does *not* address are very different data from a study by Patricia Devine and Andrew Elliot (1995), in which 45 per cent of respondents felt that African Americans were lazy, compared with Dovidio *et al.*'s figure of about 5 per cent. Working in a social cognition framework, Devine and Elliot found that more than 25 per cent of their respondents characterised African Americans as athletic and rhythmic, but also less intelligent, criminal, hostile and loud. The specific stereotypes have changed but the negativity remains.

Because blatant racism is usually illegal and socially censured, it is now more difficult to find. Most people in most contexts do not behave in this way. However, racism may actually have changed its form. New racism has a variety of names, including *aversive racism* (Gaertner & Dovidio, 1986) and *modern racism*

Figure 7.2

Decline over time of White
derogation of African Americans.

The percentage of White participants
selecting the derogatory stereotypic
traits 'superstitious', 'lazy' and
'ignorant' to describe African
Americans has diminished
dramatically since 1933.

Source: Based on data from Dovidio, Brigham,
Johnson & Gaertner (1996).

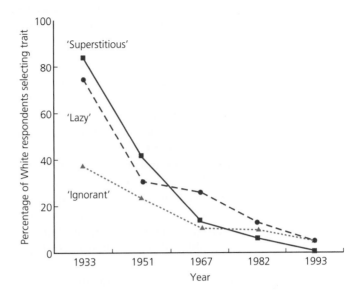

(McConahay, 1986), with essentially the same meaning. At its heart, new racism
reflects how people experience a conflict between deep-seated emotional antipathy
towards racial outgroups and values that stress equality (see the review by Hilton
& von Hippel, 1996). People prejudiced in this way resolve their problem by leading separate lives and avoiding the topic of race. They deny being prejudiced, deny
racial disadvantage, and oppose affirmative action or other measures that address
racial disadvantage.

These ideas grew from studies on race relations in the United States, but have
been applied by Peter Glick and Susan Fiske (1996) to gender, and by Tom
Pettigrew and Roel Meertens (1995) to racial attitudes in Europe.

Gender
Sex-stereotypical
attributes of a person.

Detecting racism

The challenge to social psychology, then, is to be able to *detect* new racism.
Although several scales based on questionnaires have been used with this aim,
unobtrusive measures are generally needed to detect racism in its subtle form – otherwise people may respond in a socially desirable way (Devine, 1989; Greenwald
& Banaji, 1995). See Chapter 4 for a discussion of bodily clues, action clues and
implicit measures of attitudes. Look in particular at biases in language use when
describing the actions of someone from an outgroup; and at how the implicit association test can be used to measure an attitude that some of us would rather
conceal (described in Chapter 4, Box 4.1).

Racism can also be imbedded unintentionally in the words we use, the way we
express ourselves and the way we communicate with and about racial outgroups in
our everyday language. Evidence for this comes from British work in discourse
analysis by Jonathan Potter and Margaret Wetherell (1987) and from the Dutch
work by linguist Teun van Dijk (1993). Take an example from Potter and Wetherell
where an underlying racism about Polynesian immigrants to New Zealand 'slips
out' in an interview:

Discourse analysis
A set of methods used to
analyse text, in particular,
naturally occurring
language, in order to
understand its meaning
and significance.

I'm not anti them at all you know, if they're willing to get on and be like us; but if they're just going to come here, just to be able to use our social welfares and stuff like that, then why don't they stay home. *(cited in Rogers, 2003, p. 82)*

Finally, although we have some control over what we say, we have less control over non-verbal communication channels that can be a rich indicator of responding negatively. If we consistently behave in this way towards individuals from a particular group, it probably signifies prejudice. For example, our face can betray fear or anger, sometimes quite subtly; if we stare we usually give offence; breaking eye contact too quickly can suggest avoidance. Non-verbal communication is explored in more detail in Chapter 11.

Expressions and acts reflecting racism are generally both illegal and morally condemned, and most people think and act accordingly, but their long history cannot be shrugged off so easily. The germs of racism still exist, and racism can be detected in various subtle forms. Racial and cultural resentment and partiality lurk beneath the surface – relatively dormant but ready to be activated by a social environment (e.g. a political regime) that might legitimise the expression of prejudice. The violence in Bosnia that began in 1992 and the horrors in Rwanda and the Sudan have been chilling reminders of this. There is also some concern at the increased media prominence given to the far right in Europe, since this can provide a legitimising environment for the public expression of old-fashioned racist attitudes.

In closing this section, there is an important point we need to bear in mind. Although some research suggests that overt discrimination may be on the wane in many Western democracies, this does not mean that the consequences of decades or even centuries of racism will change so quickly. For example, although attitudes towards Blacks in the United States have improved dramatically over the past twenty-five years, the physical, material and spiritual plight of Blacks in much of Europe has not.

Sexism

Sexism
Prejudice and discrimination against people based on their gender.

Kay Deaux and Marianne LaFrance (1998) have both carried out many studies relating to the psychology of gender, and noted that almost all research on sexism focuses on prejudice and discrimination against women. This is because women have historically suffered most as the victims of sexism – primarily because of their lower power position relative to men in business, government and employment. Why have subjectively constructed gender roles (as distinct from biological sex roles) persisted? A contributing reason is that they provide men with structural power, but women with interpersonal (i.e. person-oriented) power, and they are built into a conservative political ideology (Jost & Banaji, 1994; Jost, Federico & Napier, 2009). And of course, to the extent that women have power over men they are just as capable of discriminating against men.

Sex stereotypes and sex roles

Stereotypes
Widely shared and simplified evaluative image of a social group and its members.

Research on sex stereotypes has revealed that both men and women traditionally believe the same thing: men are competent and independent, and women are warm and expressive. As Susan Fiske (1998, p. 377) puts it: 'The typical woman is seen as nice but incompetent, the typical man as competent but maybe not so nice.' These beliefs have substantial cross-cultural generality. They prevail in Europe, North and South America, Australia and parts of the Middle East (Deaux, 1985; Williams & Best, 1982). These are really consensual social stereotypes.

Just because we know about such stereotypes does not mean that we personally believe them. In fact, it seems that such a correspondence between knowing and believing occurs only among highly prejudiced individuals (Devine, 1989). For the most part, men and women do not apply strong sex stereotypes to themselves, and women often say that sex discrimination is something experienced by *other* women (Martin, 1987; Crosby, Cordova & Jaskar, 1993; see below).

In Fiske's review of sex stereotypes, there are four major female subtypes in Western cultures: housewife, sexy woman, career woman and feminist/athlete/ lesbian. The first two represent an interpersonal dimension and the second two a competence dimension. The typical woman is closest to the housewife or sexy woman subtype. Male subtypes are less clear-cut, but the two main ones are businessman and macho man, and these emphasise the competence dimension. The typical man falls between the two poles.

It is tempting to argue that competence, independence, warmth and expressiveness are all highly desirable and valued human attributes. If this were true, they would be equally valued. However, one early study suggested that female-stereotypical traits are significantly less valued than male-stereotypical traits. A hospital psychologist Inge Broverman and her colleagues asked mental health clinicians (clinical psychologists, psychiatrists, social workers) to describe a healthy, mature, socially competent individual, who was (1) 'a male', (2) 'a female' or (3) 'a person'. Both male and female clinicians described a healthy adult man and a healthy adult person in almost exactly the same terms (reflecting competence). The healthy adult woman was seen to be significantly more submissive, excitable and appearance-oriented, characteristics not attached to either the healthy adult or the healthy man (Broverman *et al.*, 1970). It is ominous that women were not considered to be normal, healthy adult people!

Traditionally, men and women have occupied different sex roles in society (men pursue full-time out-of-home jobs, while females are 'homemakers'). This is sometimes called a social role theory. The assignment of roles may be determined and perpetuated by the social group that has more power – men. Alternatively, is there a biological imperative behind role assignments? This is consistent with sexual selection theory based in evolutionary social psychology. We revisit this issue in dealing with differences between men and women in relation to aggression (see Chapter 8).

Gender and power

One reason why sex stereotypes persist is that role assignment according to gender persists. In general, women make up the overwhelming majority of restaurant servers, telephone operators, secretaries, nurses, babysitters, dental hygienists, librarians and elementary/kindergarten teachers; most lawyers, dentists, truck drivers, accountants, top executives and engineers are male (Greenglass, 1982). Certain occupations become labelled as 'women's work' and are accordingly valued less.

Alice Eagly, who has a long record of research dealing with both gender and attitudes, investigated this idea with Valerie Steffen (Eagly & Steffen, 1984). They asked male and female students to rate an imaginary man or woman who was described as being either a 'homemaker' or employed full-time outside the home. In a control condition, no employment information was given. The results show that both male and female homemakers were rated as more feminine than people working full-time (see Figure 7.3). This suggests that certain roles may be sex-typed and that as women increasingly take on masculine roles there could be substantial change in sex stereotypes. However, the converse may also occur: as women take up a traditional male role, that role may become less valued.

Sex role
Behaviour deemed sex-stereotypically appropriate.

Social role theory
The argumen that sex differences in occupations are determined by society rather than one's biology.

Sexual selection theory
The argument that male–female differences in behaviour derive from human evolutionary history.

Figure 7.3

Trait ratings can be affected by knowing a person's sex and employment status.

Male and female students rated a 'homemaker' as significantly more feminine than someone described as a full-time employee, irrespective of the target's sex.

Source: Based on data from Eagly & Steffen (1984).

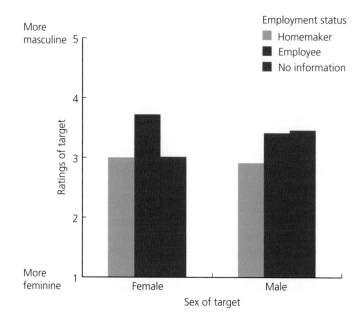

Glass ceiling
An invisible barrier that prevents women, and other minorities, from attaining top leadership positions.

Changes in access to higher-status 'masculine' occupations have been slower and less extensive outside more progressive environments such as universities, and women can still find it difficult to attain top leadership positions in large organisations. Women are well represented in middle management, but on the way up, and just within sight of the top, they hit an invisible barrier – the glass ceiling (Eagly, 2003; also see Chapter 6). One explanation is that male prejudice against women heading for power generates a backlash that constructs the glass ceiling, as evidence in Box 7.2 suggests.

The glass ceiling. Can she break through to become CEO or will a male power base resist?
Source: Pearson Online Database (POD)

Research and applications 7.2
Backlash: self-promoting women can be socially rejected

The violation of gender stereotypes can lead to reprisal or backlash. According to Laurie Rudman, women who are thought to be assertive or highly competent violate a feminine stereotype. Instead, they should be *communal* and socially oriented, such as kind, sympathetic and concerned about others. It is a man's job to be *agentic* such as forceful, decisive and independent (Rudman, 1998; Rudman & Glick, 1999, 2001).

A competent woman may therefore be disliked, viewed as lacking in interpersonal skills, and less likely to be hired than an identically qualified man. Penalising agentic women is especially pronounced if a job inherently requires being more communal. Men do not suffer in the same way: they are not perceived as less competent if they happen to be seen as highly communal. According to Rudman and Glick, this asymmetry rests on the fact that gender stereotypes put women rather than men in a straitjacket.

More evidence of backlash comes from the research of Madeline Heilman and her colleagues (Heilman, Wallen, Fuchs & Tamkins, 2004). Students who take part in a personnel decision-making task were given information about a male-stereotypical company job (Assistant Vice President for Sales) and about fictitious employees who were holding the job. These employees were described as either male or female, with a record of either clear previous success or ambiguous previous success. The students then rated the employees in terms of their competence, interpersonal liking and hostility. There were two findings:

- If previous success was clear, male and female employees were rated as equally competent; but if previous success was ambiguous, the male was rated as significantly more competent than the female.

- If previous success was clear, male employees were liked significantly more than female; but if previous success was ambiguous, males and females were equally liked.

These findings indicate that in ambiguous situations, women are denied competence in a 'male' job market. When their competence cannot be doubted, they are less liked and personally derogated. (For a review of how gender stereotypes affect women in the workplace, see Heilman & Parks-Stamm, 2007.)

In closing this section on two major 'isms', we should recall that stereotypes are based on categories – the ones that we use to attend to and distinguish between various groups in our social world (Oakes, Haslam & Turner, 1994). In this sense, stereotypes reflect the images that we have of intergroup relations (see Chapter 2). We use our stereotypes to define our identities (see Chapter 3); they reduce uncertainty and also justify the status quo. For these reasons they are notoriously difficult to change, an issue to which we will return in the later part of this chapter.

Self-fulfilling prophecy and stereotype threat

Prejudiced attitudes lead to overt or covert discriminatory behaviour, and in time this creates disadvantage. In this way, a stereotypical belief can create a material reality that confirms the belief: it is a self-fulfilling prophecy (see the review by Jussim & Fleming, 1996). For example, the organisational psychologist Dov Eden (1990) led platoon leaders in the Israeli Defence Force to believe that their subordinates had a potential to perform at a high level. Behold – after an eleven-week training programme, platoons with high-expectation leaders outperformed platoons with 'no-expectation' leaders. See Box 7.3 for the most famous of studies in this field.

Self-fulfilling prophecy
Expectations and assumptions about a person that influence our interaction with that person and eventually change their behaviour in line with our expectations.

Research classic 7.3
Pygmalion in the classroom

Dov Eden referred to the Pygmalion effect as 'a special case of the self-fulfilling prophecy'. Pygmalion was the name of a play by George Bernard Shaw, brought to the stage and screen in *My Fair Lady*, in which a simple Cockney girl is transformed into a society lady with an upper class accent. Robert Rosenthal and Lenore Jacobson brought this myth to life in their famous work, *Pygmalion in the Classroom* (1968). Their book's cover said: 'Simply put, when teachers expect students to do well and show intellectual growth, they do; when teachers do not ... [students] may in fact be discouraged in a number of ways.'

Rosenthal and Jacobson administered an IQ test to elementary school children and told their teachers that the results of the test would be a reliable predictor of which children would 'bloom' (show rapid intellectual development in the near future). The teachers were given the names of the twenty 'bloomers'; in fact, the twenty names were chosen randomly by the researchers,

and there were no IQ differences between bloomers and non-bloomers. Very quickly, the teachers rated the non-bloomers as being less curious, less interested and less happy than the bloomers: that is, the teachers developed stereotypical expectations about the two groups. Grades for work were consistent with these expectations.

Rosenthal and Jacobson measured the children's IQ at the end of the first year, and at the start and end of the second year. They found that in both years the bloomers showed a significantly greater IQ gain than the non-bloomers. Sceptics simply did not believe this, so Rosenthal and Rubin (1978) conducted a meta-analysis of 345 follow-up studies to prove that the phenomenon really exists. Rosenthal did not limit the positive potential of the effect to education. He saw how it could be applied in business and in medicine: the expectations of managers could have consequences for their employees, and those of clinicians for the mental and physical health of their patients.

Stereotype threat
Feeling that we will be judged and treated in terms of negative stereotypes of our group, and that we will inadvertently confirm these stereotypes through our behaviour.

Members of a stigmatised group know exactly the negative stereotypes that others have of them and experience what Steele and colleagues have called stereotype threat (Steele, Spencer & Aronson, 2002). Stigmatised individuals are aware that others may judge and treat them in a stereotyped way. On tasks that really matter to them, they worry that through their behaviour they may confirm the stereotypes – that their behaviour will become a self-fulfilling prophecy. American research has indicated that Black students are continually anxious that their academic failures will be seen as confirming a stereotype. Cumulatively, this produces enormous anxiety and can encourage Black students to reduce their efforts, to have lower academic ambitions and ultimately to drop out of school altogether. Similarly, stereotype threat could account for women's underachievement in mathematics and science.

These concerns not only increase anxiety but can also impair task performance. For example, an academically ambitious West Indian in London or an Algerian Arab in Paris, aware of stereotypes of intellectual inferiority, may be extremely anxious when answering a question in class – worried that the slightest mistake would be interpreted in line with the stereotype. This anxiety may actually impact adversely on behaviour.

In a test of the stereotype threat hypothesis by Steele and Aronson (1995), Black and White students anticipated taking either a 'very difficult' test that was defined as being 'diagnostic of intellectual ability', or as 'just a laboratory exercise'. They then completed a number of measures designed to assess awareness of racial stereotypes: for example, they completed ambiguous sentence fragments such as _____CE or _____ERIOR. As predicted, Black students who were anticipating a difficult test that was diagnostic of intellectual ability were more likely than other participants to complete the fragments with race-related words (e.g. race, inferior). Further, the Black students actually performed worse on these tests than White students of equivalent scholastic aptitude.

Ultimate discrimination: violence and genocide

Our focus to this point has been on indirect or subtle forms of prejudice and their effects, typified for the most part by Western democracies where antidiscrimination legislation is in place. For example, there is a lively campaign to purge language of racist and sexist terminology. However, it is important not to lose sight of the extremes of prejudiced behaviour. Prejudiced attitudes tend to have common themes: e.g. the targets of prejudice are considered to be dirty, stupid, insensitive, repulsive, aggressive and psychologically unstable (Brigham, 1971; Katz & Braly, 1933). This is a constellation that evaluates others as relatively worthless human beings who do not need or deserve to be treated with consideration, courtesy and respect. As Nick Haslam (2006) has noted in his review, these are characteristics of dehumanisation – together with fear and hatred, this is a potent mix that can foster individual violence, or encourage mass aggression or even systematic extermination.

In the absence of explicit institutional or legislative support, dehumanisation usually sponsors individual acts of violence. For example, in Britain there are attacks on Asian immigrants, in the United States the Ku Klux Klan was notorious for its lynchings of Blacks (see the powerful movie *Mississippi Burning*), in Germany there are Nazi-style attacks on Turkish immigrants, and in India female infanticide is still practised – albeit covertly (Freed & Freed, 1989). The Abu Ghraib prisoner abuse scandal which broke in 2004 is a sickening example of dehumanisation – some American guards at Abu Ghraib prison just outside Baghdad engaged in appalling acts of degradation of Iraqi prisoners of war, all caught on video.

When prejudice is morally accepted and legally endorsed in a society, then systematic acts of mass discrimination can be perpetrated. This can take the form of systems of apartheid, in which target groups are isolated from the rest of the community. South Africa from 1948 to 1994 is the most familiar recent example of this, but a similar system of segregation was practised in educational contexts in the United States until the mid-1950s, and the existence of reservations for native peoples in 'new world' countries, such as Australia and the United States, attest to a form of segregation. Apartheid and segregation often come equipped with a formidable array of social justifications in terms of benefits for the segregated group. (Perhaps you can apply this argument to the first focus question.)

The most extreme form of legitimised prejudice is genocide (Staub, 1989), where the target group is systematically exterminated. The dehumanisation process (Haslam, 2006) makes it relatively easy for people to perpetrate unimaginable acts of degradation and violence on others (see Thomas Keneally's biographical novel *Schindler's Ark* (1982), or the movie *The Killing Fields*). For example, Stalin targeted anyone he felt was plotting against him and, until his death in 1953, exiled 40 million people to brutal labour camps in Siberia (the Gulags); 15 million people died. The most chilling and best-documented instance of highly targeted genocide is the Holocaust of the early 1940s, when six million Jews were systematically exterminated by the Nazis in death camps in central Europe. At the massive Auschwitz–Birkenau complex in Poland, two million Jews were gassed between January 1942 and the summer of 1944 (a rate of 2220 men, women and children each day). See further examples of dehumanisation in Box 8.4, Chapter 8.

There are more recent examples of genocide: Pol Pot's 'killing fields' in Cambodia in the 1970s; Saddam Hussein's extermination of Kurds in northern Iraq and Shi'ites in southern Iraq; the Bosnian Serbs' campaign of 'ethnic cleansing' in Bosnia; the mutual genocide practised by the Hutu and Tutsi in Rwanda in 1994; and the ongoing systematic slaughter of non-Arabs in the western Sudanese region of Darfur.

Genocide can also be practised more indirectly, by creating conditions of massive material disadvantage in which a group effectively exterminates itself through disease, and through suicide and murder based on alcoholism, drug abuse and acute despair. The plight of the Australian Aborigines, Canadian Inuit and Brazilian Indians falls squarely into this camp.

We have discussed the nature of prejudice, its targets and some forms of discrimination that go with it. You might wonder if some people are more prejudiced than others. Do individuals vary in this way?

Prejudice and individual differences

We include here several theories of prejudice arguing that its origins lie in personality. These were popular in the mid decades of the twentieth century, but were gradually supplanted by broader explanations that we shall also consider. These have linked prejudice to differences between people in their values or ideologies.

The authoritarian personality

In their work *The Authoritarian Personality* published in 1950, Theodor Adorno, Else Frenkel-Brunswik and other colleagues described what they believed to be a personality syndrome that predisposed certain people to be authoritarian. The historical context for the concept of the authoritarian personality theory was the role of fascism, an extreme form of right-wing ideology, in the Holocaust – Adorno and Frenkel-Brunswik, who were both Jewish, had fled Hitler's regime in Germany and Austria respectively. The theory proposed that autocratic and punitive child-rearing practices were responsible for the emergence in adulthood of various clusters of beliefs. These included: ethnocentrism; an intolerance of Jews, African Americans, and other ethnic and religious minorities; a pessimistic and cynical view of human nature; conservative political and economic attitudes; and a suspicion of democracy. (Apply these ideas to the second focus question. You can check photos of the train hijacking at the Dutch site: http://gaf.zeelandnet.nl/yp408/de_punt.html.)

With the publication of their major work, Adorno reported that he and his group had constructed a questionnaire known as the California F-scale, intended at first to assess tendencies towards fascism, but turned out to be a purported measure of general authoritarianism. Despite substantial methodological and conceptual flaws (Brown, 1995; Hogg & Abrams, 1988), this work stimulated huge research interest in the 1960s and beyond.

In later years, the American Robert Altemeyer (1998) developed a more restricted but better designed measure of *right-wing authoritarianism*, conceived as an ideology that varies from person to person, and suggests that positions of power within a social hierarchy come from correct and moral behaviour (i.e. following social conventions). Questioning authority and tradition is a transgression that

Authoritarian personality
Personality syndrome originating in childhood that predisposes individuals to be prejudiced.

Ethnocentrism
Evaluative preference for all aspects of our own group relative to other groups.

ought to invite the wrath of legitimate authorities. Authoritarianism thus legitimises and maintains the status quo.

Politically-based theories

Social dominance theory

Let us propose that societies are based on, and that a society typically consists of, a hierarchy in which dominant groups have higher social status, and more political authority, power and wealth. This is the fundamental idea behind social dominance theory as developed by the political psychologist Jim Sidanius and his colleagues (Pratto, Sidanius and Levin, 2006; Sidanius & Pratto, 1999). Over time, such a hierarchical social structure might incorporate legitimising myths such as the 'divine right of kings' to suggest that inequality is actually fair. A particular society will develop a set of attitudes and values that create an ideology that entrenches social dominance. This enhances hierarchical social relations and maintains prejudice. A dominant group, such as the rich, is disproportionately advantaged (e.g. by the status or power of its members), whereas subordinate groups, such as the poor, are disproportionately disadvantaged (e.g. by lack of access to healthcare). A society's institutions can enhance the existing hierarchy. For example, the criminal justice system may be biased towards harsher penalties for members of socially disadvantaged minority groups.

Social dominance theory allows for individual differences. Some people want a society based on a hierarchy, one that supports discrimination; others want one based on equality, one that seeks fair practices. Underlying all of this is a view of intergroup relations that is exploitative and power-based. People who want their own group to be superior have a high social dominance orientation, reject equality as a virtue and are more prejudiced. People who are high in social dominance are ethnocentric, nationalistic, authoritarian, racist and sexist. They stereotype and discriminate against minorities, endorse policies such as the death penalty and reducing social welfare, and support military conquest. The character Archie Bunker in the 1970s TV series *All in the Family* springs to mind.

System justification theory

System justification theory is closely linked to social dominance theory, but is more specifically connected to people's views on politics. Its fundamental argument is that people vary along a dimension that measures the extent to which they justify the political status quo, and the social and economic policies that go with this. According to John Jost and his colleagues, most political ideologies are located on a left–right dimension (Jost & Hunyadi, 2002; Jost, Nosek & Gosling, 2008). One pole is often called *liberal*: people at this end call for social change but reject social inequality. The other pole is *conservative*: people at this end resist social change and endorse social inequality. The basis of any particular political ideology rests on the differences in the specific thinking and motivation that go with being generally either a liberal or a conservative. Liberals prefer some of the following: progress, rebelliousness, chaos, flexibility, feminism and equality; conservatives prefer some of the following: conformity, order, stability, traditional values and hierarchy. Consequently, system justification is more marked among conservatives than liberals. Conservatives justify and protect the existing social system – the status quo – even if this means upholding an unfavourable position for one's own group. There is an irony here. Why would people protect such an ideology when it maintains

Social dominance theory
An approach in which prejudice, exploitation and oppression are attributed to an ideology that legitimises a hierarchy of social groups.

System justification theory
Theory that attributes social stasis to people's adherence to an ideology that justifies and protects the status quo.

their position of disadvantage? Jost has suggested that one motivation for this may be to reduce uncertainty – better to live in reduced circumstances and be certain of one's place than to challenge the status quo and face an uncertain future. This point is closely connected to *social identity theory* and the nature of social change, which we discuss later in this chapter.

An interesting point emerges in what we have just looked at. Measures of prejudice that favoured the role of individual differences, in particular in personality, have evolved to take into account the lack of equity in social systems and the role of ideology. This has its origins in the Marxist view that people should understand that the ruling class has an ideology based on domination over subordinate classes. While there might be variations in the degree to which people hold these views, an emphasis on the social structure has intruded – a transition to the remaining sections of this chapter.

Intergroup relations and social unrest

We have noted that prejudice can be studied at an intergroup level of analysis, and we will now deal with this more explicitly. There are several theories and lines of research that view attitudes as emanating from the groups to which we belong. Since prejudice finds its targets in outgroups its origins are in ingroups. In this sense, discrimination is one kind, though a common one, of intergroup behaviour. When we deal with intergroup conflict we include both short-term misunderstandings and prolonged struggles between individuals from different groups as well as those between whole nations. We can also apply intergroup concepts to political confrontations, revolutions, inter-ethnic relations, negotiations between corporations, and competitive team sports.

Intergroup behaviour
Behaviour among individuals that is regulated by those individuals' awareness of and identification with different social groups.

Intergroup behaviour. 'Beware, Hells Angels!' The Bandidos continue a long struggle for biker gang dominance in Germany.

Source: Wolfgang Rattay/Reuters

We have visited the topic of groups, processes that occur *within* groups, in detail in Chapter 6. But wherever there is a group to which people belong (i.e. an ingroup), there are other groups to which those people do not belong (outgroups). Thus there is almost always an intergroup, or ingroup–outgroup, context for whatever happens in groups. We now make the argument that the nature of prejudice and discrimination makes better sense when examined in an intergroup context.

An old theory of aggression, the frustration–aggression hypothesis (Dollard Doob, Miller, Mowrer & Sears, 1939; also see Chapter 8), provides a starting point. Although it is remembered mostly today as an account of extreme forms of aggression, such as lynchings, the targets were usually individuals from a minority group. Leonard Berkowitz (1972a) extended the scope of the theory to account for intergroup aggression in a collective context, such as a riot. He also took into account the experience of relative deprivation.

Relative deprivation

The best-known application of this concept is to the riots that occurred during long periods of hot weather in the United States, including the Watts riots in Los Angeles in August 1965 and the Detroit riots in August 1967. The economic circumstances of Blacks were improving in the 1960s, but in a fast-growing economy not nearly as fast as for Whites. As a result, when Blacks compared their lot with Whites they experienced relative deprivation.

Relative deprivation frustrates people, and according to Iain Walker and Heather Smith (2002) it is a precondition for intergroup aggression. Heat is aversive, especially in a long, hot summer (Anderson & Anderson, 1984). It is likely to amplify existing frustration, especially in poor, overcrowded neighbourhoods with little air conditioning or cooling vegetation. This increases the prevalence of individual acts of aggression, a situation that worsens in the presence of provocative stimuli such as armed police. Widespread individual aggression now becomes true collective violence by a process of *social facilitation*: the presence of other people (in this case, on the streets) facilitates a dominant behaviour pattern (in this case, aggression). See Chapter 6 for a discussion of social facilitation.

In his treatment of political revolutions, the sociologist James Davies (1969) suggested a J-curve model to represent the way that people construct their future expectations from past and current attainments, and that under certain circumstances attainments may suddenly fall short of rising expectations. When this happens, relative deprivation is particularly acute, with the consequence of collective unrest. The shape of the line in Figure 7.4 is a J-curve (in this case, the J is rotated to the left). The 1992 Los Angeles riots provided a riveting, real-life example of relative deprivation perceived by a large group of people (see Box 7.4).

There are other historical events that seem to fit the J-curve model. For example, the Depression of the early 1930s caused a sudden fall in farm prices, which was associated with increased anti-Semitism in Poland (Keneally, 1982). Davies (1969) himself cites the French and Russian Revolutions, the American Civil War, the rise of Nazism in Germany and the growth of Black Power in the United States in the 1960s. In all these cases, a long period of increasing prosperity, lasting twenty to thirty years was followed by a steep and sudden recession. A variation on this theme puts relative deprivation squarely in an intergroup context. The British sociologist Garry Runciman (1966) has called this fraternalistic relative deprivation, in which people think that the lot of their ingroup as a whole is worse when

Frustration–aggression hypothesis
Theory that all frustration leads to aggression, and all aggression comes from frustration. Used to explain prejudice and intergroup aggression.

Relative deprivation
Perceived gap between expectations and achievements.

J-curve
A graphical figure that captures the way in which relative deprivation arises when attainments suddenly fall short of rising expectations.

Fraternalistic relative deprivation
Sense that our group has less than it is entitled to, relative to its aspirations or to other groups.

Real world 7.4
Rising expectations and collective protest

The Los Angeles riots that erupted on 29 April 1992 resulted in more than 50 dead and 2 300 injured. The immediate cause was the finding of 'not guilty' by an all-White suburban jury of four Los Angeles police officers accused of beating a Black motorist, Rodney King. The assault with which the police officers were charged had been captured on video and played on national TV. Against a background of rising unemployment and deepening disadvantage, Blacks saw this acquittal as a particularly poignant symbol of the low value placed by White America on American Blacks.

The flashpoint for the riot was the intersection of Florence and Normandie Avenues in South Central Los Angeles. Initially, there was an outbreak of stealing liquor from a nearby liquor store, breaking of car windows and throwing objects at police. The police moved in en masse

but then withdrew to try to de-escalate the tension. This left the intersection largely in the hands of the rioters, who attacked Whites and Hispanics. Reginald Denny, a White truck driver who happened to be driving through, was dragged from his cab and brutally beaten; the incident was watched live on TV by millions and has largely come to symbolise the riots.

South Central Los Angeles is relatively typical of Black ghettos in the United States. However, the junction of Florence and Normandie is not in the worst part of the ghetto by any means. It is a relatively well-off Black neighbourhood in which the poverty rate dropped during the 1980s from 33 to only 21 per cent. That the initial outbreak of rioting would occur here, rather than in a more impoverished neighbourhood, is consistent with relative deprivation theories of social unrest.

Figure 7.4

The J-curve hypothesis of relative deprivation.

Relative deprivation is particularly acute when attainments suffer a sudden setback in the context of expectations which continue to rise.

Source: Based on Davies (1969).

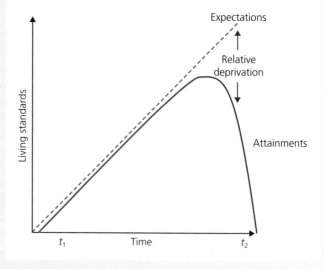

compared with other groups (see also Brewer & Brown, 1998). In this case, the emphasis is on the choice of outgroup with which to compare. In their study of German reunification, Amélie Mummendey and her colleagues observed that East Germans were partly motivated to revolt by comparing their standard of living unfavourably with that of West Germans (Mummendey, Klinke, Mielke, Wenzel & Blanz, 1999). East Germans chose *not* to compare themselves with a variety of European nations whose standard of living was even lower.

Collective protest and social change

Social unrest associated with relative deprivation often represents sustained social protest to achieve social change. However, the study of protest is complex, requiring an integration of constructs from social psychology, sociology and political science, as several European social psychologists have noted (e.g. Klandermans, 1997).

Bert Klandermans (2002) identified three concepts that are fundamental to collective protest:

1. *Injustice* – indignation about how authorities are handling a societal problem, e.g. social inequality, or a violation of human rights. To connect to an actual movement you need to be a sympathiser with a potential ingroup and be aware of a target outgroup that is responsible for your plight.
2. *Efficacy* – a conviction that the situation can be changed by collective action at a reasonable cost. Motivation to participate in action arises from the value that you place on the outcome of protest and the extent to which you believe that the protest will actually deliver the goods.
3. *Identity* – defined by group membership (i.e. social identity).

A social identity analysis, which we deal with in more detail below, has been proposed by the German social psychologists Stefan Stürmer and Bernd Simon (2004). When people identify very strongly with a group, they have a powerfully shared perception of collective injustice, needs and goals. They also share ideas about how they intend to act, they trust and like one another, and are collectively influenced by group norms and legitimate group leaders. Furthermore, group motivation eclipses personal motivation. Provided that members believe that protest is an effective way forward, these processes make participating in collective protest

Collective protest. Social unrest, in this case in Malmo, is usually grounded in a powerful, collective feeling of a minority being treated unjustly.

Source: Bob Strong / Reuters

an effective way forward, these processes make participating in collective protest more likely.

We have looked at approaches to social change against a background of large-scale unrest. In the next section we examine two social psychological theories that have made major contributions to the study of prejudice: intergroup conflict and the nature of social change.

Realistic conflict theory

Where groups compete over scarce resources, intergroup relations become marked by conflict, and ethnocentrism arises. Muzafer Sherif (1966) tested this idea in several famous field experiments at American summer camps for young boys. The general procedure involved three phases:

1. The children arrived at the camp, which, unknown to them, was run by the experimenters. They engaged in various camp-wide activities, through which they formed friendships.
2. The camp was then divided into two groups that split up friendships. The groups were isolated, with separate living quarters and daily activities, and developed their own norms and status differences. The groups made little reference to each other apart from some embryonic ethnocentrism.
3. Next, the groups met in organised intergroup contests. They competed fiercely and became antagonistic, even beyond the contests. Ethnocentrism was amplified along with intergroup aggression and ingroup solidarity. The encounters were often hostile: in one instance when the two groups ate together, the meal was an opportunity to throw food at the other group. Things became so bad that two of three experiments were hastily concluded at this point.

In one experiment, however, it was possible to proceed to a fourth phase:

Superordinate goals
Groups may desire these but they can only be achieved by intergroup cooperation.

4. The two groups were provided with superordinate goals, goals they both desired but were unable to achieve on their own. The groups had to work together in cooperation.

As an example of a superordinate goal that was beyond reach without cooperation, the groups were told that the truck delivering a movie that both groups wanted to watch had become bogged down and would need to be pulled out. It was a case of 'all hands on deck' because the truck was very heavy. Sherif had a wonderful sense of symbolism – the rope used cooperatively by the boys to pull the truck was the same rope that had previously been used in an aggressive tug-of-war between the warring groups. Sherif and colleagues found a gradual improvement in intergroup relations as there were more instances of cooperation to achieve superordinate goals.

There are some notable points about these experiments:

- There was a degree of latent ethnocentrism even before the groups competed (more of this below).
- Prejudice, discrimination and ethnocentrism arose as a consequence of real intergroup conflict.
- The boys did not have authoritarian personalities.

- The less frustrated group (the winners) was usually the one that expressed the greater intergroup aggression.
- Ingroups formed despite the fact that friends (from the first phase) were actually outgroup members.
- Simple contact between members of opposing groups did not improve intergroup relations (see below).

Sherif's explanation was a realistic conflict theory of intergroup behaviour (see Figure 7.5). As with individuals, the nature of the goal relations determines the nature of intergroup relations. Individuals who share goals that require interdependence to be achieved tend to cooperate and form a group. However, individuals who have mutually exclusive goals (i.e. a scarce resource that only one can obtain, such as winning a chess game) engage in competition. This prevents a group forming or can cause an existing group to collapse. Groups with mutually exclusive goals are heading for conflict and ethnocentrism. When shared goals require interdependence to be achieved, i.e. goals are superordinate, conflict is reduced and harmony is encouraged.

Sherif's model is generally supported by other naturalistic experiments. For example, Marilynn Brewer and Donald Campbell (1976) surveyed thirty tribal groups in Africa and found greater derogation of tribal outgroups that lived close by and were thus likely to be direct competitors for scarce resources, such as water and land. (See the third focus question. Jean and Alison have a problem since their 'tribes' live so close to each other.) Sherif's theory makes good sense, and Ronald Fisher (1990, 2005) has outlined how establishing superordinate goals can be applied to help resolve conflict between communities, and even between nations.

Realistic conflict theory
Sherif's theory of intergroup conflict that explains intergroup behaviour in terms of the nature of goal relations between groups.

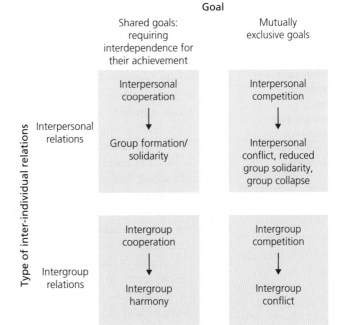

Figure 7.5

Realistic conflict theory.

Goal relations between individuals and groups determine cooperative or competitive interdependence, and thus the nature of interpersonal and intergroup behaviour.

Source: Based on Sherif (1966).

At the same time the theory has a problem: because so many variables are in play in field studies, how can we know that it is the nature of goal relations that ultimately determines intergroup behaviour? Perhaps the results are due to nothing more than the cooperative or competitive nature of a particular interaction. Or might it be merely the existence of two separate groups? These questions are pursued in the next section.

Social identity theory

In the early 1970s, researchers at Bristol developed a theoretical approach that stressed the importance of group membership per se in understanding intergroup relations. A person's membership groups in effect define crucial aspects of one's self, and play a major part in how one perceives and behaves towards members of other groups. We will deal with what is social identity theory in more detail below. Let us see how the thinking behind it came about.

Recall that embryonic ethnocentrism was found in the second phase of Sherif's summer camp studies, when groups had just been formed but there was no realistic conflict between them. Other researchers have found that competitive intergroup behaviour spontaneously emerges even when goal relations between groups are not interdependent (Rabbie & Horwitz, 1969), and even under conditions of explicitly non-competitive intergroup relations (Ferguson & Kelley, 1964). What, then, are the minimal conditions for intergroup behaviour: conditions that are both necessary and sufficient for a collection of individuals to be ethnocentric and to engage in intergroup competition?

Minimal groups

Minimal group paradigm
Experimental methodology basis used to demonstrate intergroup discrimination, even when people are categorised on random or trivial criteria.

Henri Tajfel and his colleagues devised an intriguing paradigm to answer this question based on the minimal group paradigm (Tajfel, Billig, Bundy & Flament, 1971). Schoolboys aged 14 and 15 years participated in what they believed was a study of decision making. They were assigned to one of two groups completely randomly, but allegedly because they preferred abstract paintings by one of two artists, Klee and Kandinsky. A boy knew only that he was in the Klee group or the Kandinsky group. Code numbers were used to conceal the identity of all other children in the two groups. Such groups are described in this field of research as 'minimal'.

Each boy then individually distributed points between pairs of recipients identified only by code number and by group membership (Klee versus Kandinsky). The boys understood that at the completion of the task the points would be realised as money and given to each of the two groups. This task was repeated for a number of trials, each time for a different pairing of an ingroup and an outgroup member. No points were available for oneself. Choices of how many points to allocate each time varied across a series of distribution matrices carefully designed to tease out the sort of strategies that a boy might use.

The results from an initial experiment were startling in their time. The children showed a strong bias towards their own group. This was surprising because the groups were indeed minimal. They were created on the basis of a flimsy criterion, had no past history or possible future, the children did not even know the identity of members in either group, and no self-interest was involved in the money distribution task as self was not a recipient.

Subsequent experiments in the same vein used categories that were even more minimal or more direct. For example, Billig and Tajfel (1973) explicitly randomly categorised their participants as X- or Y-group members, thereby eliminating any possibility that they might infer that people in the same group were somehow similar because they preferred the same artist. Another study used actual coins as rewards (Vaughan, Tajfel & Williams, 1981). Children who were either 7 or 12 years old simply distributed coins to unidentified ingroup and outgroup members. Marked ingroup bias was reported in these and many other studies.

For some time, research suggested that the mere act of being categorised into a group was enough to produce ethnocentrism and competitive intergroup behaviour (Bourhis, Sachdev & Gagnon, 1994; Tajfel, 1982). As it turns out, social categorisation is necessary but may not be sufficient for intergroup behaviour. It seems that one reason why people identify with groups, even minimal groups, is to reduce subjective uncertainty. By identifying with various groups we can simplify our lives and make our choices of action more predictable. (Subjective uncertainty is discussed further below.) Thus categorisation will produce identification and discrimination only if people identify with the category, and they are more likely to do so if the group categorisation reduces uncertainty.

Social categorisation
Classification of people as members of different social groups.

The upshot is that social categorisation has a pivotal role in intergroup behaviour, as the minimal group studies demonstrated. On this basis Tajfel (1974) developed the concept of social identity. This simple idea has evolved over the years to become perhaps the pre-eminent contemporary social psychological analysis of group processes, intergroup relations and the collective self – *social identity theory* (Tajfel & Turner, 1979).

Social identity and being a group member

Society is structured into distinct social groups that stand in power and status relations to one another (e.g. Blacks and Whites in the United States, Sunnis and Shi-ites in Iraq). The central premise of the social identity approach is that social categories of all kinds (e.g. a nation, a university or a hobby group) provide members with a *social identity* – a definition and evaluation of who one is. Social identities not only describe attributes. They also prescribe what one should think and how one should behave as a member. For example, Drina is Romani. She lives in Spain but she defines and evaluates herself, and thinks and behaves, in a characteristically Romani way.

Social identity is that part of the self-concept that develops from group membership. In line with what we have discussed in earlier chapters, this means that people will conform to ingroup norms and show both ingroup solidarity and ingroup favouritism. When they think about themselves, fellow ingroupers and outgroupers will use relevant group *stereotypes*.

Ingroup favouritism
Behaviour that favours one's own group over other groups.

Social identity can be distinguished from personal identity. The latter is that part of the self-concept that derives from individual traits and the unique relationships we have with other people (Turner, 1982). Personal identity is associated with individual and interpersonal behaviour rather than with group and intergroup behaviours. People have as many social identities as they have groups they identify with; they have as many personal identities as they have unique attributes or close relationships they use to define themselves. Despite our many identities, we experience the self as an integrated whole with an unbroken biography. To think of our self as fragmented rather than coherent might point to a psychopathology (see Chapter 3).

Self-categorisation theory
Turner and associates' theory of how the process of categorising oneself as a group member produces social identity and group and intergroup behaviours.

Meta-contrast principle
The prototype of a group is that position within the group that has the largest ratio of 'differences to ingroup positions' to 'differences to outgroup positions'.

Depersonalisation
The perception and treatment of self and others not as unique individual persons but as prototypical embodiments of a social group.

Self-categorisation theory

The original analysis offered by social identity theory focused on intergroup relations (Tajfel & Turner, 1979). John Turner and his colleagues later showed how self-categorisation is related to group processes as a whole – self-categorisation theory (Turner, Hogg, Oakes, Reicher & Wetherell, 1987). Both of these theories have been developed largely by social psychologists whose origins were in Europe.

People mentally represent social categories and groups as prototypes. A *prototype* is a fuzzy set of attributes (perceptions, beliefs, attitudes, feelings, behaviours) that describes one group and distinguishes it from relevant other groups. Prototypes obey the meta-contrast principle – a contrast between contrasts, e.g. chairs can be different, but they are more alike to each other than they are to tables. We form categories so that the differences between them exceed the differences within them. The content of prototypes can vary according to the social context. Take an example: Nick Hopkins and Christopher Moore (2001) found that Scots perceived themselves to be different from the English, but that this perceptual difference was diminished when they made comparisons between Scots and Germans. Even though the Scots might not like it, they saw their prototype moving a little closer to the English prototype!

When we categorise people we see them through the lens of the relevant ingroup or outgroup prototype. We view them as members of a group rather than as unique individuals, and this leads to depersonalisation. We judge them as more similar to a relevant prototype than they probably are, drawing on our group stereotypes, and in the case of outgroups we fall prey to ethnocentrism. When we categorise ourselves, exactly the same happens – we define, perceive and evaluate ourselves in terms of our ingroup prototype and behave in line with it. When we self-categorise we bring ourselves into line with the norms of our ingroup at that moment: we conform to group norms (see Chapter 5).

How social identity works

When does a particular social identity become *salient* and so trigger social categorisation? Penny Oakes and her other Bristol university colleagues (e.g. Oakes & Turner, 1990) drew on work in social cognition to answer this question, and partly on an older tradition in perception research (Bruner, 1957). Social categories are selectively activated, either because they are highly accessible to us in memory (e.g. we use them frequently or have used them recently; see Chapter 2) or because they fit well with the cues in the present context. An example of a context effect was an old questionnaire study by Lutfy Diab (1963) in Beirut. When Arab-Moslem students selected traits that applied to Americans, the stereotype for Americans was more positive when other unpopular groups were included in the same task, e.g. Algerians and Egyptians.

An individual's social identity serves two important functions:

1. *Self-enhancement*: groups stand in status and prestige relations to one another, and we recognise this. Groups compete to be different in favourable ways to achieve positive distinctiveness, and this provides a positive social identity for the individual member.
2. *Subjective uncertainty reduction*: in life, we want to know who we are. We also want to know how to relate to and what to expect from others, how to make life predictable and to plan effective action. By identifying with groups we reduce uncertainty and address these concerns (Hogg, 2007b).

Social identity and intergroup relations

In its original form, the social identity approach offered an explanation of intergroup conflict and social change (Tajfel, 1974). In pursuing positive social identity, groups and individuals can adopt various strategies. The choice is determined by what we believe about the nature of relations between our group and other groups (Ellemers, 1993; Tajfel & Turner, 1979). These strategies are shown in Figure 7.6.

Beliefs about intergroup relations are ideological constructs that may or may not accord with reality. For example, is it actually possible to 'pass' from a lower-status group to a higher-status group? A social mobility belief system inhibits *group* action by a subordinate group. Instead, it encourages individuals to break from their group and try to be accepted in the dominant group. The belief in being mobile is enshrined in political systems founded on individualism, which is more common in Western cultures (see Chapter 11). Bearing these points in mind, how would you estimate Katrina's chances of success in the fourth focus question?

People who think that an intergroup boundary is impermeable to 'passing', such as the Hindu caste system in India, have another solution: adopt a social change belief system. However, there is a proviso. Is the status quo (the status and power hierarchy) perceived to be secure or insecure? If it is secure (i.e. perceived as stable and legitimate), people may not be able to imagine an alternative social structure (i.e. no cognitive alternatives exist), let alone a path to real social change.

Social mobility belief system
Belief that intergroup boundaries are permeable. Thus, it is possible for someone to pass from a lower-status into a higher-status group to improve social identity.

Individualism
Societal structure and world view in which people prioritise standing out as an individual over fitting in as a group member.

Social change belief system
Belief that intergroup boundaries are impermeable. Therefore, a lower-status individual can improve social identity only by challenging the legitimacy of the higher-status group's position.

Cognitive alternatives
Belief that the status quo is unstable and illegitimate, and that social competition with the dominant group is the appropriate strategy to improve social identity.

Belief system	Type of strategy to improve social identity	Specific tactics
Social mobility	Individual mobility	'Exit' and 'passing': assimilation into high-status group
Social change → No cognitive alternatives	Social creativity	New dimensions of intergroup comparison
		Redefining value of existing dimensions
		Comparison with different outgroup(s)
Social change → Cognitive alternatives	Social competition	Civil rights activity, political lobbying, terrorism, revolution, war, etc.

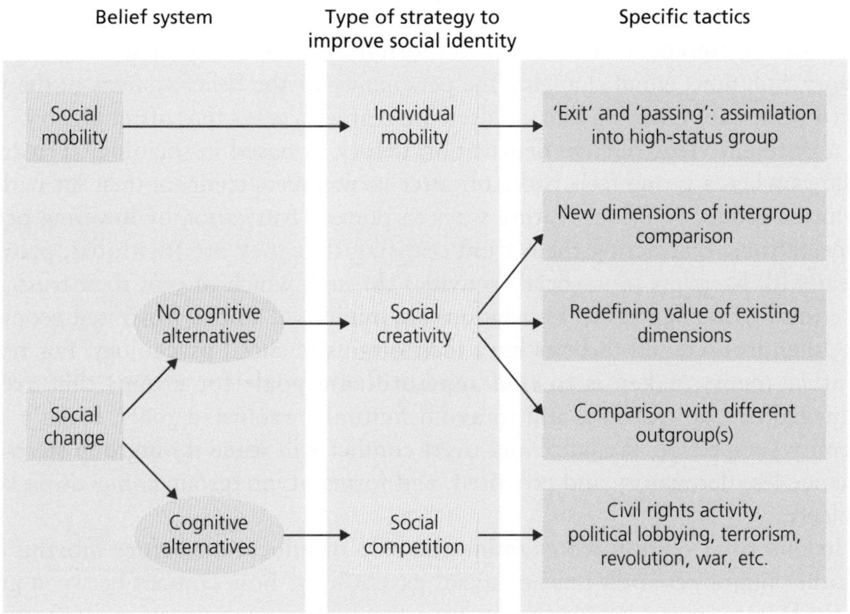

Figure 7.6

Belief structures and strategies for improving social identity.

Beliefs about the nature of intergroup relations influence the general strategies and specific tactics that group members can adopt to try to maintain or achieve positive social identity.

Social creativity
Group-based behavioural strategies that improve social identity but do not directly attack the dominant group's position.

Subordinate groups sometimes adopt social creativity strategies, such as highlighting novel features that favour their own group. For example, the French social psychologist Gerard Lemaine (1974) studied children in groups with unequal resources who were competing to build the best hut. To offset their handicap and perhaps distract the judges, disadvantaged groups would emphasise how good a garden they had made. In other contexts, creative solutions include converting an ingroup attribute from a negative to a positive (e.g. 'Black is beautiful'); or making comparisons with another group of supposedly lower status (e.g. an experienced worker feeling superior to a novice).

Social competition
Group-based behavioural strategies that improve social identity by directly confronting the dominant group's position in society.

If the status quo is insecure (perceived as unstable and illegitimate), and if cognitive alternatives exist (a different social order), then social competition follows. This means direct intergroup conflict such as political action, collective protest, revolutions and war. This is the stuff of *social protest*, the seeds of which are also described in *system justification theory*, topics that we discussed earlier in this chapter.

Social identity theory has been tested successfully in a range of laboratory and naturalistic contexts (Hogg & Abrams, 1988; Ellemers, 1993), and has been elaborated and extended in many areas of social psychology, including the study of language and ethnicity (see Chapter 11).

Improving intergroup relations

The variety of theories dealt with in this chapter spawn different emphases in solving prejudice and intergroup conflict. Some revolve around personality or individual differences, such as the authoritarian personality or social dominance theory. Solutions entail changing the personality or the belief systems of the prejudiced person, or ensuring that children are reared in ways that offset bigotry.

A different view, relative deprivation theory, is based in sociology. Frustration follows when a group feels badly off after its members compare their lot with that of an outgroup. Solutions feature ways to prevent frustration by lowering people's expectations, distracting them from realising that they are frustrated, providing them with harmless (non-social) activities through which to vent their frustration, or ensuring that aggressive associations are minimised among frustrated people.

Other group-based theories have their origins in social psychology. For realistic conflict theory, a key is to find superordinate goals for groups that are best achieved by cooperation, and to avoid mutually exclusive goals. From a social identity perspective, prejudice and overt conflict will wane if outgroup stereotypes become less derogatory and polarised, and forms of intergroup competition bypass violence.

In this final section we examine the role of education before moving on to another major research field in social psychology: how contact between groups might help to improve relations between them. (For a recent review of the contact hypothesis, educational strategies and methodological issues in prejudice reduction research, see Paluck and Green, 2009.) And last, we look at several tools that have been developed in real-life settings that try to settle intergroup disputes.

Educating for tolerance

Can reactions to others based on powerful, negative, affect-laden stereotypes be reduced? The task is difficult, given how resistant to change most extreme stereotypes and strongly held attitudes are (see Chapter 4). However, prejudice is partly based on ignorance. Education that promotes tolerance of diversity may reduce bigotry, particularly in children (Stephan & Stephan, 2001). Despite this, formal education has only a marginal impact if children remain exposed to prejudice in the world outside the classroom.

One strategy of value for children is for them to experience being stigmatised and then victimised, as demonstrated in a short movie *The Eye of the Storm* by Jane Elliot, an Iowa school teacher. She divided her class of very young children into those with blue eyes and those with brown eyes. For one day the 'brown eyes', and then for different day the 'blue eyes', were assigned inferior status: they were ridiculed, denied privileges, accused of being dull, lazy and sloppy, and made to wear a special collar. Being stigmatised was unpleasant enough to make the children think twice about being prejudiced against others.

So there is hope among the young. Children trained to be *mindful* of others – to think about others not as stereotypes but as complex, whole individuals – may well change. For example, the applied social psychologist Ellen Langer and her colleagues found that young children could be educated to be more thoughtful towards the handicapped (Langer, Bashner & Chanowitz, 1985).

Education and sex-stereotypy. Sweden debates ways to break down traditional stereotypes of how boys and girls play. Will this particular measure work?

Source: Janine Wiedel Photolibrary / Alamy

Contact between groups

Unfavourable attitudes towards outgroups are at the heart of prejudice and conflict. Negative beliefs are enshrined in widespread social ideologies and are maintained by lack of access to contrary information. In most cases, such isolation is reinforced by real social and physical isolation of different groups from one another – the Protestant–Catholic situation in Northern Ireland is a case in point (Hewstone *et al.*, 2005). There is often simply a chronic lack of intergroup contact, and little opportunity to meet real members of another group. The scenario in which two groups really do meet presents difficulties but has the potential of a better future for both (see Box 7.5).

Contact hypothesis
The view that bringing members of opposing social groups together will improve intergroup relations and reduce prejudice and discrimination.

However, issues remain about what *kind* of effects contact may have (see overviews by Brewer & Miller, 1996, and Pettigrew, 1998). There are interesting possibilities. Will intergroup contact lead people to think that the two groups are more alike? Will favourable attitudes brought about by contact between individuals generalise to attitudes between groups?

Research and applications 7.5
Can intergroup contact improve intergroup relations?

Historically, groups are kept apart by educational, occupational, cultural and material differences. Walter and Cookie Stephan (Stephan & Stephan 1985, 2000) have argued that a major concern is anxiety about negative consequences of contact for oneself. This anxiety is one of the most significant hurdles to greater intergroup contact, and arises from several sources:

- *Realistic threat* – a sense of menace to the very existence of one's group.

- *Symbolic threat* – trouble posed by an outgroup for one's norms, values and morals.

- *Intergroup anxiety* – a concern for self (e.g. embarrassment) experienced during intergroup interactions.

- *Negative stereotypes* – leading to fear of intergroup anxiety (imagined or anticipated).

Under the right circumstances, however, contact can reduce anxiety and improve intergroup relations (Pettigrew & Tropp, 2006). This is the **contact hypothesis** and was first proposed by Gordon Allport (1954b) in the very year that the United States Supreme Court paved the way for the racial desegregation of the American education system. Here are Allport's conditions for contact:

- It should be prolonged and involve cooperative activity rather than casual and purposeless interaction. It was precisely this sort of contact that improved relations in Sherif's (1966) summer camp studies.

- It should occur within the framework of official and institutional support for integration. Although legislation against discrimination, or for equal opportunities, will not in itself abolish prejudice, it provides a social climate that is conducive to the emergence of more tolerant social practices.

- It should bring together people or groups of equal social status. Unequal status contact is more likely to confirm stereotypes and thus entrench prejudices.

For the role that the Internet can play in intergroup contact, together with a review of the contact hypothesis by the Israeli social psychologists Yair Amichai-Hamburger and Katelyn McKenna (2006), go to http://jcmc.indiana.edu/vol11/issue3/amichai-hamburger.html.

Will contact lead to perceived similarity?

Contact causes people to recognise that they are in fact a great deal more similar than they had thought and hence to get to like one another (see Chapter 10). There are some problems with this perspective. Some groups such as those from different cultures can be very different, and contact may highlight more profound or more widespread differences than thought. This can reduce liking further and worsen intergroup attitudes (Bochner, 1982). Furthermore, intergroup attitudes are not merely a matter of ignorance, unfamiliarity or assumed lack of similarity. There can be a conflict of interest, such as competition for jobs, or a difference in status and power relationships (discussed earlier). New knowledge through contact is not a guarantee that attitudes will change.

Will personal experience generalise to a group?

Research indicates that when contact improves attitudes towards other individuals this does not generalise to the group as a whole (Amir, 1976; Cook, 1978). This may be because what we like to call intergroup contact is actually *interpersonal* contact. The others are treated as individual cases, not as members of a group. 'The exception proves the rule': if you like Berndt as a friend, possibly the fact that he happens to be Swedish is irrelevant.

There is some experimental evidence that it can work. If two individuals cooperate happily on a task and one sees the other as typical of an outgroup, attitudes towards that outgroup may improve (Wilder, 1984). However, where real intergroup conflict exists (e.g. between Catholics and Protestants in Northern Ireland), it may be almost impossible to distract people from their group affiliations. Research in this challenging area continues. Gaertner's common ingroup identity model (Gaertner & Dovidio, 2000; Gaertner, Rust, Dovidio, Bachman & Anastasio, 1996) suggests that if members of opposing groups can be encouraged to be more inclusive, by recategorising themselves as members of the same group, intergroup attitudes will, by definition, not only improve but actually disappear.

Common ingroup identity model
Members of two groups recategorise themselves as members of the one social entity.

Contact policy in multicultural contexts

Initially, it might seem that the most non-discriminatory and unprejudiced way to approach inter-ethnic relations is to be 'colour-blind': that is, to ignore group differences completely (Berry, 1984; Schofield, 1986). This is a 'melting-pot' policy, where all groups are ostensibly treated as equal, but it can also amount to assimilation (discussed in Chapter 11). There are problems with this approach:

Assimilation
The merging of a subordinate group or culture into a dominant group or culture.

- Discrimination has acted to disadvantage certain groups (e.g. regarding education or health). Unless corrected the disadvantage will simply persist.
- It ignores the reality of ethnic and cultural differences (e.g. the Muslim dress code for women).
- The melting pot is not really a melting pot at all, but rather a 'dissolving' pot. Ethnic minorities are dissolved, assimilated and stripped of their cultural heritage and cease to exist.

The extensive riots in France in November 2005 have been attributed to that country's adoption of cultural monism and ethnic assimilation – an approach that does not formally recognise cultural or ethnic differences within France despite the presence of huge numbers of North African Muslims. This assimilationist policy has, ironically, created ghettos of cultural disadvantage and associated discrimination and prejudice.

Multiculturalism
The way that a society manages and maintains the identity of its diverse cultures.

The alternative to assimilationism is multiculturalism, a topic analysed in depth by Maykel Verkuyten (2006) in dealing with the place of Turkish Dutch people within a dominant society of the ethnic Dutch. This approach aims for a multicultural society in which intergroup relations between the constituent groups are harmonious. However, multiculturalism may need to be implemented carefully for it not to sustain hidden conflicts and nourish separatism (also see Chapter 11). Instances of difficulties that can be experienced have occurred in Britain and Australia, two countries that in different ways provide strong political support for multiculturalism. It was disaffiliated Muslim youths who bombed public transport in London in July 2005, and in Australia there were large anti-Lebanese riots in Sydney in December 2005.

Superordinate goals

Sherif (1966) managed to improve intergroup relations between warring factions of boys by arranging for them to cooperate to achieve several superordinate goals (shared goals that were unachievable by either group alone). The European Union has provided a natural laboratory to study the effect of a superordinate identity (European) on inter-subgroup relations (between nations within Europe). Here are some examples of such work. Xenia Chryssochoou (2000) has explored what meanings Greek and French nationals give to their national identity – being 'French' or 'Greek' – but also to being 'European' as well. An interesting detail uncovered in this work was that being European allowed people to now contrast themselves with a powerful outgroup, the United States. Marco Cinnirella and Saira Hamilton (2007) asked the question 'Are all Britons reluctant Europeans?' And Carmen Huici and her colleagues investigated how salient a European identity might be among Scottish and Italian samples (Huici et al., 1997).

We noted earlier in this chapter that there is an important qualification to the use of superordinate goals. They do not reduce intergroup conflict if the groups fail to achieve the goal. Intergroup relations can worsen when groups fail to achieve a common goal: failure can be attributed, rightly or wrongly, to the other group (Worchel & Novell, 1980). Take an example. The 1982 Falklands conflict between Britain and Argentina provided an opportunity (a superordinate goal) within Argentina to reduce factional conflict. The cooperative exercise by the Argentines failed when Argentina lost the war. Because the junta could easily be blamed for the outcome, there was renewed factional conflict and the junta was overthrown (Latin American Bureau, 1982).

Groups that negotiate

Can groups negotiate their way out of trouble? In Box 7.6 we list several tools of negotiation that have been widely used in real life.

The bottom line is that negotiating to reduce conflict can be a difficult task. Impediments include the variety of individual biases that operate in perception and attribution (see Chapter 2) as well as those that serve self-interest (see Chapter 3). Add to these a common failure to adopt the perspective of another person and we have a recipe for failure. Leigh Thompson and Adam Galinksy are two experts in conflict resolution who have researched these questions extensively (e.g. Galinsky, Mussweiler & Medvec, 2002; Thompson & Loewenstein, 2003). In an intergroup context there are further complexities. A negotiator has constituents and is constrained to act on behalf of a group. Add to this, many crucial negotiations are between cultures and are beset by a host of cross-cultural communication issues (Smith, Bond & Kağitçibaşi, 2006).

Reducing intergroup conflict. Can negotiation and mediation bring intergroup cooperation to Jerusalem?

Source: Matty Stern / U.S. Embassy / Handout / Reuters

Bargaining
Process of intergroup conflict resolution where representatives reach agreement through direct negotiation.

Mediation
Process of intergroup conflict resolution where a neutral third party intervenes in the negotiation process to facilitate a settlement.

Arbitration
Process of intergroup conflict resolution in which a neutral third party is invited to impose a mutually binding settlement.

Real world 7.6
Popular tools used to reduce intergroup conflict

Bargaining

When people are bargaining on behalf of groups to which they belong, they often do so more fiercely than if they were simply bargaining for themselves, especially if they are aware of pressure from their constituents (Carnevale, Pruitt & Britton, 1979). At the intergroup level an impasse is likely, as two American presidents have found. In the media-orchestrated bargaining over the plight of Kuwait in 1990 between George Bush senior and Saddam Hussein, Bush threatened to 'kick Saddam's ass' and Hussein threatened to make 'infidel' Americans 'swim in their own blood' – a bad start. The family affair continued in 2006 when George Bush Jr and the Iranian president Mähmoud Ahmadinejad traded insults. Ahmadinejad reminded Bush that he was an infidel, and the latter accused the former of being a member of the 'axis of evil' – another bad start.

Ian Morley and his colleagues have observed that a group can be fearful of a 'sell-out' if their negotiator appears to get too friendly with the other side, and that intergroup bargaining is part of a wider context: the relationship between the groups in question (Morley & Stephenson, 1977; Morley, Webb & Stephenson, 1988). Even if a specific problem is solved, broader intergroup issues way well remain unchanged.

Mediation

Mediation by a third party can break a deadlock. Rodney Lim and Peter Carnevale (1990) found that an effective mediator needs sufficient power to exert pressure but must also be seen as impartial and trustworthy. Mediators can: reduce the heat associated with deadlock; encourage understanding and establish trust; propose novel compromises that suggest a win–win situation; help both

▶

parties to retreat gracefully from untenable positions without losing face; reduce conflict within a group and clarify how it can reach internal consensus.

History records some effective mediators. Henry Kissinger's shuttle diplomacy involved meeting each side separately over two years after the 1973 Arab–Israeli conflict. This led to Israel and its Arab neighbours reaching some agreement. Later in that decade, Jimmy Carter used the wonders of seclusion by closeting President Sadat of Egypt with Prime Minister Begin of Israel at Camp David near Washington DC. Their agreement ended a state of war that had existed between Israel and Egypt since 1948.

Arbitration

When intergroup conflict is intractable the last resort is **arbitration**. A mediator or other third party is invested with the power to impose a mutually binding settlement. Dean Pruitt (1998), a specialist in conflict resolution by negotiation, has noted that when arbitration is invoked as a looming second stage to resolve an impasse, parties in the dispute are encouraged to reach an agreement in the first stage by mediation. Arbitration is a common legal procedure, but has also an international application in peacekeeping activities controlled by the United Nations.

Summary

- Prejudice consists of derogatory attitudes that dehumanise another group. There are pervasive prejudices based on ethnicity and sex. There are more subtle forms based on age, sexual orientation, and physical and mental handicap.

- Discrimination is behaviour that often, though not always, follows from the attitudes that underlie prejudice, though legislation and social disapproval may restrict it to 'milder' forms of discrimination. In its most extreme form discrimination can lead to mass killings.

- Prejudice can be difficult to detect when it is expressed covertly or in restricted contexts. It may not be noticed as it is so often imbedded in ordinary everyday assumptions, language and discourse.

- Victims of prejudice suffer material and psychological disadvantage, low self-esteem, stigma and depressed aspirations. Although sex stereotypes are now relatively less blatant, women remain less visible in higher-status 'masculine' positions.

- Prejudice may flow from people with prejudiced personalities that develop in restrictive families. Even so, institutional factors that sustain prejudice are stronger determinants. Individual explanations do not deal well with the widespread collective nature of prejudice.

- Social unrest and collective protest happens when groups rather than individuals subjectively feel relatively deprived. This can happen when their outcomes are compared with their aspirations or the lot of their group as a whole is compared with that of another group.

- Competition for scarce resources is fertile ground for intergroup conflict. Cooperation to achieve a superordinate (shared) goal helps reduce conflict.

- Categorising people into groups may be the only necessary precondition for being a group and engaging in intergroup behaviour, provided that people identify with the category.

- When people self-categorise they identify with a group and behave as group members. Social comparison and the need for self-esteem motivate groups to compete in different ways for positive social identity.

- Prejudice, discrimination and intergroup conflict are difficult to reduce. Education and working towards shared goals may help. Contact between groups is useful under special conditions, but random contact is not effective.

- Tools that can help reduce intergroup conflict include bargaining, mediation and arbitration.

Literature, film and TV

Hotel Rwanda

Chilling 2004 film directed by Terry George, starring Don Cheadle and Nick Nolte. Set against the backdrop of the Rwandan genocide – a period of 100 days in 1994 when Hutus massacred between 500 000 and one million Tutsis. A Hutu hotel manager shelters Tutsi refugees in his Belgian-owned luxury hotel in Kigali.

Mississippi Burning

A 1988 film by Alan Parker, starring Gene Hackman and William Dafoe, is a classic portrayal of old-fashioned overt racial prejudice in the American south – Ku Klux Klan and all.

Conspiracy

This 2001 film with Kenneth Branagh and Colin Firth is a chilling dramatisation of the top-secret two-hour Nazi meeting in which fifteen men debated and ultimately agreed upon Hitler's 'Final Solution', the extermination of the entire Jewish population of Europe. The film recreates one of the most infamous gatherings in world history. This is relevant not only to topics of dehumanisation and genocide but also group decision making in general.

Far from Heaven

A 2002 film by Todd Haynes, with Dennis Quaid and Julianne Moore, is set in 1950s middle-America, this is a powerful portrayal of intolerance and prejudice (racism and homophobia) against a backdrop of ultra-conservative attitudes.

The Boy in the Striped Pyjamas

Mark Herman's 2008 film concerns a young boy, Bruno, befriending another boy, Shmuel, who wears strange striped pyjamas and lives behind an electrified fence. Bruno discovers that he is not permitted to be friends with Shmuel. Bruno is German and his father runs a World War Two prison camp for Jews awaiting extermination; and Shmuel who is Jewish is awaiting extermination. A very powerful film that engages with issues of intergroup contact and friendship across group boundaries.

Gran Torino

Clint Eastwood's 2008 film in which he also stars. Set in contemporary Detroit, Eastwood's character, Walt Kowalski, is a proud and grizzled Korean War veteran whose floridly bigoted attitudes are out of step with changing times. Walt refuses to abandon the neighbourhood he has lived in all his life, despite its changing demographics. The film is about his developing friendship with a Hmong teenage boy and his immigrant family – a poignant, and subtly uplifting, commentary on intergroup friendship and the development of intergroup tolerance and respect.

Gandhi

This 1982 classic film by Richard Attenborough, and starring Ben Kingsley as Gandhi, deals with social mobilisation, social action and collective protest. It shows how Gandhi was able to mobilise India to oust the British. The film touches on prejudice and group decision making.

Germinal

Emile Zola's 1885 novel draws attention to the misery experienced by poor French people during France's Second Empire. The descriptions of crowd behaviour are incredibly powerful, and were drawn upon by later social scientists, such as Gustave Le Bon, to develop their theories of collective behaviour.

Gulliver's Travels

Jonathan Swift's 1726 satirical commentary on the nature of human beings is relevant to virtually all the themes in our text; however, the section on Big-Endians and Little-Endians is particularly relevant to this chapter on intergroup behaviour. Swift provides a hilarious and incredibly full and insightful description of a society that is split on the basis of whether people open their boiled eggs at the big or the little end – highly relevant to the minimal group studies in this chapter.

The Road to Wigan Pier

George Orwell's 1937 novel, capturing the plight of the English working class, is a powerful, and strikingly contemporary, portrayal of relative deprivation.

Guided questions

- Blatant racism may be publicly censured yet still lurk in the background. How might you detect it? One method is the Implicit Association Test, a technique discussed by Mahzarin Banaji in Chapter 7 of MyPsychLab at www.mypsychlab.co.uk.

- What is the background to the study of the *authoritarian personality*?

- According to Sherif, prejudice arises when *intergroup goals* are incompatible. What does this mean? Did he offer a solution?

- What is *social identity*? How are minority group members' beliefs about intergroup relations important in planning for *social change*?

- Trying to reduce prejudice by simply providing *intergroup contact* between people from different groups may not work very well. Why?

- Is it possible for a teacher's expectations of a pupil's educational capacity – for better or for worse – to influence the intellectual development of that pupil? Robert Rosenthal discusses research dealing with the 'Pygmalion effect', or the self-fulfilling prophecy, in Chapter 7 of MyPsychLab at www.mypsychlab.co.uk.

Learn more

Brewer, M. B. (2003). *Intergroup relations* (2nd ed). Philadelphia, PA: Open University Press. A readable overview of research on intergroup relations, which includes coverage of issues directly relating to prejudice.

Brown, R. J. (1995). *Prejudice: Its social psychology*. Oxford, UK: Blackwell. Styled as the sequel to Allport's classic 1954 book, *The nature of prejudice*, this is an accessible, detailed and comprehensive coverage of what social psychology has learned about prejudice.

Brown, R. J., & Gaertner, S. (eds) (2001). *Blackwell handbook of social psychology: Intergroup processes*. Oxford, UK: Blackwell. An extensive collection of twenty-five chapters from leading social psychologists, covering the entire field of intergroup processes.

Dovidio, J. F., Glick, P., & Rudman, L. A. (eds) (2005). *On the nature of prejudice: Fifty years after Allport*. Malden, MA: Blackwell. In commemorating Gordon Allport's classic work on prejudice and discrimination, a group of international scholars examine the current state of knowledge in the field.

Hogg, M. A. (2006). Social identity theory. In P. J. Burke (ed), *Contemporary social psychological theories* (pp. 111–136). Palo Alto, CA: Stanford University Press. Up-to-date and easily readable overview of social identity theory.

Hogg, M. A., & Abrams, D. (eds) (2001). *Intergroup relations: Essential readings*. Philadelphia, PA: Psychology Press. Annotated collection of key publications on intergroup relations. There is an introductory overview chapter and commentary chapters introducing each reading.

Paluck, E. L., & Green, D. P. (2009). Prejudice reduction: What works? A review and assessment of research and practice. *Annual Review of Psychology*, 60, 339–360. An up-to-date review of educational approaches and interventions that have shown promise for dealing with prejudice.

Pruitt, D. G. (1998). Social conflict. In D. T. Gilbert, S. T. Fiske, & G. Lindzey (eds), *The handbook of social psychology* (4th ed, Vol. 2, pp. 470–503). New York: McGraw-Hill. Good overview that also covers sociocognitive aspects of intergroup behaviour.

Stangor, C. (ed) (2000). *Stereotypes and prejudice: Essential readings*. Philadelphia, PA: Psychology Press. Annotated collection of key publications on stereotyping and prejudice, but also covers some cognitive aspects of intergroup relations. There is an introductory overview chapter and commentary chapters introducing each reading.

Wright, S. C., & Taylor, D. M. (2003). The social psychology of cultural diversity: Social stereotyping, prejudice, and discrimination. In M. A. Hogg & J. Cooper (eds), *The Sage handbook of social psychology* (pp. 432–457). London: Sage. A comprehensive overview of the current state of research on prejudice and discrimination. It also deals with stereotyping and prejudice reduction.

Refresh your understanding, assess your progress and go further with interactive summaries, questions, podcasts, videos and much more on the website accompanying the book: **www.mypsychlab.co.uk**.

Chapter 8

Hurting other people

What to look for

- What aggression means and how can we define it

- Biological approaches: Freudian theory, ethology and the role of evolution

- How being frustrated or aroused can trigger aggression

- Learning to be aggressive

- Effects of violence in the mass media

- Trains of thought and responding aggressively

- Personal factors versus situational factors

- Aggression at the extreme: war

- Methods we can use to reduce aggression

Focus questions

1. Mary is sarcastic to her boyfriend, Tony, and circulates nasty rumours about him, but she never pushes or shoves him. Tony is never sarcastic to Mary and never circulates rumours about her, but he does push and shove her. Who is more 'aggressive'?

2. We've all seen those nature movies – a nasty looking pack of African hunting dogs viciously tearing some poor little creature to bits and snarling aggressively at each other. Are humans like this? How far does animal behaviour inform our understanding of human aggression?

3. According to your neighbour, watching violent movies and playing gory computer games is a good way to let off steam. Can you counter this view? For an example based on a correlation between childhood exposure to TV violence and levels of aggressiveness ten years later, go to Chapter 8 of MyPsychLab at www.mypsychlab.co.uk.

4. Tom has quite a collection of favourite porn sites. His girlfriend knows this and asks him to give his habit up. Tom says: 'It doesn't hurt anyone. I'm not turning in to a rapist, you know!' As a budding social psychologist, how would you advise him?

Source: Charles Platiau / Reuters

I n Chapters 8 and 9 we look at two conflicting aspects of human nature. People have a nature with different potentials – one is negative and aggressive, while the other is positive and altruistic. What we will find is that the human potential for both kinds of actions have both biological and social roots. Acts that hurt or help others have a genetic underlay, but there is also a capacity to learn and control what we do. This chapter explores how the first of these ideas unfolds.

What is aggression?

What catches your attention about aggression? Is it the latest report of casualties in one of the world's ongoing wars or of civilians killed in a terrorist attack? What about a burglary in your neighbourhood, or reported serious injuries to a child by a close relative? How about a newspaper story of a rape in a nearby town? Some of these – but perhaps not all – are criminal acts against persons or property, and may be shockingly violent. Would unkind words between two people count as aggression? As we shall see, all of these are important issues in our daily lives and qualify to varying degrees as acts of aggression, some fairly trivial and others monstrous.

Defining aggression

Many of us witness occasional aggression and most of us regularly see evidence and symbols of aggressive acts or aggressive people: graffiti, vandalism, violent arguments and weapons. Would you regard wearing a hoodie in a shopping mall as 'in your face'? A wide variety of definitions have been offered for aggression. One simple definition reflected in modern texts is 'the intentional infliction of some type of harm on others'. Consider the components listed in Box 8.1, and ask yourself if you think each qualifies. If you think you know what aggression means, how would you measure it?

Real world 8.1
What does being aggressive mean?

Which actions qualify as aggressive? Is motive important? What about the nature of the target? Are some situations more complex in reaching a decision? Consider whether the following would be included in your list:

- actual harm, but not an unsuccessful act of violence;
- physical injury, but not psychological harm (such as verbal abuse);
- harm to people, but not to animals or property;
- harm to people in war;
- harm in a rule-governed context (such as a boxing match);

- intentional harm, but not negligent harm;
- belief by a victim that harm has occurred;
- an assault in a victim's alleged 'best interests' (such as smacking a child);
- self-injury, such as self-mutilation or suicide.

This list is not exhaustive. Make a list of those that you regard as aggressive actions, and add more if they come to mind. Discuss your list with a friend. Is it difficult to agree on a definition?

Measuring aggression

What is called aggression can vary from one researcher to another, and across different cultures. For example, are bodily cues of anger directed towards someone else the same as actually fighting? Are protests by indigenous peoples about their traditional lands comparable to acts of international terrorism; or is spanking a child in the same category as the grisly deeds of a serial killer?

Even in the experimental tradition, different researchers have used different measures for the same term. Consider the following experimental measures of aggression:

- punching an inflated plastic doll (Bandura, Ross & Ross, 1963);
- pushing a button that is supposed to deliver an electric shock to someone else (Buss, 1961);
- pencil-and-paper ratings by teachers and classmates of a child's level of aggressiveness (Eron, 1982);
- written self-report by institutionalised teenage boys about their prior aggressive behaviour (Leyens, Camino, Parke & Berkowitz, 1975);
- a verbal expression of willingness to use violence in an experimental laboratory setting (Geen, 1978).

Each of these measures has been used as an analogue, or substitute, for the real thing. The major reason for this is ethical (see Chapter 1), since it is extremely difficult to justify an actual physical assault against a person in an experimental setting.

Can we generalise the findings of research using an analogue measure to a larger population in real-life settings? Consider the electric shock machine developed by Buss (1961), which is also similar to the apparatus used by Milgram (1963) in his studies of obedience (see Chapter 5). Don Cherek and his colleagues tested this device among male offenders on parole, comparing those with and those without histories of violence. They found that the violent offenders administered higher levels of shock to an experimental confederate (Cherek, Schnapp, Moeller & Dougherty, 1996). Similarly, there is a parallel between the laboratory and real life for the effects on aggression of alcohol, high temperatures, and violence in the media (topics dealt with below).

Even though this chapter explores only some of the extensive range of behaviour that is labelled 'aggressive', it will become clear that there can be no single definition for an array of complex, and perhaps qualitatively different, phenomena. (How would you address the first focus question?)

Analogue
Device or measure intended to faithfully mimic the 'real thing'.

What do the major theories say?

If aggression is omnipresent, perhaps it is an integral part of human nature? We will see that a biological approach argues that aggression is a basic human instinct, an innate and fixed action pattern that we share with other species. This reasoning can be extended to include the way humans express their emotions (see Chapter 11). It means that aggression must have a genetic basis and probably is an inevitable aspect of being human. Other theorists favour the crucial role that environmental factors play, and remain optimistic that we can prevent and even control violence, even if aggressive tendencies are part of our behavioural repertoire. We explore these different emphases concerning the origins of aggression in this chapter. The immediate challenges for psychologists are to identify the reasons why people aggress against others and to find ways of reducing the harmful effects on the victims, the aggressor and society.

Why do humans aggress against their own kind with viciousness and brutality towards one another in ways and degrees unparalleled in other animals? Explanations of aggression fall into two broad classes, the biological and the social, although this distinction is not rigid. A debate about which of the two is the crucial component is an example of the nature–nurture controversy: is human action determined by our biological inheritance or by our social environment? (This debate also applies to the origins of prosocial behaviour, dealt with in Chapter 9.)

Social theories are different. They have in common the premise that aggressive behaviour is learned, at least partly. Some favour a cognitive basis in which the reasons for and ways of expressing aggression are laid down in memory. There is also room for compromise. A biosocial approach will look for a biological basis for aggression which depends on the social context for behaviour to follow. Cues that trigger this can be quite complex and depend upon learning. We deal next with these two broad classes of explanation, one biological and social.

Biological theories of aggression

First, we consider the nature of an instinct and the way it has been used to account for aggression in the discipline known as ethology. This leads us to discuss modern developments in evolutionary theory, and to look briefly at some limitations of purely biological approaches.

An instinct refers to an innate tendency of living things to behave in a particular way. The behaviour has these characteristics. It is: *unlearned*; *directed to a goal* and terminates when it is reached (e.g. an attack); *beneficial* to the individual and to the species; *adapted* to a normal environment; *shared* by members of the species; and *develops* as the individual matures.

Three major views that deal with human aggression have shared most, if not all, of these biological attributes. All argue cogently that aggressive behaviour is an inherent part of human nature, that we are programmed at birth to act in that way. The oldest is based on psychodynamic theory and dates back to the early part of the twentieth century. More influential in the long term were ideas developed next in ethology, focusing on the behaviour of animals in their natural habitat, and in the more recent and startling field of evolutionary social psychology.

Psychodynamic theory

In *Beyond the Pleasure Principle* (1920/1990), Freud proposed that human aggression stems from an innate death instinct, which is opposed to a life instinct. The death instinct is initially directed at self-destruction, but as a child develops it becomes redirected outwards at others. Freud's background as a physician heavily influenced his theorising; his notion of the death instinct was partly a response to the large-scale destruction of the First World War (see www.historyguide.org/europe/freud_discontents.html). Like the sexual urge, which stems from the life instinct, an aggressive urge from the death instinct builds up from bodily tensions, and needs to be expressed. This is essentially a one-factor theory: aggression builds up naturally and must be released. Freud's ideas were revised by later theorists sympathetic to his position who viewed aggression as a more rational, but nonetheless innate, process whereby people sought a healthy release for primitive survival instincts that are basic to all animal species (Hartmann, Kris & Loewenstein, 1949).

Nature–nurture controversy
Classic debate about whether genetic or environmental factors determine human behaviour. Scientists generally accept that it is an interaction of both.

Ethology
Approach that argues that animal behaviour should be studied in the species' natural physical and social environment. Behaviour is genetically determined and is controlled by natural selection.

Instinct
Innate drive or impulse, genetically transmitted.

Psychodynamic theory
A general approach to human motivation in which the locus is unconscious. In the Freudian version, the underlying mental energy is instinctive and involves a dynamic interplay of the id, ego and superego.

Evolutionary social psychology
An extension of evolutionary psychology that views complex social behaviour as adaptive, helping the individual, kin and the species as a whole to survive.

We can note that Freud was considerably influenced by Charles Darwin's theory of evolution, which was also a precursor to later contributions by the ethologists.

Ethology

In the 1960s, three books made a strong case for the instinctual basis of human aggression by comparing people with animals: Konrad Lorenz's *On Aggression* (1966), Robert Ardrey's *The Territorial Imperative* (1966) and Desmond Morris's *The Naked Ape* (1967). Ethology is a branch of biology devoted to the study of instincts, or fixed action patterns, found among all members of a species when living in their natural environment.

Ethologists stressed the positive, functional aspects of aggression, but they also recognised that, while the potential or instinct for aggression may be innate, actual aggressive behaviour is elicited by specific stimuli in the environment, known as releasers. Lorenz invoked evolutionary principles to propose that aggression has survival value. An animal is considerably more aggressive towards other members of its species, which serves to distribute the individuals and/or family units in a way that makes the most efficient use of available resources, such as sexual selection and mating, food and territory. Most of the time, intraspecies aggression may not even result in actual violence, as one animal will display instinctual threat gestures that are recognised by the other animal, which can then depart the scene – 'the rottweiler growls so the chihuahua runs'. Even if fighting does break out, it is unlikely to result in death, since the losing animal can display instinctual appeasement gestures that divert the victor from actually killing: for example, some animals will lie on the ground belly up in an act of subordination. Over time, in animals such as monkeys that live in colonies, appeasement gestures can help to establish dominance hierarchies or pecking orders. This is a two-factor theory: (1) there is an innate urge to aggress, which (2) depends upon appropriate stimulation by the environmental releasers.

Lorenz extended the argument to humans, who must also have an inherited fighting instinct. Unfortunately, its survival value is much less clear than is the case for other animals. This is largely because humans lack well-developed killing appendages, such as large teeth or claws, so that clearly recognisable appeasement gestures seem not to have evolved. (This may give you a partial answer to the second focus question.)

Ethology implies that: (1) once we start being violent, we do not seem to know when to stop; and (2) in order to kill we generally need to resort to weapons. The advanced technology of our times has produced frightful devices that can slaughter people in large numbers. Furthermore, this can be accomplished at a great distance, so that even the visual and auditory feedback cues of the victim's anguish are not available to persuade the victor to desist. In short, humans have the ability to harm others easily, and with very little effort.

Releasers
Specific stimuli in the environment thought by ethologists to trigger aggressive responses.

Fighting instinct
Innate impulse to aggress which ethologists claim is shared by humans with other animals.

Evolutionary theory

Evolutionary social psychology developed out of evolutionary theory and a field known as sociobiology. It is an ambitious approach that not only assumes an innate basis for aggression but also claims a biological basis for all social behaviour. It is typified in David Buss's book, *Evolutionary Psychology: The New Science of the Mind* (1999). (We revisit the theory in relation to helping behaviour later in this chapter and also when we discuss attraction and close relationships in Chapter 10.)

The evolutionary argument is provocative: specific behaviour has evolved because it promotes the survival of genes that allow the individual to live long enough to pass the same genes on to the next generation. Aggression is adaptive because it must be linked to living long enough to procreate. As such, it is helpful to the individual and to the species. Consider the situation where danger threatens the offspring of a species. Most animals, and usually the mother, will react with a high level of aggression, often higher than they would normally exhibit in other situations. A mother bird, for example, may take life-threatening risks to protect her young. In common with the ethological view, being aggressive also increases access to resources. For humans, the goals for which aggressive behaviour is adaptive include social and economic advantage, either to defend the resources that we already have or to acquire new ones.

Limitations of biological arguments

Explaining aggression purely in terms of biology has appeal, including as it does a popular assumption that violence is part of human nature. It was the seventeenth century philosopher Thomas Hobbes who famously proclaimed that life is 'solitary, poor, nasty, brutish and short'. We have also experienced the power of strong bodily reactions that accompanies anger. Broadly speaking, however, social scientists such as Jeffrey Goldstein question the sufficiency of the explanation of aggression when it is based totally on the cornerstone of instinct, on the grounds that this concept depends on energy that is unknown, with limited observations of actual human behaviour, and of little use in preventing or controlling aggression.

On the other hand, what we do inherit can interact with factors in a social context. For example, if Igor is by nature an irritable person, it might be in his best interests not to be his usual confrontational self (a behavioural trait) when a gang of powerful bullies visit the neighbourhood bar. This is in effect a biosocial approach. We now move on to theories that are avowedly either social or biosocial in their sweep.

Social theories of aggression

While social psychologists generally have not favoured theories of aggression defined in terms of instinct, modern evolutionary psychology has stimulated a renewed interest in a biological account. We now consider approaches that emphasise the critical role of learning and of the social context. Some of these nevertheless incorporate a biological element and we refer to them as biosocial theories. The two outlined below propose that a drive (or state of arousal) is a precondition for aggression, although they differ in how internal and external factors are thought to interact to promote aggressive reactions.

Biosocial theories
In the context of aggression, theories that emphasise an innate component, though not the existence of a full-blown instinct.

Frustration and aggression

The link between these concepts was first spelled out in the *frustration–aggression hypothesis*, according to which aggression is a response to an antecedent condition of frustration. It derived from the work of a group of psychologists headed by John Dollard at Yale University in the 1930s and grew from a marriage between Freudian concepts and principles of animal learning theory (Dollard, Doob, Miller,

Mowrer & Sears, 1939). The theory, also used as an explanation of prejudice (see Chapter 7), proposed that aggression was always caused by some kind of frustrating event or situation; conversely, frustration invariably led to aggression.

Frustration-aggression hypothesis

The underlying psychodynamic assumption that a fixed amount of psychic energy is available for the human mind to perform psychological activities, and that the completion of a psychological activity is *cathartic*: that is, it dissipates aroused energy and returns the system to psychological equilibrium. (We return to the notion of catharsis later in this chapter.)

Seeking our personal goals entail the arousal of psychic energy, and if we reach them our achievement is cathartic. However, if we are blocked we become frustrated; but psychic energy remains activated, and our psychological system is in a state of disequilibrium that can be corrected only by aggression. In other words, frustration instigates us to aggress, and this is the only way to achieve catharsis.

Our target is usually the perceived agent of frustration, but in many cases the agent of frustration is amorphous (e.g. a bureaucracy), indeterminate (the economy), too powerful (someone very big and strong wielding a weapon), unavailable (a specific individual bureaucrat), or someone you love (a parent). Consequently, our attempt to aggress is inhibited, but there is a solution: we can *displace* our aggression, which has been induced by frustration, onto an alternative target. This can be a person or an inanimate object that can be legitimately aggressed against without fear. In other words, a scapegoat is found.

Scapegoat
Individual or group that becomes the target for anger and frustration caused by a different individual or group or some other set of circumstances.

The frustration–aggression hypothesis has received considerable criticism over the years. A major obstacle is that frustration is neither necessary nor sufficient for aggression. Aggression can occur in the absence of frustration, and frustration does not necessarily result in aggression (Bandura, 1973; Berkowitz, 1962).

In an attempt to rescue the frustration–aggression hypothesis, Berkowitz (1962) proposed three major changes:

1. The probability of frustration–induced aggression actually being vented is increased by the presence of situational cues to aggression, including past or present associations of a specific group (scapegoat) with conflict or dislike.
2. It is not objective frustration that instigates aggression but the subjective (cognitive) feeling of being frustrated.
3. Frustration is only one of a large number of aversive events (e.g. pain, extreme temperatures and other noxious stimuli) that can instigate aggression.

Despite Berkowitz's efforts, the debate has continued. Let us agree that frustration can make people angry. The same argument can also be true of being in a bad mood. For example, unpleasant music can have this effect – think of a genre that you really don't like. If this were to put you in a bad mood unpleasant thoughts are more likely, i.e. negative stimuli become more accessible in memory (Baumeister, Dale & Sommer, 1998; also see Chapter 2). Anger is a more accurate predictor than frustration for later aggression. Finally, there is little clear evidence that displacement of aggression will occur onto a scapegoat, someone not responsible for the original frustration.

In defence of Dollard and his colleagues, we should note that their main aim was to explain intergroup aggression – specifically, the violence and aggression associated with prejudice (see Chapter 7). An archival study by Hovland and Sears (1940) provides some support for this sort of analysis. They correlated an economic index of frustrated ambitions (the price of cotton) with an index of racial aggression (number of lynchings of Blacks) in the southern United States over a fifty-year period. The two indices were negatively correlated: as the price of cotton fell (frustration), the number of lynchings increased (displaced aggression). The links here have appeal but are also diffuse. More recently, John Dutton and his colleagues have argued that social and economic deprivation was a fact in the 'ethnic cleansing' of the Kurds in Iraq and of non-Serbs in Bosnia (Dutton, Boyanowsky & Bond, 2005).

Despite an intrinsic appeal, the application of the frustration–aggression hypothesis at an intergroup level has other limitations. What needs to be accounted for is how the attitudes and behaviour of a large number of people are regulated and directed in a uniform way against a specific target group. Critics have argued that the hypothesis has generally not worked well in this way. The reason for this is that it is a reductionist approach that tries to account for group behaviour by aggregating the emotional states of individuals who, apparently, do not even communicate with each other (Brown, 2000; Hogg & Abrams, 1988).

We have touched on terms such as anger and mood in this section. Let us see how these play their part in an approach to aggression that invokes a prior state of arousal.

Arousal and aggression

Excitation-transfer model
The expression of aggression is a function of learned behaviour, some excitation from another source, and the person's interpretation of the arousal state.

A later approach that featured a drive concept is Dolf Zillmann's (1979) excitation-transfer model, based on his research in both communication and psychology. Aggression follows when the following elements are in place:

- a learned aggressive behaviour;
- arousal (excitation), which can be from any source;
- the person's interprets this arousal in a way that it seems appropriate to be aggressive.

This arousal can persist for some time and carries over from the original situation to another potentially provoking one, making an aggressive response likely. Look at the example in Figure 8.1. A student has been exercising at the gym and is still physically aroused when driving to the local supermarket. Here, another customer's car sneaks forward into the parking space that the student is trying to reverse into. Although the event might ordinarily be mildly annoying, this time the residual excitation from the gym session (now forgotten) triggers verbal abuse from the student (not you, of course!).

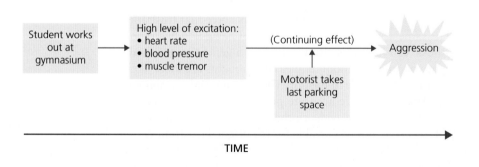

Figure 8.1

Applying the excitation-transfer model of aggression.

Source: Based on Zillmann (1979).

Arousal and aggression. Road rage is often connected with people's mood; but also with more general arousal, such as that caused by physical exercise.

Source: BAE, Inc / Alamy

Perhaps you can think of situations where this model makes sense. Heightened arousal can often lead us to be more aggressive than we are normally: for example, making gestures while driving in stressful traffic conditions; exclaiming with annoyance at our partner when we are already upset about dropping some crockery in the kitchen; severely scolding a young family member who gets lost in a department store. An extreme level of excitement at a football match can erupt in violence between rival groups of fans, as John Kerr (2005) has noted. All of these instances make some sense in terms of Zillmann's theory. It can be applied to the experience of sexual arousal as well (see the section on erotica below), or to any kind of former stimulation whose effects linger over time.

With respect to our discussion of frustration and aggression in the last section, we could now argue that frustration can indeed lead to negative mood states, either acutely (e.g. right now) or chronically (over an extended period of time). As it turns out, it is also possible that arousal which precipitates later aggression can be quite general – its cause may be pleasant, unpleasant or neither.

Learning to be aggressive

The gradual control of aggressive impulses in an infant depends upon an extensive learning process. Social learning theory is a wide-ranging behavioural approach in psychology that was also applied by Albert Bandura (1973) to an understanding of the origins of antisocial behaviour. Although he acknowledged that biological factors provide a basis, Bandura's central proposition was that experience was crucial to when and how aggression is expressed. Through socialisation, children learn to aggress because either they are directly rewarded or someone else appears to be rewarded for their actions. Experience can be direct or vicarious. The idea of learning by direct experience is based on reinforcement principles: a behaviour is maintained by rewards and punishments actually experienced by the child. For example, if Jonathan takes Margaret's biscuit from her, and no one intervenes, then

Social learning theory
The view championed by Bandura that human social behaviour is not innate but learned from appropriate models.

Learning by direct experience
Acquiring a behaviour because we were rewarded for it.

Learning by vicarious experience
Acquiring a behaviour after observing that another person was rewarded for it.

modelling
Tendency for a person to reproduce the actions, attitudes and emotional responses exhibited by a real-life or symbolic model. Also called *observational learning*.

he is reinforced by now having the biscuit. The idea of learning by vicarious experience is a particular contribution of social learning theory: learning occurs by modelling and imitating other people. There is a proviso in social learning theory: the act to be imitated must be seen to be rewarding in some way. Some models, such as parents, siblings and peers, are more appropriate for the child than others. The learning sequence of aggression can be extended beyond direct interactions between people to include media images, such as on television. It can also be applied to understanding how adults learn in later life.

Modelling by children

Children readily mimic the aggressive acts of others. An adult makes a potent model, no doubt because children perceive their elders as responsible and authoritative figures (see also helping behaviour in Chapter 9 and attitude learning in Chapter 4). It is even more disturbing that modelling has been demonstrated when an adult model was seen acting violently on television (see Box 8.2 and Figure 8.2).

The results in Figure 8.2 show that children who saw an adult behave aggressively in any condition behaved more aggressively later. The most telling was the live sequence. However, the finding that the cartoon and videotaped conditions also increased imitative aggression in children provided fuel for scientific and popular audiences who argued that graphic presentations of violence in the media could seriously affect children's later behaviour.

More recently, social learning theory has been blended to an extent with work conducted in social cognition with a particular kind of cognitive schema – the *script* (see Chapter 2). Children learn rules of conduct from those around them, such as when and how to aggress. These rules become internalised. Rowell Huesmann has shown that an aggressive sequence that has been established in childhood is persistent (Huesmann, 1988; Huesmann, Eron, Lefkowitz & Walder, 1984). It can even become a way of life, which is likely to repeat itself by imitation across generations.

The social learning approach has touched a popular chord. If violence is learned, exposure to aggressive and successful models leads people to imitate them. This does not mean that change is impossible. If aggression can be learned, it may be modified and remedied. This is the basis of behaviour modification programmes, such as anger management, used by clinical and community psychologists to help people to find more peaceful ways of dealing with others.

Our discussion of modelling sets up the next topic. We deal with the effects of models and action sequences portrayed in the media can have on others, in particular in the visual media. These effects apply to adults as well as children, and can involve both short-term and long-term behaviour and attitudes.

Role of the mass media

You may have an opinion about the impact of mass media on aggression. What does the psychological evidence say?

Mass media

The media themselves sometimes report a link, such as examples of people emulating violent acts such as assault, rape and murder in an almost identical fashion to portrayals in films or television programmes. Likewise, we hear of the disinhibiting

Research classic 8.2
Sock it to the Bobo doll!

Can merely observing an act be sufficient to learn how to perform it? Albert Bandura and his colleagues tested this idea experimentally at Stanford University. This work stimulated great interest in how social factors impact on learning, and had a long-term effect on thinking about the origins of aggression. According to social learning theory, observing an action produces a cognitive representation in the observer, who then experiences vicarious reinforcement. The outcome for whoever is the model, whether rewarding or punishing, becomes a remote reinforcement for the observer. Could this apply when the action is aggressive?

Bandura, Ross and Ross (1963) asked this question in a study of preschool children who watched a male or female adult play with a then-popular, inflated 'Bobo' doll. There were four conditions:

1 *Live*. An adult came into the room where the child was playing. After playing with some Tinker Toys, the adult then began to act aggressively – sitting on the doll, hitting its nose, banging it on the head with a mallet and kicking it around the room. The words used were 'sock him in the nose', 'pow', 'kick him', 'hit him down' and the like. The child was then left to play with the Bobo doll.

2 *Videotape*. This was the same as the live sequence but had been filmed for the child to view.

3 *Cartoon*. The model acted in the same way but was dressed in a cat uniform, and the room was decorated as if it were in a cartoon.

4 *Control*. The child skipped all of these conditions and went directly to play with the Bobo doll.

Figure 8.2

How children learn aggression through mere observation.

Source: Based on data from Bandura & Walters (1963).

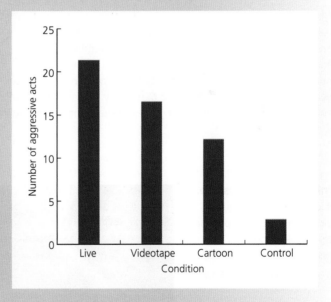

effects of watching an excessive amount of sanitised violence, mostly on television. Some of the relevant laboratory research has been flawed. For example, work on the effects of desensitisation to media violence has often involved exposure to rather mild forms of television violence for relatively short periods of time, as a review by Jonathan Freedman (1984) revealed.

Interestingly, violence can be framed in such a way by movie makers as if it is not really harmful. Bandura (1986) has shown how film and television violence distorts its perceived outcomes by sanitising both the aggressive acts and the

Desensitisation
A serious reduction in a person's responsiveness to material that usually evokes a strong emotional reaction, such as violence or sexuality.

injuries sustained by the victim. Again, an aggressor may be portrayed as the good guy and go unpunished for acts of violence. Social learning theory has taken a strong position on this point: children will readily mimic the behaviour of a model who is reinforced for aggressing, or at least escapes punishment (Bandura, 1973). There has been considerable debate about whether violent video games can also have harmful effects on children (see Box 8.3 and then consider how you would deal with the third focus question).

Research and applications 8.3
Do gory video games make young people more aggressive?

The effects of violence in video games have been frequent debated. Some say violent games make children more aggressive, and social *learning theory* is sympathetic to this view. We noted in Box 8.2, for example, that young children might even imitate cartoon characters. Others believe that children may experience the benefits of *catharsis* from playing the games, by venting some energy and then relaxing. We have already called into question the efficacy of catharsis.

Will children become desensitised to the consequences of acting aggressively in real-life situations by playing out violent scenes? Certainly, the content of the games themselves is of some concern. Sociologist Tracy Dietz (1998) found that nearly 80 per cent of thirty-three popular video games at that time

contained aggression as an immediate objective or the long-term strategy.

In a large-scale study a variety of both aggressive and non-aggressive video games played by Dutch children, Emil van Schie and Oene Wiegman (1997) found:

● no significant relationship between time spent gaming and subsequent levels of aggression;

● video gaming did not replace children's other leisure activities;

● the time spent gaming was positively correlated with the child's measured level of intelligence.

However, they also found that game playing was negatively correlated with behaving prosocially, a topic covered in Chapter 9.

Learning to be aggressive.
Social learning theory argues that violent video games provide models for behaving aggressively.

Source: Pearson Online Database (POD)

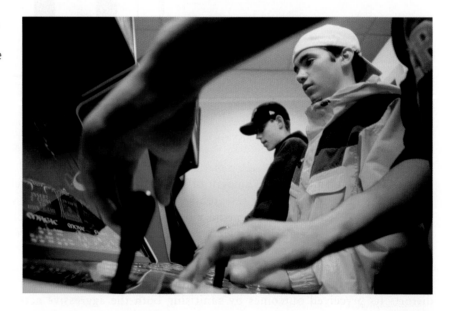

Peter Sheehan (1983) found that the television viewing habits for Australian children aged 8–10 years correlated consistently with their levels of aggressive behaviour. Similarly, longitudinal research has generally reported correlations throughout childhood between repeated exposure to media violence and aggressive behaviour (Huesmann & Miller, 1994). In a real-life setting conducted outside a cinema, Stephen Black and Susan Bevan (1992) studied the aggressive tendencies of Canadians who chose to watch either a very violent or a non-violent film. The participants completed an aggression questionnaire either entering or leaving the cinema. The researchers found higher pre-viewing aggression scores among participants who chose the violent film, and their scores were even higher after seeing the film. Gender differences were minimal (see Figure 8.3).

The bottom line in an extensive and rigorous meta-analysis by Craig Anderson and Brad Bushman (2002b) is that, regardless of how we examine the media violence/aggression link, the outcomes are the same – significant, substantial positive relations. The issue is not whether but *why* violent media increase aggression. Let us seek an answer in a social cognition framework.

Memory gets to work

Social cognition deals with how people process information (see Chapter 2). Research based on theory and techniques in this field has clarified whether aggressive media scenes or descriptions can trigger violence (Berkowitz, 1984; Huesmann, 1988). According to Leonard Berkowitz's (1984) neo-associationist analysis, exposure to real or fictional images of violence can translate later into antisocial acts. Conversely, exposure to images of people helping others can lead later to prosocial acts (see Figure 8.4).

Berkowitz drew from cognitive psychology the idea that memory is a collection of networks, each consisting of nodes. A node can include elements of thoughts and feelings, connected through associative pathways. When a thought comes into

Neo-associationist analysis
A view of aggression according to which mass media may provide images of violence to an audience that later translate into antisocial acts.

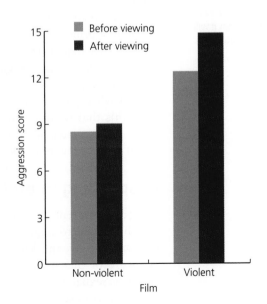

Figure 8.3

Tendency to aggress before and after watching a violent film.

- People who attend screenings of violent films may be generally more disposed to aggression, according to their scores on an aggression questionnaire.
- Viewing a violent film has additional impact, because their aggression scores rise afterwards.

Source: Based on data from Black & Bevan (1992).

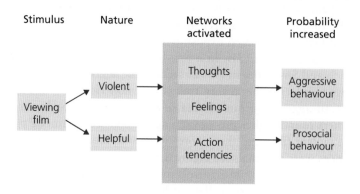

Figure 8.4

'Unconscious' effects of the media: a neo-associationist analysis.

Source: Based on Berkowitz (1984).

focus, its activation radiates out from that particular node via the associative pathways to other nodes, which in turn can lead to a *priming* effect (see Chapter 2). Imagine that Hugo has been watching a movie depicting a violent gang 'rumble'. He might then be primed to have semantically related thoughts, such as *punching, kicking* and *firing a gun*. Hugo's thinking will be mostly automatic, with little conscious awareness. He might also have feelings, such as being a little angry or perhaps even enraged. The chances of an aggressive act have been increased. Hugo will probably be generally aroused. Then, according to the sociologist David Phillips (1986), Hugo might go one step further and commit a copy-cat crime.

Weapons effect
The mere presence of a weapon increases the probability that it will be used aggressively.

Can the mere sight of a gun provoke a person to use it? Perhaps. Neo-associationism can account for the weapons effect: Berkowitz asked the question, 'Does the finger pull the trigger or the trigger pull the finger?' (Berkowitz & LePage, 1967). If weapons suggest aggressive images a person's range of attention is curtailed. In a priming experiment by Craig Anderson (Anderson, Anderson & Deuser, 1996), participants first viewed either pictures of guns or scenes of nature. Next, while reading words printed in different colours that had either aggressive or neutral meaning, they reported the colours of the words. Their response speed was slowest when pictures of weapons preceded aggressive words. We should not infer from this that weapons always invite violent associations. A gun, for example, might be associated with sport rather than being a destructive weapon (Berkowitz, 1993) – hence the more specific term 'weapons effect'.

Responding to erotic images

If exposure to erotica in magazines and videos can lead to sexual arousal, might it also be linked to aggression? A meta-analysis of forty-six studies by Oddone-Paolucci, Genuis and Violato (2000) suggests so. Their evidence indicates that the exposure of men to *pornography* (rather than erotica) is connected to sexual deviancy, sexual perpetration and attitudes to intimate relationships and rape myths.

But let us look more closely at different kinds of evidence. Data based on experiments by Robert Baron and by Dolf Zillmann, and their respective colleagues indicate that any effect on aggression depends on the kind of erotica viewed. For example, viewing pictures of attractive nudes (mild erotica) have a distracting effect – they seem to reduce aggression when compared with neutral pictures (Baron, 1979; Ramirez, Bryant & Zillmann, 1983). On the other hand, viewing images of explicit lovemaking (highly erotic) can increase aggression (Baron & Bell, 1977; Zillmann, 1984, 1996). We need to allow that sexually arousing non-violent erotica could lead to aggression because of the excitation-transfer effect discussed earlier (see Figure 8.1). However, excitation transfer includes the experience of a later frustrating event, which acts as a trigger to aggress. In short, there has not been a convincing demonstration of a direct link between erotica per se and aggression.

In a more dramatic experiment (Zillmann & Bryant, 1984), participants were first exposed to a massive amount of violent pornography, and then were actively irritated by a confederate. They became more callous about what they had seen: they viewed rape more tolerantly and became more lenient about prison sentences that they would recommend (see Figure 8.5). However, the experimental design involves a later provoking event, so this outcome could be an instance of excitation transfer.

Evidence based on correlations rather than experiments using larger population samples open up a different possibility. The clinical psychologist Michael Seto reviewed the literature dealing with a possible link between exposure to pornography and sexual offending (Seto, Maric & Barbaree, 2001). None was established. However, it is possible that men already predisposed to sexually offend are the ones most likely to be affected by pornography and to show the strongest consequences.

Edward Donnerstein's research with several colleagues has shed light on several issues:

- When violence is mixed with sex in films there is, at the very least, evidence of male desensitisation to aggression against women – this surfaced as callous and demeaning attitudes (Donnerstein & Linz, 1994).
- When women were depicted enjoying violent pornography, men were later more willing to aggress against women (although, interestingly, not against men). Perhaps just as telling are other consequences of such material: it can perpetuate the myth that women actually enjoy sexual violence (Linz, Donnerstein & Penrod, 1988).

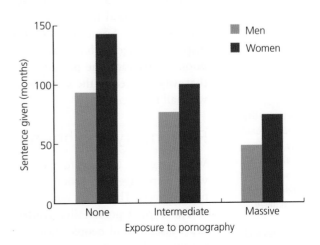

Figure 8.5

Effect of viewing pornographic films on lenience in sentencing.

Source: Based on data from Zillmann & Bryant (1984).

- It has been demonstrated that portrayals of women apparently enjoying such acts reinforce rape myths and weaken social and cognitive restraints against violence towards women (Malamuth & Donnerstein, 1982).

A *feminist perspective* emphasises two concerns about continual exposure of men to media depicting violence and/or sexually explicit material involving women:

- Exposure to violence will cause men to become callous or desensitised to violence against female victims.
- Exposure to pornography will contribute to the development of negative attitudes towards women.

In Russell Geen's (1998) review, an attitude of callousness – perhaps a value – develops by using pornography over a long period. (See the fourth focus question. What might you now tell Tom?) In summary, Daniel Linz (Linz, Wilson & Donnerstein, 1992) isolated two culprits in an otherwise confusing mix of violence, sex and women in the media:

1. The portrayal of violence can beget violence.
2. Degrading messages about women institutionalise a demeaning and one-dimensional image of women.

Much of what we have covered to this point deals in a general way with the 'average person'. We now ask the following questions. Are some people more likely to aggress than others? Can the situation change, so that the same person might be aggressive at one time but not at another?

Personal and situational variations

Common sense suggests that social behaviour is an outcome of how a person responds in a situation, as Lee Ross and Richard Nisbett (1991) have argued. In studies of aggression, separating *person* variables from *situation* variables has been a matter of convenience. This reflects how most research has been performed but it belies the reality that the causes of aggression are complex and interactive.

Consider some contexts in which aggression occurs: reacting to being teased, a carry-over from a near traffic accident, a continuing response to the burden of poverty, a method for dealing with a nagging partner, or a parent's control over a fractious child. Some of these appear to involve situational variables, but closer inspection suggests that some go with the person, or with a category of people (the poor, the partner, the parent). Moreover, not all people in a category respond in that way, or even in the same way in identical situations. With that caveat in mind, we shall move on.

Type A personality
The 'coronary-prone' personality – a behavioural correlate of heart disease characterised by striving to achieve, time urgency, competitiveness and hostility.

Personality and hormonal effects

While research looking for personality correlates of aggression has yielded little of value, there have been promising findings relating both to Type A personality and hormonal effects. The effects reported are small to moderate, however, rather than strong.

The Type A personality syndrome is associated with susceptibility to coronary heart disease, and people showing this pattern are overactive and excessively competitive in their encounters with others. Type A people:

- may be more aggressive towards others that they think compete with them on an important task (Carver & Glass, 1978);
- prefer to work alone rather than with others when they are under stress, probably to avoid exposure to incompetence in others and to feel in control of the situation (Dembroski & MacDougall, 1978).

There are downsides. For example, Type A people may be more abusive to children (Strube *et al.*, 1984). Robert Baron (1989) also found that Type A managers conflicted more with peers and subordinates, although not with their own supervisors. They apparently knew where to draw the line!

Is it a fallacy that *hormonal activity* affects the rate at which aggression occurs? There may be a real, though slight, link. The endocrinologist Brian Gladue (1991) reported higher levels of overt aggression in males than in females. Moreover, this sex difference applied equally to both heterosexual and homosexual males when compared with females – biology (i.e. being genetically male or female) rather than gender orientation was the main contributing variable. However, a meta-analysis of 45 studies by Angela Book and her colleagues (Book, Starzyk & Quinsey, 2001) found only a small correlation of 0.14 between elevated testosterone (in both males and females) and aggression – if the link is causal, testosterone would explain barely 2 per cent of variation in aggression.

Testosterone is a hormone. What effects does a drug like alcohol have?

Alcohol and the social context

Many of us might agree that alcohol befuddles the brain, which is a particular form of *disinhibition* (see below). The drug detracts from cortical control and increases activity in more primitive brain areas. As Peter Giancola (2003) has noted, the link between alcohol and aggressive behaviour seems firmly established.

In an experimental study of the effects of alcohol on aggression, Stuart Taylor and James Sears (1988) placed male students in either an alcohol or placebo condition where they each competed with another participant (who was a confederate of the experimenter) in an adjoining room on a task involving reaction time. In each pair, the slower person on a given trial would receive an electric shock from the faster person. The level of shock was selected by each person before that trial commenced. The confederate's shock settings were actually determined by the experimenter, and were always low intensity (i.e. fairly passive) with a win/loss frequency of 50 per cent. The results in Figure 8.6 show the proportions of high-intensity shocks given by participants who were in either an alcohol or a placebo condition.

There were four sequential stages (none → mild → strong → none) of social pressure in which a second confederate, who was watching the proceedings, sometimes encouraged the participant to give a shock. The results show an interaction (i.e. a difference in the slope of the lines) between taking alcohol and being pressured to aggress: participants who had imbibed were more susceptible to influence and continued to give high-intensity shocks even after the pressure was later withdrawn.

The analogy to real life is the *context* of social drinking, such as at a party or in a bar, where others may goad the drinker to be aggressive. Behaviour that is normally under control, such as acts that are antisocial, illegal or embarrassing, can be released by consuming alcohol. How many people sing karaoke only after a few drinks? We should note, however, that actual statistics on the connection between levels of alcohol consumption and aggression are suggestive, not clear-cut.

Figure 8.6

Alcohol, social pressure and willingness to give shock to a passive opponent.

Source: Based on Taylor & Sears (1988).

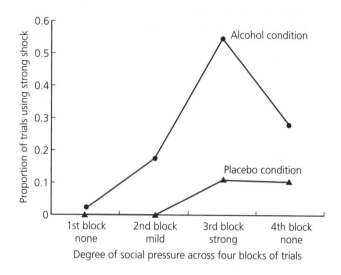

Disinhibition, deindividuation and dehumanisation

Disinhibition
A breakdown in the learned controls (social mores) against behaving impulsively or, in this context, aggressively. For some people, alcohol has a disinhibiting effect.

Deindividuation
Process whereby people lose their sense of socialised individual identity and engage in unsocialised, often antisocial, behaviours.

Dehumanisation
Stripping people of their dignity and humanity.

Collective aggression
Unified aggression by a group of individuals, who may not even know one another, against another individual or group.

Sometimes people act 'out of character'. Disinhibition refers to a reduction in the usual social forces that operate to restrain us from acting antisocially, illegally or immorally. There are several ways in which people lose their normal inhibitions against aggression, one of which is deindividuation. According to Philip Zimbardo (1970), being in a large group provides people with a cloak of anonymity that diffuses personal responsibility for the consequences of their actions. This leads to a loss of identity and a reduced concern for social evaluation. In turn, this causes people to become impulsive, irrational and disinhibited because they have lost their usual social and personal controls. In one study, Zimbardo aimed to deindividuate people by dressing them in cloaks and hoods, with overtones of the Ku Klux Klan (KKK). Deindividuated female students thought they were giving electric shocks to another female in a learning task. Those in uniforms gave shocks that lasted twice as long as those dressed in ordinary clothes. He also mimicked a prison setting, constructed in the basement of the Psychology Department of Stanford University (Zimbardo, Haney, Banks & Jaffe, 1982; see Box 6.2 in Chapter 6). Students dressed as prison guards were extremely brutal to other students who were dressed in prisoners' garb.

In Box 8.4 we look a real-life examples of both deindividuation and dehumanisation, both of which are situational variations that increase the likelihood of aggression taking place. Factors such as the presence of others or lack of identifiability lead to a deindividuated state while a perception that victims are less than human eases the way to treating them aggressively.

Leon Mann (1981) applied the concept of deindividuation to a context of collective aggression, the 'baiting crowd'. The typical situation involves a person threatening to jump from a high building, a crowd gathers below, and some begin to chant 'jump, jump'. In one dramatic case in New York in 1938, thousands of people waited at ground level, some for eleven hours, until a man jumped to his death from a seventeenth-floor hotel ledge.

Real world 8.4
Deindividuation and dehumanisation

Being deindividuated

Deindividuation brings a sense of reduced likelihood of punishment for acting aggressively. A dramatic example of how a real, or perceived, reduction in the likelihood of punishment can enhance violence took place at My Lai, during the Vietnam War, where American soldiers slaughtered an entire village of innocent civilians. According to the official inquiry detailed by Seymour Hersh (1970), the same unit had previously killed and tortured civilians without any disciplinary action; that the area was a designated 'free-fire' zone, so that it was fine to shoot at anything that moved; and indeed that the ethos of the war was one of glorified violence.

There was also a sense of anonymity, a correlate of deindividuation, that goes with being part of a large group and this further enhanced the soldiers' perception that they would not be punished as individuals. Anonymity may contribute to an emotion that translates into violence. Examples include a pack rape at a gang convention, or the wearing of white hoods by Ku Klux Klan members. A study by Neil Malamuth (1981) found that almost one-third of male students questioned at an American university admitted that they might rape if they were certain of not getting caught. Charming!

Dehumanising the victim

A variation is when the victim is anonymous or dehumanised in some way, so that the aggressor is not confronted with the victim's pain or injury, thus weakening feelings of shame and guilt. Terrible examples of this phenomenon have been documented, such as Charles Steir's (1978) report of the violent treatment of psychiatric patients and prisoners who were either kept naked or dressed identically so that they were indistinguishable as individuals.

Extreme instances of dehumanisation come from war. Carol Cohn (1987) presented a revealing analysis of the ways in which military personnel 'sanitise', and thereby justify, the use of nuclear weaponry by semantics that dehumanise the likely or actual victims, referring to them as 'targets', 'the aggressed' or even 'collateral damage'. American military personnel used the same semantic strategies during the Vietnam War to rationalise and justify the killing of Vietnamese civilians, who were known as 'gooks'.

In 1993 Bosnian Serbs, in what was once part of Yugoslavia, referred to acts of genocide against the Muslim population as 'ethnic cleansing'. The media can also unwittingly lessen the impact of the horror of large-scale killing. A phrase often used on television during the Allied bombing campaigns in Iraq in 1991 was 'theatre of war', inviting the audience to sit back and be entertained.

See Chapter 7 for other examples of dehumanisation.

Mann analysed reports of suicides reported in newspapers in the 1960s and 1970s, finding that in ten out of the twenty-one cases where there had been a crowd watching, baiting had occurred. His analysis showed that this was more likely to occur at night, when the crowd was large (more than 300 people), and when the crowd was typically a long way from the victim, usually at ground level. These features lead people to be deindividuated. The longer the crowd waited, the more likely they would bait, perhaps egged on by irritability and frustration (see Figure 8.7).

Since the early 1970s, European, but particularly English, football became associated with hooliganism. Popular views used characterisations of football fans on the rampage. Were the fans deindividuated in a crowd setting? Peter Marsh and his colleagues (Marsh, Russer & Harré, 1978) suggested a different cause. Fan violence is often orchestrated far away from the stadium and long before the match. What might appear to be a motley crowd on match day can actually consist of several groups of fans with different statuses. A faithful follower can in time be 'promoted' into a higher group and pursue a 'career structure'. Organised football

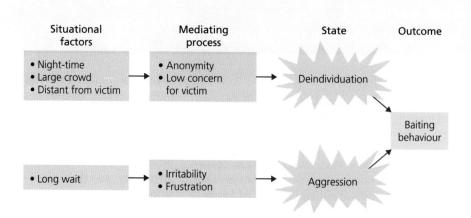

Figure 8.7

The baiting crowd: an exercise in deindividuation and frustration.

Source: Based on Mann (1981).

hooliganism is a kind of staged production rather than an example of an uncontrollable mob. Clifford Stott has pointed out that football hooliganism can also be viewed in intergroup terms, e.g. the way hooligans behave towards the police and vice versa (Stott, Hutchison & Drury, 2001).

Situations that trigger aggression

Two factors in the physical environment have been implicated in levels of aggression, *heat* and *crowding*. We deal with each of these below.

Feeling hot

Aggression is linked to ambient temperature. Even our metaphors refer to *body temperature*: we can be 'hot under the collar' or 'simmering with rage', or tell someone else to 'cool down'. As the temperature rises, studies show that domestic and collective violence increase, and frustrated motorists honk horns.

Graphically, the line fit between heat and aggression follows an inverted U: as the temperature increases, so does aggression until it peaks. When it gets very hot, aggression levels out and then declines, a trend suggesting that extreme heat saps our energy. The critical variable is the *ambient temperature*. Ellen Cohn and James Rotton (1997) tracked an inverted U-curve when they related assault rates to temperature throughout each day for two years in Minneapolis, 1987–88. See Figure 8.8. Assaults were more frequent in the later evening. Most people in Minneapolis work in temperature-controlled environments during the day; as a result, the effects of ambient temperature did not show up until people left work. Further analysis revealed that it is temperature per se that accounts for the curvilinear trend, and not simply by time of day. There was also a link with alcohol consumption. When people used alcohol in the evening to quench their thirst, it was a mediating variable leading to aggression.

Figure 8.8

Relationship between rate of assaults and outdoor temperature.

A curve has been fitted to the data. The effect is an inverted U-curve.

Source: Based on data from Cohn & Rotton (1997).

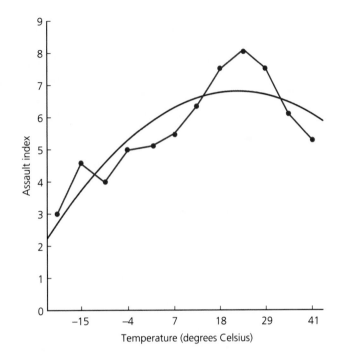

Feeling crowded

Crowding that leads to fighting has long been recognised in a variety of animal species, as the ecologist John Calhoun (1962) observed. For humans, crowding is a subjective state and is generally characterised by feeling that one's personal space has been encroached (see Chapter 11). Although the concepts of personal space and population density are distinct, in practical terms they also overlap. Urbanisation puts a premium on living space and elevates stress. Wendy Regoeczi (2003) noted that Toronto's population density as a gross measure contributed to the overall level of crime. However, variables crucial to feeling crowded are more finely grained, such as household density (persons per house) and neighbourhood density (detached housing versus high-rise housing). Both measures of density correlated positively with people's feelings of aggression and of withdrawal from strangers. In a British study, Claire Lawrence and Kathryn Andrews (2004) confirmed a consistent finding in prison contexts: feeling crowded made prisoners more likely to perceive events as aggressive and protagonists as more hostile and malevolent.

Societal influences

Gender variation

We have referred to hormonal effects in the preceding section, so we should extend the line of argument to cover a major issue: are men more aggressive than women, and if so, is this socialised?

Roles and gender

Both social and developmental psychology emphasise that becoming socialised is closely connected to gendered characteristics, such as homemaker versus worker. According to John Archer (2004), this is a crucial point that sets off social role theory from sexual selection theory, which is based in evolutionary social psychology.

Does this apply to aggression? On balance, yes – there is a wealth of evidence confirming that men are more aggressive than women across cultures and socio-economic groups. However, the size of this difference varies according to the kind and context of aggression. In a study of college students, Mary Harris (1992) reported that young men are more likely than young women to be physically violent, whereas women are almost as likely as men to use verbal attack in similar contexts, although the degree to which they aggress may be less. As children mature, girls manipulate and boys fight – the essential gender difference is that boys aggress directly whereas girls aggress indirectly: for example, by gossip and social exclusion (Archer & Coyne, 2005).

A Canadian study by Michael Conway and his colleagues noted that gender is often confounded with status in many studies of aggression, an issue that becomes important when a male–female interaction involves strangers (Conway, Irannejad & Giannopoulos, 2005). Aggression is often directed at the weaker person, who may be female or simply of lower status.

Gender stereotypes have characterised men as being much more aggressive than women. However, as gender roles in Western societies change, women have become less inhibited against violence. Emancipation may be linked to crime: in most Western societies in recent decades it is correlated with a rise in alcohol and drug abuse among women. The return of women to the workforce coincided with widespread unemployment in a number of countries, a further trigger for increased offences against persons (and property).

Although criminal violence is still more prevalent among men than women, the *rate* of violent offending has increased more rapidly among women (see the trend for young American offenders in Figure 8.9).

Social role theory
The argument that sex differences in occupations are determined by society rather than one's biology.

Sexual selection theory
The argument that male–female differences in behaviour derive from human evolutionary history.

Figure 8.9

US juvenile arrest rates for aggravated assault by sex, 1980–2004.

- The original data set is arrest rates per 100 000 for males and females aged 10–17 years from 1980 to 2004.
- The data have been converted to percentages calculated on the base rates in 1980, 239 for males and 45 for females.
- The graph shows that the relative increase in percentages of the arrest rates for aggravated assault was considerably higher for females between 1987 and 1994.

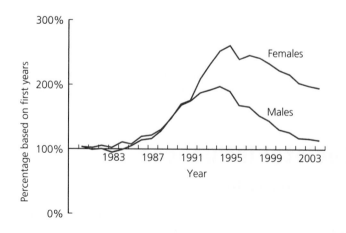

Source: Based on data from US Department of Justice (2006).

Domestic violence

Family violence is now recognised as a major public health issue with an important psychological basis. Groups at risk are women, children and elders. It is partner abuse, however, that has come so much into focus that a specialised journal *Violence Against Women* was founded in 1995. Already we can detect a gender asymmetry here: the victims are mostly women. Data relating to partner abuse have been available for many years. A survey of more than 2000 families by sociologist Murray Straus revealed that an assault with intent to injure had occurred in three out of ten of married couples, and in one out of six within the past year (Straus, Gelles & Steinmetz, 1980). The acts were pushing, hitting with the fist, slapping, kicking, throwing something and beating up; and a few were threatened with a gun or knife. Here is a sobering statistic: about one-quarter of those homicides where the killer knows the victim are spousal. According to Todd Shackelford (2001), American women in cohabiting relationships incur about nine times the risk of being murdered as women in marital relationships, a trend that is similar in Canada.

Is there a gender asymmetry? Walter DeKeseredy (2006) has pointed out that partner abuse, and *domestic violence* more generally, can work in different ways according to one's gender and also ethnicity:

- Most sexual assaults in heterosexual relationships are committed by men.
- Much of women's use of violence is in self-defence against their partner's assault.
- Men and women in different ethnic groups 'do gender' differently, including variations in perceptions of when it is appropriate to use violence.

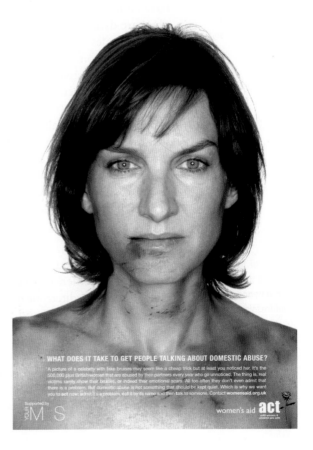

Domestic violence. Law enforcement and a helpline to deal with partner abuse are important components of strategies to combat domestic violence.

Source: The Advertising Archives

Why do people want to hurt those closest to them? There are no simple answers, but here are some influential factors:

- *learned patterns of aggression*, imitated from parents and significant others, together with low competence in responding non-aggressively; there is a generational cycle of child abuse, and the chronic repetition of violence in some families has been identified as an abuse syndrome.
- The *proximity* of family members, making them either sources or targets of annoyance or frustration.
- *Stresses*, especially financial difficulties, unemployment and illnesses (including postnatal depression).
- The division of *power* in traditional nuclear families, favouring the man.
- A high level of *alcohol* consumption, a correlate of male abuse of a spouse.

These factors can interact to mean that, ironically, those we live closest to are the likeliest targets of our aggression.

Cultural variation

If the tendency to aggress can be shaped through learning, it makes sense to extend this analysis to cultures. Are some cultures more aggressive than others?

Throughout history, there have always been differences in cultural norms and values that have shaped some societies to be more aggressive and some less aggressive than others. The reasons are usually evident. A history of repeated invasions, a geography that made some settlements more competitive or more vulnerable, and a bio-evolutionary factor of physique that permitted successful raids by some groups, have all in part shaped the social philosophies of particular societies. These philosophies are dynamic and can change rapidly according to context. Examples of this in recent decades are the development of both aggressive Zionism and a radical Islam.

There are some societies that actively practise a lifestyle of non-aggression. Bruce Bonta (1997) listed twenty-five societies with a worldview based on cooperation rather than competition. Among these are the Hutterite and Amish communities in the United States, the Inuit of the Arctic region and the Ladakhis of Tibet. Such communities are small, sometimes scattered and relatively isolated, which suggests that these may be necessary preconditions for peaceful existence.

Of greater significance from a cultural perspective is the variation of norms that support certain kinds of violence in certain contexts or certain sub-groups in many societies. Since this often is coloured by power, it applies frequently to women as victims of male violence. We turn to this next.

Culture of honour

Joseph Vandello and Dov Cohen (2003) studied the impact of a culture of honour on domestic violence. Regions that put a value on violence to restore honour include some Mediterranean countries, the Middle East and Arab countries, central and southern America, and the southern United States. They compared samples in Brazil and southern US honour cultures with northern US samples. Their major findings were:

- female infidelity damages a man's reputation, particularly in honour cultures;
- this reputation can be partly restored by using violence;
- women in honour cultures are expected to remain loyal in the face of jealousy-related violence.

Abuse syndrome
Factors of proximity, stress and power that are associated with the cycle of abuse in some families.

Cultural norms
Norms whose origin is part of the tradition of a culture.

Values
A higher-order concept thought to provide a structure for organising attitudes.

Culture of honour
A culture that endorses male violence as a way of addressing threats to social reputation or economic position.

Aggression against women is generally not a matter to display publicly. Zoe Hilton and her colleagues have suggested that, in patriarchal cultures, men and boys are proud of male violence directed at males but ashamed when it is directed at females (Hilton, Harris & Rice, 2000).

Other cultures sanction or even encourage special forms of violence. For example, Bron Ingoldsby (1991) noted the existence of machismo among Latin American families. Likewise, Giovanna Tomada and Barry Schneider (1997) reported that aggression is still expected in adolescent boys from traditional Italian villages in the belief that it shows sexual prowess and shapes a dominant male in the household. They also linked this to a higher rate of male bullying at Italian schools than in England, Spain, Norway or Japan.

Machismo
A code in which challenges, abuse and even differences of opinion must be met with fists or other weapons.

War: aggression on a grand scale

People often think that war is about victory and peace. It's not. War is the total despair of the human spirit. *(Robert Fiske)*

Tragically, large-scale aggression is part of the human condition. Its worst form is war, which is a shocking, massive stain on humanity. Two million years of human evolution, industrialisation, the communications revolution, philosophy, art and

Machismo. Perhaps 'manly' behaviour is not confined to Latin American cultures.
Source: Peter Schols / GPD / Handout / Reuters

poetry have had no effect whatsoever – collective violence continues unabated. Recent years have witnessed monstrous violence in Somalia, Bosnia, Croatia, Kosovo, Rwanda, Chechnya, Afghanistan and Iraq. While we might like to think that we have evolved gracefully from the Renaissance period, the last century was by far the bloodiest in systematic human slaughter, as Donald Dutton and his colleagues have noted (Dutton, Boyanowsky & Bond, 2005).

A way of glimpsing the continuing tragedy is to consider the incidence and severity of wars. Most of us will think of two world wars as the most obvious examples of widespread violence, but there are many others. The estimates in Figure 8.10 are drawn from a number of sources, and are limited to the twentieth century. The data include interstate wars, civil wars, wars of independence, genocide, massacres and atrocities. It remains selective by excluding other instances of mass death that numbered fewer than *one million* people!

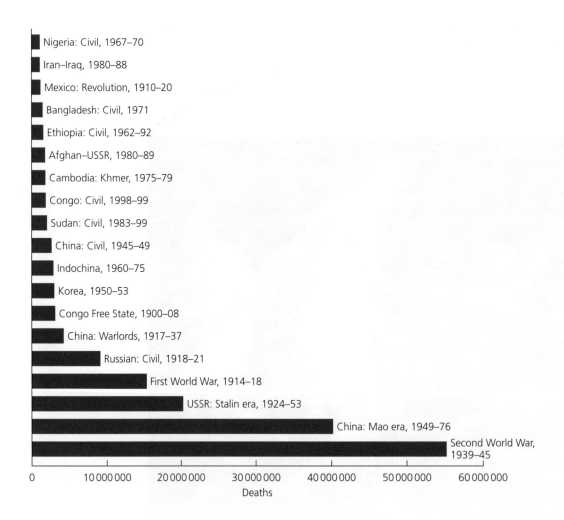

Figure 8.10

Wars, massacres and atrocities of the twentieth century: deaths exceeding one million people.

Source: Based on data from White (2004).

War is a form of institutionalised aggression and usually politically legitimised by the opposing sides. Warfare is not possible without a supporting psychological structure involving the beliefs and emotions of a people. If such a structure is lacking, leaders will use propaganda to create one (see Chapter 4). In times of war, both the soldiers who are fighting and the people at home need to maintain good morale. Genocide is a kind of legitimised prejudice translated into behaviour (see Chapter 7). Some political regimes have fostered beliefs in genetic differences between groups of people to justify oppression and slaughter. Ideologies of racial, moral and social inferiority were the cornerstones of the Nazi programmes directed against gypsies, political non-conformists, homosexuals, the mentally handicapped, ill people, African Americans and Jews.

Reducing aggression

Finally, we deal briefly with a variety of ways that aggression might be reduced. One of these is an old chestnut – by acting out some violence we can get rid of some of the bottled up (Freudian!) energy. The other methods belong properly in the province of a community: what part can it play?

Letting off steam

This suggested solution has popular appeal in accounting for some kinds of aggression, and is a latter-day derivative of psychodynamic theory covered earlier in this chapter. It is sometimes called the cathartic hypothesis, referring to the process of using our behaviour as an outlet or release for pent-up emotion.

Cathartic hypothesis
The notion that acting aggressively, or even just viewing aggressive material, reduces feelings of anger and aggression.

Although associated with Freud, the idea can be traced back to Aristotle and ancient Greek tragedy: by acting out their emotions, people can purify their feelings. Perhaps venting our feelings that arise from frustration can restore a stable level of functioning. A modern example is 'boss bashing'. In Japan, some companies provided a special room with a toy replica of the boss upon which employees can relieve their tensions by bashing it. A more common example is when a group of workers gather to share complaints and gossip about their incompetent boss – even if they don't do it face to face!

Serious doubts about the efficacy of the catharsis hypothesis have been raised. Recent experimental research has actually rejected outright the basis of catharsis in the present for reducing later aggression. Brad Bushman and his colleagues found that people who hit a punching bag, believing that it reduced stress, were more likely later to punish someone who had transgressed them (Bushman, Baumeister & Stack, 1999). The implication? Letting it 'all hang out' may be worse than useless. Bushman put it this way: 'venting to reduce anger is like using gasoline to put out a fire – it only feeds the flame'.

Community solutions

At the level of the individual aggressor, effective interventions require political decisions, a budget and a community will. There are now effective technologies deriving from behavioural and counselling psychology that involve the cooperation of regional agencies, schools and families for their implementation. There is also the cycle of violence involving the family unit to be addressed. In families, parents can raise more peaceful children by not rewarding violent acts, by rewarding behaviour that is not compatible with violence, and by minimising the use of punishment. There is room for optimism when dealing with one individual.

Psychological techniques of behaviour modification, social skills training, non-aggressive modelling, anger management and assertiveness training have been shown to be effective in enhancing personal self-control. With respect to violence in schools, educational psychologist Arnold Goldstein (1999) pointed out that aggression is multicausal and that a preventative strategy must be both broad and flexible, including a match between the techniques used and target groups selected. A successful strategy should generally avoid punitive tactics that have proved ineffective in the past, such as corporal punishment and suspension.

There are educational opportunities open to both males and females that target the betterment of women. For example, a media studies course can help develop critical skills that evaluate whether and how women are demeaned, and in what way we might undermine rape myths.

Law can play a role at a societal level. Take gun ownership law in the United States as an example. You now know something of the weapons effect. Consider this irony: guns may be kept in American homes to confer protection. According to Arthur Kellerman, these protective guns turn out to be handy when killing a family member or an intimate acquaintance, particularly in homes with a history of drug use and physical violence (Kellerman *et al.*, 1993).

Mass violence such as war is a different matter. There is of course room for peace studies in the formal education system. Peace education is more than an anti-war campaign: it has broadened to cover all aspects of peaceful relationships and coexistence. By teaching young children how to build and maintain self-esteem without being aggressive, there can be a long-term impact that will expand into all areas of people's lives. There is now a journal devoted to these and other topics, the *Journal of Peace Research*.

However, war is an institutional phenomenon, so that its prevention can be defined only partly in political terms. Wars between nations nearly always involve a complex history of intergroup relations that in turn are derived from outgroup stereotypes and prejudice (see Chapter 2 and 7) that have been perpetuated across generations.

We cannot wave a magic wand and banish violence. At both individual and societal levels, there is room for social psychologists and others to work towards harmony in a world of increasing stress and dwindling resources. Let us now turn to the kinder face of humanity in Chapter 9.

Peace studies
Multidisciplinary movement dedicated to the study and promotion of peace.

Summary

- Defining aggression will reflect differences in theories about its nature and causes. One simple definition is 'the intentional infliction of some type of harm on others'.

- There are two major classes of theory about the origins of aggression, one stressing biological origins and the other stressing social influences.

- Biological explanations, particularly those within ethology and evolutionary social psychology, emphasise genetically determined behaviour patterns that are shared by a species.

- Social explanations usually stress the roles of learning processes and societal influences. Some theories incorporate some biology, such as the frustration–aggression hypothesis and excitation–transfer theory. Social learning theory is a developmental approach that stresses reinforcement principles and the influence that models have on the young child.

- The nature of the effects of the mass media on aggression has been debated. However, the continued portrayal of violence at the very least desensitises young people to its consequences.

- Research in social cognition and human memory have helped to understand better why some media scenes can prime aggressive thoughts and sometimes lead to aggressive actions.

- The effects of non-violent pornography on male tendencies to be violent towards women are unclear. When it is distinguished from erotica, non-violent pornography can foster negative beliefs about women.

- Examples of individual differences with modest links to aggression are the Type A personality syndrome and elevated levels of testosterone.

- Situational factors that increase aggression are higher levels of heat (ambient temperature) and crowding. Drinking alcohol can disinhibit people and sometimes lead them to be more aggressive.

- Deindividuation is a psychological state that reduces the sense of being punished for acting aggressively. It has multiple causes, including the feeling of being anonymous.

- Major societal correlates of aggression are gender and cultural differences. Men are generally more violent than women and are more often responsible for domestic violence. Some cultures have norms that permit and even encourage aggression in particular contexts.

- War, the most extreme and massive form of violence, is a shocking example of institutionalised aggression and is usually politically legitimised.

- Reducing aggression has been addressed with some success by specialised psychological techniques and by community programmes that are educational and interventional.

Literature, film and TV

Syriana

A 2005 geopolitical thriller, directed by Stephen Gaghan and starring George Clooney and Matt Damon that focuses on the complexity and intrigue of petroleum politics and the Middle East. This film is also a powerful commentary on strategic state-sponsored aggression, individual suicide terrorism, and the personal cost of violence. Other recent films in the same genre include Gavin Hood's 2007 film *Rendition*, and Peter Berg's 2007 film *The Kingdom*.

A Clockwork Orange

The 1971 film directed by Stanley Kubrick is based on the novel by Anthony Burgess, and stars Malcolm McDowell. It is a powerful and classic exploration of apparently mindless violence – acts of 'ultraviolence' to the accompaniment of Beethoven's Ninth Symphony. The movie also touches on controversial ways to stop such extreme violence through flooding.

Bowling for Columbine and Elephant

Bowling for Columbine is Michael Moore's 2000 documentary about gun crime and aggression, particularly among adolescents in school settings, in the United States. It centres on the Columbine High School shooting in Littleton, Colorado, on April 20, 1999. Two students, 18-year-old Eric Harris and 17-year-old Dylan Klebold, walked into school dressed in trench coats and killed twelve of their classmates and one teacher, and then themselves. In the 2003 film, *Elephant*, director Gus Van Sant approaches the same issues in a different way. Using unknown actors and a naturalistic approach, the audience witness the build up to the massacre and the killings themselves from the students' point of view (victims, onlookers and culprits) encouraging us to make sense of the aggression and premeditated violence of the teenagers.

City of God

Fernando Meirelles's (2002) film portrays gang violence in the slums of Rio de Janeiro. In it we see how easily aggression and violence becomes a way of life when there is no protection on the streets and a gun can give you safety, power and popularity. This is most poignantly demonstrated by the story of 11-year-old Li'l Dice who murders everyone in a brothel, and goes on to become a powerful gang leader and drug dealer within a couple of years, thriving on the power afforded by his brutality.

Pulp Fiction

In Quentin Tarantino's 1994 classic, starring John Travolta, Samuel T. Jackson and Uma Thurman, the violent lives of mobsters and small-time criminals in Los Angeles are graphically dramatised; but the film is also memorable for its clever and humorous dialogue and its focus on the characters' perspectives on life and on their essential humanness.

Lock, Stock and Two Smoking Barrels and RocknRolla

Two classic Guy Ritchie films from 1998 and 2008 are set in London's underbelly of organised, though often quite disorganised, crime. These films are not only graphic portrayals of chaotic violent lifestyles but they are also very funny.

Fatal Attraction and The War of the Roses

Two films that illustrate violence in relationships, but in different ways. *Fatal Attraction* is a 1987 film starring Michael Douglas and Glenn Close. A man has a one-night stand with his work colleague, who then stalks him. This is a very tense and scary movie about violence in a relationship. In contrast, *The War of the Roses* is a 1989 black comedy in which Danny DeVito is a divorce lawyer for Michael Douglas and Kathleen Turner, who were formerly deeply in love but now dedicate their lives to harming each other. Each refuse to leave the family home – in the process they wreck the home and each other.

Guided questions

- What is the *frustration–aggression hypothesis*? Does it help to account for the origins of aggression?

- Does the incidence of aggression vary in relation to gender or culture?

- Does viewing television violence make people more aggressive?

- In what ways can the tendency to aggress be reduced?

- Can children really learn quickly how to be aggressive? See a portrayal of one of the scenarios used in Albert Bandura's famous Bobo doll experiment in Chapter 8 of MyPsychLab at www.mypsychlab.co.uk.

Learn more

Anderson, C. A., & Huesmann, L. R. (2003). Human aggression: A social-cognitive view. In M. A. Hogg & J. Cooper (eds), *The Sage handbook of social psychology* (pp. 296–323). London: Sage. Up-to-date and comprehensive overview of research on human aggression, by two of the world's leading aggression researchers.

Baron, R. A., & Richardson, D. R. (1994). *Human aggression* (2nd ed). New York: Plenum. A recognised source of psychological research findings spanning the whole field.

Berkowitz, L. (1993). *Aggression: Its causes, consequences and control*. Philadelphia, PA: Temple University Press. Another work by an authority in the field with a good coverage of the topic.

Buford, B. (1993). *Among the thugs*. New York: Vintage. An insider's perspective on the world of English football 'hooligans' in British and other European settings. The work is compelling – one reviewer described it as '*A Clockwork Orange* comes to life'.

Campbell, A. (1993). *Men, women and aggression*. New York: HarperCollins. The concepts of violence and aggression are explored, with particular focus on roles and on the implications regarding gender and culture.

Kerr, J. H. (2005). *Rethinking aggression and violence in sport*. London: Routledge. A health and sports psychologist reviews current theory in the psychology of aggression and explores how players become accustomed to violence. He also discusses psychological benefits of sanctioned and unsanctioned sport violence, moral and ethical dimensions of the debate, and spectator aggression.

Krahé, B. (1996). Aggression and violence in society. In G. R. Semin & K. Fiedler (eds), *Applied social psychology* (pp. 343–73). London: Sage. A compact introduction to problems of definition and explanation. Personal and situational variables are explored, along with the topics of domestic violence, rape and bullying.

Refresh your understanding, assess your progress and go further with interactive summaries, questions, podcasts, videos and much more on the website accompanying the book: **www.mypsychlab.co.uk**.

Chapter 9

Helping other people

What to look for

- Nature, nurture and being helpful

- The roles of empathy, learning and attribution

- Theoretical models of helping: bystander-calculus, cognitive

- Helping in an emergency

- People who are very helpful

- Encouraging people to be helpful

- Volunteers as dedicated helpers

Focus questions

1. Arthur spots this headline in his local newspaper: 'Altruistic dolphin pushes child away from shark!' Fascinating, he thinks, but that's not altruism . . . or is it?

2. Vincenzo is fit and healthy, his whole life ahead of him. His twin brother's future is uncertain. He now needs dialysis more than once a week. After months of thinking, some of it agonising, Vincenzo's mind is made up – he will donate a kidney to his brother. Would you want to help your really close kin? Does Vincenzo's choice have implications for evolutionary theory?

3. Lily is 13 years old and tall for her age. One afternoon, she confronts a suspicious-looking stranger loitering near a young girl playing in the local park. The stranger takes to his heels when Lily challenges him. It's the talk of the neighbourhood, and there's mention of a medal for bravery. Hearing this, your social psychology classmate points out: 'It's just as well that Lily's usual playmates were not around, or that little girl might not have received any help.' What could your classmate mean? For an experimental re-enactment of a similar scenario go to Chapter 9 of MyPsychLab at www.mypsychlab.co.uk.

4. You turn the corner of a city street to see a man sprawled across the footpath in front of you. What do you do? What things might you want to know more about before deciding on how to act?

his chapter stands in contrast to Chapter 8, which dealt with the human potential to be negative and aggressive. In Chapter 9 we now turn to the positive and altruistic aspect of human nature. Whether we behave aggressively or prosocially, our capacity to do so has both biological and social roots. One would be forgiven for concluding that people are basically full of hatred and aggression. Was the philosopher Thomas Hobbes right to call us nasty and brutish? At times we are not. We now ask why, when and how people decide to help others even if they in turn pay the ultimate sacrifice.

What is prosocial behaviour?

Prosocial behaviour
Acts that are positively valued by society.

Acts that benefit another person are referred to as prosocial behaviour, helping behaviour or altruism. Some use these terms interchangeably, but there are distinctions and differences as they are used in the research literature.

Prosocial behaviour can be varied

Prosocial behaviour is a broad category of acts that are valued positively by society – contrast it with antisocial behaviour. Wispé (1972) defined prosocial behaviour as behaviour that has positive social consequences, and contributes to the physical or psychological well-being of another person. It is voluntary and has the intention to benefit others (Eisenberg *et al.*, 1996). Being prosocial includes both being helpful and altruistic. It also embraces acts of charity, cooperation, friendship, rescue, sacrifice, sharing, sympathy and trust. What is thought to be prosocial is defined by a society's norms.

Helping behaviour
Acts that intentionally benefit someone else.

Helping behaviour is a subcategory of prosocial behaviour. Helping is intentional and it benefits another living being or group. If you accidentally drop £10 and someone finds it and uses it, you have not performed a helping behaviour. But if you gave £10 to Connie who really needed it, you have helped her. On the other hand, making a large public donation to a charity because you wanted to appear generous is not helping behaviour. Some corporate donations to a good cause may even be driven by product image, e.g. looking for a long-term increase in profit. Helping can sometimes be antisocial, e.g. overhelping, when giving help is designed to make others look inferior (Gilbert & Silvera, 1996).

Altruism
A special form of *helping behaviour*, sometimes costly, that shows concern for fellow human beings and is performed without expectation of personal gain.

Altruism is another subcategory of prosocial behaviour, and refers to an act that is meant to benefit another rather than oneself. In this respect, Dan Batson (1991) proposed that true altruism is selfless, although there is some difficulty with the concept. Can we demonstrate that an act does not stem from a long-term ulterior motive, such as ingratiation?

While the literature dealing with altruism is controversial, the broader topic of acting prosocially is difficult to explain using traditional theories of human behaviour. Many commentators regard human behaviour as egoistic: self-interest reigns supreme. Therefore, to call some behaviour prosocial is unusual because this suggests it does not rely on reinforcement. It also highlights an optimistic and positive view of human beings. How can effort and sacrifice for another person be reinforcing in the usual sense?

nature–nurture controversy
Classic debate about whether genetic or environmental factors determine human behaviour. Scientists generally accept that it is an interaction of both.

In dealing with aggression in Chapter 8, we referred to the nature–nurture controversy – the debate over the roles of biological versus learned determinants of behaviour. It is relevant to the origins of, and situational factors involved in, pro-social acts. The question of why people help others is important. First, we address two seemingly opposing views, *evolutionary theory* and *social learning theory*. Next, we look at biosocial views that reflect an interplay of empathy, cognition, and the context in which help is either given or not.

Biological approaches

In this section we commence with an approach that is grounded in evolutionary theory and draws analogies between animal and human behaviour. We then consider the nature of empathy to find that both cognitive and social factors are involved and therefore move us towards a biosocial approach.

A phenomenon of nature?

Put simply, the biological position is that humans have innate tendencies to eat, drink, mate and fight – and to help others. This could be why humans have been so successful in an evolutionary sense. The question whether altruism has evolutionary survival value has been asked by the social psychologist Dennis Krebs (1975), the sociobiologist Edward Wilson (1978), and the evolutionary social psychologists David Buss and Doug Kenrick (1998). Consider the next example given by Dan Batson (1983).

A small child, Margaret, and her friend, Red, were seated in the back seat of Margaret's parents' car. Suddenly the car burst into flames. Red jumped from the car but realised that Margaret was still inside. He jumped back into the burning car, grabbed Margaret by the jacket and pulled her to safety. Can we trace this sequence to an altruistic impulse inherited from our ancestors? The fact that Red was an Irish setter – yes, a dog! – lends weight to the argument that there is a genetic aspect to altruism and prosocial behaviour (see the first focus question about the dolphin). It also begs the question: can other animals be 'altruistic'?

Jeffrey Stevens and his colleagues (Stevens, Cushman & Hauser, 2005) distinguished two reliable explanations of cooperative behaviour in animals and humans:

- *Mutualism* – cooperative behaviour that benefits the cooperator as well as others; a defector will do worse than a cooperator.
- *Kin selection* – in which a cooperator is biased towards blood relatives because it helps propagate one's own genes; the lack of direct benefit to the cooperator indicates *altruism*.

Kin selection is the obvious candidate to be an evolutionary account of human altruism. Is there any such evidence?

Eugene Burnstein and his colleagues investigated 'decision rules' for being altruistic that might deal with genetic overlap between persons. Participants rated how likely they would be to help others in several situations (see Figure 9.1). People favoured the sick over the healthy in everyday situations but favoured the healthy over the sick in life-or-death situations. They gave more weight to kinship in everyday situations and the healthy in life-or-death situations. Finally, people were more likely to assist the very young or the very old in everyday situations, but under famine conditions people are more likely to help 10-year-olds or 18-year-olds than

Figure 9.1

Helping kin who are either healthy or sick: life-or-death versus everyday situations.

- There is an interaction between health, kinship and willingness to help.
- Participants chose between people who varied in kinship in two conditions: healthy versus sick individuals, and giving help in a situation that was life-or-death versus merely 'everyday'.
- They were generally more willing to help closer kin than more distant kin.
- They also preferred to help people who were sick rather than healthy in an everyday situation, but who were healthy rather than sick in a perilous situation.

Source: Burnstein, E., Crandall, C., & Kitayama, S. (1994). Some neo-Darwinian decision rules for altruism: Weighing cues for inclusive fitness as a function of the biological importance of the decision. *Journal of Personality and Social Psychology, 67*, 773–789, Reproduced with permission from Professor Eugene Burnstein and the American Psychological Association (APA).

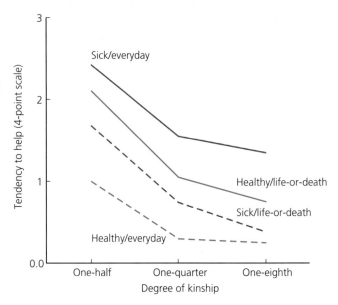

infants or older people. These data are consistent with, if not fully convincing, the idea that close kin will get crucial help when 'the chips are down'. (See the second focus question about Vincenzo's choice.)

A biological predisposition to help others, as well as kin, is a fascinating notion. However, few social psychologists accept an exclusively evolutionary explanation of human prosocial behaviour, though may accept an evolutionary basis to a limited extent.

A problem with evolutionary theory as a sole explanation of altruism is the lack of convincing human evidence; on the contrary, a case such as the failure to help the murder victim Kitty Genovese considered later (see Box 9.2) is difficult to explain at a biological level. Another criticism is the scant attention afforded by evolutionary theorists to the work of social learning theorists, in particular to the role of modelling, as we shall see.

Ross Buck and Benson Ginsburg (1991) argued that altruism depends upon the capacity for both humans and animals to communicate. Communication allows some species to pick up emotional signals (see Chapter 11), and to form social bonds (see Chapter 10), and to act prosocially based on empathy. These ideas have merit but they are a long way from an extreme evolutionary view, such as the existence of an 'altruistic gene'. Later, we will look at the practical value of social structures that promote prosocial behaviour.

Empathy
Ability to feel another person's experiences; identifying with and experiencing another person's emotions, thoughts and attitudes.

Do helpers feel empathic?

Here we consider a biosocial approach, a less extreme account of prosocial behaviour than an evolutionary one. As Sam Gaertner and John Dovidio have pointed out, a common experience before acting prosocially is a state of arousal followed by empathy (Gaertner & Dovidio, 1977). Empathy is an emotional response to someone else's distress, a reaction to witnessing a disturbing event. Adults and children respond empathically to signs of a troubled person, implying that watching someone suffer is unpleasant. Have you ever looked away when a film shows someone being tortured? At first glance this suggests that when we help we are merely trying to reduce our own unpleasant feelings. This points to the need for an extra ingredient, empathy – an ability to identify with someone else's experiences, particularly their feelings (Krebs, 1975). See how this has been formalised in a theoretical model in the next section.

Doing the maths

The bystander-calculus model of helping involves body and mind, a mixture of physiological processes and cognitive processes. According to sociologist Jane Piliavin, when we think someone is in trouble we work our way through three stages, or sets of calculations, before we respond (Piliavin *et al.*, 1981). First, we are physiologically aroused by another's distress. Second, we label this arousal as an emotion. Third, we evaluate the consequences of helping. See Box 9.1.

If the bystander-calculus model is applied strictly, it implies that 'altruism' is a misnomer because it is really motivated by self-interest, or egoism (see Maner *et al.*, 2002). However, Batson's view is that an act is truly altruistic only if the helper is *not* feeling highly distressed, such as having second thoughts and turning back to help a stranded motorist. In a German study, Hans-Werner Bierhoff and Elke Rohmann (2004) have supported this line of thinking, that true altruism will reveal itself when the potential helper could easily not help, such as just quietly slipping away.

Bystander-calculus model
In attending to an emergency, the bystander calculates the perceived costs and benefits of providing help compared with those associated with not helping.

Research and applications 9.1
Steps in the bystander-calculus model

There are three steps in Jane Piliavin's model, which is supported by the work of others:

1. Physiological arousal

Our first reaction to someone in distress is physiological, an empathic response. The greater the arousal, the more chance that a bystander will help. How quickly we react is related to the level of our body's response: e.g. the quicker our heartbeat the quicker we respond (Gaertner & Dovidio, 1977). There is also a cognitive aspect. As the victim's plight becomes clearer and more severe our physiological arousal increases.

2. Labelling the arousal

Being aroused is one thing, but feeling a specific emotion (fear, anger, love) is another. Generally, arousal does not automatically produce specific emotions; people's cognitions or thoughts about the

arousal play a critical role in determining the nature of the emotions they feel. Sometimes our response is also to feel distressed. Dan Batson suggested further that situational cues often trigger another set of responses, *empathic concern* (Batson & Coke, 1981). He also argued that when bystanders believe they are similar to a victim they are more likely to experience empathic concern.

3. Evaluating the consequences

Finally, bystanders evaluate the consequences of acting before they help a victim, choosing an action that will reduce their personal distress at the lowest cost (a cost–benefit analysis is also used in a social exchange approach to close relationships; see Chapter 10). The main costs of helping are time and effort: the greater these costs, the less likely that a bystander will help (Darley & Batson, 1973).

Perspective taking

Empathic concern
An element in Batson's theory of helping behaviour. In contrast to personal distress (which may lead us to flee from the situation), it includes feelings of warmth, being soft-hearted, and having compassion for a person in need.

To experience empathic concern requires us to demonstrate *perspective taking* – being able to see the position of another person from that person's point of view. According to Jean Decety and Klaus Lamm (2006), this capacity has evolutionary significance. Some non-human primates respond to the feelings of others, but humans can both feel and act intentionally on behalf of others. It is this capacity that may account for why empathic concern is thought by theorists such as Batson to be crucial for altruism.

Batson and his colleagues (Batson, Early & Salvarini, 1997; Batson, van Lange, Ahmad & Lishner, 2003) made a further distinction concerning perspective taking: between understanding and experiencing how another person feels and how you would feel in the same situation. Different kinds of empathy lead to different kinds of motivation to help. Their study showed that actively imagining how *another* feels produces empathy, which leads to altruistic motivation. However, actively imagining how *you* would feel produces empathy, but it also produces self-oriented distress, and involves a mix of altruism and egoism. Perhaps people who have experienced something stressful will empathise more with a person who is in a similar situation. For example, people who have been homeless or extremely ill may empathise more with a person in the same condition.

Are women more empathic?

We have seen several times in this book (e.g. Chapters 6, 7 and 8) that socialisation can shape behaviour differently for men and women in many societies. This is emphasised in *social role theory*, an approach that gives little credence to a biological explanation, for example, in terms of hormonal factors. Is there any evidence of a gender difference in the tendency to show empathy?

Batson and his colleagues took up this question. In their study, people read a same-sex adolescent's description of a stressful life event, such as being the object of ridicule and teasing because of acne, or being betrayed and rejected (Batson *et al.*, 1996). Women reported more empathy with a same-sex teenager when they had had similar experiences during their adolescence, an effect not found with men. Batson accounted for this gender difference in terms of socialisation: women value interdependence and are more other-oriented, while men value independence and are more self-oriented. See Figure 9.2.

We return to the topic of gender differences in a later section when we consider the question whether some people are more helpful than others. But next we deal with several approaches to prosocial behaviour whose origins lie squarely within social psychology.

Social approaches

In this section, we look at the role of learning. Recall that in Chapter 8 we noted how social learning theorists such as Bandura emphasised that children have a knack of learning to be aggressive and readily mimic appropriate models who act out violent sequences. A similar argument applies here: if children can learn to be aggressive in some contexts they can surely learn to be prosocial in others (see Figure 8.4 in Chapter 8). We also look at the how attributional processes can play a part, and that there are social norms for helping.

Figure 9.2

Differences between men and women in empathising with a distressed teenager.

- We might expect that people with prior experience of a stressful situation would empathise more with a same-sex teenager undergoing that same experience.
- In this study, only women with prior experience showed an increase in empathy.

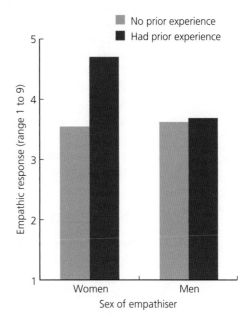

Learning to be helpful

A major explanation of helping is that displaying prosocial behaviour is intricately bound up with becoming socialised: it is learned, not inborn. Various theorists have argued that the processes of classical conditioning, instrumental conditioning and observational learning all contribute to being prosocial. In dealing with child development, Nancy Eisenberg noted a strand of research directed to the way that prosocial behaviour is acquired in childhood (Eisenberg *et al.*, 1999). The application of learning theory to prosocial behaviour has been vigorously pursued within developmental and educational research fields in recent years.

However, traditional research carried out with adults in earlier decades, some of it experimental, dealt with a variety of conditions that control the display of helping. These are covered later in this chapter. First, we deal with studies of childhood, the period in which so much important learning takes place. Carolyn Zahn-Waxler has studied the development of the emotions in children. She concluded that how we respond to distress in others is connected to the way we learn to share, help and provide comfort, and that these patterns emerge between the ages of 1 and 2 (Zahn-Waxler, Radke-Yarrow, Wagner & Chapman, 1992). There are several ways in which these actions can be learned:

- *Giving instructions.* In her studies of parenting, Joan Grusec found that simply telling children to be helpful to others actually works (Grusec, Kuczynski, Rushton & Simutis, 1978). Telling a child what is appropriate establishes an expectation and a later guide for action. However, preaching about being good is of doubtful value unless a fairly strong form of advice is used (Rice & Grusec, 1975). Furthermore, telling children to be generous if the 'preacher' behaves inconsistently is pointless: 'do as I say, not as I do' does not work. Grusec reported that when an adult acted selfishly but urged children to be generous, the children were actually less generous.

- *Using reinforcement.* Acts that are rewarded are more likely to be repeated. When young children are rewarded for offering to help, they are more likely to offer help again later. Similarly, if they are not rewarded, they are less likely to offer help again (Grusec, 1991). J. Philippe Rushton has studied this field intensively. See an example of his work in Figure 9.3.
- *Exposure to models.* In his review of factors that influence children to give help, Rushton (1976) concluded that while reinforcement is effective in shaping behaviour, modelling is even more effective. Watching someone else helping another is a powerful form of learning. This approach can be extended to other contexts. Take the case of young Johnny who first helps his mummy to carry some shopping into the house and then wants to help in putting it away, and then cleans up his/her bedroom. Well, maybe not the last bit!

Modelling
Tendency for a person to reproduce the actions, attitudes and emotional responses exhibited by a real-life or symbolic model. Also called *observational learning.*

The impact of attribution

People make attributions about helping or not helping others. To continue being helpful on more than one occasion requires a person to internalise the idea of 'being helpful' (see self-perception theory, Chapter 3). Helpfulness can then be a guide in the future when helping is an option. A self-attribution can be even more powerful than reinforcement for learning helping behaviour: young children who were told they were 'helpful people' donated more marbles to a needy child than those who were reinforced with verbal praise, and this effect persisted over time (Grusec & Redler, 1980). Indeed, David Perry and his colleagues found that children may experience self-criticism and bad feelings when they fail to live up to the standards implied by their own attributions (Perry *et al.*, 1980).

If we are wondering if we should offer help to someone in need we usually try to figure out who or what this person might be. Some observers may even blame an

Figure 9.3

The effects of reward and punishment on children's willingness to be generous.

- Boys aged 8–11 years watched an adult who played a game to win tokens.
- Then the adult generously donated some by putting them in a bowl to be given later to a child pictured in a poster, a boy who was 'poor little Bobby, who had no Mommy or Daddy to look after him'.
- Next, the child played the game. In one condition, the adult used verbal reinforcers as rewards or punishments for behaving generously (e.g. either 'good for you', or 'that's kind of silly . . . now you will have less tokens for yourself').
- Both tactics had strong effects on how the boys behaved, immediately and after a two-week interval.
- While this study employed reinforcement principles, it clearly also featured the effects of watching a model.

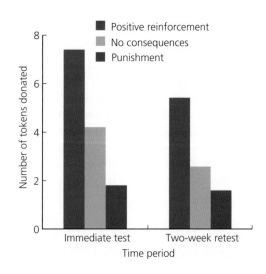

Source: Based on Rushton & Teachman (1978).

Exposure to models. Young children soon learn the value of sharing and helping one another.

Source: Pearson Online Database (POD)

innocent victim. According to the just-world hypothesis proposed by Melvin Lerner and Dale Miller (Lerner & Miller, 1978), people need to believe – perhaps for their own security – that the world is a just place where people get what they deserve (see Chapter 2). Therefore, if some victims deserve their fate, we can think 'Good, they had that coming to them!' and not help them. Perhaps a rape victim 'deserved' what happened because her clothing was too tight or revealing? Accepting that the world must necessarily be a just place begins in childhood and is a learned attribution.

Fortunately, most of us respond to evidence that suffering is undeserved. Accepting this undermines the power of belief in a just world and allows justice to be done. A necessary precondition of actually helping is to believe that the help will be effective. Miller (1977) isolated two factors that can convince a would-be helper: (1) the victim is a special case rather than one of many, and (2) the need is temporary rather than persisting. Each of these allows us to decide that giving aid 'right now' will be effective.

> **Just-world hypothesis**
> According to Lerner, people need to believe that the world is a just place where they get what they deserve. Examples of undeserved suffering undermine this belief, and people may conclude that victims deserve their fate.

Norms for helping

Often we help others simply because 'something tells us' we should. Help that little old lady cross the street, hand in a wallet we found in the supermarket, help a crying child. An important influence that develops and sustains prosocial behaviour is a cultural norm. *Norms* provide a steady check for how we should act (see Chapters 5 and 6) and are quintessentially learned rather than innate. A norm is a standard that specifies what is expected, 'normal' or proper.

Almost every culture shares a norm that 'concern for others is good; selfishness is bad'. An unwritten rule is that when the cost is not very great and another person's need is high, we should help. If a norm of social responsibility is universal, it means that it is functional and that it facilitates social life. One way to account for why we help others, therefore, is to say that it is *normative*. There are social rewards for behaving in accord with the norm and sanctions for violating the norm. Sanctions may range from mild disapproval to incarceration or worse, depending on the threat posed to the existing social order.

Two norms have been proposed as a basis for altruism:

Reciprocity norm
The principle of 'doing unto others as they do to you'. It can refer to returning a favour, mutual aggression or mutual help.

1. The reciprocity norm. We should help those who help us. It is said that this norm, also referred to as the *reciprocity principle*, is as universal as the incest taboo. However, the extent to which we should reciprocate varies. Abraham Tesser found that we feel deeply indebted when someone freely makes a big sacrifice for us but much less so if what they do is smaller and expected (Tesser, Gatewood & Driver, 1968). Further, people might help only in return for help given in the past or anticipated in the future. People driven by egoism are more likely to act prosocially when they believe their reputations are at stake (Simpson & Willer, 2008).

Social responsibility norm
The idea that we should help people who are dependent and in need. It is contradicted by another norm that discourages interfering in other people's lives.

2. The social responsibility norm. We should give help freely to those in need without regard to future exchanges. Members of a community are often willing to help the needy, even when they remain anonymous donors and do not expect any social reward (Berkowitz, 1972b). In practice, people usually apply this norm selectively, e.g. to those in need through no fault of their own rather than to callers at the front door. The extent to which people internalise as a norm beliefs about the future of our planet has been linked to environmental activism (Stern, Dietz & Guagnano, 1995; Fielding, McDonald & Louis, 2008).

Neither norm can realistically explain prosocial behaviour in animals (Stevens, Cushman & Hauser, 2005). If reciprocity applies to humans then it is distinctive to humans; and there is no room for a social responsibility norm in animals.

The next approach is also social psychological but gives greater emphasis to cognitive factors. Because of the huge effect it had on research in the field of prosocial behaviour we highlight it in a separate section.

Bystander apathy

Bystander intervention
This occurs when an individual breaks out of the role of a bystander and helps another person in an emergency.

Bystander effect
People are less likely to help in an emergency when they are with others than when alone. The greater the number, the less likely it is that anyone will help.

Recall that in the 1980s Jane Piliavin and her colleagues wanted to know how empathy impacted on whether people chose to help or not help in an emergency. However, this field of research has an older history. A single event gave it a major impetus – the murder of a young woman called Kitty Genovese in New York in 1964. Her murder appalled New York residents (see Box 9.2).

The initial frenzy of research that followed Kitty Genovese's murder focused on the situational factors that affect bystander intervention rather than on how helping behaviour is learned. Failure to intervene fairly naturally invited a focus on people's thinking processes, leading to developing a cognitive model of helping. What has this revealed? We now know that a lone bystander is more likely to help than any of several bystanders, a phenomenon known as the bystander effect. (Perhaps this applies to Lily; see the third focus question.) The most influential research was that of Latané and Darley (1970).

Real world 9.2
The Kitty Genovese murder: a trigger for research on bystander intervention

Late one night in March 1964, Kitty Genovese was on her way home from work at the time she was attacked by a knife-wielding maniac. The scene was the Kew Gardens in the borough of Queens in New York, a respectable neighbourhood. Her screams and struggles drove off the attacker at first but, seeing no one come to the woman's aid, the man attacked again. Once more she escaped, shouting and crying for help. Yet her screams were to no avail and she was soon cornered again. She was stabbed eight more times and then sexually molested. In the half-hour or so that it took for the man to kill Kitty, not one of her neighbours helped her.

About half an hour after the attack began, the local police received a call from an anonymous witness. He reported the attack but would not give his name because he did not want to 'get involved'. The next day, when the police interviewed the area's residents, thirty-eight people openly admitted to hearing the screaming. They had all had time to do something but failed to act. It is perhaps understandable that some had not rushed out into the street for fear of also being attacked, but why did they not at least call the police?

This particularly tragic and horrific event received national media attention in America, all asking why none of the neighbours had helped. Not surprisingly, there was heightened interest from social psychologists, including Latané and Darley (1976, p. 309):

> This story became the journalistic sensation of the decade. 'Apathy,' cried the newspapers. 'Indifference,' said the columnists and commentators. 'Moral callousness', 'dehumanisation', 'loss of concern for our fellow man', added preachers, professors and other sermonisers. Movies, television specials, plays and books explored this incident and many like it. Americans became concerned about their lack of concern.

Read how the story of Kitty's murder first broke at http://kewgardenshistory.com/ss-nytimes-3.html

Bystander intervention. It is an irony that your best chance of being helped in an emergency is when only one bystander is present.

Source: Pearson Online Database (POD)

Helping in an emergency

Stemming directly from the wide public discussion and concern about the Genovese case, Bibb Latané and John Darley began a programme of research (Darley & Latané, 1968), now considered a classic in social psychology. Surely, these researchers asked, empathy for another's suffering, or at the very least a sense of civic responsibility, should lead to an intervention in a situation of danger? Furthermore, where several bystanders are present, there should be a correspondingly greater probability that someone will help. Before dealing with this theory, consider the elements of an emergency situation:

- It can involve danger, for person or property.
- It is an unusual event, rarely encountered by the ordinary person.
- It can differ widely in nature, from a bank on fire to a pedestrian being mugged.
- It is not foreseen, so that prior planning of how to cope is improbable.
- It requires instant action, so that leisurely consideration of options is not feasible.

Emergency situation
Often involves an unusual event, can vary in nature, is unplanned, and requires a quick response.

It would be easy to label the failure to help a victim in an emergency as apathy, but Latané and Darley reasoned that more rational processes were involved. An early and crucial finding was that failure to help occurred more often when the size of the group of witnesses increased. Latané and Darley's cognitive model of bystander intervention proposes that whether a person helps depends on the outcomes of a series of decisions. At any point along this path, a decision could be made that would terminate a tendency to help. The steps in this model are described in Box 9.3, and the decision process is illustrated in Figure 9.4.

In one experiment (Latané & Rodin, 1969), male students were led to believe that someone had been injured. They were either alone or in pairs filling in a questionnaire when they heard what sounded like a woman in another room struggling to open a filing cabinet. Then they heard a loud crash, followed by a cry of pain and moans and groans. Those who were alone helped 70 per cent of the time but those in pairs only 40 per cent of the time. Participants who were with a passive confederate, a manipulation that suggested the situation was not critical, helped only 7 per cent of the time.

A major outcome of these studies is that personal responsibility is enhanced when there is just *one* onlooker in an emergency. (Again, this is relevant to Lily's case described in the third focus question.) Latané and Darley proposed several psychological processes that can trigger the reluctance to help when others are present. In a variety of experiments they delivered cogent evidence that *all* of these can account for bystander apathy, and that their effects are cumulative:

- *Diffusion of responsibility*. Other onlookers give an opportunity to transfer the responsibility for acting, or not acting, on to them. We may not actually see them. It is necessary only that they be available, somewhere, for action. People who are alone are most likely to help a victim because they believe they carry the entire responsibility for action. The presence of just one other witness allows diffusion of responsibility to operate.
- *Audience inhibition*. Other onlookers can make people self-conscious about an intended action; people do not want to appear foolish by overreacting. In the context of prosocial behaviour, this process is sometimes referred to as a fear of social blunders. Have you felt a dread of being laughed at for misunderstanding little crises involving others? What if things are not as they seem? What if someone is playing a joke?

Fear of social blunders
The dread of acting inappropriately or of making a foolish mistake witnessed by others. The desire to avoid ridicule inhibits effective responses to an emergency by members of a group.

Research classic 9.3
Steps in Latané and Darley's cognitive model: When will we help?

1 Do we even notice an event where helping may be required, such as an accident?

2 How do we interpret the event? We are most likely to define a situation as an emergency, and most likely to help, when we believe that the victim's condition is serious and is about to deteriorate rapidly. Findings show that people are more likely to help in emergencies (e.g. someone needs an insulin shot for diabetes) than in non-emergencies (e.g. needing some allergy medicine). Verbal distress cues (e.g. screaming) are particularly effective and increase the likelihood of bystander intervention. Bystander apathy is markedly reduced once people interpret a situation as an emergency.

3 Do we accept personal responsibility for helping? Sometimes a person witnessing an emergency knows that there are other onlookers but cannot see their reactions. This was clearly the case in the Genovese incident. Sometimes the decision to assume responsibility is determined by how competent the bystander feels in the particular situation. For both steps 2 and 3, the influence of other people is clearly a determining factor.

4 What do we decide to do?

5 Is help given? If we doubt whether the situation is an emergency, or we do not know what to do if it is, the behaviour of others around us can influence how we respond.

Source: Based on Darley & Latané (1968).

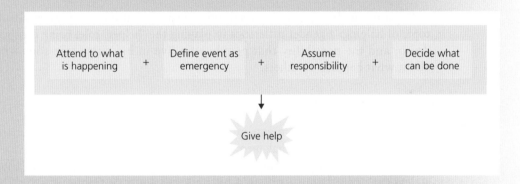

Figure 9.4

Deciding whether to help in Latané and Darley's cognitive model.

Source: Based on Latané & Darley (1970).

- *Social influence.* Other onlookers provide a model for action. If they are passive and unworried, the situation may seem less serious.

Generally speaking, bystander apathy characterises the behaviour of strangers, and is most evident when they know they will not interact later and possibly need to explain their lack of action. When bystanders know each other, help is much more likely to be given, particularly if the victim is an acquaintance, friend or relative, or is a child being abused in a public place (Christy & Voigt, 1994).

We suspect you have already thought of this question: are there some people who are usually more helpful than others? Let us see.

Who are the helpful people?

There is a psychological maxim that 'behaviour is a product of the individual and the environment'. Are there personal characteristics that are relatively independent of the situation? There is a potpourri of research findings dealing with mood and several individual differences. These include the following:

- *Mood.* When people feel good, they are more sensitive to the needs of others and therefore more helpful. For example, this can happen if you have performed well in a task and have a 'warm glow of success' (Isen, 1970). The opposite holds for people in a bad mood. In either case, giving help leads to a good mood!
- *Personality measures.* These have little or no bearing on being helpful. Further, there is no stand-alone, altruistic personality (Latané & Darley, 1970). At most, someone's personality might interact with particular aspects of the situation or of the victim.
- *The 'Good Samaritan'.* Supporting evidence is weak (Schwartz, 1977). However, people who are consistently helpful tend to be taller, heavier and physically stronger, and better trained to cope with crimes and emergencies (see Huston, Ruggiero, Conner & Geis, 1981).
- *Attachment style.* People who are secure are somewhat more compassionate and altruistic (Mikulincer & Shaver, 2005). We deal with attachment style in more detail in Chapter 10.

We continue by considering three other factors that have intriguing links to the topic of helping: a gender difference in playing the 'helper' role; being competent to do so; and the possibility that people who live in big cities care somewhat less about what happens to others.

Gender differences

Are men destined to be 'knights in shining armour'? The literature of romance but also of science indicates that men are more likely to help women than vice versa. Examples of research contexts include helping a motorist in distress (flat tyre, stalled car), or offering a ride to a hitchhiker (Latané & Dabbs, 1975). When the person in need of such help is female, passing cars are much more likely to stop than for a man or for a male–female pair. Those who stop are typically young men driving alone. A meta-analysis by Alice Eagly showed that the strongest combination was that of males being more helpful to women – and importantly, despite a baseline difference of women showing more empathy generally than men (Eagly & Crowley, 1986). Read about an interesting study that explored a connection between sexual arousal and the likelihood of helping someone of either sex who is in trouble (see Box 9.4 and Figure 9.5.)

Competence: 'have skills, will help'

Feeling competent to deal with an emergency makes it more likely that help will be given; there is the awareness that 'I know what I'm doing' (Korte, 1971).

Specific kinds of competence have increased helping in these contexts:

- People who were told they had a high tolerance for electric shock were more willing to help others move electrically charged objects (Midlarsky & Midlarsky, 1976).

Research and applications 9.4
Prosocial behaviour and male-female interactions

Might men be motivated by sexual attraction to help women in trouble? Probably so, according to Peter Benson who found that more physically attractive women received more help (Benson, Karabenick & Lerner, 1976). David Przybyla (1986) clarified the effect of sexual arousal more directly. Male and female students watched either an erotic or non-erotic video, or none at all. When leaving the laboratory, they passed either a male or a female confederate who 'accidentally' knocked over a stack of papers and cried out 'oh no!' Will the passer-by help to clean up the mess? The results are shown in Figure 9.5. Almost all the males who had seen an erotic tape were motivated to help a female. They also spent a relaxed six minutes helping a woman, but a man in need got short shrift – thirty seconds!

Przybyla noted that both men and women reported degrees of arousal when viewing the erotic tape. The more aroused the man felt, the longer he spent helping a woman, an effect not extended to another man. In contrast, the more aroused women spent less time helping anyone. It is possible that male altruism towards women is confounded with a desire to be romantic. However, women are less likely to initiate interactions with strangers (especially men), due perhaps to socialisation experiences. This is a *social role* explanation of cross-gender helping and has been supported in a recent study by Lori Karakashian (Karakashian, Walter, Christopher & Lucas, 2006).

Figure 9.5

Helping an opposite-sex stranger as a function of sexual arousal.

- Male and female students watched either an erotic or non-erotic video, or none at all.
- The use of erotic material was to induce sexual arousal and explore its consequences on helping others.
- They then saw either a male or a female confederate who needed some help.
- There was one huge sex-difference: males, but not females, were very ready to help an opposite-sex stranger.

Source: Based on data from Przybyla (1986).

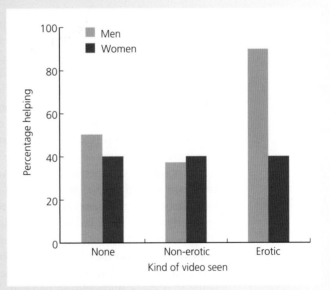

- People who were told they were good at handling rats were more likely to help recapture a 'dangerous' laboratory rat (Schwartz & David, 1976).
- The competence effect may even generalise beyond a restricted context. Kazdin and Bryan (1971) found that people who thought they had done well on a health examination, or even on a creativity task, were later more willing to donate blood.

Certain 'packages' of skills are perceived as relevant to some emergencies. In reacting to a stranger who was bleeding, people with first-aid training intervened more often than those who were untrained (Shotland & Heinold, 1985).

Competence in an emergency. 'Trust us – we know what we're doing.'

Source: Pearson Online Database (POD)

Pantin and Carver (1982) improved the level of students' competence by showing them a series of films on first aid and emergencies. Three weeks later, they had the chance to help a confederate who was apparently choking. The bystander effect was reduced by having previously seen the films. Pantin and Carver also reported that the increase in helping persisted over time. This area of skill development is at the core of Red Cross first-aid training courses for ordinary people in many countries.

The impact of skill level was tested experimentally by comparing professional help with novice help (Cramer, McMaster, Bartell & Dragna, 1988). The participants were two groups of students, one being highly competent (registered nurses) and the other less competent (general-course students). In a contrived context, each participant waited in the company of a non-helping confederate. The nurses were more likely than the general students to help a workman, seen earlier, who had apparently fallen off a ladder in an adjoining corridor (a rigged accident replete with pre-recorded moans). In responding to a post-experimental questionnaire, the nurses specified that they felt they had the skills to help.

To sum up: situations highlighting the fact that a person possesses relevant skills implies that these skills should be used. The self-perception is: 'I know what to do, so I have the responsibility to act'. Competence may be situation-specific, but there is the tantalising possibility that it may last over time and also generalise to non-related situations.

Living in big cities

Latané and Darley (1970) found that fairly obvious demographic variables, such as a parent's occupation and number of siblings, were not correlated with helping behaviour. However, there was the intriguing suggestion that size of one's home town might be connected. People from small-town backgrounds were more likely to help than those from larger cities, a finding replicated by Gelfand, Hartmann, Walder and Page (1973).

Paul Amato (1983) studied size of population in a direct fashion. He investigated people's willingness to help in fifty-five Australian cities and towns, focusing on acts such as picking up fallen envelopes, giving a donation to charity, giving a favourite colour for a student project, correcting inaccurate directions that are overheard and helping a stranger who has hurt a leg and collapsed on the footpath. With the exception of picking up the fallen envelope, the results showed that as population size rose (i.e. in the larger towns and cities), acts of helping decreased. The results for four of the helping measures are shown in Figure 9.6. Best-fit regression lines for each set of data points are shown. You can see that there is a consistent trend downwards for helping a stranger as the population level rises.

Various reasons have been advanced for rural–urban differences in helping or not helping. Perhaps rural people care more because they feel less crowded, less rushed and less affected by noise; and generally feel less 'urban overload' and environmental stress than their fellows in a big and bustling city (Bonnes & Secchiaroli, 1995; Halpern, 1995).

What motivates people to be prosocial?

In the preceding sections we have dealt with major theories and relevant research into the nature and origins of prosocial behaviour. Let us now explore how we might unlock and even promote the tendency of people to help their fellows.

The keys to being helpful

Dan Batson has argued that what prompts helping is a question of motivation, and motives involve goals. Is the action an *instrumental goal*, an intermediate step on the way to a person's ultimate self-interest? Or is it an *ultimate goal* in its own right, with any self-benefit as an unintended side effect? We summarise his ideas in Box 9.5.

Figure 9.6

Effect of population level on willingness to help a stranger.

- In cities with large populations, strangers can expect less help from the inhabitants.
- Regression lines have been fitted to the original data points for each helping measure.

Source: Based on data from Amato (1983).

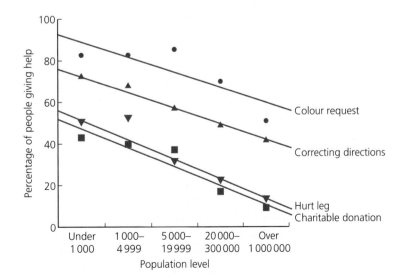

Research and applications 9.5
Four motives for helping others

His research over many years has led Dan Batson to conclude that four motives control prosocial behaviour. How often we help, and the various ways that we might help, depend on one of the following:

1 *Egoism* – prosocial acts benefit one's self. We may help others to secure material, social and self-reward; and to escape punishment.

2 *Altruism* – prosocial acts contribute to the welfare of others. Acting altruistically does not imply that someone should reciprocate. This kind of prosocial motivation is esteemed in many cultures.

3 *Collectivism* – prosocial acts contribute to the welfare of a social group, e.g. one's family, ethnic group or country. Of course, actions that benefit one's ingroup may harm an outgroup (see Chapter 7).

4 *Principlism* – prosocial acts follow a moral principle, such as 'the greatest good for the greatest number'. Although the link between moral reasoning and prosocial behaviour is not strong, the two processes are at least related (Underwood & Moore, 1982).

Sources: Based on Batson (1994); Batson, Ahmad & Tsang, (2002).

Of Batson's four motives, one serves self-interest (an instrumental goal) but the other three are linked to altruism (an ultimate goal). Next, we take some examples of where the promotion of prosocial behaviour has been dealt with in research. We should bear in mind that while all involve prosocial acts, not all are necessarily altruistic. An abiding interest for social psychologists is how to promote ideas that encourage people to be involved in their communities and how they might benefit the common good.

Promoting prosocial behaviour

We consider two particular ways that can encourage people to act prosocially. The first is how we might prevent crime by persuading people to take some personal responsibility. The second is a major issue in the educational sector: how can we reduce cheating in examinations?

Crime prevention

An interesting line of research has focused on the causes and prevention of petty and non-violent crime, such as property theft and shoplifting. Preventing crime can involve a class of prosocial behaviour. The development of neighbourhood watch schemes and accompanying media campaigns are examples of how it might be promoted.

People are most likely to engage in non-violent crime if the benefits are high and the costs are low. For example, offenders often perceive fraud and tax evasion in this way (Hassett, 1981; Lockard, Kirkevold & Kalk, 1980). A riskier crime is property theft, which is statistically more common among younger men. As individuals mature, their assessment of the costs and benefits change. Older people are more likely to deceive a customer or lie about a product or service than to actually steal something. However, research into property theft illustrates two important phenomena related to prosocial behaviour: responsibility and commitment.

People are much more likely to help others if they have a feeling of *responsibility* for providing assistance. For example, we now know that people feel responsible if they are the only witness to a crime or accident, or if they have been trained to deal with emergencies. Feeling responsible for providing aid increases the likelihood of prosocial behaviour. This is called prior commitment, a specific form of responsibility that can induce a prosocial act.

In a series of real-life encounters based on staged thefts, Thomas Moriarty (1975) chose individuals who were sitting alone on a crowded New York beach and then sat next to them with a radio and blanket. Shortly afterwards, he talked to his new neighbour and either simply asked for a match (smoking was prevalent in those days!), or asked them to watch his things while he went for a short walk. All participants agreed to the second request, thereby committing themselves to be *responsible bystanders*. Then a 'thief' (confederate) came along, picked up the radio and quickly walked away. Of participants who were only asked for a match, just 20 per cent took action by intervening, compared with 95 per cent for those specifically asked to be responsible. Most of those who helped even ran after the thief, demanding an explanation, with some even grabbing the thief's arm. Who said New Yorkers don't care!

The powerful effect of being committed has been demonstrated in other ways: for example, watching a stranger's suitcase in a laundrette or a student's books in a library.

Taking responsibility

Earlier in this book we noted that Dariusz Dolinski (2000) explored how being committed to someone enhanced the tendency to act responsibly towards them as well. His study was conducted on a street in Poland. People tried to handle a simple request but were unable to comply because it was actually impossible. Nevertheless, this trivial level of commitment led them to help with a larger but possible request. (See Figure 5.7 in Chapter 5.)

A variation on the theme of competence, commitment and responsibility has been explored in the context of acting as a leader. We might think that a leader is, by definition, more generally competent than followers and more likely to initiate all kinds of action (see Chapter 6), including helping in an emergency. The skills component of leadership could probably be used to account for some helping outcomes. Even so, a study by Roy Baumeister and his colleagues specified an additional feature of the leadership role that goes beyond the 'have skills, will help' explanation: simply being a leader acts as a cue to generalised responsibility. In an emergency situation, Baumeister hypothesised, the leader does not experience the same degree of diffusion of responsibility as ordinary group members. Read how they tested for this in Box 9.6.

Can we discourage exam cheating?

Exam cheating in schools and universities has been an interesting topic to social psychologists. These days, cheating extends to plagiarising other people's work, including material downloaded from the Internet. In a massive American survey (Gallup, 1978), about two-thirds of the population admitted that they had cheated in school at least once. Donald McCabe's review of more recent surveys confirms this trend (McCabe, Trevino & Butterfield, 2001). The link between cheating and personality measures is not strong, suggesting that transgressions are related to situational factors.

One short-term situational effect is *arousal* – a feeling of excitement or a thrill from taking a chance. Why not cheat, at least when there is little chance of being

Prior commitment
An individual's agreement in advance to be responsible if trouble occurs: for example, committing oneself to protect the property of another person against theft.

Research and applications 9.6
Acting like a leader counteracts diffusion of responsibility:
'Who's in charge around here?'

A major requirement of effective leadership is to guide decision making for a group (see Chapter 6) and, in an emergency, to provide control and direction for action. In an experiment by Baumeister, Chesner, Senders and Tice (1988) thirty-two male and female students (seven others were dropped because they suspected a deception) were led to believe they had been allocated to four-person groups, in which one member was supposedly randomly assigned to act as leader. The students were told that their task was to decide which survivors of a nuclear war should be allowed to join the group in its bomb shelter. The assistants could make recommendations, but their designated leader would make the final decision.

Participants were actually tested individually, half as leaders and half as followers, and group discussion was simulated using tape recordings over an intercommunication system. At a critical point, each participant was exposed to a simulated emergency, when the recorded voice of a male group member faltered and said, 'Somebody come help me, I'm choking!' He then had a fit of coughing and went

silent. The experimenter met those who came out of the test room to help, telling them there was no problem. All were later debriefed.

Those designated as leaders were much more likely to help than assistants: as high as 80 per cent (twelve of fifteen) leaders helped, but only 35 per cent (six of seventeen) followers did so.

Now, the leaders in this study were randomly allocated to their role, so the outcome cannot be explained in terms of their merely having a set of personal skills. In Baumeister's view, acting as a leader brings with it a generalised responsibility, which:

- goes beyond the immediate requirement of the group task to involve other external events;

- provides a buffer against the usual process of diffusion of responsibility to which ordinary members are prone, and which can mediate the seeming indifference to helping a victim.

Source: Based on Baumeister, Chesner, Senders & Tice (1988).

caught? Arousal, such as being in an exam room, may even increase cheating. The clinical psychologists Robert Lueger (1980) and Gerald Heisler (1974) have cast light on this issue. Lueger suggested that arousal is distracting and makes us less able to regulate our behaviour. In his experiment, participants saw either an arousing film or a relaxing one and then had the chance to cheat while taking a test. In the relaxed condition 43 per cent cheated, but in the aroused condition 70 per cent cheated. Paradoxically, as Heisler found, warning students about to sit an exam of the penalties for being caught cheating may actually increase cheating, perhaps because they are also more aroused.

How can we discouraging cheating? A traditional reaction is to increase the severity of punishments available. However, one estimate is that only about one in five self-reported cheaters are ever caught (Gallup, 1978). McCabe's review provided some contextual clues: less cheating occurred at universities with smaller campuses, where fewer peers cheated and where an honour code and standards of academic integrity had been highlighted. This is consistent with Batson's ideal of principlism built on moral reasoning.

People usually agree that cheating is wrong, and those who do cheat disapprove as strongly as those who do not (Hughes, 1981). Richard Dienstbier has noted that some institutions have introduced programmes to raise the ethical awareness of their pupils and to promote prosocial behaviour in various ways (Dienstbier, Kahle, Willis

& Tunnell, 1980). This study reported some success by focusing less on students' assumed lack of morality and more on how to make ethical standards salient.

Our final section in this chapter is clearly devoted to one's community and the common good.

Volunteers: the ultimate helpers

Many people now take an interest in another form of spontaneous helping – volunteering, an activity that has become more and more important for the common good in times of government retrenchment. Gil Clary and Mark Snyder have noted that retaining a high level of volunteering in any community involves earmarking situations of opportunities and enhancing a sense of personal control among the volunteers (Clary & Snyder, 1991, 1999). Volunteers commonly offer to others a sense of community, or civic participation (Omoto & Snyder, 2002). This can show itself by being a companion for the elderly, counselling troubled people, tutoring the illiterate, making home visits to the terminally ill through the hospice movement, or acting as a support person for AIDS victims. In the United States in 1998, more than one million people gave 3.5 hours per week acting in these and similar ways. Mark Davis and his colleagues have shown that voluntary activities that entail some distress, which is an example of a response invoking empathy discussed earlier, require well-designed training programmes to prepare the volunteer (Davis, Hall & Meyer, 2003).

Sometimes the idea of volunteering involves high-profile individuals who can and have done much good for many people. The humanitarian gestures of Bob Geldof, the founder of Live Aid, and of Bono spring to mind. We must add that even what is arguably the noblest of motives, altruism, continues to be questioned. Is it real? Even volunteers, it seems, may in some senses be self-serving.

Batson allows that community involvement can be driven by an egoistic motive (Batson, Ahmad & Tsang, 2002), but argues that it is just one of four, as we have discussed earlier; and that all four have both strengths and weaknesses. In recruiting

The ultimate helpers. Volunteering is a praiseworthy form of spontaneous helping – sometimes it takes a little reminder.

Source: The Advertising Archives

volunteers, an effective strategy is to steer them to supplement egoism with additional reasons based on altruism, principlism, or both. Evert van der Vliert and his colleagues also pointed to other very broad features, not located within the person as such, that affect whether egoism or altruism comes into play. In a cross-cultural comparison of volunteers in thirty-three countries, they found the two motives can be separated in some countries but not in others. The picture they paint is complex. Put simply, the weight given to each motive depends on a country's ecology (the climate) and its overall wealth (van de Vliert, Huang & Levine, 2004).

In closing, let us reflect on what we have covered in this and the preceding chapter. We have seen that both brutal and charitable aspects of humanity – hurting others versus helping others – entail strong physical reactions that are rooted in our biology. There are ways that we can reduce aggression and promote prosocial behaviour. Moreover, acting in ways that contribute to the common good can be learned and, more importantly, entrenched as social norms. One thing that social psychologists can do is to spread this message.

Summary

- When we act prosocially we do things that are positively valued by society. This includes being helpful and altruistic. Helping is acting intentionally in a way that benefits someone else.

- We are altruistic when we want to benefit another person without expecting personal gain. It is difficult to identify acts of pure altruism in someone else because their motives or rewards are often private.

- Theories of prosocial behaviour have different and occasionally contrary arguments. At the extremes are heavily biological and heavily social viewpoints.

- A biological approach grew from ethology that concentrated on animals in their natural environment. Later, evolutionary theory tried to account for 'altruism' in animals and to argue for a genetic explanation of human altruism as well.

- A moderate biosocial approach was the basis for focusing on physiological arousal and empathy, brought together in the bystander-calculus model.

- In social learning theory, prosocial behaviour is treated similarly to aggressive behaviour. As the name of the theory suggests, both kinds of behaviour can surely be learned. Other emphases in a strongly social approach are the roles of attribution and of norms.

- The Kitty Genovese murder had a huge influence on research dealing with human prosocial behaviour and unravelled the nature of bystander apathy. A theory emerged that favoured cognitive, decision-making processes thought to underlie how we respond to emergencies.

- Situational factors generally outweigh personal factors in accounting for prosocial behaviour. However, there are some personal attributes that enhance people's willingness to help others. These include good mood and a high level of competence in an individual.

- There are important gender differences. Women are usually more sensitive to the needs of others. In a mixed-sex context, men are more likely to help a woman in need than vice versa.

- Research fields dealing with prosocial behaviour have provided good examples of how social psychology can be usefully applied. These include studies of how to prevent academic cheating, and how to involve people more in their community through volunteering activities.

Literature, film and TV

Schindler's Ark

Thomas Keneally's 1982 novel about how Otto Schindler, a German living in Krakow during the Second World War, took enormous risks to save Jews from the gas chambers of Auschwitz. The book was made into a 1993 film called *Schindler's List*, directed by Stephen Spielberg, and starring Liam Neeson and Ben Kingsley.

The Girl in the Café

Although this 2005 film by David Yates, starring Bill Nighy and Kelly Macdonald, is largely a gentle love story it also has a sharper subtext. The setting is the 2005 G8 meeting in Reykjavik at which decisions are to be made about helping the developing world out of poverty. The film illustrates how difficult it can be to engineer collective prosocial behaviour.

Smallville

A popular US TV series that is based around the super-human but also altruistic actions of Clark Kent, aka Superboy!

The Trial

Franz Kafka's prophetic 1935 novel about being trapped in a monstrous bureaucratic system where it is rare to encounter a real human being and no-one and nothing seems to be designed to help you. A world devoid of prosocial behaviour.

The Bonfire of the Vanities

This powerful 1987 novel by Tom Wolfe is about greed and selfishness – the very antithesis of prosocial or altruistic behaviour. It was also made into a film directed by Brian de Palma (1990), and starring Tom Hanks, Bruce Willis and Melanie Griffiths.

Pay It Forward

A 'feel-good' film by Mimi Leder (2000), with Kevin Spacey and Helen Hunt, concerns a small boy, played by Haley Joel Osment, who takes the opportunity to make the world a better place, by starting a chain where people do an altruistic act for three other people, and each of them does it to another three, and so forth.

Secret Millionaire

A popular TV reality show first aired in 2006 in the UK. Millionaires go incognito to live like locals in impoverished communities – they identify worthy projects and individuals to donate tens of thousands of pounds of their own fortune to. On their final day the millionaires come clean and reveal their identity to the lucky people they have chosen – lots of joy and tears ensue.

Guided questions

- How is *empathy* related to helping others who are in need?

- Is there evidence that children can learn to be helpful?

- Suppose that you were in dire need of help in an *emergency*. What factors in the situation would increase your chances of receiving help? Under what conditions are you more likely to be helped?

- What advice could a social psychologist give to a school board to help reduce exam cheating?

- What factors in the situation, or what kinds of individual differences between potential helpers, would increase the chances of a child being bullied receiving help? See some relevant examples in Chapter 9 of MyPsychLab at www.mypsychlab.co.uk.

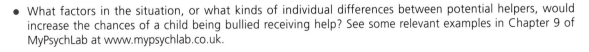

Learn more

Batson, C. D., van Lange, P. A. M., Ahmad, N., & Lishner, D. A. (2003). Altruism and helping behavior. In M. A. Hogg & J. Cooper (eds), *The Sage handbook of social psychology* (pp. 279–95). London: Sage. Comprehensive, up-to-date and easily accessible overview of research on altruism and prosocial behaviour.

Clark, M. S. (ed) (1991). *Prosocial behaviour.* Newbury Park, CA: Sage. A good coverage in its time by the major theorists who have helped to build the social psychology of helping behaviour.

Eisenberg, N., & Mussen, P. H. (1989). *The roots of prosocial behaviour in children.* Cambridge, UK: Cambridge University Press. A concise introduction to the methods and main concepts used in this field, with an emphasis on the socialisation process and the connections of prosocial behaviour to the development of moral reasoning.

Penner, L. A., Dovidio, J. F., Piliavin, J. A., & Schroeder, D. A. (2005). Prosocial behaviour. *Annual Review of Psychology*, 56, 365–392. As well as covering recent studies in the field, this review offers a 'levels of analysis' approach including helper–recipient dyads, origins of and variations in prosocial tendencies, and prosocial actions in groups and organisations.

Schroeder, D. A., Penner, L. A., Dovidio, J. F., & Piliavin, J. A. (1995). *The psychology of helping and altruism.* New York: McGraw-Hill. A good general overview of the literature dealing with prosocial behaviour.

Spacapan, S., & Oskamp, S. (eds) (1992). *Helping and being helped.* Newbury Park, CA: Sage. The contributors deal with a wide range of real-life altruism, including spouse support of stroke patients, family support for people with Alzheimer's disease and kidney donors.

 Refresh your understanding, assess your progress and go further with interactive summaries, questions, podcasts, videos and much more on the website accompanying the book: **www.mypsychlab.co.uk**.

Chapter 10

Attraction and close relationships

What to look for

- How attraction evolved
- The appealing body
- Contextual cues and attraction
- Culture intervenes
- Rewards and costs in selecting a mate
- Why we get attached
- Liking and loving
- Close relationships and well-being
- Marriage: love or a contract?
- Relationships that work
- Ending a relationship

Focus questions

1. Carol finds David more attractive than Paul but bumps into him less often. Who do you think Carol is most likely to get to like and perhaps have a relationship with?

2. Erik and Charles have been chatting over a few drinks when Erik remarks that he is 'profiting' from his latest romantic relationship. Charles doesn't know what to say, but thinks this a callous comment. Can you offer a more benign interpretation?

3. Even when they were dating, Kamesh felt that Aishani was mostly uncomfortable when they were with other people. She also avoided having other members of their families visit them. Now, Aishani does not seem very interested in their new baby. Are these events somehow connected?

4. Can we study love scientifically – or should we pack the statistics away and leave it to the poets? Robert Sternberg discusses his general approach and the main components of his triangular theory of love in Chapter 10 of MyPsychLab at www.mypsychlab.co.uk.

Source: Blend Images / Alamy

Collectively we are known as the species *Homo sapiens* – wise, knowing and judicious humans. Given the modern interest in the nature of cognition – how we think – this description might seem apt, but it is barely half the story. We live as social beings. We love and help, hate and fight. This chapter deals with the liking and the loving part, and more fundamentally with why we want to be with others. Perhaps there is a term missing from our dictionary: *Homo socius* – humans who can be allies, friends and partners. We start with the process of attraction, then take a step back to explore the reasons why we affiliate (i.e. choose the company) with and become attached to others, and ask the perennial question 'What is love?' We conclude with how our most intimate relationships can be maintained and what happens when they break down.

Attractive people

We just *know* when we are attracted to someone. We are allured, perhaps charmed, captivated, even enthralled. We want to know and spend time with that person. At one level, attraction is necessary for friendships of any kind to begin, though many first meetings are by chance. At another level, attraction can be the precursor to an intimate relationship. Do you believe in love at first sight?

Perhaps you subscribe to other popular sayings such as: *Never judge a book by its cover, beauty is only skin deep,* and *beauty is in the eye of the beholder.* Unfortunately for some of us, there is evidence that the primary cue in evaluating others is how they look. A systematic *meta-analysis* of more than one hundred studies by Judith Langlois and her colleagues (2000) found that these sayings are myths rather than maxims. As a cautionary note, the overall impact of the findings is reduced because some studies focus on just two categories – the attractive and the unattractive. Bearing this in mind, Langlois *et al.* concluded that attractive people are different from those who are unattractive in how they are judged, how they are treated and how they behave. Here are some of the major findings:

- Attractive children received higher grades from their teachers, showed higher levels of intellectual competence, and were more popular and better adjusted than their unattractive counterparts.
- Attractive adults were more successful in their jobs, liked more, more physically healthy and more sexually experienced than unattractive adults. They had had more dates, held more traditional attitudes, had more self-confidence and self-esteem, and had slightly higher intelligence and mental health.

We can add more to the advantages of having good looks:

- If you are female, babies will gaze longer (Slater *et al.*, 1998)!
- In computer-simulation studies, attractiveness is associated with some feminisation of facial features, even for male faces (Rhodes, Hickford & Jeffrey, 2000), and with having a slimmer figure (Gardner & Tockerman, 1994);
- An attractive person is a youthful person (Buss & Kenrick, 1998), is judged as more honest (Yarmouk, 2000), and, if a female defendant, gets an easier time from jurors (Sigall & Ostrove, 1975).

We have noted that attractive children receive higher grades than unattractive children. David Landy and Harold Sigall (1974) studied the last effect experimentally in university students, asking the question 'Does beauty signal talent?'. Male students graded one or other of two essays of different quality, attached to which was a photograph of the supposed writer, a female student. The same essays were also rated by control participants, but without any photograph. The 'good' and 'poor' essays were paired in turn with either an attractive photograph or a relatively unattractive photograph. The answer to the researchers' question was 'yes' – sad to relate, better grades were given to the attractive female student (see Figure 10.1).

With attractiveness being such an asset, those who spend big on cosmetics and fashion could be making a real investment in their future! Short of this, just a smile can also work wonders. Joe Forgas and his colleagues found that students who smile are punished less after a misdemeanour than those who do not (Forgas, O'Connor & Morris, 1983).

Evolution and attraction

Evolutionary theory, derived in the main from Charles Darwin, has helped by teasing out biological factors that trigger aggression, altruism and the emotions (see Chapters 8, 9 and 11). It has also offered insights that can help us understand some aspects of why we are attracted to some people, and how we might go about choosing a long-term partner. In an extreme form, David Buss (2003) used evolutionary social psychology to argue that close relationships can only be understood in terms of evolutionary theory. Let us consider what modern research has told us about our natural endowment.

Evolutionary social psychology
An extension of evolutionary psychology that views complex social behaviour as adaptive, helping the individual, kin and the species as a whole to survive.

The role of our genes

In the large-scale analysis of studies by Langlois and colleagues cited above, the way that interpersonal attraction develops is related partly to how we select a

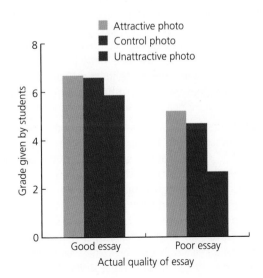

Figure 10.1

Being attractive can lead to better essay grades.

Source: Based on data from Landy & Sigall (1974)

mate. According to the evolutionary concept of *reproductive fitness*, people guess whether a prospective mate has good genes, using cues such as physical health, youthful appearance, and body and facial symmetry. Good looks can also help, since attractive children receive extra care from their parents. Humans can respond to all kinds of cues – e.g. women who sniffed T-shirts of unknown origin preferred those that had been worn by symmetrical men! And further, this was even more likely among those about to ovulate (Gangestad & Simpson, 2000)!

As you know, men 'have a thing' about women's waist-to-hip ratio (WHR). Typically, they prefer the classic hourglass figure (a ratio of 0.70), probably because it signifies youthfulness, good health and fertility. However, there are cultural and ecological effects: in foraging societies, being thin may mean being ill and so men prefer their women to be heavier (i.e. larger WHRs). In Western societies, where heaviness may indicate ill health, men prefer slimmer women (i.e smaller WHRs) (Marlowe & Wetsman, 2001). These effects point to the role of social and contextual factors that go beyond a genetic account.

Attractive faces

Averageness effect
Humans have evolved to prefer average and symmetrical faces to those with unusual or distinctive features.

How would evolutionary theory deal with the maxim *beauty is in the eye of the beholder*? Is physical attractiveness a matter of personal preference, or of fashion in a particular society and its history, or is it something else – in our genes? As part of her research programme dealing with face perception, Gill Rhodes (2006) has extensively researched the social information that our faces convey, including the cues that make a face attractive. One interesting finding is the 'pulling power' of the averageness effect (see Box 10.1 and Figure 10.2).

Research and applications 10.1
Physical appeal – evolutionary or cultural?

What kind of face do we prefer? The preferences of very young children and a high degree of cross-cultural agreement challenge the notion that standards of beauty are dictated by culture. For example, body and facial *symmetry* (of right and left halves) in both women and men contributes to standards that most people have in judging beauty. Perhaps surprisingly, facial *averageness* is another plus.

Gill Rhodes (2006), who has researched extensively how we process information about the human face, asked whether facial beauty depends more on common physical qualities than on striking features. Participants judged caricatures of faces, each of which was systematically varied from average to distinctive. She found that averageness, rather than distinctiveness, was correlated with facial attractiveness (see also Rhodes, Sumich & Byatt, 1999). The averageness effect has also been confirmed in other studies (e.g. Langlois, Roggman & Musselman, 1994).

Rhodes & Tremewan (1996) suggested an evolutionary basis for this effect: average faces draw the attention of infants to those objects in their environment that most resemble the human face – an average face is like a prototype. Face preferences may be adaptations that guide mate choice. Why would facial averageness (and also facial symmetry) make a person more attractive? One possibility is that these cues make a face seem more familiar and less strange. Another possibility is that both averageness and symmetry are signals of good health and therefore of 'good genes' – cues that we latch on to in searching for a potential mate.

See Figure 10.2 for examples of how averageness has been created by combining sets of real faces into composite faces.

Figure 10.2

What makes a face attractive?

- Landmark points were used to align features across individual photographs.

- Face composites were created by averaging the features of 24 real faces.

- These four faces are composites and are usually rated as more attractive than a real individual face.

Source: Rhodes. G. (2006). The evolutional psychology of facial beauty. *Annual review of Psychology*, 57, 199–226. Copyright © 2006 by Annual Reviews. Reproduced with permission from the Annual Review of Psychology and Professor Gill Rhodes.

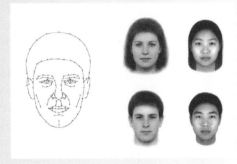

The search for ideals

There are other characteristics of being attractive that may derive *in part* from our genes. Garth Fletcher (Fletcher *et al.*, 2004; also see Buss, 2003) studied the ideals (or standards) that college students look for in a partner. In long-term relationships, three 'ideal partner' dimensions appear to guide the preferences of both men and women:

- *warmth–trustworthiness* – showing care and intimacy;
- *vitality–attractiveness* – signs of health and reproductive fitness;
- *status–resources* – being socially prominent and financially sound.

A fair conclusion is that the physicality of the human is a major cue to initial attraction and that there is an evolutionary and universal basis for some of this. Let us turn now to a number of social and contextual factors also related to what we find attractive.

What increases liking?

Suppose that someone has passed your initial 'attraction' test. What other factors encourage you to take another step? This question has been well researched and points to several crucial factors that determine how we come to like people even more:

- *Proximity* – do they live or work close by?
- *Familiarity* – do we feel that we know them?
- *Similarity* – are they people who are like us?

Proximity

There is a good chance that you will get to like people who are in a reasonable proximity to where you live or work – think of this as the neighbourhood factor. In a famous study of a housing complex led by Leon Festinger (who is also associated with the concept of cognitive dissonance discussed in Chapter 4), it emerged that people were more likely to choose as friends those living in the same building and even on the same floor (Festinger, Schachter & Back, 1950). Subtle architectural

Proximity
The factor of living close by is known to play an important role in the early stages of forming a friendship.

features, such as the location of a staircase, can also affect the process of making acquaintances and establishing friendships.

People who live close by are *accessible*, so that interacting with them requires little effort and the rewards of doing so have little cost. Consider your immediate neighbours: you expect to continue interacting with them and it is better that you are at ease when you do so rather than feeling stressed.

If at the outset you think that you are more likely to interact with John rather than Brian it is probable that you will anticipate (perhaps hope!) that you will like John more (Berscheid, Graziano, Monson & Dermer, 1976). In the first focus question, who will Carol like more, David or Paul?

Proximity became a hazier psychological concept during the twentieth century. The potentially negative impact of having a 'long-distance lover' is lessened by a phone call, an email, or better still by video contact such as 'skyping' (see the review by Bargh & McKenna, 2004). Can we actually pursue a relationship on the net? (See Box 10.2.)

Familiarity

Familiarity
As we become more familiar with a stimulus (even another person), we feel more comfortable with it and we like it more.

Proximity generally leads to greater familiarity – a friend is rather like your favourite pair of shoes, something that you feel comfortable about. Further, Robert Zajonc (1968) found that familiarity enhances liking just as repeatedly presenting stimuli increases liking for them – the basic *mere exposure effect* as used by advertisers to have us feel familiar with new products. Familiarity can account for why we gradually come to like the faces of strangers if we encounter them more often

Real world 10.2
Meeting on the net

Access to a computer and the Internet allows people to meet, form friendships, fall in love, live together or get married. A cyberspace relationship does not necessarily stop there, and some online friends actually meet.

In cyberspace, traditional variables that you would find interesting about someone else are often missing, such as seeing, hearing and touching them. Even so, cyber-relationships can progress rapidly from knowing little about the other person to being intimate; equally, they can be ended very quickly, literally with the 'click of a button'.

From the outset, Internet-mediated relationships differ markedly from offline relationships. A first meeting via the Internet does not give access to the usual range of physical and spoken linguistic cues that help to form an impression, unless the use of digital cameras to exchange images and live video over the Internet increases.

Jacobson (1999) investigated impression formation in comparing online expectation with offline experiences: that is, when people who had met online actually met in person. He found significant discrepancies – people had often formed erroneous impressions about characteristics such as talkativeness ('they seemed so quiet in person') and expansiveness ('they seemed so terse online but were very expressive offline'). People online often constructed images based on stereotypes, such as the vocation of the unseen person. One participant reported:

> I had no idea what to expect with Katya. From her descriptions I got the impression she would be overweight, kinda hackerish, but when we met, I found her very attractive. Normal sized, nice hair, not at all the stereotypical programmer.

(Jacobson, 1999, p. 13)

(Moreland & Beach, 1992). In contrast, when something familiar seems different, people feel uncomfortable. For example, people usually do not like mirror reversals of photos of their own or others' faces (Mita, Dermer & Knight, 1977).

Similarity

There are other important psychological factors that exert some control over attraction. In an early study by Theodore Newcomb (1961), students received rent-free housing in return for filling in questionnaires before they arrived about their attitudes and values. Changes in interpersonal attraction were measured over the course of a semester. Initially, attraction went hand-in-hand with proximity – students liked those who lived close by. Then another factor came into play: having compatible attitudes.

Similarity of attitudes

Newcomb found that, as the semester progressed, the focus shifted to similarity of attitudes. Students with similar pre-acquaintance attitudes became more attractive. This is logical, because in real life it usually takes some time to discover whether or not a housemate thinks and feels in the same way about a variety of social issues.

Donn Byrne and Gerald Clore have carried out extensive research dealing with the connection between sharing attitudes with another person and liking them (Byrne, 1971; Clore & Byrne, 1974). Attitudes that were markedly similar were an important ingredient in maintaining a relationship. The results were so reliable and consistent that Clore (1976) formulated a 'law of attraction' – attraction towards a person bears a linear relationship to the actual proportion of similar attitudes shared with that person. This law was thought to be applicable to more than just attitudes. Anything that other people do that agrees with your perception of things is rewarding, i.e. reinforcing. The more other people agree, the more they act as reinforcers for you and the more you like them. For example, if you suddenly discover that someone you are going out with likes the same obscure rock band as you, your liking for that person will increase.

Conversely, differences in attitudes and interests can lead to avoidance and dislike (Singh & Ho, 2000). The notion that we should be consistent in our thinking, as stressed in the theory of cognitive dissonance (see Chapter 4), may explain this. An inconsistency, such as recognising that we like something but that someone else does not, is cause for worry. A way to resolve this is to not like that person and re-establish consistency. Thus we usually choose or preserve the company of similar others – it makes us feel comfortable.

Social matching

There is an extensive interest devoted to match-making where people are paired up based on having compatible attitudes, but also on sharing demographic characteristics that we discuss further below. But even a seemingly trivial similarity such as one's name can increase attraction. See the study by Jones, Pelham, Carvallo and Mirenberg (2004) based on archival research in Box 10.3.

Similarity of attitudes
One of the most important positive, psychological determinants of attraction.

Research and applications 10.3
What's in a name? A search in the marriage archives

Marriage records that included the names of brides and grooms were downloaded from the website 'Ancestry.com', dating back to the nineteenth century. Several common names were focused on: Smith, Johnson, Williams, Jones and Brown. The researchers predicted that people would seek out others who simply resemble them, and found that people disproportionately married someone whose first or last name resembles their own. It seems that we are egotists at heart. Someone who is similar enough to activate mental associations with 'me' must be a fairly good choice!

In some initial experimental work, the researchers found that people were more attracted to someone with: (a) a random experimental code number (such as a PIN number) resembling their own birth date, (b) a

surname containing letters from their own surname, and (c) a number on a sports jersey that had been paired subliminally, on a computer screen, with their own name.

These results prompted them to carry out an *archival study* of marriage among people with matching surnames. They found the most frequent choices of a marriage partner had the same last name. More than 60% of the Smiths married another Smith, more than 50% of the Joneses married another Jones, and more than 40% of the Williamses married another Williams. All of these choices were well beyond chance.

We can note with passing interest that the senior researcher is named John Jones!

Source: Based on Jones, Pelham, Carvallo & Mirenberg (2004, Study 2).

Assortative mating

Life is not a lucky dip. People seeking a partner do not usually choose one at random, but try to *match* each other on several features. Peruse the personal columns in your local newspaper to see how people describe themselves and what they look for in a potential partner. We bring previously held beliefs to the situation – beliefs about appropriateness such as gender, physique, socioeconomic class and religion. Matching is a form of assortative mating. Susan Sprecher (1998) found that, in addition to the factors of proximity and familiarity, people who are evenly matched in their physical appearance, social background and personality, sociability and interests and leisure activities are more likely to be attracted to one another. There is perhaps some truth in the saying *birds of a feather flock together*.

Assortative mating
A non-random coupling of individuals based on their resemblance to each other on one or more characteristics.

Do cohort studies, conducted across time, support this? Ann Gruber-Baldini and her colleagues carried out such a longitudinal study of married couples over twenty-one years (Gruber-Baldini, Schaie & Willis, 1995). At the time of first testing, they found similarities in age, education, intellectual aptitude and flexibility of attitudes. An additional and interesting finding was that some spouses became even more alike over time on attitude flexibility and word fluency. Thus initial similarity in the phase of assortative mating was enhanced by their experiences together. There is also a strong element of reality testing when it comes to looks, since most usually settle on a romantic partner who is similar to their own level of physical attractiveness (Feingold, 1988).

Studies of dating across ethnic or cultural groups reveal a complex interplay of factors involving *similarity of culture* that influence attraction. A study of heterosexual dating preferences among four ethnic groups in the United States (Asian, African, Latino and Euro/White Americans) showed that participants generally preferred partners from their own ethnic group (Liu, Campbell & Condie, 1995).

Assortative mating. Similarity of age, ethnicity and culture are some factors that increase interpersonal liking, dating and mating.

Source: Pearson Online Database (POD)

Gaining approval from one's social network was the most powerful predictor for partner preferences, followed by similarity of culture and physical attractiveness. The sociologist George Yancey (2007) compared the ethnic choices of White, Black, Hispanic and Asian contributors to the Internet site *Yahoo Personals*. Willingness to meet with partners of different race varied: women were less likely than men to date interracially, while Asians were more likely than Whites or Hispanics to date Blacks. Significantly, interracial dating was lower among those who were conservative politically or high in religiosity (the religious right). On the other hand, several demographic factors (age, city size, level of education) had little influence on ethnic dating preferences.

We can reasonably conclude that, while similarity of culture and ethnicity are important determinants of partner choice, interracial studies point to other factors, particularly values, that come into play. In the world where multi-ethnic societies are increasingly more prevalent, we need to take into account differences between cultures in dating practices and how intimate relationships develop, along with the more obvious factors of proximity and similarity.

Our next section deals with several major theories of the attraction process.

Attraction and rewards

A reinforcement approach

The general idea is simple. People who reward us directly become associated with pleasure and we learn to like them. People who punish us directly become associated with pain and we dislike them, ideas that have a long heritage in philosophy, literature and general psychology. They have also been applied in social psychology to help explain interpersonal attraction (Walster, Walster & Berscheid, 1976).

In a variation related to classical or Pavlovian conditioning (also see Chapter 4), Byrne and Clore (1970) proposed a reinforcement–affect model – just as Pavlov's dog learned to associate the sound of a bell with the positive reinforcement of food, so humans can associate another person with other positive or negative aspects of the immediate environment. They proposed that any *background* (and neutral) stimulus that may be associated even accidentally with reward becomes positively valued. However, if it is associated with punishment it becomes negatively valued.

An example of this was an early environmental experiment by William Griffitt and Russell Veitch (1971) who showed how simple background features, such as feeling hot or crowded, can reduce our attraction to a stranger (see Box 10.4 and Figure 10.3).

The study of how our feelings can be conditioned is connected to another important field in social psychology, the *automatic activation* of attitudes (see Chapter 4). In short, terms such as *affect*, *stimulus value* and *attitude* are related to the fundamental psychological dimensions of *good* versus *bad*, *positive* versus *negative*, and *approach* versus *avoidance* (De Houwer & Hermans, 2001).

Relationships as a social exchange

As we have noted, reinforcement is based on patterns of rewards and punishments. When we look at how economics is applied to studying social behaviour, psychologists talk about social exchange: payoffs, costs and rewards.

Is there a relationships marketplace out there, where we humans can satisfy our needs to interact, be intimate, 'love and be loved in return'? While social exchange theory is one of a family of theories based on behaviourism, it is also an approach to studying interpersonal relationships that incorporates *interaction*. Further, it deals directly with close relationships.

Costs and benefits

If two people are to progress in a relationship it will be because they gain from the way that they exchange benefits (i.e. rewards). Social exchange is a model of behaviour introduced by the sociologist George Homans (1961): it accounts for our interpersonal relationships using economic concepts and is wedded to behaviourism. Whether we like someone is determined by the cost–reward ratio: 'What will it cost me to get a positive reward from that person?' Social exchange theory also argues that the each participant's outcomes are determined by their *joint* actions.

A relationship is an ongoing everyday activity. We seek to obtain, preserve or exchange things of value with other human beings. We bargain. What are we prepared to give in exchange for what they will give us? Some exchanges are brief and may have shallow meaning, while others are ongoing and long-term and may be extremely

Reinforcement–affect model
Model of attraction which postulates that we like people who are around when we experience a positive feeling (which itself is reinforcing).

Social exchange
People often use a form of everyday economics when they weigh up costs and rewards before deciding what to do.

Behaviourism
An emphasis on explaining observable behaviour in terms of reinforcement schedules.

Cost–reward ratio
Tenet of social exchange theory, according to which liking for another is determined by calculating what it will cost to be reinforced by that person.

Research classic 10.4
Evaluating a stranger when we feel hot and crowded

After completing a 24-item attitude scale designed to measure opinions on a variety of social issues, imagine that you were later invited to participate by completing a further series of questionnaires along with other students in an investigation of 'judgemental processes under altered environmental conditions'. You were not to know that you were in one of eight different experimental groups. Dressed lightly in cotton shorts and a cotton shirt, you and your group enter an 'environmental chamber', 3 metres long and 2.2 metres wide.

By using eight groups, the researchers were able to test three independent variables: (a) *heat*, the ambient temperature, which was either normal at 23°C or hot at 34°C; (b) *population density* which consisted of having either 3–5 group members or 12–16 group members in the chamber at one time; (c) *attitude similarity*. Note that some participants would really have experienced a degree of environmental stress by working on their questionnaires in an environment that was either hot or crowded. As a measure of attitude similarity, each participant also rated an anonymous stranger after they had first inspected the stranger's responses to the 24-item attitude scale – the same scale that the participants had completed earlier. What they saw was fictitious. The stranger had made similar responses to a proportion of the items – to either 0.25 (low similarity) or 0.75 (high similarity) of them – as those made by that participant.

Finally, the stranger was also rated in order to calculate a measure of attraction based on two questions: how much the stranger would probably be liked, and how desirable would the stranger be as a work partner.

The result for attitude similarity was striking. Not surprisingly, the stranger who was more similar to a participant was considerably more attractive than one who was less similar, confirming the importance of attitude similarity in determining initial attraction, discussed in an earlier section.

The other results show that feeling hot or feeling crowded also affected how attractive a stranger was judged. In the context of classical conditioning, this means that the mere association of a negatively valued background stimulus, in this case two different environmental stressors, can make another person seem less attractive.

Figure 10.3

Attraction and the reinforcing effects of background features.

- Students rated a fictitious stranger as more attractive when they shared a higher proportion of similar attitudes.

- Stressful background factors, such as feeling hot or feeling crowded, reduced the attractiveness of the stranger.

Source: Based on Griffitt & Veitch (1971)

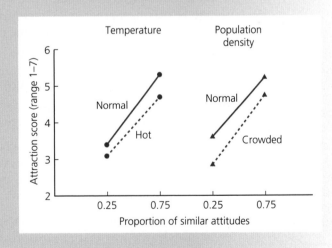

important. In all cases, we experience outcomes or payoffs that depend on what others do. Over time, we try to fashion a way of interacting that is rational and mutually beneficial. Social exchange is a give-and-take relationship between people, and relationships are examples of business transactions. So, is this a dry approach to the study of important relationships? If so, its proponents argue it is nevertheless valid.

Broadly speaking, resources exchanged include goods, information, love, money, services and status (Foa & Foa, 1975). Each can be particular, so that its value depends on who gives the reward. So a hug (a specific case of 'love') will be more valued if it comes from a special person. Each reward can also be concrete, as money clearly is. There are also costs in a relationship, such as the time it takes to pursue it or the way one's friends may frown on it. Because resources are traded with a partner, we try to use a minimax strategy – minimise costs and maximise rewards. Of course, we may not be conscious of doing so and would probably object to the idea that we do!

John Thibaut and Harold Kelley's (1959) *The social psychology of groups* was a major work that underpinned much subsequent research. They argued that we must understand the *structure* of a relationship in order to deal with the behaviour that takes place, as it is this structure that defines the rewards and punishments available. According to the minimax strategy, what follows is that a relationship is unsatisfactory when the costs exceed the rewards. In practice, people exchange resources with one another in the hope that they will earn a profit: that is, one in which the rewards exceed the costs. This is a novel way of defining a 'good relationship'. How might you interpret what Erik meant in the second focus question?

Minimax strategy
In relating to others, we try to minimise the costs and maximise the rewards that accrue.

Profit
This flows from a relationship when the rewards that accrue from continued interaction exceed the costs.

Comparison level
A standard that develops over time, allowing us to judge whether a new relationship is profitable or not.

Comparison levels

A final and important concept in social exchange theory is the part played by each person's comparison level or *CL* – a standard against which all of one's relationships are judged. People's comparison levels are the product of their past experiences with other parties in similar exchanges. If the result in a present exchange is positive (i.e. a person's profit exceeds their *CL*), the relationship will be perceived as satisfying and the other person will seem attractive. However, dissatisfaction follows if the final result is negative (i.e. the profit falls below the *CL*). There is a blessing in this model because it is possible for both people in a relationship to be making a profit and therefore to be gaining satisfaction. The *CL* concept is helpful in accounting for why some relationships might be acceptable at some times but not at others (see Box 10.5).

Does exchange theory have a future?

In summary, the answer to this question is yes. A strong feature of exchange theory is that it accommodates variations in relationships, including:

- differences between people in how they perceive rewards and costs (you might think that free advice from your partner is rewarding, others might not);
- differences within the person based on varying CLs, both over time and across different contexts (I like companionship, but I prefer to shop for clothes alone).

The theory is frequently used. For example, Caryl Rusbult has shown how *investment* includes the way that rewards, costs and CLs are related to both satisfaction and commitment in a relationship (Rusbult, Martz & Agnew, 1998).

Its connections with how we view social justice are explored next, and a review (Le & Agnew, 2003) has shown that the breakdown of a relationship often follows a lack of commitment (discussed later).

Real world 10.5
What do you get from a relationship? An exercise in social exchange

An individual's comparison level or CL is an idiosyncratic judgement point, as each person has had unique experiences. Your CL is the average value of all outcomes of relationships with others in your past, and also of outcomes for others that you may have heard about. It can vary across different kinds of relationship, so your CL for your doctor will be different from that for a lover.

Your entry point into a new relationship is seen against a backdrop of the other people you have known (or known about) in that context, together with the profits and losses you have encountered in relating to them. This running average constitutes a baseline for your relationships in that particular sphere. A new encounter could only be judged as satisfactory if it exceeded this baseline.

Take as an example a date that you have had with another person. The outcome is defined as the rewards (having a nice time, developing a potential relationship) minus the costs (how much money it cost you, how difficult or risky it was to arrange, whether you feel you blew your chance to make a good impression). The actual outcome will be determined by how it compares with other dates you have had in similar circumstances in the past or at present, and perhaps by how successful other people's dates have seemed to you.

To complicate matters a little, your CL can change over time. Although age may not make you any wiser, as you get older you are likely to expect more of some future commitment to another person than when you were younger.

There is an additional concept – the *comparison level for alternatives*. Suppose that you are in an already satisfying relationship but then meet someone new, an enticing stranger. As the saying goes, 'the grass always looks greener on the other side of the fence'. In social exchange language, there is the prospect here of an increase in rewards over costs.

Does all this sound too calculating to you? Be honest, now! Whatever the outcome, the situation has become unstable. Decisions, decisions . . .

Social exchange, equity and justice

Western society may actually be founded on a system of social exchange within which we strive for *equity*, or balance, in our relationships with others (Walster, Walster & Berscheid, 1978). Most people believe that outcomes in an exchange should be fair and just, enshrined in a society's laws and norms: we should comply with the 'rules'. What is thought to be just and fair is a feature of group life (see the role of leader in Chapter 6) and of intergroup relations (see Chapter 7). Equity and equality are not identical concepts. In a work setting, *equality* requires that all are paid the same, whereas *equity* requires that those who work hardest or do the most important jobs are paid more.

People are happiest in relationships when they believe that the give and take is approximately equal. Equity theory was developed in the context of workplace motivation and popularised in social psychology by J. Stacey Adams (1965). It covers two main situations:

Equity theory
A special case of social exchange theory that defines a relationship as equitable when the ratio of inputs to outcomes are seen to be the same by both partners.

1. a mutual exchange of resources (as in marriage);
2. an exchange where limited resources must be distributed (such as a judge awarding compensation for injury).

In both, equity theory predicts that people expect resources to be given out *fairly*, in proportion to their contribution. (See how a norm of equity has been applied to help understand *prosocial behaviour* in Chapter 9.) If we help others, it is fair to expect them to help us. Equity exists between Jack and Jill when:

$$\frac{\text{Jack's outcomes}}{\text{Jack's inputs}} = \frac{\text{Jill's outcomes}}{\text{Jill's inputs}}$$

First, Jack estimates the ratio between what he has put into his relationship with Jill and what he has received in return. Next, Jack compares this ratio with the ratio applying to Jill (see Figure 10.4). If these ratios are equal, Jack will feel that each of them is being treated fairly or equitably. Jill, of course, will have her own ideas about what is fair. Perhaps Jack is living in a dream world!

When a relationship is equitable, the participants' outcomes (rewards minus costs) are proportional to their inputs or contributions to the relationship. The underlying concept is distributive justice (Homans, 1961). It is an aspect of social justice and refers more generally to practising a norm of fairness in the sharing of goods that each member of a group receives. Equity theory can be applied to many areas of social life, such as exploitative relationships, helping relationships and intimate relationships (Walster, Walster & Berscheid, 1978). The more inequitably people are treated, the more distress they will feel. When we experience continuing inequity, the relationship is likely to end (Adams, 1965), a topic dealt with at the end of this chapter.

Distributive justice
The fairness of the outcome of a decision.

The role of norms

Although Adams (1965) thought that people always prefer an equity norm when allocating resources, this has been questioned (Deutsch, 1975). When resources are shared out according to inputs, we may evaluate our friend's inputs differently from a stranger's. Strangers tend to allocate resources on the basis of *ability*, whereas friends allocate on the basis of both *ability* and *effort* (Lamm & Kayser, 1978). A norm of mutual obligation, rather than equity, to contribute to a common cause may be triggered when a friendship is involved: we expect our friends more so than strangers to pull their weight – perhaps to help us paint our new house!

Gender plays an interesting role: women prefer an equality norm and men an equity norm (Major & Adams, 1983). Such a difference may be based on a sex-stereotyped role in which a woman strives for harmony and peace in interactions by treating people equally. In contrast, Tyler has suggested that in *groups* people actually consider procedural justice to be more important than distributive justice or equality (Tyler & Lind, 1992; also see Chapter 6).

Procedural justice
The fairness of the procedures used to make a decision.

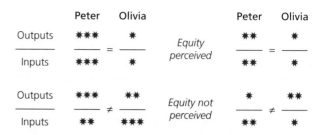

Figure 10.4

Equity theory applied to equitable and inequitable relationships.

Source: Based on Baron & Byrne (1987).

Attachment

Attachment is an increasingly important research area in social psychology. Initially focused on the bonding that occurs between infant and caregiver, the study of attachment has expanded to include the different ways that adults make connections with those who are close to them. First, we will explore an area that underpins this topic – affiliation.

Affiliation

The need to affiliate, to be with others, is powerful and pervasive, and underlies the way in which we form positive and lasting interpersonal relationships. There are, of course, times when we wish to be alone, to enjoy our own company, and there are models that deal with people's attempts to regulate their need for privacy. We start with the effects of enduring social isolation, an experience that can be dire.

Need to affiliate
The urge to form connections and make contact with other people.

Forerunners in this field

There have been many stories of people being isolated for long periods of time, such as prisoners in solitary confinement and shipwreck survivors. However, in situations such as these, isolation is often accompanied by punishment or perhaps lack of food. For this reason, the record of Admiral Byrd is perhaps the most interesting example we have – his isolation was voluntary and planned, with adequate supplies to meet his physical needs. Byrd volunteered to spend six months alone at an Antarctic weather station observing and recording conditions. His only contact was by radio with the main expedition base. At first, he wanted to 'be by myself for a while and to taste peace and quiet and solitude long enough to find out how good they really are' (Byrd, 1938, p. 4). But in the fourth week he wrote of feeling lonely, lost and bewildered. He began to spice up his experience by imagining that he was among familiar people. After nine weeks Byrd became preoccupied with religious questions and, like Monty Python, dwelt on the 'meaning of life'. His thoughts turned to ways of believing that he was not actually by himself: 'The human race, then, is not alone in the universe. Though I am cut off from human beings, I am not alone' (p. 185). After three months, he became severely depressed, apathetic and assailed by hallucinations and bizarre ideas.

The early social psychologist William McDougall (1908) suggested that humans are innately motivated to gather together and to be part of a group, as some animals do that live in herds or colonies. This was a simplistic *instinct* theory and was roundly criticised by the behaviourist John Watson (1913). He argued that accounting for herding behaviour by calling it a herding instinct was a very weak position. Later biological arguments about social behaviour were much more sophisticated (note what we have covered already about evolutionary theory and attraction). Affiliation has been extensively researched, so we have been selective in choosing just two topics. Do people want company when they become anxious? How serious are the consequences of inadequate care-giving for infants?

Modern research

In his classic work *The Psychology of Affiliation* (1959), Stanley Schachter described a connection between being isolated and feeling anxious. Being alone can lead people to want to be with others, even with strangers for a short period.

Social comparison
Comparing our behaviours and opinions with those of others in order to establish the correct or socially approved way of thinking and behaving.

Schachter surmised that having company serves to reduce anxiety, noting that two factors could be involved, either that the other person might serve as a distraction from a worrying situation, or else as a yardstick for the process of social comparison. His results confirmed the latter explanation. James Kulik has studied how social psychological processes can be used to promote recovery from surgery. See Box 10.6 for an example of how social comparison can be used to speed recovery for heart patients.

The need to affiliate can be affected by temporary states, such as fear. It is not just any person that we want to be with, but someone specific. The maxim *misery loves company* can be amended to read: *misery loves the company of those in the same miserable situation.* Reducing anxiety is only one outcome of making a social comparison. More broadly, we are making these comparisons whenever we seek the views of a special group – our friends. How people come to be part of this special group is discussed below.

Effects of social deprivation

A new insight into the nature of affiliation was provided by the study of the effects of *social deprivation in infancy.* According to the British psychiatrist John Bowlby (1988), the release of two movies had a profound effect on research workers studying children in the 1950s, one by René Spitz, *Grief: A Peril in Infancy* (1947), and the other by James Robertson, *A Two-year-old Goes to Hospital* (1952). Survival, it transpired, depends on physical needs but also on a quite independent need for care and intimate interaction.

Hospitalism
A state of apathy and depression noted among institutionalised infants deprived of close comfort with a caregiver.

The psychoanalyst Spitz (1945) reported on babies who had been in an overcrowded institution for two years, left there by mothers unable to look after them. The babies were fed but rarely handled, and were mostly confined to their cots. Compared with other institutionalised children who had been given adequate care, they were less mentally and socially advanced, and their mortality rate was extremely high. Spitz coined the term hospitalism to describe the psychological

Research and applications 10.6
Heart to heart: effects of room sharing before surgery

Kulik, Mahler and Moore (1996) recorded the verbal interactions of heart patients, studying the effects of pre-operative room-mate assignments on patterns of affiliation, including how anxious they were before the operation and their speed of recovery afterwards. If social comparison were to play a part in this context then it should reveal itself if the other person is also a cardiac patient. The results indicated that the process of social comparison was at work:

- Patients were significantly more likely to clarify their thoughts, by talking about the surgery and the prospects of recovery afterwards, when their room-mate was a cardiac rather than a non-cardiac patient.

- This effect was strongest when the room-mate had already undergone the operation. When patient A was pre-operative and patient B was post-operative, patient A would be less anxious, as measured by the number of anxiety-reducing drugs and sedatives requested by patients the night before surgery.

- Patients were also more likely to be discharged sooner if assigned to a room-mate who was cardiac rather than non-cardiac, measured by the length of stay following the procedure.

- Patients without room-mates generally had the slowest recoveries.

condition in which he found these children. Hospitalism came to life vividly with heart-wrenching television footage of little children abandoned in Romanian orphanages in the early 1990s.

Other work of that time by Harry Harlow and his colleagues at the University of Wisconsin dealt with the devastating effects of social isolation on newborn rhesus monkeys (Harlow, 1958; Harlow & Harlow, 1965). This included deprivation of contact with their mothers. A monkey mother provides more than contact, food, rocking and warmth: she is the first link in the chain of the baby's experience of socialisation. Harlow's investigation was extended to babies who were totally isolated from contact with any living being for up to 12 months. Such long periods of solitary confinement had drastic consequences. The infant monkeys would sometimes huddle in a corner, rock back and forth repetitively, and bite themselves. When later exposed to normal peers, they did not enter into the rough-and-tumble play of the others, and failed to defend themselves from attack. As adults, they were sexually incompetent.

The link to attachment

Clearly, long-term social deprivation in infants is psychologically traumatic – in particular with a long-term caregiver, typically the mother. Bowlby (1969) and his colleagues at the Tavistock Institute in England focused on the attachment behaviour of infants to their mothers, noting that young children keep close to their mothers. Young children send signals to their caregiver by crying and smiling, and maintained proximity by clinging or following, all of which Bowlby attributed to an innate affiliative drive. Compared with affiliation, attachment involves that extra step of a close relationship at a particular point in time with just a few, perhaps one, other person. For Bowlby and many other social psychologists, attachment behaviour is not limited to the mother–infant experience but can be observed throughout the life cycle. In Bowlby's words, it accompanies people 'from the cradle to the grave'.

Attachment behaviour
The tendency of an infant to maintain close physical proximity with the mother or primary caregiver.

Attachment styles

Stable adult relationships 'come from somewhere' (Berscheid, 1994). Modern research into the genesis of adult attachment in relationships is now clearly linked to the study of human social development in infancy, and Bowlby's work with young children in particular has moved on to include the study of attachment styles in their elders. In accounting for the way that we as adults experience both love and loneliness, Cindy Hazan and Phillip Shaver (1987) defined three attachment styles — secure, avoidant and anxious — that are also found in children (see Table 10.1).

Based on their studies of how important the family is to an individual's psychological development, Mary Feeney and Pat Noller (1990) found that attachment styles developed in childhood carry on to influence the way romantic relationships are formed in later life. They assessed the levels of attachment, communication patterns and relationship satisfaction of married couples, and found that securely attached individuals (comfortable with closeness and having low anxiety about relationships) were more often paired with similarly secure spouses. On the other hand, people with an avoidant style often report aversive sexual feelings and experiences, and are less satisfied and more stressed from parenting when a baby arrives (Birnbaum *et al.*, 2006; Rholes, Simpson & Friedman, 2006), and less close to their children as they grow older (Rholes, Simpson & Blakely, 1995). Now consider the

Attachment styles
Descriptions of the nature of people's close relationships, thought to be established in childhood.

A secure attachment style. Children benefit from contact with compassionate caregivers. They are more likely to be both self-sufficient and trusting of others.

Source: Pearson Online Database (POD)

Table 10.1 Characteristics of three attachment styles

Attachment style	Characteristics
Secure	Trust in others; not worried about being abandoned; belief that one is worthy and liked; find it easy to be close to others; comfortable being dependent on others, and vice versa.
Avoidant	Suppression of attachment needs; past attempts to be intimate have been rebuffed; uncomfortable when close to others; find it difficult to trust others or to depend on them; feel nervous when anyone gets close.
Anxious	Concern that others will not reciprocate one's desire for intimacy; feel that a close partner does not really offer love, or may leave; want to merge with someone and this can scare people away.

Source: Based on Hazan & Shaver (1987).

third focus question. What might have happened in Aishani's life before she met Kamesh that could account for her current predicament?

Studies in this field suggest that Bowlby was right – attachment is a process that is active throughout life rather than simply a feature of infancy, and attachment styles adopted early in life can prevail in later relationships. One study by Brennan and Shaver (1995) of attachment styles and romantic relationships found that:

• *secure* adults found it easier to get close to others and to enjoy affectionate and long-lasting relationships;

- *avoidant* adults reported discomfort in getting close to others and their relationships were hampered by jealousy and a lack of self-disclosure;
- *anxious* adults tended to fall in love easily; however, their subsequent relationships were full of emotional highs and lows, and they were more often unhappy.

Experimental data from Claudia Brumbaugh and Chris Fraley (2006) show that an attachment style in one romantic relationship is likely to carry over to another relationship. However, people's styles may not be set in concrete. Lee Kirkpatrick and Cindy Hazan's (1994) study carried out over a four-year period has shown that an insecure partner may become less so if a current partner is secure and the relationship engenders trust.

Longitudinal research

Most research into attachment styles has not examined children and therefore is not genuinely developmental. The studies to which we have referred (excluding Kirkpatrick and Hazan's) typically measure the attachment style of adult participants and have no independent estimate of children's attachment style. Even cross-sectional studies of different age groups tested at the one time are not, strictly speaking, developmental. In contrast, Eva Klohnen spearheaded a genuine longitudinal programme of research across more than thirty years. Women who had been avoidant or secure in their attachment styles in their 20s were still so in their 40s and 50s. Differences in how they related were also maintained across the years. Compared with secure women, avoidant women were more distant from others, less confident, more distrustful, but more self-reliant (Klohnen & Bera, 1998).

Attachment theory has been increasingly researched since the 1980s and has become fashionable as well in the popular literature devoted to love, our next topic.

Close relationships

What does a close relationship conjure up for you? Perhaps warm fuzzies, perhaps passion and maybe love. But when you search your memory banks, there can be other worrisome thoughts too – try jealousy for one.

Close relationships are a crucible for a host of strong emotions (Fitness, Fletcher & Overall, 2003). According to the emotion-in-relationships model, relationships pivot on strong, well-established and wide-ranging expectations about a partner's behaviour (Berscheid & Ammazzalorso, 2001). People who can express their emotions are generally valued in close relationships, particularly by others with a secure attachment style (Feeney, 1999). There is, however, a caveat. Julie Fitness (2001) has reported that the elevated tendency to feel *all* emotions in close relationships makes it important for us to manage their expression, particularly negative emotions. If I engage in an orgy of uninhibited expression of all I feel for my partner the relationship may not be long for this world. The way that I show my feelings for my partner needs to be carefully, even strategically, managed.

What is love?

We have discussed the general process of interpersonal attraction. We have explored the way we choose our acquaintances and our friends, the powerful need to affiliate with a range of people, and with how we become attached to particular individuals.

Self-disclosure
The sharing of intimate information and feelings with another person.

Emotion-in-relationships model
Close relationships provide a context that elicits strong emotions due to the increased probability of behaviour interrupting interpersonal expectations.

Love
A combination of emotions, cognitions and behaviours that can be involved in intimate relationships.

Can we extend these principles to the important topic of the very special people whom we love – and are liking and loving different? Once a neglected topic of empirical study, love is now a popular focus for research (Dion & Dion, 1996).

People commonly use terms such as passion, romance, companionship, infatuation and sexual attraction, but would have difficulty defining them. Couple this with the way that love is regarded as magical and mysterious – the stuff of poetry and song rather than science – and the difficulty of taking love into the laboratory becomes compounded. Despite this, our knowledge is growing (see the fourth focus question), but not surprisingly, most research on love has used survey and interview methods.

Zick Rubin (1973) distinguished between *liking* and *loving* and developed scales to measure each separately. Take a few examples of some of Rubin's items. Julie thinks Artie is 'unusually well adjusted', 'is one of the most likeable people' she knows, and 'would highly recommend him for a responsible job'. When it comes to Frankie, Julie 'finds it easy to ignore his faults', 'if she could never be with him she would feel miserable', and 'feels very possessive towards him'. Which one does Julie like and which one does she love? Other researchers have added that *liking* involves the desire to interact with a person, *loving* adds the element of trust, and *being in love* implies sexual desire and excitement (Regan & Berscheid, 1999).

Kinds of love

In a study of what kinds of love there might be, Beverley Fehr (1994) asked this question: do ordinary people and love researchers *think* of love in the same way? She answered this by analysing the factors underlying several love scales commonly used in psychological research, and also by having ordinary people generate ideas about the kinds of love that they thought best described various close relationships in a number of scenarios. Fehr found both a simple answer and a more complex one:

- There was reasonable agreement across her data sets that there are at least two broad categories of love: (a) *companionate love* and (b) *passionate* or *romantic love*. This result substantiated earlier, influential work by Hatfield and Walster (1981).
- The scales devised by love experts made relatively clear distinctions between types and sub-types of love, whereas the views of lay people were quite fuzzy.

Passionate love is an intensely emotional state and a confusion of feelings: tenderness, sexuality, elation and pain, anxiety and relief, altruism and jealousy. Companionate love, in contrast, is less intense, combining feelings of friendly affection and deep attachment (Hatfield, 1987). A distinction between passionate and companionate love makes good sense. There are many people with whom we are pleased and comforted by sharing time, and yet with whom we are not 'in love'. In general, love can trigger emotions such as sadness, anger, fear and happiness (discussed in Chapter 11).

Love and romance

In 1932 the American songwriters Rodgers and Hart asked the question 'Isn't it romantic?' and also tried to tell us what love is. Social psychologists have mostly been more prosaic, sticking to descriptions of acts and thoughts that point to being 'in love'. People report that they think of their lover constantly; they want to spend as much time as possible with, and are often unrealistic about, their lover (Murstein, 1980). Not surprisingly, the lover becomes the focus of the person's life, to the exclusion of other friends (Milardo, Johnson & Huston, 1983). It is a very intense emotion and almost beyond control.

In pursuing the nature of romantic love, we should note that the concepts of love and friendship almost certainly share a common root of becoming acquainted and are generally triggered by the same factors – proximity, similarity, reciprocal liking and desirable personal characteristics. Our lover is very likely to be a friend, albeit a special one!

Have you ever fallen in love? We speak of 'falling in love' as though it is an accident, something that happens rather than a process in which we actively participate. What happens when we fall in this way? Arthur Aron and his colleagues addressed this in a short-term longitudinal study of undergraduate students who completed questionnaires about their love experiences and their concept of self every two weeks for ten weeks (Aron, Paris & Aron, 1995). Those who reported that they fell in love during this period reported positive experiences that were centred on their self-concept. Since somebody now loved them their self-esteem increased. Further, their self-concept had 'expanded' by incorporating aspects of the other person; and they also reported an increase in self-efficacy, e.g. not only making plans but making the plans work.

One widely accepted claim about falling in love is that it is culture-bound: for young people to experience it, a community needs to believe in love and offer it as an option, through fiction and real-life examples. If it is an accident, then at least some people from all cultures should fall in love – but is this case? Attachment theory has argued that love is both a biological and a social process, and cannot be reduced to a historical or cultural invention (Hazan & Shaver, 1987). Indeed, there is evidence of romantic love, not necessarily linked to marriage, in the major literate civilisations of early historic times – Rome, Greece, Egypt and China (Mellen, 1981). For example, although romance was not an essential ingredient in choosing a spouse in ancient Rome, love between a husband and wife could grow (see www.womenintheancientworld.com).

Love as a label

In Elaine Hatfield and William Walster's (1981) three-factor theory of love, romantic love is a product of three interacting variables:

1. A *cultural determinant* that acknowledges love as a state.
2. An *appropriate love object* present – in most cultures, the norm is a member of the opposite sex and of similar age.
3. *Emotional arousal*, self-labelled 'love', that is felt when interacting with, or even thinking about, an appropriate love object.

Label or not, those of us who have been smitten report powerful feelings. Although the idea of labelling arousal may not seem intuitively appealing, it has a basis in research. Our physiological reactions are not always well differentiated across the emotions, such as when we describe ourselves as angry, fearful, joyful or sexually aroused (Fehr & Stern, 1970).

Recall Schachter and Singer's (1962) argument that arousal prompts us to make a causal attribution (see Chapter 2). Some cues (e.g. heightened heart rate) suggest that the cause is internal and we then label the experience as an emotion. If we feel aroused following an insult we are likely to label the feeling as anger. However, if we are interacting with an attractive member of appropriate gender we will possibly label the arousal as sexual attraction, liking and even a precursor to love. See Box 10.7 on how even danger, or at least excitement, can act as a precursor to romance!

Three-factor theory of love
Hatfield and Walster distinguished three components of what we label 'love': a cultural concept of love, an appropriate person to love and emotional arousal.

Research classic 10.7
Excitement and attraction on a suspension bridge

Donald Dutton and Arthur Aron (1974) conducted a famous experiment on a suspension bridge spanning Capilano canyon in British Columbia. They described the setting in this way:

> The 'experimental' bridge was the Capilano Canyon Suspension Bridge, a five-foot-wide, 450-foot-long, bridge constructed of wooden boards attached to wire cables that ran from one side to the other of the Capilano Canyon. The bridge has many arousal-inducing features such as a tendency to tilt, sway, and wobble, creating the impression that one is about to fall over the side; (b) very low handrails of wire cable which contribute to this impression; and (c) a 230-foot drop to rocks and shallow rapids below the bridge. *(Dutton & Aron, 1974, pp. 510–511)*

The participants were young men who crossed rather gingerly over the high and swaying suspension bridge, one at a time. An attractive young woman approached each one on the pretext of conducting research, asking if they would complete a questionnaire for her. Next, she gave them her name and her phone number in case they wanted to ask more questions later. Many called her. However, very few made the phone call if the interviewer was a man or if the setting was a lower and safer 'control' bridge. Arousal in a perilous situation, it seems, enhances romance!

The phenomenon of accidental arousal enhancing the attractiveness of an already attractive person described is reliable, according to a meta-analysis of thirty-three experimental studies (Foster, Witcher, Campbell & Green, 1998).

The three-factor theory stresses that love depends on past learning of the concept of love, the presence of someone to love, and arousal. Even if these components are necessary, they are not sufficient for love to occur. If they were, love could easily be taken into the laboratory. The ingredients would require that John's culture includes a concept of love and that Janet provides arousal by being attractive, or by chasing John around the room, or by paying him a compliment – and hey presto! 'Love'!

We know that sexual arousal itself does not define love, and that lust and love can be distinguished. Think of the anecdote in which a person is called to account for an extramarital affair by a spouse and makes the classic response 'But, dear, it didn't *mean* anything!'

Love and illusions

People bring various ideals or images into a love relationship that can impact on the way it might develop. A person can fall out of love quickly if the partner is not what (or who) they were first thought to be. The initial love was not for the partner but for some *ideal image* that the person had formed of this partner, such as 'the knight in shining armour'. Possible sources for these images are previous lovers, characters from fiction and childhood love objects such as parents. A physical characteristic similar to one contained by the image can start a chain reaction whereby other characteristics from the image are transferred on to the partner.

It is the images we hold about an ideal partner (discussed further below) that seem best to differentiate love from liking. Some of these images may be based on illusions. One of these is the belief in romantic destiny – *we were meant for each other*. This illusion can be helpful, both in feeling initially satisfied and in maintaining a relationship longer (Knee, 1998). Romance in general is most likely entwined with fantasy and positive illusions (Martz *et al.*, 1998; Murray & Holmes, 1997). A positive illusion may not be a bad thing when it comes to relationships.

Probably, the reality is that we need to be in the right relationship with the right person. There is some conviction 'from maintaining a tight, coherent, evaluatively consistent story about one's partner' (Murray, Holmes & Griffin, 2003, p. 290). When a partner falls short of one's ideals, we could highlight virtues and minimise faults. Partner ideals are a feature of the work of Fletcher and his colleagues in maintaining relationships, discussed in a later section.

No greater love

Robert Sternberg (1988) proposed what has become an influential model in which commitment and intimacy are factors as crucial as passion to some experiences of love. *Passion* is roughly equivalent to sexual attraction; *intimacy* refers to feelings of warmth, closeness and sharing; *commitment* is our resolve to maintain the relationship, even in moments of crisis. These same three dimensions have been confirmed as independent statistical factors (Aron & Westbay, 1996).

While sexual desire and romantic love are linked in experience, Lisa Diamond has pointed out that they may have evolved as different biological systems with different goals:

> Desire is governed by the *sexual mating* system, the goal of which is sexual union for the purpose of reproduction. Romantic love, however, is governed by the *attachment* or *pair-bonding* system. *(Diamond, 2003, p. 174)*

It would follow that affectional bonding can be directed towards both other-gender and same-gender partners.

In Sternberg's model, romance is exceeded by one other experience, consummate love, which includes all three factors. By systematically creating combinations of the presence or absence of each factor, we can distinguish eight cases, ranging in degree of bonding from no love at all to consummate love. Out of this some interesting relationships emerge. Fatuous love is characterised by passion and commitment but no intimacy (e.g. the 'whirlwind Hollywood romance'). The differentiation between varieties of love by Sternberg appears to be robust (Diamond, 2003). Have you experienced some of the relationships in Figure 10.5?

Consummate love
Sternberg argues that this is the ultimate form of love, involving passion, intimacy and commitment.

Love and marriage

Love and romance being the essence of deciding to get married has long been a popular theme in literature. And yet, in Western culture there appears to have been a change in attitude over time, even across a single generation. Jeffry Simpson and his colleagues compared three time samples (1967, 1976 and 1984) of people who answered this question: 'If a man (woman) had all the qualities you desired, would you marry this person if you were not in love with him (her)?' The answer 'No' was much higher in 1984, but in 1967 women were much more like to say 'Yes' (Simpson, Campbell & Berscheid, 1986). A later study documented a trend in Western cultures towards far more long-term relationships outside marriage (Hill & Peplau, 1998). Even so, American data suggest that love is still an accurate predictor of getting married or not, but is not enough to guarantee a happy and stable relationship.

Most research on marriage is Western, and may seem culturally myopic. In one sense, it is – because 'marriage', as a social contract, takes varying forms in different cultures and groups. However, almost all love relationships in all cultures and groups have some kind of public contract to identify the relationship.

Figure 10.5

The triangle of love.

- Three factors (passion, commitment and intimacy) are crucial in characterising different experiences of love. When all three are present we can speak of consummate love.

- When only one or two are present we have love in a different way. Two commonly experienced kinds include romantic love and companionate love.

Source: Sternberg, R. J. (1988). *The triangle of love*. New York: Basic Books. Reproduced with permission from Professor Robert J. Sternberg.

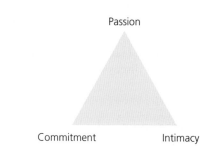

	Passion	Commitment	Intimacy
No love	✗	✗	✗
Infatuation	✓	✗	✗
Empty love	✗	✓	✗
Liking	✗	✗	✓
Fatuous love	✓	✓	✗
Romantic love	✓	✗	✓
Companionate love	✗	✓	✓
Consummate love	✓	✓	✓

Arranged marriages

Some cultures have long preferred the careful arrangement of 'suitable' partners for their children. Arranged marriages can be very successful, particularly if we judge them by their duration and social function: having children, caring for aged parents, reinforcing the extended family and building a stronger community. They can also act as treaties between communities and tribal groups. Historically, this function has been critical – it became weaker in post-industrial societies that are organised around nuclear families, including Western societies in general.

There have been several studies of arranged marriages in India. In one, mutual love was rated lower by arranged couples than by 'love' couples – at first (Gupta & Singh, 1982). Over time, this trend reversed. In a second study, female students preferred the idea of an arranged marriage, provided they consented to it; but they endorsed the 'love marriage' provided their parents consented (Umadevi, Venkataramaiah & Srinivasulu, 1992). In a third study, students who preferred love marriages were liberal in terms of their mate's sociocultural background, whereas those who preferred arranged marriages would seek a partner from within their own kin group (Saroja & Surendra, 1991).

Has the dichotomy of arranged and love marriages been oversimplified? The anthropologist Victor De Munck (1996) investigated love and marriage in a Sri Lankan Muslim community. Arranged marriages were the cultural preference. However, romantic love also contributed to the final decision, even when parents officially selected the partner.

These studies highlight the importance and respect that some cultures afford their elders as legitimate matchmakers. Many Westerners believe that they would never consider an arranged marriage. However, dating and international marriage-match agencies are growing rapidly in popularity in Western culture, perhaps reflecting diminished opportunities for people to meet, particularly those with busy lives.

Gay and lesbian relationships

Until recently, this important topic has been neglected in research, but an increase in the numbers of people 'coming out' has changed that. Lesbians and gay men are more evident in many societies, and research on same-sex couples has increased accordingly. Same-sex marriages, civil unions, gay adoption and gay/lesbian sexuality have been matters of public debate. There was once a view that same-sex couples were abnormal and their activities illegal. This has shifted – lesbians and gay men are minority groups who are now more confident in confronting social stigma and discrimination. For a discussion of psychological issues confronting people in gay and lesbian relationships, see the review by Letitia Peplau and Adam Fingerhut (2007).

Relationships that work (and those that don't)

Maintaining relationships

This literature deals mostly with marriage, as researchers no doubt assume that this is the most obvious relationship to be preserved. However, in view of what we have discussed so far, marriage is only one of a number of love relationships. In this section we do not draw a distinction between marriage, de facto relationships and other long-term intimate relationships.

Same-sex relationships. Gay and lesbian intimacy is now more evident, and is a theme commonly found in literature and films.

Source: © Focus / Everett Collection / Rex Features

Margaret Clark and Nancy Grote (1998) have used equity theory based on benefits and costs to pinpoint actions that help or hinder a relationship:

- *Benefits* help. They can be intentional (e.g. 'My husband complimented me on my choice of clothing') or unintentional (e.g. 'I like being in public with my wife because she is attractive').
- *Costs* hinder. They can be intentional (e.g. 'My wife corrected my grammar in front of other people') or unintentional (e.g. 'My husband kept me awake at night by snoring').
- *Communal behaviour* helps. Sometimes it can be a benefit to one partner but a cost to the other (e.g. 'I listened carefully to something my wife wanted to talk about even though I had no interest in the issue.')

Romance novels suggest that 'love endures', whereas TV soap operas often focus on relationship breakups. A longitudinal study spanning ten years of American newly-weds found a steady decline in marital satisfaction among both husbands and wives (Kurdeck, 1999). This decline included two accelerated downturns, one after the first year, 'the honeymoon is over', and the other in the eighth year, 'the seven year itch'!

A relationship that survives is one where partners adapt and change in what they expect of each other. Companionate love can preserve a relationship, based on deep friendship and caring, and arising from lives that are shared and the myriad experiences that only time can provide. In this way, we can get a glimpse of how both the Western 'love' marriage and the Eastern arranged marriage could each result in a similar perception of powerful bonding between partners.

For better or for worse

When do partners live up to the maxim 'For better or for worse'? Jeff Adams and Warren Jones (1997) pinpointed three factors that contribute to an ongoing relationship:

1. *Personal dedication* – positive attraction to a particular partner and relationship.
2. *Moral commitment* – a sense of obligation, religious duty or social responsibility, controlled by a person's values and moral principles.
3. *Constraint commitment* – factors that make it costly to leave a relationship, such as lack of attractive alternatives, and various social, financial or legal investments in the relationship.

Commitment
The desire or intention to continue an interpersonal relationship.

Commitment is a concept we have referred to several times in this chapter. It increases the chance that partners will stay together, and even entertaining the idea of becoming committed is important (Berscheid & Reis, 1998). Jennifer Wieselquist and her colleagues found a link between commitment and marital satisfaction, acts that promote a relationship, and trust (Wieselquist, Rusbult, Foster & Agnew, 1999).

To err is human, to forgive divine: Frank Fincham (2000) has characterised forgiveness as an interpersonal construct: *you* forgive *me*. It is a process and not an act, and resonates in histories, religions and values of many cultures. Forgiveness is a solution to estrangement, and a positive alternative to relationship breakdown.

Does your partner meet your ideals?

How well do you match the expectations of your partner, and is this important to your relationship? These are questions that Garth Fletcher and his colleagues have explored (Fletcher, Simpson, Thomas & Giles, 1999). Our ideal image of a partner has developed over time and usually predates a relationship in the present. In a study of romantic relationships by Campbell, Simpson, Kashy and Fletcher (2001), people rated their ideal romantic partners on three dimensions: warmth–trustworthiness, vitality–attractiveness and status–resources, the same dimensions proposed by Fletcher as important when selecting a mate (discussed earlier). The results were in accord with the *ideal standards model*: people who think that their current partner closely matches their image of an ideal partner are more satisfied with their relationship.

This model has been extended to include how people maintain and perhaps improve a relationship by trying to regulate or control a partner's behaviour. See how Nikola Overall and her colleagues have expanded this idea in Box 10.8.

Relationship breakdown

Levinger (1980) points to four factors that herald the end of a relationship:

1. A new life seems to be the only solution.
2. Alternative partners are available (see also Arriaga & Agnew, 2001).
3. There is an expectation that the relationship will fail.
4. There is a lack of commitment to a continuing relationship.

Rusbult and Zembrodt (1983) believe that once deterioration has been identified, it can be responded to in any of the following ways. A partner can take a passive stance and show:

- loyalty, by waiting for an improvement to occur; or
- neglect, by allowing the deterioration to continue.

Alternatively, a partner can take an active stance and show:

Partner regulation
Strategy that encourages a partner to match an ideal standard of behaviour.

Research and applications 10.8
Strategies for sustaining a long-term relationship

According to Overall, Fletcher & Simpson (2006), people use a variety of cognitive tactics to maintain their relationships when they judge their partner to be less than ideal. They may weather little storms along the way by:

- enhancing a partner's virtues and downplaying the faults (Murray & Holmes, 1999);

- lowering their expectations to fit more closely with what their partner offers (Fletcher, Simpson & Thomas, 2000);

- adjusting their perceptions so that their partner bears resemblance to their ideal (Murray, Holmes, & Griffin, 1996).

Another approach works more directly on the partner. You will recall that people use *self-regulation* when they try to rationalise perceived self-concept discrepancies between how they are and how they want to be (see

Chapter 4). Overall and her colleagues have used a similar, but more complex, concept based on the ideal standards model, with its pivotal dimensions of warmth–trustworthiness, vitality–attractiveness, and status–resources. This model throws new light on the way that we might improve and sustain a long-term relationship – partner regulation. Begin by comparing what we perceive with what we want relating to our partner – test the perception against our ideal standards. Regulation kicks in when the reality begins to fall short. Overall *et al.* give this example: Mary places considerable importance on one of the three dimensions, status/resources; but her partner John has limited potential to be financially secure; Mary encourages John to retrain or look for another job, perhaps a major challenge. But there are brownie points on offer – John's status and resources could come much closer to Mary's ideal and lift the quality of their relationship.

- voice behaviour, by working at improving the relationship; or
- exit behaviour, by choosing to end the relationship.

It is not clear whether the passive or the active approach leads to more pain at the final breakup. Other factors are involved, such as previous levels of attraction, the amount of time and effort invested and the availability of new partners. It can also depend on the person's available social contact, such as support from family and friends. It is often loneliness that adds to the pain and makes life seem unbearable; if this is minimised, recovery from the ending of a relationship can be faster.

Consequences of failure

Relationship dissolution model
Duck's proposal of the sequence through which most long-term relationships proceed if they finally break down.

A breakup is a process, not a single event. Steve Duck has offered a detailed relationship dissolution model of four phases that partners pass through (see Box 10.9 and Figure 10.6). Each phase culminates in a threshold at which a typical form of action follows.

You may well think, 'This is pretty grim stuff.' It is. Most often, the breakup of long-term relationships and marriages is extremely distressing. Partners who were close have tried hard over a long period to make it work – they have mutually reinforced each other and have had good times along with the bad. In the breakup of marriage, at least one partner has reneged on a contract (Simpson, 1987). The consequences of a family breakup can be serious for children. A longitudinal study of more than 1200 people from 1921 to 1991 showed that men and women whose parents had divorced were more likely also to experience divorce (Tucker *et al.*, 1997).

Serious domestic conflict also undermines parent–child relationships. Ronald Riggio (2004) studied young adults from families affected by divorce or chronic and high levels of conflict, finding that they more often felt lacking in social support and

Relationship breakdown. This couple will divorce. According to Duck's model, with the end in sight they will seek support from their respective social networks.

Source: Everett Collection / Rex Features

Research and applications 10.9
Phases in the breakup of a relationship

Steve Duck has described four phases that people endure when a relationship dissolves:

1 The *intrapsychic phase* starts as a period of brooding with little outward show, perhaps in the hope of putting things right. This can give way to needling the partner and seeking out a third party to be able to express one's concerns.

2 The *dyadic* (i.e two-person) *phase* leads to the point of deciding that some action should be taken, short of leaving the partner, which is usually easier said than done. Arguments point to differences in attributing responsibility for what is going wrong. With luck, they may talk their problems through.

3 The *social phase* involves a new element: in saying that the relationship is near an end, the partners

may negotiate with friends, both for support for an uncertain future and for reassurance of being right. The social network will probably take sides, pronounce on guilt and blame and, like a court, sanction the dissolution.

4 The final *grave-dressing phase* can involve more than leaving a partner. It may include the division of property, access to children, and working to assure one's reputation. Each partner wants to emerge with a self-image of reliability for a future relationship. The metaphor for the relationship is death: there is its funeral, it is buried and marked by erecting a tablet. This 'grave-dressing' activity seeks a socially acceptable version of the life and death of the relationship.

Source: Based on Duck (1982, 2007).

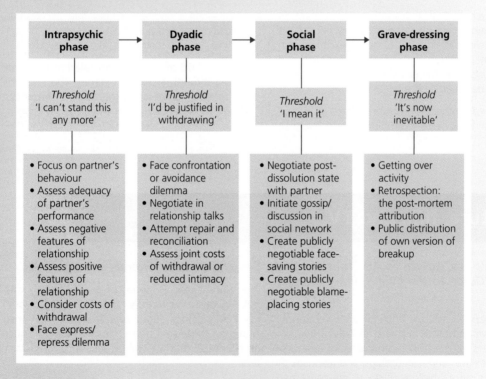

Figure 10.6

When things go wrong: phases in dissolving an intimate relationship.

Source: Based on Duck (1982).

more anxious in their own relationships. Add divorce to the mixture and the quality of the relationship with the father, though not with the mother, was also diminished, perhaps because interaction with mothers was expected to continue.

In short, most of us probably live in the hope that a long-term intimate relationship will involve loyalty, trust and commitment – forever. There is truth in the adage *look before you leap*.

Summary

- Attraction is necessary for friendships to form and is a precursor to an intimate relationship.

- Evolutionary social psychology has made strong arguments for the power of human genetic inheritance in accounting for what attracts people to each other.

- Variables that play a significant role in determining why people are attracted towards each other include physical attributes, whether they live or work close by, how familiar they are and how similar they are, especially in terms of attitudes and values.

- Social psychological explanations of attraction include: reinforcement (a person who engenders positive feelings is liked more); social exchange (an interaction is valued if it increases benefits and reduces costs); and the experience of equitable outcomes for both parties in a relationship.

- Affiliation with others is a powerful form of human motivation. Long-term separation from others can have disturbing intellectual and social outcomes, and may lead to irreversible psychological damage in young children.

- Life-cycle studies of affiliation led to research into attachment and attachment styles. The ways that children connect psychologically to their caregiver can have long-term consequences for how they establish relationships in adulthood.

- Love is distinguished from mere liking. It also takes different forms, such as romantic love and companionate love.

- Maintaining a long-term relationship involves partner regulation, strategies that a person uses to bring their partner closer to their expectations or standards.

- The breakup of a long-term relationships can be traced through a series of stages. The relationship dissolution model notes four phases: intrapsychic, dyadic (two-person), social and grave-dressing.

Literature, film and TV

Dr Tatiana's Sex Advice to All Creation: The Definitive Guide to the Evolutionary Biology of Sex

This 2006 popular science book by an evolutionary biologist, Olivia Judson, is hilarious. Dr Tatiana (Judson) receives letters from a truly bizarre array of creatures about their sex lives and relationships, and responds by explaining the surreal biology of sex to the concerned creatures. Although not directly about people, you can make comparisons, and examine your assumptions about how 'natural' the nature of human relationships and sexuality really are.

Sex and the City, Friends and Cold Feet

These are classic TV series of a genre that explores, both seriously and with wit and humour, the complexity of friendships and sexual and love relationships. Although these series have finished, they did such an excellent job that we will be seeing re-runs for some time.

When Harry met Sally

This 1989 film by Rob Reiner, starring Billy Crystal and Meg Ryan, is a classic comedy showing how love and attraction can develop between very dissimilar people.

There are lots of wonderful little vignettes of very long-term relationships and how they first started.

Scenes from a Marriage

Classic 1973 Swedish film and TV mini-series by Ingmar Bergman, and starring Liv Ullmann, is an intense and psychologically demanding film about the pain and the peace that accompanies a lifetime of loving. The film chronicles ten years of turmoil and love that bind a couple despite infidelity, divorce and subsequent marriages.

Mamma Mia

This 2008 film is a romantic comedy built around Abba's hits and stars Meryl Streep, Amanda Seyfried, Pierce Brosnan, Stellan Skarsgård and Colin Firth. About to get married, 20-year-old Sophie has never met her father, but after unearthing her mother's secret diary, she narrows the 'culprit' down to three lovers, whom she invites to her wedding. Sophie is determined to acquire a father. Attachment theory suggests that one Dad is enough, but Sophie faces a dilemma – she likes them all! Is it better to know who it is and have just one father? Or could she share all three in her life but never solve the puzzle?

Casablanca

Many film critics feel that *Casablanca* is the greatest film ever – a 1942 all-time classic directed by Michael Curtiz, starring Humphrey Bogart (as Rick) and Ingrid Bergman (as Ilsa), and also with Sydney Greenstreet and Peter Lorré. A love affair between Rick and Ilsa is disrupted by the Nazi occupation of Paris and some years later Ilsa shows up in Rick's Café in Casablanca. The film is about love, friendship and close relationships, as well as hatred and jealousy, against the background of war, chaos and other impossible obstacles. Another absolute classic in the same vein is David Lean's 1965 film, *Dr Zhivago* – based on the novel by Boris Pasternak, and starring Omar Sharif and Julie Christie.

Brokeback Mountain

This 2005 film by Ang Lee, starring Heath Ledger, Jake Gyllenhaal, Anne Hathaway and Michelle Williams is set in the period 1963–83 in the American West. A sexual encounter between two men deepens into a relationship that is not only sexual but also emotional and romantic. One of the men later marries, and his conflict between two relationships, one homosexual and the other heterosexual, is a key element in the story.

The Road

2009 John Hillcoat film based on a Cormac McCarthy novel, and starring Viggo Mortensen. A father and his young son trudge across a brutal and ruined post-apocalyptic world – the only thing that allows them to survive and keeps them sane and human is their relationship.

Guided questions

- What does evolutionary social psychology have to say about how humans select a mate?

- How can a *cost-and-benefits* analysis be applied to predict the future of an intimate relationship?

- How does a person's *attachment style* develop and can it continue later in life? A student discusses her experience of insecure attachment following years of physical and emotional abuse from her father in Chapter 10 of MyPsychLab (www.mypyschlab.co.uk)?

- What has social psychology told us about how and why some relationships work?

Learn more

Berscheid, E., & Reis, H. T. (1998). Attraction and close relationships. In D. T. Gilbert, S. T. Fiske & G. Lindzey (eds), *The handbook of social psychology* (4th ed, Vol. 2, pp. 193–281). New York: McGraw-Hill. Authoritative overview of attraction and related topics, in the most recent edition of the classic handbook – a primary source for theory and research.

Duck, S. W. (2007). *Human relationships* (4th ed). Thousand Oaks, CA: Sage. A perspective by a major theorist on people's interactions, acquaintances, friendships and relationships. Students can use the resources provided to apply the concepts in their personal lives.

Fitness, J., Fletcher, G., & Overall, N. (2003). Interpersonal attraction and intimate relationships. In M. A. Hogg & J. Cooper (eds), *The Sage handbook of social psychology* (pp. 258–278). London: Sage. Up-to-date overview of research on close relationships, including emotion in relationships and evolutionary dimensions of relationships.

Mikulincer, M., & Goodman, G. S. (eds) (2006). *Dynamics of romantic love: Attachment, caregiving, and sex*. New York: Guilford. Topics such as intimacy, jealousy, self-disclosure, forgiveness and partner violence are examined through three behavioural systems: attachment, caregiving and sex.

Rholes, W. S., & Simpson, J. A. (2004). *Adult attachment: Theory, research, and clinical implications*. New York: Guilford. Attachment theory is considered from physiological, emotional, cognitive and behavioural perspectives.

Refresh your understanding, assess your progress and go further with interactive summaries, questions, podcasts, videos and much more on the website accompanying the book: **www.mypsychlab.co.uk**.

Chapter 11

Culture and communication

What to look for

- Culture, thinking, attributing causes, and conformity

- Individualistic and collectivist cultures

- The two psyches: East and West

- Adapting to a new culture

- Multiculturalism

- How language arose and its connections to thought

- Why language is crucial to a culture

- Communicating our feelings

- Body language: using the eyes, postures and gestures

- Personal space: the bubble around our bodies

Focus questions

1. Bernice and Joeli are indigenous Fijians who have studied social psychology at the University of the South Pacific in Suva. They are concerned that what they have studied is based on Western theory, with limited relevance to the traditional group-centred values of their community. Do they have a point?

2. Daan is Dutch and has been brought up to defend openly what he believes to be true. After living in South Korea for a few months, he has noticed that the locals are more concerned about maintaining harmony in their social relationships than in deciding who is right and who is wrong. Why, he wonders, can they not just speak their minds?

3. Keiko and her new husband are Japanese. After a traditional wedding in Hokkaido, they emigrated to Oslo. Then a dilemma arose – should they maintain the customs of their homeland, or should they become entirely Norwegian? Do they have any other options?

4. Pablo, his wife Diana and young son Paulo have recently moved from Colombia to the United States. They think it is important for their son to speak both Spanish and English. Will it be useful for Paulo to be bilingual? Watch these parents discuss this real-life issue in Chapter 11 of MyPsychLab at www.mypsychlab.co.uk.

5. Santoso has recently arrived in The Hague after emigrating from Jakarta. At his first job interview, he did not make much eye contact with the human resources manager. Why might he have not done so, and will it hurt his prospects?

n this final chapter we deal with two fields that are increasingly important in social psychology. The first asks what is culture? From time to time we become aware of cultural difference in our lives. What is often neglected is that it actually permeates what we think, feel and do. The second addresses communication and distinguishes between language and non-verbal forms. Communication is the essence of interaction. Because of its juxtaposition with culture we highlight cultural variation, but also give examples of how communication interacts with other major categories such as gender and social status.

Culture

How far have you travelled recently? With relatively cheap airfares the world is increasingly at your doorstep. Most Europeans have travelled extensively within Europe; many West-coast Americans have explored islands in the Pacific, Australians head for Indonesia and Thailand. Russians live in London, Japanese chill out in Hawaii, and the Dutch head for Tuscany.

One of the first things to strike you in a foreign land is the different language or accent, along with the appearance and dress of the local people. Other differences may be more subtle and slower to emerge. These are to do with the actions and entire belief systems that underlie a country – the attitudes and values held by its people and which they use to represent and explain their world. Culture infuses behaviour and is the lifeblood of ethnic and national groups.

Culture
A set of beliefs and practices that identify a specific social group and distinguish it from others.

What we might call *our* culture provides us with an identity and a set of attributes that define that identity. Culture influences what we think, how we feel, how we dress, what and how we eat, how we speak, what values and moral principles we hold, how we interact with one another and how we understand the world around us. Culture pervades almost all aspects of our existence. Perhaps because of this, our own culture is often the taken-for-granted background to everyday life. We may only really become aware of its features when we encounter other cultures or when our own culture is threatened. Culture, like other entrenched systems of norms, may only be revealed to us by intercultural exposure, or by intercultural conflict.

In unravelling the properties and processes of groups, social psychologists have sometimes neglected culture. So let us put this right. In this chapter we ask what culture is and how it works and helps to define our self. We also deal with communication, verbal and non-verbal, and its crucial place in our everyday lives. Humans are highly complex social animals whose defining feature is the capacity to use real language, and it is usually language varieties that most obviously differentiate the inhabitants of one country from those of another.

Defining and studying culture

Culture is a pervasive but slippery construct. More than twenty years ago, Walter Lonner took stock of what had been learned after a decade of cross-cultural studies in psychology. He noted wryly that culture has been 'examined, poked at, pushed, rolled over, killed, revived and reified ad infinitum' (1984, p. 108). You will be aware of popular talk about culture, and read about cultural differences, cultural sensitivity, cultural change, culture shock, subcultures and culture contact. But what precisely is culture, and how much and through what processes does it affect people, and how in turn is it affected by people?

From a later perspective, what cross-cultural research has shown is considerable cultural variation in a range of quite basic human behaviour and social psychological processes. It has also identified a general difference between Eastern and Western cultures – indeed, the contemporary debate in social psychology about 'culture' is largely restricted to this contrast, or more accurately the contrast between (Eastern) collectivism and (Western) individualism.

The big question then is 'How deep do these differences go?' Are they simply differences in practices, or do they go much deeper to affect basic processes in thinking and perceiving? In this chapter, we also explore the role of language barriers to effective communication, the nature of acculturation, what can be done to help ease tensions in intercultural relations, and the challenge of managing cultural diversity.

The scientific study of culture is entwined with the rise of cultural anthropology in the late nineteenth century. Victorians came to learn of the ways of exotic peoples in books such as *The Mind of Primitive Man* (1911). Its author was the sociologist Franz Boas who located culture at the centre of social science, defining it as 'the social habits of a community' (Boas, 1930). He also argued that the main contribution of the growing discipline of social psychology should surely be the study of how culture influences people. In their collaborative *Social Psychology across Cultures* (1998), Peter Smith in Britain and Michael Bond in Hong Kong did not go as far as Boas. They saw social psychology as a discipline that covered a wide variety of psychological processes. Nevertheless, they argued that culture – which they defined as 'systems of shared meanings' – had been largely neglected in mainstream social psychology.

Although definitions vary, they tend to share the broad view that culture is an enduring product of and influence on human interaction. In line with this broad perspective, we view culture as the set of beliefs and practices that identify a specific social group, providing it with features that distinguish it from other groups. In the same vein, Geert Hofstede, an influential Dutch cross-cultural psychologist, referred to culture as 'the collective programming of the mind that distinguishes the members of one group or category of people from another' (2001, p. 9). In essence, culture is the expression of *group norms* (see Chapters 5 and 6), but at a national and ethnic level. Next, we look briefly at cultural variations in cognitive processes and explaining causality, and how conforming and being aggressive can mean different things in different countries.

Culture's impact on thought and action

In this section we look at cultural variations in cognition, attributing causality, conforming to one's group and aggression. Each of these takes into account a substantial body of work, and each points to important variations in the impact of culture upon humans.

A review of social psychological research by the Canadian cultural psychologist Darrin Lehman pointed to subtle but consistent differences in *thought processes* between East Asians and Americans (Lehman, Chiu & Schaller, 2004). The intellectual tradition of East Asians (and other collectivist cultures) has evolved to be generally more holistic and relationship-oriented, whereas Americans (and other individualistic cultures) are usually more analytic and linear in their thinking. In Box 11.1 we include some findings suggesting that East Asians differ in subtle ways of thinking and of attributing causes when they are compared with North Americans. We shall see in a later section that this broad East–West difference is reflected in different conceptions of the self and in the way that values are

Real world 11.1
East Asian and American differences in thinking and explaining behaviour

Is it possible that thought processes among East Asian peoples differ from those in the West? Studies by Richard Nisbett, Kaiping Peng and Incheol Choi suggest they do in subtle ways. East Asians more often:

- have a better memory for objects in their context (e.g. the *wolf* is in the *dark forest*);

- are prone to perceptual error when a stimulus object needs to be judged against a distracting background (e.g. judging if a fixed rod remains perpendicular as a frame behind it starts to rotate);

- are sensitive to people's social backgrounds when judging them;

- accept deductions when the premises are believable;

- take notice of typical examples when solving tasks based on categories;

- expect trends in behaviour in the future to be variable rather than consistent;

- accept apparent contradictions about themselves (e.g. agreeing that *equality is more important than ambition* at one moment in time but then disagreeing with this later);

- are less surprised by unexpected behaviour;

- look at arguments from both sides and compromise when there is conflict.

Sources: Based on Choi & Nisbett (2000); Masuda & Nisbett (2001); Peng & Nisbett (1999).

expressed. Richard Nisbett has referred to the 'geography of thought' and suggests that people from East Asia and those from the West have had different systems for thinking for thousands of years.

Earlier, we discussed the importance of attribution – how we go about explaining our world and the actions of people (see Chapter 2). Studies in different cultures have made it increasingly clear that *causal explanations* can be fully understood only by taking into account the wider belief and value systems of individuals. In his book *How Natives Think* (1925), the French anthropologist and sociologist Lucien Lévy-Bruhl reported that the natives of Motumotu in New Guinea attributed a pleurisy epidemic to the presence of a specific missionary, his sheep, two goats and, finally, a portrait of Queen Victoria. We can chuckle at this, but recall that in the early sixteenth century the astronomer Copernicus caused a religious storm by suggesting that the Earth was not actually the centre of the universe.

Is there cultural variation in how attributions are made, in particular with respect to the correspondence bias (or *fundamental attribution error*)? Perhaps, Ross and Nisbett (1991) suggested, North American researchers had been ethnocentric in their approach to the study of attribution. Their view was triggered in part following a study by Joan Miller (1984), who tested the limits of correspondence bias by comparing four age groups of Americans in Chicago with Indian Hindus in Mysore. Participants narrated stories of prosocial and antisocial acts and then tried to explain these acts in their own words. Miller identified the proportion of attributions that were either internal (due to the person) or external (due to the situation). The young children in Mysore responded in the same way as those in Chicago (see Figure 11.1). However, as age increased, the cultures diverged, mainly because the Americans increasingly looked for internal causes: they judged people to be responsible for how they behaved.

The reasons why and when conformity will occur were dealt with in Chapter 5. Does culture impact in these domains? Recall Asch's (1951) famous experiment of people who agreed with a majority opinion even when doing so was clearly wrong.

Correspondence bias
A general attribution bias in which people have an inflated tendency to see behaviour as reflecting (corresponding to) stable underlying personality attributes.

Conformity
Deep-seated, private and enduring change in behaviour and attitudes due to group pressure.

Figure 11.1

Effect of culture on explaining the causes of behaviour.

- As young children, North Americans and Indian Hindus do not differ in the rate at which they attribute other people's behaviour internally, i.e. believing that people are responsible for what they do.

- However, by the age of 15 there is a clear difference that strengthens in adulthood. Compared with Indians, Americans become much more inclined to see people as accountable for their own actions.

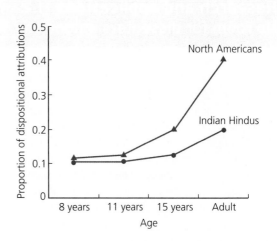

Source: Based on data from Miller (1984).

The method used in this study has been carefully replicated in other countries with results that vary in an important way. The likelihood of conforming to group pressure was highest in non-Western cultures (see Figure 11.2). This does not mean that non-Westerners give way easily to peer opinion out of weakness of character. The data could just as easily reflect embarrassment (saving face) as capitulation to the group (conformity).

Let us look at another case. The way in which people function interpersonally and in groups can be profoundly affected by where they work and live. For example, people from both Western and Eastern cultures experience considerable physical and psychological stress when they live for extended periods of time in polar regions. An early study of two subsistence cultures compared response differences in an Asch-type conformity setting. One was a food-accumulating culture, the Temne from Sierra Leone, and the other a hunter–gatherer society, the Canadian Eskimos (Inuit) (Berry, 1967; see Box 11.2).

Figure 11.2

Variations in size of conformity effect across cultures.

- This analysis of 'effect size' shows that conformity rates were lower in American and other Western samples than in samples from other parts of the world.

- The rates among Americans have also dropped since the times Asch conducted his studies.

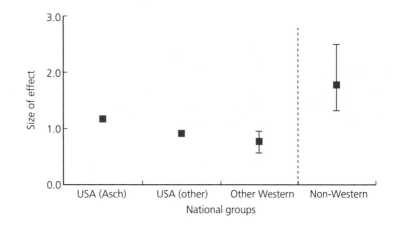

Source: Based on Smith & Bond (1998).

Research and applications 11.2
No room for dissenters among the Temne of Sierra Leone

The strength of a norm to work closely with a group can depend on the context of action, even the geographic location. Using a variant of Asch's conformity paradigm, the cross-cultural psychologist John Berry (1967) argued that a people's hunting and food-gathering practices should affect the extent that individuals conform to their group. On this basis, he compared the Temne people of Sierra Leone with the Eskimos (Inuits) of Canada and found a much higher conformity rate among the Temne.

The Temne subsist on a single crop, which they harvest in one concerted effort once a year. As this requires enormous cooperation and coordination of effort, consensus and agreement are strongly represented in Temne culture. Berry quotes one harvester as saying, 'When Temne people choose a thing, we must all agree with the decision – this is what we call cooperation' (1967, p. 417).

In contrast, the Eskimo economy involves continual hunting and gathering on a relatively individual basis. An Inuit looks after himself and his immediate family; thus, consensus is less strongly emphasised in Eskimo culture.

By the 1930s, anthropologists at Columbia University such as Franz Boas, Ruth Benedict and Margaret Mead had established that the way children develop was inextricably bound up with cultural norms. According to Margaret Mead, Samoan norms dictate that young people 'should keep quiet, wake up early, obey, and work hard and cheerfully' (1928/1961, p. 130), whereas among the Manus in New Guinea they were encouraged to be 'the aggressive, violent, overbearing type' (1930/1962, p. 233). *Aggression* by its nature catches our attention and we know that the social context makes a huge contribution to when it is triggered and how it is expressed (see Chapter 8). Let us see how culture plays its part.

In his literature search for peaceful societies, Bruce Bonta asked the question 'is it a dog-eat-dog world', one characterised by aggression rather than harmony? He managed to track down twenty-five striking exceptions to this so-called rule. In contrast to widespread examples of aggression in various societies, often featured in cross-cultural commentaries, there are some that emphasise the importance of co-operation; they devalue individual achievement because they believe it leads to violence. They are usually non-Western communities and are mostly small and isolated.

There are other cultures where violence is not only cultivated but is encouraged. One of these is prevalent in the American South where a *subculture of violence* is channelled through the family. Rates of violence have traditionally been higher in there than in other parts of the United States. The relevant trends are confined to situations involving oneself, one's family or one's possessions (see Box 11.3). Studies by Richard Nisbett and Dov Cohen use the concept of culture of honour to give meaning to a regional pattern of behaviour. In this instance, it is linked to a tradition of aggression in dealing with threat and is related clearly to *machismo* in Latin American families. It can also be linked to acts of beneficence, however: a person can be honour-bound to help as well as to hurt. The Arabic term *izzat* has the same sense.

Culture of honour
A culture that endorses male violence as a way of addressing threats to social reputation or economic position.

Real world 11.3
Honour in the American South

Does the B feature film western cliché have a basis in fact? Historically, Southern United States has had higher homicide rates than the rest of the country. Nisbett and Cohen captured the significance of this in their famous work *Culture of Honor: The Psychology of Violence in the South* (1996).

In this and other sources they link greater violence in the South to the herding economy that developed in its early settlements. In other parts of the world, herders have typically resorted to force more readily when they needed to protect their property, especially in contexts where their animals can roam widely.

When self-protection can be so important, a culture of honour may develop. An individual must let an adversary know that intrusion will not be tolerated. In old Louisiana, a wife and her lover would be surrendered by law to the husband, who might punish as he saw fit, including killing them. Even today, laws in the South relating to violent actions are more tolerant of violence than those in the North – for example, relating to gun ownership, spouse abuse, corporal punishment and capital punishment. Southern violence is not indiscriminate. For example, rates for robbery in the South are no higher than those in the North. The culture of honour would apply to self-protection, protection of the family, or when affronted.

The persistence of higher levels of violence so long after the pioneering days may follow from the use of a more violent child-rearing in the South. Boys are told to stand up for themselves and to use force in so doing, while spanking is regarded as the normal solution for misbehaviour.

Individualism, collectivism and the self

The study of what people value most has a long history in the social sciences. In psychology, values have generally been explored as properties of the individual. For example, is a person a conservative or a liberal? This is a question often posed in political psychology. In *social* psychology, however, values are thought of more broadly. They orient a whole people, pulling together their specific attitudes and behaviour, and integrating these in a meaningful way. Values are tied to groups, social categories and cultures, and are thus socially constructed and socially maintained.

Hofstede's work (1980, 2001), *Culture's Consequences*, included a major study of work values that compared forty countries on several value dimensions. One of these had opposing anchor points, individualism versus collectivism, which stimulated a large number of cross-cultural studies in the years that followed. The contrast between these reflects whether people's identity is mostly determined by personal choices or by the collective. In an organisational context, if workers have the freedom to adapt their approach to the job then the ethos of the organisation is individualistic ethos, but if they do not then the ethos is collectivist. Where Hofstede's approach was unique was his argument that the opposing values of individualism and collectivism could be applied to nations, and to cultures, as a whole. See Table 11.1 for one of his later studies using a scale measuring individualism–collectivism. The twenty countries listed were part of a larger pool of fifty, ranked here into quartiles. The most individualistic is the United States ranked first out of fifty, and the most collectivist is Colombia ranked forty-ninth (exceeded only by Venezuela, not included here).

If you look carefully at these you will see that nations of a European origin tend to be more individualistic (in quartiles 1 and 2) while those in the Middle East, East Asia and Latin America are more collectivist (in quartiles 3 and 4). However,

Individualism
Societal structure and world-view in which people prioritise standing out as an individual over fitting in as a group member.

Collectivism
Societal structure and world-view in which people prioritise group loyalty, commitment and conformity, and belonging and fitting-in to groups, over standing out as an isolated individual.

Table 11.1 Rankings of twenty nations on individualism–collectivism

| Individualism ◄───────────────────────────────► Collectivism | | | |
Quartile 1	Quartile 2	Quartile 3	Quartile 4
1. United States	13. Norway	26. Arab countries	40. Singapore
2. Australia	15. Germany	28. Turkey	40. Thailand
3. Great Britain	18. Austria	30. Greece	44. Taiwan
4. Netherlands	19. Israel	31. Philippines	48. Pakistan
9. Denmark	20. Spain	33. Portugal	49. Colombia

Source: Based on data from Hofstede (2001).

an interesting aspect is that Eastern and Western countries do not always follow a literal East–West dichotomy. We can go further to say that it is individualism–collectivism rather than Eastern–Western that captures the essence of this so-called dichotomy. Collectivism characterises traditional and agrarian societies and are based on the extended family. The very term 'tribe' has the sense of a collective. As far as we know, collectivism characterised pre-literate communities as well. A shift to individualism has been gradual and is associated with industrialisation and the growth of secularism and its base is the nuclear family. (Are Bernice and Joeli's concerns justified? See the first focus question.)

We need to add a note of caution: no single dimension of social behaviour, in this case individualism–collectivism, can hope to do justice to the range of the world's complex and varied cultures (Smith, Bond & Kağitçibaşi, 2006). By comparison with individualism–collectivism, the impact of religion and of political ideology has been neglected in the arena of cross-cultural research despite its obvious importance in national and international affairs, both past and present.

Let us now turn to the impact of what we have considered so far upon how the self is structured.

Two psyches, two selves

Hazel Markus from the United States and Shinobu Kitayama from Japan (1991) introduced the concepts of the independent self and the interdependent self that tend to predominate in certain cultures (see Table 11.2).

People in individualistic cultures (e.g. American, European) generally have an independent self, whereas people in collectivist cultures (e.g. Asian, Latin American) have an interdependent self. The independent self is an autonomous entity with clear boundaries between self and others. Internal attributes, such as thoughts, feelings and abilities, are stable and largely not affected by social context. The independent self acts primarily on one's inner thoughts and disposition. In contrast, the interdependent self has flexible and diffuse boundaries between self and others. It is tied into relationships and is highly responsive to social context. Others are seen as a part of the self, and the self is seen as a part of other people. There is no self without the collective. One's behaviour is governed and organised primarily

Ideology
A systematically interrelated set of beliefs whose primary function is explanation. It circumscribes thinking, making it difficult for the holder to escape from its mould.

Independent self
A self that is relatively separate, internal and unique.

Interdependent self
A self that is relatively dependent on social relations and has more fuzzy boundaries.

Table 11.2 Western and Eastern cultural models of the self

The independent self	The interdependent self
is bounded, stable, autonomous	is connected, fluid, flexible
has personal attributes that guide action	participates in social relationships that guide action
is achievement-oriented	is oriented to the collective
formulates personal goals	meets obligations and conforms to norms
defines life by successful goal achievement	defines life by contributing to the collective
is responsible for own behaviour	is responsible with others for joint behaviour
is competitive	is cooperative
strives to feel good about the self	subsumes self in the collective

Source: Based on Fiske, Kitayama, Markus & Nisbett (1998).

according to perception of other people's thoughts, feelings and actions. Refer back to Box 11.1 to see how this throws more light on psychological differences between East Asians and Americans.

The distinction between two kinds of self has important implications for how individuals relate to significant others in their cultures. Think back now to Daan's concern about 'speaking out' in South Korea (the second focus question). These cultural differences in how we understand our self are probably implicit – we operate the way we do with little conscious awareness (Kitayama, Snibbe, Markus & Suzuki, 2004).

A review by Vivian Vignoles and her British colleagues (Vignoles, Chryssochoou & Breakwell, 2000) concluded that despite cultural differences in self-conception, the need to have a distinctive and integrated sense of self may be universal; however, self-distinctiveness means something different in individualist and in collectivist cultures. In one it is the isolated and bounded self that gains meaning from separateness, whereas in the other it is the relational self that gains meaning from its relations with others. In answering the question 'Who am I?', people from individualist cultures consistently describe themselves as independent and autonomous individuals, whereas those from collectivist cultures use interdependent descriptions. Bettina Hannover and Ulrich Kühnen (2004) contrast the two with an example: an individualist might say 'I have a good sense of humour' while the collectivist would say 'I enjoy telling jokes with my friends'.

Acculturation

When people migrate, they find it almost impossible to avoid close contact with members of the host culture and with other immigrant cultural groups. Extended contact inevitably produces changes in behaviour and thinking among new migrants. Acculturation is the process of internalising the rules for behaving in another culture; when it applies to a whole group we have large-scale culture change. However, immigrant groups have some choice about the form that these changes take – the starkest choice is between assimilation and separatism.

Acculturation
The process whereby individuals learn about the rules of behaviour characteristics of another culture.

The Canadian cross-cultural psychologist John Berry (e.g. Berry, Trimble & Olmedo, 1986) identified four different paths to acculturation. In weighing up home culture and dominant culture, immigrants can choose between:

- *integration* – maintaining home culture but also relating to dominant culture;
- *assimilation* – giving up home culture and embracing dominant culture;
- *separation* – maintaining home culture and being isolated from dominant culture;
- *marginalisation* – giving up home culture and failing to relate properly to dominant culture.

These choices are shown in Figure 11.3. (Reflect on the dilemma faced by Keiko and her husband in the third focus question.)

The most popular path for immigrants is integration, and it is the one associated with the least stress in acculturating (Berry, Kim, Minde & Mok, 1987). However, choosing to integrate is a process that takes considerable time and, in many instances, competes with a host culture's frequent expectation of assimilation. For the second generation immigrants (the children of the settlers), conflict with their elders is minimised if all actually integrate. Integration may be a 'good' solution for the individual immigrant – is it also good for whole groups of immigrants, and indeed for the host culture? Let us see what social psychology has to say about multiculturalism.

Multicultural societies

Many societies face a challenge: can multiple cultures coexist? Should all cultural forms be permitted to flourish in your community and what spectrum of practices should be tolerated? Legal and political issues constrain how we answer these questions.

At the cultural level, the debate is largely over the relative merits of assimilationism and multiculturalism. For example, Moghaddam (1998) has contrasted assimilationist policies with those that manage cultural diversity by promoting multiculturalism (see Figure 11.4). *Assimilation* can be of two kinds, total and 'melting-pot'. The former implies the obliteration of a culture, whereas the latter is less extreme and allows a new form of the dominant culture to emerge.

Figure 11.3

Four paths to acculturation.

- Berry *et al.* pinpointed four options that immigrants can follow in reconciling their ancestral culture with the new host culture.
- The positive valence (+) indicates that, to an extent, an immigrant adopts the host culture or retains the ancestral culture – or both;
- The negative valence (–) indicates that, to an extent, an immigrant fails to adopt the host culture or to retain elements of the ancestral culture – or both.
- The optimal outcome for an immigrant is integration.

Source: Based on Berry, Trimble & Olmedo (1986).

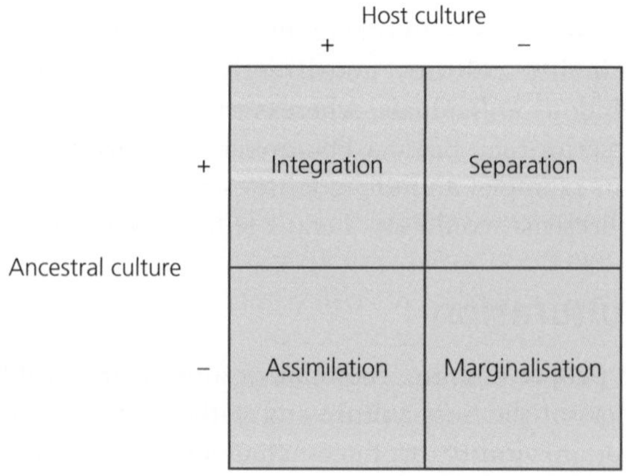

Figure 11.4

Types of assimilation and multiculturalism.

Cultural diversity is a challenge to society. Immigrant or indigenous minorities may assimilate fully or may leave some mark on the host culture in the process. Or cultural pluralism may flourish, either by accident or design.

Sources: Based on Allport (1954b) and Moghaddam (1998).

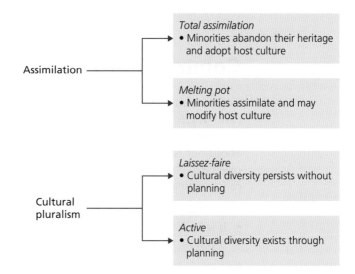

Multiculturalism is a more positive and embracing view of dominant and minority cultures. In its *laissez-faire* form, cultural diversity can continue without help from the host culture. Ethnic enclaves, such as the many Chinatowns that can be found in various cities of the world, Little India in Singapore and expatriate European communities in Dubai are examples of *laissez-faire* multiculturalism. In its active form, a nation's policy sustains cultural diversity. For example, there is government support in Canada and Australia for a variety of activities designed to sustain, to some degree, the cultural integrity of various immigrant groups. An active multiculturalism sustains cultural units that can be either individualistic or collectivist. Multiculturalism works when minority groups believe that their cherished identities and practices are respected. We have also learned that harmonious intergroup relations depend on groups to feel that they are not competitive but are more like different teams that 'pull together' (see Chapter 6).

There is, of course, another face to cultural diversity. In Western European cities such as Paris and London, high levels of immigration have coincided with a growth of intergroup confrontation and frightening acts of terror. Some commentary has simplified this to a clash between Islam and other world-views. There are other underlying causes – high rates of unemployment among youth from ethnic minorities in the West; a history of economic and political exploitation, the clamour for oil and national independence in the Middle East. To lay the major cause of conflict at the feet of centuries-old religions is naive.

Multiculturalism is not only evident but is increasing in many parts of the world. Take two instances: more business is being transacted between China and the West, and the expansion of the European community has large numbers of people relocating from Eastern to Western Europe. In addition, Internet access has made business, governmental, academic and personal communication very easy. In short, globalisation has accelerated. More than ever, these changes require psychologists to have more accurate definitions of culture, and of how it can influence the way that people think, feel and behave (Hong & Mallorie, 2004). Furthermore, cultures are not set in stone. Cultures in contact, especially living side by side, are probably

Multiculturalism
The way that a society manages and maintains the identity of its diverse cultures.

cultures that will change. A vibrant social psychology is one that can track change both within and between cultures and contribute to cooperative development.

Communication

Communication is the essence of social interaction: when we interact we communicate. Try to think of any social interaction that is free of communication. We constantly transmit information about what we sense, think and feel – indeed even about our identity – and some of our 'messages' are unintentional. We communicate through words, facial expressions, signs, bodily gestures, touch. We use phone calls, writing, emails and texts. Communication is social in several ways:

- It involves our relationships with others.
- It is built upon a shared understanding of meaning.
- It is how people influence each other.

Let us consider first the major part that language plays in human communication and how social factors, particularly culture and ethnicity, contribute to the overall picture.

Origins of language

We think of language as words, either written or spoken. However, there are a number of other ways that we communicate very effectively, as we shall see in later sections. True language is a distinctly human form of communication, although it has evolved.

Communication. We get our message across with spoken and written language and a rich mix of expressions, gestures and emblems – all contextualised by ethnicity and nationality.

Source: Graham Vaughan

Can chimps talk? Not as we know it. Animal vocalisation in general is stimulus-bound – a small number of utterances in responding to specific cues, such as a food source or a predator. Our own cries that sometimes accompany the primary emotions (treated below) may be the vestiges of the utterances of our primate ancestors. The eminent evolutionary psychologist Michael Corballis believes that hand gestures preceded spoken language in humans, and research in neuroscience indicates that only a brain as complex as yours and mine can handle what a real language depends on – syntax. See Box 11.4 for a short evolutionary history of how language came about.

Language, thought and society

Language is social in all sorts of ways: as a system of symbols, it lies at the heart of social life. We have noted that the sociologist G. H. Mead (1934) thought that our very self arises out of human interacting, i.e. communicating, with others (Chapter 3).

Have you ever had a little chat with yourself? The early Russian developmental psychologist Lev Vygotsky (1962) believed that inner speech was the medium of thought, and that it was closely connected to external speech, the medium of social communication. An extreme version of this idea was the theory of *linguistic relativity* (Whorf, 1956). This held that language entirely determines thought, so people

---

Research and applications 11.4
The hands have it: the gestural origins of language

Michael Corballis (1999) has argued that language evolved something like this:

1 Hominids diverged from the other great apes (6–7 million years ago).

2 Bipedal hominids, such as *Australopithecus*, used hand gestures (5 million years ago).

3 Syntax was added to gestures, and then vocalisation (2 million years ago).

4 Speech now dominated gesture in *Homo sapiens* (100 000 years ago).

Chimpanzees and the early hominids could undoubtedly vocalise well before the arrival of *Homo sapiens*, but this was largely involuntary. Bodily and brain changes necessary for controlling vocalisation were probably not complete until *Homo sapiens* emerged. Vocal language freed the hands for making things. It also allowed pedagogy to develop by combining speech and manual action, and enabled our forebears to communicate at night. The past 100 000 years have seen a 'human revolution', marked by technological innovation and the demise of all other hominids.

A limited use of gesture to communicate may extend back more than 25 million years to the common ancestors of humans, apes and monkeys. However, when hominids (our human line) stood up and walked, their hands were no longer instruments to move about and instead could serve extensively as tools for communicating. Like speech, gestural language in right-handed people depends on the left side of the brain.

Today, examples of gestural language include:

- sign languages used by the deaf;

- communicating with someone who speaks a different language;

- hand gestures that accompany speech, often superfluously, as when talking on the phone;

- religious communities bound by a vow of silence;

- sophisticated manual hand signs among Australian Aborigines and American Plains Indians.

Source: Based on Corballis (1999).

who speak different languages see the world in entirely different ways and effectively live in entirely different cognitive universes.

Let us take some examples. Inuit (Eskimos) have a much more textured vocabulary for snow than other people; does this mean that they actually see more differences than we do? In English, we differentiate between living and non-living flying things, while the Hopi of North America do not; does this mean that they actually see no difference between a bee and an aeroplane? Japanese personal pronouns differentiate between interpersonal relationships more subtly than do English personal pronouns; does this mean that English speakers cannot tell the difference between different relationships?

A weaker form of this theory seems to accord better with the facts. Language does *not* determine thought. What it does do is to help us communicate more easily about those aspects of our physical or social environment that really matter (see Krauss & Chiu, 1998). If I need to communicate lots of details about rice, then I will enrich my vocabulary to know about *basmati*, *jasmine* and *samba*, and perhaps a few more as well. If you find it important to discuss wine in any detail and with ease, you will taste lots of wine, have fun reading and talking about it, and master the 'lingo' of a connoisseur.

As communication researchers Mark Knapp and Judith Hall (2005) have noted, language communicates not only by *what* is said but also by *how* it is said. Paralanguage refers to all the non-linguistic accompaniments of speech – volume, stress, pitch, speed, loudness, tone of voice, pauses, throat clearing, grunts and sighs. These features can dramatically change meaning. When we end a statement with a rising tone we make it a question or show uncertainty. When we are sad or bored we use a low pitch; when we are angry, afraid or surprised we use a high pitch; and when we talk quite fast we may well be exerting power and control.

Speech contains social markers. Our social class, ethnicity, age and gender are often clearly identifiable and are clues to group membership. For instance, most Britons can quite easily identify Americans, Australians and South Africans from speech style alone, and are probably even better at identifying people who come from Exeter, Birmingham, Liverpool, Leeds and Essex! If one's speech style points to a social category it can bring a listener's attitudes towards that group into play. Recall how hard Eliza Doolittle tried in the film *My Fair Lady* to acquire a standard English accent – anything to conceal her Cockney origins!

In their influential book *Speech Style and Social Evaluation*, Howard Giles and Peter Powesland (1975) outlined how we tend to use two major dimensions to judge others on their speech:

1. *status* (a cluster of traits such as intelligent, competent, powerful);
2. *solidarity* (a cluster of traits such as close, friendly, warm).

A community's standard language variety is the one that usually reflects high economic status and power and has tended to dominate media usage. By tradition, it is called received pronunciation (RP) English in Britain and is mocked from time to time in TV comedies. Non-standard varieties include regional accents (e.g. Yorkshire), non-standard urban accents (e.g. Birmingham) and minority ethnic languages (e.g. Hindi in Britain). The status associated with standard varieties is counteracted by the down-to-earth image suggested by non-standard varieties. For example, in Switzerland more pronounced solidarity traits are attributed to non-standard Swiss German speakers than to High German speakers (Hogg, Joyce & Abrams, 1984).

The general thrust of published research is that the way we speak, our accent

Paralanguage
The non-linguistic accompaniments of speech (e.g. stress, pitch, speed, tone, pauses).

Social markers
Features of speech style that convey information about mood, context, status and group membership.

Received pronunciation (RP)
Standard, high-status, spoken variety of English.

and language, affects how others evaluate us. Some languages and certain speech styles are associated with particular social groups, and in turn are evaluated more positively or less positively in society. If your speech style suggests your status is relatively high, people are fairly naturally inclined to evaluate you in terms of a high status group. At this point, a variety of other factors linked to intergroup relations, including some that are historical, can affect how individuals are judged. A voice with a speech style, as much as a face with ethnic features, can conjure up all kinds of images (e.g. holidays, work and perhaps stories of war).

Language and culture

In this section we link language mainly to culture and ethnicity, though we can note that there is a considerable literature dealing with speech styles that differentiate us by our age or generation, or by our gender, as noted by Kimberly Noels and her colleagues (Noels, Giles & Le Poire, 2003).

Howard Giles and his colleagues applied *social identity theory* (see Chapter 7) to develop ethnolinguistic identity theory (e.g. Giles, Bourhis & Taylor, 1977). Ethnic groups can differ from one another in appearance, dress, cultural practices and religious beliefs, but also in language or speech style.

Language or speech style is often a distinct marker of *ethnic identity*. For instance, the Welsh and the English in the UK are most distinctive in terms of accent and language. Speech style can be a central property of group membership: one of the most powerful ways to display your Welshness is to speak English with a marked Welsh accent – or, even better, to speak Welsh itself. You may choose to

Ethnolinguistic identity theory
Application and extension of social identity theory to deal with language behaviour of ethnolinguistic groups.

Communication mismatch! Ayatollah Khomeini pronounced a death sentence on Salmon Rushdie 20 years ago. Does burning Danish cartoons resolve the issue?

Source: Asim Tanveer / Reuters

emphasise your ethnic language when it is a source of self-respect and pride, or tone it down when it does not. How you respond is influenced by how you perceive interethnic power and status relations in your country and in a given context. Today, almost all societies are multicultural, with a single dominant high-status group whose language is the *lingua franca* of the nation, and other ethnic groups whose languages are subordinate.

However, it is in new world immigrant countries such as the United States, Canada, Australia and Brazil that the biggest variety of large ethnic minorities occurs. Much of the research into ethnicity and language comes from these countries, particularly Australia and Canada. In Australia where sociolinguist Cindy Gallois and her colleagues have worked, English is the *lingua franca*, but there are also large ethnic Chinese, Italian, Greek and Vietnamese Australian communities. In her study, ethnic differences in communication style may have implications for a student's perceived academic ability (see Box 11.5).

Ethnolinguistic vitality
Concept describing objective features of an interethnic context that influence language, and ultimately the cultural survival or disappearance of an ethnolinguistic group.

Howard Giles and his colleagues coined the term ethnolinguistic vitality to describe features of an interethnic context that influence how much a language is used (Giles, Bourhis & Taylor, 1977). Groups that are high on status, and are supported by their demographics and by institutions, have high ethnolinguistic vitality. These features offer a future for the language and help to ensure its survival. This process protects a space for the group itself as a distinct entity. Low vitality is a mark of language decline and a portent of its disappearance. What follows is language death and perhaps the obliteration of an ethnic group (see Figure 11.5).

Research and applications 11.5
Communication mismatch

Chinese students are the largest single ethnic group of overseas students enrolled in Australian universities. Owing to cultural differences in communication styles, these students often find it difficult to adjust to local Australian communication norms, which encourage students to speak out in class and when interacting with academic staff.

Cindy Gallois and her associates studied this problem. They prepared twenty-four carefully scripted videotapes of conversation sequences between a student and a lecturer, in which the student adopted a submissive, assertive or aggressive communication style to ask for help with an assignment or to complain about a grade. The student was either a male or a female Anglo-Australian or an ethnic Chinese. The lecturer was always Anglo-Australian and the same sex as the student.

The ethnic Chinese students were either from Hong Kong, Singapore or Malaysia. The Chinese students, Australian students and lecturers viewed the videotaped vignettes and rated the students in the videotape on a number of behavioural dimensions and on the effectiveness of their communication style. All participants agreed that the aggressive style was inappropriate, ineffective and atypical of students of any ethnic background. Consistent with stereotypes, submissiveness was considered more typical of Chinese than Australian students, and assertiveness more typical of Australian than Chinese students. Chinese students felt that the submissive style was more effective than the assertive style. However, lecturers and Australian students interpreted the submissive style as being less effective and indicating less need for assistance.

The assumption by the Australian students and the lecturers that a submissive style indicates a lack of need and interest could nourish an unfortunate view that Chinese students are less talented than their Australian counterparts.

Source: Gallois, Barker, Jones & Callan (1992).

Figure 11.5

When is a language vital?

Ethnolinguistic vitality is influenced by status, demographic and institutional support variables.

Source: Based on Hogg, M. A., & Abram, D. (1988). *Social identifications: A social psychology of intergroup relations and group processes*. London: Routledge. Reproduced with permission.

Status variables

- Economic control of destiny
- Consensually high self-esteem
- Pride in the group's past
- Respected language of international repute

+

Demographic variables

- Large numbers concentrated in ancestral homeland
- Favourable ingroup–outgroup numerical proportion
- Low emigration rate
- High birth rate
- Low incidence of mixed ingroup–outgroup marriage

+

Institutional support variables

- Good representation of language in national or territorial institutions (government, media, schools, universities, church, etc.)

Ethnolinguistic vitality

Ethnolinguistic vitality. A challenge to a truly multicultural society is to find ways of preserving the ancestral languages of its citizens.

Source: Pearson Online Database (POD)

Links between using a language and having a flourishing ethnic identity have been reported in various countries. In Canada, recent decades have witnessed a strong French-language revival in the province of Quebec. Other revivals include Hebrew, considered a dead language half a century ago, in Israel; Flemish in Belgium; Hindi in India; and Welsh in both Wales and beyond (see Coupland, Bishop, Evans & Garrett, 2006; Fishman, 1989; Sachdev & Bourhis, 2005). These studies converge on a major finding: ethnolinguistic vitality is strongest among speakers who are competent in the language.

A language can also die. A loss of ethnolinguistic identity has occurred in the following: in Canada, Italian and Scottish Canadians generally consider themselves Anglo-Canadian; third-generation Japanese in Brazil have entirely lost their Japanese culture; in Australia, linguistic vitality has declined from first- to second-generation Greek, Italian and Vietnamese Australians (see Edwards & Chisholm, 1987; Hogg, D'Agata & Abrams, 1989; Kanazawa & Loveday, 1988).

In closing this section we should note that second-language learning is a vital component of acculturating for a migrant. Immigrants throughout Europe need to learn the *lingua franca* in order to be educated and to be able to participate in employment, culture and day-to-day life. Success in a new country requires more than proficiency; what is needed is the wholesale acquisition of a language imbedded in its cultural context. An immigrant should aim to speak like a native, and to do so hinges more on motivation than on linguistic aptitude or pedagogical factors (Giles & Byrne, 1982). Native-like mastery is the ideal. At the other end of the scale, a poor command of the local language can undermine self-confidence and cause physical and social isolation, leading to material hardship and psychological suffering. For example, Noels, Pon and Clément (1996) found low self-esteem and marked symptoms of stress among Chinese Canadians with poor English skills.

It could be argued that native-like mastery implies assimilation and therefore a loss of ancestral culture (see Figures 11.3 and 11.4). However, there are examples where multiculturalism can be preserved. These include English-language mastery among Japanese in the United States and Chinese in Hong Kong, and Italian language mastery among Valdotans, a French-speaking community in northern Italy (see Bond & King, 1985; Saint-Blancat, 1985: San Antonio, 1987). These groups acquired native-like mastery in the dominant language and yet maintain their own cultural and ethnolinguistic heritage. (Should Paulo become bilingual? See the fifth focus question.)

Majority group members do not generally have the motivation to acquire native-like mastery of another language. According to sociolinguist John Edwards (1994), it is precisely the international prestige and usefulness of English that make native English speakers such poor foreign-language students: they simply are not motivated to become proficient. Edwards was aware of the wry words of the poet John Milton:

We Englishmen, being far northerly, do not open our mouths in the cold air wide enough to grace a southern tongue. (*Milton, 1644, cited in Edwards, 1994, pp. 60–61*).

Itesh Sachdev and Audrey Wright (1996) pursued this point in a study in South England. They found that White English children were more motivated to learn European languages than Asian languages: the former were considered more useful and of higher status, even though the children in their sample had immeasurably more day-to-day contact with Asian than with European languages and people.

In this section we have dealt with the interplay between language and culture. Next, we now expand our view to explore non-verbal communication, featuring both cultural universals and cultural differences.

Communicating without words

Did you know that people can produce about 20 000 different facial expressions and about 1 000 different cues based on paralanguage? There are also about 700 000 different physical gestures, facial expressions and movements (see Birdwhistell, 1970; Hewes, 1957; Pei, 1965). How on earth do we cope? Even the briefest interaction can involve the fleeting and simultaneous use of a large number of these devices, making it very difficult even to code behaviour, let alone analyse the causes and consequences of particular non-verbal communications. Their importance is now well recognised in social psychology (Burgoon, Buller & Woodall, 1989; DePaulo & Friedman, 1998). However, doing research in this area is a major challenge. Non-verbal behaviour can serve a variety of purposes (Patterson, 1983). We can use it to:

Non-verbal communication Transfer of meaningful information from one person to another by means other than written or spoken language (e.g. gaze, facial expression, posture, touch).

- glean information about feelings and intentions of others (e.g. non-verbal cues are often reliable indicators of whether someone likes you);
- regulate interactions (e.g. non-verbal cues can signal the approaching end of an utterance, or that someone else wishes to speak);
- express intimacy (e.g. touching and mutual eye contact);
- establish dominance or control (non-verbal threats);
- facilitate goal attainment (e.g. pointing).

These functions will become evident in our discussion of gaze, facial expressions, body language, touch and interpersonal distance. Now here is an interesting aspect: people acquire, without any formal training, consummate mastery of a rich repertoire of non-verbal behaviour very early in life. Indeed, to do so with skill is important in becoming socially adjusted and in forming satisfactory relationships in adulthood (Schachner, Shaver & Mikulincer, 2005). Perhaps partly because we acquire non-verbal behaviour unawares, we tend not to be conscious that we are using non-verbal cues or that we are being influenced by others' use of such cues: non-verbal communication goes largely unnoticed, yet it has enormous impact.

This is not to say that non-verbal behaviour is completely uncontrolled. On the contrary, social norms can influence its expression. For example, even if delighted at the demise of a foe, we are unlikely to smile at his or her funeral. There are also individual and group differences, with some people being better than others at noticing and using non-verbal cues. Robert Rosenthal and his colleagues (1979) devised a *profile of non-verbal sensitivity* (PONS) as a test to chart some of these individual and group differences. All things being equal, non-verbal sensitivity improves with age, is more advanced among successful people and is compromised among people with a range of psychopathologies.

You may have already surmised that the emotions play a major part in communicating our feelings, and that there is a time and a place when we should do so. Keeping a 'stiff upper lip' is not always the smartest move.

Expressing our emotions

The scientific study of facial expression has largely focused on the way in which the face communicates emotions. Darwin (1872) believed that there are a small number of universal emotions, and that associated with these are universal facial expressions. Subsequent research generally identified six basic emotions (happiness, surprise, sadness, fear, disgust and anger), from which more complex or blended emotions are derived (Ekman, 1982, 2003; Scherer, 1986). There are cross-culturally stable gender differences in how often both basic and complex emotions are experienced (Fischer, Mosquera, van Vienan & Manstead, 2004). Women report more often their powerless emotions (e.g. fear, sadness, shame, guilt), while men more often report their powerful emotions (e.g. anger, hostility).

A basic emotion has a quite distinctive pattern of facial muscle activity: for instance, surprise is associated with raised eyebrows, dropped jaw, horizontal wrinkles across the forehead, raised upper eyelids and lowered lower eyelids (Ekman & Friesen, 1975). Researchers have even developed a computer program that can simultaneously vary different facial components (e.g. roundness of eyes, thickness of lips, curve of eyebrows, distance between mouth and eyes) to reproduce recognisable emotional expressions on a computer screen (Katsikitis, Pilowsky & Innes, 1990).

The human facial expressions associated with basic emotions appear to be relatively universal. Paul Ekman and his colleagues showed people a series of photographs of faces expressing the six basic emotions and had them report the emotions being expressed (Ekman, 1971; Ekman & Friesen, 1971; Ekman *et al.*, 1987). People from a variety of Western cultures (Argentina, Brazil, Chile, Germany, Greece, Italy, Scotland, the United States), Asian cultures (Hong Kong,

Six basic emotions. Anger, happiness, surprise, fear, sadness and disgust. But, which is which?

Source: Godfrey Boehnke

Japan, Sumatra, Turkey) and tribal cultures (Borneo, New Guinea) were remarkably accurate in identifying the six emotions from facial expression by people from both the same and different cultures.

There has been some criticism of Ekman's method, which depended on participants rating photographs of posed rather than natural (candid) emotional expressions. However, in contrast to Ekman's use of posed photographs, Robert Krauss and his colleagues adopted a more naturalistic technique in which people identified emotions as they occurred on videotapes of Japanese and American soap operas (Krauss, Curran & Ferleger, 1983). Like Ekman's findings, there was remarkable cross-cultural agreement.

Ekman's argument that the primary emotions are universal has also been criticised (e.g. Russell, Bachorowski & Fernandez-Dols, 2003), but his work has generated a large number of studies and continues to do so. Undeterred, Ekman has developed a Facial Action Coding System (FACS), a standardised method to measure facial movement based on small units of muscles that reflect a variety of underlying emotional states (Ekman, Friesen & Hager, 2002). This technique has even been adapted to measure facial responses in chimpanzees (Vick *et al.*, 2007). The aim of such work is to make a cross-species comparison of 'emotions' with humans, in an evolutionary quest for characteristics that are uniquely human and those that may be shared with other primates.

The apparent universality of facial expressions of emotion may either reflect universals of *ontogeny* (cross-cultural commonalities in early socialisation) or else *phylogeny* (an innate link between emotions and facial muscle activity). The contribution of phylogeny has some support from research among people born deaf, blind and without hands. Although these people have limited access to the normal cues that we would use to learn which facial expressions go with which emotions, they express basic emotions in much the same manner as people who are not handicapped in these ways (Eibl-Eibesfeldt, 1972).

Having made this argument for universals in the facial expression of the emotions, we must now make an important qualification. There are marked cultural and situational rules, called display rules, governing the expression of emotions (see Figure 11.6).

These rules exist because we also use our facial expressions to communicate with someone else, as Cindy Gallois (1993) observed. There are shades of surprise: when we 'choose' one of these, we might accompany our facial display by vocalising with something like 'oh my god' or 'whew'. In a fine-grained analysis of conversations, Sue Wilkinson and Celia Kitzinger (2006) have demonstrated that we are equipped to respond with surprise several turns in advance. Perhaps you can remember talking with a friend and can guess what is about to announced – your face begins to move . . . oh gosh, the suspense!

There are cultural, gender and situational variations in display rules. Expressing an emotion is encouraged among women and in Mediterranean cultures, but is discouraged among men and in northern European and Asian cultures (Argyle, 1975). In Japan, people are taught to control facial expressions of negative emotion and to use laughter or smiling to conceal anger or grief. In Western cultures, it is impolite to display happiness at beating an opponent in tennis by laughing, yet happy laughter is acceptable at a party. Similarly, it is fine to cry at a funeral but not on hearing disappointing news in a business setting.

In short, we are dealing with the nature–nurture controversy, a point that is nicely illustrated by James Russell's (1994) investigation of the varying success that people

Display rules
Cultural and situational rules that dictate how appropriate it is to express emotions in a given contexts.

nature–nurture controversy
Classic debate about whether genetic or environmental factors determine human behaviour. Scientists generally accept that it is an interaction of both.

Figure 11.6

The facial affect programme: expressing an emotion.

Source: Based on Ekman (1971).

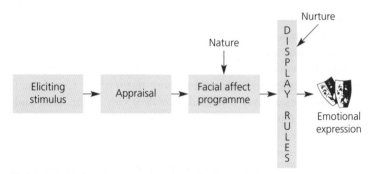

- Rapid facial signals accompany many affective states.
- These signals are the facial affect programme, or facial blueprint.
- They distinguish primary emotions from their blends.
- There is an interplay between nature and nurture:
  - signals have a genetic base, whereas
  - display rules arise from experience and provide a little control over what we show others.

from different parts of the world have in decoding (or labelling) the six primary emotions (shown in the photos on page 340). His results are shown in Figure 11.7.

Focusing on cross-cultural differences in emotional displays, Ekman (1973) monitored facial expressions of American students in America and Japanese students in Japan watching a very stressful film in private and talking about it to the experimenter afterwards. In private, both groups displayed negative emotions, but in public only the Americans gave facial expressions indicating negative emotions.

Figure 11.7

Cross-cultural success at matching primary emotions.

- People from three categories of cultures were compared: literate and from the West (20 studies) or elsewhere (11 studies), and non-literate from elsewhere (three studies).

- Recognition of happiness is high in all cultures.

- Agreement about other emotions falls away, depending on: (a) what is thought to be a culturally appropriate expression, and (b) exposure to a literature that provides models of how to express an emotion.

Source: Based on data from Russell (1994).

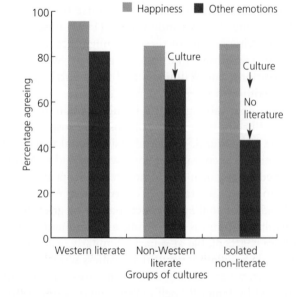

In public, the Japanese students' facial expressions were indicative of positive emotions. A meta-analysis of 162 studies by Maryanne LaFrance and her colleagues showed that Western women were encouraged to smile more often than their Asian counterparts (LaFrance, Hecht & Paluck, 2003). This finding clearly reflects the existence of different cultural (and gender) display rules.

Finally, facial movements are more than cues to our emotions; they are also used deliberately to support or even to replace spoken language. We raise our eyebrows to emphasise a question, or furrow our brows and squint our eyes to reflect doubt or scorn. A relatively new development – American Sign Language (ASL) – is linked to Ekman's work on the facial expression of basic emotions. ASL is a convention that uses a set of sign language facial expressions, which have emotional meaning and are dynamic, i.e. they occur in real time (Grossman & Kegl, 2007).

Eye contact

The eyes are often considered to be the windows of the soul, so it is not surprising to learn that people spend a great deal of time gazing at each other's eyes. In two-person settings, people spend 61 per cent of the time gazing, and a gaze lasts about three seconds (Argyle & Ingham, 1972). Eye contact refers more precisely to mutual gaze. People in pairs spend about 30 per cent of their time engaging in mutual gaze, and a mutual gaze lasts less than a second.

Gaze
Looking at someone's eyes.

According to Chris Kleinke (1986), gaze is perhaps the most information-rich and important of the non-verbal communication channels. We make inferences about their feelings, credibility, honesty, competence and attentiveness. We are driven to seek out the information communicated by others' eyes, even though under certain circumstances (e.g. passing a stranger in the street) eye contact itself is uncomfortable and even embarrassing. Absence of eye behaviour can be equally unnerving. Consider how disorienting it can be to interact with someone whose eyes you cannot see (e.g. someone wearing dark glasses) or someone who continually avoids eye contact. Conversely, obscuring from others where your own eyes are looking can increase your own sense of security and privacy: for example, female tourists visiting notably chauvinistic societies are often encouraged to wear dark glasses and to avoid eye contact with male strangers. In many societies, women secure privacy in public places by wearing a veil.

We look more at people we like than those we dislike. Greater gaze signals intimacy, particularly if the gaze is mutual. This appears to be such common knowledge that even false information that someone has looked at you quite often can increase your liking for that person.

Gaze also plays an important role in regulating the course of a conversation once started. White adults spend on average 75 per cent of the time gazing when listening and 41 per cent of the time gazing when speaking (Argyle & Ingham, 1972). We can counteract this when we are turn-taking. As a listener, you can decrease your gaze in order to show that you want to gain the floor; as a speaker, you can increase your gaze to show that you are about to stop speaking.

Gaze can communicate relative status between you and someone else. From studies of status differences between interactants that have been experimentally manipulated or are actually real-life, we now know that lower-status individuals gaze at their partners more than do higher-status individuals (e.g. Dovidio & Ellyson, 1985). Given that a traditional gender difference in power often cast women in a lower-status position, this may explain why women engage in more eye contact than men (Duncan, 1969; Henley & Harmon, 1985).

Marianne LaFrance and Clara Mayo (1976) have shown that this pattern is reversed among African Americans, who gaze more when speaking than when listening. This produces some complicated communication problems in interracial interactions. For example, a White speaker may interpret a Black listener's *low* rate of gaze as lack of interest, rudeness or an attempt to butt in and take the floor, while a Black speaker may interpret a White listener's *high* rate of gaze in the same way. From the perspective of the listener, a White may interpret a Black speaker's high rate of gaze as arrogance and/or an invitation to take the floor, while a Black may interpret a White speaker's low rate of gaze in the same way. There is less eye contact during the course of an interview in Japan than in the West. Unlike Western listeners, who are socialised to look at a speaker's eyes, Japanese listeners find it less stressful to focus on the speaker's knees (Bond & Komai, 1976), a practice that might be unnerving to some! (What do you now think about Santoso's plight? See the fifth focus question.)

Postures and gestures

Kinesics
Linguistics of body communication.

Your eyes and face communicate. Your head, hands, legs, feet and torso communicate as well. The anthropologist Ray Birdwhistell (1970) made an ambitious attempt to construct an entire linguistics of body communication, called kinesics. Working mainly in the United States, he identified up to seventy basic units of body movement (e.g. flared nostrils) and described rules of combination that produce meaningful units of body communication (e.g. the combination of a shoulder shrug, raised eyebrows and upturned palms).

We use our hands and arms to enrich the meaning of what we say (Archer, 1997; Ekman & Friesen, 1972). There are gender differences: research by Thomas Schubert (2004) indicates that men are more likely than women to raise a clenched fist as a symbol of pride or power. Some gestures are universal, such as giving directions by moving the arm and pointing with a finger or thumb. Sometimes we even continue to do so when talking on the telephone – why should technology get in our way? We have already noted that *manual gestures* are the precursor of human language (refer back to Box 11.4).

Emblems
Gestures that replace or stand in for spoken language.

Emblems, on the other hand, are special gestures that have a verbal counterpart, such as the wave of the hand in greeting, or less friendly hand signals. Some emblems are widely understood across cultures, but many are culture-specific. The same thing can be indicated by different gestures in different cultures, and the same gesture can mean different things in different cultures. For instance, we refer to 'self' by pointing at our chest, while in Japan they put a finger to the nose (DeVos & Hippler, 1969). A sideways nod of the head means 'no' in Britain but 'yes' in India, and in Turkey 'no' is indicated by moving the head backwards and rolling the eyes upwards (Rubin, 1976). In Britain, we invite people to approach by beckoning with an upturned finger, while Indians use all four downturned fingers. In Britain, if you were to draw your finger across your throat it would mean that someone was in big trouble. The same gesture in Swaziland means 'I love you' and 'I've lost my job' in Japan. Cross-cultural differences in the meaning of gestures can have serious consequences. Be careful when and where you gesture with a forefinger and thumb forming a circle: you might intend it to mean 'it's okay' or 'great'. In Brazil this means 'screw you!' (Burgoon, Buller & Woodall, 1989).

Up close and personal

We have seen how parts of our bodies can send messages. The distance between our bodies, or interpersonal distance does this as well and its study is called proxemics. Furthermore, the closer two people are, the greater the number of non-verbal cues that can be detected and 'talking' becomes richer. We use interpersonal distance to regulate privacy and intimacy: the greater the distance, the more private you can be. The influential anthropologist Edward Hall's (1966) work *The Hidden Dimension* identified four *interpersonal distance zones* – ranging from high to low intimacy, each a little more removed from our bodies (see Table 11.3).

If you feel more intimate towards someone you will move closer, but if you feel a difference in status you will keep physically further away – see Hayduk's (1983) review. Because a short distance is such a potent cue to intimacy, it can be disconcerting to be close to some people. Personal space, a now-popular term also introduced by Hall, reflects the importance that people place on their perceived body buffer zone.

Michael Argyle and Janet Dean (1965) proposed an intimacy–equilibrium theory, which predicts that when intimacy signals are increased in one modality, they are decreased in other modalities (e.g. eye contact). For instance, on approaching a stranger who is still some distance away, you might gaze discretely; as soon as the approaching stranger enters your social zone (about 3.5 metres), you look away; or on your own turf you might show a ritualised recognition (a smile or mumbled greeting). Have you had that crowded feeling in a lift? According to intimacy–equilibrium theory, we can reduce intimacy cues by assiduously staring at the

Proxemics
Study of interpersonal distance.

Personal space
Physical space around people's bodies which they treat as a part of themselves.

Personal space. These women are in what Edward Hall called a zone of intimate distance. They are comfortable with each other to the point of showing 'postural echo'.

Source: Michael Hogg

Table 11.3 Four zones of space in social interaction: how close is comfortable?

Zone	Distance	Description
Intimate distance	Up to 0.5 m	Physical contact can take place. Much is exposed about a person. Cues come from sight, sound, smell, body temperature, and depth and pace of breathing.
Personal distance	0.5–1.25 m	This transitional area between intimate contact and formal behaviour is the norm in Western countries for everyday interactions with friends and acquaintances. Touching is still possible. Although many cues are still available, the effects of body temperature, smell and breathing are greatly reduced.
Social distance	1.25–4 m	This is typical for both casual and business interactions. Many cues are lost, but verbal contact is easily maintained. Furniture arrangement helps to achieve this. In an office, the desk is about 75 cm deep, and allowing for chair space, people interacting across the desk are just over one metre apart. A bigger desk can signal rank.
Public distance	4–8 m	Communication cues now lose some impact. It is a common distance for public speakers, celebrities and lecturers. In a lecture hall, lecterns are usually placed about 3.5 m back from the first row of seats. Courtrooms use this intervening space to prevent easy exchanges with the judge. The message? Interaction is not wanted.

Source: Hall (1966).

numbers for each floor level flashing away (Zuckerman, Miserandino & Bernieri, 1983). Close seating arrangements can have a similar effect (Sommer, 1969). Look at how people usually try to create space between themselves and other passengers in an airport terminal, or read or listen to their iPods more as numbers build up.

Cultural (and gender) differences in relation to personal space and acceptable touching abound. In the United States, African Americans will stand much closer when talking than White Americans (Aiello & Jones, 1971). Likewise, people in Southern Europe, the Middle East and Latin America also stand closer, while in some tribal communities in Africa and Indonesia people will often touch while talking (Argyle & Dean, 1965).

We have referred to touch several times in this section. Social touch is perhaps the earliest form of communication we learn. Do you have flashes from your childhood, or have you watched very young children? Long before we learn language, and even before we are adept at using body illustrators or gestures, we give and receive information by touch. There are many different types of touch (e.g. brief, enduring, firm, gentle) to different parts of the body (e.g. hand, shoulder, chest). The meaning of a touch varies as a function of the type of touch, the context within which the touch occurs, who touches whom, and what the relationship is between the interactants (e.g. husband and wife, doctor and patient, strangers). As Stephen Thayer (1986) noted, our language reflects facets of its meaning – e.g. 'a soft touch', 'a gripping experience', 'deeply touched'.

Even the most incidental and fleeting touches can have significant effects. Male and female customers in a restaurant gave larger tips after their female waiting person touched them casually on the hand (Crusco & Wetzel, 1984). In another study, university library clerks briefly touched the hand of students checking out books. Women who had been touched indicated greater liking for the clerk, and even for the library, than those who had not been touched (Fisher, Rytting & Heslin, 1976). Male students were stolidly unaffected.

Finally, there is substantial cross-cultural variation in the frequency of using social touch. People from Latin American, Mediterranean and Arab countries touch a great deal, while people from northern Europe, North America, Australia and Asia do not (Argyle, 1975). From a study of the touching behaviour of couples in cafes in different countries, Sydney Jourard (1966) observed, in a one-hour period, no touching in London, 2 touches in Florida, 110 touches in Paris and 180 in Puerto Rico. Perhaps a Londoner dating in Puerto Rico or a Parisian dating in Florida might feel uncomfortable!

Concluding thoughts

Our book is an introduction to social psychology, a discipline that is a passion for us, the authors. You have joined us in this journey and we hope that you have enjoyed the ride. We will have succeeded in our purpose if you use what you have learned in your studies and later in your professional lives. We will be gratified even more if this book helps you to understand yourself a little more, appreciate your fellows as social beings, and tolerate or even nourish the myriad of groups that make up our world. Our message? Read, think and, when you can, act.

Summary

- Cultures vary considerably in social behaviour, including cognitive processes and attributional style. Norms that govern conformity and aggression also differ across cultures.

- Modern systems that characterise cultures include crucial differences in values, in particular, and a different distribution of individualism and collectivism.

- People in the East have a different way of viewing themselves and relating to each other from people in the West. Eastern people are collectivist and nurture interdependence, whereas Western people are individualistic and nurture independence.

- Acculturating groups such as migrants face different acculturative choices, varying from retaining their ethnic identity to merging with the dominant culture. Acculturative stress is a common problem.

- The world's societies are increasingly multicultural. To both foster cultural diversity and maintain intergroup harmony is a challenge.

- Communication is the basis of social interaction and language is its most sophisticated form. Speech evolved and was predated by manual gestures.

- Language does not determine thought, but it eases how we communicate with others about what is important.

- The way we speak informs others about our feelings, motives and our membership of social groups, such as gender, status, nationality and ethnicity.

- Ethnic groups may actively promote their own language, or gradually abandon it, depending on the degree of vitality they consider their ethnolinguistic group to possess in a multi-ethnic context.

- For a minority ethnolinguistic group, motivation is crucial if its members wish to master the dominant group's language as a second language.

- Non-verbal channels of communication (e.g. gaze, facial expression, posture, gesture, touch, interpersonal distance) carry important information about our emotions. They can also suggest what our attitudes might be, and contain cues to our relative status, gender and culture.

Literature, film and TV

Bend It Like Beckham and East is East

A 2002 film directed by Gurinder Chadha, starring Parminder Nagra as the Indian girl 'Jess', *Bend it Like Beckham* is a light-hearted film about the clashing of different cultures in the UK, and about how culture creates expectations and ways of doing things that seem normal – Jess is at the intersection of different role expectations based on culture and gender. In a very similar vein, *East is East* is a 1999 culture-clash comedy set in Salford in the 1970s. George Kahn is a Pakistani immigrant who runs a fish-and-chips shop and tries to bring up his sons in traditional Pakistani ways. He gradually comes to realize that his sons see themselves as British and will never conform to his strict rules on marriage, food, dress and religion.

The Kitchen God's Wife

Amy Tan's 1991 novel is about second-generation Chinese in San Francisco who are pulled between traditional Chinese culture and liberal US culture. It focuses on women, who feel the contrast more strongly because the pressure and expectations to retain relatively traditional and repressive Chinese culture are very strong.

Crash

An incredibly powerful and sophisticated 2004 Paul Haggis film about cultural diversity, starring Don Cheadle, Sandra Bullock, Matt Dillon and Jennifer Esposito and set in the cultural melting pot of Los Angeles, a sprawling city of 17 million. It shows how different cultures are often suspicious of one another and how all cultures have stereotypes of one another that can turn ugly when people are anxious and stressed. A sobering film that moves away from the old-fashioned 'white male redneck' caricature of prejudice and raises challenging questions about how and if cultures really can live in harmony in the global village.

Pygmalion

This 1938 play directed by Anthony Asquith and Leslie Howard is based on the play by George Bernard Shaw. There are many variants on this perennial theme of changing your accent and the way you speak in order to change your status in society: for example, the 1964 film *My Fair Lady*, directed by George Cukor (again based on Shaw's play), and starring Audrey Hepburn and Rex Harrison; and the 1983 film *Educating Rita*, directed by Lewis Gilbert, written by Willy Russell and starring Michael Caine and Julie Walters.

Babel

Alejandro González Inárritu 2006 film with Brad Pitt, Cate Blanchett and Gael Garcia Bernal is a powerful, atmospheric multi-narrative drama exploring the theme that cross-cultural assumptions prevent people from understanding and communicating with one another. Each sub-plot features people out of their familiar cultural context: American children lost in the Mexican borderlands, a deaf Japanese girl mourning and alone in a hearing world, and two Americans stranded in the Moroccan desert.

Lost in Translation

This 2003 film written and directed by Sofia Coppola and starring Bill Murray and Scarlet Johansson, illustrates how you can feel like a fish out of water in a foreign culture where you do not speak the language and do not really understand the culture. This is also a film about life crises – two Americans at very different stages in their lives but with similar relationship problems are marooned in a large Japanese city and are drawn to each other.

Rachel Getting Married

Jonathan Demme's 2008 film starring Anne Hathaway is a superbly powerful commentary on, among other things, culture as commodity, has as its setting a wealthy wedding party at a country mansion in the eastern US. The wedding hosts and guests are liberal, educated and politically correct – but they are cringingly pretentious and inauthentic as they cycle through different cultural practices and symbols as mere decoration and entertainment. The only authentic and genuinely human character at the wedding is the younger daughter Kym, played by Hathaway, who is just out of rehab.

Persepolis

This 2007 French film explores cultural anomie. The young Marji Statrapi celebrates the removal of the Shah in the 1979 Iranian revolution, but quickly finds herself an outsider as Iran lurches towards Islamic fundamentalism and a new form of tyranny. For her own protection her family sends her to Vienna to study and build a new life, but Marji finds it an abrasive and difficult culture that is hard to fit into. When she returns to Iran things have changed so much that she feels like a stranger in her own culture – she must decide where she belongs.

Guided questions

- What do you understand by the *independent* and *interdependent self*, and how is this related to culture?

- How are *individualism* and *collectivism* connected to the world's cultures?

- What does it mean to say that a language has *ethnolinguistic vitality* for a minority group?

- Are the ways that emotions are expressed on the face universal across cultures?

- How accurate are people in recognising basic emotions? See how students fared on this task in Chapter 11 of MyPsychLab at www.mypsychlab.co.uk.

Learn more

Adamopoulos, J., & Kashima, Y. (eds) (1999). *Social psychology and cultural context*. London: Sage. Social and cross-cultural psychologists from various countries discuss the cultural context of social psychology and how social psychological phenomena are influenced by culture.

Bayley, B., & Schechter, S. R. (eds) (2003). *Language socialization in bilingual and multilingual societies*. Clevedon, UK: Multilingual Matters. Sociolinguists, educationalists and other social scientists take an international perspective on language socialisation and bilingualism from early childhood to adulthood. Contexts include home, schools, communities and workplaces.

Chryssochoou, X. (2004). *Cultural diversity: Its social psychology*. Oxford, UK: Blackwell. This book deals with processes in multicultural societies, including the challenge of migration to a community's ethnic relations. It features text boxes that outline illustrative studies, key concepts and summaries of important studies.

Knapp, M. L., & Hall, J. A. (2005). *Nonverbal communication in human interaction* (6th ed). Belmont, CA: Wadsworth. An excellent introduction to the field, the topics include evolution, communicating with the eyes, posture and gesture, paralanguage, and the accuracy of decoding states and traits.

Noels, K. A., Giles, H., & Le Poire, B. (2003). Language and communication processes. In M. A. Hogg & J. Cooper (eds), *The Sage handbook of social psychology* (pp. 232–257). London: Sage. A very accessible review, from a social psychological perspective, of research on language and communication – includes both verbal and non-verbal communication.

Russell, J. A., & Fernandez-Dols, J. M. (eds) (1997). *The psychology of facial expression*. Cambridge, UK: Cambridge University Press. A critical overview of major theoretical perspectives on facial expression. These include ethological, neurobehavioural and developmental views.

Smith, P. B., Bond, M. H., & Kağitçibaşi, C. (2006). *Social psychology across cultures: Living and working in a changing world*. Thousand Oaks, CA: Sage. This is a substantially revised and updated version of an earlier work (Smith & Bond, 1998), organised around three sections: an overall framework, core issues, and global change.

Refresh your understanding, assess your progress and go further with interactive summaries, questions, podcasts, videos and much more on the website accompanying the book: **www.mypsychlab.co.uk**.

Glossary

Abuse syndrome Factors of proximity, stress and power that are associated with the cycle of abuse in some families.

Accentuation principle Categorisation accentuates perceived similarities within and differences between groups on dimensions that people believe are correlated with the categorisation. The effect is amplified where the categorisation and/or dimension has subjective importance, relevance or value.

Accessibility Ease of recall of categories or schemas that we already have in mind.

Acculturation The process whereby individuals learn about the rules of behaviour characteristics of another culture.

Actor–observer effect Tendency to attribute our own behaviours externally and others' behaviours internally.

Affect–infusion model Cognition is infused with affect such that social judgements reflect current mood.

Agentic state A frame of mind thought by Milgram to characterise unquestioning obedience, in which people as agents transfer personal responsibility to the person giving orders.

Altruism A special form of *helping behaviour*, sometimes costly, that shows concern for fellow human beings and is performed without expectation of personal gain.

Analogue Device or measure intended to faithfully mimic the 'real thing'.

Anchoring and adjustment A cognitive short cut in which inferences are tied to initial standards or schemas.

Arbitration Process of intergroup conflict resolution in which a neutral third party is invited to impose a mutually binding settlement.

Archival research Non-experimental method involving the assembly of data, or reports of data, collected by others.

Assimilation The merging of a subordinate group or culture into a dominant group or culture.

Associative network Model of memory in which nodes or ideas are connected by associative links along which cognitive activation can spread.

Assortative mating A non-random coupling of individuals based on their resemblance to each other on one or more characteristics.

Attachment behaviour The tendency of an infant to maintain close physical proximity with the mother or primary caregiver.

Attachment styles Descriptions of the nature of people's close relationships, thought to be established in childhood.

Attitude (a) A relatively enduring organisation of beliefs, feelings and behavioural tendencies towards socially significant objects, groups, events or symbols. (b) A general feeling or evaluation – positive or negative – about some person, object or issue.

Attitude change Any significant modification of an individual's attitude. In the persuasion process this involves the communicator, the communication, the medium used, and the characteristics of the audience. Attitude change can also occur by inducing someone to perform an act that runs counter to an existing attitude.

Attitude formation The process of forming our attitudes, mainly from our own experiences, the influences of others and our emotional reactions.

Attribution The process of assigning a cause to our own behaviour, and that of others.

Attributional style An individual (personality) predisposition to make a certain type of causal attribution for behaviour.

Audience Intended target of a persuasive communication.

Authoritarian personality Personality syndrome originating in childhood that predisposes individuals to be prejudiced.

Autokinesis Optical illusion in which a pinpoint of light shining in complete darkness appears to move about.

Automatic activation According to Fazio, attitudes that have a strong evaluative link to situational cues are more likely to automatically come to mind from memory.

Availability heuristic A cognitive short cut in which the frequency or likelihood of an event is based on how quickly instances or associations come to mind.

Averageness effect Humans have evolved to prefer average and symmetrical faces to those with unusual or distinctive features.

Bargaining Process of intergroup conflict resolution where representatives reach agreement through direct negotiation.

Basic-level categories Middle range categories that have cognitive priority because they are the most useful, e.g. a 'chair' rather than 'furniture' or a 'rocker'.

Behaviourism An emphasis on explaining observable behaviour in terms of reinforcement schedules.

Belief in a just world Belief that the world is a just and predictable place where good things happen to 'good people' and bad things to 'bad people'.

Big Five The five major personality dimensions of extraversion/surgency, agreeableness, conscientiousness, emotional stability, and intellect/openness to experience.

Biosocial theories In the context of aggression, theories that emphasise an innate component, though not the existence of a full-blown instinct.

BIRGing Basking In Reflected Glory – that is, name-dropping to link yourself with desirable people or groups and thus improve other people's impression of you.

Bogus pipeline technique A measurement technique that leads people to believe that a 'lie detector' can monitor their emotional responses, thus measuring their true attitudes.

Bottom-up processing Information is processed synthetically from specific bits of data.

Brainstorming Uninhibited generation of as many ideas as possible in a group, in order to enhance group creativity.

Bystander-calculus model In attending to an emergency, the bystander calculates the perceived costs and benefits of providing help compared with those associated with not helping.

Bystander effect People are less likely to help in an emergency when they are with others than when alone. The greater the number, the less likely it is that anyone will help.

Bystander intervention This occurs when an individual breaks out of the role of a bystander and helps another person in an emergency.

Case study In-depth analysis of a single case (or individual).

Cathartic hypothesis The notion that acting aggressively, or even just viewing aggressive material, reduces feelings of anger and aggression.

Central traits Traits that have a disproportionate influence on the configuration of final impressions, in Asch's configural model of impression formation.

Charismatic leadership Leadership style based upon the leaders (perceived) possession of charisma.

Cognitive alternatives Belief that the status quo is unstable and illegitimate, and that social competition with the dominant group is the appropriate strategy to improve social identity.

Cognitive consistency A model of social cognition in which people try to reduce inconsistency among their cognitions, because they find inconsistency unpleasant.

Cognitive dissonance State of psychological tension, produced by simultaneously having two opposing cognitions. People are motivated to reduce the tension, often by changing or rejecting one of the cognitions. Festinger proposed that we seek harmony in our attitudes, beliefs and behaviours, and try to reduce tension from inconsistency among these elements.

Cognitive miser A model of social cognition that characterises people as using the least complex and demanding cognitions that are able to produce generally adaptive behaviours.

Cohesiveness The property of a group that affectively binds people, as group members, to one another and to the group as a whole, giving the group a sense of solidarity and oneness.

Collective aggression Unified aggression by a group of individuals, who may not even know one another, against another individual or group.

Collective behaviour The behaviour of people en masse – such as in a crowd, protest or riot.

Collectivism Societal structure and world-view in which people prioritise group loyalty, commitment and conformity, and belonging and fitting-in to groups, over standing out as an isolated individual.

Commitment The desire or intention to continue an interpersonal relationship.

Common ingroup identity model Members of two groups recategorise themselves as members of the one social entity.

Communication network Set of rules governing how communication will take place between different roles in a group.

Comparison level A standard that develops over time, allowing us to judge whether a new relationship is profitable or not.

Compliance Superficial, public and transitory change in behaviour and expressed attitudes in response to requests, coercion or group pressure.

Conformity Deep-seated, private and enduring change in behaviour and attitudes due to group pressure.

Conformity bias Tendency for social psychology to treat group influence as a one-way process in which individuals or minorities always conform to majorities.

Confounding Where two or more independent variables covary in such a way that it is impossible to know which has caused the effect.

Conspiracy theories Explanations of widespread, complex and worrying events in terms of the premeditated actions of small groups of highly organised conspirators.

Constructs Abstract or theoretical concepts or variables that are not observable and are used to explain or clarify a phenomenon.

Consummate love Sternberg argues that this is the ultimate form of love, involving passion, intimacy and commitment.

Contact hypothesis The view that bringing members of opposing social groups together will improve intergroup relations and reduce prejudice and discrimination.

Contingency theories Theories of leadership that consider the leadership effectiveness of particular behaviours or behavioural styles to be contingent on the nature of leadership situation.

Conversion effect When minority influence brings about a sudden and dramatic internal and private change in the attitudes of a majority.

Coordination loss Deterioration in group performance compared with individual performance, due to problems in coordinating behaviour.

Correlation Where changes in one variable reliably map onto changes in another variable, but it cannot be determined which of the two variables *caused* the change.

Correspondence bias A general attribution bias in which people have an inflated tendency to see behaviour as reflecting (corresponding to) stable underlying personality attributes.

Correspondent inference Causal attribution of behaviour to underlying dispositions.

Cost–reward ratio Tenet of social exchange theory, according to which liking for another is determined by calculating what it will cost to be reinforced by that person.

Covariation model Kelley's theory of causal attribution – people assign the cause of behaviour to the factor that covaries most closely with the behaviour.

Cultural norms Norms whose origin is part of the tradition of a culture.

Culture A set of beliefs and practices that identify a specific social group and distinguish it from others.

Culture of honour A culture that endorses male violence as a way of addressing threats to social reputation or economic position.

Dehumanisation Stripping people of their dignity and humanity.

Deindividuation Process whereby people lose their sense of socialised individual identity and engage in unsocialised, often antisocial, behaviours.

Demand characteristics Features of an experiment that seem to 'demand' a certain response.

Dependent variables Variables that change as a consequence of changes in the independent variable.

Depersonalisation The perception and treatment of self and others not as unique individual persons but as prototypical embodiments of a social group.

Desensitisation A serious reduction in a person's responsiveness to material that usually evokes a strong emotional reaction, such as violence or sexuality.

Discourse analysis A set of methods used to analyse text, in particular, naturally occurring language, in order to understand its meaning and significance.

Disinhibition A breakdown in the learned controls (social mores) against behaving impulsively or, in this context, aggressively. For some people, alcohol has a disinhibiting effect.

Display rules Cultural and situational rules that dictate how appropriate it is to express emotions in a given context.

Distributive justice The fairness of the outcome of a decision.

Door-in-the-face tactic Multiple-request technique to gain compliance, in which the focal request is preceded by a larger request that is bound to be refused.

Drive theory Zajonc's theory that the physical presence of members of the same species instinctively causes arousal that motivates performance of habitual behaviour patterns.

Effort justification A special case of cognitive dissonance: inconsistency is experienced when a person makes a considerable effort to achieve a modest goal.

Elaboration–likelihood model Petty and Cacioppo's model of attitude change: when people attend to a message carefully, they use a central route to process it; otherwise they use a peripheral route. This model competes with the heuristic–systematic model.

Emblems Gestures that replace or stand in for spoken language.

Emergency situation Often involves an unusual event, can vary in nature, is unplanned, and requires a quick response.

Emotion-in-relationships model Close relationships provide a context that elicits strong emotions due to the increased probability of behaviour interrupting interpersonal expectations.

Empathic concern An element in Batson's theory of helping behaviour. In contrast to personal distress (which may lead us to flee from the situation), it includes feelings of warmth, being soft-hearted, and having compassion for a person in need.

Empathy Ability to feel another person's experiences; identifying with and experiencing another person's emotions, thoughts and attitudes.

Entitativity The property of a group that makes it seem like a coherent, distinct and unitary entity.

Equity theory A special case of social exchange theory that defines a relationship as equitable when the ratio of inputs to outcomes are seen to be the same by both partners.

Essentialism Pervasive tendency to consider behaviour to reflect underlying and immutable, often innate, properties of people or the groups they belong to.

Ethnocentrism Evaluative preference for all aspects of our own group relative to other groups.

Ethnolinguistic identity theory Application and extension of social identity theory to deal with language behaviour of ethnolinguistic groups.

Ethnolinguistic vitality Concept describing objective features of an interethnic context that influence language, and ultimately the cultural survival or disappearance of an ethnolinguistic group.

Ethnomethodology Method devised by Garfinkel, involving the violation of hidden norms to reveal their presence.

Ethology Approach that argues that animal behaviour should be studied in the species' natural physical and social environment. Behaviour is genetically determined and is controlled by natural selection.

Evaluation apprehension A concern about being evaluated by others who are present can lead to social facilitation.

Evolutionary social psychology An extension of evolutionary psychology that views complex social behaviour as adaptive, helping the individual, kin and the species as a whole to survive.

Excitation-transfer model The expression of aggression is a function of learned behaviour, some excitation from another source, and the person's interpretation of the arousal state.

Exemplars Specific instances of a member of a category.

Expectation states theory Theory of the emergence of roles as a consequence of people's status-based expectations about others' performance.

Experimental method Intentional manipulation of independent variables in order to investigate effects on one or more dependent variables.

Experimental realism Psychological impact of the manipulations in an experiment.

External (or situational) attribution Assigning the cause of our own or others' behaviour to external or environmental factors.

False consensus effect Seeing our own behaviour as being more typical than it really is.

Familiarity As we become more familiar with a stimulus (even another person), we feel more comfortable with it and we like it more.

Family resemblance Defining property of category membership.

Fear of social blunders The dread of acting inappropriately or of making a foolish mistake witnessed by others. The desire to avoid ridicule inhibits effective responses to an emergency by members of a group.

Field study The gathering of animal or human behavioural data in a natural setting.

Fighting instinct Innate impulse to aggress which ethologists claim is shared by humans with other animals.

Foot-in-the-door tactic Multiple-request technique to gain compliance, in which the focal request is preceded by a smaller request that is bound to be accepted.

Forewarning Advance knowledge that one is to be the target of a persuasion attempt. Forewarning often produces resistance to persuasion.

Frame of reference Complete range of subjectively conceivable positions that relevant people can occupy in that context on some attitudinal or behavioural dimension.

Fraternalistic relative deprivation Sense that our group has less than it is entitled to, relative to its aspirations or to other groups.

Frustration–aggression hypothesis Theory that all frustration leads to aggression, and all aggression comes from frustration. Used to explain prejudice and intergroup aggression.

Fuzzy sets Categories are considered to be fuzzy sets of features organised around a prototype.

Gaze Looking at someone's eyes.

Gender Sex-stereotypical attributes of a person.

Genocide The ultimate expression of prejudice by exterminating an entire social group.

Glass ceiling An invisible barrier that prevents women, and other minorities, from attaining top leadership positions.

Group mind McDougall's idea that people adopt a qualitatively different mode of thinking when in a group.

Group polarisation Tendency for group discussion to produce more extreme group decisions than the mean of members' pre-discussion opinions, in the direction favoured by the mean.

Group socialisation Dynamic relationship between the group and its members that describes the passage of members through a group in terms of commitment and of changing roles.

Group structure Division of a group into different roles that often differ with respect to status and prestige.

Groupthink A mode of thinking in highly cohesive groups in which the desire to reach unanimous agreement overrides the motivation to adopt proper rational decision-making procedures.

Helping behaviour Acts that intentionally benefit someone else.

Heuristics Cognitive short cuts that provide adequately accurate inferences for most of us most of the time.

Heuristic–systematic model Chaiken's model of attitude change: when people attend to a message carefully, they use systematic processing; otherwise they process information by using heuristics, or 'mental short cuts'. This model competes with the elaboration–likelihood model.

Hospitalism A state of apathy and depression noted among institutionalised infants deprived of close comfort with a caregiver.

Hypotheses Empirically testable predictions about what goes with what, or what causes what.

Ideology A systematically interrelated set of beliefs whose primary function is explanation. It circumscribes thinking, making it difficult for the holder to escape from its mould.

Idiosyncrasy credit Hollander's transactional theory, that followers reward leaders for achieving group goals by allowing them to be relatively idiosyncratic.

Illusion of control Belief that we have more control over our world than we really do.

Illusion of group effectivity Experience-based belief that we produce more and better ideas in groups than alone.

Illusory correlation Cognitive exaggeration of the degree of co-occurrence of two stimuli or events, or the perception of a co-occurrence where none exists.

Implicit association test Reaction-time test to measure attitudes – particularly unpopular attitudes that people might conceal.

Implicit personality theories Idiosyncratic and personal ways of characterising other people and explaining their behaviour.

Impression management People's use of various strategies to get other people to view them in a positive light.

Independent self A self that is relatively separate, internal and unique.

Independent variables Features of a situation that change of their own accord, or can be manipulated by an experimenter to have effects on a dependent variable.

Individualism Societal structure and world-view in which people prioritise standing out as an individual over fitting in as a group member.

Induced compliance A special case of cognitive dissonance: inconsistency is experienced when a person is persuaded to behave in a way that is contrary to an attitude.

Informational influence An influence to accept information from another as evidence about reality.

Ingratiation Strategic attempt to get someone to like you in order to obtain compliance with a request.

Ingroup favouritism Behaviour that favours one's own group over other groups.

Initiation rites Often painful or embarrassing public procedure to mark group members' movements from one role to another.

Inoculation A way of making people resistant to persuasion. By providing them with a diluted counter-argument, they can build up effective refutations to a later, stronger argument.

Instinct Innate drive or impulse, genetically transmitted.

Interdependent self A self that is relatively dependent on social relations and has more fuzzy boundaries.

Intergroup attributions Process of assigning the cause of one's own or others' behaviour to group membership.

Intergroup behaviour Behaviour among individuals that is regulated by those individuals' awareness of and identification with different social groups.

Internal (or dispositional) attribution Process of assigning the cause of our own or others' behaviour to internal or dispositional factors.

J-curve A graphical figure that captures the way in which relative deprivation arises when attainments suddenly fall short of rising expectations.

Just-world hypothesis According to Lerner, people need to believe that the world is a just place where they get what they deserve. Examples of undeserved suffering undermine this belief, and people may conclude that victims deserve their fate.

Kinesics Linguistics of body communication.

Leader categorisation theory We have a variety of schemas about how different types of leaders behave in different leadership situations. When a leader is categorised as a particular type of leader, the schema fills in details about how that leader will behave.

Leader–member exchange (LMX) theory Theory of leadership in which effective leadership rests on the ability of the leader to develop good-quality personalised exchange relationships with individual members.

Leadership Getting group members to achieve the group's goals.

Learning by direct experience Acquiring a behaviour because we were rewarded for it.

Learning by vicarious experience Acquiring a behaviour after observing that another person was rewarded for it.

Least-preferred co-worker (LPC) scale Fiedler's scale for measuring leadership style in terms of favourability of attitude towards one's least-preferred co-worker.

Level of analysis (or explanation) The types of concepts, mechanisms and language used to explain a phenomenon.

Looking-glass self The self derived from seeing ourselves as others see us.

Love A combination of emotions, cognitions and behaviours that can be involved in intimate relationships.

Low-ball tactic Technique for inducing compliance in which a person who agrees to a request still feels committed after finding that there are hidden costs.

Machismo A code in which challenges, abuse and even differences of opinion must be met with fists or other weapons.

Mediation Process of intergroup conflict resolution where a neutral third party intervenes in the negotiation process to facilitate a settlement.

Mere exposure effect Repeated exposure to an object results in greater attraction to that object.

Message Communication from a source directed to an audience.

Meta-analysis Statistical procedure that combines data from different studies to measure the overall reliability and strength of specific effects.

Meta-contrast principle The prototype of a group is that position within the group that has the largest ratio of 'differences to ingroup positions' to 'differences to outgroup positions'.

Minimal group paradigm Experimental methodology used to demonstrate intergroup discrimination, even when people are categorised on random or trivial criteria.

Minimax strategy In relating to others, we try to minimise the costs and maximise the rewards that accrue.

Minority influence Social influence processes whereby numerical or power minorities change the attitudes of the majority.

Modelling Tendency for a person to reproduce the actions, attitudes and emotional responses exhibited by a real-life or symbolic model. Also called *observational learning*.

Motivated tactician A model of social cognition that characterises people as having multiple cognitive strategies available, which they choose among on the basis of personal goals, motives and needs.

Multiculturalism The way that a society manages and maintains the identity of its diverse cultures.

Multiple requests Tactics for gaining compliance using a two-step procedure: the first request functions as a set-up for the second, real request.

Mundane realism Similarity between circumstances surrounding an experiment and circumstances encountered in everyday life.

Naive scientist (or psychologist) Model of social cognition that characterises people as using rational, scientific-like, cause–effect analyses to understand their world.

Nature–nurture controversy Classic debate about whether genetic or environmental factors determine human behaviour. Scientists generally accept that it is an interaction of both.

Need to affiliate The urge to form connections and make contact with other people.

Neo-associationist analysis A view of aggression according to which mass media may provide images of violence to an audience that later translate into antisocial acts.

Non-verbal communication Transfer of meaningful information from one person to another by means other than written or spoken language (e.g. gaze, facial expression, posture, touch).

Normative influence An influence to conform with the positive expectation of others, to gain social approval or to avoid social disapproval.

Norms Attitudinal and behavioural uniformities that define group membership and differentiate between groups.

Optimal distinctiveness People strive to achieve a balance between conflicting motives for inclusiveness and separateness, expressed in groups as a balance between intragroup differentiation and intragroup homogenisation.

Overjustification effect In the absence of obvious external determinants of our behaviour, we assume that we freely choose the behaviour because we enjoy it.

Paralanguage The non-linguistic accompaniments of speech (e.g. stress, pitch, speed, tone, pauses).

Partner regulation Strategy that encourages a partner to match an ideal standard of behaviour.

Path-goal theory (PGT) A contingency theory of leadership that can also be classified as a transactional theory – it focuses on how 'structuring' and 'consideration' behaviours motivate followers.

Peace studies Multidisciplinary movement dedicated to the study and promotion of peace.

Peripheral traits Traits that have an insignificant influence on the configuration of final impressions, in Asch's configural model of impression formation.

Personal constructs Idiosyncratic and personal ways of characterising other people.

Personal identity The self defined in terms of unique personal attributes or unique interpersonal relationships.

Personal space Physical space around people's bodies which they treat as a part of themselves.

Persuasive arguments theory View that people in groups are persuaded by novel information that supports their initial position, and thus become more extreme in their endorsement of their initial position.

Persuasive communication Message intended to change an attitude and related behaviours of an audience.

Pluralistic ignorance A situation where people in a group privately reject a norm but assume that others accept it.

Post-decisional conflict The dissonance associated with behaving in a counter-attitudinal way. Dissonance can be reduced by bringing the attitude into line with the behaviour.

Prejudice An unfavourable and sometimes hostile attitude towards a social group and its members.

Primacy An order of presentation effect in which earlier presented information has a disproportionate influence on social cognition.

Priming Activation of accessible categories or schemas in memory that influence how we process new information.

Prior commitment An individual's agreement in advance to be responsible if trouble occurs: for example, committing oneself to protect the property of another person against theft.

Procedural justice The fairness of the procedures used to make a decision.

Production blocking Reduction in individual creativity and productivity in brainstorming groups due to interruptions and turn-taking.

Profit This flows from a relationship when the rewards that accrue from continued interaction exceed the costs.

Prosocial behaviour Acts that are positively valued by society.

Protection motivation theory Adopting a healthy behaviour requires cognitive balancing between the perceived threat of illness and one's capacity to cope with the health regimen.

Prototype Cognitive representation of the typical/ideal defining features of a category.

Proxemics Study of interpersonal distance.

Proximity The factor of living close by is known to play an important role in the early stages of forming a friendship.

Psychodynamic theory A general approach to human motivation in which the locus is unconscious. In the Freudian version, the underlying mental energy is instinctive and involves a dynamic interplay of the id, ego and superego.

Racism Prejudice and discrimination against people based on their ethnicity or race.

Reactance Brehm's theory that people try to protect their freedom to act. When they perceive that this freedom has been curtailed, they will act to regain it.

Realistic conflict theory Sherif's theory of intergroup conflict that explains intergroup behaviour in terms of the nature of goal relations between groups.

Received pronunciation (RP) Standard, high-status, spoken variety of English.

Recency An order of presentation effect in which later presented information has a disproportionate influence on social cognition.

Reciprocity norm The principle of 'doing unto others as they do to you'. It can refer to returning a favour, mutual aggression or mutual help.

Reciprocity principle The law of 'doing unto others as they do to you'. It can refer to an attempt to gain compliance by first doing someone a favour, or to mutual aggression or mutual attraction.

Reductionism A phenomenon in terms of the language and concepts of a lower level of analysis, usually with a loss of explanatory power.

Referent informational influence Pressure to conform to a group norm that defines oneself as a group member.

Regulatory focus theory People use self-regulation to bring themselves into line with their standards and goals, using either a promotion system or a prevention system.

Reinforcement–affect model Model of attraction which postulates that we like people who are around when we experience a positive feeling (which itself is reinforcing).

Relationship dissolution model Duck's proposal of the sequence through which most long-term relationships proceed if they finally break down.

Relative deprivation Perceived gap between expectations and achievements.

Releasers Specific stimuli in the environment thought by ethologists to trigger aggressive responses.

Representativeness heuristic A cognitive short cut in which instances are assigned to categories or types on the basis of overall similarity or resemblance to the category.

Role congruity theory Mainly applied to the gender gap in leadership – because social stereotypes of women are inconsistent with people's schemas of effective leadership, women are evaluated as poor leaders.

Roles Patterns of behaviour that distinguish between different activities within the group, and that interrelate to one another for the greater good of the group.

Rumours Unverified accounts passed between individuals who try to make sense of events that are uncertain or confusing.

Salience Property of a stimulus that makes it stand out in relation to other stimuli and attract attention.

Scapegoat Individual or group that becomes the target for anger and frustration caused by a different individual or group or some other set of circumstances.

Schema Cognitive structure that represents knowledge about a concept or type of stimulus, including its attributes and the relations among those attributes.

Schism Division of a group into subgroups that differ in their attitudes, values or ideology.

Science Method for studying nature that involves the collecting of data to test hypotheses.

Self-affirmation theory The theory that people reduce the impact of threat to their self-concept by focusing on and affirming their competence in some other area.

Self-assessment The motivation to seek out new information about ourselves in order to find out what sort of person we really are.

Self-categorisation theory Turner and associates' theory of how the process of categorising oneself as a group member produces social identity and group and intergroup behaviours.

Self-disclosure The sharing of intimate information and feelings with another person.

Self-discrepancy theory Higgins' theory about the consequences of making actual–ideal and actual–'ought' self comparisons that reveal self-discrepancies.

Self-efficacy Expectations that we have about our capacity to succeed in particular tasks.

Self-enhancement The motivation to develop and promote a favourable image of self.

Self-esteem Feelings about and evaluations of oneself.

Self-evaluation maintenance model People who are constrained to make esteem-damaging upward comparisons can underplay or deny similarity to the target, or they can withdraw from their relationship with the target.

Self-fulfilling prophecy Expectations and assumptions about a person that influence our interaction with that person and eventually change their behaviour in line with our expectations.

Self-handicapping Publicly making advance external attributions for our anticipated failure or poor performance in a forthcoming event.

Self-monitoring Carefully controlling how we present ourselves. There are situational differences and individual differences in self-monitoring.

Self-perception theory Bem's idea that we gain knowledge of ourselves only by making self-attributions: for example, we infer our own attitudes from our own behaviour.

Self-presentation A deliberate effort to act in ways that create a particular impression, usually favourable, of ourselves.

Self-regulation Strategies that we use to match our behaviour to an ideal or 'ought' standard.

Self-serving biases Attributional distortions that protect or enhance self-esteem or the self-concept.

Self-verification Seeking out information that verifies and confirms what we already know about ourselves.

Sexism Prejudice and discrimination against people based on their gender.

Sex role Behaviour deemed sex-stereotypically appropriate.

Sexual selection theory The argument that male–female differences in behaviour derive from human evolutionary history.

Similarity of attitudes One of the most important positive, psychological determinants of attraction.

Situational control Fiedler's classification of task characteristics in terms of how much control effective task performance requires.

Social categorisation Classification of people as members of different social groups.

Social change belief system Belief that intergroup boundaries are impermeable. Therefore, a lower-status individual can improve social identity only by challenging the legitimacy of the higher-status group's position.

Social cognition Cognitive processes and structures that influence and are influenced by social behaviour.

Social comparison Comparing our behaviours and opinions with those of others in order to establish the correct or socially approved way of thinking and behaving.

Social comparison/cultural values Through group discussion people shift their views towards what others think or what is culturally valued.

Social compensation Increased effort on a collective task to compensate for other group members' actual, perceived or anticipated lack of effort or ability.

Social competition Group-based behavioural strategies that improve social identity by directly confronting the dominant group's position in society.

Social creativity Group-based behavioural strategies that improve social identity but do not directly attack the dominant group's position.

Social decisions schemes Explicit or implicit decision-making rules that relate individual opinions to a final group decision.

Social dominance theory An approach in which prejudice, exploitation and oppression are attributed to an ideology that legitimises a hierarchy of social groups.

Social exchange People often use a form of everyday economics when they weigh up costs and rewards before deciding what to do.

Social facilitation An improvement in the performance of well-learned/easy tasks and a deterioration in the performance of poorly learned/difficult tasks in the mere presence of members of the same species.

Social identity That part of the self-concept that derives from our membership of social groups.

Social identity theory Theory of group membership and intergroup relations based on self-categorisation, social comparison and the construction of a shared self-definition in terms of ingroup-defining properties.

Social identity theory of leadership Development of social identity theory to explain leadership as an identity process in which in salient groups prototypical leaders are more effective than less prototypical leaders.

Social impact The effect that other people have on our attitudes and behaviour, usually as a consequence of factors such as group size, and temporal and physical immediacy.

Social influence Process whereby attitudes and behaviour are influenced by the real or implied presence of other people.

Social learning theory The view championed by Bandura that human social behaviour is not innate but learned from appropriate models.

Social loafing A reduction in individual effort when working on a collective task (one in which our outputs are pooled with those of other group members) compared with working either alone or co-actively (our outputs are not pooled).

Social markers Features of speech style that convey information about mood, context, status and group membership.

Social mobility belief system Belief that intergroup boundaries are permeable. Thus, it is possible for someone to pass from a lower-status into a higher-status group to improve social identity.

Social neuroscience The exploration of the neurological underpinnings of the processes traditionally examined by social psychology.

Social ostracism Exclusion from a group by common consent.

Social psychology Scientific investigation of how the thoughts, feelings and behaviour of individuals are influenced by the actual, imagined or implied presence of others.

Social representations Collectively elaborated explanations of unfamiliar and complex phenomena that transform them into a familiar and simple form.

Social responsibility norm The idea that we should help people who are dependent and in need. It is contradicted by another norm that discourages interfering in other people's lives.

Social role theory The argument that sex differences in occupations are determined by society rather than one's biology.

Source The point of origin of a persuasive communication.

Status Consensual evaluation of the prestige of a role or role occupant in a group, or of the prestige of a group and its members as a whole.

Stereotype Widely shared and simplified evaluative image of a social group and its members.

Stereotype threat Feeling that we will be judged and treated in terms of negative stereotypes of our group, and that we will inadvertently confirm these stereotypes through our behaviour.

Subjective group dynamics A process in which deviant group members threaten a group's norms and its unity.

Superordinate goals Groups may desire these but they can only be achieved by intergroup cooperation.

Survey research Method in which a large and representative sample of people answer direct questions about their attitudes or behaviour.

Symbolic interactionism Theory of how the self emerges from human interaction that involves people trading symbols (through language and gesture) that are usually consensual, and represent abstract properties rather than concrete objects.

System justification theory Theory that attributes social stasis to people's adherence to an ideology that justifies and protects the status quo.

Terror management theory The notion that the most fundamental human motivation is to reduce the terror of the inevitability of death. Self-esteem may be centrally implicated in effective terror management.

Theory Set of interrelated concepts and principles that explain a phenomenon.

Theory of planned behaviour Modification by Ajzen of the *theory of reasoned action*. It suggests that predicting a behaviour from an attitude measure is improved if people believe they have control over that behaviour.

Theory of reasoned action Fishbein and Ajzen's model of the links between attitude and behaviour. A major feature is the proposition that the best way to predict a behaviour is to ask whether the person intends to do it.

Three-component attitude model An attitude consists of cognitive, affective and behavioural components. This three-fold division has an ancient heritage, stressing thought, feeling and action as basic to human experience.

Three-factor theory of love Hatfield and Walster distinguished three components of what we label 'love': a cultural concept of love, an appropriate person to love and emotional arousal.

Tokenism Practice of publicly making small concessions to a minority group in order to deflect accusations of prejudice and discrimination.

Top-down processing Information is processed analytically from psychological constructs or theories.

Transactional leadership Approach to leadership that focuses on the transaction of resources between leader and followers. Also a style of leadership.

Transactive memory Group members have a shared memory for who within the group remembers what and is the expert on what.

Transformational leadership Approach to leadership that focuses on the way that leaders transform group goals and actions – mainly through the exercise of charisma. Also a style of leadership based on charisma.

Type A personality The 'coronary-prone' personality – a behavioural correlate of heart disease characterised by striving to achieve, time urgency, competitiveness and hostility.

Ultimate attribution error Tendency to internally attribute bad outgroup and good ingroup behaviour, and to externally attribute good outgroup and bad ingroup behaviour.

Uncertainty-identity theory People are motivated to reduce uncertainty about who they are, or about their thoughts or actions that reflect on who they are.

Unobtrusive measures Observational approaches that neither intrude on the processes being studied nor cause people to behave unnaturally.

Values A higher-order concept thought to provide a structure for organising attitudes.

Weapons effect The mere presence of a weapon increases the probability that it will be used aggressively.

References

A

Abelson, R. P. (1972). Are attitudes necessary? In B. T. King (ed), *Attitudes, conflict and social change* (pp. 19–32). New York: Academic Press.

Abelson, R. P. (1981). The psychological status of the script concept. *American Psychologist, 36,* 715–729.

Abelson, R. P., Aronson, E., McGuire, W. J., Newcomb, T. M., Rosenberg, M. J., & Tannenbaum, P. H. (eds) (1968). *Theories of cognitive consistency: A sourcebook.* Chicago: Rand McNally.

Abrams, D., & Hogg, M. A. (2001). Collective identity: Group membership and self-conception. In M. A. Hogg & R. S. Tindale (eds), *Blackwell handbook of social psychology: Group processes* (pp. 425–460). Oxford, UK: Blackwell.

Adamopoulos, J., & Kashima, Y. (1999). *Social psychology and cultural context.* London: Sage.

Adams, J. (1965). Inequity in social exchange. In L. Berkowitz (ed), *Advances in experimental social psychology* (Vol. 2, pp. 267–299). New York: Academic Press.

Adams, J. M., & Jones, W. H. (1997). The conceptualisation of marital commitment: An integrative analysis. *Journal of Social and Personal Relationships, 11,* 1177–1196.

Adorno, T. W., Frenkel-Brunswik, E., Levinson, D. J., & Sanford, R. M. (1950). *The authoritarian personality.* New York: Harper.

Aiello, J. R., & Jones, S. E. (1971). Field study of the proxemic behaviour of young children in three subcultural groups. *Journal of Personality and Social Psychology, 19,* 351–356.

Ajzen, I. (1989). Attitude structure and behaviour. In A. R. Pratkanis, S. J. Breckler, & A. G. Greenwald (eds), *Attitude structure and function* (pp. 241–274). Hillsdale, NJ: Erlbaum.

Ajzen, I., & Madden, T. J. (1986). Prediction of goal-directed behaviour: Attitudes, intentions and perceived behavioural control. *Journal of Experimental Social Psychology, 22,* 453–474.

Aldag, R. J., & Fuller, S. R. (1993). Beyond fiasco: A reappraisal of the groupthink phenomenon and a new model of group decision processes. *Psychological Bulletin, 113,* 533–552.

Alexander, C. N., Zucker, L. G., & Brody, C. L. (1970). Experimental expectations and autokinetic experiences: Consistency theories and judgemental convergence. *Sociometry, 33,* 108–122.

Alexander, S., & Ruderman, M. (1987). The role of procedural and distributive justice in organizational behavior. *Social Justice Research, 1,* 177–198.

Allen, V. L. (1975) Social support for non-conformity. In L. Berkowitz (ed) *Advances in experimental social psychology* (Vol. 8, pp. 1–41). New York: Academic Press.

Allen, V. L., & Levine, J. M. (1971). Social support and conformity: The role of independent assessment of reality. *Journal of Experimental Social Psychology, 7,* 48–58.

Allport, F. H. (1920). The influence of the group upon association and thought. *Journal of Experimental Psychology, 3,* 159–182.

Allport, F. H. (1924). *Social psychology.* Boston, MA: Houghton Mifflin.

Allport, G. W. (1935). Attitudes. In C. M. Murchison (ed), *Handbook of social psychology* (pp. 789–844). Worcester, MA: Clark University Press.

Allport, G. W. (1954a). The historical background of modern social psychology. In G. Lindzey (ed), *Handbook of social psychology* (Vol. 1, pp. 3–56). Reading, MA: Addison-Wesley.

Allport, G. W. (1954b). *The nature of prejudice*. Reading, MA: Addison-Wesley.

Allport, G. W., & Postman, L. J. (1945). Psychology of rumour. *Transactions of the New York Academy of Sciences, 8*, 61–81.

Allyn, J., & Festinger, L. (1961). The effectiveness of unanticipated persuasive communications. *Journal of Abnormal and Social Psychology, 62*, 35–40.

Altemeyer, B. (1998). The other 'authoritarian personality'. In M. Zanna (ed), *Advances in experimental social psychology* (Vol. 30, pp. 47–92). Orlando, FL: Academic Press.

Amato, P. R. (1983). Helping behavior in urban and rural environments: Field studies based on a taxonomic organisation of helping episodes. *Journal of Personality and Social Psychology, 45*, 571–586.

American Psychological Association (2002). Ethical principles of psychologists and code of conduct. *American Psychologist, 57(12)*.

Amichai-Hamburger, Y., & McKenna, K. Y. A. (2006). The contact hypothesis reconsidered: Interacting via the Internet. *Journal of Computer-Mediated Communication, 11*(3), article 7. [http://jcmc.indiana.edu/vol11/issue3/amichai-hamburger.html]

Amir, Y. (1976). The role of intergroup contact in change of prejudice and ethnic relations. In P. A. Katz (ed), *Towards the elimination of racism* (pp. 245–308). Elmsford, NY: Pergamon Press.

Anderson, C. A., & Anderson, D. C. (1984). Ambient temperature and violent crime: Tests of the linear and curvilinear hypothesis. *Journal of Personality and Social Psychology, 46*, 91–97.

Anderson, C. A., Anderson, K. B., & Deuser, W. E. (1996). Examining an affective framework: Weapon and temperature effects on aggressive thoughts, affect, and attitudes. *Personality and Social Psychology Bulletin, 22*, 366–376.

Anderson, C. A., & Bushman, B. J. (2002). The effects of media violence on society. *Science, 295*, 2377–2378.

Anderson, C. A., & Huesmann, L. R. (2003). Human aggression: A social-cognitive view. In M. A. Hogg & J. Cooper (eds), *The Sage handbook of social psychology* (pp. 296–323). London: Sage.

Anderson, J. R. (1990). *Cognitive psychology and its implications* (3rd ed). New York: Freeman.

Anderson, J., & McGuire, W. J. (1965). Prior reassurance of group consensus as a factor in producing resistance to persuasion. *Sociometry, 28*, 44–56.

Antonakis, J., & House, R. J. (2003). An analysis of the full-range leadership theory: The way forward. In B. J. Avolio & F. J. Yammarino (eds), *Transformational and charismatic leadership: The road ahead* (pp. 3–33). New York: Elsevier.

Archer, D. (1997). Unspoken diversity: Cultural differences in gestures. *Qualitative Sociology, 20*, 79–105.

Archer, J. (2004). Sex differences in aggression in real-world settings: A meta-analytic review. *Review of General Psychology, 8*, 291–322.

Archer, J., & Coyne, S. M. (2005). An integrated review of indirect, relational, and social aggression. *Personality and Social Psychology Review, 9*, 212–230.

Ardrey, R. (1966). *The territorial imperative*. New York: Atheneum.

Arendt, H. (1963). *Eichmann in Jerusalem: A report on the banality of evil*. New York: Viking.

Argote, L., Insko, C. A., Yovetich, N., & Romero, A. A. (1995). Group learning curves: The effects of turnover and task complexity on group performance. *Journal of Applied Social Psychology, 25*, 512–529.

Argyle, M. (1975). *Bodily communication*. London: Methuen.

Argyle, M., & Dean, J. (1965). Eye-contact, distance and affiliation. *Sociometry, 28*, 289–304.

Argyle, M., & Ingham, R. (1972). Gaze, mutual gaze, and proximity. *Semiotica, 6*, 32–49.

Aron, A., Paris, M., & Aron, E. N. (1995). Falling in love: Prospective studies of self-concept change. *Journal of Personality and Social Psychology, 69*, 1102–1112.

Aron, A., & Westbay, L. (1996). Dimensions of the prototype of love. *Journal of Personality and Social Psychology, 70*, 535–551.

Aronson, E., Ellsworth, P. C., Carlsmith, J. M., & Gonzales, M. H. (1990). *Methods of research in social psychology* (2nd ed). New York: McGraw-Hill.

Aronson, E., & Mills, J. (1959). The effects of severity of initiation on liking for a group. *Journal of Abnormal and Social Psychology, 59*, 177–181.

Arriaga, X. B., & Agnew, C. R. (2001). Being committed: Affective, cognitive, and conative components of relationship commitment. *Personality and Social Psychology Bulletin, 27,* 1190–1203.

Asch, S. E. (1946). Forming impressions of personality. *Journal of Abnormal and Social Psychology, 41,* 258–290.

Asch, S. E. (1951). Effects of group pressure upon the modification and distortion of judgements. In H. Guetzkow (ed), *Groups, leadership and men* (pp. 177–190). Pittsburgh, PA: Carnegie Press.

Asch, S. E. (1952). *Social psychology.* Englewood Cliffs, NJ: Prentice Hall.

Atkin, C. K. (1980). *Effects of the mass media.* New York: McGraw-Hill.

B

Bales, R. F. (1950). *Interaction process analysis: A method for the study of small groups.* Reading, MA: Addison-Wesley.

Bandura, A. (1973). *Aggression: A social learning analysis.* Englewood Cliffs, NJ: Prentice Hall.

Bandura, A. (1986). *Social foundations of thought and action: A social cognitive theory.* Englewood Cliffs, NJ: Prentice Hall.

Bandura, A., Ross, D., & Ross, S. A. (1963). Imitation of film-mediated aggressive models. *Journal of Abnormal and Social Psychology, 66,* 3–11.

Bandura, A., & Walters, R. H. (1963). *Social learning and personality development.* New York: Holt, Rinehart & Winston.

Bargh, J. A. (1984). Automatic and conscious processing of social information. In R. S. Wyer, Jr, & T. K. Srull (eds), *Handbook of social cognition* (Vol. 3, pp. 1–44). Hillsdale, NJ: Erlbaum.

Bargh, J. A., Lombardi, W. J., & Higgins, E. T. (1988). Automaticity of chronically accessible constructs in person X situation effects on person perception: It's just a matter of time. *Journal of Personality and Social Psychology, 55,* 599–605.

Bargh, J. A., & McKenna, K. Y. A. (2004). The internet and social life. *Annual Review of Psychology, 55,* 573–590.

Baron, R. A. (1979). Aggression, empathy, and race: Effects of victim's pain cues, victim's race, and level of instigation on physical aggression. *Journal of Applied Social Psychology, 9,* 103–114.

Baron, R. A. (1989). Personality and organisational conflict: The type A behavior pattern and self-monitoring. *Organisational Behavior and Human Decision Processes, 44,* 281–297.

Baron, R. A., & Bell, P. (1977). Sexual arousal and aggression by males: Effects of types of erotic stimuli and prior provocation. *Journal of Personality and Social Psychology, 35,* 79–87.

Baron, R. A., & Byrne, D. (1987). *Social psychology: Understanding human interaction* (5th ed). Boston, MA: Allyn & Bacon.

Baron, R. A., & Richardson, D. R. (1994). *Human aggression* (2nd ed). New York: Plenum.

Baron, R. S. (1986). Distraction–conflict theory: Progress and problems. In L. Berkowitz (ed), *Advances in experimental social psychology* (Vol. 20, pp. 1–40). New York: Academic Press.

Baron, R. S., & Kerr, N. (2003). *Group process, group decision, group action* (2nd ed). Buckingham, UK: Open University Press.

Barron, F. (1953). Some personality correlates of independence of judgment. *Journal of Personality, 21,* 287–297.

Bass, B. M. (1985). *Leadership and performance beyond expectations.* New York: Free Press.

Bass, B. M., & Riggio, R. E. (2006). *Transformational leadership* (2nd ed). Mahwah, NJ: Lawrence Erlbaum Associates.

Batson, C. D. (1983). Sociobiology and the role of religion in promoting prosocial behavior: An alternative view. *Journal of Personality and Social Psychology, 45,* 1380–1385.

Batson, C. D. (1991). The altruism question: *Toward a social-psychological answer.* Hillsdale, NJ: Lawrence Erlbaum.

Batson, C. D. (1994). Why act for the public good? Four answers. *Personality and Social Psychology Bulletin, 20,* 603–610.

Batson, C. D., Ahmad, N., & Tsang, J. (2002). Four motives for community involvement. *Journal of Social Issues 58,* 429-445.

Batson, C. D., & Coke, J. S. (1981). Empathy: A source of altruistic motivation for helping? In J. P. Rushton & R. M. Sorrentino (eds), *Altruism and helping behavior: Social, personality, and developmental perspectives* (pp. 167–183). Hillsdale, NJ: Erlbaum.

Batson, C. D., Early, S., & Salvarani, G. (1997). Perspective taking: Imagining how another feels versus imagining how you would feel. *Personality and Social Psychology Bulletin, 23,* 751–758.

Batson, C. D., Sympson, S. C., Hindman, J. L., Decruz, P., Todd, R. M., Weeks, J. L., Jennings, G., & Burris, C. T. (1996). 'I've been there, too': Effect on empathy of prior experience with a need *Personality and Social Psychology Bulletin, 22,* 474–482.

Batson, C. D., van Lange, P. A. M., Ahmad, N., & Lishner, D. A. (2003). Altruism and helping behavior. In M. A. Hogg & J. Cooper (eds), *The Sage handbook of social psychology* (pp. 279–295). London: Sage.

Baumeister, R. F. (1987). How the self became a problem: A psychological review of historical research. *Journal of Personality and Social Psychology, 52,* 163–176.

Baumeister, R. F. (1991). *Escaping the self: Alcoholism, spirituality, masochism, and other flights from the burden of selfhood.* New York: Basic Books.

Baumeister, R. F. (1998). The self. In D. T. Gilbert, S. T. Fiske, & G. Lindzey (eds), *Handbook of social psychology* (4th ed, Vol. 1, pp. 680–740). New York: McGraw-Hill.

Baumeister, R. F., Chesner, S. P., Senders, P. S., & Tice, D. M. (1988). Who's in charge here? Group leaders do lend help in emergencies. *Personality and Social Psychology Bulletin, 14,* 17–22.

Baumeister, R. F., Dale, K., & Sommer, K. L. (1998). Freudian defense mechanisms and empirical findings in modern social psychology: Reaction formation, projection, displacement, undoing, isolation, sublimation, and denial. *Journal of Personality, 66,* 1081–1124.

Baumeister, R. F., & Darley, J. M. (1982). Reducing the biasing effect of perpetrator attractiveness in jury simulation. *Personality and Social Psychology Bulletin, 8,* 286–292.

Baumeister, R. F., & Leary, M. R. (1995). The need to belong: Desire for interpersonal attachments as a fundamental human motivation. *Psychological Bulletin, 117,* 497–529.

Baumeister, R. F., Smart, L., & Boden, J. M. (1996). Relation of threatened egotism to violence and aggression: The dark side of high self-esteem. *Psychological Review, 103,* 5–33.

Baumeister, R. F., Tice, D. M., & Hutton, D. G. (1989). Self-presentational motivations and personality differences in self-esteem. *Journal of Personality, 57,* 547–579.

Baumeister, R., & Vohs, K. (eds) (2007). *Encyclopedia of social psychology.* Thousand Oaks, CA: Sage.

Baumrind, D. (1964). Some thoughts on ethics of research: After reading Milgram's 'Behavioral study of obedience'. *American Psychologist, 19,* 421–443.

Bavelas, A. (1950). Communications patterns in task-oriented groups. *Journal of the Acoustical Society of America, 22,* 725–730.

Bavelas, A. (1968). Communications patterns in task-oriented groups. In P. Cartwright & A. Zander (eds) *Group dynamics: Research and Theory,* (3rd ed, pp. 503–511). London: Tavistock.

Bayley, B., & Schechter, S. R. (eds) (2003). *Language socialization in bilingual and multilingual societies.* Clevedon, UK: Multilingual Matters.

Belch, G. E., & Belch, M. A. (2007). *Advertising and promotion: An integrated marketing communications perspective* (7th ed). New York: McGraw-Hill/Irwin.

Bem, D. J. (1967). Self perception: An alternative interpretation of cognitive dissonance. *Psychological Review, 74,* 183–200.

Bem, D. J. (1972). Self-perception theory. In L. Berkowitz (ed), *Advances in experimental social psychology* (Vol. 6, pp. 1–62). New York: Academic Press.

Benson, P. L., Karabenick, S. A., & Lerner, R. M. (1976). Pretty pleases: The effects of physical attractiveness, race, and sex on receiving help. *Journal of Experimental Social Psychology, 12,* 409–415.

Berglas, S., & Jones, E. E. (1978). Drug choice as a self-handicapping strategy in response to noncontingent success. *Journal of Personality and Social Psychology, 36,* 405–417.

Berkowitz, L. (1962). *Aggression: A social psychological analysis.* New York: McGraw-Hill.

Berkowitz, L. (1972a). Frustrations, comparisons, and other sources of emotion arousal as contributors to social unrest. *Journal of Social Issues, 28,* 77–91.

Berkowitz, L. (1972b). Social norms, feelings, and other factors affecting helping and altruism. In L. Berkowitz (ed), *Advances in experimental social psychology* (Vol. 6, pp. 63–108). New York: Academic Press.

Berkowitz, L. (1984). Some effects of thoughts on anti- and pro-social influences of media events: A cognitive-neoassociation analysis. *Psychological Bulletin, 95*, 410–427.

Berkowitz, L. (1993). *Aggression: Its causes, consequences and control*. Philadelphia, PA: Temple University Press.

Berkowitz, L., & LePage, A. (1967). Weapons as aggression-eliciting stimuli. *Journal of Personality and Social Psychology, 7*, 202–207.

Bernard, M. M., Maio, G. R., & Olson, J. M. (2003). The vulnerability of values to attack: Inoculation of values and value-relevant attitudes. *Personality and Social Psychology Bulletin, 29*, 63–75.

Bernbach, W. (2002). *Bill Bernbach said*. New York: DDB Needham Worldwide.

Berry, J. W. (1967). Independence and conformity in subsistence level societies. *Journal of Personality and Social Psychology, 7*, 415–418.

Berry, J. W. (1984). Multicultural policy in Canada: A social psychological analysis. *Canadian Journal of Behavioural Science, 16*, 353–370.

Berry, J. W., Kim, U., Minde, T., & Mok, D. (1987). Comparative studies of acculturative stress. *International Migration Review, 21*, 491–511.

Berry, J. W., Trimble, J. E., & Olmedo, E. L. (1986). Assessment of acculturation. In W. J. Lonner & J. W. Berry (eds), *Field methods in cross-cultural research* (pp. 290–327). Beverly Hills, CA: Sage.

Berscheid, E. (1994). Interpersonal relationships. *Annual Review of Psychology, 45*, 79–129.

Berscheid, E., & Ammazzalorso, H. (2001). Emotional experience in close relationships. In G. J. O. Fletcher & M. Clark (eds), *Blackwell handbook of social psychology: Interpersonal processes* (pp. 253–278). Oxford, UK: Blackwell Publishers.

Berscheid, E., Graziano, W., Monson, T., & Dermer, M. (1976). Outcome dependency: Attention, attribution, and attraction. *Journal of Personality and Social Psychology, 34*, 978–989.

Berscheid, E., & Reis, H. T. (1998). Attraction and close relationships. In D. T. Gilbert, S. T. Fiske & G. Lindzey (eds), *The handbook of social psychology* (4th ed, Vol. 2, pp. 193–281). New York: McGraw-Hill.

Bierhof, H.-W., & Rohmann, E. (2004) Altruistic personality in the context of the empathy-altruism hypothesis. *European Journal of Personality, 18*, 351–365.

Billig, M. (1976). *Social psychology and intergroup relations*. London: Academic Press.

Billig, M. (1978). *Fascists: A social psychological view of the National Front*. London: Harcourt Brace Johanovich.

Billig, M., & Tajfel, H. (1973). Social categorisation and similarity in intergroup behaviour. *European Journal of Social Psychology, 3*, 27–52.

Birdwhistell, R. (1970). *Kinesics and context: Essays on body movement communication*. Philadelphia, PA: University of Pennsylvania Press.

Birnbaum, G. E., Reis, H. T., Mikulincer, M., Gillath, O., & Orpaz, A. (2006). When sex is more than just sex: Attachment orientations, sexual experience, and relationship quality. *Journal of Personality and Social Psychology, 91*, 929–943.

Black, S. L., & Bevan, S. (1992). At the movies with Buss and Durkee: A natural experiment on film violence. *Aggressive Behavior, 18*, 37–45.

Blankenship, K. L., & Holtgraves, T. (2005). The role of different markers of linguistic powerlessness in persuasion. *Journal of Language and Social Psychology, 24*, 3–24.

Blumer, H. (1969). *Symbolic interactionism: Perspective and method*. Englewood Cliffs, NJ: Prentice Hall.

Boas, F. (1911). *The mind of primitive man*. New York: Macmillan.

Boas, F. (1930). Anthropology. *Encyclopedia of the Social Sciences, 2*, 73–110.

Bochner, S. (1982). The social psychology of cross-cultural relations. In S. Bochner (ed), *Cultures in contact: Studies in cross-cultural interaction*. Oxford, UK: Pergamon Press.

Bohner, G., Bless, H., Schwarz, N., & Strack, F. (1988). What triggers causal attributions? The impact of valence and subjective probability. *European Journal of Social Psychology, 18*, 335–345.

Bohner, G., & Wänke, M. (2002). *Attitudes and attitude change*. Hove, UK: Psychology Press.

Bond, C. F., Jr (1982). Social facilitation: A self-presentational view. *Journal of Personality and Social Psychology, 42,* 1042–1050.

Bond, C. F., Jr and Titus, L. J. (1983). Social facilitation: A meta-analysis of 241 studies. *Psychological Bulletin, 94,* 265–292.

Bond, M. H., & King, A. Y. C. (1985). Coping with the threat of Westernisation in Hong Kong. *International Journal of Intercultural Relations, 9,* 351–364.

Bond, M. H., & Komai, H. (1976). Targets of gazing and eye contact during interviews: Effects on Japanese nonverbal behaviour. *Journal of Personality and Social Psychology, 34,* 1276–1284.

Bonnes, M., & Secchiaroli, G. (1995). *Environmental psychology: A psycho-social introduction.* London: Sage.

Bonta, B. D. (1997). Cooperation and competition in peaceful societies. *Psychological Bulletin, 121,* 299–320.

Book, A. S., Starzyk, K. B., & Quinsey, V. L. (2001). The relationship between testosterone and aggression: A meta-analysis. *Aggression and Violent Behavior, 6,* 579–599.

Borden, R. J. (1980). Audience influence. In P. B. Paulus (ed), *Psychology of group influence* (pp. 99–131). Hillsdale, NJ: Erlbaum.

Bornstein, R. F. (1989). Exposure and affect: Overview and meta-analysis of research, 1968–1987. *Psychological Bulletin, 106,* 265–289.

Bourhis, R. Y., Sachdev, I., & Gagnon, A. (1994). Intergroup research with the Tajfel matrices: Methodological notes. In M. Zanna & J. Olson (eds), *The psychology of prejudice: The Ontario symposium* (Vol. 7, pp. 209–232). Hillsdale, NJ: Erlbaum.

Bowlby, J. (1969). *Attachment and loss*: (Vol. 1) *Attachment.* London: Hogarth Press.

Bowlby, J. (1988). *A secure base: Parent–child attachment and healthy human development.* New York: Basic Books.

Bowles, H. R., & McGinn, K. L. (2005). Claiming authority: Negotiating challenges for women leaders. In D. M. Messick & R. M. Kramer (eds), *The psychology of leadership: New perspectives and research* (pp. 191–208). Mahwah, NJ: Erlbaum.

Brauer, M., Judd, C. M., & Gliner, M. D. (1995). The effects of reoperated expressions on attitude polarisation during group discussion. *Journal of Personality and Social Psychology, 68,* 1014–1029.

Breakwell, G. M., & Canter, D. V. (1993). *Empirical approaches to social representations.* Oxford, UK: Clarendon Press.

Brehm, J. W. (1966). *A theory of psychological reactance.* New York: Academic Press.

Brennan, K. A., & Shaver, P. R. (1995). Dimensions of adult attachment, affect regulation, and romantic relationship functioning. *Personality and Social Psychology Bulletin, 21,* 267–283.

Brewer, M. B. (1988). A dual process model of impression formation. In T. K. Srull & R. S. Wyer (eds), *Advances in social cognition: A dual process model of impression formation* (Vol. 1, pp. 1–36). Hillsdale, NJ: Erlbaum.

Brewer, M. B. (1991). The social self: On being the same and different at the same time. *Personality and Social Psychology Bulletin, 17,* 475–482.

Brewer, M. B. (2003). *Intergroup relations* (2nd ed). Philadelphia, PA: Open University Press.

Brewer, M. B., & Brown, R. J. (1998). Intergroup relations. In D. T. Gilbert, S. T. Fiske & G. Lindzey (eds), *The handbook of social psychology* (4th ed, Vol. 2, pp. 554–594). Mahwah, NJ: Erlbaum.

Brewer, M. B., & Campbell, D. T. (1976). *Ethnocentrism and intergroup attitudes: East African evidence.* New York: Sage.

Brewer, M. B., & Gardner, W. (1996). Who is this 'We'? Levels of collective identity and self representation. *Journal of Personality and Social Psychology, 71,* 83–93.

Brewer, M. B., & Miller, N. (1996). *Intergroup relations.* Buckingham, UK: Open University Press.

Brief, A. P., Dukerich, J. M., & Doran, L. I. (1991). Resolving ethical dilemmas in management: Experimental investigation of values, accountability, and choice. *Journal of Applied Social Psychology, 21,* 380–396.

Brigham, J. C. (1971). Ethnic stereotypes. *Psychological Bulletin, 76,* 15–38.

Broverman, I. K., Broverman, D. M., Clarkson, F., Rosencrantz, P. S., & Vogel, S. (1970). Sex-role stereotypes and clinical judgments of mental health. *Journal of Consulting and Clinical Psychology, 34,* 1–7.

Brown, R. J. (1995). *Prejudice: Its social psychology.* Oxford, UK: Blackwell.

Brown, R. J. (2000). *Group processes* (2nd ed). Oxford, UK: Blackwell.

Brown, R. J., & Gaertner, S. (eds) (2001). *Blackwell handbook of social psychology: Intergroup processes*. Oxford, UK: Blackwell.

Brumbaugh, C. C., & Fraley, R. C. (2006). Transference and attachment: How do attachment patterns get carried forward from one relationship to the next? *Personality and Social Psychology Bulletin, 32,* 552–560.

Bruner, J. S. (1957). On perceptual readiness. *Psychological Review, 64,* 123–152.

Buck, R., & Ginsburg, B. (1991). Spontaneous communication and altruism: The communicative gene hypothesis. In M. S. Clark (ed), *Prosocial behaviour* (pp. 149–175). Newbury Park, CA: Sage.

Buford, B. (1993). *Among the thugs*. New York: Vintage.

Burgoon, J. K., Buller, D. B., & Woodall, W. G. (1989). *Nonverbal communication: The unspoken dialogue*. New York: Harper and Row.

Burgoon, M., Pfau, M., & Birk, T. S. (1995). An inoculation theory explanation for the effects of corporate issue/advocacy advertising campaigns. *Communication Research, 22,* 485–505.

Burnstein, E., Crandall, C., & Kitayama, S. (1994). Some neo-Darwinian decision rules for altruism: Weighing cues for inclusive fitness as a function of the biological importance of the decision. *Journal of Personality and Social Psychology, 67,* 773–789.

Burnstein, E., & Vinokur, A. (1977). Persuasive argumentation and social comparison as determinants of attitude polarisation. *Journal of Experimental Social Psychology, 13,* 315–332.

Bushman, B. J. (1984). Perceived symbols of authority and their influence on compliance. *Journal of Applied Social Psychology, 14,* 501–508.

Bushman, B. J. (1988). The effects of apparel on compliance: A field experiment with a female authority figure. *Personality and Social Psychology Bulletin, 14,* 459–467.

Bushman, B. J., & Baumeister, R. F. (1998). Threatened egotism, narcissism, self-esteem, and direct and displaced aggression: Does self-love or self-hate lead to violence? *Journal of Personality and Social Psychology, 75,* 219–229.

Bushman, B. J., Baumeister, R. F., & Stack, A. D. (1999). Catharsis, aggression, and persuasive influence: Self-fulfilling or self-defeating prophecies? *Journal of Personality and Social Psychology, 76,* 367–376.

Bushman, B. J., & Stack, A. D. (1996). Forbidden fruit versus tainted fruit: Effects of warning labels on attraction to television violence. *Journal of Experimental Psychology: Applied, 2,* 207–226.

Buss, A. H. (1961). *The psychology of aggression*. New York: Wiley.

Buss, D. M. (1999). *Evolutionary psychology: The new science of the mind*. Boston, MA: Allyn & Bacon.

Buss, D. M. (2003). *The evolution of desire: Strategies of human mating* (rev. ed). New York: Free Press.

Buss, D. M., & Kenrick, D. T. (1998). Evolutionary social psychology. In D. T. Gilbert, S. T. Fiske & G. Lindzey (eds), *The handbook of social psychology* (4th ed, Vol. 2, pp. 982–1026). New York: McGraw-Hill.

Byrd, R. E. (1938). *Alone*. New York: Putnam.

Byrne, D. (1971). *The attraction paradigm*. New York: Academic Press.

Byrne, D., & Clore, G. L. (1970). A reinforcement model of evaluative responses. *Personality: An International Journal, 1,* 103–128.

C

Cacioppo, J. T., & Petty, R. E. (1981). Electromyograms as measures of extent and affectivity of information processing. *American Psychologist, 36,* 441–456.

Calhoun, J. B. (1962). Population density and social pathology. *Scientific American, 206,* 139–148.

Callaway, M. R., Marriott, R. G., & Esser, J. K. (1985). Effects of dominance on group decision making: Towards a stress-reduction explanation of groupthink. *Journal of Personality and Social Psychology, 49,* 949–952.

Campbell, A. (1993). *Men, women and aggression*. New York: HarperCollins.

Campbell, J. D., & Fairey, P. J. (1985). Effects of self-esteem, hypothetical explanations, and verbalisations of expectancies on future performance. *Journal of Personality and Social Psychology, 48,* 1097–1111.

Campbell, L., Simpson, J.A., Kashy, D.A., & Fletcher, G.J.O. (2001). Ideal standards, the self, and flexibility of ideals in close relationships. *Personality and Social Psychology Bulletin, 27,* 447–462.

Cantor, N., & Kihlstrom, J. F. (1987). *Personality and social intelligence.* Englewood Cliffs, NJ: Prentice Hall.

Carlsmith, J. M., & Gross, A. E. (1969). Some effects of guilt on compliance. *Journal of Personality and Social Psychology, 37,* 337–344.

Carnevale, P. J. D., Pruitt, D. G., & Britton, S. D. (1979). Looking tough: The negotiator under constituent surveillance. *Personality and Social Psychology Bulletin, 5,* 118–121.

Carter, L. F., & Nixon, M. (1949). An investigation of the relationship between four criteria of leadership ability for three different tasks. *The Journal of Psychology, 27,* 245–261.

Carver, C. S., & Glass, D. C. (1978). Coronary-prone behavior pattern and interpersonal aggression. *Journal of Personality and Social Psychology, 36,* 361–366.

Carver, C. S., & Scheier, M. F. (1981). *Attention and self-regulation: A control theory approach to human behavior.* New York: Springer.

Chacko, T. I. (1982). Women and equal employment opportunity: Some unintended effects. *Journal of Applied Psychology, 67,* 119–123.

Chaffee, S. H., Jackson-Beeck, M., Durall, J., & Wilson, D. (1977). Mass communication in political communication. In S. A. Renshon (ed), *Handbook of political socialization: Theory and research* (pp. 223–258). New York: Free Press.

Chaiken, S. (1980). Heuristic versus systematic information processing and the use of source versus message cues in persuasion. *Journal of Personality and Social Psychology, 39,* 752–766.

Chaplin, W. F., John, O. P., & Goldberg, L. R. (1988). Conceptions of states and traits: Dimensional attributes with ideals as prototypes. *Journal of Personality and Social Psychology, 54,* 541–557.

Chapman, L. J. (1967). Illusory correlation in observational report. *Journal of Verbal Learning and Verbal Behavior, 6,* 151–155.

Chemers, M. M. (2001). Leadership effectiveness: An integrative review. In M. A. Hogg & R. S. Tindale (eds), *Blackwell handbook of social psychology: Group processes* (pp. 376–399). Oxford, UK: Blackwell.

Cherek, D. R., Schnapp, W., Moeller, F., & Dougherty, D. M. (1996). Laboratory measures of aggressive responding in male parolees with violent and nonviolent histories. *Aggressive Behaviour, 22,* 27–36.

Choi, I., & Nisbett, R. E. (2000). Cultural psychology of surprise: Holistic theories and recognition of contradiction. *Journal of Personality and Social Psychology, 79,* 890–905.

Christy, C. A., & Voigt, H. (1994). Bystander responses to public episodes of child abuse. *Journal of Applied Social Psychology, 24,* 824–847.

Chryssochoou, X. (2000) Memberships in a superordinate level: Re-thinking European Union as a multi-national society. *Journal of Community and Applied Social Psychology, 10,* 403–420.

Chryssochoou, X. (2004). *Cultural diversity: Its social psychology.* Oxford, UK: Blackwell.

Cialdini, R. B., Borden, R. J., Thorne, A., Walker, M. R., Freeman, S., & Sloan, L. R. (1976). Basking in reflected glory: Three (football) field studies. *Journal of Personality and Social Psychology, 34,* 366–375.

Cialdini, R. B., Cacioppo, J. T., Bassett, R., & Miller, J. A. (1978). Low-balling procedure for producing compliance: Commitment then cost. *Journal of Personality and Social Psychology, 36,* 463–476.

Cialdini, R. B., & Goldstein, N. J. (2004). Social influence: compliance and conformity. *Annual Review of Psychology, 55,* 591–621.

Cialdini, R. B., & Petty, R. E. (1979). Anticipatory opinion effects. In R. Petty, T. Ostrom & T. Brock (eds), *Cognitive responses in persuasion.* Hillsdale, NJ: Erlbaum.

Cialdini, R. B., & Trost, M. R. (1998). Social influence: Social norms, conformity, and compliance. In D. Gilbert, S. T. Fiske & G. Lindzey (eds), *The handbook of social psychology* (4th ed, Vol. 2, pp. 151–192). New York: McGraw-Hill.

Cialdini, R. B., Vincent, J. E., Lewis, S. K., Catalan, J., Wheeler, D., & Darby, B. L. (1975). Reciprocal concessions procedure for inducing compliance: The door-in-the-face technique. *Journal of Personality and Social Psychology, 31,* 206–215.

Cinnirella, M., & Hamilton, S. (2007). Are all Britons reluctant Europeans? Exploring European identity and attitudes to Europe amongst British citizens of South Asian ethnicity. *Ethnic and Racial Studies, 30*, 481–501.

Clark, M. S. (ed) (1991). *Prosocial behaviour.* Newbury Park, CA: Sage.

Clark, M. S., & Grote, N. K. (1998). Why aren't indices of relationship costs always negatively related to indices of relationship quality? *Personality and Social Psychology Review, 2*, 2–17.

Clark, N. K., & Stephenson, G. M. (1995). Social remembering: Individual and collaborative memory for social information. *European Review of Social Psychology, 6*, 127–160.

Clary, E. G., & Snyder, M. (1991). A functional analysis of altruism and prosocial behaviour: The case of volunteerism. In M. S. Clarke (ed), *Prosocial behaviour* (pp. 119–147). Newbury Park, CA: Sage.

Clary, E. G., & Snyder, M. (1999). Considerations of community: The context and process of volunteerism. *Current Directions in Psychological Science, 8*, 156–159.

Clore, G. L. (1976). Interpersonal attraction: An overview. In J. W. Thibaut, J. T. Spence & R. C. Carson (eds), *Contemporary topics in social psychology* (pp. 135–175). Morristown, NJ: General Learning Press.

Clore, G. L., & Byrne, D. (1974). A reinforcement–affect model of attraction. In T. L. Huston (ed), *Foundations of interpersonal attraction* (pp. 143–165). New York: Academic Press.

Codol, J.-P. (1975). On the so-called 'superior conformity of the self' behaviour: Twenty experimental investigations. *European Journal of Social Psychology, 5*, 457–501.

Cohn, C. (1987). Slick'ems, glick'ems, Christmas trees and cookie cutters: Nuclear language and how we learned to pat the bomb. *Bulletin of Atomic Scientists, 43*, 17–24.

Cohn, E. G., & Rotton, J. (1997). Assault as a function of time and temperature: A moderator-variable time-series analysis. *Journal of Personality and Social Psychology, 72*, 1322–1334.

Cohn, N. (1966). *Warrant for genocide: The myth of the Jewish world conspiracy and the Protocol of the Elders of Zion.* New York: Harper & Row.

Condry, J. (1977). Enemies of exploration: Self-initiated versus other-initiated learning. *Journal of Personality and Social Psychology, 35*, 459–477.

Conger, J. A., & Kanungo, R. N. (1998). *Charismatic leadership in organizations.* Thousand Oaks, CA: Sage.

Conway, M., Irannejad, S., & Giannopoulos, C. (2005). Status-based expectancies for aggression, with regard to gender differences in aggression in social psychological research. *Aggressive Behaviour, 31*, 381-398.

Cook, S. W. (1978). Interpersonal and attitudinal outcomes in cooperating interracial groups. *Journal of Research and Development in education, 12*, 97–113.

Cooper, C. D., & Kurland, N. B. (2002). Telecommuting, professional isolation, and employee development in public and private organizations. *Journal of Organizational Behavior, 23*, 511–532.

Cooper, J., & Axsom, D. (1982). Effort justification in psychotherapy. In G. Weary & H. Mirels (eds), *Integrations of Clinical and Social Psychology.* London: Oxford University Press.

Corballis, M. C. (1999). The gestural origins of language. *American Scientist, 87*, 138–145.

Costanzo, P. R. (1970). Conformity development as a function of self-blame. *Journal of Personality and Social Psychology, 14*, 366–374.

Cottrell, N. B. (1972). Social facilitation. In C. McClintock (ed), *Experimental social psychology* (pp. 185–236). New York: Holt, Rinehart & Winston.

Coupland, N., Bishop, H., Evans, B., & Garrett, P. (2006). Imagining Wales and the Welsh language: Ethnolinguistic subjectivities and demographic flow. *Journal of Language and Social Psychology, 25*, 351–376.

Cramer, R. E., McMaster, M. R., Bartell, P. A., & Dragna, M. (1988). Subject competence and minimization of the bystander effect. *Journal of Applied Social Psychology, 18*, 1133–1148.

Crano, W. D. (2001). Social influence, social identity, and ingroup leniency. In C. W. K. de Dreu & N. K. de Vries (eds), *Group consensus and minority influence: Implications for innovation* (pp. 122–143). Oxford: Blackwell.

Crano, W. D., & Brewer, M. B. (2002). *Principles and methods of social research* (2nd ed). Mahwah, NJ: Erlbaum.

Crano, W. D., & Prislin, R. (2006). Attitudes and persuasion. *Annual Review of Psychology, 57,* 345–374.

Crisp, R. J., & Hewstone, M. (2007). Multiple social categorization. In M. P. Zanna (ed), *Advances in experimental social psychology* (vol. 39). San Diego, CA: Academic Press.

Crosby, F., Cordova, D., & Jaskar, K. (1993). On the failure to see oneself as disadvantaged: Cognitive and emotional components. In M. A. Hogg & D. Abrams (eds), *Group motivation: Social psychological perspectives* (pp. 87–104). London: Harvester Wheatsheaf.

Cross, P. (1977). Not can but will college teaching be improved? *New Directions for Higher education, 17,* 1–15.

Crusco, A. H., & Wetzel, C. G. (1984). The Midas touch: The effects of interpersonal touch on restaurant tipping. *Personality and Social Psychology Bulletin, 10,* 512–517.

Crutchfield, R. A. (1955). Conformity and character. *American Psychologist, 10,* 191–198.

D

Darley, J. M., & Batson, C. D. (1973). From Jerusalem to Jericho: A study of situational and dispositional variables in helping behavior. *Journal of Personality and Social Psychology, 27,* 100–108.

Darley, J. M., & Latané, B. (1968). Bystander intervention in emergencies: Diffusion of responsibility. *Journal of Personality and Social Psychology, 8,* 377–383.

Darlington, R. B., & Macker, D. F. (1966). Displacement of guilt-produced altruistic behaviour. *Journal of Personality and Social Psychology, 4,* 442–443.

Darwin, C. (1872). *The expression of emotions in man and animals.* Chicago: University of Chicago Press.

Davies, J. C. (1969). The J-curve of rising and declining satisfaction as a cause of some great revolutions and a contained rebellion. In H. D. Graham & T. R. Gurr (eds), *The history of violence in America: Historical and comparative perspectives* (pp. 690–730). New York: Praeger.

Davis, J. H. (1973). Group decision and social interaction: A theory of social decision schemes. *Psychological Review, 80,* 97–125.

Davis, M. H., Hall, J. A., & Meyer, M. (2003). The first year: Influences on the satisfaction, involvement, and persistence of new community volunteers. *Personality and Social Psychology Bulletin, 29,* 248–260.

De Cremer, D., & van Knippenberg, D. (2003). Cooperation with leaders in social dilemmas: On the effects of procedural fairness and outcome favorability in structural cooperation. *Organizational Behavior and Human Decision Processes, 91,* 1–11.

De Houwer, J., & Hermans, D. (2001). editorial: Automatic affective processing. *Cognition and Emotion, 15,* 113–114.

de Jong, P. F., Koomen, W., & Mellenbergh, G. J. (1988). Structure of causes for success and failure: A multi-dimensional scaling analysis of preference judgments. *Journal of Personality and Social Psychology, 55,* 1024–1037.

De Munck, V. C. (1996). Love and marriage in a Sri Lankan Muslim community: Toward an evaluation of Dravidian marriage practices. *American Ethnologist, 23,* 698–716.

Deaux, K. (1985). Sex and gender. *Annual Review of Psychology, 36,* 49–81.

Deaux, K., & LaFrance, M. (1998). Gender. In D. T. Gilbert, S. T. Fiske & G. Lindzey (eds), *The handbook of social psychology* (4th ed, Vol. 1, pp. 788–827). New York: McGraw-Hill.

Deaux, K., Reid, A., Mizrahi, K. & Ethier, K. A. (1995). Parameters of social identity. *Journal of Personality and Social Psychology, 68,* 280–291.

Decety, J., & Lamm, C. (2006). Human empathy through the lens of social neuroscience. *The Scientific World Journal, 6,* 1146–1163.

Deci, E. L., & Ryan, R. M. (1985). *Intrinsic motivation and self-determination in human behavior.* New York: Plenum.

DeJong, W. (1979). An examination of self-perception mediation of the foot in the door effect. *Journal of Personality and Social Psychology, 37,* 2171–2180.

DeKeseredy, W. S. (2006). Future directions. *Violence against women, 12,* 1078–1085.

Dembrowski, T. M., & MacDougall, J. M. (1978). Stress effects on affliation preferences among subjects possessing the Type A coronary-prone behavior pattern. *Journal of Personality and Social Psychology, 36,* 23–33.

DePaulo, B., & Friedman, H. S. (1998). Nonverbal communication. In D. T. Gilbert, S. T. Fiske, & G. Lindzey (eds), *The handbook of social psychology* (4th ed, Vol. 2, pp. 3–40). New York: McGraw-Hill.

Deutsch, M. (1975). Equity, equality and need: What determines which value will be used as a basis of distributive justice? *Journal of Social Issues, 31*, 137–149.

Deutsch, M., & Gerard, H. B. (1955). A study of normative and informational social influences upon individual judgment. *Journal of Abnormal and Social Psychology, 51*, 629–636.

Devine, P. G. (1989). Stereotypes and prejudice: Their automatic and controlled components. *Journal of Personality and Social Psychology, 56*, 5–18.

Devine, P. G., & Elliot, A. (1995). Are racial stereotypes really fading? The Princeton trilogy revisited *Personality and Social Psychology Bulletin, 22*, 22–37.

Devine, P. G., Hamilton, D. L., & Ostrom, T. M. (eds) (1994). *Social cognition: Impact on social psychology.* San Diego, CA: Academic Press.

DeVos, G. A., & Hippler, A. E. (1969). Cultural psychology: Comparative studies of human behavior. In G. Lindzey & E. Aronson (eds), *Handbook of social psychology* (2nd ed, Vol. 4, pp. 322–417). Reading, MA: Addison-Wesley.

Diab, L. (1963). Factors affecting studies of national stereotypes. *Journal of Social Psychology, 59*, 29–40.

Diamond, L. M. (2003). What does sexual orientation orient? A biobehavioral model distinguishing romantic love and sexual desire. *Psychological Review, 110*, 173–192.

Dienstbier, R. A., Kahle, L. R., Willis, K. A., & Tunnell, G. B. (1980). The impact of moral theories on cheating: Studies of emotion attribution and schema activation. *Motivation and Emotion, 4*, 193–216.

Dietz, T. L. (1998). An examination of violence and gender role portrayals in video games: Implications for gender socialization and aggressive behavior. *Sex Roles, 38*, 425–442.

Dion, K. L. (2000). Group cohesion: From 'field of forces' to multidimensional construct. *Group Dynamics, 4*, 7–26.

Dion, K. K., & Dion, K. L. (1996). Toward understanding love. *Personal Relationships, 3*, 1–3.

Dittmar, H., (ed) (2008). *Consumer culture, identity and well-being.* New York: Psychology Press.

Doise, W. (1986). *Levels of explanation in social psychology.* Cambridge, UK: Cambridge University Press.

Doise, W., Clémence, A., & Lorenzi-Cioldi, F. (1993) *The quantitative analysis of social representations.* London: Harvester Wheatsheaf.

Dolinski, D. (2000). On inferring one's beliefs from one's attempt and consequences for subsequent compliance. *Journal of Personality and Social Psychology, 78*, 260–272.

Dollard, J., Doob, L. W., Miller, N. E., Mowrer, O. H., & Sears, R. R. (1939). *Frustration and aggression.* New Haven, CT: Yale University Press.

Donnerstein, E., & Linz, D. (1994). Sexual violence in the mass media. In M. Costanzo and S. Oskamp (eds), *Violence and the law* (pp. 9–36). Thousand Oaks, CA: Sage.

Dovidio, J. F., Brigham, J. C., Johnson, B. T., & Gaertner, S. L. (1996). Stereotyping, prejudice, and discrimination: Another look. In C. N. Macrae, C. Stangor, & M. Hewstone (eds), *Stereotypes and stereotyping* (pp. 276–319). New York: Guilford Press.

Dovidio, J. F., & Ellyson, S. L. (1985). Patterns of visual dominance behavior in humans. In S. Ellyson & J. Dovidio (eds), *Power, dominance, and nonverbal behavior* (pp. 129–149). New York: Springer.

Dovidio, J. F., Glick, P., & Rudman, L. A. (eds) (2005). *On the nature of prejudice: Fifty years after Allport.* Malden, MA: Blackwell.

Dovidio, J., Hewstone, M., Glick, P., & Esses, V. (eds) (in press). *Handbook of prejudice, stereotyping and discrimination.* London: Sage.

Duck, S. (ed) (1982). *Personal relationships, 4: Dissolving personal relationships.* London: Academic Press.

Duck, S. (2007). *Human relationships* (4th ed). Thousand Oaks, CA: Sage.

Duncan, S. (1969). Nonverbal communication. *Psychological Bulletin, 72*, 118–137.

Durkheim, E. (1898). Représentations individuelles et représentations collectives. *Revue de Metaphysique et de Morale, 6*, 273–302.

Dutton, D. G., & Aron, A. P. (1974). Some evidence for heightened sexual attraction under conditions of high anxiety. *Journal of Personality and Social Psychology, 30*, 510–517.

Dutton, D. G., Boyanowsky, E. H., & Bond, M. H. (2005). Extreme mass homicide: From military massacre to genocide. *Aggression and Violent Behavior, 10,* 437–473.

Duval, S., & Wicklund, R. A. (1972). *A theory of objective self-awareness.* New York: Academic Press.

Dvir, T., eden, D., Avolio, B. J., & Shamir, B. (2002). Impact of transformational leadership training on follower development and performance: A field experiment. *Academy of Management Journal, 45,* 735–744.

E

Eagly, A. H. (2003). Few women at the top: How role incongruity produces prejudice and the glass ceiling. In D. van Knippenberg & M. A. Hogg (eds), *Leadership and power: Identity processes in groups and organizations* (pp. 79–93). London: Sage.

Eagly, A. H., & Chaiken, S. (1993). *The psychology of attitudes.* San Diego, CA: Harcourt Brace Johanovich.

Eagly, A. H., & Chaiken, S. (1998). Attitude structure and function. In D. T. Gilbert, S. T. Fiske & G. Lindzey (eds), *The handbook of social psychology* (Vol. 1, pp. 269–322). Boston, MA: McGraw-Hill.

Eagly, A. H., & Chaiken, S. (2005). Attitude research in the 21st century: The current state of knowledge. In D. Albarracín, B. T. Johnson & M. P. Zanna (eds), *The handbook of attitudes* (pp. 742–767). Mahwah, NJ: Erlbaum.

Eagly, A. H., & Crowley, M. (1986). Gender and helping behavior: A meta-analytic review of the social psychological literature. *Psychological Review, 100,* 283–308.

Eagly, A. H., & Karau, S. J. (2002). Role congruity theory of prejudice toward female leaders. *Psychological Review, 109,* 573–598.

Eagly, A. H., Makhijani, M. G., & Klonsky, B. G. (1992). Gender and the evaluation of leaders: A meta-analysis. *Psychological Bulletin, 111,* 3–22.

Eagly, A. H., & Steffen, V. J. (1984). Gender stereotypes stem from the distribution of women and men into social roles. *Journal of Personality and Social Psychology, 46,* 735–754.

Earley, P. C. (1989). Social loafing and collectivism: A comparison of the United States and the People's Republic of China. *Administrative Science Quarterly, 34,* 565–581.

eden, D. (1990). Pygmalion without interpersonal contrast effects: Whole groups gain from raising manager expectations. *Journal of Applied Psychology, 75,* 394–398.

edwards, J. (1994). *Multilingualism.* London: Routledge.

edwards, J., & Chisholm, J. (1987). Language, multiculturalism and identity: A Canadian study. *Journal of Multilingual and Multicultural Development, 8,* 391–407.

Eibl-Eibesfeldt, I. (1972). Similarities and differences between cultures in expressive movements. In R. Hinde (ed), *Non-verbal communication* (pp. 297–314). Cambridge, UK: Cambridge University Press.

Eisenberg, N., Fabes, R. A., Karbon, M., Murphy, B. C., Wosinski, M., Polazzi, L., *et al.* (1996). The relationship of children's dispositional prosocial behaviour to emotionality, regulation, and social functioning. *Child Development, 67,* 974–992.

Eisenberg, N., Guthrie, I. K., Murphy, B. C., Shepard, S. A., Cumberland, A., & Carlo, G. (1999). Consistency and development of prosocial dispositions: A longitudinal study. *Child Development, 70,* 1360–1372.

Eisenberg, N., & Mussen, P. H. (1989). *The roots of prosocial behaviour in children.* Cambridge, UK: Cambridge University Press.

Ekman, P. (1971). Universals and cultural differences in facial expressions of emotion. In J. K. Cole (ed), *Nebraska symposium on motivation* (Vol. 19, pp. 207–284). Lincoln, NE: University of Nebraska Press.

Ekman, P. (1973). Cross-cultural studies of facial expression. In P. Ekman (ed), *Darwin and facial expression* (pp. 169–222). New York: Academic Press.

Ekman, P. (1982). *Emotion in the human face.* New York: Cambridge University Press.

Ekman, P. (2003). *Emotions revealed* New York: Times Books.

Ekman, P., & Friesen, W. V. (1971). Constants across cultures in the face and emotion. *Journal of Personality and Social Psychology, 17,* 124–129.

Ekman, P., & Friesen, W. V. (1972). Hand movements. *Journal of Communication, 22,* 353–374.

Ekman, P., & Friesen, W. V. (1975). *Unmasking the face.* Englewood Cliffs, NJ: Prentice Hall.

Ekman, P., Friesen, W. V., & Hager, J. C. (2002). *Facial action coding system*. Salt Lake City: Research Nexus.

Ekman, P., Friesen, W. V., O'Sullivan, M., Chan, A., Diacoyanni-Tarlatzis, I., Heider, K., *et al.*, (1987). Universals and cultural differences in the judgements of facial expressions of emotion. *Journal of Personality and Social Psychology, 53*, 712–717.

Ellemers, N. (1993). The influence of socio-structural variables on identity management strategies. *European Review of Social Psychology, 4*, 27–57.

Ellis, R. J., Olson, J. M., & Zanna, M. P. (1983). Stereotypic personality inferences following objective versus subjective judgments of beauty. *Canadian Journal of Behavioral Science, 15*, 35–42.

Elms, A. C. (1982). Keeping deception honest: Justifying conditions for social scientific research strategies. In T. L. Beauchamp & R. Faden (eds), *Ethical issues in social science research*. Baltimore: Johns Hopkins University Press.

Emler, N., & Reicher, S. D. (1995*). Adolescence and delinquency: The collective management of reputation*. Oxford, UK: Blackwell.

Eron, L. D. (1982). Parent–child interaction, television violence, and aggression of children. *American Psychologist, 37*, 197–211.

Evans, B. K., & Fischer, D. G. (1992). A hierarchical model of participatory decision-making, job autonomy, and perceived control. *Human Relations, 45*, 1169–1189.

F

Fajardo, D. M. (1985). Author race, essay quality, and reverse discrimination. *Journal of Applied Social Psychology, 15*, 255–268.

Farr, R. M. (1996). *The roots of modern social psychology: 1872–1954*. Oxford, UK: Blackwell.

Fazio, R. H. (1986). How do attitudes guide behavior? In R. M. Sorrentino & E. T. Higgins (eds), *The handbook of motivation and cognition*. New York: Guilford Press.

Fazio, R. H. (1989). On the power and functionality of attitudes: The role of attitude accessibility. In A. R. Pratkanis, S. Breckler & A. G. Greenwald (eds), *Attitude structure and function* (pp. 153–179). Hillsdale, NJ: Erlbaum.

Fazio, R. H. (1995). Attitudes as object-evaluation associations: Determinants, consequences, and correlates of attitude accessibility. In R. E. Petty & J. A. Krosnick (eds), *Attitude strength: Antecedents and consequences* (pp. 247–282). Mahwah, NJ: Erlbaum.

Fazio, R. H., Effrein, E. A., & Falender, V. J. (1981). Self-perceptions following social interactions. *Journal of Personality and Social Psychology, 41*, 232–242.

Fazio, R. H., Jackson, J. R., Dunton, B. C., & Williams, C. J. (1995). Variability in automatic activation as an unobtrusive measure of racial attitudes: A bona fide pipeline. *Journal of Personality and Social Psychology, 69*, 1013–1027.

Feather, N. T. (1985). Attitudes, values, and attributions: Explanations of unemployment. *Journal of Personality and Social Psychology, 48*, 876–889.

Feeney, J. A. (1999). Adult attachment, emotional control, and marital satisfaction. *Personal Relationships, 6*, 169–185.

Feeney, J. A., & Noller, P. (1990). Attachment style as a predictor of adult romantic relationships. *Journal of Personality and Social Psychology, 58*, 281–291.

Fehr, B. (1994). Prototype based assessment of laypeople's views of love. *Personal Relationships, 1*, 309–331.

Fehr, R. S., & Stern, J. A. (1970). Peripheral physiological variables and emotion: The James–Lange theory revisited *Psychological Bulletin, 74*, 411–424.

Feingold, A. (1988). Matching for attractiveness in romantic partners and same-sex friends: a meta-analysis and theoretical critique. *Psychological Bulletin, 104*, 226–235.

Fenigstein, A. (1984). Self-consciousness and the overperception of self as a target. *Journal of Personality and Social Psychology, 47*, 860–870.

Ferguson, C. K., & Kelley, H. H. (1964). Significant factors in overevaluation of own group's product. *Journal of Abnormal and Social Psychology, 69*, 223–228.

Festinger, L. (1954). A theory of social comparison processes. *Human Relations, 7*, 117–140.

Festinger, L. (1957). *A theory of cognitive dissonance*. Stanford, CA: Stanford University Press.

Festinger, L., & Carlsmith, J. M. (1959). Cognitive consequences of forced compliance. *Journal of Abnormal and Social Psychology, 58*, 203–210.

Festinger, L., Schachter, S., & Back, K. (1950). *Social pressures in informal groups: A study of human factors in housing.* New York: Harper.

Fiedler, F. E. (1964). A contingency model of leadership effectiveness. In L. Berkowitz (ed), *Advances in experimental social psychology* (Vol. 1, pp. 149–190). New York: Academic Press.

Fielding, K. S., & Hogg, M. A. (2000). Working hard to achieve self-defining group goals: A social identity analysis. *Zeitschrift für Sozialpsychologie, 31*, 191–203.

Fielding, K. S., McDonald R., & Louis, W. R. (2008). Theory of planned behaviour, identity and intentions to engage in environmental activism. *Journal of Environmental Psychology, 28*, 318–326.

Fincham, F. D. (2000). The kiss of the porcupines: From attributing responsibility to forgiving. *Personal Relationships, 7*, 1–23.

Fincham, F. D., & Bradbury, T. N. (1993). Marital satisfaction, depression, and attributions: A longitudinal analysis. *Journal of Personality and Social Psychology, 64*, 442–452.

Fischer, A. H., Mosquera, P. M. R., van Vienan, A. E. M., & Manstead, A. S. R. (2004). Gender and culture differences in emotion. *Emotion, 4*, 87–94.

Fishbein, H. D. (2002). *Peer prejudice and discrimination: The origins of prejudice.* Mahwah, NJ: Erlbaum.

Fishbein, M., & Ajzen, I. (1974). Attitudes toward objects as predictors of single and multiple behavior criteria. *Psychological Review, 81*, 59–74.

Fishbein, M., Ajzen, I., & Hinkle, R. (1980). Predicting and understanding voting in American elections: Effects of external variables. In I. Ajzen & M. Fishbein (eds), *Understanding attitudes and predicting human behavior* (pp. 173–195). Englewood Cliffs, NJ: Prentice Hall.

Fisher, J. D., Rytting, M., & Heslin, R. (1976). Hands touching hands: Affective and evaluative effects of an interpersonal touch. *Sociometry, 39*, 416–421.

Fisher, R. J. (1990). *The social psychology of intergroup and international conflict resolution.* New York: Springer.

Fisher, R. J. (ed) (2005). *Paving the way: Contributions of interactive conflict resolution to peacemaking.* Rowman & Littlefield: Lanham, MD.

Fishman, J. A. (1989). *Language and ethnicity in minority sociolinguistic perspective.* Clevedon, UK: Multilingual Matters.

Fiske, A. P., Kitayama, S., Markus, H. R., & Nisbett, R. E. (1998). The cultural matrix of social psychology. In D. T. Gilbert, S. T. Fiske & G. Lindzey (eds), *The handbook of social psychology* (4th ed, Vol. 2, pp. 915–981). New York: McGraw-Hill.

Fiske, S. T. (1998). Stereotyping. prejudice, and discrimination. In D. T. Gilbert, S. T. Fiske & G. Lindzey (eds), *The handbook of social psychology* (4th ed, Vol. 2, pp. 357–414). New York: McGraw-Hill.

Fiske, S. T., Gilbert, D. T., & Lindzey, G. (eds) (in press). *The handbook of social psychology* (5th ed). New York: Wiley.

Fiske, S. T., & Neuberg, S. L. (1990). A continuum of impression formation, from category-based to individuating processes: Influences of information and motivation on attention and interpretation. In L. Berkowitz (ed), *Advances in experimental social psychology* (Vol. 23, pp. 1–74). New York: Academic Press.

Fiske, S. T., & Taylor, S. E. (1991). *Social cognition* (2nd ed). New York: McGraw-Hill.

Fiske, S. T., & Taylor, S. E. (2008). *Social cognition: From brains to culture.* New York: McGraw-Hill.

Fitness, J. (2001). Emotional intelligence in intimate relationships. In J. Ciarrochi, J. Forgas & J. Mayer (eds), *Emotional intelligence in everyday life: A scientific enquiry* (pp. 98–112). Philadelphia, PA: Taylor & Francis.

Fitness, J., Fletcher, G., & Overall, N. (2003). Interpersonal attraction and intimate relationships. In M. A. Hogg & J. Cooper (eds), *The Sage handbook of social psychology* (pp. 258–278). London: Sage.

Fletcher, G. J. O., Simpson, J. A., Thomas, G., & Giles, L. (1999). Ideals in intimate relationships. *Journal of Personality and Social Psychology, 76*, 72–89.

Fletcher, G. J. O., Simpson, J. A., & Thomas, G. (2000). Ideals, perceptions, and evaluations in early relationship development. *Journal of Personality and Social Psychology, 79*, 933–940.

Fletcher, G. J. O., Tither, J. M., O'Loughlin, C., Friesen, M., & Overall, N. (2004). Warm and homely or cold and beautiful? Sex differences in trading off traits in mate selection. *Personality and Social Psychology Bulletin, 30*, 659–672.

Fletcher, G. J. O., & Ward, C. (1988). Attribution theory and processes: A cross-cultural perspective. In M. H. Bond (ed), *The cross-cultural challenge to social psychology* (pp. 230–244). Newbury Park, CA: Sage.

Floyd, D. L., Prentice-Dunn, S., & Rogers, R. W. (2000). A meta-analysis of research on protection motivation theory. *Journal of Applied Social Psychology, 30*, 407–429.

Foa, E. B., & Foa, U. G. (1975). *Resource theory of social exchange.* Morristown NJ: General Learning Press.

Forgas, J. P. (1983). The effects of prototypicality and cultural salience on perceptions of people. *Journal of Research in Personality, 17*, 153–173.

Forgas, J. P. (1995). Mood and judgment: The affect infusion model. *Psychological Bulletin, 117*, 39–66.

Forgas, J. P., O'Connor, K., & Morris, S. (1983). Smile and punishment: The effects of facial expression on responsibility attributions by groups and individuals. *Personality and Social Psychology Bulletin, 9*, 587–596.

Forgas, J. P., & Smith, C. A. (2003). Affect and emotion. In M. A. Hogg & J. Cooper (eds), *The Sage handbook of social psychology* (pp. 161–189). London: Sage.

Forsterling, F. (1988). *Attribution theory in clinical psychology.* Chichester, UK: Wiley.

Forsterling, F., & Rudolph, U. (1988). Situations, attributions and the evaluation of reactions. *Journal of Personality and Social Psychology, 54*, 225–232.

Forsyth, D. R. (2006). *Group dynamics* (4th ed). Pacific Grove, CA: Brooks/Cole. A comprehensive and accessible coverage of the social psychology of processes within groups.

Foss, R. D., & Dempsey, C. B. (1979). Blood donation and the foot-in-the-door technique. *Journal of Personality and Social Psychology, 37*, 580–590.

Foster, C. A., Witcher, B. S., Campbell, W. K., & Green, J. D. (1998). Arousal and attraction: Evidence for automatic and controlled processes. *Journal of Personality and Social Psychology, 74*, 86–101.

Fox, S., & Hoffman, M. (2002). Escalation behavior as a specific case of goal-directed activity: A persistence paradigm. *Basic and Applied Social Psychology, 24*, 273–285.

Freed, R. S., & Freed, S. A. (1989). Beliefs and practices resulting in female deaths and fewer females than males in India. *Population and Environment, 10*, 144–161.

Freedman, J. L. (1984). Effect of television violence on aggressiveness. *Psychological Bulletin, 96*, 227–246.

Freedman, J. L., & Fraser, S. C. (1966). Compliance without pressure: The foot-in-the-door technique. *Journal of Personality and Social Psychology, 4*, 195–202.

Freedman, J. L., Wallington, S. A., & Bless, E. (1967). Compliance without pressure: The effect of guilt. *Journal of Personality and Social Psychology, 7*, 117–124.

Freeman, S., Walker, M. R., Bordon, R., & Latané, B. (1975). Diffusion of responsibility and restaurant tipping: Cheaper by the bunch. *Personality and Social Psychology Bulletin, 1*, 584–587.

Freides, D. (1974). Human information processing and sensory modality: Cross-modal functions, information complexity, memory, and deficit. *Psychological Bulletin, 81*, 284–310.

Freud, S. (1920/1990). *Beyond the pleasure principle.* New York: W. W. Norton.

Freud, S. (1921). Group psychology and the analysis of the ego. In J. Strachey (ed), *Standard edition of the complete psychological works* (Vol. 18, pp. 1953–1964). London: Hogarth Press.

Funder, D. C. (1987). Errors and mistakes: Evaluating the accuracy of social judgment. *Psychological Bulletin, 101*, 75–90.

Furnham, A. (1983). Attributions for affluence. *Personality and Individual Differences, 4*, 31–40.

Furnham, A. (2003). Belief in a just world: Research progress over the past decade. *Personality and Individual Differences, 34*, 795–817.

G

Gaertner, S. L., & Dovidio, J. F. (1977). The subtlety of white racism, arousal, and helping behavior. *Journal of Personality and Social Psychology, 35*, 691–707.

Gaertner, S. L., & Dovidio, J. F. (1986). The aversive form of racism. In J. F. Dovidio & S. L.

Gaertner (eds), *Prejudice, discrimination, and racism* (pp. 61–89). New York: Academic Press.

Gaertner S. L., & Dovidio, J. F. (2000). *Reducing intergroup bias: The common ingroup identity model.* New York: Psychology Press.

Gaertner, S. L., Rust, M. C., Dovidio, J. F., Bachman, B. A., & Anastasio, P. A. (1996). The contact hypothesis: The role of a common ingroup identity on reducing intergroup bias among majority and minority group members. In J. L. Nye & A. M. Bower (eds), *What's social about social cognition: Research on socially shared cognition in small groups* (pp. 230–260). Thousand Oaks, CA: Sage.

Galinsky, A. D., Mussweiler, T., & Medvec, V. H. (2002). Disconnecting negotiated outcomes and evaluations: The role of negotiator focus. *Journal of Personality and Social Psychology, 83,* 1131–1140.

Gallois, C. (1993). The language and communication of emotion: Interpersonal, intergroup, or universal. *American Behavioral Scientist, 36,* 309–338.

Gallois, C., Barker, M., Jones, E., & Callan, V. J. (1992). Intercultural communication: Evaluations of lecturers and Australian and Chinese students. In S. Iwawaki, Y. Kashima, & K. Leung (eds), *Innovations in cross-cultural psychology* (pp. 86–102). Amsterdam: Swets & Zeitlinger.

Gallup, G. (1978). Gallup youth survey. *Indianapolis Star,* 18 October.

Gangestad, S. W., & Simpson, J. A. (2000). The evolution of human mating: Trade-offs and strategic pluralism. *Behavioral and Brain Sciences, 23,* 573–644.

Gardner, R. M., & Tockerman, Y. R. (1994). A computer–TV methodology for investigating the influence of somatotype on perceived personality traits. *Journal of Social Behavior and Personality, 9,* 555–563.

Garfinkel, H. (1967). *Studies in ethnomethodology.* Englewood Cliffs, NJ: Prentice Hall.

Gawronski, B. (2003). Implicational schemata and the correspondence bias: On the diagnostic value of situationally constrained behavior. *Journal of Personality and Social Psychology, 84,* 1154–1171.

Geen, R. G. (1978). Some effects of observing violence on the behaviour of the observer. In B. A. Maher (ed), *Progress in experimental personality research* (Vol. 8, pp. 49–93). New York: Academic Press.

Geen, R. G. (1991). Social motivation. *Annual Review of Psychology, 42,* 377–399.

Geen, R. G. (1998). Aggression and antisocial behaviour. In D. T. Gilbert, S. T. Fiske & G. Lindzey (eds), *The handbook of social psychology* (4th ed, Vol. 2, pp. 317–356). New York: McGraw-Hill.

Gelfand, D. M., Hartmann, D. P., Walder, P., & Page, B. (1973). Who reports shoplifters? A field-experimental study. *Journal of Personality and Social Psychology, 25,* 276–285.

Genovese, M. A. (1993). Women as national leaders: What do we know? In M. A. Genovese (ed), *Women as national leaders* (pp. 177–210). Newbury Park, CA: Sage.

Gerard, H. B., & Mathewson, G. C. (1966). The effects of severity of initiation on liking for a group: A replication. *Journal of Experimental Social Psychology, 2,* 278–287.

Gergen, K. J. (1971). *The concept of self.* New York: Holt, Rinehart & Winston.

Gersick, C. J., & Hackman, J. R. (1990). Habitual routines in task performing groups. *Organizational Behavior and Human Decision Processes, 47,* 65–97.

Giancola, P. R. (2003). Individual difference and contextual factors contributing to the alcohol-aggression relation: diverse populations, diverse methodologies: An introduction to the special issue. *Aggressive Behavior, 29,* 285–287.

Gigone, D., & Hastie, R. (1993). The common knowledge effect: Information sharing and group judgment. *Journal of Personality and Social Psychology, 65,* 959–974.

Gilbert, D. T. (1998). Ordinary personology. In D. T. Gilbert, S. T. Fiske & G. Lindzey (eds), *The handbook of social psychology* (4th ed, Vol. 2, pp. 89–150). New York: McGraw-Hill.

Gilbert, D. T., & Malone, P. S. (1995). The correspondence bias. *Psychological Bulletin, 117,* 21–38.

Gilbert, D. T., & Silvera, D. H. (1996). Overhelping. *Journal of Personality and Social Psychology, 70,* 678–690.

Giles, H., Bourhis, R. Y., & Taylor, D. M. (1977). Towards a theory of language in ethnic group relations. In H. Giles (ed), *Language, ethnicity, and intergroup relations* (pp. 307–48). London: Academic Press.

Giles, H., & Byrne, J. L. (1982). The intergroup model of second language acquisition. *Journal of Multilingual and Multicultural Development, 3,* 17–40.

Giles, H., & Coupland, N. (1991). *Language: Contexts and consequences.* Milton Keynes, UK: Open University Press.

Giles, H., & Powesland, P. F. (1975). *Speech style and social evaluation.* London: Academic Press.

Gladue, B. (1991). Aggressive behavioural characteristics, hormones, and sexual orientation in men and women. *Aggressive Behavior, 17,* 313–326.

Glick, P., & Fiske, S. T. (1996). The ambivalent sexism inventory: Differentiating hostile and benevolent sexism. *Journal of Personality and Social Psychology, 70,* 491–512.

Goffman, E. (1959). *The presentation of self in everyday life.* New York: Doubleday/Anchor Books.

Goldberg, M. E., & Gorn, G. J. (1974). Children's reactions to television advertising: An experimental approach. *Journal of Consumer Research, 1,* 69–75.

Goldman, M., Creason, C. R., & McCall, C. G. (1981). Compliance employing a two-feet-in-the-door procedure. *Journal of Social Psychology, 114,* 259–265.

Goldstein. A. P. (1987). Aggression. In R. J. Corsini (ed). *Concise encyclopedia of psychology* (pp. 35–39). New York: Wiley.

Goldstein, A. P. (1999). Aggression reduction strategies: Effective and ineffective. *School Psychology Quarterly, 14,* 40–58.

Gorassini, D. R., & Olson, J. M. (1995). Does self-perception change explain the foot-in-the-door effect? *Journal of Personality and Social Psychology, 69,* 91–105.

Gordon, R. A. (1996). Impact of ingratiation on judgments and evaluations: A meta-analytic investigation. *Journal of Personality and Social Psychology, 71,* 54–70.

Graen, G. B., & Uhl-Bien, M. (1995). Relationship-based approach to leadership: Development of leader–member exchange (LMX) theory of leadership over 25 years: Applying a multi-level multi-domain approach. *The Leadership Quarterly, 6,* 219–247.

Greenberg, J., Solomon, S., & Pyszczynski, T. (1997). Terror management theory of self-esteem and cultural worldviews: Empirical assessments and conceptual refinements. In M. Zanna (ed), *Advances in experimental social psychology* (Vol. 29, pp. 61–139). Orlando, FL: Academic Press.

Greenberg, J., Solomon, S., Pyszczynski, T., Rosenblatt, A., Burling, J., Lyon, D., *et al.* (1992). Why do people need self-esteem? Converging evidence that self-esteem serves an anxiety-buffering function. *Journal of Personality and Social Psychology, 63,* 913–922.

Greenglass, E. R. (1982). A world of difference: Gender roles in perspective. Toronto: Wiley.

Greenwald, A. G. (1980). The totalitarian ego: Fabrication and revision of personal history. *American Psychologist, 35,* 603–618.

Greenwald, A. G., & Banaji, M. R. (1995). Implicit social cognition: Attitudes, self-esteem, and stereotypes. *Psychological Review, 102,* 4–27.

Greenwald, A. G., McGhee, D. E., & Schwartz, J. L. K. (1998). Measuring individual differences in implicit cognition: The implicit association test. *Journal of Personality and Social Psychology, 74,* 1464–1480.

Griffitt, W., & Veitch, R. (1971). Hot and crowded: Influence of population density and temperature on interpersonal affective behavior. *Journal of Personality and Social Psychology, 17,* 92–98.

Gross, A. E., & Fleming, J. (1982). Twenty years of deception in social psychology. *Personality and Social Psychology Bulletin, 8,* 402–408.

Grossman, R. B., & Kegl, J. (2007). Moving faces: Categorization of dynamic facial expressions in American Sign Language by deaf and hearing participants. *Journal of Nonverbal Behavior, 31,* 23–38.

Gruber-Baldini, A. L., Schaie, K. W., & Willis, S. L. (1995). Similarity in married couples: A longitudinal study of mental abilities and rigidity–flexibility. *Journal of Personality and Social Psychology, 69,* 191–203.

Grusec, J. E. (1991). The socialisation of altruism. In M. S. Clark (ed), *Prosocial behaviour* (pp. 9–33). Newbury Park, CA: Sage.

Grusec, J. E., Kuczynski, L., Rushton, J. P., & Simutis, Z. M. (1978). Modelling, direct instruction, and attributions: Effects on altruism. *Developmental Psychology, 14,* 51–57.

Grusec, J. E., & Redler, E. (1980). Attribution, reinforcement and altruism: A developmental analysis. *Developmental Psychology, 16*, 525–534.

Guerin, B. (1993). *Social facilitation*. Cambridge, UK: Cambridge University Press.

Gupta, U., & Singh, P. (1982). An exploratory study of love and liking and types of marriages. *Indian Journal of Applied Psychology, 19*, 92–97.

H

Hackman, J. R. (2002). *Leading teams: Setting the stage for great performances*. Boston, MA: Harvard Business School Press.

Hains, S. C., Hogg, M. A., & Duck, J. M. (1997). Self-categorization and leadership: Effects of group prototypicality and leader stereotypicality. *Personality and Social Psychology Bulletin, 23*, 1087–1100.

Hall, E. T. (1966). *The hidden dimension*. New York: Doubleday.

Halpern, D. (1995). *Mental health and the built environment*. London: Taylor & Francis.

Hamilton, D. L., & Gifford, R. K. (1976). Illusory correlation in interpersonal personal perception: A cognitive basis of stereotypic judgments. *Journal of Experimental Social Psychology, 12*, 392–407.

Hamilton, D. L., & Sherman, S. J. (1996). Perceiving persons and groups. *Psychological Review, 103*, 336–335.

Hamilton, D. L., & Stroessner, S. (in press). *Social cognition*. London: Sage.

Haney, C., Banks, C., & Zimbardo, P. (1973). Interpersonal dynamics in a simulated prison. *International Journal of Criminology and Penology, 1*, 69–97.

Hannover, B., & Kühnen, U. (2004). Culture, context, and cognition: The semantic procedural interface model of the self. *European Review of Social Psychology, 15*, 297–333.

Hans, V. P. (2008). Jury systems around the world. *Annual Review of Law and Social Science, 4*, 275–297.

Harlow, H. F. (1958). The nature of love. *American Psychologist, 13*, 673–685.

Harlow, H. F., & Harlow, M. K. (1965). The affectional systems. In A. M. Schrier, H. F. Harlow & F. Stollnitz (eds), *Behavior of non-human primates* (Vol. 2). New York: Academic Press.

Harmon-Jones, E., & Winkielman, P. (eds) (2007). *Social neuroscience: Integrating biological and psychological explanations of social behavior*. New York: Guildford.

Harré, N., Foster, S., & O'Neill, M. (2005). Self-enhancement, crash-risk optimism and the impact of safety advertisements on young drivers. *British Journal of Psychology, 96*, 215–230.

Harris, M. B. (1992). Sex, race, and experiences of aggression. *Aggressive Behavior, 18*, 201–217.

Hartmann, H., Kris, E., & Loewenstein, R. M. (1949). Notes on a theory of aggression. *Psychoanalytic Study of the Child, 3–4*, 9–36.

Haslam, N. (2006). Dehumanization: An integrative review. *Personality and Social Psychology Review, 10*, 252–264.

Haslam, N., Bastian, B., Bain, P., & Kashima, Y. (2006). Psychological essentialism, implicit theories, and intergroup relations. *Group Processes and Intergroup Relations, 9*, 63–76.

Haslam, N., Rothschild, L., & Ernst, D. (1998). Essentialist beliefs about social categories. *British Journal of Social Psychology, 39*, 113–127.

Haslam, S. A., & Platow, M. J. (2001). Your wish is our command: The role of shared social identity in translating a leader's vision into followers' action. In M. A. Hogg & D. J. Terry (eds), *Social identity processes in organizational contexts* (pp. 213–228). Philadelphia, PA: Psychology Press.

Hassett, J. (1981). But that would be wrong . . . *Psychology Today*, November, 34–50.

Hastie, R. (1984). Causes and effects of causal attribution. *Journal of Personality and Social Psychology, 46*, 44–56.

Hastie, R., & Park, B. (1986). The relationship between memory and judgment depends on whether the judgment task is memory-based or on-line. *Psychological Review, 93*, 258–268.

Hatfield, E. (1987). Love. In R. J. Corsini (ed), *Concise encyclopedia of psychology* (pp. 676–677). New York: Wiley.

Hatfield, E., & Walster, G. W. (1981). *A new look at love*. Reading, MA: Addison-Wesley.

Hayduk, L. A. (1983). Personal space: Where we now stand. *Psychological Bulletin, 94*, 293–335.

Hazan, C., & Shaver, P. (1987). Romantic love conceptualized as an attachment process. *Journal of Personality and Social Psychology, 52*, 511–524.

Heider, F. (1946). Attitudes and cognitive organisation. *Journal of Psychology, 21,* 107–112.

Heider, F. (1958). *The psychology of interpersonal relations.* New York: Wiley.

Heilman, M. E., & Parks-Stamm, E. J. (2007). Gender stereotypes in the workplace: Obstacles to women's career progress. *Advances in Group Processes, 24,* 47–77.

Heilman, M. E., & Stopeck, M. H. (1985). Attractiveness and corporate success: Different causal attributions for males and females. *Journal of Applied Psychology, 70,* 379–388.

Heilman, M. E., Wallen, A. S., Fuchs, D., & Tamkins, M. M. (2004) Penalties for success: Reactions to women who succeed at male gender-typed tasks. *Journal of Applied Psychology, 89,* 416–427.

Heisler, G. (1974). Ways to deter law violators: Effects of levels of threat and vicarious punishment on cheating. *Journal of Consulting and Clinical Psychology, 42,* 577–582.

Henderson, J., & Taylor, J. (1985). Study finds bias in death sentences: Killers of whites risk execution. *Times Union,* 17 November, A19.

Henley, N. M., & Harmon, S. (1985). The nonverbal semantics of power and gender: A perceptual study. In S. L. Ellyson & J. F. Dovidio (eds), *Power, dominance, and nonverbal behavior* (pp. 151–164). New York: Springer.

Herek, G. (2000). Sexual prejudice and gender: Do heterosexuals' attitudes toward lesbians and gay men differ? *Journal of Social Issues, 56,* 251–256.

Herman, C. P., Roth, D. A., & Polivy, J. (2003). Effects of the presence of others on food intake: A normative interpretation. *Psychological Bulletin, 129,* 873–886.

Hersh, S. (1970). *My Lai: A report on the massacre and its aftermath.* New York: Vintage Books.

Heuer, L., & Penrod, S. (1994). Trial complexity: A field investigation of its meaning and its effect. *Law and Human Behavior, 18,* 29–51.

Hewes, G. W. (1957). The anthropology of posture. *Scientific American, 196,* 123–132.

Hewstone, M. (1989). *Causal attribution: From cognitive processes to collective beliefs.* Oxford, UK: Blackwell.

Hewstone, M., Cairns, E., Voci, A., Paolini, S., McLernon, F., Crisp, R. J., *et al.* (2005). Intergroup contact in a divided society: Challenging segregation in Northern Ireland. In D. Abrams, J. M. Marques, & M. A. Hogg (eds), *The social psychology of inclusion and exclusion* (pp. 265–292). New York: Psychology Press.

Hewstone, M., & Ward, C. (1985). Ethnocentrism and causal attribution in Southeast Asia. *Journal of Personality and Social Psychology, 48,* 614–623.

Higgins, E. T. (1987). Self-discrepancy: A theory relating self and affect. *Psychological Review, 94,* 319–340.

Higgins, E. T. (1996). Knowledge activation: Accessibility, applicability, and salience. In E. T. Higgins & A. W. Kruglanski (eds), *Social psychology: Handbook of basic principles* (pp. 133–168). New York: Guilford Press.

Higgins, E. T. (1997). Beyond pleasure and pain. *American Psychologist, 52,* 1280–1300.

Higgins, E. T., Bond, R. N., Klein, R., & Strauman, T. (1986). Self-discrepancies and emotional vulnerability: How magnitude, accessibility, and type of discrepancy influence affect. *Journal of Personality and Social Psychology, 51,* 5–15.

Higgins, E. T., & Silberman, I. (1998). Development of regulatory focus: Promotion and prevention as ways of living. In J. Heckhausen & C. S. Dweck (eds), *Motivation and self-regulation across the lifespan* (pp. 78–113). New York: Cambridge University Press.

Hill, C., & Peplau, L. (1998). Premarital predictors of relationship outcomes: A 15-year follow up of the Boston couples study. In T. N. Bradbury *et al.* (eds), *The developmental course of marital dysfunction* (pp. 237–278). New York: Cambridge University Press.

Hilton, D. (2007). Casual explanation: From social perception to knowledge-based causal attribution. In A. W. Kruglanski & E. T. Higgins (eds), *Social psychology: Handbook of basic principles* (2nd ed, pp. 232–253). New York: Guilford.

Hilton, D. J. (1990). Conversational processes and causal explanation. *Psychological Bulletin, 107,* 65–81.

Hilton, J. L., & von Hippel, W. (1996). Stereotypes. *Annual Review of Psychology, 47,* 237–271.

Hilton, N. Z., Harris, G. T., & Rice, M. E. (2000). The functions of aggression by male teenagers. *Journal of Personality and Social Psychology, 79,* 988–994.

Hitler, A. (1933). *Mein Kampf.* Retrieved November 11, 2003, from http://www.stormfront.org/books/mein_kampf/mkv1ch06.html

Hoffman, C., Mischel, W., & Mazze, K. (1981). The role of purpose in the organisation of information about behavior: Trait-based versus goal-based categories in person cognition. *Journal of Personality and Social Psychology, 40,* 211–225.

Hofstede, G. (1980). *Culture's consequences: International differences in work-related values.* Beverly Hills, CA: Sage.

Hofstede, G. (2001). *Culture's consequences: Comparing values, behaviours, institutions and organizations across nations* (2nd ed). Thousand Oaks, CA: Sage.

Hogg, M. A. (1992). *The social psychology of group cohesiveness: From attraction to social identity.* London: Harvester Wheatsheaf.

Hogg, M. A. (1993). Group cohesiveness: A critical review and some new directions. *European Review of Social Psychology, 4,* 85–111.

Hogg, M. A. (2000). Social identity and social comparison. In J. Suls & L. Wheeler (eds), *Handbook of social comparison: Theory and research* (pp. 401–421). New York: Kluwer/Plenum.

Hogg, M. A. (2001). A social identity theory of leadership. *Personality and Social Psychology Review, 5,* 184–200.

Hogg, M. A. (2006). Social identity theory. In P. J. Burke (ed), *Contemporary social psychological theories* (pp. 111–136). Palo Alto, CA: Stanford University Press.

Hogg, M. A. (2007a). Social psychology of leadership. In A. W. Kruglanski & E. T. Higgins (eds), *Social psychology: A handbook of basic principles* (2nd ed). New York: Guilford.

Hogg, M. A. (2007b). Uncertainty-identity theory. In M. P. Zanna (ed), *Advances in experimental social psychology* (Vol. 39, pp. 69–126). San Diego, CA: Academic Press.

Hogg, M. A. (in press). Influence and leadership. In S. T. Fiske, D. T. Gilbert, & G. Lindzey (eds), *Handbook of social psychology* (5th ed). New York: Wiley.

Hogg, M. A., & Tindale, R. S. (2005). Social identity, influence, and communication in small groups. In J. Harwood & H. Giles (eds), *Intergroup communication: Multiple perspectives* (pp. 141–164). New York: Peter Lang.

Hogg, M. A., & Abrams, D. (1988). *Social identifications: A social psychology of intergroup relations and group processes.* London: Routledge.

Hogg, M. A., & Abrams, D. (eds) (2001). *Intergroup relations: Essential readings.* Philadelphia, PA: Psychology Press.

Hogg, M. A., & Cooper, J. (eds) (2007). *The Sage handbook of social psychology: Concise student edition.* London: Sage.

Hogg, M. A., D'Agata, P., & Abrams, D. (1989). Ethnolinguistic betrayal and speaker evaluations among Italian Australians. *Genetic, Social and General Psychology Monographs, 115,* 153–181.

Hogg, M. A., & Hains, S. C. (1998). Friendship and group identification: A new look at the role of cohesiveness in groupthink. *European Journal of Social Psychology, 28,* 323–341.

Hogg, M. A., Joyce, N., & Abrams, D. (1984). Diglossia in Switzerland? A social identity analysis of speaker evaluations. *Journal of Language and Social Psychology, 3,* 185–196.

Hogg, M. A., Kelley, J., & Williams K. (in press), *Group processes and intergroup relations.* London: Sage.

Hogg, M. A., & Tindale, R. S. (2005). Social identity, influence and communication in small groups. In J. Harwood & H. Giles (eds), *Intergroup communication: Multiple perspectives* (pp. 141–164). New York: Peter Lang.

Hogg, M. A., & Turner, J. C. (1987). Social identity and conformity: A theory of referent informational influence. In W. Doise & S. Moscovici (eds), *Current issues in European social psychology* (Vol. 2, pp. 139–182). Cambridge: Cambridge University Press.

Hogg, M. A., & van Knippenberg, D. (2003). Social identity and leadership processes in groups. In M. P. Zanna (ed), *Advances in experimental social psychology* (Vol. 35, pp. 1–52). San Diego, CA: Academic Press.

Hogg, M. A., & Vaughan, G. M. (2008). *Social psychology* (5th ed). London: Prentice Hall.

Holland, R. B., Verplanken, B., & Van Knippenberg, A. (2002). On the nature of attitude–behavior relations: The strong guide, the weak follow. *European Journal of Social Psychology, 32,* 869–876.

Hollander, E. P. (1958). Conformity, status, and idiosyncrasy credit. *Psychological Review, 65,* 117–127.

Hollingshead, A. B. (1998). Retrieval processes in transactive memory systems. *Journal of Personality and Social Psychology, 74, 659–671.*

Hollingshead, A. B., & McGrath, J. E. (1995). Computer-assisted groups: A critical review of the empirical research. In R. A. Guzzo & E. Salas (eds), *Team effectiveness and decision making in organizations* (pp. 46–78). San Francisco, CA: Jossey-Bass.

Homans, G. C. (1961). *Social behavior: Its elementary forms.* New York: Harcourt, Brace and World.

Hong, Y.-Y., & Mallorie, L. M. (2004). A dynamic constructivist approach to culture: Lessons learned from personality psychology. *Journal of Research in Personality, 38, 59–67.*

Hopkins, N., & Moore, C. (2001). Categorizing the neighbors: Identity, distance, and stereotyping. *Social Psychology Quarterly, 64, 239–252.*

Hornsey, M. J. (2005). Why being right is not enough: Predicting defensiveness in the face of group criticism. *European Review of Social Psychology, 16, 301–334.*

Horowitz, I. A., & Bordens, K. S. (1990). An experimental investigation of procedural issues in complex tort trials. *Law and Human Behavior, 14, 269–285.*

House, R. J. (1977). A 1976 theory of charismatic leadership. In J. G. Hunt & L. Larson (eds), *Leadership: The cutting edge* (pp. 189–207). Carbondale, IL: Southern Illinois University Press.

House, R. J. (1996). Path-goal theory of leadership: Lessons, legacy, and a reformulated theory. *The Leadership Quarterly, 7, 323–352.*

Hovland, C. I., Janis, I. L., & Kelley, H. H. (1953). *Communication and persuasion.* New Haven, CT: Yale University Press.

Hovland, C. I., & Sears, R. R. (1940). Minor studies in aggression: VI. Correlation of lynchings with economic indices. *Journal of Psychology, 9, 301–310.*

Hovland, C. I., & Weiss, W. (1952). The influence of source credibility in communication effectiveness. *Public Opinion Quarterly, 15, 635–650.*

Huesmann, L. R. (1988). An information processing model for the development of aggression. *Aggressive Behavior, 14, 13–24.*

Huesmann, L. R., Eron, L. D., Lefkowitz, M. M., & Walder, L. O. (1984). Stability of aggression over time and generations. *Developmental Psychology, 20, 1120–1134.*

Huesmann, L. R., & Miller, L. S. (1994). Long-term effects of repeated exposure to media violence in childhood. In L. R. Huesmann (ed), *Aggressive behaviour: Current perspectives* (pp. 153–186). New York: Plenum.

Hughes, M. T. (1981). To cheat or not to cheat? *Albany Times–Union,* 26 July, pp. B-1, B-3.

Huguet, P., Galvaing, M. P., Monteil, J. M., & Dumas, F. (1999). Social presence effects in the Stroop task: Further evidence for an attentional view of social facilitation. *Journal of Personality and Social Psychology, 77, 1011–1025.*

Huici, C., Ros, M., Cano, I., Hopkins, N., Emler, N., & Carmona, M. (1997). Comparative identity and evaluation of socio-political change: Perceptions of the European Community as a function of the salience of regional identities. *European Journal of Social Psychology, 27, 97–113.*

Huston, T. L., Ruggiero, M., Conner, R., & Geis, G. (1981). Bystander intervention into crime: A study based on naturally occurring episodes. *Social Psychology Quarterly, 44, 14–23.*

I

Ingham, A. G., Levinger, G., Graves, J., & Peckham, V. (1974). The Ringelmann effect: Studies of group size and group performance. *Journal of Experimental Social Psychology, 10, 371–384.*

Ingoldsby, B. B. (1991). The Latin American family: Familism vs machismo. *Journal of Comparative Family Studies, 23, 47–62.*

Isen, A. M. (1970). Success, failure, attention, and reaction to others: The warm glow of success. *Journal of Personality and Social Psychology, 15, 294–301.*

Islam, M., & Hewstone, M. (1993). Intergroup attributions and affective consequences in majority and minority groups. *Journal of Personality and Social Psychology, 65, 936–950.*

J

Jacks, Z. J., & Cameron , K. A. (2003). Strategies for resisting persuasion. *Basic and Applied Social Psychology, 25, 145–161.*

Jacobson, D. (1999). Impression formation in cyberspace: Online expectations and offline experiences in textbased virtual communities. *Journal of Computer-Mediated Communication* [online serial], *5* (1). http://www.ascusc.org/jcmc/vol5/issue1/jacobson.html

James, W. (1890). *The principles of psychology* (Vol. 1). New York: Holt.

Jamieson, D. W., & Zanna, M. P. (1989). Need for structure in attitude formation and expression. In A. R. Pratkanis, S. J. Breckler & A. G. Greenwald (eds), *Attitude structure and function* (pp. 383–406). Hillsdale, NJ: Erlbaum.

Janis, I. L. (1954). Personality correlates of susceptibility to persuasion. *Journal of Personality, 22,* 504–518.

Janis, I. L. (1972). *Victims of groupthink: A psychological study of foreign policy decisions and fiascoes.* Boston, MA: Houghton Mifflin.

Janis, I. L., & Feshbach, S. (1953). Effects of fear-arousing communications. *Journal of Abnormal and Social Psychology, 48,* 78–92.

Janis, I. L., & Mann, L. (1977). *Decision making.* New York: Free Press.

Janis, I. L., Kaye, D., & Kirschner, P. (1965). Facilitating effects of 'eating-while-reading' on responsiveness to persuasive communications. *Journal of Personality and Social Psychology, 1,* 181–186.

Jaspars, J. M. F. (1980). The coming of age of social psychology in Europe. *European Journal of Social Psychology, 10,* 421–428.

Jaspars, J. M. F. (1986). Forum and focus: A personal view of European social psychology. *European Journal of Social Psychology, 16,* 3–15.

Jennings, M. K., & Niemi, R. G. (1968). The transmission of political values from parent to child. *American Political Science Review, 62,* 546–575.

Jodelet, D. (1991). *Madness and social representations.* Hemel Hempstead, UK: Harvester Wheatsheaf.

Jones, E. E. (1990). *Interpersonal perception.* New York: Freeman.

Jones, E. E. (1998). Major developments in five decades of social psychology. In D. T. Gilbert, S. T. Fiske & G. Lindzey (eds), *The handbook of social psychology* (4th ed, Vol. 1, pp. 3–57). New York: McGraw-Hill.

Jones, E. E., & Berglas, S. (1978). Control of attributions about the self through self-handicapping: The appeal of alcohol and the role of underachievement. *Personality and Social Psychology Bulletin,* 200–206.

Jones, E. E., & Davis, K. E. (1965). From acts to dispositions: The attribution process in person perception. In L. Berkowitz (ed), *Advances in experimental social psychology* (Vol. 2, pp. 219–266). New York: Academic Press.

Jones, E. E., & Goethals, G. R. (1972). Order effects in impression formation: Attribution context and the nature of the entity. In E. E. Jones, D. E. Kanouse, H. H. Kelley, R. E. Nisbett, S. Valins & B. Weiner (eds), *Attribution: Perceiving the causes of behavior* (pp. 27–46). Morristown, NJ: General Learning Press.

Jones, E. E., & Harris, V. A. (1967). The attribution of attitudes. *Journal of Experimental Social Psychology, 3,* 1–24.

Jones, E. E., & McGillis, D. (1976). Correspondent inferences and the attribution cube: A comparative reappraisal. In J. H. Harvey, W. J. Ickes, & R. F. Kidd (eds), *New directions in attribution research* (Vol. 1, pp. 389–420). Hillsdale, NJ: Erlbaum.

Jones, E. E., & Nisbett, R. E. (1972). The actor and the observer: Divergent perceptions of the causes of behavior. In E. E. Jones, D. E. Kanouse, H. H. Kelley, R. E. Nisbett, S. Valins, & B. Weiner (eds), *Attribution: Perceiving the causes of behavior* (pp. 79–94). Morristown, NJ: General Learning Press.

Jones, E. E., & Pittman, T. S. (1982). Toward a general theory of strategic self-presentation. In J. Suls (ed), *Psychological perspectives on the self* (Vol. 1, pp. 231–262). Hillsdale, NJ: Erlbaum.

Jones, J. T., Pelham, B. W., Carvallo, M., & Mirenberg, M. C. (2004). How do I love thee? Let me count the Js: Implicit egotism and interpersonal attraction. *Journal of Personality and Social Psychology, 87,* 665–683.

Jost, J. T., & Banaji, M. R. (1994). The role of stereotyping in system-justification and the production of false consciousness. *British Journal of Social Psychology, 33,* 1–27.

Jost, J., Federico, C. M., & Napier, J. L. (2009). Political ideology: Its structure, functions, and elective affinities. *Annual Review of Psychology, 60,* 307–337.

Jost, J. T., & Hunyadi, O. (2002). The psychology of system justification and the palliative function of ideology. *European Review of Social Psychology, 13*, 111–153.

Jost, J. T., Nosek, B. A., & Gosling, S. D. (2008). Ideology: Its resurgence in social, personality, and political psychology. *Perspectives on Psychological Science*, 2008, 126–136.

Jourard, S. M. (1966). An exploratory study of body-accessibility. *British Journal of Social and Clinical Psychology, 5*, 221–231.

Judge, T. A., & Bono, J. E. (2000). Five-factor model of personality and transformational leadership. *Journal of Applied Psychology, 85*, 751–765.

Judge, T. A., Bono, J. E., Ilies, R., & Gerhardt, M. W. (2002). Personality and leadership: A qualitative and quantitative review. *Journal of Applied Psychology, 87*, 765–780.

Jussim, L., & Fleming, C. (1996). Self-fulfilling prophecies and the maintenance of social stereotypes: The role of dyadic interactions and social forces. In C. N. Macrae, C. Stangor, & M. Hewstone (eds), *Stereotypes and stereotyping* (pp. 161–192). New York: Guilford Press.

K

Kanazawa, H., & Loveday, L. (1988). The Japanese immigrant community in Brazil: Language contact and shift. *Journal of Multilingual and Multicultural Development, 9*, 423–435.

Kaplan, M. F., & Miller, L. E. (1978). Reducing the effects of juror bias. *Journal of Personality and Social Psychology, 36*, 1443–1455.

Kapogiannis, D., Barbey, A. K., Su, M., Zamboni, G., et al. (2009). Cognitive and neural foundations of religious belief. *Proceedings of the Royal Academy of Sciences*, March 9. [Online: http://www.pnas.org/cgi/content/full/0811717106/DCSupplemental]

Karakashian, L. M., Walter, M. I., Christopher, A. N., & Lucas, T. (2006). Fear of negative evaluation affects helping behavior: The bystander effect revisited *North American Journal of Psychology, 8*, 13–32.

Karau, S. J., & Hart, J. W. (1998). Group cohesiveness and social loafing: Effects of a social interaction manipulation on individual motivation within groups. *Group Dynamics, 2*, 185–191.

Kassin, S. M. (1979). Consensus information, prediction and causal attribution: A review of the literature and issues. *Journal of Personality and Social Psychology, 37*, 1966–1981.

Katsikitis, M., Pilowsky, I., & Innes, J. M. (1990). The quantification of smiling using a microcomputer-based approach. *Journal of Nonverbal Behavior, 14*, 3–17.

Katz, D., & Braly, K. (1933). Racial stereotypes of one hundred college students. *Journal of Abnormal and Social Psychology, 28*, 280–290.

Kazdin, A. E., & Bryan, J. H. (1971). Competence and volunteering. *Journal of Experimental Social Psychology, 7*, 87–97.

Kellerman, A. L., Rivara, F. P., Rushforth, N. B., Banton, J. G., Reay, D. T., Francisco, J. T., et al. (1993). Gun ownership as a risk factor for homicide in the home. *New England Journal of Medicine, 329*, 1084–1091.

Kelley, H. H. (1967). Attribution theory in social psychology. In D. Levine (ed), *Nebraska symposium on motivation* (pp. 192–238). Lincoln, NE: University of Nebraska Press.

Kellstedt, P. M. (2003). *The mass media and the dynamics of American racial attitudes.* Cambridge, UK: Cambridge University Press.

Kelly, G. A. (1955). *The psychology of personal constructs.* New York: Norton.

Kelman, H. C. (1967). Human use of human subjects: The problem of deception in social psychology. *Psychological Bulletin, 67*, 1–11.

Keneally, T. (1982). *Schindler's ark.* Washington: Hemisphere Press.

Kenny, D. A., & DePaulo, B. M. (1993). Do people know how others view them? An empirical and theoretical account. *Psychological Bulletin, 114*, 145–161.

Kernis, M. H., Granneman, B. D., & Barclay, L. C. (1989). Stability and level of self-esteem as predictors of anger arousal and hostility. *Journal of Personality and Social Psychology, 56*, 1013–1022.

Kerr, J. H. (2005). *Rethinking aggression and violence in sport.* London: Routledge.

Kerr, N. L. (1978). Beautiful and blameless: Effects of victim attractiveness and responsibility on mock jurors' verdicts. *Journal of Personality and Social Psychology, 4*, 479–482.

Kerr, N. L., Niedermeier, K. E., & Kaplan, M. F. (1999). Bias in jurors vs bias in juries: New evidence from the SDS perspective. *Organizational Behavior and Human Decision Processes, 80*, 70–86.

Kerr, N. L., & Tindale, R. S. (2004). Group performance and decision making. *Annual Review of Psychology, 55*, 623–655.

Kiesler, C. A., & Kiesler, S. B. (1969). *Conformity.* Reading, MA: Addison-Wesley.

Kirkpatrick, L. A., & Hazan, C. (1994). Attachment styles and close relationships: A four-year prospective study. *Personal Relationships, 1*, 123–142.

Kitayama, S., Markus, H. R., Matsumoto, H., and Norasakkunkit, V. (1997). Individual and collective processes in the construction of the self: Self-enhancement in the United States and self-criticism in Japan. *Journal of Personality and Social Psychology, 72*, 1245–1267.

Kitayama, S., Snibbe, A. C., Markus, H. M., & Suzuki, T. (2004). Is there any 'free' choice? Self and dissonance in two cultures. *Psychological Science, 15*, 527–533.

Kite, M. E., Stockdale, G. D., Whiteley, B. E. Jr. & Johnson, B. T. (2005). Attitudes toward younger and older adults: An updated meta-analytic review. *Journal of Social Issues, 61*, 241–266.

Klandermans, B. (1997). *The social psychology of protest.* Oxford, UK: Blackwell.

Klandermans, B. (2002). How group identification helps to overcome the dilemma of collective action. *American Behavioral Scientist, 45*, 887–900.

Klein, S. B., Loftus, J., Trafton, J. G., & Fuhrman, R. W. (1992). Use of exemplars and abstractions in trait judgments: A model of trait knowledge about self and others. *Journal of Personality and Social Psychology, 63*, 739–753.

Kleinke, C. L. (1986). Gaze and eye contact: A research review. *Psychological Bulletin, 100*, 78–100.

Klohnen, E. C., & Bera, S. (1998). Behavioural and experiential patterns of avoidantly and securely attached women across adulthood: A 31-year longitudinal perspective. *Journal of Personality and Social Psychology, 74*, 211–223.

Knapp, M. L. (1978). *Nonverbal communication in human interaction* (2nd ed). New York: Holt, Rinehart & Winston.

Knapp, M. L., & Hall, J. (2005). *Nonverbal communication in human interaction* (6th ed). Belmont, CA: Wadsworth.

Knee, C. R. (1998). Implicit theories of relationships: Assessment and prediction of romantic relationship initiation, coping, and longevity. *Journal of Personality and Social Psychology, 74*, 360–370.

Knowles, E. S., & Linn, J. A. (eds). (2004). *Resistance and persuasion.* Mahwah, NJ: Erlbaum.

Korte, C. (1971). Effects of individual responsibility and group communication on help-giving in an emergency. *Human Relations, 24*, 149–159.

Krahé, B. (1996). Aggression and violence in society. In G. R. Semin & K. Fiedler (eds), *Applied social psychology* (pp. 343–373). London: Sage.

Krauss, R. M., & Chiu, C. Y. (1998). Language and social behavior. In D. T. Gilbert, S. T. Fiske & G. Lindzey (eds), *The handbook of social psychology* (4th ed, Vol. 2, pp. 41–88). New York: McGraw-Hill.

Krauss, R. M., Curran, N. M., & Ferleger, N. (1983). Expressive conventions and the cross-cultural perception of emotion. *Basic and Applied Social Psychology, 4*, 295–305.

Krebs, D. L. (1975). Empathy and altruism. *Journal of Personality and Social Psychology, 32*, 1134–1146.

Krosnick, J. A., & Alwin, D. F. (1989). Attitude and susceptibility to attitude change. *Journal of Personality and Social Psychology, 57*, 416–425.

Kruger, J., & Dunning, D. (1999). Unskilled and unaware of it: How difficulties in recognizing one's own incompetence lead to inflated self-assessments. *Journal of Personality and Social Psychology, 77*, 1121–1134.

Kulik, J. A., Mahler, H. I. M., & Moore, P. J. (1996). Social comparison and affiliation under threat: Effects on recovery from major surgery. *Journal of Personality and Social Psychology, 71*, 967–979.

Kunda, Z. (1990). The case for motivated reasoning. *Psychological Bulletin, 108*, 480–498.

Kurdeck, L. A. (1999). The nature and predictors of the trajectory of change in marital quality for husbands and wives over the first 10 years of marriage. *Developmental Psychology, 35*, 1283–1296.

L

LaFrance, M., Hecht, M. A., & Paluck, E. L. (2003). The contingent smile: A meta-analysis of sex differences in smiling. *Psychological Bulletin, 129*, 305–334.

LaFrance, M., & Mayo, C. (1976). Racial differences in gaze behavior during conversations: Two systematic observational studies. *Journal of Personality and Social Psychology, 33*, 547–552.

Lamm, H., & Kayser, E. (1978). The allocation of monetary gain and loss following dyadic performance: The weight given effort and ability under conditions of low and high intradyadic attraction. *European Journal of Social Psychology, 8*, 275–278.

Landy, D., & Sigall, H. (1974). Beauty is talent: Task evaluation as a function of the performer's physical attractiveness. *Journal of Personality and Social Psychology, 29*, 299–304.

Langer, E. J. (1975). The illusion of control. *Journal of Personality and Social Psychology, 32*, 311–328.

Langer, E. J., Bashner, R. S., & Chanowitz, B. (1985). Decreasing prejudice by increasing discrimination. *Journal of Personality and Social Psychology, 49*, 113–120.

Langlois, J. H., Kalakanis, L., Rubenstein, A. J., Larson, A., Hallam M., & Smoot, M. (2000). Maxims or myths of beauty? A meta-analytic and theoretical review. *Psychological Bulletin, 126*, 390–423.

Langlois, J. H., Roggman, L. A., & Musselman, L. (1994). What is average and what is not average about attractive faces? *Psychological Science, 5*, 214–220.

LaPiere, R. T. (1934). Attitudes vs actions. *Social Forces, 13*, 230–237.

LaPiere, R. T., & Farnsworth, P. R. (1949). *Social psychology* (3rd ed). New York: McGraw-Hill.

Latané, B., & Dabbs, J. M. Jr (1975). Sex, group size and helping in three cities. *Sociometry, 38*, 180–194.

Latané, B., & Darley, J. M. (1970). *The unresponsive bystander: Why doesn't he help?* New York: Appleton-Century-Crofts.

Latané, B., & Darley, J. M. (1976). Help in a crisis: Bystander response to an emergency. In J. W. Thibaut & J. T. Spence (eds), *Contemporary topics in social psychology* (pp. 309–332). Morristown, NJ: General Learning Press.

Latané, B., & Rodin, J. (1969). A lady in distress: Inhibiting effects of friends and strangers on bystander intervention. *Journal of Experimental Social Psychology, 5*, 189–202.

Latané, B., Williams, K. D., & Harkins, S. G. (1979). Many hands make light the work: The causes and consequences of social loafing. *Journal of Personality and Social Psychology, 37*, 822–832.

Latané, B., & Wolf, S. (1981). The social impact of majorities and minorities. *Psychological Review, 88*, 438–453.

Latin American Bureau (1982). *Falklands/ Malvinas: Whose crisis?* London: Latin American Bureau.

Lawrence, C., & Andrews, K. (2004). The influence of perceived prison crowding on male inmates' perception of aggressive events. *Aggressive Behavior, 30*, 273–283.

Le, B., & Agnew, C. R. (2003). Commitment and its theorized determinants: A meta-analysis of the investment model. *Personal Relationships, 10*, 37–57.

Leary, M. R. (1995). *Self-presentation: Impression management and interpersonal behavior.* Madison, WI: Brown & Benchmark.

Leary, M. R., Tambor, E. S., Terdal, S. K., & Downs, D. L. (1995). Self-esteem as an interpersonal monitor: The sociometer hypothesis. *Journal of Personality and Social Psychology, 68*, 518–530.

Leary, M. R., & Tangney, J. P. (2003). *Handbook of self and identity.* New York: Guilford.

LeBon, G. (1908). *The crowd: A study of the popular mind.* London: Unwin (original work published 1896). Online: http://cupid.ecom.unimelb.edu.au/ het/lebon/ crowds.pdf

Lehman, D. R., Chiu, C.-Y., & Schaller, M. (2004). Psychology and culture. *Annual Review of Psychology, 55*, 689–714.

Lemaine, G. (1974). Social differentiation and social originality. *European Journal of Social Psychology, 4*, 17–52.

Lepper, M. R., Greene, D., & Nisbett, R. E. (1973). Undermining children's intrinsic interest with extrinsic reward: A test of the over-justification hypothesis. *Journal of Personality and Social Psychology, 28*, 129–137.

Lerner, M. J., & Miller, D. T. (1978). Just-world research and the attribution process: Looking back and ahead. *Psychological Bulletin, 85,* 1030–1051.

Lesar, T. S., Briceland, L., & Stein, D. S. (1997). Factors related to errors in medication prescribing. *Journal of the American Medical Association, 277,* 312–317.

Leventhal, H., Singer, R., & Jones, S. (1965). Effects of fear and specificity of recommendations upon attitudes and behavior. *Journal of Personality and Social Psychology, 2,* 20–29.

Levine, J. M., & Moreland, R. L. (1994). Group socialization: Theory and research. *European Review of Social Psychology, 5,* 305–336.

Levinger, G. (1980). Toward the analysis of close relationships. *Journal of Experimental Social Psychology, 16,* 510–544.

Lévy-Bruhl, L. (1925). *How natives think.* New York: Alfred A. Knopf.

Lewin, K. (1951). *Field theory in social science.* New York: Harper.

Lewin, K., Lippitt, R., & White, R. K. (1939). Patterns of aggressive behavior in experimentally created 'social climates'. *Journal of Social Psychology, 10,* 271–299.

Lewis, B. (2004). *The crisis of Islam: Holy war and unholy terror.* London: Phoenix.

Leyens, J.-P., Camino, L., Parke, R. D., & Berkowitz, L. (1975). Effects of movie violence on aggression in a field setting as a function of group dominance and cohesion. *Journal of Personality and Social Psychology, 32,* 346–360.

Lieberman, M. D., Gaunt, R., Gilbert, D. T., & Trope, Y. (2002). Reflexion and reflection: A social cognitive neuroscience approach to attributional inference. In M. P. Zanna (ed), *Advances in experimental social psychology* (Vol. 34, pp. 199–249). San Diego, CA: Academic Press.

Lim, R. G., & Carnevale, P. J. D. (1990). Contingencies in the mediation of disputes. *Journal of Personality and Social Psychology, 58,* 259–272.

Linville, P. W. (1985). Self-complexity and affective extremity: Don't put all of your eggs in one cognitive basket. *Social Cognition, 3,* 94–120.

Linz, D. G., Donnerstein, E., & Penrod, S. (1988). Effects of long-term exposure to violent and sexually degrading depictions of women. *Journal of Personality and Social Psychology, 55,* 758–768.

Linz, D., Wilson, B. J., & Donnerstein, E. (1992). Sexual violence in the mass media: Legal solutions, warnings, and mitigation through education. *Journal of Social Issues, 48,* 145–171.

Liu, J. H., Campbell, S. M., & Condie, H. (1995). Ethnocentrism in dating preferences for an American sample: The ingroup bias in social context. *European Journal of Social Psychology, 25,* 95–115.

Liu, T. J., & Steele, C. M. (1986). Attributional analysis and self-affirmation. *Journal of Personality and Social Psychology, 51,* 531–540.

Lockard, J. S., Kirkevold, B. C., & Kalk, D. F. (1980). Cost–benefit indexes of deception in nonviolent crime. *Bulletin of the Psychonomic Society, 16,* 303–306.

Lockwood, P., Jordan, C. H., & Kunda, Z. (2002). Motivation by positive or negative role models: Regulatory focus determines who will best inspire us. *Journal of Personality and Social Psychology, 83,* 854–864.

Lonner, W. J. (ed) (1984). Differing views on 'culture.' *Journal of Cross-Cultural Psychology, 15,* 107–109.

Lord, R. G., & Brown, D. J. (2004). *Leadership processes and follower identity.* Mahwah, NJ: Erlbaum.

Lorenz, K. (1966). *On aggression.* New York: Harcourt, Brace and World.

Lorenzi-Cioldi, F., & Clémence, A. (2001). Group processes and the construction of social representations. In M. A. Hogg & R. S. Tindale (eds), *Blackwell handbook of social psychology: Group processes* (pp. 311–333). Oxford, UK: Blackwell.

Lorge, I., & Solomon, H. (1955). Two models of group behavior in the solution of eureka-type problems. *Psychometrika, 20,* 139–148.

Lott, A. J., & Lott, B. E. (1965). Group cohesiveness as interpersonal attraction. *Psychological Bulletin, 64,* 259–309.

Lueger, R. J. (1980). Person and situation factors influencing transgression in behavior-problem adolescents. *Journal of Abnormal Psychology, 89,* 453–458.

M

Maass, A. (1999). Linguistic intergroup bias: Stereotype-perpetuation through language. In M. P. Zanna (ed), *Advances in experimental social psychology* (Vol. 31, pp. 79–121). San Diego, CA: Academic Press.

Maass, A., & Clark, R. D., III (1983). Internalisation versus compliance: Differential processes underlying minority influence and conformity. *European Journal of Social Psychology, 13*, 197–215.

Maass, A., Clark, R. D., III and Haberkorn, G. (1982). The effects of differential ascribed category membership and norms on minority influence. *European Journal of Social Psychology, 12*, 89–104.

Mackie, D. M. (1986). Social identification effects in group polarization. *Journal of Personality and Social Psychology, 50*, 720–728.

Mackie, D. M., & Worth, L. T. (1989). Processing deficits and the mediation of positive affect in persuasion. *Journal of Personality and Social Psychology, 57*, 27–40.

MacNeil, M., & Sherif, M. (1976). Norm change over subject generations as a function of arbitrariness of prescribed norms. *Journal of Personality and Social Psychology, 34*, 762–773.

Maio, G., & Haddock, G. (in press). *The science of attitudes*. London: Sage.

Major, B., & Adams, J. B. (1983). Role of gender, interpersonal orientation, and self-presentation in distributive justice behaviour. *Journal of Personality and Social Psychology, 45*, 598–608.

Malamuth, N. M. (1981). Rape proclivity among males. *Journal of Social Issues, 37*, 138–157.

Malamuth, N. M., & Donnerstein, E. (1982). The effects of aggressive-pornographic mass media stimuli. In L. Berkowitz (ed), *Advances in experimental social psychology* (Vol. 15, pp. 104–136). New York: Academic Press.

Malkin, P. Z., & Stein, H. (1990). *Eichmann in my hands*: New York: Warner Books.

Mandela, N. (1994). *The long walk to freedom: The autobiography of Nelson Mandela*. London: Little, Brown.

Maner, J. K., Luce, C. L., Neuberg, S. L., Cialdini, R. B., Brown, S., & Sagarin, B. J. (2002). The effects of perspective taking on motivations for helping: Still no evidence for altruism. *Personality and Social Psychology Bulletin, 28*, 1601–1610.

Mann, L. (1981). The baiting crowd in episodes of threatened suicide. *Journal of Personality and Social Psychology, 41*, 703–709.

Marks, G., & Miller, N. (1987). Ten years of research on the false-consensus effect: An empirical and theoretical review. *Psychological Bulletin, 102*, 72–90.

Markus, H. (1977). Self-schemata and processing information about the self. *Journal of Personality and Social Psychology, 35*, 63–78.

Markus, H., & Kitayama, S. (1991). Culture and the self: Implications for cognition, emotion, and motivation. *Psychological Review, 98*, 224–253.

Markus, H., Kitayama, S., & Heiman, R. J. (1996). Culture and basic psychological principles. In E. T. Higgins & A. W. Kruglanski (eds), *Social psychology: Handbook of basic principles* (pp. 857–914). New York: Guilford.

Markus, H., & Nurius, P. (1986). Possible selves. *American Psychologist, 41*, 954–969.

Markus, H., & Wurf, E. (1987). The dynamic self-concept: A social-psychological perspective. *Annual Review of Psychology, 38*, 299–337.

Marlowe, F., & Wetsman, A. (2001). Preferred waist-to-hip ratio and ecology. *Personality and Individual Differences, 30*, 481–489.

Marques, J. M., Abrams, D., & Serodio, R. (2001). Being better by being right: Subjective group dynamics and derogation of in-group deviants when generic norms are undermined *Journal of Personality and Social Psychology, 81*, 436–447.

Marques, J. M., & Páez, D. (1994). The 'black sheep effect': Social categorisation, rejection of ingroup deviates and perception of group variability. *European Review of Social Psychology, 5*, 37–68.

Marrow, A. J. (1969). *The practical theorist: The life and work of Kurt Lewin*. New York: Basic Books.

Marsh, P., Russer, E., & Harré, R. (1978). *The rules of disorder*. Milton Keynes, UK: Open University Press.

Martin, R. (1987). Influence minorité et relations entre groupe. In S. Moscovici & G. Mugny (eds), *Psychologie de la conversion*. Paris: Cossett de Val.

Martin, R., & Hewstone, M. (2003). Social influence processes of control and change: Conformity, obedience to authority, and innovation. In M. A. Hogg & J. Cooper (eds), *The Sage handbook of social psychology* (pp. 347–366). London: Sage.

Martz, J. M., Verette, J., Arriaga, X. B., Slovic, L. F., Cox, C. L., & Rusbult, C. E. (1998). Positive illusion in close relationships. *Personal Relationships, 5*, 159–181.

Masuda, T., & Nisbett, R. E. (2001). Attending holistically versus analytically: Comparing the context sensitivity of Japanese and Americans. *Journal of Personality and Social Psychology, 81*, 922–934.

Matsui, T., Kakuyama, T., & Onglatco, M. L. (1987). Effects of goals and feedback on performance in groups. *Journal of Applied Psychology, 72*, 407–415.

McArthur, L. A. (1972). The how and what of why: Some determinants of consequences of causal attributions. *Journal of Personality and Social Psychology, 22*, 171–193.

McCabe, D. L., Trevino, L. K., & Butterfield, K. D. (2001). Cheating in academic institutions: A decade of research. *Ethics & Behavior, 11*, 219–232.

McConahay, J. G. (1986). Modern racism, ambivalence, and the modern racism scale. In J. F. Dovidio & S. L. Gaertner (eds), *Prejudice, discrimination, and racism* (pp. 91–125). New York: Academic Press.

McDougall, W. (1908). *An introduction to social psychology*. London: Methuen.

McDougall, W. (1920). *The group mind*. London: Cambridge University Press.

McGuire, W. J. (1969). The nature of attitudes and attitude change. In G. Lindzey & E. Aronson (eds), *Handbook of social psychology* (2nd ed, Vol. 3, pp. 136–314). Reading, MA: Addison-Wesley.

McGuire, W. J., & Papageorgis, D. (1961). The relative efficacy of various types of prior belief-defence in producing immunity against persuasion. *Journal of Abnormal and Social Psychology, 62*, 327–337.

Mead, G. H. (1934). *Mind, self and society*. Chicago: University of Chicago Press.

Mead, M. (1928/1961). *Coming of age in Samoa*. New York: Morrow.

Mead, M. (1930/1962). *Growing up in New Guinea*. New York: Morrow.

Medvec, V. H., Madley, S. F., & Gilovich, T. (1995). When less is more: Counterfactual thinking and satisfaction among Olympic medalists. *Journal of Personality and Social Psychology, 69*, 603–610.

Mellen, S. L. W. (1981). *The evolution of love*. Oxford, UK: W. H. Freeman.

Messick, D. M. (2005). On the psychological exchange between leaders and followers. In

D. M. Messick & R. M. Kramer (eds), *The psychology of leadership: New perspectives and research* (pp. 81–96). Mahwah, NJ: Erlbaum.

Michelini, R. L., & Snodgrass, S. R. (1980). Defendant characteristics and juridic decisions. *Journal of Research in Personality, 14*, 340–350.

Middleton, D., & edwards, D. (eds) (1990). *Collective remembering*. London: Sage.

Midlarsky, M., & Midlarsky, E. (1976). Status inconsistency, aggressive attitude, and helping behavior. *Journal of Personality, 44*, 371–391.

Mikulincer, M., & Goodman, G. S. (eds). (2006). *Dynamics of romantic love: Attachment, caregiving, and sex*. New York: Guilford.

Mikulincer, M., & Shaver, P. (2005). Attachment security, compassion, and altruism. *Current Directions in Psychological Science, 14*, 34–38.

Milardo, R. M., Johnson, M. P., & Huston, T. L. (1983). Developing close relationships: Changing patterns of interaction between pair members and social networks. *Journal of Personality and Social Psychology, 44*, 964–976.

Milgram, S. (1963). Behavioral study of obedience. *Journal of Abnormal and Social Psychology, 67*, 371–378.

Milgram, S. (1974). *Obedience to authority*. London: Tavistock.

Milgram, S. (1992). *The individual in a social world: Essays and experiments* (2nd ed). New York: McGraw-Hill.

Miller, C. E. (1989). The social psychological effects of group decision rules. In P. B. Paulus (ed), *Psychology of group influence* (2nd ed, pp. 327–355). Hillsdale, NJ: Erlbaum.

Miller, D. T. (1977). Altruism and the threat to a belief in a just world. *Journal of Experimental Social Psychology, 13*, 113–124.

Miller, D. T., & McFarland, C. (1987). Pluralistic ignorance: When similarity is interpreted as dissimilarity. *Journal of Personality and Social Psychology, 53*, 298–305.

Miller, D. T., & Porter, C. A. (1983). Self-blame in victims or violence. *Journal of Social Issues, 39*, 139–152.

Miller, D. T., & Ross, M. (1975). Self-serving biases in the attribution of causality: Fact or fiction? *Psychological Bulletin, 82*, 213–225.

Miller, J. G. (1984). Culture and the development of everyday social explanation. *Journal of Personality and Social Psychology, 46*, 961–978.

Miller, N., Maruyama, G., Beaber, R. J., & Valone, K. (1976). Speed of speech and persuasion. *Journal of Personality and Social Psychology, 34*, 615–625.

Mita, T. H., Dermer, M., & Knight, J. (1977). Reversed facial images and the mere exposure hypothesis. *Journal of Personality and Social Psychology, 35*, 597–601.

Moghaddam, F. M. (1998). *Social psychology: Exploring universals across cultures*. New York: Freeman.

Moreland, R. L., Argote, L., & Krishnan, R. (1996). Socially shared cognition at work: Transactive memory and group performance. In J. L. Nye & A. M. Bower (eds), *What's social about social cognition: Research on socially shared cognition in small groups* (pp. 57–84). Thousand Oaks, CA: Sage.

Moreland, R. L., & Beach, S. R. (1992). Exposure effects in the classroom: The development of affinity among students. *Journal of Experimental Social Psychology, 28*, 255–276.

Moreland, R. L., & Levine, J. M. (1982). Socialization in small groups: Temporal changes in individual–group relations. In L. Berkowitz (ed), *Advances in experimental social psychology* (Vol. 15, pp. 137–192). New York: Academic Press.

Moriarty, T. (1975). Crime, commitment and the responsive bystander: Two field experiments. *Journal of Personality and Social Psychology, 31*, 370–376.

Morley, I. E., & Stephenson, G. M. (1977). *The social psychology of bargaining*. London: Allen and Unwin.

Morley, I. E., Webb, J., & Stephenson, G. M. (1988) Bargaining and arbitration in the resolution of conflict. In W. Stroebe, A. W. Kruglanski, D. Bar-Tal & M. Hewstone (eds), *The social psychology of intergroup conflict: Theory, research and applications* (pp. 117–134). Berlin: Springer-Verlag.

Morris, D. (1967). *The naked ape*. New York: McGraw-Hill.

Morris, M. W., & Peng, K. P. (1994). Culture and cause: American and Chinese attributions for social and physical events. *Journal of Personality and Social Psychology, 67*, 949–971.

Moscovici, S. (1961). *La psychanalyse: Son image et son public*. Paris: Presses Universitaires de France.

Moscovici, S. (1972). Society and theory in social psychology. In J. Israel & H. Tajfel (eds), *The context of social psychology: A critical assessment* (pp. 17–68). New York: Academic Press.

Moscovici, S. (1980). Toward a theory of conversion behavior. In L. Berkowitz (ed), *Advances in experimental social psychology* (Vol. 13, pp. 202–239). New York: Academic Press.

Moscovici, S. (1982). The coming era of representations. In J.-P. Codol & J. P. Leyens (eds), *Cognitive analysis of social behaviour* (pp. 115–150). The Hague: Martinus Nijhoff.

Moscovici, S. (1988). Notes towards a description of social representations. *European Journal of Social Psychology, 18*, 211–250.

Moscovici, S., & Faucheux, C. (1972). Social influence, conforming bias, and the study of active minorities. In L. Berkowitz (ed), *Advances in experimental social psychology* (Vol. 6, pp. 149–202). New York: Academic Press.

Moscovici, S., & Lage, E. (1976). Studies in social influence: III. Majority vs. minority influence in a group. *European Journal of Social Psychology, 6*, 149–174.

Moscovici, S., Lage, E., & Naffrechoux, M. (1969). Influence of a consistent minority on the responses of a majority in a colour perception task. *Sociometry, 32*, 365–380.

Moscovici, S., & Zavalloni, M. (1969). The group as a polarizer of attitudes. *Journal of Personality and Social Psychology, 12*, 125–135.

Moskowitz, G. B. (2005). *Social cognition: Understanding self and others*. New York: Guilford.

Mucchi-Faina, A., Maass, A., & Volpato, C. (1991). Social influence: The role of originality. *European Journal of Social Psychology, 21*, 183–197.

Mudrack, P. E. (1989). Defining group cohesiveness: A legacy of confusion. *Small Group Behavior, 20*, 37–49.

Mugny, G., & Pérez, J. A. (1991). *The social psychology of minority influence*. Cambridge, UK: Cambridge University Press.

Mullen, B., & Copper, C. (1994). The relation between group cohesiveness and performance: An integration. *Psychological Bulletin, 115*, 210–227.

Mummendey, A., Klink, A., Mielke, R., Wenzel, M., & Blanz, M. (1999). Socio-structural characteristics of intergroup relations and identity management strategies: Results from a field study in East Germany. *European Journal of Social Psychology, 29,* 259–286.

Murphy, G., & Murphy, L. B. (1931). *Experimental social psychology.* New York: Harper (rev. ed published with T. M. Newcomb in 1937).

Murray, S. L., & Holmes, J. G. (1997). A leap of faith? Positive illusions in romantic relationships. *Personality and Social Psychology Bulletin, 23,* 586–604.

Murray, S. L., & Holmes, J. G. (1999). The mental ties that bind: Cognitive structures that predict relationship resilience. *Journal of Personality and Social Psychology, 77,* 1228–1244.

Murray, S. L., Holmes, J. G., & Griffin, D. W. (1996). The self-fulfilling nature of positive illusions in romantic relationships: Love is not blind, but prescient. *Journal of Personality and Social Psychology, 71,* 1155–1180.

Murray, S. L., Holmes, J. G., & Griffin, D. W. (2003). Reflections on the self-fulfilling effects of positive illusions. *Psychological Inquiry, 14,* 289–295.

Murstein, B. I. (1980). Love at first sight: A myth. *Medical Aspects of Human Sexuality, 14* (34), 39–41.

N

Nemeth, C. (1986). Differential contributions of majority and minority influence. *Psychological Review, 93,* 23–32.

Neuberg, S. L., & Fiske, S. T. (1987). Motivational influences on impression formation: Outcome dependency, accuracy-driven attention, and individuating processes. *Journal of Personality and Social Psychology, 53,* 431–444.

Newcomb, T. M. (1961). *The acquaintance process.* New York: Holt, Rinehart & Winston.

Newcomb, T. M. (1965). Attitude development as a function of reference groups: The Bennington study. In H. Proshansky & B. Seidenberg (eds), *Basic studies in social psychology* (pp. 215–225). New York: Holt, Rinehart & Winston.

Nisbett, R. E., & Cohen, D. (1996). *Culture of honor: The psychology of violence in the South.* Boulder, CO: Westview Press.

Nisbett, R. E., Krantz, D. H., Jepson, C., & Fong, G. T. (1982). Improving inductive inference. In D. Kahneman, P. Slovic & A. Tversky (eds), *Judgment under uncertainty: Heuristics and biases* (pp. 445–462). New York: Cambridge University Press.

Nisbett, R. E., & Ross, L. (1980). *Human inference: Strategies and shortcomings of social judgment.* Englewood Cliffs, NJ: Prentice Hall.

Nisbett, R. E., & Wilson, T. D. (1977). Telling more than we can know: Verbal reports on mental behavior. *Psychological Review, 84,* 231–259.

Noels, K. A., Giles, H., & Le Poire, B. (2003). Language and communication processes. In M. A. Hogg & J. Cooper (eds), *The Sage handbook of social psychology* (pp. 232–257). London: Sage.

Noels, K. A., Pon, G., & Clément, R. (1996). Language and adjustment: The role of linguistic self-confidence in the acculturation process. *Journal of Language and Social Psychology, 15,* 246–264.

Northouse, P. G. (2007). *Leadership: Theory and practice* (4th ed). Thousand Oaks, CA: Sage.

O

Oakes, P. J., Haslam, S. A., & Turner, J. C. (1994). *Stereotyping and social reality.* Oxford, UK: Blackwell.

Oakes, P. J., & Turner, J. C. (1990). Is limited information processing capacity the cause of social stereotyping? *European Review of Social Psychology, 1,* 111–135.

Oddone-Paolucci, E., Genuis, M., & Violato, C. (2000). A meta-analysis of the published research on the effects of pornography. In C. Violato, E. Oddone-Paolucci & M. Genuis (eds), *The changing family and child development* (pp. 48–59). Aldershot, UK: Ashgate.

Olson, J. M. (1988). Misattribution, preparatory information, and speech anxiety. *Journal of Personality and Social Psychology, 54,* 758–767.

Omoto, A. M., & Snyder, M. (2002). Considerations of community: The context and process of volunteerism. *American Behavioral Scientist, 45,* 846–867.

Orne, M. T. (1962). On the social psychology of the psychology experiment: With particular reference to demand characteristics and their implications.

American Psychologist, 17, 776–783.

Osborn, A. F. (1957). *Applied imagination* (rev. ed). New York: Charles Scribner's Sons.

Oskamp, S. (1977). *Attitudes and opinions.* Englewood Cliffs, NJ: Prentice Hall.

Overall, N. C., Fletcher, G. J. O., & Simpson, J. A. (2006). Regulation processes in intimate relationships: The role of ideal standards. *Journal of Personality and Social Psychology, 91,* 662–685.

P

Paluck, E. L., & Green, D. P. (2009). Prejudice reduction: What works? A review and assessment of research and practice. *Annual Review of Psychology, 60,* 339–360.

Pandey, J., Sinha, Y., Prakash, A., & Tripathi, R. C. (1982). Right–left political ideologies and attribution of the causes of poverty. *European Journal of Social Psychology, 12,* 327–331.

Pantin, H. M., & Carver, C. S. (1982). Induced competence and the bystander effect. *Journal of Applied Social Psychology, 12,* 100–111.

Parducci, A. (1968). The relativism of absolute judgments. *Scientific American, 219,* 84–90.

Park, B. (1986). A method for studying the development of impressions of real people. *Journal of Personality and Social Psychology, 51,* 907–917.

Parkinson, B. (1985). Emotional effects of false autonomic feedback. *Psychological Bulletin, 98,* 471–494.

Patch, M. E. (1986). The role of source legitimacy in sequential request strategies of compliance. *Personality and Social Psychology Bulletin, 12,* 199–205.

Patterson, M. L. (1983). *Nonverbal behavior: A functional perspective.* New York: Springer.

Paulhus, D. L., & Levitt, K. (1987). Desirable responding triggered by affect: Automatic egotism. *Journal of Personality and Social Psychology, 52,* 245–259.

Paulus, P. B., Dzindolet, M. T., Poletes, G., & Camacho, L. M. (1993). Perception of performance in group brainstorming: The illusion of group productivity. *Personality and Social Psychology Bulletin, 19,* 78–89.

Pei, M. (1965). *The story of language* (2nd ed). Philadelphia, PA: Lippincott.

Peng, K., & Nisbett, R. E. (1999). Culture, dialectics, and reasoning about contradiction. *American Psychologist, 54,* 741–754.

Pennebaker, J. W. (1997). Writing about emotional experiences as a therapeutic process. *Psychological Science, 8,* 162–166.

Penner, L. A., Dovidio, J. F., Piliavin, J. A., & Schroeder, D. A. (2005). Prosocial behavior: Multilevel perspectives. *Annual Review of Psychology, 56,* 365–392.

Peplau, L. A., & Fingerhut, A. W. (2007). The close relationships of lesbians and gay men. *Annual Review of Psychology, 58,* 400–424.

Perry, D. G., Perry, L., Bussey, K., English, D., & Arnold, G. (1980). Processes of attribution and children's self-punishment following misbehaviour. *Child Development, 51,* 545–551.

Pettigrew, T. F. (1979). The ultimate attribution error: Extending Allport's cognitive analysis of prejudice. *Personality and Social Psychology Bulletin, 5,* 461–476.

Pettigrew, T. F. (1998). Intergroup contact theory. *Annual Review of Psychology, 49,* 65–85.

Pettigrew, T. F., & Meertens, R. W. (1995). Subtle and blatant prejudice in Western Europe. *European Journal of Social Psychology, 25,* 57–75.

Pettigrew, T. F., & Tropp, L. R. (2006). A meta-analytic test of intergroup contact theory. *Journal of Personality and Social Psychology, 90,* 751-783.

Petty, R. E., & Cacioppo, J. T. (1986). The elaboration likelihood model of persuasion. In L. Berkowitz (ed), *Advances in experimental social psychology* (Vol. 19, pp. 123–205). New York: Academic Press.

Petty, R. E., & Wegener, D. (1998) Attitude change: Multiple roles for persuasion variables. In D. T. Gilbert, S. T. Fiske & G. Lindzey (eds) *The handbook of social psychology* (4th ed, Vol. 2, pp. 323–390). New York: McGraw-Hill.

Phillips, D. P. (1986). Natural experiments on the effects of mass media violence on fatal aggression: Strengths and weaknesses of a new approach. In L. Berkowitz (ed), *Advances in experimental social psychology* (Vol. 19, pp. 207–250). New York: Academic Press.

Piliavin, J. A., Piliavin, I. M., Dovidio, J. F., Gaertner, S. L., & Clark, R. D., III (1981). *Emergency intervention.* New York: Academic Press.

Pittinsky, T. L., & Simon, S. (2007). Intergroup leadership. *Leadership Quarterly, 18,* 586–605.

Plous, S., & Williams, T. (1995). Racial stereotypes from the days of American slavery: A continuing legacy. *Journal of Applied Social Psychology, 25,* 795–817.

Potter, J., Stringer, P., & Wetherell, M. S. (1984). *Social texts and context: Literature and social psychology.* London: Routledge and Kegan Paul.

Potter, J., & Wetherell, M. S. (1987). *Discourse and social psychology: Beyond attitudes and behaviour.* London: Sage.

Powell, M. C., & Fazio, R. M. (1984). Attitude accessibility as a function of repeated attitudinal expression. *Personality and Social Psychology Bulletin, 10,* 139–148.

Pratto, F., Sidanius, J., & Levin, S. (2006). Social dominance theory and the dynamics of intergroup relations: Taking stock and looking forward. *European Review of Social Psychology, 17,* 271–320.

Pruitt, D. G. 1998). Social conflict. In D. T. Gilbert, S. T. Fiske & G. Lindzey (eds), *The handbook of social psychology* (4th ed, Vol. 2, pp. 470–503). New York: McGraw-Hill.

Przybyla, D. P. (1986). The effects of exposure to erotica on prosocial behavior. *Dissertation Abstracts International. B, The Sciences and Engineering* [0419–4217], 46 (11-B), 4067.

R

Rabbie, J. M., & Horwitz, M. (1969). Arousal of ingroup–outgroup bias by a chance win or loss. *Journal of Personality and Social Psychology, 13,* 269–277.

Ramirez, J., Bryant, J., & Zillman, D. (1983). Effects of erotica on retaliatory behavior as a function of level of prior provocation. *Journal of Personality and Social Psychology, 43,* 971–978.

Regan, D. T., & Fazio, R. H. (1977). On the consistency of attitudes and behavior: Look to the method of attitude formation. *Journal of Experimental Social Psychology, 13,* 38–45.

Regan, J. (1971). Guilt, perceived injustice, and altruistic behaviour. *Journal of Personality and Social Psychology, 18,* 124–132.

Regan, P. C., & Berscheid, E. (1999). *Lust: What we know about human sexual desire.* Thousand Oaks, CA: Sage.

Regoeczi, W. C. (2003). When context matters: A multilevel analysis of household and neighbourhood crowding on aggression and withdrawal. *Journal of Environmental Psychology, 23,* 457–470.

Reicher, S. D., & Haslam, S. A. (2006). Rethinking the psychology of tyranny: The BBC prison study. *British Journal of Social Psychology, 45,* 1–40.

Reicher, S. D., & Potter, J. (1985). Psychological theory as intergroup perspective: A comparative analysis of 'scientific' and 'lay' accounts of crowd events. *Human Relations, 38,* 167–189.

Reisenzein, R. (1983). The Schachter theory of emotion: Two decades later. *Psychological Bulletin, 94,* 239–264.

Rhodes, G. (2006). The evolutionary psychology of facial beauty. *Annual Review of Psychology, 57,* 199–226.

Rhodes, G., Hickford, C., & Jeffrey, L. (2000). Sex-typicality and attractiveness: Are supermale and superfemale faces super-attractive? *British Journal of Psychology, 91,* 125–140.

Rhodes, G., Sumich, A., & Byatt, G. (1999). Are average facial configurations attractive only because of their symmetry? *Psychological Science, 10,* 52–58.

Rhodes, G., & Tremewan, T. (1996). Averageness, exaggeration, and facial attractiveness. *Psychological Science, 2,* 105–110.

Rhodewalt, F., Madrian, J. C., & Cheney, S. (1998). Narcissism, self-knowledge, organization, and emotional reactivity: The effects of daily experiences on self-esteem and affect. *Personality and Social Psychology Bulletin, 24,* 75–86.

Rholes, W. S., & Pryor, J. B. (1982). Cognitive accessibility and causal attributions. *Personality and Social Psychology Bulletin, 8,* 719–727.

Rholes, W. S., & Simpson, J. A. (2004). *Adult attachment: Theory, research, and clinical implications.* New York: Guilford.

Rholes, W. S., Simpson, J. A., & Blakely, B. S. (1995). Adult attachment styles and mothers' relationships with their young children. *Personal Relationships, 2,* 35–54.

Rholes, W. S., Simpson, J. A., & Friedman, M. (2006). Avoidant attachment and the experience of parenting. *Personality and Social Psychology Bulletin, 32,* 275–285.

Rice, M. E., & Grusec, J. E. (1975). Saying and doing: Effects on observer performance. *Journal of Personality and Social Psychology, 32,* 584–593.

Ridgeway, C. L. (2001). Social status and group structure. In M. A. Hogg & R. S. Tindale (eds), *Blackwell handbook of social psychology: Group processes* (pp. 352–375). Oxford, UK: Blackwell.

Riggio, H. R. (2004). Parental marital conflict and divorce, parent-child relationships, social support, and relationship anxiety in young adulthood. *Personal Relationships, 11,* 99–114.

Riggio, R. E., & Carney, D. R. (2003). *Social skills inventory manual* (2nd ed). Redwood City, CA: MindGarden.

Rogers, W. S. (2003). *Social psychology: Experimental and critical approaches.* Maidenhead, UK: Open University Press.

Rosch, E. (1978). Principles of categorization. In E. Rosch and B. B. Lloyd (eds), *Cognition and categorization* (pp. 27–48). Hillsdale, NJ: Erlbaum.

Rosenberg, M. J., & Hovland, C. I. (1960). Cognitive, affective, and behavioral components of attitude. In M. J. Rosenberg, C. I. Hovland, W. J. McGuire, R. P. Abelson, & J. W. Brehm (eds), *Attitude organization and change: An analysis of consistency among attitude components.* New Haven, CT: Yale University Press.

Rosenfield, D., Greenberg, J., Folger, R., & Borys, R. (1982). Effect of an encounter with a Black panhandler on subsequent helping for Blacks: Tokenism or conforming to a negative stereotype? *Personality and Social Psychology Bulletin, 8,* 664–671.

Rosenthal, R., Hall, J. A., DiMatteo, M. R., Rogers, P. L., & Archer, D. (1979). *Sensitivity to nonverbal communication: The PONS test.* Baltimore: Johns Hopkins University Press.

Rosenthal, R., & Jacobson, L. F. (1968). *Pygmalion in the classroom.* New York: Holt, Rinehart & Winston.

Rosenthal, R., & Rubin, D. B. (1978). Interpersonal expectancy effects: The first 345 studies. *Behavioral and Brain Sciences, 3,* 377–386.

Rosnow, R. L. (1980). Psychology of rumour reconsidered *Psychological Bulletin, 87,* 578–591.

Rosnow, R. L., & Rosenthal, R. (1997). *People studying people: Artifacts and ethics in behavioural research.* New York: Freeman.

Ross, E. A. (1908). *Social psychology.* New York: Macmillan.

Ross, L. (1977). The intuitive psychologist and his shortcomings. In L. Berkowitz (ed), *Advances in experimental social psychology* (Vol. 10, pp. 174–220). New York: Academic Press.

Ross, L., Greene, D., & House, P. (1977). The 'false consensus effect': An egocentric bias in social perception and attribution processes. *Journal of Experimental Social Psychology, 13,* 279–301.

Ross, L., Lepper, M. R., & Hubbard, M. (1975). Perseverance in self-perception and social perception: Biased attribution processes in the debriefing paradigm. *Journal of Personality and Social Psychology, 32,* 880–892.

Ross, L., & Nisbett, R. E. (1991). *The person and the situation: Perspectives of social psychology.* New York: McGraw-Hill.

Rothbart, M. (1981). Memory processes and social beliefs. In D. L. Hamilton (ed), *Cognitive processes in stereotyping and intergroup behavior* (pp. 145–182). Hillsdale, NJ: Erlbaum.

Rotter, J. B. (1966). Generalized expectancies for internal versus external control of reinforcement. *Psychological Monographs, 80,* whole no. 609.

Rubin, J. (1976). How to tell when someone is saying no. *Topics in Culture Learning, 4,* 61–65.

Rubin, Z. (1973). *Liking and loving: An invitation to social psychology.* New York: Holt, Rinehart and Winston.

Ruckmick, C. A. (1912). The history and status of psychology in the United States. *American Journal of Psychology, 23,* 517–531.

Rudman, L. A (1998). Self-promotion as a risk factor for women: The costs and benefits of counter-stereotypical impression management. *Journal of Personality and Social Psychology, 74,* 629–645.

Rudman, L. A., & Glick, P. (1999). Feminized management and backlash toward agentic women: The hidden costs to women of a kinder, gentler image of middle managers. *Journal of Personality and Social Psychology, 75,* 1004–1010.

Rudman, L. A., & Glick, P. (2001). Prescriptive gender stereotypes and backlash against agentic women. *Journal of Social Issues, 57,* 743–762.

Runciman, W. G. (1966). *Relative deprivation and social justice.* London: Routledge and Kegan Paul.

Rusbult, C. E., Martz, J. M., & Agnew, C. R. (1998). The Investment Model Scale: Measuring commitment level, satisfaction level, quality of alternatives, and investment size. *Personal Relationships, 5,* 357–391.

Rusbult, C. E., & Zembrodt, I. M. (1983). Responses to dissatisfaction in romantic involvements: A multi-dimensional scaling analysis. *Journal of Experimental Social Psychology, 19,* 274–293.

Rushton, J. P. (1976). Socialization and the altruistic behavior of children. *Psychological Bulletin, 83,* 898–913.

Rushton, J. P., & Teachman, G. (1978). The effects of positive reinforcement, attributions, and punishment on model induced altruism in children. *Personality and Social Psychology Bulletin, 4,* 322–325.

Russell, J. A. (1994). Is there universal recognition of emotion from facial expressions? A review of the cross-cultural studies. *Psychological Bulletin, 115,* 102–141.

Russell, J. A., Bachorowski, J.-A., & Fernandez-Dols, J.-M. (2003). Facial and vocal expressions of emotion. *Annual Review of Psychology, 54,* 329–349.

Russell, J. A., & Fernandez-Dols, J. M. (eds) (1997). *The psychology of facial expression: Studies in emotion and social interaction.* Cambridge, UK: Cambridge University Press.

Rutland, A. (1999). The development of national prejudice, ingroup favouritism and self-stereotypes in British children. *British Journal of Social Psychology, 38,* 55–70.

S

Sachdev, I., & Bourhis, R. Y. (2005). Multilingual communication and social identification. In J. Harwood & H. Giles (eds), *Intergroup communication: Multiple perspectives* (pp. 65–91). New York: Peter Lang.

Sachdev, I., & Wright, A. (1996). Social influence and language learning: An experimental study. *Journal of Language and Social Psychology, 15,* 230–245.

Saint-Blancat, C. (1985). The effect of minority group vitality upon its sociopsychological behaviour and strategies. *Journal of Multilingual and Multicultural Development, 6,* 31–44.

Saks, M. J. (1978). Social psychological contributions to a legislative committee on organ and tissue transplants. *American Psychologist, 33,* 680–690.

Saks, M. J., & Marti, M. W. (1997). A meta-analysis of the effects of jury size. *Law and Human Behavior, 21,* 451–467.

San Antonio, P. M. (1987). Social mobility and language use in an American company in Japan. *Journal of Language and Social Psychology, 6,* 191–200.

Sanders, G. S., & Baron, R. S. (1977). Is social comparison relevant for producing choice shift? *Journal of Experimental Social Psychology, 13,* 303–314.

Sani, F., & Reicher, S. D. (2000). Contested identities and schisms in groups: Opposing the ordination of women as priests in the Church of England. *British Journal of Social Psychology, 39,* 95–112.

Sansone, C., Weir, C., Harpster, L., & Morgan, C. (1992). Once a boring task always a boring task? Interest as a self-regulatory mechanism. *Journal of Personality and Social Psychology, 63,* 379–390.

Saroja, K., & Surendra, H. S. (1991). A study of postgraduate students' endogamous preference in mate selection. *Indian Journal of Behaviour, 15,* 1–13.

Schachner, D. A., Shaver, P. R., & Mikulincer, M. (2005). Patterns of non-verbal behavior and sensitivity in the context of attachment relationships. *Journal of Nonverbal Behavior, 29,* 141–169.

Schachter, S. (1959). *The psychology of affiliation.* Stanford, CA: Stanford University Press.

Schachter, S. (1964). The interaction of cognitive and physiological determinants of emotional state. In L. Berkowitz (ed), *Advances in experimental social psychology* (Vol. 1, pp. 49–80). New York: Academic Press.

Schachter, S., & Singer, J. E. (1962). Cognitive, social and physiological determinants of emotional state. *Psychological Review, 69,* 379–399.

Schaller, M., Simpson, J. A., & Kenrick, D. T. (eds) (2006). *Evolution and social psychology.* Madison, CT: Psychosocial Press.

Scherer, K. R. (1978). Personality inference from voice quality: The loud voice of extroversion. *European Journal of Social Psychology, 8,* 467–488.

Scherer, K. R. (1986). Vocal affect expression: A review and model for future research. *Psychological Bulletin, 99,* 143–165.

Schlenker, B. R. (1980*). Impression management: The self-concept, social identity, and interpersonal relations*. Monterey, CA: Brooks/Cole.

Schlenker, B. R., Weingold, M. F., & Hallam, J. R. (1990). Self-serving attributions in social context: Effects of self-esteem and social pressure. *Journal of Personality and Social Psychology, 58*, 855–863.

Schmitt, B. H., Gilovich, T., Goore, N., & Joseph, L. (1986). Mere presence and socio-facilitation: One more time. *Journal of Experimental Social Psychology, 22*, 242–248.

Schneider, D. J. (1973). Implicit personality theory: A review. *Psychological Bulletin, 79*, 294–309.

Schneider, D. J., Hastorf, A. H., & Ellsworth, P. C. (1979). *Person perception*. Reading, MA: Addison-Wesley.

Schofield, J. W. (1986). Black–White contact in desegregated schools. In M. Hewstone & R. J. Brown (eds), *Contact and conflict in intergroup encounters* (pp. 79–92). Oxford, UK: Blackwell.

Schriesheim, C. A., Tepper, B. J., & Tetrault, L. A. (1994). Least preferred co-worker score, situational control, and leadership effectiveness: A meta-analysis of contingency model performance predictions. *Journal of Applied Psychology, 79*, 561–573.

Schroeder, D. A., Penner, L. A., Dovidio, J. F., & Piliavin, J. A. (1995). *The psychology of helping and altruism*. New York: McGraw-Hill.

Schubert, T. W. (2004). The power in your hand: Gender differences in bodily feedback from making a fist. *Personality and Social Psychology Bulletin, 30*, 757–769.

Schul, Y., & Burnstein, E. (1985). The informational basis of social judgments: Using past impression rather than the trait description in forming new impression. *Journal of Experimental Social Psychology, 21*, 421–439.

Schwartz, S. H. (1977). Normative influences on altruism. In L. Berkowitz (ed), *Advances in experimental social psychology* (Vol. 10, pp. 222–279). New York: Academic Press.

Schwartz, S. H., & David, T. B. (1976). Responsibility and helping in an emergency: Effects of blame, ability and denial of responsibility. *Sociometry, 39*, 406–415.

Sears, D. O. (1986). College sophomores in the laboratory: Influences of a narrow data base on social psychology's view of human nature. *Journal of Personality and Social Psychology, 51*, 515–530.

Sedikides, C. (1993). Assessment, enhancement, and verification determinants of the self-evaluation process. *Journal of Personality and Social Psychology, 65*, 317–338.

Sedikides, C., & Brewer, M. B. (eds) (2001). *Individual self, relational self, and collective self*. Philadelphia, PA: Psychology Press.

Sedikides, C., & Gregg, A. P. (2003). Portraits of the self. In M. A. Hogg & J. Cooper (eds), *The Sage handbook of social psychology* (pp. 110–138). London: Sage.

Sedikides, C., & Ostrom, T. M. (1988). Are person categories used when organizing information about unfamiliar sets of persons? *Social Cognition, 6*, 252–267.

Seeley, E., Gardner, W., Pennington, G., & Gabriel, S. (2003). Circle of friends or members of a group? Sex differences in relational and collective attachment to groups. *Group Processes and Intergroup Relations, 6*, 251–263.

Semin, G. R. (1980). A gloss on attribution theory. *British Journal of Social Psychology, 19*, 291–300.

Seto, M. C., Maric, A., & Barbaree, H. E. (2001). The role of pornography in the etiology of sexual aggression. *Aggression and Violent Behaviour, 6*, 35–53.

Shackelford, T. K. (2001). Cohabitation, marriage, and murder: Woman-killing by male romantic partners. *Aggressive Behavior, 274*, 284–291.

Shapiro, P. N., & Penrod, S. (1986). Meta-analysis of facial identification studies. *Psychological Bulletin, 100*, 139–156.

Sharpe, D., Adair, J. G., & Roese, N. J. (1992). Twenty years of deception research: A decline in subjects' trust? *Personality and Social Psychology Bulletin, 18*, 585–590.

Sheehan, P. W. (1983). Age trends and the correlates of children's television viewing. *Australian Journal of Psychology, 35*, 417–431.

Sheppard, J. A. (1993). Productivity loss in performance groups: A motivational analysis. *Psychological Bulletin, 113*, 67–81.

Sherif, M. (1935). A study of some social factors in perception. *Archives of Psychology, 27*, 1–60.

Sherif, M. (1936). *The psychology of social norms*. New York: Harper.

Sherif, M. (1966). *In common predicament: Social psychology of intergroup conflict and cooperation*. Boston, MA: Houghton Mifflin.

Sherif, M., Harvey, O. J., White, B. J., Hood, W., & Sherif, C. (1961). *Intergroup conflict and cooperation: The Robbers Cave experiment*. Norman, OK: University of Oklahoma Institute of Intergroup Relations.

Sherif, M., & Sherif, C. W. (1953). *Groups in harmony and tension: An integration of studies in intergroup relations*. New York: Harper & Row.

Sherman, D. K., & Cohen, G. L. (2006). The psychology of self-defense: Self-affirmation theory. In M. P. Zanna (ed), *Advances in experimental social psychology* (Vol. 38, pp. 183–242). San Diego, CA: Academic Press.

Shibutani, T. (1966). *Improvised news: A sociological study of rumor*. Indianapolis: Bobbs-Merrill.

Shotland, R. L., & Heinold, W. D. (1985). Bystander response to arterial bleeding: Helping skills, the decision-making process, and differentiating the helping response. *Journal of Personality and Social Psychology, 49*, 347–356.

Showers, C. (1992). Compartmentalization of positive and negative self-knowledge: Keeping bad apples out of the bunch. *Journal of Personality and Social Psychology, 62*, 1036–1049.

Showers, C., & Cantor, N. (1985). Social cognition: A look at motivated strategies. *Annual Review of Psychology, 36*, 275–305.

Shrauger, J. S., & Schoeneman, T. J. (1979). Symbolic interactionist view of self-concept: Through the looking glass darkly. *Psychological Bulletin, 86*, 549–573.

Sidanius, J., & Pratto, F. (1999). *Social dominance: An intergroup theory of social hierarchy and oppression*. New York: Cambridge University Press.

Sigall, H., & Ostrove, N. (1975). Beautiful but dangerous: Effects of offender attractiveness and the nature of the crime on juristic judgment. *Journal of Personality and Social Psychology, 31*, 410–414.

Simmonds, D. B. (1985). The nature of the organizational grapevine. *Supervisory Management*, 39–42.

Simpson, B., & Willer, R. 2008. Altruism and indirect reciprocity: The interaction of person and situation in prosocial behavior. *Social Psychology Quarterly, 71*, 37–52.

Simpson, J. A. (1987). The dissolution of romantic relationships: Factors involved in relationship stability and emotional distress. *Journal of Personality and Social Psychology, 53*, 683–692.

Simpson, J. A., Campbell, B., & Berscheid, E. (1986). The association between romantic love and marriage: Kephart (1967) twice revisited *Personality and Social Psychology Bulletin, 12*, 363–372.

Singh, R., & Ho, S. Y. (2000). Attitudes and attraction: A new test of the attraction, repulsion and similarity–dissimilarity asymmetry hypotheses. *British Journal of Social Psychology, 39*, 197–211.

Sistrunk, F., & McDavid, J. W. (1971). Sex variable in conforming behavior. *Journal of Personality and Social Psychology, 2*, 200–207.

Skowronski, J. J., & Carlston, D. E. (1989). Negativity and extremity biases in impression formation: A review of explanations. *Psychological Bulletin, 105*, 131–142.

Slater, A., Von der Schulenburg, C., Brown, E., Badenoch, M., Butterworth, G., Parsons, S., & Samuels, C. (1998). Newborn infants prefer attractive faces. *Infant Behavior & Development, 21*, 345–354.

Slater, P. E. (1955). Role differentiation in small groups. *American Sociological Review, 20*, 300–310.

Smith, C. A., & Lazarus, R. S. (1990). Emotion and adaption. In L. A. Pervin (ed.), *Handbook of personality: Theory and research* (pp. 609–637). New York: Guilford.

Smith, D. L., Pruitt, D. G., & Carnevale, P. J. D. (1982). Matching and mismatching: The effect of own limit, other's toughness, and time pressure on concession rate in negotiation. *Journal of Personality and Social Psychology, 42*, 876–883.

Smith, E. R., Fazio, R. H., & Cejka, M. A. (1996). Accessible attitudes influence categorization of multiply categorizable objects. *Journal of Personality and Social Psychology, 71*, 888–898.

Smith, E. R., & Zárate, M. A. (1992). Exemplar-based model of social judgment. *Psychological Review, 99*, 3–21.

Smith, M. B., Bruner, J. S., & White, R. W. (1956). *Opinions and personality*. New York: Wiley.

Smith, P. B., & Bond, M. H. (1998). *Social*

psychology across cultures (2nd ed). London: Prentice Hall Europe.

Smith, P. B., Bond, M. H., & Kağitçibaşi, Ç. (2006). *Understanding social psychology across cultures: Living and working in a changing world.* London: Sage.

Sniderman, P. M., Hagen, M. G., Tetlock, P. E., & Brady, H. E. (1986). Reasoning chains: Causal models of policy reasoning in mass publics. *British Journal of Political Science, 16,* 405–430.

Snyder M. (1974). The self-monitoring of expressive behavior. *Journal of Personality and Social Psychology, 30,* 526–537.

Snyder, M. (1984). When belief creates reality. In L. Berkowitz (ed), *Advances in experimental social psychology* (Vol. 18, pp. 248–306). New York: Academic Press.

Sommer, R. (1969). *Personal space: The behavioral basis of design.* Englewood Cliffs, NJ: Prentice Hall.

Spacapan, S., & Oskamp, S. (eds) (1992). *Helping and being helped* Newbury Park, CA: Sage.

Sparrowe, R. T., & Liden, R. C. (1997). Process and structure in leader-member exchange. *Academy of Management Review, 22,* 522–552.

Spitz, R. A. (1945). Hospitalism: An inquiry into the genesis of psychiatric conditions in early childhood. In A. Freud, H. Hartman & E. Kris (eds), *The psychoanalytic study of the child* (Vol. 1, pp. 53–74). New York: International University Press.

Sprecher, S. (1998). Insiders' perspectives on reasons for attraction to a close other. *Social Psychology Quarterly, 61,* 287–300.

Srull, T. K., & Wyer, R. S. (1989). Person memory and judgement. *Psychological Review, 96,* 58–83.

Stangor, C. (1988). Stereotype accessibility and information processing. *Personality and Social Psychology Bulletin, 14,* 694–708.

Stangor, C. (ed) (2000). *Stereotypes and prejudice: Essential readings.* Philadelphia, PA: Psychology Press.

Stangor, C. (2004). *Social groups in action and interaction.* New York: Psychology Press.

Stasser, G., Kerr, N. L., & Bray, R. M. (1982). The social psychology of jury deliberations: Structure, process, and product. In N. Kerr & R. Bray (eds), *The psychology of the courtroom* (pp. 221–256). New York: Academic Press.

Stasser, G., Kerr, N. L., & Davis, J. H. (1989). Influence processes and consensus models in decision-making groups. In P. B. Paulus (ed), *Psychology of group influence* (2nd ed, pp. 279–326). Hillsdale, NJ: Erlbaum.

Staub, E. (1989). *The roots of evil: The psychological and cultural origins of genocide and other forms of group violence.* New York: Cambridge University Press.

Steele, C. M. (1975). Name-calling and compliance. *Journal of Personality and Social Psychology, 31,* 361–369.

Steele, C. M. (1988). The psychology of self-affirmation: Sustaining the integrity of the self. In L. Berkowitz (ed), *Advances in experimental social psychology* (Vol. 21, pp. 261–302). New York: Academic Press.

Steele, C. M., & Aronson, J. (1995). Stereotype vulnerability and the intellectual test performance of African-Americans. *Journal of Personality and Social Psychology, 69,* 797–811.

Steele, C. M., Spencer, S. J., & Aronson, J. (2002). Contending with group image: The psychology of stereotype and social identity threat. In M. P. Zanna (ed), *Advances in experimental social psychology* (Vol. 34, pp. 379–440). San Diego, CA: Academic Press.

Steiner, I. D. (1976). Task-performing groups. In J. W. Thibaut & J. T. Spence (eds), *Contemporary topics in social psychology* (pp. 393–422). Morristown, NJ: General Learning Press.

Steir, C. (1978). *Blue jolts: True stories from the cuckoo's nest.* Washington, DC: New Republic Books.

Stephan, W. G., & Stephan, C. W. (1985). Intergroup anxiety. *Journal of Social Issues, 41,* 157–175.

Stephan, W. G., & Stephan, C. W. (2000). An integrated threat theory of prejudice. In S. Oskamp (ed), *Reducing prejudice and discrimination* (pp. 23–46). Mahwah, NJ: Erlbaum.

Stephan, W. G., & Stephan, C. W. (2001). *Improving intergroup relations.* Thousand Oaks, CA: Sage.

Stern, P. C., Dietz, T., & Guagnano, G. A. (1995). The new ecological paradigm in social psychological context. *Environment and Behavior, 27,* 723–743.

Sternberg, R. J. (1988). *The triangle of love*. New York: Basic Books.

Stevens, J. R., Cushman, F. A., & Hauser, M. D. (2005). Evolving the psychological mechanisms for cooperation. *Annual Review of Ecology, Evolution and Systematics, 36*, 499–518.

Stewart, J. E. (1980). Defendant's attractiveness as a factor in the outcome of criminal trials: An observational study. *Journal of Applied Social Psychology, 10*, 348–361.

Stogdill, R. (1974). *Handbook of leadership*. New York: Free Press.

Stogdill, R. M. (1948). Personal factors associated with leadership: A survey of the literature. *Journal of Psychology, 25*, 35–71.

Storms, M. D. (1973). Videotape and the attribution process: Reversing actor's and observer's points of view. *Journal of Personality and Social Psychology, 27*, 165–175.

Stott, C. J., Hutchison, P., & Drury, J (2001). 'Hooligans' abroad? Intergroup dynamics, social identity and participation in collective disorder at the 1998 world cup finals. *British Journal of Social Psychology, 40*, 359–384.

Strauman, T. J., Lemieux, A. M., & Coe, C. L. (1993). Self-discrepancy and natural killer cell activity: Immunological consequences of negative self-evaluation. *Journal of Personality and Social Psychology, 64*, 1042–1052.

Straus, M. A., Gelles, R. J., & Steinmetz, S. K. (1980). *Behind closed doors: Violence in the American family*. Garden City, NY: Anchor Books.

Strodtbeck, F. L., James, R., & Hawkins, C. (1957). Social status in jury deliberations. *American Sociological Review, 22*, 713–718.

Strodtbeck, F. L., & Lipinski, R. M. (1985). Becoming first among equals: Moral considerations in jury foreman selection. *Journal of Personality and Social Psychology, 49*, 927–936.

Stroebe, W., & Diehl, M. (1994). Why groups are less effective than their members: On productivity losses in idea-generating groups. *European Review of Social Psychology, 5*, 271–303.

Stroebe, W., Diehl, M., & Abakoumkin, G. (1992). The illusion of group effectivity. *Personality and Social Psychology Bulletin, 18*, 643–650.

Strube, M. J., Turner, C. W., Cerro, D., Stevens, J., & Hinchey, F. (1984). Interpersonal aggression and the type A coronary-prone behavior pattern: A theoretical distinction and practical implications. *Journal of Personality and Social Psychology, 47*, 839–847.

Surowiecki, J. (2004). *The wisdom of crowds: Why the many are smarter than the few and how collective wisdom shapes business, economies, societies, and nations*. New York: Doubleday.

Stürmer, S., & Simon, B. (2004). Collective action: Towards a dual-pathway model. *European Review of Social Psychology, 15*, 59–99.

Swann, W. B. Jr (1984). Quest for accuracy in person perception: A matter of pragmatics. *Psychological Review, 91*, 457–477.

Swann, W. B. Jr (1987). Identity negotiation: Where two roads meet. *Journal of Personality and Social Psychology, 53*, 1038–1051.

Swann, W. B. Jr (in press). The Self. In D. T. Gilbert, S. T. Fiske & G. Lindzey (eds), *Handbook of social psychology* (5th ed). Hoboken, NJ: Wiley.

T

Tajfel, H. (1959). Quantitative judgement in social perception. *British Journal of Psychology, 50*, 16–29.

Tajfel, H. (1969). Social and cultural factors in perception. In G. Lindzey & E. Aronson (eds), *Handbook of social psychology* (Vol. 3, pp. 315–394). Reading, MA: Addison-Wesley.

Tajfel, H. (1970). Experiments in intergroup discrimination. *Scientific American, 223*, 96–102.

Tajfel, H. (1972). Experiments in a vacuum. In J. Israel & H. Tajfel (eds), *The context of social psychology: A critical assessment*. London: Academic Press.

Tajfel, H. (1974). Social identity and intergroup behaviour. *Social Science Information, 13*, 65–93.

Tajfel, H. (1982). Social psychology of intergroup relations. *Annual Review of Social Psychology, 33*, 1–39.

Tajfel, H., Billig, M., Bundy, R. P., & Flament, C. (1971). Social categorization and intergroup behaviour. *European Journal of Social Psychology, 1*, 149–177.

Tajfel, H., & Turner, J. C. (1979). An integrative theory of intergroup conflict. In W. G. Austin & S. Worchel (eds), *The social psychology of intergroup relations* (pp. 33–47). Monterey, CA: Brooks/Cole.

Tajfel, H., & Wilkes, A. L. (1963). Classification

and quantitative judgement. *British Journal of Psychology, 54*, 101–114.

Tanford, S., & Penrod, S. (1984). Social influence model: A formal integration of research on majority and minority influence processes. *Psychological Bulletin, 95*, 189–225.

Tarde, G. (1898). *Etudes de psychologie sociale.* Paris: V. Giard & E. Briére.

Taylor, D. M., & Jaggi, V. (1974). Ethnocentrism and causal attribution in a S. Indian context. *Journal of Cross-cultural Psychology, 5*, 162–171.

Taylor, D. M., & Brown, R. J. (1979). Towards a more social social psychology. *British Journal of Social and Clinical Psychology, 18*, 173–179.

Taylor, S. E. (1998). The social being in social psychology. In D. T. Gilbert, S. T. Fiske & G. Lindzey (eds), *The handbook of social psychology* (4th ed, Vol. 1, pp. 58–95). New York: McGraw-Hill.

Taylor, S. E., & Brown, J. D. (1988). Illusion and well-being: A social psychological perspective on mental health. *Psychological Bulletin, 103*, 193–210.

Taylor, S. E., Fiske, S. T., Etcoff, N. L., & Ruderman, A. J. (1978). Categorical and contextual bases of person memory and stereotyping. *Journal of Personality and Social Psychology, 36*, 778–793.

Taylor, S. P., & Sears, J. D. (1988). The effects of alcohol and persuasive social pressure on human physical aggression. *Aggressive Behavior, 14*, 237–243.

Tennen, H., & Affleck, G. (1993). The puzzles of self-esteem: A clinical perspective. In R. F. Baumeister (ed), *Self-esteem: The puzzle of low self-esteem* (pp. 241–262). New York: Plenum.

Terry, D. J., Carey, C. J., & Callan, V. J. (2001). Employee adjustment to an organizational merger: An intergroup perspective. *Personality and Social Psychology Bulletin, 27*, 267–280.

Terry, D., Gallois, C., & McCamish, M. (1993). The theory of reasoned action and health care behaviour. In D. Terry, C. Gallois & M. McCamish (eds), *The theory of reasoned action: Its application to AIDS-preventive behaviour* (pp. 1–27). Oxford, UK: Pergamon Press.

Tesser, A. (1988). Toward a self-evaluation maintenance model of social behavior. In L. Berkowitz (ed), *Advances in experimental social psychology* (Vol. 21, pp. 181–227). San Diego, CA: Academic Press.

Tesser, A., & Bau, J. J. (2002). Social psychology: Who we are and what we do. *Personality and Social Psychology Review, 6*, 72–85.

Tesser, A., Gatewood, R., & Driver, M. (1968). Some determinants of gratitude. *Journal of Personality and Social Psychology, 9*, 233–236.

Tesser, A., & Schwartz, N. (eds) (2001). *Blackwell handbook of social psychology: Intra-individual processes.* Oxford: Blackwell.

Tetlock, P. E., & Boettger, R. (1989). Accountability: A social magnifier of the dilution effect. *Journal of Personality and Social Psychology, 57*, 388–398.

Thayer, S. (1986). Touch: The frontier of intimacy. *Journal of Nonverbal Behaviour, 10*, 7–11.

Thibaut, J. W., & Kelley, H. H. (1959). *The social psychology of groups.* New York: Wiley.

Thomas, W. I., & Znaniecki, F. (1918). *The Polish peasant in Europe and America* (Vol. 1). Boston: Badger.

Thompson, L., & Loewenstein, J. (2003). Mental models of negotiation: Descriptive, prescriptive, and paradigmatic implications. In M. A. Hogg & J. Cooper (eds), *The Sage handbook of social psychology* (pp. 494–511). London: Sage.

Thompson, W. C., Fong, G. T., & Rosenhan, D. L. (1981). Inadmissible evidence and juror verdicts. *Journal of Personality and Social Psychology, 40*, 453–463.

Thompson, W. C., & Fuqua, J. (1998). 'The jury will disregard …': A brief guide to inadmissible evidence. In J. M. Golding & C. M. MacLeod (eds), *Intentional forgetting: Interdisciplinary approaches* (pp. 133–154). Mahwah, NJ: Erlbaum.

Thurstone, L. L. (1928). Attitudes can be measured *American Journal of Sociology, 33*, 529–554.

Tice, D. M. (1992). Self-presentation and self-concept change: The looking-glass self as magnifying glass. *Journal of Personality and Social Psychology, 63*, 435–451.

Tindale, R. S., Nadler, J., Krebel, A., & Davis, J. H. (2001). Procedural mechanisms and jury behavior. In M. A. Hogg & R. S. Tindale (eds), *Blackwell handbook of social psychology: Group processes* (pp. 574–602). Oxford, UK: Blackwell.

Tomada, G., & Schneider, B. H. (1997). Relational aggression, gender, and peer acceptance: Invariance across culture, stability over time, and concordance among informants. *Developmental Psychology, 33*, 601–609.

Tourangeau, R., Smith, T. W., & Rasinski, K. A. (1997). Motivation to report sensitive behaviours on surveys: Evidence from a bogus pipeline experiment. *Journal of Applied Social Psychology, 27,* 209–222.

Trafimow, D. (2000). Habit as both a direct cause of intention to use a condom and as a moderator of the attitude–intention and the subjective norm–intention relations. *Psychology and Health, 15,* 383–395.

Triplett, N. (1898). The dynamogenic factors in pacemaking and competition. *American Journal of Psychology, 9,* 507–533.

Trope, Y. (1986). Self-enhancement and self-assessment in achievement behavior. In R. Sorrentino & E. T. Higgins (eds), *Handbook of motivation and cognition* (Vol. 2, pp. 350–378). New York: Guilford Press.

Trope, Y., & Gaunt, R. (2007). Attribution and person perception. In M. A. Hogg & J. Cooper (eds), *The Sage handbook of social psychology: Concise student edition* (pp. 176–194). London: Sage.

Tucker, J. S., Friedman, H. S., Schwartz, J. E., Criqui, M. H., Tomlinson-Keasey, C., Wingard, D. L., *et al.* (1997). Parental divorce: Effects on individual behavior and longevity. *Journal of Personality and Social Psychology, 73,* 381–391.

Turner, J. C. (1982). Towards a cognitive redefinition of the social group. In H. Tajfel (ed), *Social identity and intergroup relations* (pp. 15–40). Cambridge, UK: Cambridge University Press.

Turner, J. C. (1991). *Social influence.* Buckingham, UK: Open University Press.

Turner, J. C., Hogg, M. A., Oakes, P. J., Reicher, S. D., & Wetherell, M. S. (1987). *Rediscovering the social group: A self-categorization theory.* Oxford, UK: Blackwell.

Turner, J. C., & Oakes, P. J. (1989). Self-categorization and social influence. In P. B. Paulus (ed), *The psychology of group influence* (2nd ed, pp. 233–275). Hillsdale, NJ: Erlbaum.

Turner, J. C., Wetherell, M. S., & Hogg, M. A. (1989). Referent informational influence and group polarization. *British Journal of Social Psychology, 28,* 135–147.

Tversky, A., & Kahneman, D. (1974). Judgment under uncertainty: Heuristics and biases. *Science, 185,* 1124–1131.

Tyler, T. R. (1997). The psychology of legitimacy: A relational perspective on voluntary deference to authorities. *Personality and Social Psychology Review, 1,* 323–345.

Tyler, T. R. (2003). Justice, identity, and leadership. In D. van Knippenberg & M. A. Hogg (eds) *Leadership and power: Identity processes in groups and organizations* (pp. 94–108). London: Sage.

Tyler, T. R., & Lind, E. A. (1992). A relational model of authority in groups. In M.P. Zanna (ed), *Advances in experimental social psychology* (Vol. 25, pp. 115–191). New York: Academic Press.

Tyler, T., & Sears, D. O. (1977). Coming to like obnoxious people when we have to live with them. *Journal of Personality and Social Psychology, 35,* 200–211.

U

Umadevi, L., Venkataramaiah, P., & Srinivasulu, R. (1992). A comparative study on the concept of marriage by professional and non-professional degree students. *Indian Journal of Behaviour, 16,* 27–37.

Underwood, B., & Moore, B. (1982). Perspective-taking and altruism. *Psychological Bulletin, 91,* 143–173.

US Department of Justice (2006). Office of juvenile justice and delinquency prevention: *Law enforcement and juvenile crime.* Retrieved 3 April, 2007 from http://ojjdp.ncjrs.org/ojstatbb/crime/JAR_Display.asp?ID=qa05235

V

Valentine, T., Pickering, A., & Darling, S. (2003). Characteristics of eyewitness identification that predict the outcome of real lineups. *Applied Cognitive Psychology, 17,* 969–993.

Valins, S., & Nisbett, R. E. (1972). Attribution processes in the development and treatment of emotional disorders. In E. E. Jones, D. E. Kanouse, H. H. Kelley, R. E. Nisbett, S. Valins & B. Weiner (eds), *Attribution: Perceiving the causes of behavior* (pp. 137–150). Morristown, NJ: General Learning Press.

van de Vliert, E., Huang, X., & Levine, R. V. (2004). National wealth and thermal climate as predictors of motives for volunteer work. *Journal of Cross-Cultural Psychology, 35,* 62–73.

van Dijk, T. A. (1987). *Communicating racism: Ethnic prejudice in thought and talk*. Newbury Park, CA: Sage.

van Dijk, T. A. (1993). *Elite discourse and racism*. Newbury Park, CA: Sage.

van Gyn, G. H., Wenger, H. A., & Gaul, C. A. (1990). Imagery as a method of enhancing transfer from training to performance. *Journal of Sport and Exercise Psychology, 12*, 366–375.

van Knippenberg, D., van Knippenberg, B., De Cremer, D., & Hogg, M. A. (2004). Leadership, self, and identity: A review and research agenda. *The Leadership Quarterly, 15*, 825–856.

van Schie, E. C. M., & Wiegman, O. (1997). Children and videogames: Leisure activities, aggression, social integration, and school performance. *Journal of Applied Social Psychology, 27*(13), 1175–1194.

Vandello, J. A., & Cohen, D. (2003). Male honor and female fidelity: Implicit cultural scripts that perpetuate domestic violence. *Journal of Personality and Social Psychology, 84*, 997–1010.

Vaughan, G. M. (1964). The trans-situational aspect of conforming behavior. *Journal of Personality, 32*, 335–354.

Vaughan, G. M., Tajfel, H., & Williams, J. (1981). Bias in reward allocation in an intergroup and an interpersonal context. *Social Psychology Quarterly, 44*, 37–42.

Verkuyten, M. (2006). Multiculturalism and social psychology. *European Review of Social Psychology, 17*, 148–184.

Vick, S.-J., Waller, B. M., Parr, L. A., Pasqualini, M. C. S., & Bard, K. A. (2007). A cross-species comparison of facial morphology and movement in humans and chimpanzees using the Facial Action Coding System (FACS). *Journal of Nonverbal Behavior, 31*, 1–20.

Vignoles, V. L., Chryssochoou, X., & Breakwell, G. M. (2000). The distinctiveness principle: Identity, meaning, and the bounds of cultural relativity. *Personality and Social Psychology Review, 4*, 337–354.

Visser, P. S., & Cooper, J. (2003). Attitude change. In M. A. Hogg & J. Cooper (eds), *The Sage handbook of social psychology* (pp. 211–231). London: Sage.

Vygotsky, L. S. (1962). *Thought and language*. New York: Wiley. (Original work published 1934.)

W

Walker, I., & Smith, H. J. (eds) (2002). *Relative deprivation: Specification, development, and integration*. Cambridge, UK: Cambridge University Press.

Walster, E., & Festinger, L. (1962). The effectiveness of 'overheard' persuasive communications. *Journal of Abnormal and Social Psychology, 65*, 395–402.

Walster, E., Walster, G. W., & Berscheid, E. (1978). *Equity theory and research*. Boston, MA: Allyn & Bacon.

Watson, D. (1982). The actor and the observer: How are the perceptions of causality divergent? *Psychological Bulletin, 92*, 682–700.

Watson, J. B. (1913). Psychology as a behaviourist views it. *Psychological Review, 20*, 158–177.

Webb, E. J., Campbell, D. T., Schwartz, R. D., & Sechrest, L. (1969). *Unobtrusive measures: Nonreactive research in the social sciences*. Chicago: Rand McNally.

Weber, R., & Crocker, J. (1983). Cognitive processes in the revision of stereotypic beliefs. *Journal of Personality and Social Psychology, 45*, 961–977.

Wegener, D. T., Petty, R. E., & Smith, S. M. (1995). Positive mood can increase or decrease message scrutiny: The hedonic contingency view of mood and message processing. *Journal of Personality and Social Psychology, 69*, 5–15.

Wegner, D. M. (1987). Transactive memory: A transactive analysis of the group mind. In B. Mullen & G. R. Goethals (eds), *Theories of group behavior* (pp. 185–208). New York: Springer.

Weiner, B. (1979). A theory of motivation for some classroom experiences. *Journal of educational Psychology, 71*, 3–25.

Weiner, B. (1986). *An attributional theory of motivation and emotion*. New York: Springer.

Wells, G. L., Memon, A., & Penrod, S. D. (2006). Eye witness evidence: Improving its probative value. *Psychological Science in the Public Interest, 7*, 45–75.

Wetherell, M. S., Taylor, S., & Yates, S. J. (2001). *Discourse as data: A guide for analysis*. London: Sage.

White, M. (2004). 30 worst atrocities of the 20th century [electronic version], http://users.erols.com/mwhite28/atrox.htm. Retrieved 25 October, 2006.

Whorf, B. L. (1956). *Language, thought and reality*. Cambridge, MA: MIT Press.

Wicker, A. W. (1969). Attitudes versus actions: The relationship of verbal and overt behavioral responses to attitude objects. *Journal of Social Issues, 25*, 41–78.

Wieselquist, J., Rusbult, C. E., Foster, C. A., & Agnew, C. R. (1999). Commitment, prorelationship behavior, and trust in close relationships. *Journal of Personality and Social Psychology, 77*, 942–966.

Wilder, D. A. (1984). Predictions of belief homogeneity and similarity following social categorization. *British Journal of Social Psychology, 23*, 323–333.

Wilder, D. A., & Shapiro, P. N. (1989). Role of competition-induced anxiety in limiting the beneficial impact of positive behavior by an outgroup member. *Journal of Personality and Social Psychology, 56*, 60–69.

Wilkinson, S., & Kitzinger, C. (2006). Surprise as an interactional achievement: Reaction tokens in conversation. *Social Psychology Quarterly, 69*, 150–182.

Williams, J. E., & Best, D. L. (1982). *Measuring sex stereotypes: A thirty nation study*. Beverly Hills, CA: Sage.

Williams, K. D. (2002). *Ostracism: The power of silence*. New York: Guilford.

Williams, K. D., Cheung, C. K. T., & Choi, W. (2000). Cyberostracism: Effects of being ignored over the internet. *Journal of Personality and Social Psychology, 79*, 748–762.

Williams, K. D., Harkins, S. G., & Karau, S. J. (2003). Social performance. In M. A. Hogg & J. Cooper (eds), *The Sage handbook of social psychology* (pp. 327–346). London: Sage.

Williams, K. D., & Karau, S. J. (1991). Social loafing and social compensation: The effects of expectations of co-worker performance. *Journal of Personality and Social Psychology, 61*, 570–581.

Williams, K. D., Shore, W. J., & Grahe, J. E. (1998). The silent treatment: Perceptions of its behaviors and associated feelings. *Group Processes and Intergroup Relations, 1*, 117–141.

Wills, T. A. (1981). Downward comparison principles in social psychology. *Psychological Bulletin, 90*, 245–271.

Wilson, E. O. (1978). *On human nature*. Cambridge, MA: Harvard University Press.

Wispé, L. G. (1972). Positive forms of social behavior: An overview. *Journal of Social Issues, 28*, 1–19.

Wood, G. S. (1982). Conspiracy and the paranoid style: Causality and deceit in the eighteenth century. *William and Mary Quarterly, 39*, 401–441.

Wood, J. V. (1989). Theory and research concerning social comparisons of personal attributes. *Psychological Bulletin, 106*, 231–248.

Worchel, S., & Novell, N. (1980). Effect of perceived environmental conditions during cooperation on intergroup attraction. *Journal of Personality and Social Psychology, 38*, 764–772.

Worchel, S., Rothgerber, H., Day, E. A., Hart, D., & Butemeyer, J. (1998). Social identity and individual productivity within groups. *British Journal of Social Psychology, 37*, 389–413.

Wright, S. C., & Taylor, D. M. (2003). The social psychology of cultural diversity: Social stereotyping, prejudice, and discrimination. In M. A. Hogg & J. Cooper (eds), *The Sage handbook of social psychology* (pp. 432–457). London: Sage.

Wyer, R. S., Jr & Gordon, S. E. (1984). The cognitive representation of social information. In R. S. Wyer Jr & T. K. Srull (eds), *Handbook of social cognition* (Vol. 2, pp. 73–150). Hillsdale, NJ: Erlbaum.

Y

Yancy, G. (2007). Homogamy over the net: Using internet advertisements to discover who interracially dates. *Journal of Social and Personal Relationships, 24*, 913–930.

Yarmouk, U. (2000). The effect of presentation modality on judgements of honesty and attractiveness. *Social Behavior and Personality, 28*, 269–278.

Younger, J. C., Walker, L., & Arrowood, A. J. (1977). Post-decision dissonance at the fair. *Personality and Social Psychology Bulletin, 3*, 247–287.

Yuki, M. (2003). Intergroup comparison versus intragroup relationships: A cross-cultural examination of social identity theory in North American and East Asian cultural contexts. *Social Psychology Quarterly, 66*, 166–183.

Yukl, G. (2005). *Leadership in organizations* (6th ed). Upper Saddle River, NJ: Prentice Hall.

Z

Zaccaro, S. J. (1984). Social loafing: The role of task attractiveness. *Personality and Social Psychology Bulletin, 10,* 99–106.

Zahn-Waxler, C., Radke-Yarrow, M., Wagner, E., & Chapman, M. (1992). Development of concern for others. *Developmental Psychology, 28,* 126–136.

Zajonc, R. B. (1965). Social facilitation. *Science, 149,* 269–274.

Zajonc, R. B. (1968). Attitudinal effects of mere exposure. *Journal of Personality and Social Psychology, 9,* 1–27.

Zanna, M. P., & Hamilton, D. L. (1972). Attribute dimensions and patterns of trait inferences. *Psychonomic Science, 27,* 353–354.

Zebrowitz, L. A. (1996). Physical appearance as a basis of stereotyping. In C. N. Macrae, C. Stangor, & M. Hewstone (eds), *Stereotypes and stereotyping* (pp. 79–120). New York: Guilford Press.

Zebrowitz, L. A., & Collins, M. A. (1997). Accurate social perception at zero acquaintance: The affordances of a Gibsonian approach. *Personality and Social Psychology Review, 1,* 204–223.

Zillmann, D. (1979). *Hostility and aggression.* Hillsdale, NJ: Erlbaum.

Zillmann, D. (1984). *Connections between sex and aggression.* Hillsdale, NJ: Erlbaum.

Zillmann, D. (1996). Sequential dependencies in emotional experience and behavior. In R. D. Kavanaugh, B. Zimmerberg, & S. Fein (eds), *Emotion: Interdisciplinary perspectives* (pp. 243–272). Mahwah, NJ: Erlbaum.

Zillmann, D., & Bryant, J. (1984). Effects of massive exposure to pornography. In N. M. Malamuth & E. Donnerstein (eds), *Pornography and sexual aggression* (pp. 115–138). New York: Academic Press.

Zimbardo, P. G. (1970). The human choice: Individuation, reason, and order versus deindividuation, impulse, and chaos. In W. J. Arnold & D. Levine (eds), *Nebraska symposium on motivation 1969* (Vol. 17, pp. 237–307). Lincoln, NE: University of Nebraska Press.

Zimbardo, P. G. (1971). *The Stanford prison experiment.* Script of the slide show.

Zimbardo, P. G., Ebbesen, E. E., & Maslach, C. (1977). *Influencing attitudes and changing behavior.* Reading, MA: Addison-Wesley.

Zimbardo, P. G., Haney, C., Banks, W. C., & Jaffe, D. (1982). The psychology of imprisonment. In J. C. Brigham & L. Wrightsman (eds), *Contemporary issues in social psychology* (4th ed, pp. 230–235). Monterey, CA: Brooks/Cole.

Zimbardo, P. G., Weisenberg, M., Firestone, I., & Levy, B. (1965). Communication effectiveness in producing public conformity and private attitude change. *Journal of Personality, 33,* 233–256.

Zuckerman, M., Miserandino, M., & Bernieri, F. (1983). Civil inattention exists – in elevators. *Personality and Social Psychology Bulletin, 9,* 578–586.

Author Index

Subject Index

British Psychological Society

Standards in Social Psychology

The British Psychological Society (BPS) accredits psychology degree programmes across the UK. It has set guidelines as to which major topics should be covered within social psychology. We have listed these topics below and indicated where in this textbook each is covered most fully.

BPS guidelines	Coverage in Hogg and Vaughan
Social perception including:	
• person perception	Chapter 2
• attitudes	Chapter 4
• attribution	Chapter 2
Intergroup processes including:	
• prejudice	Chapter 7
• intergroup conflict	Chapter 7
• social identification	Chapters 3 and 7
Small group processes including:	
• norms	Chapters 5 and 6
• leadership	Chapter 6
• decision making	Chapter 6
• productivity	Chapter 6
Social influence including:	
• conformity and obedience	Chapter 5
• majority and minority influence	Chapter 5
• the bystander effect	Chapter 9
Close relationships including:	
• interpersonal attraction	Chapter 10
• relationships	Chapter 10